FOUNDATIONS
of MORAL
PHILOSOPHY

Readings in Metaethics

Edited by

STEVEN M. CAHN *and*
ANDREW T. FORCEHIMES

New York　　Oxford
OXFORD UNIVERSITY PRESS

Oxford University Press is a department of the University of Oxford.
It furthers the University's objective of excellence in research,
scholarship, and education by publishing worldwide.
Oxford is a registered trade mark of Oxford University Press
in the UK and certain other countries.

Published in the United States of America by
Oxford University Press
198 Madison Avenue, New York, NY 10016,
United States of America.

For titles covered by Section 112 of the US Higher Education
Opportunity Act, please visit www.oup.com/us/he for the
latest information about pricing and alternate formats.

Library of Congress Cataloging-in-Publication Data

Names: Cahn, Steven M. editor. | Forcehimes, Andrew
Title: Foundations of moral philosophy : readings in metaethics / edited by
   Steven M. Cahn and Andrew T. Forcehimes.
Description: New York City : Oxford University Press, 2016.
Identifiers: LCCN 2016024540 | ISBN 9780190623074 (pbk.)
Subjects: LCSH: Metaethics.
Classification: LCC BJ1012 .F6384 2016 | DDC 170/.42--dc23 LC record available
   at https://lccn.loc.gov/2016024540

Printing number: 9 8 7 6 5 4 3 2 1
Printed by LSC Communications, Inc.

Contents

PART IV NON-COGNITIVISM

PART V ERROR THEORY

PART VI RELATIVISM

PART VII RESPONSE DEPENDENCE

PART VIII CONSTRUCTIVISM

PART IX   THEISTIC VOLUNTARISM

PART X   EPISTEMOLOGY

PART XI   MORAL EXPLANATIONS

PART XII   REASONS & MOTIVES

Preface

Metaethics investigates the most fundamental questions about the nature of morality. While the field is challenging, in recent years it has enjoyed much attention among theorists.

This collection covers all aspects of the subject. The readings have been chosen for their importance and, wherever appropriate, edited to enhance their accessibility. Further assistance is provided by an extended general introduction, a detailed glossary, as well as introductions and study questions accompanying each selection. Unlike other anthologies, almost all of which focus exclusively on work since 1900, we have included relevant writings by leading philosophers of the past whose work forms the basis for subsequent inquiry. Of the contemporary articles, approximately thirty percent are authored by women.

We wish to express appreciation to our editor, Robert Miller, for his guidance and support. We also wish to thank assistant editor Alyssa Palazzo for her generous help, manuscript editor Marianne Paul for her conscientiousness, and the staff of Oxford University Press for kind assistance throughout the production and presentation of the book.

We are grateful for suggestions from reviewers chosen by the Press: Caroline Arruda, University at Texas, El Paso; James Bruce, John Brown University; Patricia Greenspan, University of Maryland, College Park; Lawrence Jost, University of Cincinnati; Fritz McDonald, Oakland University; Douglas Portmore, Arizona State University; Michael Smith, Princeton University; Kyle Yrigoyen, San Jose State University.

A final note: Some of the selections were written when the custom was to use the noun "man" and the pronoun "he" to refer to all persons regardless of gender, and we have retained the authors' original wording. With this proviso, we begin our readings.

Part I

INTRODUCTION

The Driving Forces of Metaethics

Andrew T. Forcehimes

§0. INTRODUCTION

Whereas theories in normative ethics ask questions concerning what we are required to do and who we are required to be, theories in metaethics ask questions *about* ethics. Metaethics, that is, investigates the nature of ethics. Unfortunately, unless you are already acquainted with metaethics, this quick gloss is not terribly informative. To get a more informative characterization, however, we need some background.

In college, I played a game that combined Charades, Pictionary, and Telephone. For the unfamiliar, the game goes like this. A team of three—an actor, a drawer, and a guesser—stand in a line. Everyone except the last person in the line, the actor, is equipped with a piece of paper and pen. In a bowl are a number of folded cards with statements describing scenes such as "a man flying a kite," "a child chasing butter-flies," or "a sailor watching a sunset." The actor selects one of these cards and silently performs it for the second-to-last person, the drawer, who sketches the charade. The drawer then passes the sketch to the third person in line, the guesser, who writes down what the picture is about. If the guesser's statement matches the statement selected from the bowl, the team gets a point.

I didn't reflect much on the game at the time, but now it seems to me a helpful way of understanding the question that arguably stands at the heart of philosophy: What is the relationship between language, mind, and the world?

A natural answer is suggested by the game. Part of what our minds do is function like the drawer. They try to capture, or represent, the world—the charade—of our immediate experience. Part of the job of language, similarly, is to describe the world, and it is successful—we get a point—when it does so accurately. So the answer suggested by the game can be visualized as follows:

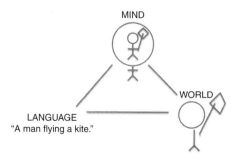

Of course, how this natural answer gets filled in—and the answer itself—is controversial. But for all that, it's a good place to start. For it makes clear how our commitments at one vertex of the triangle entail commitments at the others.

Suppose, for example, we start with the world. That is, we start with metaphysical questions. What is there? And what is it like? And suppose further that, as an answer to these questions, we were committed to a scientific conception of the world, according to which reality—all that exists—is limited to what is recognized by the natural and social sciences. We would then face a serious restriction on what our minds and language could be about while still accurately describing reality. Returning to our analogy with the game, we can clarify how the implications of this metaphysical commitment limit what we can say later about language and the mind. All cards are natural cards—cards that describe things studied by the natural and social sciences. Accordingly, we would know upfront that we could not get points for drawings or sentences of things that did not fit within a scientific worldview. Yet even if we were told that all cards met this restriction, we might raise questions as to whether certain cards made it in. Would we find cards describing qualitative experiences, modals, or mathematics? A compelling theory would be able to justify the restriction while providing answers to this and other questions that might crop up on the mind and language fronts.

Ultimately, then, we seek a unified and compelling theory of language, mind, and world. And it is here that specific, vexing subjects come into play. Take, for instance, mathematics. We might ask: What does the utterance "three is prime" mean? What mental states are we in when we think that three is prime? Are we trying to represent some part of reality, the part with the number three? These questions concerning mathematical talk, thought, and reality are questions in the Philosophy of Mathematics. Philosophers working in this field ask questions *about* mathematics. They are informed by mathematicians working *within* mathematics and by the best extant theories of language, mind, and metaphysics. If successful, they are able to explain how our talk and thought about mathematics works and what it refers to (if it refers at all).

We are now in a better position to answer the question: What is metaethics? Metaethicists are to ethics what philosophers of mathematics are to mathematics. Metaethicists ask second-order questions about the language, psychology, and metaphysics of ethics. What do utterances like "adultery is impermissible" mean? What mental state are we in when we think that adultery is impermissible? Is ethical thought and talk made true, if it is apt for truth, by accurately describing some part of reality? If so, what part? In addressing these questions, the commitments that ethicists take on while doing normative ethics provide crucial data. Like philosophers of mathematics, metaethicists are thus informed by those working within the subject matter under investigation.

As this characterization suggests, locating a compelling metaethical theory is a trying task. A compelling theory should be able to fit within our best theories of language, psychology, and metaphysics while avoiding being overly revisionary to ethics itself. Metaethical theories, in other words, not only face *outside pressure* from the best going theories in philosophy of language, mind, and metaphysics, but they also face *inside pressure* from the central features concerning the presumed nature of the subject matter—i.e., what ethicists take ethics to be like. These pressures are the driving forces of metaethical inquiry.

My aim in this introduction is to make explicit the outside and inside pressures that a compelling metaethical theory needs to accommodate, and to show how these pressures motivate the main contenders. To this end, we will make two passes through the language, metaphysics, and psychology of ethics. One path toward accommodation is to mold a theory to fit the existing outside and inside pressures. Our first pass will thus be non-revisionary. But, as we shall see, the pressures generated by our initial thoughts about ethics, language, metaphysics, and psychology pull in different directions. Something must give. Not all of the appearances can be saved. A second path toward accommodation is redirecting the pressure or showing its force to be illusory. Our second pass will thus be revisionary. We will see how one might release the pressure generated in one area to make room for the pressure created in another.

As this brief sketch of what's to come indicates, metaethical theorizing is trying in a second way. Even the best theories fail to get everything we want. After reading this anthology, you will probably have a preferred theory. But chances are, in your honest moments, you take your preferred theory to be a failure; it's simply that you think rival theories fail worse. Nevertheless, you should not be disheartened. Though metaethics is difficult, we can make progress. As you make your way through the readings, you shall see that in just the last decade significant advances in metaethics have taken place. And much work remains. Given this possibility of progress, metaethics is an exciting enterprise. Yet in order to recognize these developments and carry forward metaethical inquiry, you must first understand the pressures driving the historically dominant theories.

§1. LANGUAGE: NON-REVISIONARY

Let's begin with language. We can do a number of different things with words. We *describe*—e.g., we assert that "the man is flying a kite"—which implies we are committed to the world being a certain way. We also *express* our attitudes, as, when confronted with the prospect of kite flying, we voice our joy by shouting "Yippee!" Language plays roles beyond describing and expressing, but these will suffice to motivate our first question: What function do ethical utterances have?

Strong inside pressure pushes us in favor of thinking of ethical utterances as on par with descriptive utterances. Ethicists declare claims that their interlocutors make true and false, and everyday ethical discourse follows suit. But the most compelling evidence in favor of thinking that ethical language mimics descriptive language comes from the surface grammar and logic of our ethical talk. The grammar and logic of ethical utterances behaves exactly like run-of-the-mill descriptive utterances. To see this parallel in action, contrast the following lists:

NON-ETHICAL
- "The man is flying a kite."
- "It is not the case that the man is flying a kite."
- "If the man is flying a kite, then he's going to miss lunch."
- "My friend thinks that the man is flying a kite."
- "I wonder whether the man is flying a kite."

ETHICAL
- "Adultery is impermissible."
- "It is not the case that adultery is impermissible."
- "If adultery is impermissible, then tempting someone to commit adultery is impermissible."
- "My friend thinks that adultery is impermissible."
- "I wonder whether adultery is impermissible."

The utterances on the ethical list above are perfectly ordinary. You may have even said such things. And taken as attempting to describe ethical reality—as functioning like the utterances on the non-ethical list—it is easy to account for the various forms these utterances take. However, if we try to create elliptical constructions, treating the items on the ethical list as non-descriptive expressions, we run into problems. If we took someone who says "adultery is impermissible" to be expressing a negative attitude toward adultery, how would we create a parallel construction for "I wonder whether adultery is impermissible"? In making such an utterance, we are not, or so it seems, expressing any attitude, negative or positive, toward adultery whatsoever. Hence there is strong inside pressure for holding that ethical utterances mirror descriptions.

We can call the view that takes ethical utterances to describe or represent reality *Descriptivism*. The central commitment of Descriptivism is that ethical utterances attempt to be about the way the world is ethically. And, we might hasten to add, if the description is accurate, our utterances are true. If not, they are false.

Descriptivism is a broad doctrine. Even if Descriptivism is accepted, questions concerning ethical language remain. The most significant among these remaining questions concerns the meaning, or semantics, of ethical terms. Of particular importance is whether or not ethical terms have the same meaning as natural terms—roughly, those terms we use to describe the world studied by the natural and social sciences. The view that answers Yes, we might call *Descriptive Naturalism*. The view that answers No, we might call *Descriptive Non-Naturalism*, which holds that ethical terms are terms of their own kind—they do not have the same meaning as any non-ethical terms. In deciding between the two, strong outside pressure pushes us toward Descriptive Non-Naturalism.

A prominent principle in semantics holds that the meaning of a complex utterance is determined by its structure and the meanings of its component terms. This principle, known as *compositionality*, offers a powerful explanation for our ability to understand utterances that we have never heard before. To see that you have this ability, imagine someone you know who talks very, very slowly. Suppose this slow-talker is telling you a story, which begins "The other day . . . I went to the cafeteria and ate . . ." Imagine this pause goes on for quite some time. One interesting thing to note, during this pause, is that your slow-talking acquaintance could tell you something unexpected, could have eaten something so bizarre, that the utterance is one you've never heard before. Nonetheless, as long as your acquaintance uses words you already know, you would understand the meaning of what was said. For instance, the story might end with your acquaintance eating three crackers folded into origami cranes. Now, the utterance "The other day I went to the cafeteria and ate three crackers folded into origami cranes" is probably completely novel to you. But you understand its meaning. Compositionality delivers a neat explanation of this phenomenon.

Compositionality also delivers a test for identifying whether two terms have the same meaning. Begin with two identical utterances. Next, replace one term in one of the utterances with a new term. If the two utterances differ in meaning, then, since the utterances have the same structure, the substituted term cannot mean the same as the original term.

By applying this test, we can determine whether an ethical term means the same thing as a natural term. Suppose we want to know if "right" means the same thing as the naturalistically acceptable "pleasure maximizing." To test for synonymy, we can start with the question:

"Is every right action one that is right?"

Any competent speaker of English, merely by understanding the terms involved, knows the answer to this question. Nonetheless, the utterance is meaningful. It just happens that, since the answer is trivially true, the question is *closed*. Continuing our test, we could then ask:

"Is every right action one that is pleasure maximizing?"

This second question is identical to the first except for the substitution of "pleasure maximizing" for "right." However, this second question is, to competent speakers of English, *open*. Even though we fully understand the meaning of the question, we might wonder whether every right action is one that is pleasure maximizing. This difference between the two questions—that one is open while the other closed—implies that their meanings are different. Accordingly, by compositionality, "right" and "pleasure maximizing" are non-synonymous.

Although the case of "right" and "pleasure maximizing" is only one instance where an ethical term does not mean the same as a natural term, the argument can be extended. For any proposed synonymy between an ethical term and a natural term, we can, by repeating the test provided by compositionality, show that the two terms do not have the same meaning. We are thus pushed toward Descriptive Non-Naturalism.

Our first pass over the language of ethics leaves us with the view that ethical utterances function like descriptive utterances, and that ethical terms are terms of their own kind—they do not have the same meaning as natural terms. Having arrived at Descriptive Non-Naturalism, our next questions are metaphysical: If our ethical language is descriptive and non-naturalistic, what are we attempting to accurately describe? To what do our ethical terms refer?

§2. METAPHYSICS: NON-REVISIONARY

If the language of ethics presents strong pressure toward Descriptive Non-Naturalism, we might think that our metaphysics should follow suit. Perhaps we should hold that what our ethical language is about is not part of the world as described by the natural and social sciences but, instead, a distinctively ethical realm. That is, perhaps we should be *Metaphysical Non-Naturalists*.

One tempting idea that could get us from Descriptive Non-Naturalism to Metaphysical Non-Naturalism is that non-synonymous terms cannot have the same referent. This idea would give us a semantic test for property identity: If two predicate terms have different meanings, they refer to different properties. For instance, since, as we saw, "right" and "pleasure maximizing" have different meanings, they have different referents. And combined with the argument from compositionality, this tempting idea yields Metaphysical Non-Naturalism. When our ethical utterances are true, what makes them true is accurately describing a part of reality that is distinctively ethical, and not the empirically discoverable features of the natural world.

Still, Metaphysical Non-Naturalism is met by strong external pressure. Naturalism is the dominant position in metaphysics. *Metaphysical Naturalism* is the view that all facts (true statements) are natural facts, and that all properties (features of things) are natural properties. Metaphysical Naturalism dominates for good reason. After all, what things could exist apart from the world studied by the natural and social sciences? Where would they be? If they are causally inert and not part of the spatiotemporal world, how could we interact with them? To put it bluntly, how could we form beliefs about something that never made causal contact with our brains? These questions drive us away from Metaphysical Non-Naturalism and into the arms of Metaphysical Naturalism.

But Metaphysical Naturalism still needs to address the tempting idea that a difference in meaning entails a difference in reference. An answer, however, appears ready to hand. If we can show that two terms with different meanings refer to the same thing outside of ethics, then we can simply port over this strategy to the case of ethical terms. And the natural sciences are ripe with examples that call into question the semantic test for property identity.

Scientific discoveries often produce surprising identity claims. Take, for instance, the term "water." Pre-scientifically, the meaning of "water" was "the stuff we call water—what falls from the sky, and fills lakes and streams, and so on." And the meaning of "H_2O" was "the stuff composed of two hydrogen atoms bounded with one oxygen atom." It was thus a surprising discovery when we found out that "water" and "H_2O" both refer to the same stuff.

To see how this discovery calls into question the idea that a difference in meaning entails a difference in reference, we can return to our compositionality test. To test for synonymy, we can start with the question:

"Is water water?"

This question, like our previous first question, is closed. We can next ask:

"Is water H_2O?"

This question is open. Pre-scientifically, a competent speaker of English could understand the meaning of the term "water" and understand the meaning of the term "H_2O" but genuinely ask whether water is H_2O. Indeed, that is precisely the question scientists asked when they investigated the chemical composition of water. Accordingly, since these questions have different meanings, by compositionality the term "water" does not mean the same thing as the term "H_2O." Now, if we combine this result with the idea that a difference in meaning entails a difference in reference, we are left with the regrettable conclusion that being water is not being H_2O.

Armed with this example, we seem well equipped to block the transition from Descriptive Non-Naturalism to Metaphysical Non-Naturalism. And, given the external pressure to be naturalists generally, Metaphysical Naturalism beckons. Yet Metaphysical Non-Naturalists should not despair. It still needs to be shown that the terms involved in cases of scientific discoveries are analogous to ethical terms.

Two points count in favor of thinking that the case of ethical terms is relevantly different. First, part of what makes scientific cases compelling is that the identity is surprising. But notice, we could have recognized, pre-scientifically, that such surprises were in the offing. There is a recognizable lack of specificity in the characterization of "water" as "the stuff that falls from the sky, and fills lakes and streams, and so on," which is what sent scientists looking for what all this stuff we call "water" had in common. Second, part of the reason why the specification of H_2O is surprising is the thought that, had our world been slightly different, it might not have been. That is, we could have discovered, were our natural environment not as it is, that the referent of "water" is something else entirely. Hence, if Metaphysical Naturalists hope to use the analogy provided by surprising scientific discoveries, it needs to be shown that these features hold for ethical terms as well.

When it comes to ethical terms, however, there does not appear to be a recognizable lack of specificity. And, more importantly, it does not seem that, were our natural environment different, the referent of our ethical terms would be different. Return to the case of "water." Imagine an alternative world, identical to our own, except that the stuff discovered to be the referent of "water" was something other than H_2O. When we contrast speakers on this imagined world with speakers on our actual world, we are inclined to say that utterances with the term "water" are indexed to the world on which they are made. Speakers on both worlds could make utterances with the term "water" and still speak truly, even though the referent of "water" across worlds is different. But, if we try to imagine a parallel case for ethical terms like "right," we get a different result. We are prone to say that whatever "right" refers to, it holds across all possible worlds. As a result, once we accept that the term "right" refers to, say, pleasure maximizing on one world, we do not think that it admits of a different referent on a second world. We are thus not inclined to think that utterances with the term "right" are indexed to the world on which they are made. Whether the world is actual or possible, what "right" picks out remains fixed. If speakers on our world speak truly when they say "the acts that maximize pleasure are right," then speakers on the alternative world speak falsely when they say "it is not the case that acts that maximize pleasure are right." So it appears that cases of surprising discoveries in the natural sciences are disanalogous to cases in ethics.

Where does this leave us? The language of ethics points us in the direction of Descriptive Non-Naturalism. Yet Naturalism is the default view in metaphysics. And Metaphysical Naturalists seem to have at least the beginnings of a response to the argument from compositionality. The inside and outside pressures pull us in different directions. Luckily, we have one more area left to investigate: ethical psychology. Perhaps the pressures surrounding ethical thought can push us decisively toward one of these two positions.

§3. PSYCHOLOGY: NON-REVISIONARY

The primary question in ethical psychology is: What mental state are we in when we make an ethical judgment? If our ethical talk is descriptive, then the obvious candidate for the corresponding mental state is a belief. For when we make a descriptive utterance such as "the man is flying a kite," we are committed to the truth of the utterance. And to hold that something is true is just to have a belief that reality is a certain way. Accordingly, if we adopt Descriptivism, we should hold that the mental states we are in when making ethical judgments are beliefs. Since we call mental states that are belief-like "cognitive," we can name the view that treats ethical judgments as beliefs *Cognitivism*.

Cognitivism has a certain appeal. It gives credence to the phenomenology of making ethical decisions. Just as you feel you might be mistaken about whether the man really is flying a kite, it feels like you could be making a mistake when you think about what you are required to do or who you are required to be. Cognitivism makes room for this possibility.

However, because Descriptivism and Cognitivism are intimately linked, all of the views we've looked at thus far are committed to Cognitivism. The benefits of Cognitivism are shared. Whether we thought our ethical beliefs were about the natural or non-natural world, we could think that, in arriving at an ethical judgment, we might be making a mistake. So the appeal of Cognitivism does not help break the stalemate we were left with at the end of the previous section.

Fortunately, another salient question in ethical psychology remains: What is the connection between ethical judgments and motivation? Unfortunately, an investigation into this connection will not help us decide between the various Cognitivist views. In fact, investigating the link between ethical judgments and motivation reveals that inside and outside pressures unite against Cognitivism.

We can start with the inside pressure. Imagine that you and a married friend go out for a night on the town. Imagine further that a third party proposes a romantic encounter with your friend. This invitation prompts a heated debate on the permissibility of adultery. In the end, your friend judges that adultery is impermissible. Having reached this judgment, you would then be shocked if your friend, without hesitation, got up, accepted the third party's offer, and went off to commit adultery. You would think that your friend was merely paying lip service to the verdict that adultery is impermissible. Why? Because when people change their mind about what they are required to do, their actions tend to follow suit. And such changes do not seem to be accidental. To be sure, if you think it would be incoherent for your friend to have made the judgment sincerely while lacking the corresponding motivation, then the connection between ethical judgments and motivation is particularly strong. It's conceptual. This view, known as *Judgment Internalism*, can be stated precisely as follows: If a person makes an ethical judgment that acting in some way is required, then it is conceptually necessary that the person is (somewhat) motivated to act in conformity with this judgment.

We can next turn to the outside pressure. Return to the game I mentioned playing in college. The drawer's role was to make a picture of the world. The drawer serves as a good analogy for what our minds do when forming beliefs. They attempt to make a picture of reality, and are successful if this picture is accurate. In forming beliefs, we try to get our minds to conform to the world, and when we achieve this fit, our beliefs are true. Belief-like mental states, that is, have *mind-to-world* direction of fit. But this is only part of what our minds do.

To see what else our minds do, imagine a reversed version of the game. We could, to get things going, substitute a director for the guesser. On cards, directors write sentences of scenes they desire to be acted out. A card is then handed to the drawer, who converts it to a picture for the actor, who in turn tries to get the charade to match the card. If the actor's charade matches the sentence written on the card, the team gets a point. On this reversed model of the game, the picture is not of the world as it currently is. Rather, the picture depicts the way the drawer desires it to be. Another function our minds perform is like the drawer on this reversed model of the game. Our desire-like mental states do not try to make an accurate map of the world. Instead, they present how we want the world to be. When we desire, for instance, that the man fly a kite, we take the world to be a certain way—devoid of the man flying a kite—and we want it to be different. We want it to be a world with the man flying a kite. When we have a desire, we try to get the world to conform to our minds, and we are successful—our desires are satisfied—when we get the world to so conform. Desire-like mental states, in other words, have *world-to-mind* direction of fit.

Our minds can thus perform at least two functions. We have mental states—e.g., beliefs—with mind-to-world direction of fit that, if accurate, are true. And we have mental states—e.g., desires—with world-to-mind direction of fit that, because they are not trying to accurately represent the world, are not apt for truth. These two functions are very different. So different that it is hard to imagine how a mental state could have both directions of fit. What mental state do we have that both tries to conform to the world and tries to get the world to conform to it? It thus seems safe to conclude that beliefs cannot also be desires, and that desires cannot be beliefs.

We are now in a position to see how Judgment Internalism can be marshaled against Cognitivism. Cognitivism holds that our ethical judgments are beliefs. So, according to Cognitivism, when we make an ethical judgment, the mental state involved has mind-to-world direction of fit. Judgment Internalism, however, forges a conceptual link between ethical judgments and motivation. But could a belief, by itself, be inherently motivating? Think on a belief you probably have: The sky is blue. Does this belief alone motivate you to action? Presumably not. If, perchance, you have a desire to look upon something blue, then, paired with this belief, you would be motivated to go look at the sky. But if you lack this desire, then your belief that the sky is blue does not motivate you in the slightest. This example suggests that mental states, like beliefs, with mind-to-world direction of fit, are motivationally inert. Not so for mental states, like desires, with world-to-mind direction of fit.

Putting the forgoing line of thought together, we can say, via Judgment Internalism, that ethical judgments necessarily motivate. But beliefs, by themselves, do not necessarily motivate. Hence, ethical judgments are not beliefs. They are instead desire-like mental states with world-to-mind direction of fit. Since such mental states do not have to do with beliefs, the view this argument supports we can call *Non-Cognitivism.*

At the end of our first pass through the language, metaphysics, and psychology of ethics, the inside and outside pressures do not drive us toward a single view. Instead, the language of ethics pulls us toward Descriptive Non-Naturalism. The metaphysics of ethics pulls us towards Metaphysical Naturalism. And the psychology of ethics pulls us toward Non-Cognitivism. We should thus take a second look to see if we can't resolve, by revisionary means, the tension generated by these conflicting pressures.

§4. LANGUAGE: REVISIONARY

Since we ended the previous section with an argument for Non-Cognitivism, the place to begin is with its linguistic counterpart: *Non-Descriptivism.* According to Non-Descriptivism, our ethical utterances do not attempt to represent ethical reality. Instead, following the most popular version of Non-Descriptivism, ethical utterances are expressions of the speaker's non-cognitive attitudes. Let's call this species of the theory *Non-Descriptive Expressivism.*

In understanding Non-Descriptive Expressivism, it is crucial to recognize a subtle shift that takes place in our theory of semantics. In the versions of Descriptivism we have looked at thus far, we took it for granted that it's the business of a theory of meaning to assign truth conditions to our utterances. That is, we explained the meaning of a given utterance in terms of what it takes for the utterance to be true. (Recall our discussion of a term picking out a property.) So we took it for granted that to be in the business of meaning is to be in the business of identifying the conditions requisite for the meaning of a term to align with its extension—i.e., the set of things to which the term applies (or extends). We looked, for example, at what it takes for "right" to pick out all acts that are right. But in accepting Non-Descriptivism, we've gotten out of the business of ethical truths altogether. Accordingly, we need to rethink the business of semantics. Non-Descriptive Expressivism's radical idea is to take each term and map it on to a mental state. When your friend says "adultery is impermissible," what is meant does not come from what it takes for the utterance to be true—that adultery has the property of being impermissible—but from the mental state associated with *thinking* that adultery is impermissible.

One attractive feature of this radical idea is that it turns out not to be so radical after all. Given the connection between our thought and talk, treating the meaning of the utterance "the man is flying a kite" as determined by what it is to think that the man is flying a kite is not a serious departure from treating its meaning as determined by what it is for the utterance to be true. Thus holding that utterances mean what they do in virtue of the mental states they express is not terribly revisionary.

This last example—a descriptive utterance—highlights another attractive feature of the semantics adopted by Non-Descriptive Expressivism. Though, on this theory, meaning is no longer beholden to the extension of terms, we can still capture the various functions of our utterances while treating all utterances as expressions. To do so, we let the associated mental state do the work of distinguishing the nature of the utterance. We associate utterances that function like descriptions with mental states that have mind-to-world direction of fit, and associate utterances that do not function like descriptions—as when we voice certain positive or negative attitudes—with mental states that have world-to-mind direction of fit. Expressivism can thus give us an entirely unified account of semantics. Indeed, we could give an expressivist reading to an entire language by mapping each utterance to the mental state it expresses.

We are now able to see how Non-Descriptive Expressivism can accommodate the inside and outside pressures from ethical psychology and metaphysics. Concerning psychology, thinking of ethical utterances as expressions of mental states with world-to-mind direction of fit gives a nice explanation of Judgment Internalism. For if ethical utterances express motivationally efficacious attitudes, we ensure a conceptual connection between ethical judgments and motivation. Furthermore, thought of in this way, we no longer face the daunting challenge of fitting ethics in a naturalistic worldview. The Non-Descriptive Expressivist denies that ethical judgments involve being in a cognitive state. Accordingly, there is nothing—neither facts nor properties—that our ethical thought and talk are about. The absence of ethical reality is perfectly compatible with Metaphysical Naturalism. Nothing can't conflict with anything.

Yet, Non-Descriptive Expressivism faces the inside pressure from the language of ethics that initially pushed us toward Descriptivism. In everyday discourse, we make a number of utterances that are easily handled as descriptions but hard to square with expressions of a speaker's non-cognitive attitudes. There exists a recipe for generating these problems. Start with a non-complex utterance—for example, "adultery is impermissible." Then, ask the Non-Descriptive Expressivist for an account of its meaning. As a toy answer, suppose that the utterance expresses the speaker's desire that no adulteries take place. We then turn to a complex utterance with the first utterance embedded within it—for instance, "If adultery is impermissible, then tempting someone to commit adultery is impermissible." We next ask the Non-Descriptive Expressivist for an account of the meaning of this complex utterance. "Adultery is impermissible" is mentioned in the antecedent of the conditional, but it does not seem that a speaker uttering this conditional is expressing a desire that no adulteries take place. So it seems that "adultery is impermissible" has a different meaning once it gets embedded.

This change in meaning yields an unintuitive result. It entails that if a speaker were to give the following argument, it would be invalid.

1. Adultery is impermissible.
2. If adultery is impermissible, then tempting someone to commit adultery is impermissible.
3. Hence, tempting someone to commit adultery is impermissible.

Insofar as Non-Descriptive Expressivism maintains that meaning changes in and out of embedded contexts, the conclusion of this argument does not follow. The meaning of "adultery is impermissible" in premise (1) is not the same as "adultery is impermissible" in premise (2). The argument commits the fallacy of equivocation. Premise (1) expresses the speaker's desire that no adulteries take place. Premise (2) does not. The reasoning of the speaker, nevertheless, looks impeccable. Non-Descriptive Expressivists thus owe us an explanation as to why such an argument is invalid, or they need to figure out how to map the meaning of what is expressed by premise (1) so that it holds for premise (2). The former is unpromising. So Non-Descriptive Expressivists need to show that their semantics can work just as well as a truth-conditional theory of meaning in and out of embedded contexts.

Thus far, we've noted that, according to Non-Descriptive Expressivism, we link utterances to mental states. But, up to this point, we've said little concerning the nature of the mental state associated with ethical utterances. Nailing down the precise content of ethical utterances might proffer a solution. Think first about a non-ethical example. What is the content of the utterance "the man is flying a kite"? The answer for the expressivist looks relatively clear. The content of the utterance "the man is flying a kite" is the content of the belief that the man is flying a kite. Things are not so clear, however, when it comes to "adultery is impermissible." When we make such an ethical utterance, what precise attitude are we expressing?

In answering this question, the Non-Descriptive Expressivists confront two problems. To illustrate these problems, return to the toy mental state we used above: desiring. Desires are untenable because they are going to massively overgenerate. We are going to get too many expressions counting as ethical expressions. We express our desires all the time in cases where no ethical utterances are in play. Children make this problem particularly vivid. Long before we are inclined to attribute ethical thought or talk to children, they express their desires. A tenable account of the mental state associated with ethical utterances thus needs to be sufficiently refined to exclude the expressions made by young children from counting as ethical. We might call this the *vertical* refinement problem, since it arises in cases where the purported attitude is possessed by the ethically underdeveloped. The second problem stems from the wide variety of ethical utterances that need to be captured: "adultery is permissible," "adultery is optional," "adultery is required," "adultery is supererogatory," "adultery is good," and so forth. If we use a blanket attitude, like desiring, we'll lack the resources to capture the different meanings these utterances have. The associated mental states must be sufficiently refined, across diverse utterances, to capture the rich diversity of ethical utterances we make. We might call this the *horizontal* refinement problem, since it arises in cases where the purported attitude is incapable of individuating the variety of expressions we find in ethical discourse.

In determining what attitude we are expressing when making ethical utterances, Non-Descriptive Expressivism thus faces three problems: it needs to keep meaning fixed in and out of embedded contexts, it needs to solve the vertical refinement problem, and it needs to solve the horizontal refinement problem. Though not insurmountable, these three worries might give us pause. Perhaps we jumped too quickly from Judgment Internalism to Non-Cognitivism. Maybe we can accommodate the apparent conceptual connection between judgment and motivation while still accepting Cognitivism.

§5. METAPHYSICS: REVISIONARY

On our previous pass through Descriptivism and Cognitivism, we took our ethical thought and talk to be about the world, broadly construed. Moreover, in the same way that we tend to think that, in the non-ethical case, whether or not the man is flying a kite is independent of us, we assumed our descriptions and beliefs attempt to capture an ethical reality independent of us. But this assumption of subject independence got us in trouble when confronted with the pressure generated by Judgment Internalism. For just as our thoughts about the external world fail to be inherently motivating, our thoughts about ethical reality, with the assumption of subject independence in place, fail to motivate. But what if this assumption were dropped? We could avoid the move to Non-Cognitivism and Non-Descriptivism, while accommodating Judgment Internalism, by holding that ethical reality does not stand apart from us—as something we reflect—but instead depends on our motivating attitudes. Let's call accounts that make this move *Subject-Dependent Theories*.

Before moving on, it's worth heading off a potential misunderstanding. It's tempting to think that Non-Descriptive Expressivism, given that it uses the mental to map meaning, is a Subject-Dependent Theory. You can disabuse yourself of this seductive thought by returning to the distinction between *describing* and *expressing*. Imagine you are chatting again with your slow-talking acquaintance. As the conversation drags on, at a certain point, you yawn. The mental state associated with your yawning is boredom. The yawn expresses this boredom. Alternatively, if you said, "I am bored," you would be describing what mental state you are in. Your yawn expresses what "I am bored" describes. Of course, yawning is not apt for truth. Nor is the associated mental state—that is, your attitude toward what is being said. Boredom is not truth-apt. But the description that you are bored is; and it is true, if you are actually bored. As its name suggests, Non-Descriptive Expressivism maintains that all ethical utterances are expressions, not descriptions, of non-cognitive mental states. Subject-Dependent Theories, by contrast, maintain that ethical utterances are descriptions.

Despite holding that ethical utterances are descriptions, certain Subject-Dependent Theories are well suited to accommodate Judgment Internalism. These theories hold that ethical facts depend on psychological features with world-to-mind direction of fit. On a simple version of this theory, an agent's actual desires determine the ethical facts. Ethical facts simply are facts about what the agent desires. This Subject-Dependent Theory we can call *Simple Subjectivism*. According to Simple Subjectivism, when you say or judge that "adultery is impermissible," what you mean is "I desire that no adulteries take place." Ethical judgments are cognitive—they are beliefs about an agent's desires—and are true when the agent in fact has the relevant desires.

Given this characterization, Simple Subjectivism entails that true ethical judgments are motivationally efficacious. If ethical facts simply are facts about the agent's desires, and if desires are motivationally efficacious, then true judgments will be conceptually tied to motivation. In addition to accommodating Judgment Internalism, Simple Subjectivism fits comfortably into a naturalistic worldview. Human beings, and our psychologies, are part of the world studied by the natural and social sciences.

Yet Simple Subjectivism also comes with a number of vices. Though Cognitivist, the theory gives up an important benefit of Cognitivism. Previously, we noted that Cognitivism accommodates the possibility of error. Intuitively, when making an ethical decision, we think we could be making a mistake. Simple Subjectivism gives up this possibility. For in order to establish the link between facts about our motivating attitudes and ethical judgments, we need to assume that agents are transparent to themselves. That is, we need to assume that agents always know what they desire. If people were not so transparent, then we might make ethical judgments—form beliefs about our desires—but fail to notice that our desires actually cut in the opposite direction. Once transparency is assumed, however, we need only search our own minds when it comes to making ethical decisions. We could know the thing to do by introspection alone. Thus, Simple Subjectivism clashes with the inside pressure generated by the phenomenology of our ethical decision-making.

But the theory has an even more damning vice. Simple Subjectivism holds ethical facts hostage to people's actual desires. And people's actual psychologies can be, to put it mildly, disturbing. If an agent's desires determine what it is for something to be ethically required, we are going to get, with depressing regularity, the unacceptable result that acts promoting the object of very disturbing desires are required. To avoid these unacceptable results, we need a more sophisticated Subject-Dependent Theory.

To block the problem posed by those with disturbing desires, we could impose certain idealizations on the agents whose desires we look to in determining the ethical facts. Some disturbing desires are a product of misinformation. In response, we might build a clause that agents must be apprised of all relevant non-ethical facts. Some disturbing desires are a product of improper reasoning. Accordingly, we might demand that agents be perfectly rational. We could thus develop a sophisticated Subject-Dependent Theory along these lines by holding that fully informed and rational agents' desires determine the ethical facts. We can call this view *Sophisticated Subjectivism*.

One immediate benefit of Sophisticated Subjectivism is that, insofar as it makes ethical facts depend on idealized agents, we cannot know what to do by introspection alone. The ethical facts are not determined by *your* present desires (assuming you are not fully informed and rational). By moving away from your actual desires, we get a gap between you and the ethical facts. The desires of a fully informed and procedurally rational agent are not transparent to you. Your ethical judgments can be mistaken. The upside this brings is that Sophisticated Subjectivism does not clash with the phenomenology of making ethical decisions.

The downside is that the theory introduces a gap between ethical judgments and motivation. Simple Subjectivism accommodates Judgment Internalism by holding that ethical judgments are judgments about our desires, and then holding that our desires are transparent to us. In other words, we guarantee a convergence between the ethical facts, judgments, and motivation by holding that the ethical facts are determined by our actual desires, and that our beliefs about our desires are always, given transparency, accurate. Our actual desires are motivationally efficacious, so this gives us a tidy explanation of Judgment Internalism. But once we turn to Sophisticated Subjectivism, things get messy. What secures the conceptual connection between our judgments concerning the desires of the fully informed and procedurally rational and our motivation to act in accordance with such judgments? To be sure, why should we care about these idealized agents at all? Sophisticated Subjectivists need to find a way to ensure the conceptual link between ethical judgments about ideal agents and the motivations of actual agents in the real world. Otherwise, they forfeit Judgment Internalism.

Subject-Dependent Theorists have many resources at their disposal to ensure this conceptual link: other ways of idealizing, counterfactuals, constitutive features of agency, and so on. But at this point, it should be clear that the twin goals of trying to accommodate Judgment Internalism and trying to avoid unacceptable results in normative ethics are difficult to mutually satisfy. Judgment Internalism puts pressure on the Subject-Dependent Theorist to keep the features determining the ethical facts close to the agent's psychology, yet keeping them too close to the psychologies of agents and their idiosyncratic constitutions will make unacceptable actions permissible. Maybe this tightrope cannot be walked. Perhaps these pressures are irreconcilable.

We've let the pressure of Judgment Internalism drive the discussion for the last two sections. Given the problems encountered, maybe it's time to rethink our ethical psychology.

§6. PSYCHOLOGY: REVISIONARY

In support of Judgment Internalism, we cited the fact that when people arrive at ethical judgments, their actions tend to follow suit. A conceptual connection between judgment and motivation would guarantee this connection. But perhaps it was a mistake to think the connection is this strong. A conceptual necessity makes it impossible for one to make an ethical judgment without the motivation to act accordingly.

We can call Judgment Internalism into question by showing that it is possible for someone to make an ethical judgment without the accompanying motivation. Consider, for example, people who suffer from bouts of depression so extreme that when it hits, they do not care about anything at all—they have no mental states with world-to-mind direction of fit. Prior to their depression, we can imagine these people make a variety of ethical judgments and are motivated accordingly. But then depression strikes, and they lose all motivation. Finally, the depression passes, and their motivational capacities return. What Judgment Internalism says about these people is that, initially, they made bona fide ethical judgments, then they lost them, and finally, they regained them. This losing and regaining of ethical judgments might strike you as puzzling. Isn't it possible that, even in their darkest hour, these depressed people could retain their ethical judgments?

If we answer this question affirmatively, then we should take the link between ethical judgments and motivation to be psychological rather than conceptual. On this view, known as *Judgment Externalism*, the tie between ethical judgment and motivation is contingent. Non-depressed people have, while depressed people lack, an aspect of their psychology that connects judgments to motivation. Given that the connection is psychological, we could also say that depressed people do not lose and regain their ethical judgments. They instead lose and regain the aspect of their psychology that links ethical judgment and motivation.

To assess the merits of Judgment Externalism, we need to clarify the precise aspect of our psychology that establishes the link between ethical judgment and motivation. To clarify this psychological link, it will help to consider other apparent exceptions to Judgment Internalism besides the depressed. Another possible exception are amoralists, those who, like psychopaths, make ethical judgments yet have no motivation whatsoever to act in conformity with them. Another possible exception are anti-moralists, those who, like the downright evil, make ethical judgments and are motivated to do precisely the opposite. So, in clarifying Judgment Externalism, we can ask: What do the depressed, amoralists, and anti-moralists lack that everyday people possess?

The answer needs to involve some aspect of our psychology that ensures motivation. Let us thus say, as a first approximation, that what all of these people lack is a desire. The depressed lack all desires, so they are little help in specifying further. The amoralists and the anti-moralists, however, lack a specific desire: the desire to be ethical. The amoralist is indifferent to ethics. The anti-moralist has a desire not to be ethical. The desire to be ethical also fits nicely with the idea that the aspect of our psychology we are looking for is something that everyday people possess. Everyday people tend to care (at least somewhat) about being ethical. One plausible way of filling out the account of Judgment Externalism, then, is to maintain that ethical judgments combine with a standing desire to be ethical and thereby motivate agents to action.

Judgment Externalism sits well with Descriptivism and Cognitivism. Yet inside pressure forces us to reconsider its merits. Think about the kind of person who desires to do what ethics demands *whatever that is*. Imagine your spouse said, "Last night I didn't commit adultery, because I desire to do what ethics tells me to do (whatever that turns out to be). Fortunately for you, one of the things that ethics tells me is that adultery is impermissible." You probably would not be filled with glowing admiration for your spouse. Your spouse's ultimate desire is being ethical; you merely play an incidental, derivative role in your spouse's fidelity. As this story illustrates, a standing desire to be ethical can reliably motivate people to act in accordance with their judgments, but only at the cost of turning people into fetishizers of ethics.

To be a viable alternative to Judgment Internalism, Judgment Externalists must explain why ethical fetishism is unproblematic, or identify a different aspect of our psychology that can ensure the regular connection between ethical judgment and motivation. A formidable task, either way.

§7. OVERVIEW AND OMISSIONS

We've now taken two passes through the language, metaphysics, and psychology of ethics. We covered the central positions one might take in each of these areas. These positions form the building blocks of metaethics. By conjoining these blocks in various ways, we can generate different theories. In the middle column of the diagram below, you will find what we might call standard package theories. Once one block of the theory is taken on board, the rest of the blocks of the theory fall in place. In the left column, you will find the inside and outside pressures driving us toward the different positions; in the right column, you will find the inside and outside pressures that drive us away.

The accompanying diagram should help you navigate the theories presented in this anthology. Many theories and issues in metaethics, however, have not been addressed here. This should not be taken as evidence of their unimportance. They were difficult to fit in the narrative I've been telling. My aim was to introduce the driving forces of metaethics and describe how they might push us toward, or away from, the various positions we might take.

It is worth stressing, as I have throughout, that none of the standard package views accommodates all inside and outside pressures. This inability to get all that we want might invite a pessimistic thought. Thus far, we've optimistically assumed that the inside and outside pressures can somehow be reconciled. That is, we have assumed that the presumed nature of ethics can be reconciled with the best going theories in language, metaphysics, and psychology. Yet we've now seen the difficulty of accommodating the various pressures. Perhaps what these conflicting forces show is that ethics rests on a set of mistaken presuppositions. Maybe the presumed nature of ethics is like the presumed nature of witches: systematically in error. Such a conclusion might strike you as alarming. But to avoid an *Error Theory*, it needs to be shown that the pressures driving metaethics can be tamed.

In response to this pessimistic thought, we can note that one of the most exciting trends in recent theorizing is the creative and unexpected ways we might combine the building blocks of metaethics. To cite one example, a growing number of theorists are attracted to *Hybrid-Expressivist Theories*, which take ethical utterances to express both cognitive and non-cognitive mental states. Perhaps such a hybrid theory can reconcile the seemingly conflicting pressures. Maybe not. We'll need to see the details.

We can end by returning to a point mentioned at the outset: Metaethics is a trying enterprise. But it is an enterprise well worth engaging. After all, what could be more valuable than figuring out the nature of value? What could be more important to do than figuring out the nature of the thing to do?

Here, then, is to taming the pressures!

Pressure Toward	Standard Package View	Pressure Against
Inside Grammar and logic of ethical talk is descriptive and subject independent. *Outside* Compositionality test for sameness of meaning. Semantic test for property identity. *Inside* Phenomenology of ethical decision-making.	**NON-NATURALISTIC REALISM** Language: Descriptivism Metaphysics: Non-Naturalism 　　　　　Subject Independence Psychology: Cognitivism 　　　　　Judgment Externalism	*Outside* All that exists is what is studied by the natural and social sciences—the empirically discoverable world. *Inside* The regular connection between ethical judgment and motivation.
Inside Grammar and logic of ethical talk is descriptive and subject independent. *Outside* All that exists is what is studied by the natural and social sciences—the empirically discoverable world. *Inside* Phenomenology of ethical decision-making.	**SUBJECT-INDEPENDENT NATURALISTIC REALISM** Language: Descriptivism Metaphysics: Naturalism 　　　　　Subject Independence Psychology: Cognitivism 　　　　　Judgment Externalism	*Outside* Compositionality test for sameness of meaning. Semantic test for property identity. *Inside* The regular connection between ethical judgment and motivation.
Outside All that exists is what is studied by the natural and social sciences—the empirically discoverable world. *Inside* The regular connection between ethical judgment and motivation.	**EXPRESSIVISM** Language: Non-Descriptivism Metaphysics: No ethical facts or 　　　　　properties 　　　　　Compatible with Naturalism Psychology: Non-Cognitivism 　　　　　Judgment Internalism	*Inside* Grammar and logic of ethical talk is descriptive and subject independent. *Outside* Keeping meaning fixed across embedded and unembedded contexts.
Outside All that exists is what is studied by the natural and social sciences—the empirically discoverable world. *Inside* The regular connection between ethical judgment and motivation.	**SUBJECT-DEPENDENT NATURALISTIC REALISM** Language: Descriptivism Metaphysics: Naturalism 　　　　　Subject Dependence Psychology: Cognitivism 　　　　　Judgment Internalism	*Inside* Grammar and logic of ethical talk is descriptive and subject independent. *Inside* Holding deontic verdicts in normative ethics hostage to our psychology. *Inside* Phenomenology of ethical decision-making.

Part II

HISTORICAL SOURCES

The Republic

Plato

Plato (c. 428–347 BCE), the famed Athenian philosopher, wrote a series of dialogues, most of which feature his teacher Socrates (469–399 BCE), who himself wrote nothing but in conversation was able to befuddle the most powerful minds of his day. *The Republic*, regarded by most as Plato's greatest work, presents a unified view of central issues in virtually every area of philosophy. Plato's central concern, however, is the relationship between justice and happiness. Acting morally often appears to conflict with pursuing our own interests. So why be moral? This question is posed to Socrates by Glaucon, Plato's brother and a representative of the Athenian aristocracy. Glaucon draws a distinction between intrinsic goods, such as pleasure, which we value for their own sake, and instrumental goods, such as exercise, which we value for their consequences. Glaucon asks Socrates to consider cases where none of the usual benefits accompanies being moral. Suppose, for example, those who act justly appear as if they were unjust and those who act unjustly appear as if they were just. Under those circumstances, would acting justly be the wisest course?

Our excerpt ends with one of the most famous passages in the history of philosophy, the parable of the cave. Socrates compares the good to the sun, shedding light on our lives. Unlike the sun, however, the good is not part of the spatiotemporal world but exists in the world of forms: invisible, immutable, and intelligible.

BOOK II

Glaucon, with that eminent courage which he displays on all occasions, . . . began thus: Socrates, do you wish really to convince us that it is on every account better to be just than to be unjust, or only to seem to have convinced us?

If it were up to me, I replied, I should prefer convincing you really.

Then, he proceeded, you are not doing what you wish. Let me ask you, Is there, in your opinion, a class of good things of such a kind that we are glad to possess them, not because we desire their consequences, but simply welcoming them for their own sake? Take, for example, the feelings of enjoyment and all those pleasures that are harmless, and that are followed by no consequences, beyond simple enjoyment in their possession.

Yes, I certainly think there is a class of this description.

Well, is there another class, do you think, of those which we value, both for their own sake and

From Plato, *The Republic,* trans. John Llewelyn Davies and David James Vaughan, rev. by Andrea Tschemplik (Oxford: Rowman & Littlefield Publishers, 2005). Reprinted with permission from the publisher.

for their results? Such as intelligence, and sight, and health—all of which we surely welcome on both accounts.

Yes.

And do you further recognize a third class of good things, which would include gymnastics training, and submission to medical treatment in illness, as well as the practice of medicine, and all other means of making money? Things like these we should describe as irksome, and yet beneficial to us; and while we should reject them viewed simply in themselves, we accept them for the sake of the rewards, and of the other consequences which result d   from them.

Yes, undoubtedly there is such a third class also; but what then?

In which of these classes do you place justice?

358   I should say in the highest—that is, among the good things which will be valued by one who is in the pursuit of true happiness, alike for their own sake and for their consequences.

Then your opinion is not that of the many, by whom justice is ranked in the irksome class, as a thing which in itself, and for its own sake, is disagreeable and repulsive, but which it is well to practice for the advantages to be had from it, with an eye to rewards and to a good name.

I know it is so . . .

b   Listen to my proposal then, and tell me whether you agree to it. . . . I am not satisfied as yet with the exposition that has been given of justice and injus-

c   tice; for I long to be told what they respectively are, and what force they exert, taken simply by themselves, when residing in the soul, dismissing the consideration of their rewards and other consequences. This shall be my plan then, if you do not object. I will . . . first state the common view respecting what kind of thing justice is and how it came to be; in the second place, I will maintain that all who practice it do so against their will, because it is indispensable, not because it is a good thing; and thirdly, that they act reasonably in so doing, because the life of the unjust man is, as men say, far better than that of the just. Not that I think so myself, Socrates; only my ears are ringing so with what I d   hear . . . that I am puzzled. Now I have never heard

the argument for the superiority of justice over injustice maintained to my satisfaction; for I should like to hear it praised, considered simply in itself; and from you if from anyone, I should expect such a treatment of the subject. Therefore I will speak as forcibly as I can in praise of an unjust life, and I shall thus display the manner in which I wish to hear you afterwards blame injustice and praise justice. See whether you approve of my plan.

Indeed I do, for on what other subject could a sensible man like better to talk and to hear others talk, again and again?

Most beautifully spoken! So now listen to me   e while I speak on my first theme, what kind of thing justice is and how it came to be.

To commit injustice is, they say, in its nature, a good thing, and to suffer it a bad thing; but the bad of suffering injustice exceeds the good of doing injustice; and so, after the two-fold experience of both   359 doing and suffering injustice, those who cannot avoid the latter and choose the former find it expedient to make a contract of neither doing nor suffering injustice. Hence arose legislation and contracts between man and man, and hence it became the custom to call that which the law enjoined just, as well as lawful. Such, they tell us, is justice, and so it came into being; and it stands midway between that which is best, to commit injustice with impunity, and that which is worst, to suffer injustice without any power of retaliating. And being a mean between these two extremes, the just is cared for, not as good in itself, but is honored because of the inability to commit   b injustice; for they say that one who had it in his power to be unjust, and who deserved the name of a man, would never be so weak as to contract with anyone neither to commit injustice nor to suffer it. Such is the current account, Socrates, of the nature of justice, and of the circumstances in which it originated.

Even those men who practice justice do so unwillingly, because they lack the power to violate it, will be most readily perceived, if we use the following reasoning. Let us give full liberty to the just man   c and to the unjust alike, to do whatever they please, and then let us follow them, and see whither the inclination of each will lead him. In that case we shall surprise the just man in the act of traveling in the same direction as the unjust, owing to that desire to gain more, the gratification of which every creature naturally pursues as a good, only that it is forced out of its path by law, and constrained to respect the principle of equality. That full liberty of action would, perhaps, be most effectively realized if they were invested with a power which they say was in old times possessed by the ancestor of Gyges the

d   Lydian. He was a shepherd, so the story runs, in the service of the reigning sovereign of Lydia, when one day a violent storm of rain fell, the ground was rent asunder by an earthquake, and a yawning gulf appeared on the spot where he was feeding his flocks. Seeing what had happened, and wondering at it, he went down into the gulf, and among other marvelous objects he saw, as the legend relates, a hollow bronze horse, with windows in its sides, through which he looked, and beheld in the interior a corpse, apparently of superhuman size; from which he took the only thing remaining, a golden ring on the hand, and

e   therewith made his way out. Now when the usual meeting of the shepherds occurred, for the purpose of sending to the king their monthly report of the state of his flocks, this shepherd came with the rest, wearing the ring. And, as he was seated with the company, he happened to turn the hoop of the ring

360   round towards himself, until it came to the inside of his hand. Whereupon he became invisible to his neighbors, who were talking about him as if he were gone away. While he was marveling at this, he again began playing with the ring, and turned the hoop to the outside, upon which he became once more visible. Having noticed this effect, he made experiments with the ring, to see whether it possessed this power. And so it was, that when he turned the hoop inwards he became invisible, and when he turned it outwards he was again visible. After this discovery, he immediately contrived to be appointed one of the messengers to carry the report to the king; and upon his arrival he seduced the queen, and conspiring with

b   her, slew the king, and took possession of the throne.

If then there were two such rings in existence, and if the just and the unjust man were each to put on one, it is to be thought that no one would be so steeled against temptation as to abide in the practice

of justice, and resolutely to abstain from touching the property of his neighbors, when he had it in his power to help himself without fear to anything he pleased in the market, or to go into private houses and have intercourse with whom he would, or to kill and release from prison according to his own plea-   c sure, and in everything else to act among men with the power of a god. And in thus following out his desires the just man will be doing precisely what the unjust man would do; and so they would both be pursuing the same path. Surely this will be allowed to be strong evidence that none are just willingly, but only by compulsion, because to be just is not a good to the individual; for all violate justice whenever they imagine that there is nothing to hinder them. And they do so because everyone thinks that, in the individual case, injustice is much more profitable than justice; and they are right in so thinking, as the speaker of this speech will maintain. For if anyone having this license within his grasp were to refuse to   d do any injustice, or to touch the property of others, all who were aware of it would think him a most pitiful and irrational creature, though they would praise him before each other's faces, deceiving one another, through their fear of suffering injustice. And so much for this topic.

But in actually deciding between the lives of the   e two persons in question, we shall be enabled to arrive at a correct conclusion, by contrasting together the thoroughly just and the thoroughly unjust man, and only by so doing. Well then, how are we to contrast them? In this way. Let us take nothing away from the injustice of the unjust or from the justice of the just, but let us suppose each to be perfect in his own line of conduct. First of all then, the unjust man must act as clever craftsmen do. For a first-rate pilot or physician perceives the difference between what is possible and what is impossible in his art; and while he attempts the former, he leaves the latter   361 alone; and moreover, should he happen to make a false step, he is able to recover himself. In the same way, if we are to form a conception of a consummately unjust man, we must suppose that he makes no mistake in the prosecution of his unjust enterprises, and that he escapes detection. But if he be found out, we must look upon him as a bungler, for it is the perfection of injustice to seem just without really being so. We must therefore grant to the perfectly unjust man, without taking anything away, the most perfect injustice; and we must concede to him,

b that while committing the grossest acts of injustice he has won himself the highest reputation for justice; and that should he make a false step, he is able to recover himself, partly by a talent for speaking with effect in case he be called in question for any of his misdeeds, and partly because his courage and strength, and his command of friends and money, enable him to employ force with success, whenever force is required. Such being our unjust man, let us, in speech, place the just man by his side, a man of true simplicity and nobleness, resolved, as Aeschylus says, not to seem, but to be, good. We must certainly take away the seeming, for if he be thought to

c be a just man, he will have honors and gifts on the strength of this reputation, so that it will be uncertain whether it is for justice's sake, or for the sake of the gifts and honors, that he is what he is. Yes, we must strip him bare of everything but justice, and make his whole case the reverse of the former. Without being guilty of one unjust act, let him have the worst reputation for injustice, so that his justice may be thoroughly tested, and shown to be proof against infamy and all its consequences; and let him go on until the day of his death, steadfast in his justice, but with a lifelong reputation for injustice, in

d order that, having brought both the men to the utmost limits of justice and of injustice respectively, we may then give judgment as to which of the two is the happier. . . .

BOOK VII

514 Now then, I proceeded to say, compare our natural condition, as far as education and the lack of education are concerned, to a state of things like the following. Imagine a number of human beings living in an underground cave-like chamber, with an entrance open to the light, extending along the entire length of the cave, in which they have been confined, from their childhood, with their legs and necks so shackled, that they are obliged to sit still and look straight forward, because their chains make it impossible for b them to turn their heads round. And imagine a bright fire burning some way off, above and behind them, and a kind of roadway above which passes between the fire and the prisoners, with a low wall built along it, like the screens which puppeteers put up in front of their audience, and above which they exhibit their puppets.

I see, he replied.

Also picture to yourself a number of persons c walking behind this wall, and carrying with them statues of men, and images of other animals, fash- 515 ioned in wood and stone and all kinds of materials, together with various other articles, which are above the wall. And, as you might expect, let some of the passers-by be talking, and others silent.

You are describing a strange scene, and strange prisoners.

They resemble us, I replied. For let me ask you, in the first place, whether persons so confined could have seen anything of themselves or of each other, beyond the shadows thrown by the fire upon the part of the cave facing them?

Certainly not, if you suppose them to have been compelled all their lifetime to keep their heads unmoved. b

And what about the things carried past them? Is not the same true with regard to them?

Unquestionably it is.

And if they were able to converse with one another, do you not think that they would be in the habit of giving names to the things which they saw before them?

Doubtless they would.

Again, if their prison-house returned an echo from the part facing them, whenever one of the passers-by opened his lips, to what, let me ask you, could they refer the voice, if not to the shadow which was passing?

They would refer it to that, by Zeus.

Then surely such persons would hold the shad- c ows of those manufactured articles to be the only truth.

Without a doubt they would.

Now consider what would happen if the course of nature brought them a release from their fetters, and a remedy for their foolishness, in the following manner. Let us suppose that one of them has been released, and compelled suddenly to stand up, and turn his head around and walk with open eyes towards the light—and let us suppose that he goes through all these actions with pain, and that the dazzling splendor renders him incapable of perceiving those things of which he formerly used to see only d the shadows. What answer should you expect him to give, if someone were to tell him that in those days he was watching foolery, but that now he is somewhat nearer to reality, and is turned towards things more real, and sees more correctly? Above all, what would you expect if he were to point out to him the several objects that are passing by, and question him, and compel him to answer what they are? Should you not expect him to be puzzled, and to regard his old visions as truer than the things now shown?

Yes, much truer.

e   And if he were further compelled to gaze at the light itself, would not his eyes be distressed, do you think, and would he not shrink and turn away to the things which he could see distinctly, and consider them to be really clearer than the things pointed out to him?

Just so.

And if someone were to drag him violently up the rough and steep ascent from the cave, and refuse 516 to let him go until he had drawn him out into the light of the sun, do you not think that he would be vexed and indignant at such treatment, and on reaching the light, would he not find his eyes so dazzled by the glare as to be incapable of making out so much as one of the objects that are now called true?

Yes, he would find it so at first.

Hence, I suppose, it will be necessary for him to become accustomed before he is able to see the things above. At first he will be most successful in distinguishing shadows, then he will discern the images of men and other things in water, and afterwards the things themselves? And after this he will b raise his eyes to encounter the light of the moon and stars, finding it less difficult to study the heavenly bodies and the heaven itself by night, than the sun and the sun's light by day.

Doubtless.

Last of all, I imagine, he will be able to observe and contemplate the nature of the sun, not as it appears in water or on alien ground, but as it is in itself in its own region.

Of course.

His next step will be to draw the conclusion, that the sun is the provider of the seasons and the c years, and the guardian of all things in the visible world, and in a manner the cause of all those things which he and his companions used to see.

Obviously, this will be his next step.

What then? When he recalls to mind his first home, and the wisdom of the place, and his old fellow-prisoners, do you not think he will think himself happy on account of the change, and pity them?

Assuredly he will.

And if it was their practice in those days to receive honor and praise one from another, and to give prizes to him who had the keenest eye for the things passing by, and who remembered best all that used to precede and follow and accompany d it, and from these divined most ably what was going to come next, do you imagine that he will desire these prizes, and envy those who receive honor and exercise authority among them? Do you not rather imagine that he will feel what Homer describes, to "drudge on the lands of a master, serving a man of no great estate," and be ready to go through anything, rather than entertain those opinions, and live in that fashion?

For my own part, he replied, I am quite of that e opinion. I believe he would consent to go through anything rather than live in that way.

And now consider what would happen if such a man were to descend again and seat himself on his old seat? Coming so suddenly out of the sun, would he not find his eyes blinded with the darkness of the place?

Certainly, he would.

And if he were forced to form a judgment again, about those previously mentioned shadows, and to compete earnestly against those who had always been prisoners, while his sight continued dim, and 517 his eyes unsteady, and if he needed quite some time to get adjusted—would he not be made a laughingstock, and would it not be said of him, that he had gone up only to come back again with his eyesight destroyed, and that it was not worthwhile even to attempt the ascent? And if anyone endeavored to set them free and carry them to the light, would they not go so far as to put him to death, if they could only manage to get their hands on him?

Yes, that they would.

Now this imaginary case, my dear Glaucon, you must apply in all its parts to our former statements, by comparing the region which the eye reveals to the prison-house, and the light of the fire to the power of the sun. And if, by the upward ascent and the contemplation of the things above, you understand the journeying of the soul into the intelligible region, you will not disappoint my hopes, since you desire to be told what they are; though, indeed, god only knows whether they are true. But, be that as it may, the view which I take of the phenomena is the following: In the world of knowledge, the idea of the good is the limit of what can be seen, and it can barely be seen; but, when seen, we cannot help concluding that it is in every case the source of all that is right and beautiful, in the visible world giving birth to light and its master, and in the intelligible world, as master, providing truth and mind—and that whoever would act prudently, either in private or in public, must see it.

To the best of my power, said he, I quite agree with you.

STUDY QUESTIONS

1. Might the same goods be intrinsic in one situation and instrumental in another?
2. What points are illustrated by the story of the ring of Gyges?
3. Can you appear to be moral without being moral?
4. Can you be happy without being moral?

Nicomachean Ethics

Aristotle

Aristotle (384–322 BCE), a student of Plato, made extraordinary contributions in virtually every area of philosophy. Aristotle grounds morality in human nature, viewing the good as the fulfillment of the human potential to live well. To live well is to live in accordance with virtue. But how does one acquire virtue? Aristotle's answer depends on his distinction between moral and intellectual virtue. Moral virtue, which we might call "goodness of character," is formed by habit. One becomes good by doing good. Repeated acts of justice and self-control result in a just, self-controlled person who not only performs just, self-controlled actions but does so from a fixed character. Intellectual virtue, on the other hand, we might refer to as "wisdom." It requires sophisticated intelligence and is acquired by teaching. Virtuous activities are those that avoid the two extremes of excess and deficiency. For example, if you fear too much, you become cowardly; if you fear too little, you become rash. The mean is courage. To achieve the mean, you need to make a special effort to avoid that extreme to which you are prone. Thus, if you tend to be foolhardy, aim at timidity, and you will achieve the right measure of boldness.

BOOK I

094a1 Every art and every inquiry, and similarly every action and choice, is thought to aim at some good; and for this reason the good has rightly been declared to be that at which all things aim. . . .

094a18 If, then, there is some end of the things we do, which we desire for its own sake (everything else being desired for the sake of this), and if we do not choose everything for the sake of something else (for at that rate the process would go on to infinity, so that our desire would be empty and vain), clearly this must be the good and the chief good. Will not the knowledge of it, then, have a great influence on life? Shall we not, like archers who have a mark to aim at, be more likely to hit upon what we should? If so, we must try, in outline at least, to determine what it is. . . .

Let us resume our inquiry and state, in view of 1095a14 the fact that all knowledge and choice aims at some good, what it is that we say political science aims at and what is the highest of all goods achievable by action. Verbally there is very general agreement; for both the general run of men and people of superior refinement say that it is happiness, and identify living well and faring well with being happy; but with regard to what happiness is they differ, and the many do not give the same account as the wise. For

From Aristotle, *Nicomachean Ethics*, trans. David Ross, rev. J. L Ackrill and J. O. Urmson (New York: Oxford University Press, 1998). Reprinted by permission of the publisher.

the former think it is some plain and obvious thing, like pleasure, wealth, or honor; they differ, however, from one another—and often even the same man identifies it with different things, with health when he is ill, with wealth when he is poor. . . .

1095b14   To judge from the lives that men lead, most men, and men of the most vulgar type, seem (not without some reason) to identify the good, or happiness, with pleasure; which is the reason why they love the life of enjoyment. For there are, we may say, three prominent types of life—that just mentioned, the political, and thirdly the contemplative life. Now the mass of mankind are evidently quite slavish in their tastes, preferring a life suitable to beasts . . . [P]eople of superior refinement and of active disposition identify happiness with honor; for this is, roughly speaking, the end of the political life. But it seems too superficial to be what we are looking for, since it is thought to depend on those who bestow honor rather than on him who receives it, but the good we divine to be something of one's own and not easily taken from one. . . . Third comes the contemplative life, which we shall consider later.

1096a6 ①   The life of money-making is one undertaken under compulsion, and wealth is evidently not the good we are seeking: for it is merely useful and for the sake of something else. . . .

1097a15   Let us again return to the good we are seeking, and ask what it can be. It seems different in different actions and arts; it is different in medicine, in strategy, and in the other arts likewise. What then is the good of each? Surely that for whose sake everything else is done. In medicine this is health, in strategy victory, in architecture a house, in any other sphere something else, and in every action and choice the end: for it is for the sake of this that all men do whatever else they do. Therefore, if there is an end for all that we do, this will be the good achievable by action, and if there are more than one, these will be the goods achievable by action.

1097a24   So the argument has by a different course reached the same point; but we must try to state this even more clearly. Since there are evidently more than one end, and we choose some of these (e.g.,

wealth, flutes, and in general instruments) for the sake of something else, clearly not all ends are complete ends; but the chief good is evidently something complete. Therefore, if there is only one complete end, this will be what we are seeking, and if there are more than one, the most complete of these will be what we are seeking. Now we call that which is in itself worthy of pursuit more complete than that which is worthy of pursuit for the sake of something else, and that which is never desirable for the sake of something else more complete than the things that are desirable both in themselves and for the sake of that other thing, and therefore we call complete without qualification that which is always desirable in itself and never for the sake of something else.

     Now such a thing happiness, above all else, is held to be; for this we choose always for itself and never for the sake of something else, but honor, pleasure, reason, and every excellence we choose indeed for themselves (for if nothing resulted from them we should still choose each of them), but we choose them also for the sake of happiness, judging that through them we shall be happy. Happiness, on the other hand, no one chooses for the sake of these, nor in general, for anything other than itself.   1097a3

     From the point of view of self-sufficiency the same result seems to follow: for the complete good is thought to be self-sufficient. Now by self-sufficient we do not mean that which is sufficient for a man by himself, for one who lives a solitary life, but also for parents, children, wife, and in general for his friends and fellow citizens, since man is sociable by nature. . . . [T]he self-sufficient we now define as that which when isolated makes life desirable and lacking in nothing: and such we think happiness to be; and further we think it most desirable of all things, without being counted as one good thing among others—if it were so counted it would clearly be made more desirable by the addition of even the least of goods; for that which is added becomes an excess of goods, and of goods the greater is always more desirable. Happiness, then, is something complete and self-sufficient, and is the end of action.   1097b

[handwritten marginal notes: "3 types of life", "seeking the GOOD =", "end of something else", "for sake of something else", "conclusion on the good we seek", "eudaimonia", "argument"]

what it is is defined by man's fn

097b23   Presumably, however, to say that happiness is the chief good seems a platitude, and a clearer account of what it is is still desired. This might perhaps be given, if we could first ascertain the function of man. For just as for a flute-player, a sculptor, or any artist, and, in general, for all things that have a function or activity, the good and the "well" is thought to reside in the function, so would it seem to be for man, if he has a function. Have the carpenter, then, and the tanner certain functions or activities, and has man none? Is he naturally functionless? Or as eye, hand, foot, and in general each of the parts evidently has a function, may one lay it down that man similarly has a function apart from all these? What then can this be? Life seems to be common even to plants, but we are seeking what is peculiar to man. Let us exclude, therefore, the life of nutrition and growth. Next there would be a life of perception, but *it* also seems to be common even to the horse, the ox, and every animal. There remains, then, an active life of the element that has a rational principle (of this, one part has such a principle in the sense of being obedient to one, the other in the sense of possessing one and exercising thought): and as this too can be taken in two ways, we must state that life in the sense of activity is what we mean; for this seems to be the more proper sense of the term. Now if the function of man is an activity of soul in accordance with, or not without, rational principle, and if we say a so-and-so and a good so-and-so have a function which is the same in kind, e.g., a lyre-player and a good lyre-player, and so without qualification in all cases, eminence in respect of excellence being added to the function (for the function of a lyre-player is to play the lyre, and that of a good lyre-player is to do so well): if this is the case, [and we state the function of man to be a certain kind of life, and this to be an activity or actions of the soul implying a rational principle, and the function of a good man to be the good and noble performance of these, and if any action is well performed when it is performed in accordance with the appropriate excellence: if this is the case,] human good turns out to be activity of soul in conformity with excellence, and if there are more than one excellence, in conformity with the best and most complete.

     But we must add "in a complete life." For one 1098a17 swallow does not make a summer, nor does one day; and so too one day, or a short time, does not make a man blessed and happy. . . .

BOOK II

(B) Virtue, then, being of two kinds, ①intellectual and 1103a14 moral, intellectual virtue in the main owes both its birth and its growth to teaching (for which reason it requires experience and time), while ②moral virtue comes about as a result of habit. . . . From this it is also plain that none of the moral virtues arises in us by nature; for nothing that exists by nature can form a habit contrary to its nature. For instance, the stone which by nature moves downwards cannot be habituated to move upwards, not even if one tries to train it by throwing it up ten thousand times; nor can fire be habituated to move downwards, nor can anything else that by nature behaves in one way be trained to behave in another. Neither by nature, then, nor contrary to nature do the virtues arise in us; rather we are adapted by nature to receive them, and are made perfect by habit.

     Again, of all the things that come to us by nature 1103a26 we first acquire the potentiality and later exhibit the activity (this is plain in the case of the senses; for it was not by often seeing or often hearing that we got these senses, but on the contrary we had them before we used them, and did not come to have them by using them); but the virtues we get by first exercising them, as also happens in the case of the arts as well. For the things we have to learn before we can do them, we learn by doing them, e.g., men become builders by building and lyre-players by playing the lyre; so too we become just by doing just acts, temperate by doing temperate acts, brave by doing brave acts. . . .

     It makes no small difference, then, whether we form habits of one kind or of another from our very youth; it makes a very great difference, or rather *all* the difference.

     Since, then, the present inquiry does not aim at 1103b27 theoretical knowledge like the others (for we are inquiring not in order to know what virtue is, but in

time and repetition is interesting

→ virtue definition?

↓ but I wanna know what virtue IS, I know it is useful

life thrives on the mean
YET institutes operate @ the extremes

order to become good, since otherwise our inquiry would have been of no use), we must examine the nature of actions, namely, how we ought to do them; for these determine also the nature of the states of character that are produced, as we have said. . . .

1104a11 (a) First, then, let us consider this, that it is the nature of such things to be destroyed by defect and excess, as we see in the case of strength and of health (for to gain light on things imperceptible we must use the evidence of sensible things); exercise either excessive or defective destroys the strength, and similarly drink or food which is above or below a certain amount destroys the health, while that which is proportionate both produces and increases and preserves it. So too is it, then, in the case of temperance and courage and the other virtues. For the man who flies from and fears everything and does not stand his ground against anything becomes a coward, and the man who fears nothing at all but goes to meet every danger becomes rash; and similarly the man who indulges in every pleasure and abstains from none becomes self-indulgent, while the man who shuns every pleasure, as boors do, becomes in a way insensible; temperance and courage, then, are destroyed by excess and defect, and preserved by the mean.

why make that to equal?

not necessarily & who said that those are virtues?

1104a28 But not only are the sources and causes of their origination and growth the same as those of their destruction, but also the sphere of their actualization will be the same; for this is also true of the things which are more evident to sense, e.g., of strength; it is produced by taking much food and undergoing much exertion, and it is the strong man that will be most able to do these things. So too is it with the virtues; by abstaining from pleasures we become temperate, and it is when we have become so that we are most able to abstain from them; and similarly too in the case of courage; for by being habituated to despise things that are fearful and to stand our ground against them we become brave, and it is when we have become so that we shall be most able to stand our ground against them. . . .

1105a18 (b) The question might be asked what we mean by saying that we must become just by doing just acts, and temperate by doing temperate acts; for if men

do just and temperate acts, they are already just and temperate, exactly as if they do what is in accordance with the laws of grammar and of music, they are grammarians and musicians.

Or is this not true even of the arts? It is possible 1105a2? to do something that is in accordance with the laws of grammar, either by chance or under the guidance of another. A man will be a grammarian, then, only when he has both said something grammatical and said it grammatically; and this means doing it in accordance with the grammatical knowledge in himself.

Again, the case of the arts and that of the vir- 1105a2? tues are not similar; for the products of the arts have their goodness in themselves, so that it is enough that they should have a certain character, but if the acts that are in accordance with the virtues have themselves a certain character it does not follow that they are done justly or temperately. The agent also must be in a certain condition when he does them; in the first place he must have knowledge, secondly he must choose the acts, and choose them for their own sakes, and thirdly his action must proceed from a firm and unchangeable character. These are not reckoned in as conditions of the possession of the arts, except the bare knowledge, but as a condition of the possession of the virtues knowledge has little or no weight, while the other conditions count not for a little but for everything, i.e., the very conditions which result from often doing just and temperate acts.

Actions, then, are called just and temperate 1105b when they are such as the just or the temperate man would do; but it is not the man who does these that is just and temperate, but the man who also does them *as* just and temperate men do them. It is well said, then, that it is by doing just acts that the just man is produced, and by doing temperate acts the temperate man; without doing these no one would have even a prospect of becoming good.

But most people do not do these, but take refuge 1105b in theory and think they are being philosophers and will become good in this way, behaving somewhat like patients who listen attentively to their doctors, but do none of the things they are ordered to do. As the latter will not be made well in body by such a

social component

I feel SEEN

Q: how one gains the just or temperate attribute? → games / scouts do thing get) skill → social component externally attributed course of treatment, the former will not be made well in soul by such a course of philosophy. . . .

106a15 [E]very virtue or excellence both brings into good condition the thing of which it is the excellence and makes the work of that thing be done well; e.g., the excellence of the eye makes both the eye and its work good; for it is by the excellence of the eye that we see well. Similarly the excellence of the horse makes a horse both good in itself and good at running and at carrying its rider and at awaiting the attack of the enemy. Therefore, if this is true in every case, the virtue of man also will be the state of character which makes a man good and which makes him do his own work well.

106a24 How this is to happen we have stated already, but it will be made plain also by the following consideration of the specific nature of virtue. In everything that is continuous and divisible it is possible to take more, less, or an equal amount, and that either in terms of the thing itself or relatively to us; and the equal is an intermediate between excess and defect. By the intermediate in the object I mean that which is equidistant from each of the extremes, which is one and the same for all men; by the intermediate relatively to us that which is neither too much nor too little—and this is not one, nor the same for all. For instance, if ten is many and two is few, six is the intermediate, taken in terms of the object; for it exceeds and is exceeded by an equal amount; this is intermediate according to arithmetical proportion. But the intermediate relatively to us is not to be taken so; if ten pounds are too much for a particular person to eat and two too little, it does not follow that the trainer will order six pounds; for this also is perhaps too much for the person who is to take it, or too little—too little for Milo, too much for the beginner in athletic exercises. The same is true of running and wrestling. Thus a master of any art avoids excess and defect, but seeks the intermediate and chooses this—the intermediate not in the object but relatively to us.

106b8 If it is thus, then, that every art does its work well—by looking to the intermediate and judging its works by this standard (so that we often say of good works of art that it is not possible either to take away or to add anything, implying that excess and

defect destroy the goodness of works of art, while the mean preserves it; and good artists, as we say, look to this in their work), and if, further, virtue is more exact and better than any art, as nature also is, then virtue must have the quality of aiming at the intermediate. I mean moral virtue; for it is this that is concerned with passions and actions, and in these there is excess, defect, and the intermediate. For instance, both fear and confidence and appetite and anger and pity and in general pleasure and pain may be felt both too much and too little, and in both cases not well; but to feel them at the right times, with reference to the right objects, towards the right people, with the right motive, and in the right way, is what is both intermediate and best, and this is characteristic of virtue. Similarly with regard to actions also there is excess, defect, and the intermediate. Now virtue is concerned with passions and actions, in which excess is a form of failure, and so is defect, while the intermediate is praised and is a form of success; and being praised and being successful are both characteristics of virtue. Therefore virtue is a kind of mean, since, as we have seen, it aims at what is intermediate. . . .

1107a9 But not every action nor every passion admits of a mean; for some have names that already imply badness, e.g., spite, shamelessness, envy, and in the case of actions adultery, theft, murder; for all of these and suchlike things imply by their names that they are themselves bad, and not the excesses or deficiencies of them. It is not possible, then, ever to be right with regard to them; one must always be wrong. Nor does goodness or badness with regard to such things depend on committing adultery with the right woman, at the right time, and in the right way, but simply to do any of them is to go wrong. . . .

1109a20 The moral virtue is a mean, then, and in what sense it is so, and that it is a mean between two vices, the one involving excess, the other deficiency, and that it is such because its character is to aim at what is intermediate in passions and in actions, has been sufficiently stated. Hence also it is no easy task to be good. For in everything it is no easy task to find the middle, e.g., to find the middle of a circle is not for everyone but for him who knows; so too anyone can get angry—that is easy—or give or spend money; but to do this to the right person, to the right extent, at the right time, with the right motive, and in the right way, *that* is not for everyone, nor is it easy; wherefore goodness is both rare and laudable and noble. . . .

1109b2   But we must consider the things towards which we ourselves also are easily carried away; for some of us tend to one thing, some to another; and this will be recognizable from the pleasure and the pain we feel. We must drag ourselves away to the contrary extreme; for we shall get into the intermediate state by drawing well away from error. . . .

So much, then, is plain, that the intermediate state is in all things to be praised, but that we must incline sometimes towards the excess, sometimes towards the deficiency; for so shall we most easily hit the mean and what is right.

STUDY QUESTIONS

1. According to Aristotle, what is the function of a human being?
2. How does moral virtue differ from intellectual virtue?
3. How is moral virtue acquired?
4. What is Aristotle's doctrine of the mean?

Leviathan

Thomas Hobbes

Thomas Hobbes (1588–1679) was an English philosopher who played a crucial role in the history of social thought. He believes that our desires move us, and the objects that satisfy those desires are for that reason judged to be good. Because we are roughly equal in our mental and physical powers, so we are roughly equal in our ability to gain the scarce goods we seek, thus leading to distrust and violence. According to Hobbes, the result is "a war, as is of every man, against every man," and a life that is "solitary, poor, nasty, brutish, and short." In this state of war, we have no property, justice has no meaning, and no limits are placed on each person's doing whatever is necessary to achieve self-preservation. Assuming this bleak picture, Hobbes develops a moral and political theory that views justice and other ethical ideals as resting on an implied agreement among individuals. He argues that reason requires us to relinquish the right to do whatever we please in exchange for all others limiting their rights in a similar manner, thus achieving security for all.

CHAPTER VI

Of the Interior Beginnings of Voluntary Motions: Commonly Called the Passions; and the Speeches by Which They Are Expressed

There be in animals, two sorts of *motions* peculiar to them: one called *vital*; begun in generation, and continued without interruption through their whole life; such as are the *course* of the *blood*, the *pulse*, the *breathing*, the *concoction, nutrition, excretion,* &c. . . . to which motions there needs no help of imagination: the other is *animal motion,* otherwise called *voluntary motion*; as to *go,* to *speak,* to *move* any of our limbs, in such manner as is first fancied in our minds. That sense is motion in the organs and interior parts of man's body, caused by the action of the things we see, hear, &c. . . . And because *going, speaking,* and the like voluntary motions, depend always upon a precedent thought of *whither, which way,* and *what*; it is evident, that the imagination is the first internal beginning of all voluntary motion. And although unstudied men do not conceive any motion at all to be there, where the thing moved is invisible; or the space it is moved in, is (for the shortness of it) insensible; yet that doth not hinder, but that such motions are. For let a space be never so little, that which is moved over a greater space, whereof that little one is part, must first be moved over that. These small beginnings of motion, within the body of man, before they appear in walking, speaking, striking, and other visible actions, are commonly called ENDEAVOUR.

From Thomas Hobbes, *Leviathan* (1651).

This endeavour, when it is toward something which causes it, is called APPETITE, or DESIRE; the latter, being the general name; and the other, oftentimes restrained to signify the desire of food, namely *hunger* and *thirst.* And when the endeavour is fromward something, it is generally called AVERSION. . . .

That which men desire, they are also said to LOVE: and to HATE those things for which they have aversion. So that desire and love are the same thing; save that by desire, we always signify the absence of the object; by love, most commonly the presence of the same. So also by aversion, we signify the absence; and by hate, the presence of the object. . . .

And because the constitution of a man's body is in continual mutation, it is impossible that all the same things should always cause in him the same appetites, and aversions: much less can all men consent, in the desire of almost any one and the same object.

But whatsoever is the object of any man's appetite or desire, that is it which he for his part calleth *good*: and the object of his hate and aversion, *evil*; and of his contempt, *vile* and *inconsiderable.* For these words of good, evil, and contemptible, are ever used with relation to the person that useth them: there being nothing simply and absolutely so; nor any common rule of good and evil, to be taken from the nature of the objects themselves: but from the person of the man (where there is no commonwealth;) or, (in a commonwealth,) from the person that representeth it; or from an arbitrator or judge, whom men disagreeing shall by consent set up, and make his sentence the rule thereof. . . .

Continual success in obtaining those things which a man from time to time desireth, that is to say, continual prospering, is that men call FELICITY; I mean the felicity of this life. For there is no such thing as perpetual tranquillity of mind, while we live here; because life itself is but motion, and can never be without desire, nor without fear, no more than without sense. . . .

CHAPTER XI

Of the Difference of Manners

By manners, I mean not here, decency of behaviour, as how one man should salute another, or how a man should wash his mouth, or pick his teeth before company, and such other points of the *small morals*; but those qualities of mankind, that concern their living together in peace, and unity. To which end we are to consider, that the felicity of this life, consisteth not in the repose of a mind satisfied. For there is no such *finus ultimus,* (utmost aim,) nor *summum bonum,* (greatest good,) as is spoken of in the books of the old moral philosophers. Nor can a man any more live, whose desires are at an end, than he, whose senses and imaginations are at a stand. Felicity is a continual progress of the desire, from one object to another; the attaining of the former, being still but the way to the latter. The cause whereof is, that the object of man's desire, is not to enjoy once only, and for one instant of time; but to assure for ever, the way of his future desire. And therefore the voluntary actions, and inclinations of all men, tend, not only to the procuring, but also to the assuring of a contented life; and differ only in the way: which ariseth partly from the diversity of passions, in diverse men; and partly from the difference of the knowledge, or opinion each one has of the causes, which produce the effect desired.

So that in the first place, I put for a general inclination of all mankind, a perpetual and restless desire of power after power, that ceaseth only in death. And the cause of this, is not always that a man hopes for a more intensive delight, than he has already attained to; or that he cannot be content with a moderate power: but because he cannot assure the power and means to live well, which he hath present, without the acquisition of more. And from hence it is, that kings, whose power is greatest, turn their endeavors to the assuring it at home by laws, or abroad by wars: and when that is done, there succeedeth a new desire; in some, of fame from new conquest; in others, of ease and sensual pleasure; in others, of admiration, or being flattered for excellence in some art, or other ability of the mind.

CHAPTER XIII

Of the Natural Condition of Mankind as Concerning Their Felicity, and Misery

Nature hath made men so equal, in the faculties of the body, and mind; as that though there be found one man sometimes manifestly stronger in body, or of quicker mind than another; yet when all is reckoned together, the difference between man, and man, is not so considerable, as that one man can thereupon claim to himself any benefit, to which another may not pretend, as well as he. For as to the strength of body, the weakest has strength enough to kill the strongest, either by secret machination, or by confederacy with others, that are in the same danger with himself.

And as to the faculties of the mind, setting aside the arts grounded upon words, and especially that skill of proceeding upon general, and infallible rules, called science; which very few have, and but in few things; as being not a native faculty, born with us; nor attained, as prudence, while we look after somewhat else, I find yet a greater equality amongst men, than that of strength. For prudence, is but experience; which equal time, equally bestows on all men, in those things they equally apply themselves unto. That which may perhaps make such equality incredible, is but a vain conceit of one's own wisdom, which almost all men think they have in a greater degree, than the vulgar; that is, than all men but themselves, and a few others, whom by fame, or for concurring with themselves, they approve. For such is the nature of men, that howsoever they may acknowledge many others to be more witty, or more eloquent, or more learned; yet they will hardly believe there be many so wise as themselves; for they see their own wit at hand, and other men's at a distance. But this proveth rather that men are in that point equal, than unequal. For there is not ordinarily a greater sign of the equal distribution of any thing, than that every man is contented with his share.

From this equality of ability, ariseth equality of hope in the attaining of our ends. And therefore if any two men desire the same thing, which nevertheless they cannot both enjoy, they become enemies; and in the way to their end, which is principally their own conservation, and sometimes their delectation only, endeavour to destroy, or subdue one another. And from hence it comes to pass, that where an invader hath no more to fear, than another man's single power; if one plant, sow, build, or possess a convenient seat, others may probably be expected to come prepared with forces united, to dispossess, and deprive him, not only of the fruit of his labour, but also of his life, or liberty. And the invader again is in the like danger of another.

And from this diffidence of one another, there is no way for any man to secure himself, so reasonable, as anticipation; that is, by force, or wiles, to master the persons of all men he can, so long, till he see no other power great enough to endanger him: and this is no more than his own conservation requireth, and is generally allowed. Also because there be some, that taking pleasure in contemplating their own power in the acts of conquest, which they pursue farther than their security requires; if others, that otherwise would be glad to be at case within modest bounds, should not by invasion increase their power, they would not be able, long time, by standing only on their defence, to subsist. And by consequence, such augmentation of dominion over men being necessary to a man's conservation, it ought to be allowed him.

Again, men have no pleasure, but on the contrary a great deal of grief, in keeping company, where there is no power able to over-awe them all. For every man looketh that his companion should value him, at the same rate he sets upon himself: and upon all signs of contempt, or undervaluing, naturally endeavours, as far as he dares, (which amongst them that have no common power to keep them in quiet, is far enough to make them destroy each other), to extort a greater value from his contemners, by damage; and from others, by the example.

So that in the nature of man, we find three principal causes of quarrel. First, competition; secondly, diffidence; thirdly, glory.

The first, maketh man invade for gain; the second, for safety; and the third, for reputation. The first use violence, to make themselves masters of other men's persons, wives, children, and cattle; the second, to defend them; the third, for trifles, as a word, a smile, a different opinion, and any other sign of undervalue, either direct in their persons, or by reflection in their kindred, their friends, their nation, their profession, or their name.

Hereby it is manifest, that during the time men live without a common power to keep them all in awe, they are in that condition which is called war; and such a WAR, as is of every man, against every man. For war, consisteth not in battle only, or the act of fighting; but in a tract of time, wherein the will to contend by battle is sufficiently known: and therefore the notion of *time,* is to be considered in the nature of war; as it is in the nature of weather. For as the nature of foul weather, lieth not in a shower or two of rain; but in an inclination thereto of many days together: so the nature of war, consisteth not in actual fighting; but in the known disposition thereto, during all the time there is no assurance to the contrary. All other time is PEACE.

Whatsoever therefore is consequent to a time of war, where every man is enemy to every man; the same is consequent to the time, wherein men live without other security, than what their own strength, and their own invention shall furnish them withal. In such condition, there is no place for industry; because the fruit thereof is uncertain: and consequently no culture of the earth; no navigation nor use of the commodities that may be imported by sea; no commodious building: no instruments of moving, and removing, such things as require much force; no knowledge of the face of the earth; no account of time; no arts; no letters; no society; and which is worst of all, continual fear, and danger of violent death; and the life of man, solitary, poor, nasty, brutish, and short.

It may seem strange to some man, that has not well weighed these things; that nature should thus dissociate, and render men apt to invade, and destroy one another: and he may therefore, not trusting to this inference, made from the passions, desire perhaps to have the same confirmed by experience. Let him therefore consider with himself, when taking a journey, he arms himself, and seeks to go well accompanied; when going to sleep, he locks his doors; when even in his house he locks his chests; and this when he knows there be laws, and public offices, armed, to revenge all injuries shall be done him; what opinion he has of his fellow-subjects, when he rides armed; of his fellow citizens, when he locks his doors; and of his children, and servants, when he locks his chests. Does he not there as much accuse mankind by his actions, as I do by my words?

But neither of us accuse man's nature in it. The desires, and other passions of man, are in themselves no sin. No more are the actions, that proceed from those passions, till they know a law that forbids them: which till laws be made they cannot know: nor can any law be made, till they have agreed upon the person that shall make it.

It may peradventure be thought, there was never such a time, nor condition of war as this; and I believe it was never generally so, over all the world: but there are many places, where they live so now, For the savage people in many places of America, except the government of small families, the concord whereof dependeth on natural lust, have no government at all; and live at this day in that brutish manner, as I said before. Howsoever, it may be perceived what manner of life there would be, where there were no common power to fear, by the manner of life, which men that have formerly lived under a peaceful government, use to degenerate into, in a civil war.

But though there had never been any time, wherein particular men were in a condition of war one against another; yet in all times, kings, and persons of sovereign authority, because of their independency, are in continual jealousies, and in the state and posture of gladiators; having their weapons pointing, and their eyes fixed on one another; that is, their forts, garrisons, and guns upon the frontiers of their kingdoms; and continual spies upon their neighbours; which is a posture of war. But because they uphold thereby, the industry of their subjects; there does not follow from it, that misery, which accompanies the liberty of particular men.

To this war of every man, against every man, this also is consequent; that nothing can be unjust. The notions of right and wrong, justice and injustice have there no place, where there is no common power, there is no law: where no law, no injustice. Force, and fraud, are in war the two cardinal virtues. Justice, and injustice are none of the faculties neither of the body, nor mind. If they were, they might be in a man that were alone in the world, as well as his senses, and passions. They are qualities, that relate to men in society, not in solitude. It is consequent also to the same condition, that there be no propriety, no dominion, no *mine* and *thine* distinct; but only that to be every man's, that he can get: and for so long, as he can keep it. And thus much for the ill condition, which man by mere nature is actually placed in; though with a possibility to come out of it, consisting partly in the passions, partly in his reason.

The passions that incline men to peace, are fear of death; desire of such things as are necessary to commodious living; and a hope by their industry to obtain them. And reason suggesteth convenient articles of peace, upon which men may be drawn to agreement. These articles, are they, which otherwise are called the Laws of Nature: whereof I shall speak more particularly, in the two following chapters.

CHAPTER XIV

Of the First and Second Natural Laws, and of Contracts

The RIGHT OF NATURE, which writers commonly call *jus naturale,* is the liberty each man hath, to use his own power, as he will himself, for the preservation of his own nature; that is to say, of his own life; and consequently, of doing any thing, which in his own judgment, and reason, he shall conceive to be the aptest means thereunto.

By LIBERTY, is understood, according to the proper signification of the word, the absence of external impediments: which impediments, may oft take away part of a man's power to do what he would; but cannot hinder him from using the power left him, according as his judgment, and reason shall dictate to him.

A LAW OF NATURE, *lex naturalis,* is a precept or general rule, found out by reason, by which a man is forbidden to do that, which is destructive of his life, or taketh away the means of preserving the same; and to omit that, by which he thinketh it may be best preserved. For though they that speak of this subject, use to confound *jus,* and *lex, right* and *law:* yet they ought to be distinguished; because right, consisteth in liberty to do, or to forbear: whereas LAW, determineth, and hindeth to one of them: so that law, and

right, differ as much, as obligation, and liberty; which in one and the same matter are inconsistent.

And because the condition of man, as hath been declared in the precedent chapter, is a condition of war of every one against every one; in which case every one is governed by his own reason; and there is nothing he can make use of, that may not be a help unto him, in preserving his life against his enemies; it followeth, that in such a condition, every man has a right to every thing; even to one another's body. And therefore, as long as this natural right of every man to every thing endureth, there can be no security to any man, how strong or wise soever he be, of living out the time, which nature ordinarily alloweth men to live. And consequently it is a precept, or general rule of reason, *that every man, ought to endeavour peace, as far as he has hope of obtaining it; and when he cannot obtain it, that he may seek, and use, all helps, and advantages of war.* The first branch of which rule, containeth the first, and fundamental law of nature; which is, to *seek peace, and follow it.* The second, the sum of the right of nature; which is, *by all means we can, to defend ourselves.*

From this fundamental law of nature, by which men are commanded to endeavour peace, is derived this second law; *that a man be willing, when others are so too, as far-forth, as for peace, and defence of himself he shall think it necessary, to lay down this right to all things; and be contented with so much liberty against other men; as he would allow other men against himself.* For as long as every man holdeth this right, of doing any thing he liketh; so long are all men in the condition of war. But if other men will not lay down their right, as well as he; then there is no reason for any one, to divest himself of his; for that were to expose himself to prey, which no man is bound to, rather than to dispose himself to peace. This is that law of the Gospel; *whatsoever you require that others should do to you, that do yet to them. . . .*

To *lay down* a man's *right* to any thing, is to *divest* himself of the *liberty,* of hindering another of the benefit of his own right to the same. For he that renounceth, or passeth away his right, giveth not to any other man a right which he had not before; because there is nothing to which every man had not right by nature: but only standeth out of his way, that he may enjoy his own original right, without hindrance from him: not without hindrance from another. So that the effect which redoundeth to one man, by another man's defect of right, is but so much diminution of impediments to the use of his own right original. Right is laid aside, either by simply renouncing it; or by transferring it to another. By *simply* RENOUNCING; when he cares not to whom the benefit thereof redoundeth. By TRANSFERRING; when he intendeth the benefit thereof to some certain person, or persons. And when a man hath in either manner abandoned, or granted away his right; then he is said to be OBLIGED, or BOUND, not to hinder those, to whom such right is granted, or abandoned, from the benefit of it; and that he *ought,* and it is his DUTY, not to make void that voluntary act of his own: and that such hindrance is INJUSTICE, and INJURY, as being *sine jure*; the right being before renounced, or transferred. So that *injury, or injustice,* in the controversies of the world, is somewhat like to that, which in the disputations of scholars is called absurdity. For as it is there called an *absurdity,* to contradict what one maintained in the beginning: so in the world, it is called injustice, and injury, voluntarily to undo that, which from the beginning he had voluntarily done. The way by which a man either simply renounceth, or transferreth his right, is a declaration, or signification, by some voluntary and sufficient sign, or signs, that he doth so renounce, or transfer; or hath so renounced, or transferred the same, to him that accepteth it. And these signs are either words only, or actions only; or, as it happeneth most often, both words, and actions. And the same are the BONDS, by which men are bound, and obliged; bonds, that have their strength, not from their own nature, for nothing is more easily broken than a man's word, but from fear of some evil consequences upon the rupture.

Whensoever, a man transferreth his right, or renounceth it; it is either in consideration of some right reciprocally transferred to himself; or for some other good he hopeth for thereby. For it is a voluntary act: and of the voluntary acts of every man, the object is some *good to himself.* And therefore there be some rights, which no man can be understood by any words, or other signs, to have abandoned, or transferred. As first a man cannot lay down the right of resisting them, that assault him by force, to take away his life; because he cannot be understood to aim thereby, at any good to himself. The same may be said of wounds, and chains, and imprisonment; both because there is no benefit consequent to such patience; as there is to the patience of suffering another to be wounded, or imprisoned; as also because a man cannot tell, when he seeth men proceed against him by violence, whether they intend his death or not. And lastly the motive, and end for which this renouncing, and transferring of right is introduced, is nothing else but the security of a man's person, in his life, and in the means of so preserving life, as not to be weary of it. And therefore if a man by words, or other signs, seem to despoil himself of the end, for which those signs were intended; he is not to be understood as if he meant it, or that it was his will; but that he was ignorant of how such words and actions were to be interpreted.

The mutual transferring of right, is that which men call CONTRACT. . . .

CHAPTER XV

Of Other Laws of Nature

From that law of nature, by which we are obliged to transfer to another, such rights, as being retained, hinder the peace of mankind, there followeth a third; which is this, *that men perform their covenants made*: without which, covenants are in vain, and but empty words; and the right of all men to all things remaining, we are still in the condition of war.

And in this law of nature, consisteth the fountain and original of JUSTICE. For where no covenant hath preceded, there hath no right been transferred, and every man has right to every thing; and consequently, no action can be unjust. But when a covenant is made, then to break it is *unjust*: and the definition of INJUSTICE, is no other than *the not performance of covenant.* And whatsoever is not unjust, is *just.*

But because covenants of mutual trust, where there is a fear of not performance on either part, as hath been said in the former chapter, are invalid; though the original of justice be the making of covenants; yet injustice actually there can be none, till the cause of such fear be taken away; which while men are in the natural condition of war, cannot be done. Therefore before the names of just, and unjust can have place, there must be some coercive power, to compel men equally to the performance of their covenants, by the terror of some punishment, greater than the benefit they expect by the breach of their covenant; and to make good that propriety, which by mutual contract men acquire, in recompense of the universal right they abandon: and such power there is none before the erection of a commonwealth. And this is also to be gathered out of the ordinary definition of justice in the Schools: for they say, that *justice is the constant will of giving to every man his own.* And therefore where there is no *own,* that is no propriety, there is no injustice; and where there is no coercive power erected, that is, where there is no commonwealth, there is no propriety; all men having right to all things: therefore where there is no commonwealth, there nothing is unjust. So that the nature of justice, consisteth in keeping of valid covenants: but the validity of covenants begins not but with the constitution of a civil power, sufficient to compel men to keep them: and then it is also that propriety begins.

The fool hath said in his heart, there is no such thing as justice; and sometimes also with his tongue; seriously alleging, that every man's conservation, and contentment, being committed to his own care, there could be no reason, why every man might not do what he thought conduced thereunto: and therefore also to make, or not make; keep, or not keep covenants, was not against reason, when it conduced to one's benefit. He does not therein deny, that there be covenants; and that they are sometimes broken, sometimes kept; and that such breach of them may be called injustice, and the observance of them justice: but he questioneth, whether injustice, taking away the fear of God, (for the same fool hath said in his heart there is no God,) may not sometimes stand with that reason, which dictateth to every man his own good; and particularly then, when it conduceth to such a benefit, as shall put a

man in a condition, to neglect not only the dispraise, and revilings, but also the power of other men. . . . This specious reasoning is nevertheless false.

For the question is not of promises mutual, where there is no security of performance on either side; as when there is no civil power erected over the parties promising; for such promises are no covenants: but either where one of the parties has performed already; or where there is a power to make him perform; there is the question whether it be against reason, that is, against the benefit of the other to perform, or not. And I say it is not against reason. For the manifestation whereof, we are to consider; first, that when a man doth a thing, which notwithstanding any thing can be foreseen, and reckoned on, tendeth to his own destruction, howsoever some accident which he could not expect, arriving may turn it to his benefit; yet such events do not make it reasonably or wisely done. Secondly, that in a condition of war, wherein every man to every man, for want of a common power to keep them all in awe, is an enemy, there is no man can hope by his own strength, or wit, to defend himself from destruction, without the help of confederates; where every one expects the same defence by the confederation, that any one else does: and therefore he which declares he thinks it reason to deceive those that help him, can in reason expect no other means of safety, than what can be had from his own single power. He therefore that breaketh his covenant, and consequently declareth that he thinks he may with reason do so, cannot be received into any society, that unite themselves for peace and defence, but by the error of them that receive him; nor when he is received, be retained in it, without seeing the danger of their error; which errors a man cannot reasonably reckon upon as the means of his security: and therefore if he be left, or cast out of society, he perisheth; and if he live in society, it is by the errors of other men, which he could not foresee, nor reckon upon; and consequently against the reason of his preservation; and so, as all men that contribute not to his destruction, forbear him only out of ignorance of what is good for themselves.

STUDY QUESTIONS

1. According to Hobbes, what is "good"?
2. What does Hobbes mean by a "law of nature"?
3. According to Hobbes, what does the "fool" believe?
4. Does Hobbes provide a satisfying response to the fool?

Fifteen Sermons

Joseph Butler

Joseph Butler (1692–1752), a bishop of the Church of England, offers an account of morality based on human nature. Arguing against egoism, he maintains that human beings act from a wide variety of motives. In addition to self-love, humans feel benevolence and esteem for others, love of society, and indignation at successful vice. Although we might do harm to one another when our desires are unchecked, no one acts simply from ill-will for another. Moreover, human beings not only seek their own gratification but also the public good. Indeed, because human beings are all part of a common humanity, morality and self-interest do not conflict but, instead, converge.

SERMON I: UPON HUMAN NATURE

For as we have many members in one body, and all members have not the same office: so we, being many, are one body in Christ, and every one members one of another.

(Rom. 12:4, 5)

[4.] The relation which the several parts or members of the natural body have to each other and to the whole body, is here compared to the relation which each particular person in society has to other particular persons and to the whole society; and the latter is intended to be illustrated by the former. And if there be a likeness between these two relations, the consequence is obvious: that the latter shows us we were intended to do good to others, as the former shows us that the several members of the natural body were intended to be instruments of good to each other and to the whole body. . . .

[5.] From this review and comparison of the nature of man as respecting self, and as respecting society, it will plainly appear, that there are as real and the same kind of indications in human nature, that we were made for society and to do good to our fellow-creatures; as that we were intended to take care of our own life and health and private good: and that the same objections lie against one of these assertions, as against the other. For,

[6.] First, There is a natural principle of *benevolence* in man; which is in some degree to *society,* what *self-love* is to the *individual.* And if there be in mankind any disposition to friendship; if there be any such thing as compassion, for compassion is momentary love; if there be any such thing as the paternal or filial affections; if there be any affection in human nature, the object and end of which is the good of another; this is itself benevolence, or the love of another. Be it ever so short, be it in ever so low a degree, or ever so unhappily confined; it proves the assertion, and points out what we were

From Joseph Butler, *Fifteen Sermons* (1726).

designed for, as really as though it were in a higher degree and more extensive. I must however remind you that though benevolence and self-love are different; though the former tends most directly to public good, and the latter to private: yet they are so perfectly coincident, that the greatest satisfactions to ourselves depend upon our having benevolence in a due degree, and that self-love is one chief security of our right behavior towards society. It may be added, that their mutual coinciding, so that we can scarce promote one without the other, is equally a proof that we were made for both.

[7.] Secondly, This will further appear, from observing that the *several passions and affections,* which are distinct both from benevolence and self-love, do in general contribute and lead us to *public* good as really as to *private.* It might be thought too minute and particular, and would carry us too great a length, to distinguish between and compare together the several passions or appetites distinct from benevolence, whose primary use and intention is the security and good of society; and the passions distinct from self-love, whose primary intention and design is the security and good of the individual. It is enough to the present argument, that desire of esteem from others, contempt and esteem of them, love of society as distinct from affection to the good of it, indignation against successful vice, that these are public affections or passions; have an immediate respect to others, naturally lead us to regulate our behavior in such a manner as will be of service to our fellow-creatures. If any or all of these may be considered likewise as private affections, as tending to private good; this does not hinder them from being public affections too, or destroy the good influence of them upon society, and their tendency to public good. . . . The sum is, men have various appetites, passions, and particular affections, quite distinct both from self-love and from benevolence: all of these have a tendency to promote both public and private good, and may be considered as respecting others and ourselves equally and in common: but some of them seem most immediately to respect others, or tend to public good; others of them most immediately to respect self, or tend to private good: as the former are not benevolence, so the latter are not self-love:

neither sort are instances of our love either to ourselves or others; but only instances of our Maker's care and love both of the individual and the species, and proofs that He intended we should be instruments of good to each other, as well as that we should be so to ourselves.

[8.] Thirdly, There is a principle of reflection in men, by which they distinguish between, approve and disapprove their own actions. We are plainly constituted such sort of creatures as to reflect upon our own nature. The mind can take a view of what passes within itself, its propensions, aversions, passions, affections, as respecting such objects, and in such degrees; and of the several actions consequent thereupon. In this survey it approves of one, disapproves of another, and towards a third is affected in neither of these ways, but is quite indifferent. This principle in man, by which he approves or disapproves his heart, temper, and actions, is conscience; for this is the strict sense of the word, though sometimes it is used so as to take in more. And that this faculty tends to restrain men from doing mischief to each other, and leads them to do good, is too manifest to need being insisted upon. . . . It cannot possibly be denied, that there is this principle of reflection or conscience in human nature. Suppose a man to relieve an innocent person in great distress; suppose the same man afterwards, in the fury of anger, to do the greatest mischief to a person who had given no just cause of offence; to aggravate the injury, add the circumstances of former friendship, and obligation from the injured person; let the man who is supposed to have done these two different actions, coolly reflect upon them afterwards, without regard to their consequences to himself: to assert that any common man would be affected in the same way towards these different actions, that he would make no distinction between them, but approve or disapprove them equally, is too glaring a falsity to need being confuted. There is therefore this principle of reflection or conscience in mankind. It is needless to compare the respect it has to private good, with the respect it has to public; since it plainly tends as much to the latter as to the former, and is commonly thought to tend chiefly to the latter. This faculty is now mentioned merely as another part in the inward frame of man, pointing out to us in some degree what we are intended for, and as what will naturally and of course have some influence. The particular place assigned to it by nature, what authority it has, and how great influence it ought to have, shall be hereafter considered.

[9.] From this comparison of benevolence and self-love, of our public and private affections, of the courses of life they lead to, and of the principle of reflection or conscience as respecting each of them, it is as manifest, that we were made for society, and to promote the happiness of it; as that we were intended to take care of our own life, and health, and private good.

SERMON II: UPON HUMAN NATURE

For when the Gentiles, which have not the law, do by nature the things contained in the law, these, having not the law, are a law unto themselves.
(Rom. 2:14)

[3.] But it may be said, "What is all this, though true, to the purpose of virtue and religion? these require, not only that we do good to others, when we are led this way, by benevolence or reflection, happening to be stronger than other principles, passions, or appetites; but likewise that the *whole* character be formed upon thought and reflection; that *every* action be directed by some determinate rule, some other rule than the strength and prevalency of any principle or passion. What sign is there in our nature (for the inquiry is only about what is to be collected from thence) that this was intended by its Author? Or how does so various and fickle a temper as that of man appear adapted thereto? It may indeed be absurd and unnatural for men to act without any reflection; nay, without regard to that particular kind of reflection which you call conscience; because this does belong to our nature. For as there never was a man but who approved one place, prospect, building, before another: so it does not appear that there ever was a man who would not have approved an action of humanity rather than of cruelty, interest and passion being quite

out of the case. But interest and passion do come in, and are often too strong for and prevail over reflection and conscience. Now as brutes have various instincts, by which they are carried on to the end the Author of their nature intended them for: is not man in the same condition; with this difference only, that to his instincts (*i.e.*, appetites and passions) is added the principle of reflection or conscience? And as brutes act agreeably to their nature, in following that principle or particular instinct which for the present is strongest in them: does not man likewise act agreeably to his nature, or obey the law of his creation, by following that principle, be it passion or conscience, which for the present happens to be strongest in him? . . .

[4.] Now all this licentious talk entirely goes upon a supposition, that men follow their nature in the same sense, in violating the known rules of justice and honesty for the sake of a present gratification, as they do in following those rules when they have no temptation to the contrary. And if this were true, that could not be so which St. Paul asserts, that men are "by nature a law to themselves." . . . the objection will be fully answered, and the text before us explained, by observing that *nature* is considered in different views, and the words used in different senses; and by showing in what view it is considered, and in what sense the word is used, when intended to express and signify that which is the guide of life, that by which men are a law to themselves. I say, the explanation of the term will be sufficient, because from thence it will appear, that in some senses of the word *nature* cannot be, but that in another sense it manifestly is, a law to us.

[5.] I. By nature is often meant no more than some principle in man, without regard either to the kind or degree of it. Thus the passion of anger, and the affection of parents to their children, would be called equally *natural*. And as the same person hath often contrary principles, which at the same time draw contrary ways, he may by the same action both follow and contradict his nature in this sense of the word; he may follow one passion and contradict another.

[6.] II. *Nature* is frequently spoken of as consisting in those passions which are strongest, and most influence the actions; which being vicious ones, mankind is in this sense naturally vicious, or vicious by nature. Thus St. Paul says of the Gentiles, "who were dead in trespasses and sins, and walked according to the spirit of disobedience, that they were by nature the children of wrath."[1] They could be no otherwise *children of wrath* by nature, than they were vicious by nature.

[7.] Here then are two different senses of the word *nature,* in neither of which men can at all be said to be a law to themselves. They are mentioned only to be excluded; to prevent their being confounded, as the latter is in the objection, with another sense of it, which is now to be inquired after and explained.

[8.] III. . . . What that is in man by which he is *naturally a law to himself,* is explained in the following words: "which show the work of the law written in their hearts, their conscience also bearing witness, and their thoughts the meanwhile accusing or else excusing one another."[2] If there be a distinction to be made between the *works written in their hearts,* and the *witness of conscience;* by the former must be meant the natural disposition to kindness and compassion, to do what is of good report, to which this apostle often refers: that part of the nature of man, treated of in the foregoing discourse, which with very little reflection and of course leads him to society, and by means of which he naturally acts a just and good part in it, unless other passions or interest lead him astray. Yet since other passions, and regards to private interest, which lead us (though indirectly, yet they lead us) astray, are themselves in a degree equally natural, and often most prevalent; and since we have no method of seeing the particular degrees in which one or the other is placed in us by nature; it is plain the former, considered merely as natural, good and right as they are, can no more be a law to us than the latter. But there is a superior principle of reflection or conscience in every man, which distinguishes between the internal principles of his heart, as well as his external actions: which passes judgment upon himself and them; pronounces determinately some actions to be in themselves just, right, good; others to be in themselves evil, wrong, unjust; which, without being consulted, without being advised with, magisterially exerts itself, and approves or condemns him the doer of them

accordingly: and which, if not forcibly stopped, naturally and always of course goes on to anticipate a higher and more effectual sentence, which shall hereafter second and affirm its own. But this part of the office of conscience is beyond my present design explicitly to consider. It is by this faculty, natural to man, that he is a moral agent, that he is a law to himself: by this faculty, I say, not to be considered merely as a principle in his heart, which is to have some influence as well as others; but considered as a faculty in kind and in nature supreme over all others, and which bears its own authority of being so.

[9.] This *prerogative,* this *natural supremacy,* of the faculty which surveys, approves or disapproves the several affections of our mind and actions of our lives, being that by which men *are a law to themselves,* their conformity or disobedience to which law of our nature renders their actions, in the highest and most proper sense, natural or unnatural; it is fit it be further explained to you: and I hope it will be so, if you will attend to the following reflections.

[10.] Man may act according to that principle or inclination which for the present happens to be strongest, and yet act in a way disproportionate to, and violate his real proper nature. Suppose a brute creature by any bait to be allured into a snare, by which he is destroyed. He plainly followed the bent of his nature, leading him to gratify his appetite: there is an entire correspondence between his whole nature and such an action: such action therefore is natural. But suppose a man, foreseeing the same danger of certain ruin, should rush into it for the sake of a present gratification; he in this instance would follow his strongest desire, as did the brute creature: but there would be as manifest a disproportion, between the nature of a man and such an action, as between the meanest work of art and the skill of the greatest master in that art: which disproportion arises, not from considering the action singly in *itself,* or in its *consequences;* but from comparison of it with the nature of the agent. And since such an action is utterly disproportionate to the nature of man, it is in the strictest and most proper sense unnatural; this word expressing that disproportion. Therefore instead of the words *disproportionate to his nature,* the word *unnatural* may now be put; this being more familiar to us: but let it be observed, that it stands for the same thing precisely.

[11.] Now what is it which renders such a rash action unnatural? Is it that he went against the principle of reasonable and cool self-love, considered *merely* as a part of his nature? No: for if he had acted the contrary way, he would equally have gone against a principle, or part of its nature, namely, passion or appetite. But to deny a present appetite, from foresight that the gratification of it would end in immediate ruin or extreme misery, is by no means an unnatural action: whereas to contradict or go against cool self-love for the sake of such gratification, is so in the instance before us. Such an action then being unnatural; and its being so not arising from a man's going against a principle or desire barely, nor in going against that principle or desire which happens for the present to be strongest; it necessarily follows, that there must be some other difference or distinction to be made between these two principles, passion and cool self-love, than what I have yet taken notice of. And this difference, not being a difference in strength or degree, I call a difference in *nature* and in *kind*. And since, in the instance still before us, if passion prevails over self-love, the consequent action is unnatural; but if self-love prevails over passion, the action is natural: it is manifest that self-love is in human nature a superior principle to passion. This may be contradicted without violating that nature; but the former cannot. So that, if we will act conformably to the economy of man's nature, reasonable self-love must govern. Thus, without particular consideration of conscience, we may have a clear conception of the *superior nature* of one inward principle to another; and see that there really is this natural superiority, quite distinct from degrees of strength and prevalency.

[13.] Passion or appetite implies a direct simple tendency towards such and such objects, without distinction of the means by which they are to be obtained. Consequently it will often happen there will be a desire of particular objects, in cases where they cannot be obtained without manifest injury to others. Reflection or conscience comes in, and disapproves the pursuit of them in these circumstances; but the desire remains. Which is to be obeyed,

appetite or reflection? Cannot this question be answered, from the economy and constitution of human nature merely, without saying which is strongest? Or need this at all come into consideration? Would not the question be intelligibly and fully answered by saying, that the principle of reflection or conscience being compared with the various appetites, passions, and affections in men, the former is manifestly superior and chief, without regard to strength? And how often soever the latter happens to prevail, it is mere usurpation: the former remains in nature and in kind its superior; and every instance of such prevalence of the latter is an instance of breaking in upon and violation of the constitution of man.

[14.] All this is no more than the distinction, which everybody is acquainted with, between *mere power* and *authority*: only instead of being intended to express the difference between what is possible, and what is lawful in civil government; here it has been shown applicable to the several principles in the mind of man. Thus that principle, by which we survey, and either approve or disapprove our own heart, temper, and actions, is not only to be considered as what is in its turn to have some influence; which may be said of every passion, of the lowest appetites: but likewise as being superior; as from its very nature manifestly claiming superiority over all others: insomuch that you cannot form a notion of this faculty, conscience, without taking in judgment, direction, superintendency. This is a constituent part of the idea, that is, of the faculty itself: and to preside and govern, from the very economy and constitution of man, belongs to it. Had it strength, as it has right; had it power, as it has manifest authority, it would absolutely govern the world.

SERMON III: UPON HUMAN NATURE

For when the Gentiles, which have not the law, do by nature the things contained in the law, these, having not the law, are a law unto themselves.
(Rom. 2:14)

[1.] The natural supremacy of reflection or conscience being thus established; we may from it form a distinct notion of what is meant by *human nature,* when virtue is said to consist in following it, and vice in deviating from it.

[2.] As the idea of a civil constitution implies in it united strength, various subordinations, under one direction, that of the supreme authority; the different strength of each particular member of the society not coming into the idea; whereas, if you leave out the subordination, the union, and the one direction, you destroy and lose it: so reason, several appetites, passions, and affections, prevailing in different degrees of strength, is not *that* idea or notion of *human nature*; but *that nature* consists in these several principles considered as having a natural respect to each other, in the several passions being naturally subordinate to the one superior principle of reflection or conscience. Every bias, instinct, propension within, is a real part of our nature, but not the whole: add to these the superior faculty, whose office it is to adjust, manage, and preside over them, and take in this its natural superiority, and you complete the idea of human nature. And as in civil government the constitution is broken in upon, and violated by power and strength prevailing over authority; so the constitution of man is broken in upon and violated by the lower faculties or principles within prevailing over that which is in its nature supreme over them all. Thus, when it is said by ancient writers, that tortures and death are not so contrary to human nature as injustice; by this to be sure is not meant, that the aversion to the former in mankind is less strong and prevalent than their aversion to the latter; but that the former is only contrary to our nature considered in a partial view, and which takes in only the lowest part of it, that which we have in common with the brutes; whereas the latter is contrary to our nature, considered in a higher sense, as a system and constitution contrary to the whole economy of man.

[3.] And from all these things put together, nothing can be more evident, than that, exclusive of revelation, man cannot be considered as a creature left by his Maker to act at random, and live at large up to the extent of his natural power, as passion, humor, wilfulness, happen to carry him; which is the condition brute creatures are in: but that from his make, constitution, or nature, he is in the strictest and most proper sense a law to himself. He hath the rule of right within: what is wanting is only that he honestly attend to it.

[4.] The inquiries which have been made by men of leisure, after some general rule, the conformity to, or disagreement from which, should denominate our actions good or evil, are in many respects of great service. Yet let any plain honest man, before he engages in any course of action, ask himself, Is this I am going about right, or is it wrong? Is it good, or is it evil? I do not in the least doubt, but that this question would be answered agreeably to truth and virtue, by almost any fair man in almost any circumstance. Neither do there appear any cases which look like exceptions to this; but those of superstition, and of partiality to ourselves. Superstition may perhaps be somewhat of an exception: but partiality to ourselves is not; this being itself dishonesty. For a man to judge that to be the equitable, the moderate, the right part for him to act, which he would see to be hard, unjust, oppressive in another; this is plain vice, and can proceed only from great unfairness of mind.

[5.] But allowing that mankind hath the rule of right within himself, yet it may be asked, "What obligations are we under to attend to and follow it?" I answer: it has been proved that man by his nature is a law to himself, without the particular distinct consideration of the positive sanctions of that law; the rewards and punishments which we feel, and those which from the light of reason we have ground to believe are annexed to it. The question then carries its own answer along with it. Your obligation to obey this law, is its being the law of your nature. That your conscience approves of and attests to such a course of action, is itself alone an obligation. Conscience does not only offer itself to show us the way we should walk in, but it likewise carries its own authority with it, that it is our natural guide; the guide assigned us by the Author of our nature: it therefore belongs to our condition of being, it is our duty to walk in that path, and follow this guide, without looking about to see whether we may not possibly forsake them with impunity.

SERMON XI: UPON THE LOVE OF OUR NEIGHBOR

And if there be any other commandment, it is briefly comprehended in this saying, namely, Thou shalt love thy neighbor as thyself.

(Rom. 13:9)

[5.] Every man hath a general desire of his own happiness; and likewise a variety of particular affections, passions, and appetites to particular external objects. The former proceeds from, or is self-love; and seems inseparable from all sensible creatures, who can reflect upon themselves and their own interest or happiness, so as to have that interest an object to their minds: what is to be said of the latter is, that they proceed from, or together make up that particular nature, according to which man is made. The object the former pursues is somewhat internal, our own happiness, enjoyment, satisfaction; whether we have, or have not, a distinct particular perception what it is, or wherein it consists: the objects of the latter are this or that particular external thing, which the affections tend towards, and of which it hath always a particular idea or perception. The principle we call self-love never seeks anything external for the sake of the thing, but only as a means of happiness or good: particular affections rest in the external things themselves. One belongs to man as a reasonable creature reflecting upon his own interest or happiness. The other, though quite distinct from reason, are as much a part of human nature.

[6.] That all particular appetites and passions are towards *external things themselves,* distinct from the *pleasure arising from them,* is manifested from hence; that there could not be this pleasure, were it not for that prior suitableness between the object and the passion: there could be no enjoyment or delight from one thing more than another, from eating food more than from swallowing a stone, if there were not an affection or appetite to one thing more than another.

[7.] Every particular affection, even the love of our neighbor, is as really our own affection, as self-love; and the pleasure arising from its gratification is as much my own pleasure, as the pleasure self-love would have, from knowing I myself should be happy some time hence, would be my own pleasure. And if, because every particular affection is a man's own, and the pleasure arising from its gratification his own pleasure, or pleasure to himself, such particular affection must be called self-love; according to this way of speaking, no creature whatever can possibly act but merely from self-love; and every action and every affection whatever is to be resolved up into this one principle. But then this is not the language of mankind: or if it were, we should want words to express the difference, between the principle of an action, proceeding from cool consideration that it will be to my own advantage; and an action, suppose of revenge, or of friendship, by which a man runs upon certain ruin, to do evil or good to another. It is manifest the principles of these actions are totally different, and so want different words to be distinguished by: all that they agree in is, that they both proceed from, and are done to gratify an inclination in a man's self. But the principle or inclination in one case is self-love; in the other, hatred or love of another. There is then a distinction between the cool principle of self-love, or general desire of our happiness, as one part of our nature, and one principle of action; and the particular affections towards particular external objects, as another part of our nature, and another principle of action. How much soever therefore is to be allowed to self-love, yet it cannot be allowed to be the whole of our inward constitution; because, you see, there are other parts or principles which come into it.

[8.] Further, private happiness or good is all which self-love can make us desire, or be concerned about: in having this consists its gratification: it is an affection to ourselves; a regard to our own interest, happiness, and private good: and in the proportion a man hath this, he is interested, or a lover of himself. Let this be kept in mind; because there is commonly, as I shall presently have occasion to observe, another sense put upon these words. On the other hand, particular affections tend towards particular external things: these are their objects; having these is their end: in this consists their gratification: no matter whether it be, or be not, upon the whole, our interest or happiness. An action done from the former of these principles is called an interested action. An action proceeding from any of the latter has its denomination of passionate, ambitious, friendly, revengeful, or any other, from the particular appetite or affection from which it proceeds. Thus self-love as one part of human nature, and the several particular principles as the other part, are, themselves, their objects and ends, stated and shown.

[11.] Self-love and interestedness was stated to consist in or be an affection to ourselves, a regard to our own private good: it is therefore distinct from benevolence, which is an affection to the good of our fellow-creatures. But that benevolence is distinct from, that is, not the same thing with self-love, is no reason for its being looked upon with any peculiar suspicion; because every principle whatever, by means of which self-love is gratified, is distinct from it; and all things which are distinct from each other are equally so. A man has an affection or aversion to another: that one of these tends to, and is gratified by doing good, that the other tends to, and is gratified by doing harm, does not in the least alter the respect which either one or the other of these inward feelings has to self-love. We use the word *property* so as to exclude any other persons having an interest in that of which we say a particular man has the property. And we often use the word *selfish* so as to exclude in the same manner all regards to the good of others. But the cases are not parallel: for though that exclusion is really part of the idea of property; yet such positive exclusion, or bringing this peculiar disregard to the good of others into the idea of self-love, is in reality adding to the idea, or changing it from what it was before stated to consist in, namely, in an affection to ourselves. This being the whole idea of self-love, it can no otherwise exclude good-will or love of others, than merely by not including it, no otherwise, than it excludes love of arts or reputation, or of anything else. Neither on the other hand does benevolence, any more than love of arts or of reputation, exclude self-love. Love of our neighbor then has just the same respect to, is no more distant from, self-love, than hatred of our neighbor, or than love or hatred of anything else. . . .

[12.] Thus it appears that there is no peculiar contrariety between self-love and benevolence; no greater competition between these, than between any other particular affections and self-love. This relates to the affections themselves. Let us now see whether there be any peculiar contrariety between the respective courses of life which these affections lead to; whether there be any greater competition between the pursuit of private and of public good, than between any other particular pursuits and that of private good.

[16.] The short of the matter is no more than this. Happiness consists in the gratification of certain affections, appetites, passions, with objects which are by nature adapted to them. Self-love may indeed set us on work to gratify these: but happiness or enjoyment has no immediate connexion with self-love, but arises from such gratification alone. Love of our neighbor is one of those affections. This, considered as a *virtuous principle,* is gratified by a consciousness of endeavoring to promote the good of others; but considered as a *natural affection,* its gratification consists in the actual accomplishment of this endeavour. Now indulgence or gratification of this affection, whether in that consciousness, or this accomplishment, has the same respect to interest, as indulgence of any other affection; they equally proceed from or do not proceed from self-love, they equally include or equally exclude this principle. Thus it appears, that benevolence and the pursuit of public good hath at least as great respect to self-love and the pursuit of private good, as any other particular passions, and their respective pursuits.

[20.] And to all these things may be added, that religion, from whence arises our strongest obligation to benevolence, is so far from disowning the principle of self-love, that it often addresses itself to that very principle, and always to the mind in that state when reason presides; and there can no access be had to the understanding, but by convincing men, that the course of life we would persuade them to is not contrary to their interest. It may be allowed, without any prejudice to the cause of virtue and religion, that our ideas of happiness and misery are of all our ideas the nearest and most important to us; that they will, nay, if you please, that they ought to prevail over those of order, and beauty, and harmony, and proportion, if there should ever be, as it is impossible there ever should be, any inconsistence between them: though these last too, as expressing the fitness of actions, are real as truth itself. Let it be allowed, though virtue or moral rectitude does indeed consist in affection to and pursuit of what is right and good as such; yet, that when we sit down in a cool hour, we can neither justify to ourselves this or any other pursuit, till we are convinced that it will be for our happiness, or at least not contrary to it.

NOTES

1. [Eph. 2:3—Eds.]
2. [Rom. 2:15]

STUDY QUESTIONS

1. What is a selfish action?
2. Is acting in one's self-interest always selfish?
3. Do morality and self-interest ever conflict?
4. If human nature were different, would morality be different?

A Treatise of Human Nature

David Hume

David Hume (1711–1776), the influential Scottish philosopher, maintains that morality is based on sentiment, not reason. He argues that while moral judgments motivate us to act, reason is inert, helping us make inferences but not producing passions for action. In other words, because moral judgments are motivating while the products of reason are not, moral judgments are not based on reason. Moreover, no factual statements by themselves imply any moral claims. In short, "is" does not imply "ought." Hume's position can be summed up in his famous words: "Reason is, and ought to be, the slave of the passions, and can never pretend to any other office than to serve and obey them."

BOOK II OF THE PASSIONS

Part III Of the Will and Direct Passions

Section III Of the Influencing Motives of the Will

Nothing is more usual in philosophy, and even in common life, than to talk of the combat of passion and reason, to give the preference to reason, and assert that men are only so far virtuous as they conform themselves to its dictates. Every rational creature, it is said, is obliged to regulate his actions by reason; and if any other motive or principle challenge the direction of his conduct, he ought to oppose it, till it be entirely subdued, or at least brought to a conformity with that superior principle. On this method of thinking the greatest part of moral philosophy, ancient and modern, seems to be founded; nor is there an ampler field, as well for metaphysical arguments, as popular declamations, than this supposed preëminence of reason above passion. The eternity, invariableness, and divine origin of the former, have been displayed to the best advantage: the blindness, inconstancy, and deceitfulness of the latter, have been as strongly insisted on. In order to show the fallacy of all this philosophy, I shall endeavor to prove, *first,* that reason alone can never be a motive to any action of the will; and *secondly,* that it can never oppose passion in the direction of the will.

The understanding exerts itself after two different ways, as it judges from demonstration or probability: as it regards the abstract relations of our ideas, or those relations of objects of which experience only gives us information. I believe it scarce will be asserted, that the first species of reasoning alone is ever the cause of any action. As its proper province is the world of ideas, and as the will always places us in that of realities, demonstration and volition seem upon that account to be totally removed from each other. Mathematics, indeed, are useful in all mechanical operations, and arithmetic in almost every

From David Hume, *A Treatise of Human Nature* (1739–40).

art and profession: but it is not of themselves they have any influence. Mechanics are the art of regulating the motions of bodies *to some designed end or purpose*; and the reason why we employ arithmetic in fixing the proportions of numbers, is only that we may discover the proportions of their influence and operation. A merchant is desirous of knowing the sum total of his accounts with any person: why? but that he may learn what sum will have the same *effects* in paying his debt, and going to market, as all the particular articles taken together. Abstract or demonstrative reasoning, therefore, never influences any of our actions, but only as it directs our judgment concerning causes and effects; which leads us to the second operation of the understanding.

It is obvious, that when we have the prospect of pain or pleasure from any object, we feel a consequent emotion of aversion or propensity, and are carried to avoid or embrace what will give us this uneasiness or satisfaction. It is also obvious, that this emotion rests not here, but, making us cast our view on every side, comprehends whatever objects are connected with its original one by the relation of cause and effect. Here then reasoning takes place to discover this relation; and according as our reasoning varies, our actions receive a subsequent variation. But it is evident, in this case, that the impulse arises not from reason, but is only directed by it. It is from the prospect of pain or pleasure that the aversion or propensity arises towards any object: and these emotions extend themselves to the causes and effects of that object, as they are pointed out to us by reason and experience. It can never in the least concern us to know, that such objects are causes, and such others effects, if both the causes and effects be indifferent to us. Where the objects themselves do not affect us, their connection can never give them any influence; and it is plain that, as reason is nothing but the discovery of this connection, it cannot be by its means that the objects are able to affect us.

Since reason alone can never produce any action, or give rise to volition, I infer, that the same faculty is as incapable of preventing volition, or of disputing the preference with any passion or emotion. This consequence is necessary. It is impossible reason could have the latter effect of preventing volition, but by giving an impulse in a contrary direction to our passions; and that impulse, had it operated alone, would have been ample to produce volition. Nothing can oppose or retard the impulse of passion, but a contrary impulse; and if this contrary impulse ever arises from reason, that latter faculty must have an original influence on the will, and must be able to cause, as well as hinder, any act of volition. But if reason has no original influence, it is impossible it can withstand any principle which has such an efficacy, or ever keep the mind in suspense a moment. Thus, it appears, that the principle which opposes our passion cannot be the same with reason, and is only called so in an improper sense. We speak not strictly and philosophically, when we talk of the combat of passion and of reason. Reason is, and ought only to be, the slave of the passions, and can never pretend to any other office than to serve and obey them. As this opinion may appear somewhat extraordinary, it may not be improper to confirm it by some other considerations.

A passion is an original existence, or, if you will, modification of existence, and contains not any representative quality, which renders it a copy of any other existence or modification. When I am angry, I am actually possessed with the passion, and in that emotion have no more a reference to any other object, than when I am thirsty, or sick, or more than five feet high. It is impossible, therefore, that this passion can be opposed by, or be contradictory to truth and reason; since this contradiction consists in the disagreement of ideas, considered as copies, with those objects which they represent.

What may at first occur on this head is, that as nothing can be contrary to truth or reason, except what has a reference to it, and as the judgments of our understanding only have this reference, it must follow that passions can be contrary to reason only, so far as they are *accompanied* with some judgment or opinion. According to this principle, which is so obvious and natural, it is only in two senses that any affection can be called unreasonable. First, When a passion, such as hope or fear, grief or joy, despair or security, is founded on the supposition of the existence of objects, which really do not exist. Secondly, When in exerting any passion in action, we choose means sufficient for the designed end, and deceive ourselves in our judgment of causes and effects. Where a passion is neither founded on false suppositions, nor chooses means insufficient for the end, the understanding can neither justify nor condemn it. It is not contrary to reason to prefer the destruction of the whole world to the scratching of my finger. It is not contrary to reason for me to choose my total ruin, to prevent the least uneasiness of an Indian, or person wholly unknown to me. It is as little contrary to reason to prefer even my own acknowledged lesser good to my greater, and have a more ardent affection for the former than the latter. A trivial good may, from certain circumstances, produce a desire superior to what arises from the greatest and most valuable enjoyment; nor is there anything more extraordinary in this, than in mechanics to see one pound weight raise up a hundred by the advantage of its situation. In short, a passion must be accompanied with some false judgment, in order to its being unreasonable; and even then it is not the passion, properly speaking, which is unreasonable, but the judgment.

The consequences are evident. Since a passion can never, in any sense, be called unreasonable, but when founded on a false supposition, or when it chooses means insufficient for the designed end, it is impossible that reason and passion can ever oppose each other, or dispute for the government of the will and actions. The moment we perceive the falsehood of any supposition, or the insufficiency of any means, our passions yield to our reason without any opposition. I may desire any fruit as of an excellent relish; but whenever you convince me of my mistake, my longing ceases. I may will the performance of certain actions as means of obtaining any desired good; but as my willing of these actions is only secondary, and founded on the supposition that they are causes of the proposed effect; as soon as I discover the falsehood of that supposition, they must become indifferent to me.

It is natural for one, that does not examine objects with a strict philosophic eye, to imagine, that those actions of the mind are entirely the same, which produce not a different sensation, and are not immediately distinguishable to the feeling and perception.

Reason, for instance, exerts itself without producing any sensible emotions; and except in the more sublime disquisitions of philosophy, or in the frivolous subtilties of the schools, scarce ever conveys any pleasure or uneasiness. Hence it proceeds, that every action of the mind which operates with the same calmness and tranquillity, is confounded with reason by all those who judge of things from the first view and appearance. Now it is certain there are certain calm desires and tendencies, which, though they be real passions, produce little emotion in the mind, and are more known by their effects than by the immediate feeling or sensation. These desires are of two kinds; either certain instincts originally implanted in our natures, such as benevolence and resentment, the love of life, and kindness to children: or the general appetite to good, and aversion to evil, considered merely as such. When any of these passions are calm, and cause no disorder in the soul, they are very readily taken for the determinations of reason, and are supposed to proceed from the same faculty with that which judges of truth and falsehood. Their nature and principles have been supposed the same, because their sensations are not evidently different.

Besides these calm passions, which often determine the will, there are certain violent emotions of the same kind, which have likewise a great influence on that faculty. When I receive any injury from another, I often feel a violent passion of resentment, which makes me desire his evil and punishment, independent of all considerations of pleasure and advantage to myself. When I am immediately threatened with any grievous ill, my fears, apprehensions, and aversions rise to a great height, and produce a sensible emotion.

The common error of metaphysicians has lain in ascribing the direction of the will entirely to one of these principles, and supposing the other to have no influence. Men often act knowingly against their interest: for which reason, the view of the greatest possible good does not always influence them. Men often counteract a violent passion in prosecution of their interests and designs: it is not, therefore, the present uneasiness alone which determines them. In general we may observe that both these principles operate on the will; and where they are contrary, that either of them prevails, according to the *general* character or *present* disposition of the person. What we call strength of mind, implies the prevalence of the calm passions above the violent; though we may easily observe, there is no man so constantly possessed of this virtue as never on any occasion to yield to the solicitations of passion and desire. From these variations of temper proceeds the great difficulty of deciding concerning the actions and resolutions of men, where there is any contrariety of motives and passions.

BOOK III OF MORALS

Part I Of Virtue and Vice in General

Section I *Moral Distinctions Not Derived from Reason*

There is an inconvenience which attends all abstruse reasoning, that it may silence, without convincing an antagonist, and requires the same intense study to make us sensible of its force, that was at first requisite for its invention. When we leave our closet, and engage in the common affairs of life, its conclusions seem to vanish like the phantoms of the night on the appearance of the morning; and it is difficult for us to retain even that conviction which we had attained with difficulty. This is still more conspicuous in a long chain of reasoning, where we must preserve to the end the evidence of the first propositions, and where we often lose sight of all the most received maxims, either of philosophy or common life. I am not, however, without hopes, that the present system of philosophy will acquire new force as it advances; and that our reasonings concerning *morals* will corroborate whatever has been said concerning the *understanding* and the *passions*. Morality is a subject that interests us above all others; we fancy the peace of society to be at stake in every decision concerning it; and it is evident that this concern must make our speculations appear more real and solid, than where the subject is in a great measure indifferent to us. What affects us, we conclude, can never be a chimera; and, as our passion is engaged on the one side

or the other, we naturally think that the question lies within human comprehension; which, in other cases of this nature, we are apt to entertain some doubt of. Without this advantage, I never should have ventured upon a third volume of such abstruse philosophy, in an age wherein the greatest part of men seem agreed to convert reading into an amusement, and to reject everything that requires any considerable degree of attention to be comprehended.

It has been observed, that nothing is ever present to the mind but its perceptions; and that all the actions of seeing, hearing, judging, loving, hating, and thinking, fall under this denomination. The mind can never exert itself in any action which we may not comprehend under the term of *perception*; and consequently that term is no less applicable to those judgments by which we distinguish moral good and evil, than to every other operation of the mind. To approve of one character, to condemn another, are only so many different perceptions.

Now, as perceptions resolve themselves into two kinds, viz. *impressions* and *ideas,* this distinction gives rise to a question, with which we shall open up our present inquiry concerning morals, *whether it is by means of our* ideas *or* impressions *we distinguish betwixt vice and virtue, and pronounce an action blamable or praiseworthy?* This will immediately cut off all loose discourses and declamations, and reduce us to something precise and exact on the present subject.

Those who affirm that virtue is nothing but a conformity to reason; that there are eternal fitnesses and unfitnesses of things, which are the same to every rational being that considers them; that the immutable measure of right and wrong impose an obligation, not only on human creatures, but also on the Deity himself: all these systems concur in the opinion, that morality, like truth, is discerned merely by ideas, and by their juxtaposition and comparison. In order, therefore, to judge of these systems, we need only consider whether it be possible from reason alone, to distinguish betwixt moral good and evil, or whether there must concur some other principles to enable us to make that distinction,

If morality had naturally no influence on human passions and actions, it were in vain to take such pains to inculcate it; and nothing would be more fruitless than that multitude of rules and precepts with which all moralists abound. Philosophy is commonly divided into *speculative* and *practical*; and as morality is always comprehended under the latter division, it is supposed to influence our passions and actions, and to go beyond the calm and indolent judgments of the understanding. And this is confirmed by common experience, which informs us that men are often governed by their duties, and are deterred from some actions by the opinion of injustice, and impelled to others by that of obligation.

Since morals, therefore, have an influence on the actions and affections, it follows that they cannot be derived from reason; and that because reason alone, as we have already proved, can never have any such influence. Morals excite passions, and produce or prevent actions. Reason of itself is utterly impotent in this particular. The rules of morality, therefore, are not conclusions of our reason.

No one, I believe, will deny the justness of this inference; nor is there any other means of evading it, than by denying that principle on which it is founded. As long as it is allowed, that reason has no influence on our passions and actions, it is in vain to pretend that morality is discovered only by a deduction of reason. An active principle can never be founded on an inactive; and if reason be inactive in itself, it must remain so in all its shapes and appearances, whether it exerts itself in natural or moral subjects, whether it considers the powers of external bodies, or the actions of rational beings.

It would be tedious to repeat all the arguments by which I have proved that reason is perfectly inert, and can never either prevent or produce any action or affection. It will be easy to recollect what has been said upon that subject. I shall only recall on this occasion one of these arguments, which I shall endeavor to render still more conclusive, and more applicable to the present subject.

Reason is the discovery of truth or falsehood, Truth or falsehood consists in an agreement or disagreement either to the *real* relations of ideas, or to *real* existence and matter of fact. Whatever therefore is not susceptible of this agreement or disagreement, is incapable of being true or false, and can

never be an object of our reason. Now, it is evident our passions, volitions, and actions, are not susceptible of any such agreement or disagreement; being original facts and realities, complete in themselves, and implying no reference to other passions, volitions, and actions. It is impossible, therefore, they can be pronounced either true or false, and be either contrary or conformable to reason.

This argument is of double advantage to our present purpose. For it proves *directly,* that actions do not derive their merit from a conformity to reason, nor their blame from a contrariety to it; and it proves the same truth more *indirectly,* by showing us, that as reason can never immediately prevent or produce any action by contradicting or approving of it, it cannot be the source of moral good and evil, which are found to have that influence. Actions may be laudable or blamable; but they cannot be reasonable or unreasonable: laudable or blamable, therefore, are not the same with reasonable or unreasonable. The merit and demerit of actions frequently contradict, and sometimes control our natural propensities. But reason has no such influence. Moral distinctions, therefore, are not the offspring of reason. Reason is wholly inactive, and can never be the source of so active a principle as conscience, or a sense of morals.

But perhaps it may be said, that though no will or action can be immediately contradictory to reason, yet we may find such a contradiction in some of the attendants of the actions, that is, in its causes or effects. The action may cause a judgment, or may be *obliquely* caused by one, when the judgment concurs with a passion; and by an abusive way of speaking, which philosophy will scarce allow of, the same contrariety may, upon that account, be ascribed to the action. How far this truth or falsehood may be the source of morals, it will now be proper to consider.

It has been observed that reason, in a strict and philosophical sense, can have an influence on our conducts only after two ways: either when it excites a passion, by informing us of the existence of something which is a proper object of it; or when it discovers the connection of causes and effects, so as to afford us means of exerting any passion. These are the only kinds of judgment which can accompany our actions, or can be said to produce them in any manner; and it must be allowed, that these judgments may often be false and erroneous. A person may be affected with passion, by supposing a pain or pleasure to lie in an object which has no tendency to produce either of these sensations, or which produces the contrary to what is imagined. A person may also take false measures for the attaining of his end, and may retard, by his foolish conduct, instead of forwarding the execution of any object. These false judgments may be thought to affect the passions and actions, which are connected with them, and may be said to render them unreasonable, in a figurative and improper way of speaking. But though this be acknowledged, it is easy to observe, that these errors are so far from being the source of all immorality, that they are commonly very innocent, and draw no manner of guilt upon the person who is so unfortunate as to fall into them. They extend not beyond a mistake of *fact,* which moralists have not generally supposed criminal, as being perfectly involuntary. I am more to be lamented than blamed, if I am mistaken with regard to the influence of objects in producing pain or pleasure, or if I know not the proper means of satisfying my desires. No one can ever regard such errors as a defect in my moral character. A fruit, for instance, that is really disagreeable, appears to me at a distance, and, through mistake, I fancy it to be pleasant and delicious. Here is one error. I choose certain means of reaching this fruit, which are not proper for my end. Here is a second error; nor is there any third one, which can ever possibly enter into our reasonings concerning actions. I ask, therefore, if a man in this situation, and guilty of these two errors, is to be regarded as vicious and criminal, however unavoidable they might have been? Or if it be possible to imagine that such errors are the sources of all immorality?

And here it may be proper to observe, that if moral distinctions be derived from the truth or falsehood of those judgments, they must take place wherever we form the judgments; nor will there be any difference, whether the question be concerning an apple or a kingdom, or whether the error be avoidable or unavoidable.

For as the very essence of morality is supposed to consist in an agreement or disagreement to reason, the other circumstances are entirely arbitrary, and can never either bestow on any action the character of virtuous or vicious, or deprive it of that character. To which we may add, that this agreement or disagreement, not admitting of degrees, all virtues and vices would of course be equal.

Should it be pretended, that though a mistake of *fact* be not criminal, yet a mistake of *right* often is; and that this may be the source of immorality: I would answer, that it is impossible such a mistake can ever be the original source of immorality, since it supposes a real right and wrong; that is, a real distinction in morals, independent of these judgments. A mistake, therefore, of right, may become a species of immorality; but it is only a secondary one, and is founded on some other antecedent to it.

As to those judgments which are the *effects* of our actions, and which, when false, give occasion to pronounce the actions contrary to truth and reason; we may observe, that our actions never cause any judgment, either true or false, in ourselves, and that it is only on others they have such an influence. It is certain that an action, on many occasions, may give rise to false conclusions in others; and that a person, who, through a window, sees any lewd behaviour of mine with my neighbor's wife, may be so simple as to imagine she is certainly my own. In this respect my action resembles somewhat a lie or falsehood; only with this difference, which is material, that I perform not the action with any intention of giving rise to a false judgment in another, but merely to satisfy my lust and passion. It causes, however, a mistake and false judgment by accident; and the falsehood of its effects may be ascribed, by some odd figurative way of speaking, to the action itself. But still I can see no pretext of reason for asserting, that the tendency to cause such an error is the first spring or original source of all immorality.

Thus, upon the whole, it is impossible that the distinction betwixt moral good and evil can be made by reason; since that distinction has an influence upon our actions, of which reason alone is incapable. Reason and judgment may, indeed, be the mediate cause of an action, by prompting or by directing a passion; but it is not pretended that a judgment of this kind, either in its truth or falsehood, is attended with virtue or vice. And as to the judgments, which are caused by our judgments, they can still less bestow those moral qualities on the actions which are their causes.

But, to be more particular, and to show that those eternal immutable fitnesses and unfitnesses of things cannot be defended by sound philosophy, we may weigh the following considerations.

If the thought and understanding were alone capable of fixing the boundaries of right and wrong, the character of virtuous and vicious either must lie in some relations of objects, or must be a matter of fact which is discovered by our reasoning. This consequence is evident. As the operations of human understanding divide themselves into two kinds, the comparing of ideas, and the inferring of matter of fact, were virtue discovered by the understanding, it must be an object of one of these operations; nor is there any third operation of the understanding which can discover it. There has been an opinion very industriously propagated by certain philosophers, that morality is susceptible of demonstration; and though no one has ever been able to advance a single step in those demonstrations, yet it is taken for granted that this science may be brought to an equal certainty with geometry or algebra. Upon this supposition, vice and virtue must consist in some relations; since it is allowed on all hands, that no matter of fact is capable of being demonstrated. Let us therefore begin with examining this hypothesis, and endeavor, if possible, to fix those moral qualities which have been so long the objects of our fruitless researches; point out distinctly the relations which constitute morality or obligation, that we may know wherein they consist, and after what manner we must judge of them.

If you assert that vice and virtue consist in relations susceptible of certainty and demonstration, you must confine yourself to those *four* relations which alone admit at that degree of evidence: and in that case you run into absurdities from which you will never be able to extricate yourself. For as you make the very essence of morality to lie in the relations, and as there is no one of these relations but what is applicable, not only to all irrational but also to an inanimate object, it follows that even such objects must be susceptible of merit or demerit. *Resemblance, contrariety, degrees in quality,* and *proportions in quantity and number;* all these relations belong as properly to matter as to our actions, passions, and volitions. It is unquestionable, therefore, that morality lies not in any of these relations, nor the sense of it in their discovery.

Should it be asserted, that the sense of morality consists in the discovery of some relation distinct from these, and that our enumeration was not complete when we comprehended all demonstrable relations under four general heads: to this I know not what to reply, till some one be so good as to point out to me this new relation. It is impossible to refute a system which has never yet been explained. In such a manner of lighting in the dark, a man loses his blows in the air, and often places them where the enemy is not present.

I must therefore, on this occasion, rest contented with requiring the two following conditions of any one that would undertake to clear up this system. *First,* as moral good and evil belong only to the actions of the mind, and are derived from our situation with regard to external objects, the relations from which these moral distinctions arise must lie only betwixt internal actions and external objects, and must not be applicable either to internal actions, compared among themselves, or to external objects, when placed in opposition to other external objects. For as morality is supposed to attend certain relations, if these relations could belong to internal actions considered singly, it would follow, that we might be guilty of crimes in ourselves, and independent of our situation with respect to the universe; and in like manner, if these moral relations could be applied to external objects, it would follow that even inanimate beings would be susceptible of moral beauty and deformity. Now, it seems difficult to imagine that any relation can be discovered betwixt our passions, volitions, and actions, compared to external objects, which relation might not belong either to these passions and volitions, or to these external objects, compared among *themselves.*

But it will be still more difficult to fulfil the *second* condition, requisite to justify this system.

According to the principles of those who maintain an abstract rational difference betwixt moral good and evil, and a natural fitness and unfitness of things, it is not only supposed, that these relations, being eternal and immutable, are the same, when considered by every rational creature, but their *effects* are also supposed to be necessarily the same; and it is concluded they have no less, or rather a greater, influence in directing the will of the Deity, than in governing the rational and virtuous of our own species. These two particulars are evidently distinct. It is one thing to know virtue, and another to conform the will to it. In order, therefore, to prove that the measures of right and wrong are eternal laws, *obligatory* on every rational mind, it is not sufficient to show the relations upon which they are founded: we must also point out the connection betwixt the relation and the will; and must prove that this connection is so necessary, that in every well-disposed mind, it must take place and have its influence; though the difference betwixt these minds be in other respects immense and infinite. Now, besides what I have already proved, that even in human nature no relation can ever alone produce any action; besides this, I say, it has been shown, in treating of the understanding, that there is no connection of cause and effect, such as this is supposed to be, which is discoverable otherwise than by experience, and of which we can pretend to have any security by the simple consideration of the objects. All beings in the universe, considered in themselves, appear entirely loose and independent of each other. It is only by experience we learn their influence and connection; and this influence we ought never to extend beyond experience.

Thus it will be impossible to fulfil the *first* condition required to the system of eternal rational measures of right and wrong; because it is impossible to show those relations, upon which such a distinction may be founded: and it is as impossible to fulfil the *second* condition; because we cannot prove *a priori,* that these relations, if they really existed and were perceived, would be universally forcible and obligatory.

But to make these general reflections more clear and convincing, we may illustrate them by some particular instances, wherein this character of moral good or evil is the most universally acknowledged. Of all crimes that human creatures are capable of committing, the most horrid and unnatural is ingratitude, especially when it is committed against parents, and appears in the more flagrant instances of wounds and death. This is acknowledged by all mankind, philosophers as well as the people: the question only arises among philosophers, whether the guilt or moral deformity of this action be discovered by demonstrative reasoning, or be felt by an internal sense, and by means of some sentiment, which the reflecting on such an action naturally occasions. This question will soon be decided against the former opinion, if we can show the same relations in other objects, without the notion of any guilt or iniquity attending them. Reason or science is nothing but the comparing of ideas, and the discovery of their relations; and if the same relations have different characters, it must evidently follow, that those characters are not discovered merely by reason. To put the affair, therefore, to this trial, let us choose any inanimate object, such as an oak or elm; and let us suppose, that, by the dropping of its seed, it produces a sapling below it, which, springing up by degrees, at last overtops and destroys the parent tree: I ask, if, in this instance, there be wanting any relation which is discoverable in parricide or ingratitude? Is not the one tree the cause of the other's existence; and the latter the cause of the destruction of the former, in the same manner as when a child murders his parent? It is not sufficient to reply, that a choice or will is wanting. For in the case of parricide, a will does not give rise to any *different* relations, but is only the cause from which the action is derived; and consequently produces the *same* relations, that in the oak or elm arise from some other principles. It is a will or choice that determines a man to kill his parent: and they are the laws of matter and motion that determine a sapling to destroy the oak from which it sprung. Here then the same relations have different causes; but still the relations are the same: and as their discovery is not in both cases attended with a notion of immorality, it follows, that that notion does not arise from such a discovery.

But to choose an instance still more resembling: I would fain ask any one, why incest in the human species is criminal, and why the very same action, and the same relations in animals, have not the smallest moral turpitude and deformity? If it be answered, that this action is innocent in animals, because they have not reason sufficient to discover its turpitude; but that man, being endowed with that faculty, which *ought* to restrain him to his duty, the same action instantly becomes criminal to him. Should this be said, I would reply, that this is evidently arguing in a circle. For, before reason can perceive this turpitude, the turpitude must exist; and consequently is independent of the decisions of our reason, and is their object more properly than their effect. According to this system, then, every animal that has sense and appetite and will, that is, every animal must be susceptible of all the same virtues and vices, for which we ascribe praise and blame to human creatures. All the difference is, that our superior reason may serve to discover the vice or virtue, and by that means may augment the blame or praise: but still this discovery supposes a separate being in these moral distinctions, and a being which depends only on the will and appetite, and which, both in thought and reality, may be distinguished from reason. Animals are susceptible of the same relations with respect to each other as the human species, and therefore would also be susceptible of the same morality, if the essence of morality consisted in these relations. Their want of a sufficient degree of reason may hinder them from perceiving the duties and obligations of morality, but can never hinder these duties from existing; since they must antecedently exist, in order to their being perceived. Reason must find them, and can never produce them. This argument deserves to be weighed, as being, in my opinion, entirely decisive.

Nor does this reasoning only prove, that morality consists not in any relations that are the objects of science; but if examined, will prove with equal certainty, that it consists not in any *matter of fact,* which can be discovered by the understanding. This is the *second* part of our argument; and if it can be made evident, we may conclude that morality is not an object of reason. But can there be any difficulty in proving that vice and virtue are not matters of fact, whose existence we can infer by reason? Take any action allowed to be vicious; wilful murder, for instance. Examine it in all lights, and see if you can find that matter of fact, or real existence, which you call *vice.* In whichever way you take it, you find only certain passions, motives, volitions, and thoughts. There is no other matter of fact in the case. The vice entirely escapes you, as long as you consider the object. You never can find it, till you turn your reflection into your own breast, and find a sentiment of disapprobation, which arises in you, towards this action. Here is a matter of fact; but it is the object of feeling, not of reason. It lies in yourself, not in the object. So that when you pronounce any action or character to be vicious, you mean nothing, but that from the constitution of your nature you have a feeling or sentiment of blame from the contemplation of it. Vice and virtue, therefore, may be compared to sounds, colors, heat, and cold, which, according to modern philosophy, are not qualities in objects, but perceptions in the mind: and this discovery in morals, like that other in physics, is to be regarded as a considerable advancement of the speculative sciences; though, like that too, it has little or no influence on practice. Nothing can be more real, or concern us more, than our own sentiments of pleasure and uneasiness; and if these be favorable to virtue, and unfavorable to vice, no more can be requisite to the regulation of our conduct and behaviour.

I cannot forbear adding to these reasonings an observation, which may, perhaps, be found of some importance. In every system of morality which I have hitherto met with, I have always remarked, that the author proceeds for some time in the ordinary way of reasoning, and establishes the being of a God, or makes observations concerning human affairs; when of a sudden I am surprised to find, that instead of the usual copulations of propositions, *is,* and *is not,* I meet with no proposition that is not connected with an *ought,* or an *ought not.* This change is imperceptible; but is, however, of the last consequence. For as this *ought,* or *ought not,* expresses some new relation or affirmation, it is necessary that it should be observed and explained; and at the same time that a reason should be given, for what seems altogether inconceivable, how this new relation can be a deduction from others, which are entirely different from it. But as authors do not commonly use this precaution. I shall presume to recommend it to the readers; and am persuaded, that this small attention would subvert all the vulgar systems of morality, and let us see that the distinction of vice and virtue is not founded merely on the relations of objects, nor is perceived by reason.

STUDY QUESTIONS

1. If you judge that an action is moral, are you motivated to perform it?
2. Does Hume believe that virtue is the same as what is natural?
3. Do statements of fact alone ever imply statements of value?
4. According to Hume, what is the ultimate source of morality?

Groundwork for the Metaphysics of Morals

Immanuel Kant

Immanuel Kant (1724–1804) was a dominant figure in the history of modern philosophy, making groundbreaking contributions in virtually every area of the subject. He argues that the moral worth of an action is to be judged not by its consequences but by the nature of the maxim or principle that motivated the action. Thus right actions are not necessarily those with favorable consequences but those performed in accord with correct maxims. But which maxims are correct? According to Kant, the only correct ones are those that can serve as universal laws because they are applicable without exception to every person at any time. In other words, you should act only on a maxim that can be universalized without contradiction. Kant refers to his supreme moral principle as the "categorical imperative," categorical because it does not depend on anyone's particular desires and imperative because it is a command of reason. Kant also claims that the categorical imperative can be reformulated as follows: Act in such a way that you treat humanity, whether in your own person or in any other person, always at the same time as an end, never merely as a means. In short, treat others as rational beings worthy of respect. Kant believes that acting otherwise is immoral and irrational.

4:393

SECTION ONE

Transition from the Common Rational Knowledge of Morality to the Philosophical

It is impossible to imagine anything at all in the world, or even beyond it, that can be called good without qualification—except a *good will*. Intelligence, wit, judgment, and the other mental talents, whatever we may call them, or courage, decisiveness, and perseverance, are, as qualities of *temperament,* certainly good and desirable in many respects; but they can also be extremely bad and harmful when the will which makes use of these *gifts of nature* and whose specific quality we refer to as *character,* is not good. It is exactly the same with *gifts of fortune.* Power, wealth, honor, even health and that total well-being and contentment with one's condition which we call "happiness," can make a person bold but consequently often reckless as well, unless a good will is present to correct their influence on the mind, thus adjusting the whole principle of one's action to render it conformable to universal ends. It goes without saying that the sight of a creature enjoying uninterrupted prosperity, but never feeling the slightest pull of a pure and good will,

From Immanuel Kant, *Groundwork for the Metaphysics of Morals* translated by Thomas E. Hill Jr. and Arnulf Zweig. (New York: Oxford University Press, 2002). Reprinted by permission of the publisher.

cannot excite approval in a rational and impartial spectator. Consequently, a good will seems to constitute the indispensable condition even of our worthiness to be happy.

Some qualities, even though they are helpful to this good will and can make its task very much easier, nevertheless have no intrinsic unconditional 4:394 worth. Rather, they presuppose a good will which puts limits on the esteem in which they are rightly held and forbids us to regard them as absolutely good. Moderation in emotions and passions, self-control, and sober reflection are not only good in many respects: they may even seem to constitute part of the inner worth of a person. Yet they are far from being properly described as good without qualification (however unconditionally they were prized by the ancients). For without the principles of a good will those qualities may become exceedingly bad; the passionless composure of a villain makes him not merely more dangerous but also directly more detestable in our eyes than we would have taken him to be without it.

A good will is not good because of its effects or accomplishments, and not because of its adequacy to achieve any proposed end: it is good only by virtue of its willing—that is, it is good in itself. Considered in itself it is to be treasured as incomparably higher than anything it could ever bring about merely in order to satisfy some inclination or, if you like, the sum total of all inclinations. Even if it were to happen that, because of some particularly unfortunate face or the miserly bequest of a step-motherly nature, this will were completely powerless to carry out its aims; if with even its utmost effort it still accomplished nothing, so that only good will itself remained (not, of course, as a mere wish, but as the summoning of every means in our power), even then it would still, like a jewel, glisten in its own right, as something that has its full worth in itself. . . .

397 We must thus develop the concept of a will estimable in itself and good apart from any further aim. This concept is already present in the natural, healthy mind, which requires not so much instruction as merely clarification. It is this concept that always holds the highest place in estimating the total worth of our actions and it constitutes the condition of all the rest. Let us then take up the concept of *duty,* which includes that of a good will, the latter however being here under certain subjective limitations and obstacles. These, so far from hiding a good will or disguising it, rather bring it out by contrast and make it shine forth more brightly. . . .

It is a duty to help others where one can, and besides this many souls are so compassionately disposed that, without any further motive of vanity or self-interest, they find an inner pleasure in spreading joy around them, taking delight in the contentment of others, so far as they have brought it about. Yet I maintain that, however dutiful and kind an action of this sort may be, it still has no genuinely moral worth. It is on a level with other inclinations—for example, the inclination to pursue honor, which if fortunate enough to aim at something generally useful and consistent with duty, something consequently honorable, deserves praise and encouragement but not esteem. For its maxim lacks the moral merit of such actions done not out of inclination but out of *duty.* Suppose then that the mind of this humanitarian were overclouded by sorrows of his own which extinguished all compassion for the fate of others, but that he still had the power to assist others in distress; suppose though that their adversity no longer stirred him, because he is preoccupied with his own; and now imagine that, though no longer moved by any inclination, he nevertheless tears himself out of this deadly apathy and does the action without any inclination, solely out of duty. Then for the first time his action has its genuine moral worth. Furthermore, if nature had put little sympathy into this or that person's heart; if he, though an honest man, were cold in temperament and indifferent to the sufferings of others—perhaps because he has the special gifts of patience and fortitude in his own sufferings and he assumes or even demands the same of others; if such a man (who would in truth not be the worst product of nature) were not exactly fashioned by nature to be a humanitarian, would he not still find in himself a source from which he might give himself a worth far higher than that of a good-natured temperament? Assuredly he would. It is precisely in this that the worth of character begins 4:399

to show—a moral worth, and incomparably the highest—namely, that he does good, not out of inclination, but out of duty. . . .

The moral worth of an action done out of duty has its moral worth, not *in the objective* to be reached by that action, but in the maxim in accordance with which the action is decided upon; it depends, therefore, not on actualizing the object of the action, but

4:400 solely on the *principle of volition* in accordance with which the action was done, without any regard for objects of the faculty of desire. It is clear from our previous discussion that the objectives we may have in acting, and also our actions' effects considered as ends and as what motivates our volition, can give to actions no unconditional or moral worth. Where then can this worth be found if not in the willing of the action's hoped for effect? It can be found nowhere but *in the principle of the will,* irrespective of the ends that can be brought about by such action. . . .

Duty is the necessity of an act done out of respect for the law. While I can certainly have an *inclination* for an object that results from my proposed action, I can never *respect* it, precisely because it is nothing but an effect of a will and not its activity. Similarly I cannot respect any inclination whatsoever, whether it be my own inclination or that of another. At most I can approve of that towards which I feel an inclination, and occasionally I can like the object of somebody else's inclination myself—that is, see it as conducive to my own advantage. But the only thing that could be an object of respect (and thus a commandment) for me is something that is conjoined with my will purely as a ground and never as a consequence, something that does not serve my inclination but overpowers it or at least excludes it entirely from my decision-making—consequently, nothing but the law itself. Now if an action done out of duty is supposed to exclude totally the influence of inclination, and, along with inclination, every object of volition, then nothing remains that could determine the will except objectively *the law* and subjectively *pure respect* for this practical law. What is left therefore is the maxim, to obey this sort

4:401 of law even when doing so is prejudicial to all my inclinations.

Thus the moral worth of an action depends neither on the result expected from that action nor on any principle of action that has to borrow its motive from this expected result. For all these results (such as one's own pleasurable condition or even the promotion of the happiness of others) could have been brought about by other causes as well. It would not require the will of a rational being to produce them, but it is only in such a will that the highest and unconditional good can be found. That pre-eminent good which we call "moral" consists therefore in nothing but *the idea of the law* in itself, which certainly *is present only in a rational being*—so far as that idea, and not an expected result, is the determining ground of the will. And this pre-eminent good is already present in the person who acts in accordance with this idea: we need not await the result of the action in order to find it

SECTION TWO

4:406

Transition from Popular Moral Philosophy to a Metaphysics of Morals

. . . Everything in nature works in accordance with laws. Only a rational being has the power to act in accordance with the idea of laws—that is, in accordance with principles—and thus has a will. . . .

The idea of an objective principle, in so far as it constrains a will, is called a commandment (of reason), and the formulation of this commandment is called an Imperative. . . .

All imperatives command either hypothetically or categorically. Hypothetical imperatives declare a possible action to be practically necessary as a means to the attainment of something else that one wants (or that one may want). A categorical imperative would be one that represented an action as itself objectively necessary, without regard to any further end.

Since every practical law presents a possible action as good and therefore as necessary for a subject whose actions are determined by reason, all imperatives are therefore formulae for determining an action which is necessary according to the principle of a will in some way good. If the action would be good only as a means to something else, the imperative is hypothetical; if the action is thought of as good in itself and therefore as necessary for a will which of itself conforms to reason as its principle, then the imperative is categorical. . . .

There is, however, *one* end that we may presuppose as actual in all rational beings (so far as they are dependent beings to whom imperatives apply); and thus there is one aim which they not only *might* have, but which we can assume with certainty that they all *do* have by a necessity of nature and that aim is *perfect happiness.* The hypothetical imperative which affirms the practical necessity of an action as a means to the promotion of perfect happiness is an assertoric imperative. We must not characterize it as necessary merely for some uncertain, merely possible purpose, but as necessary for a purpose that we can presuppose a priori and with certainty to be present in everyone because it belongs to the essence of human beings. Now we can call skill in the choice of the means to one's own greatest well-being "prudence" in the narrowest sense of the word. So the imperative concerning the choice of means to one's own happiness—that is, the precept of prudence—still remains hypothetical; the action is commanded not absolutely but only as a means to a further end.

Finally, there is one imperative which commands a certain line of conduct directly, without assuming or being conditional on any further goal to be reached by that conduct. This imperative is categorical. It is concerned not with the material of the action and its anticipated result, but with its form and with the principle from which the action itself results. And what is essentially good in the action consists in the [agent's] disposition, whatever the result may be. This imperative may be called the imperative of morality. . . .

The question now arises "How are all these imperatives possible?" This question does not ask how an action commanded by the imperative can be performed, but merely how we can understand the constraining of the will, which imperatives express in setting us a task. How an imperative of skill is possible requires no special discussion. Whoever wills

the end also wills (so far as reason has decisive influence on his actions) the means which are indispensably necessary and in his power. . . .

By contrast, "How is the imperative of morality possible?" is beyond all doubt the one question in need of solution. For the moral imperative is in no way hypothetical, and consequently the objective necessity, which it affirms, cannot be supported by any presupposition, as was the case with hypothetical imperatives. But we must never forget that it is impossible to settle by any example, i.e., empirically, whether there is any imperative of this kind at all; we should rather worry that all imperatives that seem to be categorical may yet be hypothetical in some hidden way. For example, when it is said, "You must abstain from making deceitful promises," one assumes that the necessity for this abstention is not mere advice so as to avoid some further evil—as though the meaning of what was said was, You ought not to make a deceitful promise lest, when it comes to light, you destroy your credit. On the contrary, an action of this kind would have to be considered as bad in itself, and the imperative of the prohibition would be therefore categorical. Even so, no example can show with certainty that the will would be determined here solely by the law without any further motivation, although it may appear to be so; for it is always possible that fear of disgrace, perhaps also hidden dread of other risks, may unconsciously influence the will. Who can prove by experience the non-existence of a cause? For experience shows only that we do not perceive it. In such a case, however, the so-called moral imperative, which as such appears to be categorical and unconditional, would in fact be only a pragmatic prescription calling attention to our own advantage and merely instructing us to take this into account. . . .

If I think of a *hypothetical* imperative as such, I do not know beforehand what it will contain—not until I am given its condition. But if I think of a *categorical imperative,* I know right away what it contains. For since this imperative contains, besides the law, only the necessity that the maxim conform to this law, while the law, as we have seen, contains no condition limiting it, there is nothing left over

4:416

4:421

to which the maxim of action should conform except the universality of a law as such; and it is only this conformity that the imperative asserts to be necessary.

There is therefore only one categorical imperative and it is this: "Act only on that maxim by which you can at the same time will that it should become a universal law." . . .

We shall now enumerate some duties. . . .

1. A man feels sick of life as the result of a mounting series of misfortunes that has reduced him to hopelessness, but he still possesses enough of his reason to ask himself whether it would not be contrary to his duty to himself to take his own life. Now he tests whether the maxim of his action could really become a universal law of nature. His maxim, however, is: "I make it my principle out of self-love to shorten my life if its continuance threatens more evil than it promises advantage." The only further question is whether this principle of self-love can become a universal law of nature. But one sees at once that a nature whose law was that the very same feeling meant to promote life should actually destroy life would contradict itself, and hence would not endure as nature. The maxim therefore could not possibly be a general law of nature and thus it wholly contradicts the supreme principle of all duty.

2. Another finds himself driven by need to borrow money. He knows very well that he will not be able to pay it back, but he sees too that nobody will lend him anything unless he firmly promises to pay it back within a fixed time. He wants to make such a promise, but he still has enough conscience to ask himself, "Isn't it impermissible and contrary to duty to get out of one's difficulties this way?" Suppose, however, that he did decide to do it. The maxim of his action would run thus: "When I believe myself short of money, I will borrow money and promise to pay it back, even though I know that this will never be done." Now this principle of self-love or personal advantage is perhaps quite compatible with my own entire future welfare; only there remains the question "Is it right?" I therefore transform the unfair demand of self-love into a universal law and frame my question thus: "How would things stand if my maxim became a universal

law?" I then see immediately that this maxim can never qualify as a self-consistent universal law of nature, but must necessarily contradict itself. For the universality of a law that permits anyone who believes himself to be in need to make any promise he pleases with the intention of not keeping it would make promising, and the very purpose one has in promising, itself impossible. For no one would believe he was being promised anything, but would laugh at any such utterance as hollow pretense.

3. A third finds in himself a talent that, with a certain amount of cultivation, could make him a useful man for all sorts of purposes. But he sees himself in comfortable circumstances, and he prefers to give himself up to pleasure rather than to bother about increasing and improving his fortunate natural aptitudes. Yet he asks himself further "Does my maxim of neglecting my natural gifts, besides agreeing with my taste for amusement, agree also with what is called duty?" He then sees that a nature could indeed endure under such a universal law, even if (like the South Sea Islanders) every man should let his talents rust and should be bent on devoting his life solely to idleness, amusement, procreation—in a word, to enjoyment. Only he cannot possibly *will* that this should become a universal law of nature or should be implanted in us as such a law by a natural instinct. For as a rational being he necessarily wills that all his powers should be developed, since they are after all useful to him and given to him for all sorts of possible purposes.

4. A fourth man, who is himself flourishing but sees others who have to struggle with great hardships (and whom he could easily help) thinks to himself: "What do I care? Let every one be as happy as Heaven intends or as he can make himself; I won't deprive him of anything; I won't even envy him; but I don't feel like contributing anything to his well-being or to helping him in his distress!" Now admittedly if such an attitude were a universal law of nature, the human race could survive perfectly well and doubtless even better than when everybody chatters about sympathy and good will, and even makes an effort, now and then, to practice them, but, when one can get away with it, swindles, traffics in human rights, or violates them in other ways. But although it is possible that a universal law of nature

4:422

4:423

in accord with this maxim could exist, it is impossible to *will* that such a principle should hold everywhere as a law of nature. For a will that intended this would be in conflict with itself, since many situations might arise in which the man needs love and sympathy from others, and in which, by such a law of nature generated by his own will, he would rob himself of all hope of the help he wants.

These are some of the many actual duties—or at least of what we take to be actual—whose derivation from the single principle cited above is perspicuous. We must be able to will that a maxim of our action should become a universal law—this is the authoritative model for moral judging of action generally. Some actions are so constituted that we cannot even *conceive* without contradiction that their maxim be a universal law of nature, let alone that we could *will* that it *ought* to become one. In the case of other actions, we do not find this inner impossibility, but it is still impossible to *will* that their maxim should be raised to the universality of a law of nature, because such a will would contradict itself. . . .

If we now look at ourselves whenever we transgress a duty, we find that we in fact do not intend that our maxim should become a universal law. For this is impossible for us. What we really intend is rather that its opposite should remain a law generally; we only take the liberty of making an *exception* to it, for ourselves or (of course just this once) to satisfy our inclination. Consequently if we weighed it all up from one and the same perspective—that of reason—we should find a contradiction in our own will, the contradiction that a certain principle should be objectively necessary as a universal law and yet subjectively should not hold universally but should admit of exceptions. . . .

We have thus at least shown this much—that if duty is a concept that is to have meaning and actual legislative authority for our actions, it can be expressed only in categorical imperatives and not at all in hypothetical ones. At the same time—and this is already a great deal—we have set forth clearly, and defined for every use, the content of the categorical imperative, which must contain the principle of all duty (if there is to be such a thing at all). But we are still not so far advanced as to prove a priori that

there actually is an imperative of this kind—that there is a practical law which by itself commands absolutely and without any further motivation, and that it is our duty to follow this law.

If we really intend to arrive at this proof it is extremely important to remember that we should not let ourselves think for a moment that the reality of this principle can be derived from *the particular characteristics of human nature.* For duty has to be a practical, unconditional necessity of action; it must therefore hold for all rational beings (to whom alone an imperative can apply at all), and *only for that reason* a law that holds also for all human wills. Whatever, on the other hand, is derived from the special predisposition of humanity, from certain feelings and propensities, and even, if this were possible, from some special bent peculiar to human reason and not holding necessarily for the will of every rational being—all this can indeed supply a personal maxim, but not a law: it can give us a subjective principle—one on which we have a natural disposition and inclination to act—but not an objective principle on which we should be directed to act even though our every propensity, inclination, and natural bent were opposed to it. This is so much the case that the sublimity and inner dignity of the commandment is even more manifest in a duty, the fewer subjective causes there are for obeying it and the more there are against it, but without this weakening in the slightest the constraint exercised by the law or diminishing its validity.

Here we see philosophy placed in what is actually a precarious position, a position that is supposed to be firm though it is neither suspended from heaven nor supported by the earth. Here she must show her purity as the sustainer of her own laws—not as the herald of laws that some implanted sense or who knows what guardian-like nature has whispered to her. Such laws, though perhaps always better than nothing, can never furnish us with fundamental principles dictated by reason, principles whose origin must be completely a priori and, because of this, have commanding authority. Such fundamental principles expect nothing from human inclinations but everything from the supremacy of the law and the respect owed it. Without this they condemn human beings to self-contempt and inner disgust.

4:424

4:425

4:426

Everything empirical is thus not only wholly unfit to contribute to the principle of morality; it is highly damaging to the purity of moral practices themselves. For, in morality, the proper worth of an absolutely good will, a worth exalted above all price, lies precisely in the freedom of its principle of action from any influence by contingent reasons that only experience can provide. We cannot warn too strongly or too often against the slack, or indeed vulgar, attitude which searches among empirical motives and laws for the principle; for human reason in its weariness is glad to rest on this cushion, and in a dream of sweet illusions (which allow it to embrace a cloud instead of Juno) to substitute for morality a bastard patched up from limbs of very diverse parentage, looking like anything one wishes to see in it, only not resembling virtue to anyone who has once beheld her in her true form.

Our question then is this: "Is it a necessary law *for all rational beings* to judge their actions always in accordance with those maxims which they can themselves will that they should serve as universal laws?" If it is a necessary law, it must already be connected (entirely a priori) with the concept of the will of a rational being as such. But in order to discover this connection we must, however reluctantly, venture into metaphysics, although into a region of metaphysics different from that of speculative philosophy, namely, the metaphysics of morals. In a practical philosophy we are not concerned with assuming reasons for what happens, but with acknowledging laws for what ought to happen, even if it may never happen—that is, objective practical laws. And here we have no need to investigate the reasons why anything pleases or displeases, how the pleasure of mere sensation differs from taste, and whether the latter is distinct from general satisfaction of reason. We need not inquire on what the feelings of pleasure and displeasure are based, or how from these feelings there arise desires and inclinations; and how from these, with the co-operation of reason, there arise maxims. For all this belongs to empirical psychology, which would constitute the second part of the study of nature, if we regard the latter as the *philosophy of nature* to the extent to which it rests on *empirical laws.* Here, however, we are discussing

4:427

objective practical laws, and consequently the relation of a will to itself insofar as it determines itself solely by reason. Everything related to the empirical then falls away of itself; for if *reason all by itself* determines conduct (and the possibility of this is what we now wish to investigate), it must necessarily do so a priori.

We think of the will as a power of determining oneself to act *in conformity with the idea of certain laws.* And such a power can be found only in rational beings. Now, what serves the will as the objective ground of its self-determining is an *end*; and this end, if it is given by reason alone, must be equally valid for all rational beings. On the other hand, something that contains merely the ground of the possibility of an action, where the result of that action is the end, is called a *means.* The subjective ground of desiring is a *driving-spring*; the objective ground of willing is a *motivating reason.* Hence the difference between subjective ends, which depend on driving-springs, and objective ends, which depend on motivating reasons that are valid for every rational being. Practical principles are *formal* if they abstract from all subjective ends; they are *material,* on the other hand, if they are based on subjective ends and consequently on certain driving-springs. Those ends that a rational being at his own discretion sets for himself as *what he intends to accomplish* through his action (material ends) are in every case only relative; for what gives them worth is only their relation to some subject's particularly constituted faculty of desire. Such worth can therefore provide no universal principles, no principles valid and necessary for all rational beings and for every act of will—that is, it can provide no practical laws. Consequently all these relative ends are only the ground of hypothetical imperatives.

Suppose, however, there were something *whose existence in itself* had an absolute worth, something that, as an end *in itself,* could be a ground of definite laws. Then in it and in it alone, would the ground of a possible categorical imperative, that is, of a practical law, reside.

Now, I say, a human being, and in general every rational being, *does exist* as an end in himself, *not merely as a means* to be used by this or that will as it pleases. In all his actions, whether they are directed

4:428

to himself or to other rational beings, a human being must always be viewed *at the same time as an end.* All the objects of inclination have only a conditional worth; for if these inclinations and the needs based on them did not exist, their object would be worthless. But inclinations themselves, as sources of needs, are so far from having absolute value to make them desirable for their own sake that it must rather be the universal wish of every rational being to be wholly free of them. Thus the value of any object *that is to be acquired* by our action is always conditional. Beings whose existence depends not on our will but on nature still have only a relative value as means and are therefore called *things,* if they lack reason. Rational beings, on the other hand, are called *persons,* because their nature already marks them out as ends in themselves—that is, as something which ought not to be used *merely* as a means—and consequently imposes restrictions on all choice making (and is an object of respect). Persons, therefore, are not merely subjective ends whose existence as an effect of our actions has a value *for us.* They are *objective ends*—that is, things whose existence is in itself an end, and indeed an end such that no other end can be substituted for it, no end to which they should serve *merely* as a means. For if this were not so, there would be nothing at all having *absolute value* anywhere. But if all value were conditional, and thus contingent, then no supreme principle could be found for reason at all.

If then there is to be a supreme practical principle and a categorical imperative for the human will, it must be such that it forms an objective principle of the will from the idea of something which is necessarily an end for everyone because *it is an end in itself,* a principle that can therefore serve as a universal practical law. The ground of this principle is: *Rational nature exists as an end in itself.* This is the way in which a human being necessarily conceives his own existence, and it is therefore a *subjective* principle of human actions. But it is also the way in which every other rational being conceives his existence, on the same rational ground which holds also for me; hence it is at the same time an *objective* principle from which, since it is a supreme practical ground, it must be possible to derive all laws of the will. The practical imperative will therefore be the following: *Act in such*

4:429

a way that you treat humanity, whether in your own person or in any other person, always at the same time as an end, never merely as a means. We will now see whether this can be carried out in practice.

Let us keep to our previous examples.

First, as regards the concept of necessary duty to oneself, the man who contemplates suicide will ask himself whether his action could be compatible with the Idea of humanity as *an end in itself.* If he damages himself in order to escape from a painful situation, he is making use of a person *merely as a means* to maintain a tolerable state of affairs till the end of his life. But a human being is not a thing—not something to be used *merely* as a means: he must always in all his actions be regarded as an end in himself. Hence I cannot dispose of a human being in my own person, by maiming, corrupting, or killing him. (I must here forego a more precise definition of this principle that would forestall any misunderstanding—for example, as to having limbs amputated to save myself or exposing my life to danger in order to preserve it, and so on—this discussion belongs to ethics proper.)

Secondly, as regards necessary or strict duty owed to others, the man who has in mind making a false promise to others will see at once that he is intending to make use of another person *merely as a means* to an end which that person does not share. For the person whom I seek to use for my own purposes by such a promise cannot possibly agree with my way of treating him, and so cannot himself share the end of the action. This incompatibility with the principle of duty to others can be seen more distinctly when we bring in examples of attacks on the freedom and property of others. For then it is manifest that a violator of the rights of human beings intends to use the person of others merely as a means without taking into consideration that, as rational beings, they must always at the same time be valued as ends—that is, treated only as beings who must themselves be able to share in the end of the very same action.

Thirdly, as regards contingent (meritorious) duty to oneself, it is not enough that an action not conflict with humanity in our own person as an end in itself: it must also *harmonize with this end.* Now there are in humanity capacities for greater perfection that form part of nature's purpose for humanity in our

4:430

own person. To neglect these can perhaps be compatible with the *survival* of humanity as an end in itself, but not with the *promotion* of that end.

Fourthly, as regards meritorious duties to others, the natural end that all human beings seek is their own perfect happiness. Now the human race might indeed exist if everybody contributed nothing to the happiness of others but at the same time refrained from deliberately impairing it. This harmonizing with humanity *as an end in itself* would, however, be merely negative and not positive, unless everyone also endeavors, as far as he can, to further the ends of others. For the ends of any person who is an end in himself must, if this idea is to have its full effect in me, be also, as far as possible, *my* ends.

This principle of humanity, and in general of every rational agent, *as an end in itself* (a principle which is the supreme limiting condition on every person's freedom of action) is not borrowed from experience: first, because it is universal, applying to all rational beings generally, and no experience is sufficient to determine anything about all such beings; secondly, because in this principle we conceive of humanity not as an end that one happens to have (a subjective end)—that is, as an object which people, as a matter of fact, happen to make their end. We conceive of it rather as an objective end—one that, as a law, should constitute the supreme limiting condition on all subjective ends, whatever those ends may be. This principle must therefore spring from pure reason.

That is to say, the ground of all practical legislation lies *objectively in the rule* and in the form of universality that (according to our first principle) makes the rule fit to be a law (and possibly a law of nature); *subjectively,* however, the ground of practical legislating lies in the *end.* But, according to our second principle, the *subject* of all ends is every rational being as an end in itself. From this there follows our third practical principle of the will: the supreme condition of the will's harmony with universal practical reason is the Idea of *the will of every rational being as a will that legislates universal law.*

By this principle all maxims are rejected which are inconsistent with the will's own universal lawgiving. The will is therefore not merely subject to the law, but subject in such a way that it must be

4:431

considered as also *giving the law to itself* and only for this reason as first of all subject to the law (of which it can regard itself as the author).

Imperatives as formulated above excluded from their legislative authority every admixture of interest as a motivation. They either commanded a conformity of actions to universal law, a conformity analogous to a *natural order,* or they asserted the prerogative of rational beings to be regarded universally as *supreme ends* in themselves. (This followed from the mere fact that these imperatives were conceived as categorical.) But the imperatives were only *assumed* to be categorical because we had to make this assumption if we wished to explain the concept of duty. That there were practical propositions that command categorically could not itself be proved, any more than it can be proved here in this chapter. But one thing might have been done—namely, to show that in willing something just out of duty the renunciation of all interest is the specific mark distinguishing a categorical from a hypothetical imperative. This is what we are doing in the present third formulation of the principle—namely, in the Idea of the will of every rational being as *a will that legislates universal law.*

For once we think of a will of this kind, it becomes clear that while a will *that is subject to laws* may be bound to this law by some interest, a will that is itself a supreme lawgiver cannot possibly depend on any interest; for such a dependent will would itself require yet another law in order to restrict the interest of self-love by the condition that this interest must be valid as a universal law.

Thus the *principle* that every human will is *a will that enacts universal laws in all its maxims would be well adapted* to be a categorical imperative, provided only that this principle is correct in other ways. Because of the Idea of giving universal law, it is *based on no interest,* and consequently, of all possible imperatives it alone can be *unconditional.* Or better still, let us take the converse of this proposition: if there is a categorical imperative (a law that applies to the will of every rational being), it can command us only to act always on the maxim of its will as one which could at the same time look upon itself as giving universal laws. For only then is the

4:432

practical principle, and the imperative that the will obeys, unconditional, because the imperative cannot be based on any interest.

If we look back on all the previous efforts to discover the principle of morality, it is no wonder that they have all had to fail. One saw that human beings are bound to laws by their duty, but it never occurred to anyone that they are subject only to *laws which they themselves have given* but which are nevertheless *universal,* and that people are bound only to act in conformity with a will that is their own but that is, according to nature's purpose, a will that gives universal law. For when one thought of human beings 4:433 merely as subject to a law (whatever it might be), the law had to carry with it some interest, as stimulus or compulsion to obedience, because it did not spring as law from their *own* will: in order to conform to the law, their will had to be compelled by *something else* to act in a certain way. But this strictly necessary consequence meant that all the labor spent in trying to find a supreme foundation for duty was irrevocably lost. For what one discovered was never duty, but only the necessity of acting from a certain interest. This interest might be one's own or another's. But the resulting imperative was bound to be always a conditional one and could not at all serve as a moral commandment. I therefore want to call my principle the principle of the *Autonomy* of the will in contrast with all others, which I therefore count as *Heteronomy.*

The concept of every rational being as a being who must regard itself as making universal law by all the maxims of its will, and must seek to judge itself and its actions from this standpoint, leads to a closely connected and very fruitful concept— namely, that of *a kingdom of ends.*

I understand by a "kingdom" the systematic union of different rational beings under common laws. Now since laws determine ends as regards their universal validity, we can—if we abstract from the personal differences between rational beings, and also from the content of their private ends—conceive a whole of all ends systematically united (a whole composed of rational beings as ends in themselves and also of the personal ends which each may set for himself); that is, we can conceive of a kingdom of ends which is possible in accordance with the aforesaid principles.

For rational beings all stand under the *law* that each of them should treat himself and all others *never merely as a means* but always *at the same time as an end in himself.* But from this there arises a systematic union of rational beings through shared objective laws—that is, a kingdom. Since these laws aim precisely at the relation of such beings to one another as ends and means, this kingdom may be called a kingdom of ends (admittedly only an ideal).

A rational being, however, belongs to the kingdom of ends as a *member,* if, while legislating its universal laws, he is also subject to these laws. He belongs to the kingdom as its *head,* if, as legislating, he is not subject to the will of any other being.

4:434

A rational being must always regard himself as lawgiving in a kingdom of ends made possible through freedom of the will—whether as member or as head. But he cannot maintain the position of head merely through the maxim of his will, but only if he is a completely independent being, without needs and with an unlimited power adequate to his will.

Thus morality consists in the relation of all action to just that lawgiving through which a kingdom of ends is made possible. But this lawgiving must be found in every rational being itself and must be capable of arising from the will of that being. The principle of its will is therefore this: never to perform any action except one whose maxim could also be a universal law, and thus to act only on a maxim *through which the will could regard itself at the same time as enacting universal law.* If maxims are not already by their very nature in harmony with this objective principle of rational beings as legislating universal law, the necessity of acting on this principle is called a constraint on the choice of actions, i.e., *duty.* Duty does not apply to the head in a kingdom of ends, but it does apply to every member and to all of them in equal measure.

The practical necessity of acting on this principle—that is, duty—is not based at all on feelings, impulses, and inclinations, but only on the relation of rational beings to one another, a relation in which the will of a rational being must always be regarded as *lawgiving,* because otherwise it could not be thought of as *an end in itself.* Reason thus relates every maxim of a universally legislating will to every other will and also to every action towards oneself: it does so, not because of any further motive or future advantage, but from the Idea of the *dignity* of a rational being who obeys no law other than one which he himself also enacts.

In the kingdom of ends everything has either a *price* or a *dignity.* Whatever has a price can be replaced by something else as *equivalent.* Whatever by contrast is exalted above all price and so admits of no equivalent has a dignity.

Whatever is relative to universal human inclinations and needs has a *market price.* Whatever, even 4:435 without presupposing a need, accords with a certain taste—that is, with satisfaction in the mere random play of our mental powers—has an *attachment price.* But that which constitutes the sole condition under which anything can be an end in itself has not mere relative worth, i.e., a price, but an inner worth—i.e., *dignity.*

Now morality is the only condition under which a rational being can be an end in itself; for only through this is it possible to be a lawgiving member in the kingdom of ends. Therefore morality, and humanity so far as it is capable of morality, is the only thing that has dignity. Skill and diligence in work have a market price; wit, lively imagination, and humor have an attachment price but fidelity to promises and benevolence out of basic principles (not out of instinct) have an inner worth. Nature and art alike offer nothing that could replace their lack; for their worth consists not in the effects which result from them, not in the advantage or profit they produce, but in the intentions—that is, in the maxims of the will—which are ready in this way to reveal themselves in action even if they are not favored by success. Such actions too need no recommendation from any subjective disposition or taste in order to be regarded with immediate favor and approval; they need no direct predilection or feeling for them. They exhibit as an object of immediate respect the will that performs them; since nothing but reason is required in order to *impose* them on the will. Nor is the will to be *coaxed* into them, which would anyhow be a contradiction in the case of duties. This assessment lets us recognize the value of such a mental attitude as dignity and puts it infinitely above all price, with

which it cannot be brought into comparison or computation without, as it were, violating its holiness.

And what is it then that justifies a morally good disposition, or virtue, in making such lofty claims? It is nothing less than the *sharing* which it allows to a rational being in *giving universal laws,* which therefore renders him fit to be a member in a possible kingdom of ends. His own nature as an end in himself already marked out this fitness and therefore his status as lawgiver in a kingdom of ends and as free from all laws of nature, obedient only to those laws which he himself prescribes, laws according to which his maxims can participate in the making of universal law (to which he at the same time subjects himself). For nothing can have worth other than that determined for it by the law. But the lawgiving that determines all worth must therefore have a dignity, 4:436 i.e., an unconditional and incomparable worth. The word "*respect*" is the only suitable expression for the esteem that a rational being must necessarily feel for such lawgiving. *Autonomy* is thus the basis of the dignity of human nature and of every rational nature.

Our three ways of presenting the principle of morality are basically only so many formulations of precisely the same law, each one of them by itself uniting the other two within it. There is nevertheless a difference among them, which, however, is more subjectively than objectively practical: that is to say, the different formulations aim to bring an Idea of reason closer to intuition (by means of a certain analogy) and thus nearer to feeling. All maxims have:

(1) A *form,* which consists in universality; and in this respect the formula of the moral imperative is expressed thus: "Maxims must be chosen as if they were to hold as universal laws of nature."

(2) A *matter*—that is, an end; and in this respect the formula says: "A rational being, as by its very nature an end and thus an end in itself, must serve every maxim as the limiting condition restricting the pursuit of all merely relative and arbitrary ends."

(3) A *complete determination* of all maxims by means of the following formula: "All maxims which stem from autonomous lawgiving are to harmonize with a possible kingdom of ends and

with a kingdom of nature." Progression that takes place here as elsewhere is through the categories of unity, plurality, and totality: *unity* of the form of the will (its universality); *plurality* of its matter (its objects—that is, its ends); and the totality or *all-comprehensiveness* of its system of ends. It is, however, better if in moral *judgement* one proceeds always in accordance with the strict method and takes as one's basic principle the universal formula of the categorical imperative: *"Act on that maxim that can at the same time make itself into a universal law."* If, however, we wish also to *gain a hearing* for the moral law, it is very useful to bring one and the same action under the three stated formulae and thereby, as far as possible, bring the moral law closer to intuition.

We can now end at the point from which we began—namely, with the concept of an unconditionally good will. A *will* is *absolutely good* if it cannot be evil—that is, if its maxim, when made into a universal law, can never be in conflict with itself. This principle is therefore also its supreme law: "Act always on that maxim whose universality as a law you can at the same time will." This is the one principle on which a will can never be in conflict with itself, and such an imperative is categorical. Since the validity of the will, as a universal law for possible actions, is analogous to the universal connection of the existence of things under universal laws, which is the formal aspect of nature in general, we can also express the categorical imperative as follows: *"Act on maxims which can at the same time have as their object [making] themselves into universal laws of nature."* This then gives us the formula for an absolutely good will.

A rational nature distinguishes itself from others by the fact that it sets itself an end. That end would be the matter for every good will. But in the idea of an absolutely good will, good without any limiting condition (the attaining of this or that end), we must abstract completely from every end that has to be *brought about* (for such an end would make any will only relatively good). Hence the proposed end must here be conceived, not as an end to be produced, *but as a self-sufficient* end It must therefore be conceived only negatively—that is, as an end which we should

never act against, and consequently one which in all our willing we must never value merely as a means, but always at the same time as an end. Now this end can be nothing other than the subject of all possible ends itself, because this subject is also the subject of a will that may be absolutely good; for such a will cannot without contradiction be subordinated to any other object. The principle "So act in relation to every rational being (both yourself and others) that this being may at the same time count in your maxim as an end in itself" is thus basically the same as the principle "Act on a maxim which at the same time embodies in itself its own universal validity for every rational being." For to say that, in using means to any end, I ought to restrict my maxim by the condition that it should also be universally valid as a law for every subject, is just the same as to say this: a subject of ends, i.e., a rational being itself, must be made the foundation of all maxims of action, and must thus be treated never merely as a means, but as the supreme condition restricting the use of all means—that is, always at the same time as an end.

Now from this it unquestionably follows that every rational being, as an end in itself, must be able to regard himself as also the maker of universal law in respect of any law whatever to which he may be subject; for it is precisely the fitness of his maxims to make universal law that marks him out as an end in himself. It follows equally that this dignity (or prerogative) he possesses above all merely natural beings carries with it the necessity of always choosing his maxims from the point of view of himself, but also of every other rational being (which is why they are called persons) as lawgiving beings. It is in this way that a world of rational beings (*mundus intelligibilis*) [intelligible world] is possible as a kingdom of ends—possible, that is, through the giving of their own laws by all persons as its members. Accordingly every rational being must act as if he were always by his maxims a lawgiving member in the universal kingdom of ends. The formal principle of such maxims is "Act as if your maxims had to serve at the same time as a universal law (for all rational beings)." A kingdom of ends is thus possible only by analogy with a kingdom of nature. A kingdom of ends is possible only through maxims—that is, self-imposed rules—while nature is possible only through laws of efficient causes externally necessitated. In spite of this difference, we give to nature as a whole, even though it is regarded as a machine, the name of a "kingdom of nature" so far as and because rational beings are its ends. Now a kingdom of ends would actually come into existence through maxims whose rule the categorical imperative prescribes for all rational beings, *if these maxims were universally followed.* Yet even if a rational being were himself to follow such a maxim strictly, he cannot count on everybody else therefore being faithful to the same maxim, nor can he count on the kingdom of nature and its purposive order harmonizing with him, as a fitting member, towards a kingdom of ends made possible through himself, i.e., that the kingdom of nature will favor his expectations of perfect happiness. Nevertheless the law "Act on the maxims of a universally lawgiving member of a merely possible kingdom of ends" remains in full force, because it commands categorically. And precisely here we encounter the paradox that, without any further end or advantage to be attained by it, the mere dignity of humanity as rational nature—and consequently respect for a mere Idea—should serve as an inflexible precept for the will; and that it is just this independence from any motivations based on his expectations of perfect happiness that constitutes the sublimity of a maxim and the worthiness of every rational subject to be a lawgiving member in the kingdom of ends; for otherwise he would have to be regarded as subject only to the natural law of his own needs. Even if both the kingdom of nature and the kingdom of ends were imagined to be united under one head and thus the kingdom of ends ceased to be a mere Idea and achieved genuine reality, the Idea would indeed gain additional motivating power by this, but no increase in its inner worth. For, even if this were so, this unique and absolute lawgiver

4:439

would have to be conceived as judging the worth of rational beings solely by the disinterested behavior they prescribed to themselves from this Idea alone. The essence of things is not changed by their external relations; and, leaving aside such relations, whatever constitutes by itself the absolute worth of human beings is that by which they must be judged—by everyone whatsoever, even by the Supreme Being. *Morality* is thus the relation of actions to the autonomy of the will—that is, to a possible universal lawgiving by means of its maxims. An action that is compatible with the autonomy of the will is *permitted*; one that does not harmonize with it is *forbidden*. A will whose maxims necessarily agree with the laws of autonomy is a *holy*, absolutely good will. The dependence of a will not absolutely good on the principle of autonomy (that is, moral necessitation) is *obligation*. Obligation can thus not apply to a holy being. The objective necessity of an action out of obligation is called *duty*.

From what has just been said we can now easily explain how it happens that, although the concept of duty includes the idea of a person's subjection to the law, we nevertheless attribute a certain sublimity and *dignity* to the person who fulfils all his duties. For although there is nothing sublime about him just in so far as he is *subject* to the law, there is sublimity to him in his being at the same time its *author* and being subordinated only for this reason to this very same law. We have also shown above how neither fear nor inclination, but only respect for the law, is the motivation that can give an action moral worth. Our own will, provided it would act only under the condition of being able to give universal law by means of its maxims—this ideal will, which is possible for us, is the proper object of respect. The dignity of humanity consists precisely in this power of giving universal law, though only on condition of also being subject to this same lawgiving.

4:44⬤

STUDY QUESTIONS

1. According to Kant, is anything unconditionally good?
2. What is Kant's distinction between a hypothetical and a categorical imperative?
3. According to Kant, why does empirical inquiry not provide a sound basis for morality?
4. Does Kant believe that acting immorally is ever reasonable?

Utilitarianism

John Stuart Mill

John Stuart Mill (1806–1873), the most prominent English philosopher of the nineteenth century, published widely in philosophy, political theory, and economics. He defends utilitarianism, the view that "actions are right in proportion as they tend to promote happiness and wrong as they tend to produce the reverse of happiness," each person to be counted equally. By "happiness," Mill means pleasure and the absence of pain. He grants, however, that some pleasures are more valuable than others, and these higher pleasures are those that would be chosen by knowledgeable judges. Mill maintains that utilitarianism cannot be strictly proven, yet some considerations can be presented in its favor. In particular, he argues that our desiring something is evidence that the thing is desirable. Thus, because happiness is the only end that people desire for its own sake, the evidence suggests that happiness is, in fact, intrinsically desirable.

CHAPTER TWO

What Utilitarianism Is

. . . The creed which accepts as the foundation of morals "utility" or the "greatest happiness principle" holds that actions are right in proportion as they tend to promote happiness; wrong as they tend to produce the reverse of happiness. By happiness is intended pleasure and the absence of pain; by unhappiness, pain and the privation of pleasure. To give a clear view of the moral standard set up by the theory, much more requires to be said; in particular, what things it includes in the ideas of pain and pleasure, and to what extent this is left an open question. But these supplementary explanations do not affect the theory of life on which this theory of morality is grounded—namely, that pleasure and freedom from pain are the only things desirable as ends; and that all desirable things (which are as numerous in the utilitarian as in any other scheme) are desirable either for pleasure inherent in themselves or as means to the promotion of pleasure and the prevention of pain.

Now such a theory of life excites in many minds, and among them in some of the most estimable in feeling and purpose, inveterate dislike. To suppose that life has (as they express it) no higher end than pleasure—no better and nobler object of desire and pursuit—they designate as utterly mean and groveling, as a doctrine worthy only of swine. . . .

But there is no known . . . theory of life which does not assign to the pleasures of the intellect, of the feelings and imagination, and of the moral sentiments a much higher value as pleasures than to those of mere sensation. It must be admitted, however, that utilitarian writers in general have placed the

From John Stuart Mill, *Utilitarianism* (1863).

superiority of mental over bodily pleasures chiefly in the greater permanency, safety, uncostliness, etc., of the former—that is, in their circumstantial advantages rather than in their intrinsic nature. And on all these points utilitarians have fully proved their case; but they might have taken the other and, as it may be called, higher ground with entire consistency. It is quite compatible with the principle of utility to recognize the fact that some kinds of pleasure are more desirable and more valuable than others. It would be absurd that, while in estimating all other things quality is considered as well as quantity, the estimation of pleasure should be supposed to depend on quantity alone.

If I am asked what I mean by difference in quality in pleasures, or what makes one pleasure more valuable than another, merely as a pleasure, except its being greater in amount, there is but one possible answer. Of two pleasures, if there be one to which all or almost all who have experience of both give a decided preference, irrespective of any feeling of moral obligation to prefer it, that is the more desirable pleasure. If one of the two is, by those who are competently acquainted with both, placed so far above the other that they prefer it, even though knowing it to be attended with a greater amount of discontent, and would not resign it for any quantity of the other pleasure which their nature is capable of, we are justified in ascribing to the preferred enjoyment a superiority in quality so far outweighing quantity as to render it, in comparison, of small account.

Now it is an unquestionable fact that those who are equally acquainted with and equally capable of appreciating and enjoying both do give a most marked preference to the manner of existence which employs their higher faculties. Few human creatures would consent to be changed into any of the lower animals for a promise of the fullest allowance of a beast's pleasures; no intelligent human being would consent to be a fool, no instructed person would be an ignoramus, no person of feeling and conscience would be selfish and base, even though they should be persuaded that the fool, the dunce, or the rascal is better satisfied with his lot than they are with theirs. They would not resign what they possess more than he for the most complete satisfaction of all the desires which they have in common with him. If they ever fancy they would, it is only in cases of unhappiness so extreme that to escape from it they would exchange their lot for almost any other, however undesirable in their own eyes. A being of higher faculties requires more to make him happy, is capable probably of more acute suffering, and certainly accessible to it at more points, than one of an inferior type; but in spite of these liabilities, he can never really wish to sink into what he feels to be a lower grade of existence. . . .

It is better to be a human being dissatisfied than a pig satisfied; better to be Socrates dissatisfied than a fool satisfied. And if the fool, or the pig, are of a different opinion, it is because they only know their own side of the question. The other party to the comparison knows both sides.

It may be objected that many who are capable of the higher pleasures occasionally, under the influence of temptation, postpone them to the lower. But this is quite compatible with a full appreciation of the intrinsic superiority of the higher. Men often, from infirmity of character, make their election for the nearer good, though they know it to be the less valuable; and this no less when the choice is between two bodily pleasures than when it is between bodily and mental. They pursue sensual indulgences to the injury of health, though perfectly aware that health is the greater good. It may be further objected that many who begin with youthful enthusiasm for everything noble, as they advance in years, sink into indolence and selfishness. But I do not believe that those who undergo this very common change voluntarily choose the lower description of pleasures in preference to the higher. I believe that, before they devote themselves exclusively to the one, they have already become incapable of the other. Capacity for the nobler feelings is in most natures a very tender plant, easily killed, not only by hostile influences, but by mere want of sustenance; and in the majority of young persons it speedily dies away if the occupations to which their position in life has devoted them, and the society into which it has thrown them, are not favorable to keeping that higher capacity in exercise. Men lose their high aspirations as they lose their intellectual tastes, because they have not time

[margin, handwritten:] good to a cow's closest good

[margin, handwritten:] "try to a cow's closest good"

[margin, handwritten:] ranking of goods

or opportunity for indulging them; and they addict themselves to inferior pleasures, not because they deliberately prefer them, but because they are either the only ones to which they have access or the only ones which they are any longer capable of enjoying. It may be questioned whether anyone who has remained equally susceptible to both classes of pleasures ever knowingly and calmly preferred the lower, though many, in all ages, have broken down in an ineffectual attempt to combine both.

From this verdict of the only competent judges, I apprehend there can be no appeal. On a question which is the best worth having of two pleasures, or which of the two modes of existence is the most grateful to the feelings, apart from its moral attributes and from its consequences, the judgment of these who are qualified by knowledge of both, or, if they differ, that of the majority among them, must be admitted as final. And there needs to be the less hesitation to accept this judgment respecting the quality of pleasures, since there is no other tribunal to be referred to even on the question of quantity. What means are there of determining which is the acutest of two pains, or the intensest of two pleasurable sensations, except the general suffrage of those who are familiar with both? . . .

I must again repeat what the assailants of utilitarianism seldom have the justice to acknowledge, that the happiness which forms the utilitarian standard of what is right in conduct is not the agent's own happiness but that of all concerned. As between his own happiness and that of others, utilitarianism requires him to be as strictly impartial as a disinterested and benevolent spectator. In the golden rule of Jesus of Nazareth, we read the complete spirit of the ethics of utility. "To do as you would be done by," and "to love your neighbor as your self," constitute the ideal perfection of utilitarian morality. As the means of making the nearest approach to this ideal, utility would enjoin, first, that laws and social arrangements should place the happiness or (as, speaking practically, it may be called) the interest of every individual as nearly as possible in harmony with the interest of the whole; and, secondly, that education and opinion, which have so vast a power over human character, should

so use that power as to establish in the mind of every individual an indissoluble association between his own happiness and the good of the whole, especially between his own happiness and the practice of such modes of conduct, negative and positive, as regard for the universal happiness prescribes; so that not only he may be unable to conceive the possibility of happiness to himself, consistently with conduct opposed to the general good, but also that a direct impulse to promote the general good may be in every individual one of the habitual motives of action, and the sentiments connected therewith may fill a large and prominent place in every human being's sentient existence. If the impugners of the utilitarian morality represented it to their own minds in this its true character, I know not what recommendation possessed by any other morality they could possibly affirm to be wanting to it; what more beautiful or more exalted developments of human nature any other ethical system can be supposed to foster; or what springs of action, not accessible to the utilitarian, such systems rely on for giving effect to their mandates. . . .

CHAPTER FOUR

Of What Sort of Proof the Principle of Utility Is Susceptible

. . . Questions about ends are . . . questions about what things are desirable. The utilitarian doctrine is that happiness is desirable and the only thing desirable as an end, all other things being only desirable as means to that end. What ought to be required of the doctrine, what conditions is it requisite that the doctrine should fulfill—to make good its claim to be believed?

The only proof capable of being given that an object is visible is that people actually see it. The only proof that a sound is audible is that people hear it; and so of the other sources of our experience. In like manner, I apprehend, the sole evidence it is possible to produce that anything is desirable is that people do actually desire it. If the end which the utilitarian doctrine proposes to itself were not, in theory and in practice, acknowledged to be an end, nothing could ever convince any person that it was so. No reason can be given why the general happiness is desirable, except that each person, so far as he believes it to be attainable, desires his own happiness. This, however, being a fact, we have not only all the proof which the case admits of, but all which it is possible to require, that happiness is a good, that each person's happiness is a good to that person, and the general happiness, therefore, a good to the aggregate of all persons. Happiness has made out its title as *one* of the ends of conduct and, consequently, one of the criteria of morality.

But it has not, by this alone, proved itself to be the sole criterion. To do that it would seem, by the same rule, necessary to show not only that people desire happiness but that they never desire anything else. Now it is palpable that they do desire things which, in common language, are decidedly distinguished from happiness. They desire, for example, virtue and the absence of vice no less really than pleasure and the absence of pain. The desire of virtue is not as universal, but it is as authentic a fact as the desire of happiness. And hence the opponents of the utilitarian standard deem that they have a right to infer that there are other ends of human action besides happiness, and that happiness is not the standard of approbation and disapprobation.

But does the utilitarian doctrine deny that people desire virtue, or maintain that virtue is not a thing to be desired? The very reverse. It maintains not only that virtue is to be desired, but that it is to be desired disinterestedly, for itself. Whatever may be the opinion of utilitarian moralists as to the original conditions by which virtue is made virtue, however they may believe (as they do) that actions and dispositions are only virtuous because they promote another end than virtue, yet this being granted, and it having been decided, from considerations of this description, what *is* virtuous, they not only place virtue at the very head of the things which are good as means to the ultimate end, but they also recognize as a psychological fact the possibility of its being, to the individual, a good in itself, without looking to any end beyond it; and hold that the mind is not in a right state, not in a state conformable to utility, not in the state most conducive to the general happiness, unless it does love virtue in this manner—as a thing desirable in itself, even

although, in the individual instance, it should not produce those other desirable consequences which it tends to produce, and on account of which it is held to be virtue. This opinion is not, in the smallest degree, a departure from the happiness principle. The ingredients of happiness are very various, and each of them is desirable in itself, and not merely when considered as swelling an aggregate. The principle of utility does not mean that any given pleasure, as music, for instance, or any given exemption from pain, as for example health, is to be looked upon as means to a collective something termed happiness, and to be desired on that account. They are desired and desirable in and for themselves; besides being means, they are a part of the end. Virtue, according to the utilitarian doctrine, is not naturally and originally part of the end, but it is capable of becoming so; and in those who live it disinterestedly it has become so, and is desired and cherished, not as a means to happiness, but to a part of their happiness.

To illustrate this further, we may remember that virtue is not the only thing originally a means, and which if it were not a means to anything else would be and remain indifferent, but which by association with what it is a means to comes to be desired for itself, and that too with the utmost intensity. What, for example, shall we say of the love of money? There is nothing originally more desirable about money than about any heap of glittering pebbles. Its worth is solely that of the things which it will buy; the desires for other things than itself, which it is a means of gratifying. Yet the love of money is not one of the strongest moving forces of human life, but money is, in many cases, desired in and for itself; the desire to possess it is often stronger than the desire to use it, and goes on increasing when all the desires which point to ends beyond it, to be compassed by it, are falling off. It may, then, be said truly that money is desired not for the sake of an end, but as part of the end. From being a means to happiness, it has come to be itself a principal ingredient of the individual's conception of happiness. The same may be said of the majority of the great objects of human life: power, for example, or fame, except that to each of these there is a certain amount of immediate pleasure annexed, which has at least the semblance of being naturally inherent in them—a thing which cannot be said of money. Still, however, the strongest natural attraction, both of power and of fame, is the immense aid they give to the attainment of our other wishes; and it is the strong association thus generated between them and all our objects of desire which gives to the direct desire of them the intensity it often assumes, so as in some characters to surpass in strength all other desires. In these cases the means have become a part of the end, and a more important part of it than any of the things which they are means to. What was once desired as an instrument for the attainment of happiness has come to be desired for its own sake. In being desired for its own sake it is, however, desired as *part* of happiness. The person is made, or thinks he would be made, happy by its mere possession and is made unhappy by failure to obtain it. The desire of it is not a different thing from the desire of happiness any more than the love of music or the desire of health. They are included in happiness. They are some of the elements of which the desire of happiness is made up. Happiness is not an abstract idea but a concrete whole; and these are some of its parts. And the utilitarian standard sanctions and approves their being so. Life would be a poor thing, very ill provided with sources of happiness, if there were not this provision of nature by which things originally indifferent, but conducive to, or otherwise associated with, the satisfaction of our primitive desires, become in themselves sources of pleasure more valuable than the primitive pleasures, both in permanency, in the space of human existence that they are capable of covering, and even in intensity.

Virtue, according to the utilitarian conception, is a good of this description. There was no original desire of it, or motive to it, save its conduciveness to pleasure, and especially to protection from pain.

But through the association thus formed it may be felt a good in itself, and desired as such with as great intensity as any other good; and with this difference between it and the love of money, of power, or of fame—that all of these may, and often do, render the individual noxious to the other members of the society to which he belongs, whereas there is nothing which makes him so much a blessing to them as the cultivation of the disinterested love of virtue. And consequently, the utilitarian standard, while it tolerates and approves those other acquired desires, up to the point beyond which they would be more injurious to the general happiness than promotive of it, enjoins and requires the cultivation of the love of virtue up to the greatest strength possible, as being above all things important to the general happiness.

It results from the preceding considerations that there is in reality nothing desired except happiness. Whatever is desired otherwise than as a means to some end beyond itself, and ultimately to happiness, is desired as itself a part of happiness, and is not desired for itself until it has become so. Those who desire virtue for its own sake desire it either because the consciousness of it is a pleasure, or because the consciousness of being without it is a pain, or for both reasons united, as in truth the pleasure and pain seldom exist separately, but almost always together— the same person feeling pleasure in the degree of virtue attained, and pain in not having attained more. If one of these gave him no pleasure, and the other no pain, he would not love or desire virtue, or would desire it only for the other benefits which it might produce to himself or to persons whom he cared for.

We have now, then, an answer to the question, of what sort of proof the principle of utility is susceptible.

STUDY QUESTIONS

1. According to Mill, what is utilitarianism?
2. If people knowledgeable about both poetry and video games prefer the latter, are video games therefore more worthwhile?
3. Does Mill believe the principle of utilitarianism can be proven?
4. What evidence do we have that the general happiness is intrinsically desirable?

The Methods of Ethics

Henry Sidgwick

Henry Sidgwick (1838–1900) was Knightbridge Professor of Philosophy at Trinity College, Cambridge. He argues that ethical terms such as "ought" and "right" are primitive or unanalyzable—that is, not admitting of any definition in simpler terms. Because ethical judgments are beliefs, Sidgwick names the faculty of cognition that makes these judgments "Reason." It attempts to locate certain self-evident moral axioms, which need to meet four conditions: (1) the terms must be clear and precise, (2) it must be ascertained by careful reflection, (3) it must be consistent with other self-evident truths, and (4) it must attract consensus. Sidgwick argues that one principle that meets all four conditions is the axiom of universal benevolence: "the good of any one individual is of no more importance, from the point of view . . . of the Universe, than the good of any other; unless, that is, there are special grounds for believing that more good is likely to be realized in the one case than in the other."

BOOK I

Chapter III

Ethical Judgments

§ 1. . . . [W]e commonly think that wrong conduct is essentially irrational, and can be shown to be so by argument; and though we do not conceive that it is by reason alone that men are influenced to act rightly, we still hold that appeals to the reason are an essential part of all moral persuasion, and that part which concerns the moralist or moral philosopher as distinct from the preacher or moral rhetorician. On the other hand it is widely maintained that, as Hume says, "Reason, meaning the judgment of truth and falsehood, can never of itself be any motive to the Will"; and that the motive to action is in all cases some Non-rational Desire, including under this term the impulses to action given by present pleasure and pain. It seems desirable to examine with some care the grounds of this contention before we proceed any further.

Let us begin by defining the issue raised as clearly as possible. Every one, I suppose, has had experience of what is meant by the conflict of non-rational or irrational desires with reason: most of us (*e.g.*) occasionally feel bodily appetite prompting us to indulgences which we judge to be imprudent, and anger prompting us to acts which we disapprove as unjust or unkind. It is when this conflict occurs that the desires are said to be irrational, as impelling us to volitions opposed to our deliberate judgments; sometimes we yield to such seductive impulses, and sometimes not; and it is perhaps when we do *not* yield that the impulsive force of such irrational desires is most definitely felt, as we have to exert in resisting them

From Henry Sidgwick, *The Methods of Ethics*, 7th ed. (1907).

a voluntary effort somewhat analogous to that involved in any muscular exertion. Often, again—since we are not always thinking either of our duty or of our interest—desires of this kind take effect in voluntary actions without our having judged such actions to be either right or wrong, either prudent or imprudent; as (*e.g.*) when an ordinary healthy man eats his dinner. In such cases it seems most appropriate to call the desires "non-rational" rather than "irrational." Neither term is intended to imply that the desires spoken of—or at least the more important of them—are not normally accompanied by intellectual processes. It is true that some impulses to action seem to take effect, as we say "blindly" or "instinctively," without any definite consciousness either of the end at which the action is aimed, or of the means by which the end is to be attained: but this, I conceive, is only the case with impulses that do not occupy consciousness for an appreciable time, and ordinarily do not require any but very familiar and habitual actions for the attainment of their proximate ends. In all other cases—that is, in the case of the actions with which we are chiefly concerned in ethical discussion—the result aimed at, and some part at least of the means by which it is to be realized, are more or less distinctly represented in consciousness, previous to the volition that initiates the movements tending to its realization. Hence the resultant forces of what I call "non-rational" desires, and the volitions to which they prompt, are continually modified by intellectual processes in two distinct ways; first by new perceptions or representations of means conducive to the desired ends, and secondly by new presentations or representations of facts actually existing or in prospect—especially more or less probable consequences of contemplated actions—which rouse new impulses of desire and aversion.

The question, then, is whether the account just given of the influence of the intellect on desire and volition is not exhaustive; and whether the experience which is commonly described as a "conflict of desire with reason" is not more properly conceived as merely a conflict among desires and aversions; the sole function of reason being to bring before the mind ideas of actual or possible facts, which modify

in the manner above described the resultant force of our various impulses.

I hold that this is not the case; that the ordinary moral or prudential judgments which, in the case of all or most minds, have some—though often an inadequate—influence on volition, cannot legitimately be interpreted as judgments respecting the present or future existence of human feelings or any facts of the sensible world; the fundamental notion represented by the word "ought" or "right," which such judgments contain expressly or by implication, being essentially different from all notions representing facts of physical or psychical experience. The question is one on which appeal must ultimately be made to the reflection of individuals on their practical judgments and reasonings: and in making this appeal it seems most convenient to begin by showing the inadequacy of all attempts to explain the practical judgments or propositions in which this fundamental notion is introduced, without recognizing its unique character as above negatively defined. There is an element of truth in such explanations, in so far as they bring into view feelings which undoubtedly accompany moral or prudential judgments, and which ordinarily have more or less effect in determining the will to actions judged to be right; but so far as they profess to be interpretations of what such judgments mean, they appear to me to fail altogether.

In considering this question it is important to take separately the two species of judgments which I have distinguished as "moral" and "prudential." Both kinds might, indeed, be termed "moral" in a wider sense; and, as we saw, it is a strongly supported opinion that all valid moral rules have ultimately a prudential basis. But in ordinary thought we clearly distinguish cognitions or judgments of duty from cognitions or judgments as to what "is right" or "ought to be done" in view of the agent's private interest or happiness: and the depth of the distinction will not, I think, be diminished by the closer examination of these judgments on which we are now to enter.

This very distinction, however, suggests an interpretation of the notion of rightness which denies its peculiar significance in moral judgments. It is urged that "rightness" is properly an attribute of means, not of ends: so that the attribution of it merely implies that the act judged right is the fittest or only fit means to the realization of some end understood if not expressly stated: and similarly that the affirmation that anything 'ought to be done' is always made with at least tacit reference to some ulterior end. And I grant that this is a legitimate interpretation, in respect of a part of the use of either term in ordinary discourse. But it seems clear (1) that certain kinds of actions—under the names of Justice, Veracity, Good Faith, etc.—are commonly held to be right unconditionally, without regard to ulterior results: and (2) that we similarly regard as "right" the adoption of certain ends—such as the common good of society, or general happiness. In either of these cases the interpretation above suggested seems clearly inadmissible.[1]

We have therefore to find a meaning for "right" or "what ought to be" other than the notion of fitness to some ulterior end. Here we are met by the suggestion that the judgments or propositions which we commonly call moral—in the narrower sense— really affirm no more than the existence of a specific emotion in the mind of the person who utters them; that when I say 'Truth ought to be spoken' or 'Truth-speaking is right,' I mean no more than that the idea of truthspeaking excites in my mind a feeling of approbation or satisfaction. And probably some degree of such emotion, commonly distinguished as 'moral sentiment,' ordinarily accompanies moral judgments on real cases. But it is absurd to say that a mere statement of my approbation of truth-speaking is properly given in the proposition 'Truth ought to be spoken'; otherwise the fact of another man's disapprobation might equally be expressed by saying 'Truth ought not to be spoken'; and thus we should have two coexistent facts stated in two mutually contradictory propositions. This is so obvious, that we must suppose that those who hold the view which I am combating do not really intend to deny it: but rather to maintain that this subjective fact of my approbation is all that there is any *ground* for stating, or perhaps that it is all that any reasonable person is prepared on reflection to affirm. And no doubt there is a large class of statements, in form objective, which yet we are not commonly prepared to maintain as more than subjective if their validity is questioned. If I say that 'the air is sweet,' or 'the food disagreeable,' it would not be exactly true to say that I mean no more than that I like the one or dislike the other: but if my statement is challenged, I shall probably content myself with affirming the existence of such feelings in my own mind. But there appears to me to be a fundamental difference between this case and that of moral feelings. The peculiar emotion of moral approbation is, in my experience, inseparably bound up with the conviction, implicit or explicit, that the conduct approved is 'really' right—*i.e.* that it cannot, without error, be disapproved by any other mind. If I give up this conviction because others do not share it, or for any other reason, I may no doubt still retain a sentiment prompting to the conduct in question, or—what is perhaps more common—a sentiment of repugnance to the opposite conduct: but this sentiment will no longer have the special quality of 'moral sentiment' strictly so called. This difference between the two is often overlooked in ethical discussion: but any experience of a change in moral opinion produced by argument may afford an illustration of it. Suppose (*e.g.*) that any one habitually influenced by the sentiment of Veracity is convinced that under certain peculiar circumstances in which he finds himself, speaking truth is not right but wrong. He will probably still feel a repugnance against violating the rule of truthspeaking: but it will be a feeling quite different in kind and degree from that which prompted him to veracity as a department of virtuous action. We might perhaps call the one a 'moral' and the other a 'quasi-moral' sentiment.

The argument just given holds equally against the view that approbation or disapprobation is not the mere liking or aversion of an individual for certain kinds of conduct, but this [is] complicated by a sympathetic representation of similar likings or aversions felt by other human beings. No doubt such sympathy is a normal concomitant of moral emotion, and when the former is absent there is much greater difficulty in maintaining the latter: this, however, is partly because our moral beliefs commonly agree with those of other members of our society, and on this agreement depends to an important extent our confidence in the truth of these beliefs. But if, as in the case just supposed, we are really led by argument to a new moral belief, opposed not only to our own habitual sentiment but also to that of the society in which we live, we have a crucial experiment proving the existence in us of moral sentiments as I have defined them, colliding with the represented sympathies of our fellow-men no less than with our own mere likings and aversions. And even if we imagine the sympathies opposed to our convictions extended until they include those of the whole human race . . . ; still, so long as our conviction of duty is firm, the emotion which we call moral stands out in imagination quite distinct from the complex sympathy opposed to it, however much we extend, complicate and intensify the latter.

§ 2. So far, then, from being prepared to admit that the proposition 'X ought to be done' *merely* expresses the existence of a certain sentiment in myself or others, I find it strictly impossible so to regard my own moral judgments without eliminating from the concomitant sentiment the peculiar quality signified by the term 'moral.' There is, however, another interpretation of 'ought,' in which the likings and aversions that men in general feel for certain kinds of conduct are considered not as sympathetically represented in the emotion of the person judging, and thus constituting the moral element in it, but as causes of pain to the person of whom 'ought' or 'duty' is predicated. On this view, when we say that a man 'ought' to do anything, or that it is his 'duty' to do it, we mean that he is bound under penalties to do it; the particular penalty considered being the pain that will accrue to him directly or indirectly from the dislike of his fellow-creatures.

I think that this interpretation expresses a part of the meaning with which the words 'ought' and 'duty' are used in ordinary thought and discourse. For we commonly use the term 'moral obligation' as equivalent to 'duty' and expressing what is implied in the verb 'ought,' thus suggesting an analogy between this notion and that of legal obligation; and in the case of positive law we cannot refuse to recognize the connection of 'obligation' and 'punishment': a law cannot be properly said to be actually established in a society if it is habitually violated with impunity. But a more careful reflection on the relation of Law to Morality, as ordinarily conceived, seems to show that this interpretation of 'ought'— though it cannot be excluded—must be distinguished from the special ethical use of the term. For the ideal distinction taken in common thought between legal and merely moral rules seems to lie in just this connexion of the former but not the latter with punishment: we think that there are some things which a man ought to be compelled to do, or forbear, and others which he ought to do or forbear without compulsion, and that the former alone fall properly within the sphere of law. No doubt we also think that in many cases where the compulsion of law is undesirable, the fear of moral censure and its consequences supplies a normally useful constraint on the will of any individual. But it is evident that what we mean when we say that a man is "morally though not legally bound" to do a thing is not merely that he "will be punished by public opinion if he does not"; for we often join these two statements, clearly distinguishing their import: and further (since public opinion is known to be eminently fallible) there are many things which we judge men 'ought' to do, while perfectly aware that they will incur no serious social penalties for omitting them. In such cases, indeed, it would be commonly said that social disapprobation 'ought' to follow on immoral conduct; and in this very assertion it is clear that the term 'ought' cannot mean that social penalties are to be feared by those who do not disapprove. Again, all or most men in whom the moral consciousness is strongly developed find themselves from time to time in conflict with the commonly received morality of the society to which they belong: and thus—as was before said—have a crucial experience proving that duty does not mean *to them* what other men will disapprove of them for not doing. . . .

There is, however, another way of interpreting 'ought' as connoting penalties, which is somewhat less easy to meet by a crucial psychological experiment. The moral imperative may be taken to be a law of God, to the breach of which Divine penalties are annexed; and these, no doubt, in a Christian society, are commonly conceived to be adequate and universally applicable. Still, it can hardly be said that this belief is shared by all the persons whose conduct is influenced by independent moral convictions, occasionally unsupported either by the law or the public opinion of their community. And even in the case of many of those who believe fully in the moral government of the world, the judgment "I ought to do this" cannot be identified with the judgment "God will punish me if I do not"; since the conviction that the former proposition is true is distinctly recognized as an important part of the grounds for believing the latter. . . .

§ 3. It seems then that the notion of 'ought' or 'moral obligation' as used in our common moral judgments, does not merely import (1) that there exists in the mind of the person judging a specific emotion (whether complicated or not by sympathetic representation of similar emotions in other minds); nor (2) that certain rules of conduct are supported by penalties which will follow on their violation (whether such penalties result from the general liking or aversion felt for the conduct prescribed or forbidden, or from some other source). What then, it may be asked, does it import? What definition can we give of 'ought,' 'right,' and other terms expressing the same fundamental notion? To this I should answer that the notion which these terms have in common is too elementary to admit of any formal definition. In so saying, I do not mean to imply that it belongs to the "original constitution of the mind"; *i.e.* that its presence in consciousness is not the result of a process of development. I do not doubt that the whole fabric of human thought—including the conceptions that present themselves as most simple and elementary—has been developed, through a gradual process of psychical change, out of some lower life in which thought, properly speaking, had no place. But it is not therefore to be inferred, as regards this or any other notion, that it has not really the simplicity which it appears to have when we now reflect upon it. It is sometimes assumed that if we can show how thoughts have grown up—if we can point to the psychical antecedents of which they are the natural consequents—we may conclude that the thoughts in question are really compounds containing their antecedents as latent elements. But I know no justification for this transference of the conceptions of

chemistry to psychology; I know no reason for considering psychical antecedents as really constitutive of their psychical consequents, in spite of the apparent dissimilarity between the two. In default of such reasons, a psychologist must accept as elementary what introspection carefully performed declares to be so; and, using this criterion, I find that the notion we have been examining, as it now exists in our thought, cannot be resolved into any more simple notions: it can only be made clearer by determining as precisely as possible its relation to other notions with which it is connected in ordinary thought, especially to those with which it is liable to be confounded.

In performing this process it is important to note and distinguish two different implications with which the word "ought" is used; in the narrowest ethical sense what we judge 'ought to be' done, is always thought capable of being brought about by the volition of any individual to whom the judgment applies. I cannot conceive that I 'ought' to do anything which at the same time I judge that I cannot do. In a wider sense, however,—which cannot conveniently be discarded—I sometimes judge that I 'ought' to know what a wiser man would know, or feel as a better man would feel, in my place, though I may know that I could not directly produce in myself such knowledge or feeling by any effort of will. In this case the word merely implies an ideal or pattern which I 'ought'—in the stricter sense—to seek to imitate as far as possible. And this wider sense seems to be that in which the word is normally used in the precepts of Art generally, and in political judgments: when I judge that the laws and constitution of my country 'ought to be' other than they are, I do not of course imply that my own or any other individual's single volition can directly bring about the change. In either case, however, I imply that what ought to be is a possible object of knowledge: *i.e.* that what I judge ought to be must, unless I am in error, be similarly judged by all rational beings who judge truly of the matter.

In referring such judgments to the 'Reason,' I do not mean here to prejudge the question whether valid moral judgments are normally attained by a process of reasoning from universal principles or axioms, or by direct intuition of the particular duties of individuals. It is not uncommonly held that the moral faculty deals primarily with individual cases as they arise, applying directly to each case the general notion of duty, and deciding intuitively what ought to be done by this person in these particular circumstances. And I admit that on this view the apprehension of moral truth is more analogous to Sense-perception than to Rational Intuition (as commonly understood):[2] and hence the term Moral Sense might seem more appropriate. But the term Sense suggests a capacity for feelings which may vary from A to B without either being in error, rather than a faculty of cognition:[3] and it appears to me fundamentally important to avoid this suggestion. I have therefore thought it better to use the term Reason with the explanation above given, to denote the faculty of moral cognition: adding, as a further justification of this use, that even when a moral judgment relates primarily to some particular action we commonly regard it as applicable to any other action belonging to a certain definable class: so that the moral truth apprehended is implicitly conceived to be intrinsically universal, though particular in our first apprehension of it.

Further, when I speak of the cognition or judgment that 'X ought to be done'—in the stricter ethical sense of the term ought—as a 'dictate' or 'precept' of reason to the persons to whom it relates, I imply that in rational beings as such this cognition gives an impulse or motive to action: though in human beings, of course, this is only one motive among others which are liable to conflict with it, and is not always—perhaps not usually—a predominant motive. In fact, this possible conflict of motives seems to be connoted by the term 'dictate' or 'imperative,' which describes the relation of Reason to mere inclinations or non-rational impulses by comparing it to the relation between the will of a superior and the wills of his subordinates. This conflict seems also to be implied in the terms 'ought,' 'duty,' 'moral obligation,' as used in ordinary moral discourse: and hence these terms cannot be applied to the actions of rational beings to whom we cannot attribute impulses conflicting with reason. We may, however, say of such beings that their actions are 'reasonable,' or (in an absolute sense) 'right.' . . .

BOOK II

Chapter XI

Review of the Morality of Common Sense

§2. There seem to be four conditions, the complete fulfilment of which would establish a significant proposition, apparently self-evident, in the highest degree of certainty attainable: and which must be approximately realized by the premises of our reasoning in any inquiry, if that reasoning is to lead us cogently to trustworthy conclusions.

I. The terms of the proposition must be clear and precise. . . .

II. The self-evidence of the proposition must be ascertained by careful reflection. It is needful to insist on this, because most persons are liable to confound intuitions, on the one hand with mere impressions or impulses, which to careful observation do not present themselves as claiming to be dictates of Reason; and on the other hand, with mere opinions, to which the familiarity that comes from frequent hearing and repetition often gives a false appearance of self-evidence which attentive reflection disperses. . . . A rigorous demand for self-evidence in our premises is a valuable protection against the misleading influence of our own irrational impulses on our judgments: while at the same time it not only distinguishes as inadequate the mere external support of authority and tradition, but also excludes the more subtle and latent effect of these in fashioning our minds to a facile and unquestioning admission of common but unwarranted assumptions.

And we may observe that the application of this test is especially needed in Ethics. For, on the one hand, it cannot be denied that any strong sentiment, however purely subjective, is apt to transform itself into the semblance of an intuition; and it requires careful contemplation to detect the illusion. Whatever we desire we are apt to pronounce desirable: and we are strongly tempted to approve of whatever conduct gives us keen pleasure. And on the other hand, among the rules of conduct to which we customarily conform, there are many which reflection shows to be really derived from some external authority: so that even if their obligation be unquestionable, they cannot be intuitively ascertained. . . .

We may illustrate this by referring to two systems of rules . . . compared with Morality; the Law of Honor, and the Law of Fashion or Etiquette. I noticed that there is an ambiguity in the common terms 'honorable' and 'dishonorable'; which are no doubt sometimes used, like ethical terms, as implying an absolute standard. Still, when we speak of the Code of Honor we seem to mean rules of which the exact nature is to be finally determined by an: appeal to the general opinion of well-bred persons: we admit that a man is in a sense 'dishonored' when this opinion condemns him, even though we may think his conduct unobjectionable or even intrinsically admirable. Similarly, when we consider from the point of view of reason the rules of Fashion or Etiquette, some may seem useful and commendable, some indifferent and arbitrary, some perhaps absurd and burdensome: but nevertheless we recognize that the final authority on matters of Etiquette is the custom of polite society; which feels itself under no obligation of reducing its rules to rational principles. Yet it must be observed that each individual in any society commonly finds in himself a knowledge not obviously incomplete of the rules of Honor and Etiquette, and an impulse to conform to them without requiring any further reason for doing so. Each often seems to see at a glance what is honorable and polite just as clearly as he sees what is right: and it requires some consideration to discover that in the former cases custom and opinion are generally the final authority from which there is no appeal. And even in the case of rules regarded as distinctly moral, we can generally find an element that seems to us as clearly conventional as the codes just mentioned, when we contemplate the morality of other men, even in our own age and country. Hence we may reasonably suspect a similar element in our own moral code: and must admit the great importance of testing rigorously any rule which we find that we have a habitual impulse to obey; to see whether it really expresses or can be referred to a clear intuition of rightness.

III. The propositions accepted as self-evident must be mutually consistent. Here . . . it is obvious that any collision between two intuitions is a proof that there is error in one or the other, or in both. Still, we frequently find ethical writers treating this point very lightly. They appear to regard a conflict of ultimate rules as a difficulty that may be ignored or put aside for future solution, without any slur being thrown on the scientific character of the conflicting formulae. Whereas such a collision is absolute, proof that at least one of the formulae needs qualification: and suggests a doubt whether the correctly qualified proposition will present itself with the same self-evidence as the simpler but inadequate one; and whether we have not mistaken for an ultimate and independent axiom one that is really derivative and subordinate.

IV. Since it is implied in the very notion of Truth that it is essentially the same for all minds, the denial by another of a proposition that I have affirmed has a tendency to impair my confidence in its validity. And in fact 'universal' or 'general' consent has often been held to constitute by itself a sufficient evidence of the truth of the most important beliefs; and is practically the only evidence upon which the greater part of mankind can rely. A proposition accepted as true upon this ground alone has, of course, neither self-evidence nor demonstrative evidence for the mind that so accepts it; still, the secure acceptance that we commonly give to the generalizations of the empirical sciences rests—even in the case of experts—largely on the belief that other experts have seen for themselves the evidence for these generalizations, and do not materially disagree as to its adequacy. And it will be easily seen that the absence of such disagreement must remain an indispensable negative condition of the certainty of our beliefs. For if I find any of my judgments, intuitive or inferential, in direct conflict with a judgment of some other mind, there must be error somewhere: and if I have no more reason to suspect error in the other mind than in my own, reflective comparison between the two judgments necessarily reduces me temporarily to a state of neutrality. And though the total result in my mind is not exactly suspense of judgment, but an alternation and conflict between positive affirmation by one act of thought and the neutrality that is the result of another, it is obviously something very different from scientific certitude. . . .

BOOK III

Chapter XIII

Philosophical Intuitionism

§ 3. Can we [avoid] on the one hand doctrines that merely bring us back to common opinion with all its imperfections, and on the other hand doctrines that lead us round in a circle, find any way of obtaining self-evident moral principles of real significance? It would be disheartening to have to regard as altogether illusory the strong instinct of Common Sense that points to the existence of such principles, and the deliberate convictions of the long line of moralists who have enunciated them. At the same time, the more we extend our knowledge of man and his environment, the more we realize the vast variety of human natures and circumstances that have existed in different ages and countries, the less disposed we are to believe that there is any definite code of absolute rules, applicable to all human beings without exception. And we shall find, I think, that the truth lies between these two conclusions. There are certain absolute practical principles, the truth of which, when they are explicitly stated, is manifest; but they are of too abstract a nature, and too universal in their scope, to enable us to ascertain by immediate application of them what we ought to do in any particular case; particular duties have still to be determined by some other method.

One such principle [is] . . . that whatever action any of us judges to be right for himself, he implicitly judges to be right for all similar persons in similar circumstances. Or, as we may otherwise put it, 'if a kind of conduct that is right (or wrong) for me is not right (or wrong) for some one else, it must be on the ground of some difference between the two cases, other than the fact that I and he are different persons.' A corresponding proposition may be stated with equal truth in respect of what ought to be done *to*—not *by*—different individuals. These principles have been most widely recognized, not in their most abstract and universal form, but in their special application to the situation of two (or more) individuals similarly related to each other: as so applied, they appear in what is popularly known as the Golden

Rule, 'Do to others as you would have them do to you.' This formula is obviously unprecise in statement; for one might wish for another's co-operation in sin, and be willing to reciprocate it. Nor is it even true to say that we ought to do to others only what we think it right for them to do to us; for no one will deny that there may be differences in the circumstances—and even in the natures—of two individuals, *A* and *B*, which would make it wrong for *A* to treat *B* in the way in which it is right for *B* to treat *A*. In short the self-evident principle strictly stated must take some such negative form as this; 'it cannot be right for *A* to treat *B* in a manner in which it would be wrong for *B* to treat *A*, merely on the ground that they are two different individuals, and without there being any difference between the natures or circumstances of the two which can be stated as a reasonable ground for difference of treatment.' Such a principle manifestly does not give complete guidance—indeed its effect, strictly speaking, is merely to throw a definite *onus probandi* on the man who applies to another a treatment of which he would complain if applied to himself; but Common Sense has amply recognized the practical importance of the maxim: and its truth, so far as it goes, appears to me self-evident.

A somewhat different application of the same fundamental principle that individuals in similar conditions should be treated similarly finds its sphere in the ordinary administration of Law, or (as we say) of 'Justice.' . . . [I]mpartiality in the application of general rules,' [is] an important element in the common notion of Justice; indeed, . . . no other element . . . could be intuitively known with perfect clearness and certainty. . . . [I]t must be plain that this precept of impartiality is insufficient for the complete determination of just conduct, as it does not help us to decide what kind of rules should be thus impartially applied; though all admit the importance of excluding from government, and human conduct generally, all conscious partiality and 'respect of persons.'

The principle just discussed, which seems to be more or less clearly implied in the common notion of 'fairness' or 'equity,' is obtained by considering the similarity of the individuals that make up a Logical Whole or Genus. There are others, no less important, which emerge in the consideration of the similar parts of a Mathematical or Quantitative Whole. Such a Whole is presented in the common notion of the Good—or, as is sometimes said, 'good on the whole'—of any individual human being. The proposition 'that one ought to aim at one's own good' is sometimes given as the maxim of Rational Self-love or Prudence: but as so stated it does not clearly avoid tautology; since we may define 'good' as 'what one ought to aim at.' If, however, we say 'one's good on the whole,' the addition suggests a principle which, when explicitly stated, is, at any rate, not tautological. . . . [T]his principle . . . that 'of impartial concern for all parts of our conscious life':—we might express it concisely by saying 'that Hereafter as such is to be regarded neither less nor more than Now.' It is not, of course, meant that the good of the present may not reasonably be preferred to that of the future on account of its greater certainty: or again, that a week ten years hence may not be more important to us than a week now, through an increase in our means or capacities of happiness. All that the principle affirms is that the mere difference of priority and posteriority in time is not a reasonable ground for having more regard to the consciousness of one moment that to that of another. The form in which it practically presents itself to most men is 'that a smaller present good is not to be preferred to a greater future good' (allowing for difference of certainty): since Prudence is generally exercised in restraining a present desire (the object or satisfaction of which we commonly regard as *pro tanto* 'a good'), on account of the remoter consequences of gratifying it. The commonest view of the principle would no doubt be that the present pleasure or happiness is reasonably to be foregone with the view of obtaining greater pleasure or happiness hereafter: but the principle need not be restricted to a hedonistic application; it is equally applicable to any other interpretation of 'one's own good,' in which good is conceived as a mathematical whole, of which the integrant parts are realized in different parts or moments of a lifetime. And therefore it is perhaps better to distinguish it here from the principle 'that Pleasure is the sole Ultimate Good,' which does not seem to have any logical connexion with it.

So far we have only been considering the 'Good on the Whole' of a single individual: but just as this notion is constructed by comparison and integration of the different 'goods' that succeed one another in the series of our conscious states, so we have formed the notion of Universal Good by comparison and integration of the goods of all individual human—or sentient—existences. And here again, just as in the former case, by considering the relation of the integrant parts to the whole and to each other, I obtain the self-evident principle that the good of any one individual is of no more importance, from the point of view (if I may say so) of the Universe, than the good of any other; unless, that is, there are special grounds for believing that more good is likely to be realized in the one case than in the other. And it is evident to me that as a rational being I am bound to aim at good generally—so far as it is attainable by my efforts—not merely at a particular part of it.

From these two rational intuitions we may deduce, as a necessary inference, the maxim of Benevolence in an abstract form: viz. that each one is morally bound to regard the good of any other individual as much as his own, except in so far as he judges it to be less, when impartially viewed, or less certainly knowable or attainable by him. I before observed that the duty of Benevolence as recognized by common sense seems to fall somewhat short of this. But I think it may be fairly urged in explanation of this that *practically* each man, even with a view to universal Good, ought chiefly to concern himself with promoting the good of a limited number of human beings, and that generally in proportion to the closeness of their connexion with him. I think that a 'plain man,' in a modern civilized society, if his conscience were fairly brought to consider the hypothetical question, whether it would be morally right for him to seek his own happiness on any occasion if it involved a certain sacrifice of the greater happiness of some other human being—without any counterbalancing gain to any one else—would answer unhesitatingly in the negative.

I have tried to show how in the principles of Justice, Prudence, and Rational Benevolence as commonly recognized there is at least a self-evident element, immediately cognizable by abstract intuition; depending in each case on the relation which individuals and their particular ends bear as parts to their wholes, and to other parts of these wholes. I regard the apprehension, with more or less distinctness, of these abstract truths, as the permanent basis of the common conviction that the fundamental precepts of morality are essentially reasonable. No doubt these principles are often placed side by side with other precepts to which custom and general consent have given a merely illusory air of self-evidence: but the distinction between the two kinds of maxims appears to me to become manifest by merely reflecting upon them. I know by direct reflection that the propositions, 'I ought to speak the truth,' 'I ought to keep my promises'—however true they may be—are not self-evident to me; they present themselves as propositions requiring rational justification of some kind. On the other hand, the propositions, 'I ought not to prefer a present lesser good to a future greater good,' and 'I ought not to prefer my own lesser good to the greater good of another,[4] do present themselves as self-evident; as much (*e.g.*) as the mathematical axiom that 'if equals be added to equals the wholes are equal.'

NOTES

1. As, for instance, when Bentham explains (*Principles of Morals and Legislation,* chap. i. § i. note) that his fundamental principle "states the greatest happiness of all those whose interest is in question as being the right and proper end of human action," we cannot understand him really to *mean* by the word "right" "conducive to the general happiness," though his language in other passages of the same chapter (§§ ix. and x.) would seem to imply this; for the proposition that it is conducive to general happiness to take general happiness as an end of action, though not exactly a tautology, can hardly serve as the fundamental principle of a moral system.
2. We do not commonly say that particular physical facts are apprehended by the Reason: we consider this faculty to be conversant in its discursive operation with the relation of judgments or propositions: and the intuitive reason (which is here rather in question) we restrict to the apprehension of universal truths, such as the axioms of Logic and Mathematics.
3. By cognition I always mean what some would rather call "apparent cognition"—that is, I do not mean to affirm the *validity* of the cognition, but only its existence as a psychical fact, and its claim to be valid.
4. To avoid misapprehension I should state that in these propositions the consideration of the different degrees of *certainty* of Present and Future Good, Own and Others' Good respectively, is supposed to have been fully taken into account *before* the future or alien Good is judged to be greater.

STUDY QUESTIONS

1. According to Sidgwick, what are ethical judgments?
2. According to Sidgwick, how should terms like "ought" and "right" be defined?
3. According to Sidgwick, what conditions need to be met for a principle to qualify as self-evident?
4. Do you believe any moral principles are self-evident?

Beyond Good and Evil

Friedrich Nietzsche

Friedrich Nietzsche (1844–1900) was a German philosopher and classical scholar. Because of his unconventional views and aphoristic style of writing, he is regarded as one of the most controversial figures in the history of philosophy. He argues that originally the term "good" was associated with nobility and power, but this "master morality" was replaced by "slave morality," which celebrates altruism and self-denial. Nietzsche maintains that slave morality needs to be transcended by a higher form of humanity that will lead toward superior forms of life in a world without God.

259

To refrain from injuring, abusing, or exploiting one another; to equate another person's will with our own: in a certain crude sense this can develop into good manners between individuals, if the preconditions are in place (that is, if the individuals have truly similar strength and standards and if they are united within one single social body). But if we were to try to take this principle further and possibly even make it the *basic principle of society,* it would immediately be revealed for what it is: a will to *deny* life, a principle for dissolution and decline. We must think through the reasons for this and resist all sentimental frailty: life itself *in its essence* means appropriating, injuring, overpowering those who are foreign and weaker; oppression, harshness, forcing one's own forms on others, incorporation, and at the very least, at the very mildest, exploitation—but why should we keep using this kind of language, that has from time immemorial been infused with a slanderous intent? Even that social body whose individuals, as we have just assumed above, treat one another as equals (this happens in every healthy aristocracy) must itself, if the body is vital and not moribund, do to other bodies everything that the individuals within it refrain from doing to one another: it will have to be the will to power incarnate, it will want to grow, to reach out around itself, pull towards itself, gain the upper hand—not out of some morality or immorality, but because it is *alive,* and because life simply *is* the will to power. This, however, more than anything else, is what the common European consciousness resists learning; people everywhere are rhapsodizing, even under the guise of science, about future social conditions that will have lost their "exploitative character"—to my ear that sounds as if they were promising to invent a life form that would refrain from all organic functions. "Exploitation" is not part of a decadent or imperfect, primitive society: it is part of the *fundamental nature* of living things, as its fundamental organic function; it is a consequence of the true will to power, which is simply the will to life.

From Friedrich Nietzsche, *Beyond Good and Evil*, trans. Marion Faber (New York: Oxford University Press, 1998). Reprinted by permission of the publisher.

Assuming that this is innovative as theory—as reality it is the *original fact* of all history: let us at least be this honest with ourselves!

260

While perusing the many subtler and cruder moral codes that have prevailed or still prevail on earth thus far, I found that certain traits regularly recurred in combination, linked to one another—until finally two basic types were revealed and a fundamental difference leapt out at me. There are *master moralities* and *slave moralities.* I would add at once that in all higher and more complex cultures, there are also apparent attempts to mediate between the two moralities, and even more often a confusion of the two and a mutual misunderstanding, indeed sometimes even their violent juxtaposition—even in the same person, within one single breast. Moral value distinctions have emerged either from among a masterful kind, pleasantly aware of how it differed from those whom it mastered, or else from among the mastered, those who were to varying degrees slaves or dependants. In the first case, when it is the masters who define the concept "good," it is the proud, exalted states of soul that are thought to distinguish and define the hierarchy. The noble person keeps away from those beings who express the opposite of these elevated, proud inner states: he despises them. Let us note immediately that in this first kind of morality the opposition "good" and "bad" means about the same thing as "noble" and "despicable"—the opposition "good" and "*evil*" has a different origin. The person who is cowardly or anxious or petty or concerned with narrow utility is despised; likewise the distrustful person with his constrained gaze, the self-disparager, the craven kind of person who endures maltreatment, the importunate flatterer, and above all the liar: all aristocrats hold the fundamental conviction that the common people are liars. "We truthful ones"—that is what the ancient Greek nobility called themselves. It is obvious that moral value distinctions everywhere are first attributed to *people* and only later and in a derivative fashion applied to *actions*: for that reason moral

historians commit a crass error by starting with questions such as: "Why do we praise an empathetic action?" The noble type of person feels *himself* as determining value—he does not need approval, he judges that "what is harmful to me is harmful per se," he knows that he is the one who causes things to be revered in the first place, he *creates values.* Everything that he knows of himself he reveres: this kind of moral code is self-glorifying. In the foreground is a feeling of fullness, of overflowing power, of happiness in great tension, an awareness of a wealth that would like to bestow and share—the noble person will also help the unfortunate, but not, or not entirely, out of pity, but rather from the urgency created by an excess of power. The noble person reveres the power in himself, and also his power over himself, his ability to speak and to be silent, to enjoy the practice of severity and harshness towards himself and to respect everything that is severe and harsh. "Wotan placed a harsh heart within my breast," goes a line in an old Scandinavian saga: that is how it is written from the heart of a proud Viking—and rightly so. For this kind of a person is proud *not* to be made for pity; and so the hero of the saga adds a warning: "If your heart is not harsh when you are young, it will never become harsh." The noble and brave people who think like this are the most removed from that other moral code which sees the sign of morality in pity or altruistic behavior or *désintéressement*;[1] belief in ourselves, pride in ourselves, a fundamental hostility and irony towards "selflessness"—these are as surely a part of a noble morality as caution and a slight disdain towards empathetic feelings and "warm hearts."

It is the powerful who *understand* how to revere, it is their art form, their realm of invention. Great reverence for old age and for origins (all law is based upon this twofold reverence), belief in ancestors and prejudice in their favor and to the disadvantage of the next generation—these are typical in the morality of the powerful; and if, conversely, people of "modern ideas" believe in progress and "the future" almost by instinct and show an increasing lack of respect for old age, that alone suffices to reveal the ignoble origin of these "ideas." Most of all, however, the master morality is foreign and embarrassing to current taste because of the severity of its fundamental principle: that we have duties only towards our peers, and that we may treat those of lower rank, anything foreign, as we think best or "as our heart dictates" or in any event "beyond good and evil"—pity and the like should be thought of in this context. The ability and duty to feel enduring gratitude or vengefulness (both only within a circle of equals), subtlety in the forms of retribution, a refined concept of friendship, a certain need for enemies (as drainage channels for the emotions of envy, combativeness, arrogance—in essence, in order to be a good *friend*): these are the typical signs of a noble morality, which, as we have suggested, is not the morality of "modern ideas" and is therefore difficult to sympathize with these days, also difficult to dig out and uncover.

It is different with the second type of morality, *slave morality.* Assuming that the raped, the oppressed, the suffering, the shackled, the weary, the insecure engage in moralizing, what will their moral value judgments have in common? They will probably express a pessimistic suspicion about the whole human condition, and they might condemn the human being along with his condition. The slave's eye does not readily apprehend the virtues of the powerful: he is skeptical and distrustful, he is *keenly* distrustful of everything that the powerful revere as "good"—he would like to convince himself that even their happiness is not genuine. Conversely, those qualities that serve to relieve the sufferers' existence are brought into relief and bathed in light: this is where pity, a kind, helpful hand, a warm heart, patience, diligence, humility, friendliness are revered—for in this context, these qualities are most useful and practically the only means of enduring an oppressive existence. Slave morality is essentially a morality of utility. It is upon this hearth that the famous opposition "good" and "*evil*" originates—power and dangerousness, a certain fear-inducing, subtle strength that keeps contempt from surfacing, are translated by experience into evil. According to slave morality, then, the "evil" person evokes fear; according to master morality, it is exactly the "good" person who evokes fear and wants to evoke it, while the "bad" person is felt to be despicable. The opposition comes to a head when, in terms of slave morality, a hint of condescension (it may be slight and well intentioned) clings even to those whom this morality designates as "good," since within a slave mentality a good person must in any event be *harmless*: he is good-natured, easily deceived, perhaps a bit stupid, a *bonhomme*.[2] Wherever slave morality gains the upper hand, language shows a tendency to make a closer association of the words "good" and "stupid."

A last fundamental difference: the longing for *freedom,* an instinct for the happiness and nuances of feeling free, is as necessarily a part of slave morals and morality as artistic, rapturous reverence and devotion invariably signal an aristocratic mentality and judgement.

NOTES

1. [Disinterestedness—Eds.]
2. [Simple man.]

STUDY QUESTIONS

1. What is the difference between "slave" and "master" morality?
2. What does Nietzsche mean by his claim that slave morality is a "morality of utility"?
3. Does pride in oneself have any role in morality?
4. Does master morality have any place for concern about others?

Part III

REALISM

Principia Ethica

G. E. Moore

George Edward Moore (1873–1958), Professor of Mental Philosophy and Logic at the University of Cambridge, was one of the most influential philosophers of the twentieth century. He argues that goodness, like the color yellow, is simple and, having no parts, unanalyzable. According to Moore, previous philosophers have failed to recognize the irreducibility of goodness because they conflate goodness with things that are good. Moore labels this alleged error the "naturalistic fallacy."

To defend his view that goodness cannot be analyzed in natural terms, Moore deploys what has come to be known as the "open-question argument." For any proposed definition of good, we can always sensibly ask whether things of that sort are good. For instance, consider these two questions:

> Going to the movies is pleasant, but is it pleasant?

> Going to the movies is pleasant, but is it good?

The first is trivial and therefore a closed question. The second, however, is an open question, because we can grant that something is pleasant but still appropriately wonder if it is good. Thus "good" and "pleasant" do not have the same meaning. Moore contends that by using the open-question argument, we can undermine any proposed definition of goodness, thus demonstrating that goodness cannot be identical with a natural property.

Much of the work in the remainder of this volume can be seen as a reaction to the open-question argument.

---

5. . . . [H]ow "good" is to be defined, is the most fundamental question in all Ethics. That which is meant by "good" is, in fact, except its converse "bad," the *only* simple object of thought which is peculiar to Ethics. Its definition is, therefore, the most essential point in the definition of Ethics; and moreover a mistake with regard to it entails a far larger number of erroneous ethical judgments than any other. Unless this first question be fully understood, and its true answer clearly recognized, the rest of Ethics is as good as useless from the point of view of systematic knowledge. True ethical judgments, of the two kinds last dealt with, may indeed be made by those who do not know the answer to this question

From G. E. Moore, *Principia Ethica* (Cambridge: Cambridge University Press, 1903). Reprinted with the permission of the publisher.

as well as by those who do; and it goes without saying that the two classes of people may lead equally good lives. But it is extremely unlikely that the *most general* ethical judgments will be equally valid, in the absence of a true answer to this question: I shall presently try to show that the gravest errors have been largely due to beliefs in a false answer. And, in any case, it is impossible that, till the answer to this question be known, any one should know *what is the evidence* for any ethical judgment whatsoever. But the main object of Ethics, as a systematic science, is to give correct *reasons* for thinking that this or that is good; and, unless this question be answered, such reasons cannot be given. Even, therefore, apart from the fact that a false answer leads to false conclusions, the present enquiry is a most necessary and important part of the science of Ethics.

6. What, then, is good? How is good to be defined? Now, it may be thought that this is a verbal question. A definition does indeed often mean the expressing of one word's meaning in other words. But this is not the sort of definition I am asking for. Such a definition can never be of ultimate importance in any study except lexicography. If I wanted that kind of definition I should have to consider in the first place how people generally used the word "good"; but my business is not with its proper usage, as established by custom. I should, indeed, be foolish, if I tried to use it for something which it did not usually denote: if, for instance, I were to announce that, whenever I used the word "good," I must be understood to be thinking of that object which is usually denoted by the word "table." I shall, therefore, use the word in the sense in which I think it is ordinarily used; but at the same time I am not anxious to discuss whether I am right in thinking that it is so used. My business is solely with that object or idea, which I hold, rightly or wrongly, that the word is generally used to stand for. What I want to discover is the nature of that object or idea, and about this I am extremely anxious to arrive at an agreement.

But, if we understand the question in this sense, my answer to it may seem a very disappointing one. If I am asked "What is good?" my answer is that good is good, and that is the end of the matter. Or if I am asked "How is good to be defined?" my answer is that it cannot be defined, and that is all I have to say about it. But disappointing as these answers may appear, they are of the very last importance. To readers who are familiar with philosophic terminology, I can express their importance by saying that they amount to this: That propositions about the good are all of them synthetic and never analytic; and that is plainly no trivial matter. And the same thing may be expressed more popularly, by saying that, if I am right, then nobody can foist upon us such an axiom as that "Pleasure is the only good" or that "The good is the desired" on the pretence that this is "the very meaning of the word."

7. Let us, then, consider this position: My point is that "good" is a simple notion, just as "yellow" is a simple notion; that, just as you cannot, by any manner of means, explain to any one who does not already know it, what yellow is, so you cannot explain what good is. Definitions of the kind that I was asking for, definitions which describe the real nature of the object or notion denoted by a word, and which do not merely tell us what the word is used to mean, are only possible when the object or notion in question is something complex. You can give a definition of a horse, because a horse has many different properties and qualities, all of which you can enumerate. But when you have enumerated them all, when you have reduced a horse to his simplest terms, then you can no longer define those terms. They are simply something which you think of or perceive, and to any one who cannot think of or perceive them, you can never, by any definition, make their nature known. It may perhaps be objected to this that we are able to describe to others, objects which they have never seen or thought of. We can, for instance, make a man understand what a chimera is, although he has never heard of one or seen one. You can tell him that it is an animal with a lioness's head and body, with a goat's head growing from the middle of its back, and with a snake in place of a tail. But here the object which you are describing is a complex object; it is entirely composed of parts, with which we are all perfectly familiar—a snake, a goat, a lioness; and we know,

too, the manner in which those parts are to be put together, because we know what is meant by the middle of a lioness's back, and where her tail is wont to grow. And so it is with all objects, not previously known, which we are able to define: they are all complex; all composed of parts, which may themselves, in the first instance, be capable of similar definition, but which must in the end be reducible to simplest parts, which can no longer be defined. But yellow and good, we say, are not complex: they are notions of that simple kind, out of which definitions are composed and with which the power of further defining ceases.

8. When we say, as Webster says, "The definition of horse is 'A hoofed quadruped of the genus Equus,'" we may, in fact, mean three different things. (1) We may mean merely: "When I say 'horse,' you are to understand that I am talking about a hoofed quadruped of the genus Equus." This might be called the arbitrary verbal definition: and I do not mean that good is indefinable in that sense. (2) We may mean, as Webster ought to mean: "When most English people say 'horse,' they mean a hoofed quadruped of the genus Equus." This may be called the verbal definition proper, and I do not say that good is indefinable in this sense either; for it is certainly possible to discover how people use a word: otherwise, we could never have known that "good" may be translated by "gut" in German and by "bon" in French. But (3) we may, when we define horse, mean something much more important. We may mean that a certain object, which we all of us know, is composed in a certain manner: that it has four legs, a head, a heart, a liver, etc., etc., all of them arranged in definite relations to one another. It is in this sense that I deny good to be definable. I say that it is not composed of any parts, which we can substitute for it in our minds when we are thinking of it. We might think just as clearly and correctly about a horse, if we thought of all its parts and their arrangement instead of thinking of the whole: we could, I say, think how a horse differed from a donkey just as well, just as truly, in this way, as now we do, only not so easily; but there is nothing whatsoever which we could so substitute for good; and that is what I mean, when I say that good is indefinable.

9. But I am afraid I have still not removed the chief difficulty which may prevent acceptance of the proposition that good is indefinable. I do not mean to say that *the* good, that which is good, is thus indefinable; if I did think so, I should not be writing on Ethics, for my main object is to help towards discovering that definition. It is just because I think there will be less risk of error in our search for a definition of "the good," that I am now insisting that *good* is indefinable. I must try to explain the difference between these two. I suppose it may be granted that "good" is an adjective. Well "the good," "that which is good," must therefore be the substantive to which the adjective "good" will apply: it must be the whole of that to which the adjective will apply, and the adjective must *always* truly apply to it. But if it is that to which the adjective will apply, it must be something different from that adjective itself; and the whole of that something different, whatever it is, will be our definition of *the* good. Now it may be that this something will have other adjectives, besides "good," that will apply to it. It may be full of pleasure, for example; it may be intelligent: and if these two adjectives are really part of its definition, then it will certainly be true, that pleasure and intelligence are good. And many people appear to think that, if we say "Pleasure and intelligence are good," or if we say "Only pleasure and intelligence are good," we are defining "good." Well, I cannot deny that propositions of this nature may sometimes be called definitions; I do not know well enough how the word is generally used to decide upon this point. I only wish it to be understood that that is not what I mean when I say there is no possible definition of good, and that I shall not mean this if I use the word again. I do most fully believe that some true proposition of the form "Intelligence is good and intelligence alone is good" can be found; if none could be found, our definition of *the* good would be impossible. As it is, I believe *the* good to be definable; and yet I still say that good itself is indefinable.

10. "Good," then, if we mean by it that quality which we assert to belong to a thing, when we say that the thing is good, is incapable of any definition, in the most important sense of that word. The most important sense of "definition" is that in which a

definition states what are the parts which invariably compose a certain whole; and in this sense "good" has no definition because it is simple and has no parts. It is one of those innumerable objects of thought which are themselves incapable of definition, because they are the ultimate terms by reference to which whatever *is* capable of definition must be defined. That there must be an indefinite number of such terms is obvious, on reflection; since we cannot define anything except by an analysis, which, when carried as far as it will go, refers us to something, which is simply different from anything else, and which by that ultimate difference explains the peculiarity of the whole which we are defining: for every whole contains some parts which are common to other wholes also. There is, therefore, no intrinsic difficulty in the contention that "good" denotes a simple and indefinable quality. There are many other instances of such qualities.

Consider yellow, for example. We may try to define it, by describing its physical equivalent; we may state what kind of light-vibrations must stimulate the normal eye, in order that we may perceive it. But a moment's reflection is sufficient to show that those light-vibrations are not themselves what we mean by yellow. *They* are not what we perceive. Indeed we should never have been able to discover their existence, unless we had first been struck by the patent difference of quality between the different colors. The most we can be entitled to say of those vibrations is that they are what corresponds in space to the yellow which we actually perceive.

Yet a mistake of this simple kind has commonly been made about "good." It may be true that all things which are good are *also* something else, just as it is true that all things which are yellow produce a certain kind of vibration in the light. And it is a fact, that Ethics aims at discovering what are those other properties belonging to all things which are good. But far too many philosophers have thought that when they named those other properties they were actually defining good; that these properties, in fact, were simply not "other," but absolutely and entirely the same with goodness. This view I propose to call the "naturalistic fallacy" and of it I shall now endeavor to dispose.

11. Let us consider what it is such philosophers say. And first it is to be noticed that they do not agree among themselves. They not only say that they are right as to what good is, but they endeavor to prove that other people who say that it is something else, are wrong. One, for instance, will affirm that good is pleasure, another, perhaps, that good is that which is desired; and each of these will argue eagerly to prove that the other is wrong. But how is that possible? One of them says that good is nothing but the object of desire, and at the same time tries to prove that it is not pleasure. But from his first assertion, that good just means the object of desire, one of two things must follow as regards his proof:

(1) He may be trying to prove that the object of desire is not pleasure. But, if this be all, where is his Ethics? The position he is maintaining is merely a psychological one. Desire is something which occurs in our minds, and pleasure is something else which so occurs; and our would-be ethical philosopher is merely holding that the latter is not the object of the former. But what has that to do with the question in dispute? His opponent held the ethical proposition that pleasure was the good, and although he should prove a million times over the psychological proposition that pleasure is not the object of desire, he is no nearer proving his opponent to be wrong. The position is like this. One man says a triangle is a circle: another replies "A triangle is a straight line, and I will prove to you that I am right: *for*" (this is the only argument) "a straight line is not a circle." "That is quite true," the other may reply; "but nevertheless a triangle is a circle, and you have said nothing whatever to prove the contrary. What is proved is that one of us is wrong, for we agree that a triangle cannot be both a straight line and a circle: but which is wrong, there can be no earthly means of proving, since you define triangle as straight line and I define it as circle."—Well, that is one alternative which any naturalistic Ethics has to face; if good is *defined* as something else, it is then impossible either to prove that any other definition is wrong or even to deny such definition.

(2) The other alternative will scarcely be more welcome. It is that the discussion is after all a verbal one. When A says "Good means pleasant" and

B says "Good means desired," they may merely wish to assert that most people have used the word for what is pleasant and for what is desired respectively. And this is quite an interesting subject for discussion: only it is not a whit more an ethical discussion than the last was. Nor do I think that any exponent of naturalistic Ethics would be willing to allow that this was all he meant. They are all so anxious to persuade us that what they call the good is what we really ought to do. "Do pray, act so, because the word 'good' is generally used to denote actions of this nature": such, on this view, would be the substance of their teaching. And in so far as they tell us how we ought to act, their teaching is truly ethical, as they mean it to be. But how perfectly absurd is the reason they would give for it! "You are to do this, because most people use a certain word to denote conduct such as this." "You are to say the thing which is not, because most people call it lying." That is an argument just as good!—My dear sirs, what we want to know from you as ethical teachers, is not how people use a word; it is not even, what kind of actions they approve, which the use of this word "good" may certainly imply: what we want to know is simply what *is* good. We may indeed agree that what most people do think good, is actually so; we shall at all events be glad to know their opinions: but when we say their opinions about what is good, we do mean what we say; we do not care whether they call that thing which they mean "horse" or "table" or "chair," "gut" or "bon" or "ἀγαθός"; we want to know what it is that they so call. When they say "Pleasure is good," we cannot believe that they merely mean "Pleasure is pleasure" and nothing more than that.

12. Suppose a man says "I am pleased"; and suppose that is not a lie or a mistake but the truth. Well, if it is true, what does that mean? It means that his mind, a certain definite mind, distinguished by certain definite marks from all others, has at this moment a certain definite feeling called pleasure. "Pleased" *means* nothing but having pleasure, and though we may be more pleased or less pleased, and even, we may admit for the present, have one or another kind of pleasure; yet in so far as it is pleasure we have, whether there be more or less of it, and whether it be of one kind or another, what we have is

one definite thing, absolutely indefinable, some one thing that is the same in all the various degrees and in all the various kinds of it that there may be. We may be able to say how it is related to other things: that, for example, it is in the mind, that it causes desire, that we are conscious of it, etc., etc. We can, I say, describe its relations to other things, but define it we can *not*. And if anybody tried to define pleasure for us as being any other natural object; if anybody were to say, for instance, that pleasure *means* the sensation of red, and were to proceed to deduce from that that pleasure is a color, we should be entitled to laugh at him and to distrust his future statements about pleasure. Well, that would be the same fallacy which I have called the naturalistic fallacy. That "pleased" does not mean "having the sensation of red," or anything else whatever, does not prevent us from understanding what it does mean. It is enough for us to know that "pleased" does mean "having the sensation of pleasure," and though pleasure is absolutely indefinable, though pleasure is pleasure and nothing else whatever, yet we feel no difficulty in saying that we are pleased. The reason is, of course, that when I say "I am pleased," I do *not* mean that "I" am the same thing as "having pleasure." And similarly no difficulty need be found in my saying that "pleasure is good" and yet not meaning that "pleasure" is the same thing as "good," that pleasure *means* good, and that good *means* pleasure. If I were to imagine that when I said "I am pleased," I meant that I was exactly the same thing as "pleased," I should not indeed call that a naturalistic fallacy, although it would be the same fallacy as I have called naturalistic with reference to Ethics. The reason of this is obvious enough. When a man confuses two natural objects with one another, defining the one by the other, if for instance, he confuses himself, who is one natural object, with "pleased" or with "pleasure" which are others, then there is no reason to call the fallacy naturalistic. But if he confuses "good," which is not in the same sense a natural object, with any natural object whatever, then there is a reason for calling that a naturalistic fallacy; its being made with regard to "good" marks it as something quite specific, and this specific mistake deserves a name because it is so common.

As for the reasons why good is not to be considered a natural object, they may be reserved for discussion in another place. But, for the present, it is sufficient to notice this: Even if it were a natural object, that would not alter the nature of the fallacy nor diminish its importance one whit. All that I have said about it would remain quite equally true: only the name which I have called it would not be so appropriate as I think it is. And I do not care about the name: what I do care about is the fallacy. It does not matter what we call it, provided we recognize it when we meet with it. It is to be met with in almost every book on Ethics; and yet it is not recognized: and that is why it is necessary to multiply illustrations of it, and convenient to give it a name. It is a very simple fallacy indeed. When we say that an orange is yellow, we do not think our statement binds us to hold that "orange" means nothing else than "yellow," or that nothing can be yellow but an orange. Supposing the orange is also sweet! Does that bind us to say that "sweet" is exactly the same thing as "yellow," that "sweet" must be defined as "yellow"? And supposing it be recognized that "yellow" just means "yellow" and nothing else whatever, does that make it any more difficult to hold that oranges are yellow? Most certainly it does not: on the contrary, it would be absolutely meaningless to say that oranges were yellow, unless yellow did in the end mean just "yellow" and nothing else whatever—unless it was absolutely indefinable. We should not get any very clear notion about things, which are yellow—we should not get very far with our science, if we were bound to hold that everything which was yellow, *meant* exactly the same thing as yellow. We should find we had to hold that an orange was exactly the same thing as a stool, a piece of paper, a lemon, anything you like. We could prove any number of absurdities; but should we be the nearer to the truth? Why, then, should it be different with "good"? Why, if good is good and indefinable, should I be held to deny that pleasure is good? Is there any difficulty in holding both to be true at once? On the contrary, there is no meaning in saying that pleasure is good, unless good is something different from pleasure. It is absolutely useless, so far as Ethics is concerned, to prove, as Mr Spencer tries to do, that increase of pleasure coincides with

increase of life, unless good *means* something different from either life or pleasure. He might just as well try to prove that an orange is yellow by showing that it always is wrapped up in paper.

13. In fact, if it is not the case that "good" denotes something simple and indefinable, only two alternatives are possible: either it is a complex, a given whole, about the correct analysis of which there may be disagreement; or else it means nothing at all, and there is no such subject as Ethics. In general, however, ethical philosophers have attempted to define good, without recognizing what such an attempt must mean. They actually use arguments which involve one or both of the absurdities considered in §11. We are, therefore, justified in concluding that the attempt to define good is chiefly due to want of clearness as to the possible nature of definition. There are, in fact, only two serious alternatives to be considered, in order to establish the conclusion that "good" does denote a simple and indefinable notion. It might possibly denote a complex, as "horse" does; or it might have no meaning at all. Neither of these possibilities has, however, been clearly conceived and seriously maintained, as such, by those who presume to define good; and both may be dismissed by a simple appeal to facts.

(1) The hypothesis that disagreement about the meaning of good is disagreement with regard to the correct analysis of a given whole, may be most plainly seen to be incorrect by consideration of the fact that, whatever definition be offered, it may be always asked, with significance, of the complex so defined, whether it is itself good. To take, for instance, one of the more plausible, because one of the more complicated, of such proposed definitions, it may easily be thought, at first sight, that to be good may mean to be that which we desire to desire. Thus if we apply this definition to a particular instance and say "When we think that A is good, we are thinking that A is one of the things which we desire to desire," our proposition may seem quite plausible. But, if we carry the investigation further, and ask ourselves "Is it good to desire to desire A?" it is apparent, on a little reflection, that this question is itself as intelligible, as the original question "Is A good?"—that we are, in fact, now asking for exactly the same

information about the desire to desire A, for which we formerly asked with regard to A itself. But it is also apparent that the meaning of this second question cannot be correctly analyzed into "Is the desire to desire A one of the things which we desire to desire?": we have not before our minds anything so complicated as the question "Do we desire to desire to desire A?" Moreover any one can easily convince himself by inspection that the predicate of this proposition—"good"—is positively different from the notion of "desiring to desire" which enters into its subject: "That we should desire to desire A is good" is *not* merely equivalent to "That A should be good is good." It may indeed be true that what we desire to desire is always also good; perhaps, even the converse may be true: but it is very doubtful whether this is the case, and the mere fact that we understand very well what is meant by doubting it, shows clearly that we have two different notions before our minds.

(2) And the same consideration is sufficient to dismiss the hypothesis that "good" has no meaning whatsoever. It is very natural to make the mistake of supposing that what is universally true is of such a nature that its negation would be self-contradictory: the importance which has been assigned to analytic propositions in the history of philosophy shows how easy such a mistake is. And thus it is very easy to conclude that what seems to be a universal ethical principle is in fact an identical proposition; that, if, for example, whatever is called "good" seems to be pleasant, the proposition "Pleasure is the good"

does not assert a connection between two different notions, but involves only one, that of pleasure, which is easily recognized as a distinct entity. But whoever will attentively consider with himself what is actually before his mind when he asks the question "Is pleasure (or whatever it may be) after all good?" can easily satisfy himself that he is not merely wondering whether pleasure is pleasant. And if he will try this experiment with each suggested definition in succession, he may become expert enough to recognize that in every case he has before his mind a unique object, with regard to the connection of which with any other object, a distinct question may be asked. Every one does in fact understand the question "Is this good?" When he thinks of it, his state of mind is different from what it would be, were he asked "Is this pleasant, or desired, or approved?" It has a distinct meaning for him, even though he may not recognize in what respect it is distinct. Whenever he thinks of "intrinsic value," or "intrinsic worth," or says that a thing "ought to exist," he has before his mind the unique object—the unique property of things—which I mean by "good." Everybody is constantly aware of this notion, although he may never become aware at all that it is different from other notions of which he is also aware. But, for correct ethical reasoning, it is extremely important that he should become aware of this fact; and, as soon as the nature of the problem is clearly understood, there should be little difficulty in advancing so far in analysis.

STUDY QUESTIONS

1. According to Moore, what is the most fundamental question in ethics?
2. How does Moore answer the fundamental question?
3. According to Moore, what is the naturalistic fallacy?
4. What does Moore mean when he claims that goodness is indefinable?

Naturalism and Prescriptivity

Peter Railton

Challenging G. E. Moore's open-question argument, Peter Railton, Professor of Philosophy at the University of Michigan, develops naturalist realism, a position which argues for the existence of facts that are both normative and natural.

Railton models his view on the identity holding between "water" and "H_2O." That water is H_2O is not known *a priori*, simply by the meaning of words, but only *a posteriori*, through empirical investigation. Thus a competent user of the word "water" could sensibly ask: "Does this cup of water contain H_2O?" This question is open, yet water is identical with H_2O. Hence the open-question argument, supposedly proving in this case that water is not identical with H_2O, fails. Similarly, the normative and the natural could be identical despite the challenge posed by the open question argument.

Turning to hedonism, Railton argues that reducing "what is good for a person" to "what is pleasurable" links five important elements. First, the reduction preserves the idea that our discourse about a person's good expresses beliefs; it is cognitive. Second, the property of being pleasurable plays an explanatory role in everyday experience; we often explain our behavior in terms of seeking pleasure. Third, the property of being pleasurable plays a normative role; we regulate our behavior in line with what would bring about pleasurable experiences. Fourth, the account of a person's good in terms of pleasure does not distort beyond recognition our pre-theoretical idea of what is good for a person. Fifth, accepting the reduction would not eliminate the normative role of a person's good. Railton thus concludes that naturalist realism should be seen as a research program with great promise and not, as the open-question argument suggests, a philosophical non-starter.

INTRODUCTION: SETTING THE PROBLEM

Statements about a person's good slip into and out of our ordinary discourse about the world with nary a ripple. Such statements are objects of belief and assertion, they obey the rules of logic, and they are often defended by evidence and argument. They even participate in common-sense explanations, as when we say of some person that he has been less subject to wild swings of enthusiasm and disappointment now that, with experience, he has gained a clearer idea of what is good for him. Statements about a person's good present themselves as being

From Peter Railton, "Naturalism and Prescriptivity," *Social Philosophy & Policy* 7 (1989). Reprinted by permission of the publisher.

about something with respect to which our beliefs can be true or false, warranted or unwarranted. Let us speak of these features as the *descriptive* side of discourse about a person's good.

Discourse about a person's good also has another, *prescriptive* side, for to make or accept a judgment that something is good for someone is in some sense to recommend that thing to him and to those who care about him. Such a recommendation need not be overriding—there often is more to be considered in any given deliberation than the good of one particular individual. But someone who spoke in earnest to others about their own good, and then was simply puzzled when they took his remarks to be any sort of recommendation, would betray a lack of full competence with such discourse.

Philosophers have been struck by the difficulty of understanding how evaluative language, such as discourse about a person's good, could be at once essentially descriptive and essentially prescriptive. To be sure, there is no difficulty in seeing how a descriptive statement might come to function prescriptively. Suppose that I am looking for a lawyer and I overhear you say that Hoolihan always wins his cases. Your statement can function as a recommendation—once I have heard it—even though its content appears to be flatly descriptive. Its commending force appears not to reside essentially in the content of the statement itself, but rather depends upon a context in which my interest in finding a successful lawyer is already independently given.[1]

Similarly, there is no difficulty in seeing how a prescriptive judgment might come to function descriptively. A child soon learns that those things that an adult goes out of the way to label 'good for you' have certain characteristic features. When a child hears his parents prescribe taking a medicine, saying that it will be 'good for you,' he effectively acquires the information that something unpleasant is in the offing. It would, however, be odd indeed to say that 'unpleasant' is part of the meaning of 'good for you.'

One can, then, use a description to recommend, or use a prescription to convey information. Discourse about a person's good seems to presuppose something more: an inherent, necessary connection between the content of the description and the force

of the prescription. Yet G. E. Moore's "open question" argument has convinced many philosophers of the impossibility of finding a connection of this kind between good and any property captured entirely in descriptive, non-evaluative terms.[2] If any such property were constitutive of the meaning of 'good for so-and-so,' the argument runs, then a statement identifying this property with a person's good would be a mere tautology, analytically true, and no more sense could be made of questioning it than of questioning the statement 'The good of a person is identical with that person's good.' But even if we consider 'The good of a person is identical with that person's pleasure' (which, of all such equations, has had the most philosophical advocates), it seems clear that to question this statement would not be absurd and would not betray a simple failure to grasp the meaning of its terms.

Very grand claims have been made on behalf of Moore's argument. Moore himself thought it to show that all attempts to define 'good' or to identify it with some natural property would involve outright fallacy. Such claims seem much too strong. We can, however, say at least this much: application of the argument to every purported analysis of 'good' yet given has shown none of them to be utterly incontestable, so that none is obviously successful in stating an analytic truth.[3]

Moore believed that the failure of descriptive analyses of 'good' was no barrier to capturing what we above called the descriptive side of talk about good, because he held that 'good' refers to a non-natural property with which we have direct acquaintance by a kind of intellectual intuition. But most contemporary philosophers are unhappy with the Moorean idea of non-natural properties that are intuitively known, and many have concluded that the failure of descriptive analyses of 'good' raises fundamental questions about the status of value judgments. After all, it seems clear that most judgments of the goodness of particular things are synthetic statements, not tautologies. But, typically, synthetic statements concern natural properties, and our knowledge of their truth or falsity derives from experience. If all known attempts to identify the property of being good with some or other natural property have failed—as Moore's "open question" argument might be used to argue—then where in the world does the property of being good fit, and how on earth can we come to have knowledge of it? . . .

[T]he theory of value . . . I will be examining in this paper . . . seeks an epistemically respectable explanation of value discourse. . . . [I]t treats the cognitive character of value discourse—its descriptive side, as we have called it—as essential to it, and then seeks to account for the prescriptive force of value judgments as arising from the substantive content of such judgments. Unlike Moore's cognitivist position, however, the approach in question does not treat value properties as non-natural and *sui generis,* and therefore avoids the problems confronting Moore's account of the semantics and epistemology of value. Instead, the approach we will consider attempts to locate value properties among features of the world that are accessible to us through ordinary experience and that play a role in empirical explanations. It therefore treats value properties as *natural* properties, and so is a form of *naturalism* about value.[4]

. . . [T]he naturalistic cognitivist faces the . . . problem of explaining how an essentially descriptive use of language could have the prescriptive force of value discourse. . . . The difficulty is in locating a tight, "internal," and necessary—or quasi-necessary—connection between the particular content attributed by the naturalist to judgments of value and some appropriate commending force. The principal concern of this paper will be with that difficulty, and with a possible strategy for contending with it. Some version of this strategy is available to various forms of naturalism, but it is most readily and conspicuously available to a certain class of hedonistic naturalists, who hold that the experience of happiness—viewed as a kind of psychological state—is the only thing intrinsically good for a person.[5] Although I do not find hedonism the most plausible naturalistic doctrine about a person's good, I do think it underrated, and it does nicely exhibit the strategy I wish to discuss.

However, before discussing this strategy . . ., a few preliminary remarks about . . . naturalism . . . may be in order. . . .

II. THE NATURE OF NATURALISM

Two Kinds of Naturalism

Since I propose to discuss a naturalistic approach to the particular species of value that constitutes a person's intrinsic non-moral good, some initial explanation is needed of what naturalism in value theory might amount to, and why one might pursue it. . . .

Naturalism can be a doctrine about either method or substance. *Methodological naturalism* holds that philosophy does not possess a distinctive, *a priori* method able to yield substantive truths that, in principle, are not subject to any sort of empirical test. Instead, a methodological naturalist believes that philosophy should proceed *a posteriori,* in tandem with—perhaps as a particularly abstract and general part of—the broadly empirical inquiry carried on in the natural and social sciences.

Substantive naturalism, in contrast, is not in the first instance a view about philosophical methods, but about philosophical conclusions. A substantive naturalist advances a philosophical account of some domain of human language or practice that provides an interpretation of its central concepts in terms amenable to empirical inquiry.

How are these two forms of naturalism related? One need not be a methodological naturalist in order to advocate substantive naturalism, and, indeed, substantive naturalistic interpretations have at times been defended by the claim that their statements have the status of analytic truths, arrived at by *a priori* conceptual analysis. A substantive naturalist of this stripe—an "analytic naturalist"—is unlikely to be a methodological naturalist, for methodological naturalists have characteristically viewed interpretive tasks as substantive, rather than merely formal, and have therefore denied that interpretations can be defended by entirely *a priori* means.

Equally, a methodological naturalist need not arrive at substantive naturalist conclusions. . . .

The two forms of naturalism are therefore not essentially connected. Although, as it happens, the contemporary naturalism with which we will be concerned here is both methodological and substantive, its primary allegiance is owed to methodological naturalism. It is not a view driven by metaphysical considerations about what sorts of entities do or can exist, and so it does not start out with a definition of 'natural property' meant to divide the realm of possible being into the Real and the Unreal. Rather, our naturalist is impressed by the fact that claims about the world which have, historically, been deemed by philosophers to be *a priori* true—the principle of sufficient reason, the Euclidean structure of space, the restriction of mechanical interaction to local contact, the non-existence of vacua, and so on—have, with distressing regularity, been revised or abandoned in the face of emerging scientific theories. What is striking here is not that allegedly *a priori* philosophical statements which were believed true in the eighteenth century are now rejected, since, after all, many of the *a posteriori* statements of eighteenth-century science are also now heartily disbelieved. The striking thing is that the development of scientific theory has shown us how claims which seemed logically or conceptually true when matters were viewed in a strictly philosophical way could nonetheless come to seem empirically false as a result of the effort to construct powerful explanatory empirical theories. In such cases, it often seems possible in retrospect to account for the *sense* of logical or quasi-logical necessity that attended certain claims in this way: the conceptual categories embedded in language at any given time characteristically present themselves as fixed and definitive—for example, the history of linguistic revision that lies behind existing categories typically is no longer visible to contemporary users of the language.

Methodological naturalism owes its inspiration, in part, to the thought that, although the remedy for the inadequacies of eighteenth-century science seems to have been the ever-more-ambitious pursuit of systematic science, the inadequacies of eighteenth-century philosophy have not been remedied by an ever-more-ambitious pursuit of systematic philosophy. It seems to the methodological naturalist, therefore, that philosophers who can see from a historical perspective the danger of becoming entrapped by treating evolving linguistic categories as fixed should resist the temptation to view philosophical inquiry as somehow methodologically prior to science, and should instead attempt as best they can to integrate their work with the ongoing development of empirical theory. This is not a recommendation of philosophical passivity, but instead an effort to identify a more productive direction for philosophical activism to take.

Thus, when the naturalist with whom we will be concerned puts forward his substantive naturalistic theory of value, he does so as part of an attempt to develop a good explanatory account of what is going on in evaluative practices involving claims about a person's own good. Our naturalist's central claims hence are, at bottom, synthetic rather than analytic. This would be so even if he put forward his naturalistic interpretation using *reforming definitions,* for a reforming definition is revisable as well as revisionist, and must earn its place by facilitating the construction of worthwhile theories.

The "Open Question" Argument Revisited

One important consequence of the fact that our naturalist's interpretation of discourse about a person's good is put forward on methodologically naturalistic grounds is that Moore's open question argument no longer applies directly to it. For the naturalist's interpretation is based, however indirectly, upon experience, and does not purport to be strictly analytic or utterly incontestable—indeed, it presents itself as remaining open to further challenges.

Our naturalist's interpretation is hedonistic; that is, he claims that the experience of happiness alone constitutes a person's intrinsic non-moral good. This claim is put forward as part of a methodologically naturalistic project, for example, as a reforming definition or an *a posteriori* statement of property identity. What would such a claim be like?

A more familiar example may help. Consider the scientific identification of water with H_2O. It was, of course, a significant empirical discovery—not a result of *a priori* analysis—that water is a compound of two parts hydrogen and one part oxygen. If it be said that this claim now has the status of a definition, then surely it is a reforming definition, for an important revision in thinking about water—and about chemistry in general—was required in order to deny water the status of an element, and to introduce the principle of distinguishing chemicals by their molecular composition rather than their macroscopic features. Competent eighteenth-century speakers could learn the meaning of 'water' as it occurred in ordinary language, and could later be introduced to the meaning of 'H_2O' as it occurs in chemistry, and still find the question whether water is H_2O *conceptually* open. So, for them, the identity statement 'Water is H_2O' would fail the "open question" test. This did not, however, rule out the identity statement, because it was not among the ambitions of scientists making this statement to state a conceptual truth.

Of course, once 'Water is H_2O' has been introduced as a reforming definition—for example, in the teaching of chemistry—then the expression 'Water is H_2O' becomes true-by-virtue-of-meaning in a clear sense, and so the question of whether water is H_2O becomes, in this sense, conceptually closed. But this reforming definition could itself be altered or dropped under the pressure of further empirical discoveries or theoretical developments, and so it does not really purport to close the question with conceptual necessity.

In a similar way, a hedonistic naturalism based upon *a posteriori* identity claims or reforming definitions would not purport conceptually to close the question of whether a person's good is identical to the experience of happiness. And because conceptual closure is not among its ambitions, the "open question" argument could not properly be used to refute it, either.

Revisionism

Even if Moore's "open question" argument cannot be deployed directly against an interpretation of discourse about a person's good that does not purport to express analytic truths, a significant critical function may still be served by pressing Moorean questions against such interpretations. For it would

be a challenge to any theoretical identification or reforming definition of P in terms of Q to argue that there is something central to the notion of P that does not appear to be captured by Q; this would make the question "I can see that this is Q, but is it P?" genuinely compelling, not just barely possible. How troublesome such open questions may be will depend, of course, upon the character of the alternative accounts in the offing for P—and also upon whether we think P is clear enough as it stands, or conceptually basic, or so unlikely to be amenable to clear, unambiguous explication in terms we find less problematic that we are prepared to do without any analysis of P at all.

Since almost any notion P found in natural language will draw its meaning from multiple sources, and will have taken on diverse functions—and possessed diverse relations to other concepts—at various points in its evolution, it is to be expected that any rendering of that concept intended to make it sufficiently clear to suit purposes of theory construction will be, to some degree, revisionist. So it was with water and H_2O, and so it will be with any significant evaluative concept. This revisionism means that some open questions will remain. It lies among the tasks of a philosophical theory to shed light upon the ways in which a discourse has functioned and evolved, and to motivate the particular rectification of discourse effected by theory. To accomplish these tasks, a theory must explain how those features upon which it fixes afford the most compelling understanding of the discourse. . . .

Revisionism may reach a point where it becomes more perspicacious to say that a concept has been abandoned, rather than revised. No sharp line separates tolerable revisionism and outright abandonment, but if our naturalist wishes to make his case compelling, he must show that his account of a person's good is a rather clear case of tolerable revision, at worst.

. . . The contemporary naturalist we will consider here is prepared to contemplate some degree of revisionism about the meanings that have been attached to evaluative terms as part of his effort to construct a theory of value discourse that will preserve its cognitive character.

Is the Naturalist's Account Scientistic?

Now it is fair enough at this point to ask "What is all this talk of 'theory construction'? And what thought animates the naturalist's attempt to assimilate the assessment and attribution of value to empirical inquiry and judgment?" One might fear that the naturalist is somehow seeking to objectify value and agency in such a way that he can turn over to the physical and social sciences the business of judging what makes a good life. More broadly, the worry here is *scientism,* which perhaps can be thought of as the view that everything worth knowing or saying about the world and our place in it—with the possible exception of some colorful emoting—belongs to scientific theory. Scientism is a remarkably crude and hasty view, which no doubt owes whatever hold it may have on the contemporary imagination to the impressive gains of scientific knowledge in comparison to other areas of inquiry. But what argument can be offered to show that every meaningful part of human inquiry can simply be turned over to science? Thomas Nagel puts a similar worry concerning a "test of reality":

> . . . it begs the question to assume that this [scientific] sort of *explanatory* necessity is the test of reality for values. . . . To assume that only what has to be included in the best causal theory of the world is real is to assume that there are no irreducibly normative truths.[6]

Yet a naturalist, especially a methodological naturalist, need not proceed in the hegemonic spirit suggested by talk of a "test of reality." His perspective can instead be experimental: let us see how far we can go in understanding a domain of judgment and purported knowledge by applying to it a form of inquiry based upon empirical models, and asking where the judgments and knowledge-claims of this area might fit within a scheme of empirical inquiry. A non-hegemonic naturalist pursues his interpretive and explanatory project without assuming in advance that his success or failure will decide the genuineness of a domain of discourse, and so his approach need not be question-begging. It is obvious to most of us that assessments of value are bound up with a great many empirical considerations. What is less obvious is how far these empirical considerations might take us. The effort to answer this question, not to legislate other approaches out of philosophy, is the primary concern of a non-hegemonic naturalist. . . .

Reductionism

Our naturalist believes that the distinction between prescriptive and descriptive uses of languages does not preclude his project. Does it follow that he must therefore in some sense be a *reductionist* about value, someone who believes that the content of statements of value can be captured by statements which contain no expressly evaluative terms?

He needn't be, for he may hold that value properties are *sui generis* natural properties, though perhaps he would also hold that they supervene upon descriptive properties, such that no two states of affairs could differ in their value properties without also differing in their descriptive properties. But the naturalist who would vindicate the cognitive status of value judgments is not required to deny the possibility of reduction, for some reductions are vindications—they provide us with reason to think the reduced phenomena are genuine. The successful reduction of water to H_2O reinforces, rather than impugning, our sense that there really is water. By contrast, the reduction of "polywater"—a peculiar form of water thought to have been observed in scientific laboratories in the late 1960s—to ordinary water-containing-some-impurities-from-improperly-washed-glassware contributed to the conclusion that there really is no such substance as polywater. Whether a reduction is vindicative or eliminative will depend upon the specific character of what is being reduced and what the reduction basis looks like. Even the reduction of water to H_2O was in part revisionist, as we noted, of both common-sense notions and previous chemistry. No general assumption can be made that reduction must be eliminativist or otherwise undermining.

The vindicative reduction of water to H_2O has another feature worth remarking upon here for the sake of parallelism with what our naturalist is attempting to achieve in the domain of value. Because the form of the reduction of water to H_2O is that of an identification, it makes no sense to ask of a causal role assigned to water (as in "This erosion was caused by water") whether the causal work is "really" being done by water or by H_2O. There can be no competition here: the causal work is done by water; the causal work is done by H_2O. In a similar way, if a naturalist in value theory identifies value with a—possibly complex—descriptive property, then it would make no sense to ask of a causal role assigned to value (as in "He gave that up because he discovered that it was no good for him") whether the causal work is "really" being done by value or by its reduction basis. The causal work is done by value; the causal work is done by the reduction basis.

As a result, the naturalist in value theory is able to make use of naturalistic accounts in epistemology and semantics to explain access to value properties, for the identification he furnishes can afford the ground for the requisite causal-explanatory role for value. For example, a naturalistic epistemology may require that, if p is to be an object of knowledge, then the fact p must be part of an explanation of our belief p. If value is identical with a—possibly complex—property which can appropriately participate in the explanation of our beliefs, then it can be an object of knowledge. And once again, it will make no sense to ask whether it is the reducing property or the value property that explains the beliefs in question—if the identification holds, then each does.

Confirmationalism

One last initial matter about our naturalist concerns his relation to a position that might be called *confirmationalism*. The confirmationalist, as I understand him, is a particularly one-dimensional sort of naturalist. He holds that, to warrant acceptance of an account of the good, it suffices to confirm empirically the existence and explanatory efficacy of that notion of the good. The confirmationalist therefore believes that the importance of the current debate about whether or not so-called "moral explanations" can be genuine is this: once it can be established that some property that we have designated 'moral' can

play an explanatory role, then we will be justified in accepting that property for normative guidance.

But here is a quick argument against the confirmationalist. Suppose a puckish naturalist, exasperated with the "Personal Health" column in the *Times*, identifies the property of being intrinsically good with the property of being *cholesterol-laden*. There is no problem now about showing that good in this sense exists (there are things laden with cholesterol) and has an explanatory role (the fact that a foodstuff is cholesterol-laden can help explain how its presence in the human diet leads to heart disease). So, if the confirmationalist is right, shouldn't we now regulate our lives in accord with this fatty notion of a person's good?

Obviously, confirmationalism thus baldly put is not a plausible form of naturalism. For to find an explanatory role for a property that simply is stipulated to be identical with goodness would not, in itself, tend to show that this property affords a satisfactory interpretation of 'good.' Good has a distinctive role in deliberation and action, and it must be shown that the reducing property is a plausible candidate for this role. "Being cholesterol-laden" would appear to have no hope of being seen as a tolerable revision of our concept of good.

We can put the point another way with more direct reference to naturalism. On various naturalistic theories of reference, the reference of a term is partly constrained by which actual phenomena were present—and, perhaps, playing a causal role—when a term has been introduced or used. The puckish confirmationalist would have to show that a common property uniting a great range of the uses of the term 'a person's own good' is "cholesterol-laden." Similarly, on various naturalistic theories of reference, certain stereotypes and truisms are associated with given expressions, and also serve to constrain its possible reference. For 'good,' it is a truism that anything intrinsically good for a person is desirable for its own sake. And it further is truistic, as John Stuart Mill noticed, that the preferences of an experienced individual give some evidence about what is desirable for him. But however much we may be drawn to foodstuffs containing cholesterol, it would be unavailing to contend, on the basis of actual preferences, that it is the cholesterol in these food-stuffs that we desire, regardless of how they taste.

Now we can begin to see how the naturalist must proceed. To achieve a vindicating reduction of good, he must identify it with a natural property (or complex of properties) that, to a significant extent, permits one to account for the correlations and truisms associated with 'good'—i.e., is at most tolerably revisionist—and that at the same time can plausibly serve as the basis of the normative function of this term. The confirmationalist's view of things is correct only insofar as it would be part of a vindicating naturalistic reduction to provide evidence for the existence of, and for our access to, the reducing property as a part of empirical reality. Whether that part deserves to be called 'good' is a larger matter.

Can a property (or complex of properties) be found that both meets naturalistic conditions on existence and access, on the one hand, and possesses the requisite normativity, on the other? Let me try to indicate how such a project might be undertaken, and where some of its difficulties might lie, by considering one version of a hedonistic theory of a person's good.

III. A STRATEGY FOR NATURALISM

The general strategy for naturalism about a person's good that I will be discussing involves the linking together of five elements: (1) locating a (possibly complex) property that is claimed by an *identificatory reduction* to underlie the cognitive content of discourse about a person's good; (2) providing evidence to the effect that this property plays an *explanatory role* of an appropriate sort to warrant saying that the property is both (potentially) empirically accessible and actually exemplified in our experience; (3) providing an account of how this property, given its character, could come in a non-accidental way to play a significant *normative role* in the regulation of human practices corresponding to the normative role played by the concept of a person's good; (4) developing an argument to the effect that the

account this property affords of a person's good is, if revisionist, at worst *tolerably revisionist*; and (5) developing a further argument to the effect that recognizing this property as underlying discourse about a person's good would not undermine the normative role of such discourse, so that the reduction is *vindicative upon critical reflection.* . . .

Hedonism

Let us now consider briefly how the hedonist might adopt this five-element strategy in his account of a person's good. I should say again that I focus upon hedonism not because I find it the most plausible doctrine about a person's good, but because it enables us to construct a relatively straightforward (and not entirely implausible) example of the strategy at work. Let us take the five elements in order.

(1) *Identificatory reduction.* The sort of hedonist we will be considering identifies the good of a person with his being in a distinctive experiential state: happiness. A person's well-being, on this view, is increased to the extent (and only to the extent) that he has more extensive or intensive experience of this state. The hedonist claims that this psychological property underlies our discourse about a person's good.

It has often been remarked, against hedonism, that when we reflect upon what is desirable for its sake we find a plurality of ends, not happiness alone. Why say that talk of a person's good has tracked happiness, rather than some broader constellation of ends?

Our hedonist offers the following reply. We have supposed happiness to be a distinctive experiential state. Let us suppose, further, that anyone who has experienced both happiness and unhappiness will have a settled preference, other things equal, for the former. Then the hedonist might propose the following simple model for the evolution of desires. When a given set of desires leads us to act in a way that brings with it the attainment of happiness, these desires are positively reinforced; conversely, when other desires lead us to act in ways that lead to unhappiness, they are negatively reinforced. Over time, for any given individual and relative to the range of behaviors he undertakes, individuals will tend to possess and act on desires that have brought happiness in the past. Quite likely, most of these desires will have immediate objects other than happiness, and many will involve intrinsic interest in ends other than happiness. What evolves in the individual, then, is a set of desires, including intrinsic desires, that can be explained in part as tracing a path oriented toward the experience of happiness, even though individuals often do not aim at happiness.

A similar evolution can, according to the hedonist, be found at the social level as well. Across societies and across time within a society, significant variation can be found in the range of behaviors and activities deemed to be part of an individual's good. The hedonist wishes to account for these variations and changes by noting the quite different circumstances that tend to promote the experience of happiness in different societies, and by noting the effects of changing beliefs about the likely consequences of various behaviors. At the same time, there are a great many similarities across societies and time, and so the hedonist draws our attention to the widespread agreement that certain activities or states, such as eating and drinking, or having friends and lovers, contribute to a person's good. In general, the hedonist's idea is to explain inter- and intrasocial variations and constancies in discourse about what is good for individuals as tending to follow those circumstances or activities in which the experience of happiness is produced—or seems likely to be produced according to prevailing beliefs.

(2) *Explanatory role.* If the hedonist's account of the evolution of discourse about what is good for individuals is correct—and I do not claim that it is—then he has already found an explanatory role for the property of being happy: it helps account for the sorts of things we desire and deem desirable. Here it is important to see that the explanation's informativeness depends upon our hedonist's substantive conception of happiness. Were he to treat happiness as "the satisfaction of desire," then it could not play this particular role in explaining the evolution of desires, for that role depends upon the shaping of desire by the experience of happiness.

If the hedonist's explanations are to some degree successful, then that will suffice to warrant calling happiness, so conceived, a natural property. It is a complex matter to assess the explanatory claims of the hedonist, and the naturalist should be content to leave such assessment largely to the development of psychological theory—does psychological theory find that it makes use of a substantive, experiential conception of happiness in accounting for human behavior? Let us suppose for the sake of argument that it does, and therefore that worries about the reality and naturalness of the hedonist's reduction basis can be met.

(3) *Normative role.* Elements (1) and (2) of the hedonist's task required that he give us reason to think that there really is such a thing as substantive happiness, and that discourse about a person's good appropriately tracks it. For element (3), it is necessary that he give us reason to think that this very thing, substantive happiness, has the capacity to play the normative role of a person's intrinsic non-moral good. To accomplish this, a sufficiently tight, "internal" connection must be found between the experience of happiness and an appropriate recommending force.

Such a connection can be effected by the very feature of substantive happiness that underlies its explanatory use: what the experience of happiness itself is like. On a substantive conception of happiness, such as the one appealed to by our hedonist, the connection between happiness and what we find motivating is not logically tight. It is not definitionally true on such a conception, as it is on some non-substantive conceptions of happiness, that we find happiness desirable. However, our hedonist can argue that the connection is as tight as need be; he claims it is psychologically (or perhaps even metaphysically) impossible for a person to have the peculiar experience that is happiness and not be drawn to it. . . .

(4) *Tolerable revisionism.* The hedonist's proffered explanation of the evolution of desires leaves us with the expectation that his account of a person's good will involve some degree of revisionism. We possess, according to his proffered explanation, intrinsic desires for a range of things other than happiness, and so when we consult our intuitive views about whether happiness alone is good in itself for a person, the answer appears to be no. Although the hedonist has no problem in convincing us that a person's happiness is among the things good in themselves for him—here intuition readily concurs—the hedonist faces great difficulty in convincing us that happiness is the only thing intrinsically good for a person.

The most characteristic philosophical counter to hedonism is to construct examples or thought-experiments that serve to make us ask whether we would indeed want considerations of our own happiness alone to govern our choices. Such an appeal to intuition can put considerable pressure on the hedonist's claim to be, at worst, tolerably revisionist. How might our naturalistic hedonist respond?

To defend a claim of tolerable revisionism he must, in some direct or indirect way, capture most of the central intuitions in this area, and must do something to lessen the force of those which he cannot capture. If this sounds more like old-fashioned philosophy than new-fangled naturalism, that is as it should be. For the naturalist is trying to show that assessments of a natural property can have the appropriate character to take on the familiar normative function of 'good' in our deliberative practices.

Perhaps the most central intuition about a person's good is the one directly captured by the hedonist: if anything is good for a person, the experience of happiness is. But with regard to other ends that, intuitively, appear intrinsically desirable, the hedonist must follow a more indirect route, via his claims about the psychology of desire. If diverse intuitive views about what is desirable for its own sake can be explained in a unified way by invoking a substantive conception of happiness—along with variation in belief and circumstance—then the hedonist can claim that, despite appearances, these other ends owe their hold upon us to the role they have played in the creation of happiness. Thus, the hedonist claims, to take our theoretically-unexamined intuitions at face value would be to misunderstand the character of our own motivational system.

To make this claim more plausible, the hedonist must rehearse in detail the sort of argument made earlier to defend the claim that our discourse about an individual's good tracks happiness. Suppose, for example, he finds philosophers (and others) at some particular juncture in history claiming that end E, distinct from happiness, is part of an individual's intrinsic non-moral good. He would then attempt to show that the sorts of activities that typically followed from an intrinsic interest in E in that society were such as to yield—or to seem likely to yield—substantive happiness. By comparison, he could consider other societies in which intrinsic interest in E would have no characteristic tendency to produce—or seem likely to produce—substantive happiness, and show that in such societies E typically is not regarded as intrinsically desirable. For example, individual autonomy, which in contemporary Western societies is sometimes held up as an intrinsic good, has been said not to be deemed a good at all in other, more communitarian societies.

In this way, the hedonist would attempt to convince us that the usage of 'good'—our practice of identifying things as good to have or to seek—has been driven fundamentally by the property of substantive happiness, so that we should not be captivated by the surface diversity of our intuitive notions about good. Our initial confidence that ends other than happiness figure in their own right in a person's good might in this way be undermined by reflection upon how those other ends came to seem desirable to us. . . .

And so the hedonist shifts from the task of indirectly capturing intuitive judgments (by showing how they can be explained within a hedonistic scheme) to the task of explaining away intuitive judgments (when they cannot be fit within this scheme). To explain away an intuition is not always to show that it is somehow ill-grounded; instead, it can be a matter of showing that the intuition is really about something else. . . .

I will not attempt to say whether the hedonist's attempt to respond to intuitive counterexamples is generally effective, since I seek only to exhibit an available theoretical response. And, in any event, we now must move on to consider another kind of argument that hedonism is not tolerably revisionist, an argument that is itself theoretical.

According to a well-developed tradition in the theory of value, internalism, it is essential to the concept of intrinsic goodness that nothing can be of intrinsic value unless it has a necessary connection to the grounds of action. The need for such a connection is defended as truistic—we simply could not make sense of a claim that something is someone's intrinsic good if that thing could not afford that person positive grounds for action. An account of intrinsic good that purports to be no more than tolerably revisionist must, it is argued, capture this truism. . . .

According to our hedonist, the experience of happiness *is* intrinsically motivating—anyone who is capable of such an experience will, once he has tasted it, want more rather than less of it, other things being equal. Does this suffice to accommodate the internalist truism?

Difficulty arises in at least two cases, both of which depend upon adopting rather powerful, non-instrumental conceptions of reasons. First, suppose there to be rational agents—perhaps even humans—who cannot experience happiness. Now on some conceptions of reasons for action, nothing could count as a reason for action unless it would, necessarily, engage the will of *all* rational agents as such. But if there are some rational agents who cannot experience happiness, then there are some rational agents whose will would not be engaged by happiness in the manner that our hedonist envisages, and this would disqualify happiness as a reason for action for any rational agent. Second, suppose that the possession of a motive does not *automatically* generate a reason for action. Then even if all rational agents were capable of happiness, the intrinsically motivating character of the experience of happiness would still not provide the guarantee necessary—according to the second reading of internalism—that happiness will always furnish an appropriate reason for action.

The question now becomes whether these two possibilities are genuinely damaging to the hedonist's claim of tolerable revision. Perhaps they are not. With regard to the first possibility—that rational agents might exist who are incapable of experiencing happiness—the hedonist can argue, not implausibly, that the compelling idea underlying internalism is that a being X's good must be such as to engage X positively, at least once X has full understanding and awareness. Is it further necessary, in order that something be X's good, that this thing similarly engage all rational beings, no matter how arbitrarily different those beings are from X? To give up this further condition may be revisionist with regard to a certain philosophical conception of intrinsic good as "rationally commanding" on a substantive view of reasons. But it is doubtful whether this philosophical conception is somehow contained within the truism that internalism takes as its starting point and that must be accommodated by any tolerably revisionist account of a person's good.[7]

A similar response is available to the second possibility—the possibility that, on a substantive conception of reasons, a motive may fail to produce even a *prima facie* reason for action. As long as the hedonist is able to draw upon a respectable philosophical conception of reasons—the broadly Humean account—to accommodate the internalist truism, then the fact that he is at odds with an alternative (and, it must be said, rather esoteric) philosophical conception of reasons need not be a sign of more-than-tolerable revisionism. Moreover, the hedonist might claim, it may be important in avoiding significant revisionism that one *not* entirely accommodate this alternative philosophical account of reasons. It is, for example, truistic that if a course of action promises great unhappiness or pain, then an agent has a *prima facie* reason to avoid it. A philosophical conception of reasons which would permit us to assert that the prospect of great unhappiness or pain could fail to count at all as a reason for an agent may have such difficulty convincing us of its correctness as a theory of reasons that it cannot be used to undermine hedonism.

(5) *Vindication upon critical reflection.* To ask whether a reductive account of a discourse is vindicative is to ask, roughly, to what extent the discourse can retain its pre-reductive functions—descriptive and normative—when exposed to critical reflection with the reduction fully in view. Our discussion of revisionism is relevant to answering this question, because what is at stake in assessing the extent of revisionism is the degree of fit between the reductive account and the pre-reductive discourse. If the fit is reasonably close in many essentials, then there may be a good chance that the reductive account will be vindicatory.

But the issue of revisionism cannot be decisive, for vindication depends upon more than fit. A closely-fitting reduction might reveal the nature and origin of an area of discourse to be such that we are led to change our views about whether the phenomena to which that discourse purports to refer are genuine, or about whether we are willing to allow the properties which that discourse effectively tracks to regulate our decisions normatively. In the case of a hedonistic reduction of a person's good, success in claiming tolerable revisionism might be matched with failure at vindication if, upon critical reflection, we found the prospect of happiness vs. unhappiness or pleasure vs. pain so insignificant that we would no longer be inclined to give considerations of our own good much, if any, consideration in deliberation.

It is important to see that there would be no logical absurdity in accepting the hedonist's reduction of discourse about a person's own good as well as his claim that happiness is intrinsically motivating, while at the same time believing that happiness, however attractive it may be, is not worth seeking. If other ends can be pursued, they can be put forward as more worthy of pursuit than one's own good or happiness. Alternatively, one might survey the scene of human motivation and opportunity and conclude that nothing, not even one's own good, is really worth seeking.

. . . Is there some . . . interest in the case of one's own good? Yes, although the term 'interest' seems excessively mediating. From all appearances it matters to people—no matter how clearly or dimly they see things—whether or not they are happy or unhappy, experiencing pleasure or pain. We must be careful here to remain faithful to the substantive character of our hedonist's account of happiness. We cannot, for example, claim it as definitional that happiness matters, i.e., that that which left us indifferent would not, by definition, be happiness. Instead, we must rely upon (what the hedonist must hope is) a deep fact about us and about the quality of the experience of happiness (or of pain): no one who has that experience (an experience like *that*) can be

altogether indifferent to it. We are such, and the experience is such, that we are moved in a way that does not depend upon possession of any particular ideology, interests, or attitudes. This resilience of the attractiveness of happiness and the aversiveness of pain is what underwrote the hedonist's confidence that he had discovered a sufficiently tight connection between the underlying descriptive content attributed by his reduction and the commending force that accompanies genuine acceptance of a judgment that something is good for one. This resilience is now used to underwrite the hedonist's confidence that, even if his account of a person's good is tolerably revisionist and somewhat deflationary, it remains true that acceptance of it would alter neither the appeal of happiness nor our willingness to allow considerations of our own happiness to figure importantly in our deliberations, so that the reduction he has effected can be substantially vindicative.

CONCLUSION

We have seen a five-element strategy that the naturalist who accepts hedonism might follow in order to accommodate both the descriptive and prescriptive side of discourse about a person's good. How successful this strategy may be depends, of course, upon how compelling the arguments for hedonism are, and here I have limited myself largely to setting these arguments down without evaluating them. A further question is whether this strategy can be generalized to non-hedonistic forms of naturalism, since at crucial points appeal has been made to (what the hedonist has alleged to be) the specific character of happiness and its interaction with human motivational systems. It seems to me that certain other forms of naturalism about a person's good—in particular, those that appeal to the reduction basis of informed desires—may be able to follow this strategy, while others, lacking a suitable connection to motivational systems, almost certainly cannot. My chief aim, however, has been to suggest how something thought by many to be, in principle, beyond the reach of cognitive naturalism might, nonetheless, be possible for at least one form.

The hedonist who would be a vindicating reductionist, then, must satisfy both the confirmationalist demands for a real, accessible property, and also the further demand that the property he fixes upon be able to explain and capture—within the limits of tolerable revisionism—the prescriptivity of discourse about a person's good. Naturalism of the sort discussed here therefore is not a way of avoiding difficult issues about prescriptivity or stopping us from asking familiar normative questions, but a way of thinking about such issues and questions—a way that seeks to come to terms with normative institutions while accepting the challenge of showing how these institutions might have epistemic standing in a domain where genuine cognition is possible for beings like us.

NOTES

1. Are there prescriptions whose action-guiding force for agents depends upon no interest at all? There could be if a substantive theory of rationality were correct, for then there would be commands of reason that depend upon no interest or motivational state of the agent. However, part of the circumstances that constitute the setting for the problem discussed in this paper is a sense that no substantive theory of rationality can be made to work.

2. G. E. Moore, *Principia Ethica* (Cambridge: Cambridge University Press, 1903), esp. p. 15.

3. I say 'obviously successful' because it remains possible that once some existing analysis has been fully understood and assimilated, and once all accidental connotations of the notion of 'good' have been stripped away (assuming such a thing to be possible), the analysis could emerge as incontestable.

4. I certainly do not mean to have given a definition of 'natural property' or 'naturalism' in this way. More will be said about naturalism in subsequent sections.

For now, let me note only that what seems to me to be of interest in naturalism is not a metaphysical doctrine about what sorts of things are part of—or not part of—"Nature," but rather a methodological stance reflecting our experience of the ways in which useful predictive and explanatory theories have been achieved. Anyone who would be a naturalist in this methodological sense must regard it as a matter for inquiry, not definition, what sorts of properties can figure in developed, explanatory empirical theories—that is, what sorts of properties are "natural."

5. I use the expression 'happiness' rather than 'pleasure' in characterizing hedonism because of the unfortunately narrow connotations of the latter. I do intend 'happiness' to pick out a class of experiential states.

6. Thomas Nagel, *The View from Nowhere* (New York: Oxford University Press, 1987), p. 144.

7. At this point, it might be argued that in adopting a broadly Humean account of reasons and abandoning stronger notions of "rational command," the hedonist has already adopted a form of skepticism about intrinsic good, skepticism of the kind that philosophers have often attributed to Hume himself. According to this argument, the idea of "rational command," though esoteric, was in fact discovered by philosophers to be a logical presupposition of ordinary discourse about good. When the hedonist gives it up, he in effect engages in a quite extensive revisionism, so much so that he changes the subject.

The hedonist, for his part, can reply that he is unconvinced that the philosopher's idea of "rational command" is at the core of ordinary discourse about a person's good, and that, in any event, the fact that the doctrine of "rational command" leads to so powerful and revisionist a conclusion as skepticism about intrinsic good should suggest that this doctrine stands in need of much greater support than it has thus far received. The need for support will be larger still if the hedonist can make good his attempt to give a naturalistic account of prescriptivity.

STUDY QUESTIONS

1. What is the difference between methodological and substantive naturalism?
2. Why does Railton believe his version of naturalism is immune to Moore's open-question argument?
3. What is the difference between vindicative and eliminative reduction?
4. Is the reduction of a person's good to pleasure vindicative or eliminative?

Against Non-Analytic Naturalism

Derek Parfit

Reductive normative naturalists maintain that normative facts are identical to natural facts. Some, known as "analytical naturalists," argue that normative facts can be reduced to natural facts by definition, as "vixen" can be reduced by definition to "female fox." Analytical naturalism will be defended in a later selection by Frank Jackson and Philip Pettit. First, however, we consider the view known as "non-analytical naturalism," presented by Peter Railton in our previous selection, according to which normative facts can be reduced to natural facts, as "water" can be reduced to "H_2O."

Derek Parfit, Emeritus Senior Research Fellow at All Souls College, Oxford, presents several arguments against non-analytical naturalism. The first is that some proposed reductions of one sort of concept to another are category mistakes. For example, rivers and squares are too different for the one to be the same as the other. Similarly, he claims that normative facts and natural facts are too different to be identical.

Because Parfit anticipates that this objection will not convince many naturalists, he offers several other lines of argument. Regarding the sort of analogues with scientific discoveries, such as that "water" is "H_2O," Parfit argues that such substantive claims tell us about the relations between different properties, while the naturalist's claim about normativity does not.

Another argument Parfit offers starts by noting that were a theory such as utilitarianism true, then non-analytical naturalists would maintain that an act's maximizing happiness is the same as that act's being what we ought to do. Parfit claims, however, that this view is mistaken. For if maximizing happiness is the same as what we ought to do, then utilitarianism would not tell us how the property of maximizing happiness is related to some other, different normative property; instead, utilitarianism would be trivial. But utilitarianism is not trivial. If true, it would give us positive, substantive information. Hence Parfit concludes that non-analytic naturalism is false.

From Derek Parfit, *On What Matters*, vol. 2 (Oxford: Oxford University Press, 2011). Reprinted by permission of the publisher.

91 THE NORMATIVITY OBJECTION

According to

> *Non-Analytical Naturalists*: Though we make some irreducibly normative claims, there are no irreducibly normative facts. When such normative claims are true, these claims state facts that could also be stated by making other, non-normative and naturalistic claims. These facts are both normative and natural.

Such views, I shall now start to argue, cannot be true. I believe that

> (A) normative and natural facts are in two quite different, non-overlapping categories.

Many kinds of thing, event, or fact are . . . undeniably in different categories. Rivers could not be sonnets, experiences could not be stones, and justice could not be—as some Pythagoreans were said to have believed—the number 4. To give some less extreme examples, it could not be a physical or legal fact that $7 \times 8 = 56$, nor could it be a legal or arithmetical fact that galaxies rotate, nor could it be a physical or arithmetical fact that perjury is a crime. It is similarly true, I believe, that when we have decisive reasons to act in some way, or we should or ought to act in this way, this fact could not be the same as, or consist in, some natural fact, such as some psychological or causal fact.

In defending this belief, I must appeal to what I mean when I use the words "reason," "should," and "ought." Some Naturalists would reply that they are not discussing the meanings of our words. When these people claim that normative facts might be natural facts, their claim is not intended to be analytic, or a claim whose truth is implied by what it means. These people might again cite the discoveries that water is H_2O and that heat is molecular kinetic energy. When scientists made these discoveries, they were not appealing to the pre-scientific meanings of the words "water" and "heat."

These analogies . . . do not support Naturalism. . . . [T]hough these discoveries were not implied by the meanings of these words, these scientists *did* appeal to these meanings. That is why these scientific discoveries were about *water* and *heat.* Of the reductive views that are both plausible and interesting, most are not analytical. But these views must still be constrained by the relevant concepts. These views are not analytical because the relevant concepts leave open various possibilities, between which we must decide on non-conceptual grounds. Many other possibilities are, however, conceptually excluded. Thus, on a wider pre-scientific version of the concept of *heat,* it was conceptually possible that heat should turn out to be molecular kinetic energy, or should instead turn out to be, or to involve, a substance, as the *phlogiston theory* claimed. But heat could not have turned out to be a shade of blue, or a medieval king. And if we claimed that rivers were sonnets, or that experiences were stones, we could not defend these claims by saying that they were not intended to be analytic, or conceptual truths. Others could rightly reply that, given the meaning of these claims, they could not possibly be true. This, I believe, is the way in which, though *much* less obviously, Normative Naturalism could not be true. Natural facts could not be normative in the reason-implying sense. . . .

If, as I believe, reason-involving normative facts are in a separate, distinctive category, there is no close analogy for their irreducibility to natural facts. These normative facts are in some ways like certain other kinds of necessary truths. One example are mathematical truths, such as the fact that $7 \times 8 = 56$. According to some empiricists, this fact is some natural fact, such as the fact that, when people multiply 7 by 8, the result of their calculation is nearly always 56. This view misunderstands arithmetic, and the way in which mathematical claims can be true. Nor could logical truths be natural facts about the ways in which people think. In the same way, I believe, normative and natural facts differ too deeply for any form of Normative Naturalism to succeed.

To give one example, . . . *Burning Hotel,* you will die unless you jump into the canal. Since your life is worth living, it is clear that

> (B) you ought to jump.

This fact, some Naturalists claim, is the same as the fact that

(C) jumping would do most to fulfil your present fully informed desires, or is what, if you deliberated in certain naturalistically describable ways, you would choose to do.

Given the difference between the meanings of claims like (B) and (C), such claims could not, I believe, state the same fact. Suppose that you are in the top storey of your hotel, and you are terrified of heights. You know that, unless you jump, you will soon be overcome by smoke. You might then believe, and tell yourself, that you have *decisive reasons* to jump, that you *should, ought to,* and *must* jump, and that if you don't jump you would be making a *terrible mistake.* If these normative beliefs were true, these truths could not possibly be the same as, or consist in, some merely natural fact, such as the causal and psychological facts stated by (C). We can call this *the Normativity Objection.*

This objection, we can add, could take a wider and less controversial form. In arguing against Naturalism, we need not claim that there are some irreducibly normative *facts.* It would be enough to claim that

(D) natural facts could not be normative.

. . .

93 THE ANALOGIES WITH SCIENTIFIC DISCOVERIES

. . . I shall . . . say some more about the analogies to which many Naturalists appeal. . . . [I]t will be enough to discuss Act Utilitarianism, since our conclusions would apply to other moral views. These Utilitarians claim that

(A) when some act would maximize happiness, this act is what we ought to do.

This view can take two forms. Non-Naturalists like Sidgwick claim that

(B) when some act would maximize happiness, this fact would make this act have the different, normative property of being what we ought to do.

Utilitarian Naturalists reject (B), claiming instead that

(C) when some act would maximize happiness, this property of this act is the same as the property of being what we ought to do.

When Gibbard argues that Utilitarian Naturalism might be true, he compares (C) with the discovery that water is the same as H2O. Other Naturalists appeal to the discovery that heat is the same as molecular kinetic energy. Such analogies can seem to support the view that some form of Naturalism is true. But if we look more closely, I believe, we find that these analogies partly fail.

True claims about the *identity* of some property use two words or phrases that refer to the same property, and tell us that this property is the same as itself. When that is *all* that such claims tell us, these claims are trivial. We already know that every property—like everything else—is the same as itself. But some of these claims use certain concepts that enable them also to state important facts. That is true of the claim that

(D) molecular kinetic energy is the same as heat.

This claim gives us important information because the word "heat," in its relevant sense, expresses the complex concept that can be more fully expressed with the phrase:

the property that can make objects have certain other properties by turning solids into liquids, turning liquids into gases, causing us to have certain sensations, etc.

(D) can be restated as

> (E) molecular kinetic energy is the property that can make objects have these other, different properties.

As a Non-Naturalist, Sidgwick could restate his view in the same way. Sidgwick could appeal to the concept that we can express with the phrase:

> *the natural property that makes an act have the different, normative property of being what we ought to do.*

Sidgwick's claim could become

> (F) being an act that would maximize happiness is the natural property that makes an act have this other, normative property.

Return next to Gibbard's suggestion that Utilitarian Naturalism is like the claim that

> (G) water is the same as H2O.

This claim, as Gibbard writes, has "great explanatory power." Unlike heat, water isn't a property but a stuff, substance, or kind of matter. But that difference is irrelevant here. In its pre-scientific sense, the word "water" refers to

> the stuff that has the properties of quenching thirst, falling from the clouds as rain, filling lakes and rivers, etc.

"H2O" refers to

> the stuff that is composed of molecules each of which contains two hydrogen atoms and one oxygen atom.

What scientists discovered is that

> (H) the stuff that has the properties of quenching thirst, falling from the clouds as rain, etc., is the same as the stuff that has the different property of being composed of such molecules.

This claim is informative because (H) tells us about the relation between various properties. Sidgwick's (F) could be similarly restated as

> (I) the property of being an act that would maximize happiness is the same as the property that makes an act have the different property of being what we ought to do.

This claim would also be informative, by telling us about the relation between different properties. Utilitarian Naturalists claim instead that

> (C) the property of being an act that would maximize happiness is the same as the property of being what we ought to do.

Unlike Sidgwick's (F) and (I), however, (C) is *not* relevantly like the scientific claims about heat and water. (C) could not, I believe, be true. But we can try to suppose that (C) is true. We can then claim that, *if* (C) were true, (C) would not tell us about the relation between different properties. For this reason, as I shall argue further below, (C) could not be an informative claim about what we ought to do. As these remarks imply, these scientific analogies do not support Naturalism. On the contrary, these analogies remind us that substantive claims like (D) and (G)—or their fuller statements (E) and (H)—tell us about the relations between different properties. The Naturalist's (C) does *not* do that. Since it is only Sidgwick's Non-Naturalist view which is relevantly like these scientific discoveries, these analogies give us some reason to reject Naturalism. . . .

95 THE TRIVIALITY OBJECTION

We can now turn to another . . . argument. . . . As before, we can discuss Hedonistic Act Utilitarianism, since our conclusions would apply to other views. These Utilitarians claim that

> (A) when some act would maximize happiness, this act is what we ought to do.

This view can take two forms. Non-Naturalists like Sidgwick claim that

> (B) when some act would maximize happiness, this fact would make this act have the *different* property of being what we ought to do.

Utilitarian Naturalists reject (B), claiming instead that

> (C) when some act would maximize happiness, that is the same as this act's being what we ought to do.

Suppose that you are a Utilitarian doctor. The Ethics Committee of your hospital asks you to imagine that, in

> *Transplant,* you know that, if you secretly killed one of your patients, this person's transplanted organs would be used to save the lives of five other young people, who would then live long and happy lives.

You admit that, on your view,

> (D) you ought to kill this patient, since this act would maximize happiness.

The Ethics Committee is horrified, and its legal adviser proposes that you be dismissed and debarred from any medical post. If you were a Naturalist, you might reply:

> When I claimed that I ought to kill this patient, I was only stating the fact that this act would maximize happiness. On my view, that is the property to which the concept *ought* refers. I was not claiming that this act would have some *different* property of being what I ought to do. On my view, there is no such different property. The property of maximizing happiness is the *same* as the property of being what we ought to do.

You might add:

> If I believed that killing some patient would have this property, that would not lead me to act

in this way. My aim is to be a successful doctor. I want to cure my patients, whether or not my acts would maximize happiness. So my moral beliefs give you no reason to dismiss me.

These remarks might satisfy the Ethics Committee, since they might show that you do not have an unacceptable moral view.

These remarks should, however, worry Naturalists. We can object that, as your remarks suggest, you do not really have *any* moral view. Normative claims are, in my sense,

> *substantive* when these claims are significant, because we might disagree with them, or they might tell us something that we didn't already know.

Such normative claims are

> *positive* when they state or imply that, when something has certain natural properties, this thing has some other, different, normative property.

When such claims are true, they state positive substantive normative facts. Utilitarian Naturalists claim both that

> (A) when some act would maximize happiness, this act is what we ought to do,

and that

> (C) when some act would maximize happiness, this property of this act is the same as the property of being what we ought to do.

We can argue:

> (1) (A) is a substantive normative claim, which might state a positive substantive normative fact.

> (2) If, impossibly, (C) were true, (A) could not state such a fact. (A) could not be used to imply

that, when some act would maximize happiness, this act would have the different property of being what we ought to do, since (C) claims that there is no such different property. Though (A) and (C) have different meanings, (A) would be only another way of stating the trivial fact that, when some act would maximize happiness, this act would maximize happiness.

Therefore

This form of Naturalism is not true.

We can call this the Triviality Objection.

This objection might be misunderstood. We are not claiming that this form of *Naturalism* is trivial. (C) is a substantive claim. And (C) is, in one way, normative, since this claim is about the property of being what we ought to do. But (C) is a *negative* normative claim, since (C) implies that, when some act would have the natural property of being an act that would maximize happiness, this act could *not* have the *different,* normative property of being what we ought to do, since there would be no such different property. Though (C) is a significant substantive claim, we are arguing that, *if* (C) were true, (*A*) would be trivial. Since (A) is *not* trivial, (C) cannot be true.

. . . The Triviality Objection applies only to [those] Naturalists, who believe that claims like (A) would, if they were true, give us positive substantive normative information. . . .

. . . Naturalists might challenge premise (2). These people might say:

(3) If (A) and (C) were true, these claims would not merely tell us that, when some act would maximize happiness, this act would maximize happiness. In telling us that we *ought* to act in this way, these claims would give us further information about such acts.

Any such information must be statable, however, as the claim that such acts would have one or more other, different properties. And these Naturalists are trying to show that (A) and (C) are substantive normative claims. So, to defend (3), these people would have to defend the claim that

(4) (A) and (C) would state or imply that, when some act would maximize happiness, this act would have some other, different, normative property.

It is not obvious what this other property could be. When we ask what is the best candidate for the different, normative property which (A) might tell us that such acts would have, the obvious answer is: the property of being what we ought to do. By claiming (C), however, these Naturalists lose this obvious candidate, since (C) denies that being what we ought to do is a *different* property. To defend (4), these people would have to find some other normative property to play this role. We can call this the *Lost Property Problem.*

There is another problem. If these Naturalists could find some other property to play this role, they would have to apply their Naturalism to this property. These people would have to claim that, when some act would have this other *normative* property, this fact would be the same as this act's having one or more other *natural* properties. These people would then have to defend another version of (4), which referred to some *other,* different, *normative* property. They would then have to apply their Naturalism to this other property, and so on for ever. This defense of (4) could not succeed.

These Naturalists might now challenge premise (2) in a different and more radical way. According to

(C) when some act would maximize happiness, that is the same as this act's being what we ought to do.

These people might say

(5) If (C) were true, as we believe, (A) would be a positive, substantive normative claim. (C) *itself* would be such a claim.

. . . On this view, Utilitarians do not *need* to claim that, when some act would maximize happiness, this fact would make this act have a *different,* normative property of being what we ought to do. . . . If (C)'s truth explained why we ought to maximize happiness, what would this explanation be?

Utilitarian Naturalists might claim

> We ought to maximize happiness because, when we use the phrase "what we ought to do," we are referring to the property of being an act that would maximize happiness.

As Moore remarks, however, when we believe that we ought to do something, we are not merely believing that "the word 'ought' is generally used to denote actions of this nature." No such fact about what this word denotes, or refers to, could tell us what we ought to do. To support this objection, we can turn to the claim that

> (E) when some act has the property of being what would maximize happiness, we can also refer to this property by using the phrase "being maximally felicific."

This claim is true, because "felicific" means "produces happiness." But (E) is not a substantive normative claim. It is a merely linguistic fact that the property of maximizing happiness can also be referred to with the phrase "being maximally felicific." These Utilitarian Naturalists appeal to the similar claim that

> (F) when some act has the property of being what would maximize happiness, we can also refer to this property by using the phrase "being what we ought to do."

For these Naturalists to defend their view, they must claim that (F) is relevantly *unlike* (E), since it is *not* a merely linguistic fact that the property of maximizing happiness can also be referred to with the phrase "being what we ought to do." Naturalists must explain how, if (F) were true, this claim would give us important normative information. Here is another way to make this point. According to these Naturalists,

> (C) being an act that would maximize happiness is the same as being what we ought to do.

This claim is like

> (G) being an act that would maximize happiness is the same as being maximally felicific.

(G) is not an important substantive claim. (G) merely refers to the same property in two different ways, and tells us that this property is the same as itself. These Naturalists must therefore claim that (C) is in one way *unlike* (G), since (C) gives us further, non-linguistic information.

There is one obvious difference to which these Naturalists might appeal. These people might say:

> (G) is trivial because this claim uses two phrases that mean the same. When we say that some act is maximally felicific, that is just another way of saying that this act would maximize happiness. No such claim applies to (C). When we say that we *ought* to do something, we do not mean that this act would maximize happiness. That is how, unlike (G), (C) gives us important, non-linguistic information.

We can reply:

> There is indeed such a difference. Because (C) uses phrases with quite different meanings, (C) *might* tell us about the relation between different properties. If that were true, however, we would need to be told what these different properties are, and how they are related. What *is* this important, non-linguistic information?

Since these Naturalists are discussing what we *ought* to do, they might be tempted to answer

> (C) tells us that, when some act would maximize happiness, this act would have the different property of being what we ought to do.

But Naturalists cannot give this answer. According to (C), *there is no such different property.* Being an act that would maximize happiness is the *same* as being what we ought to do. So we can repeat our question. We already know that some acts would maximize happiness. What else do these Naturalists tell us to believe? Which *other* property would such acts have?

This question is entirely open. As I use the concept of a *property,* any information about such acts could be stated as the claim that these acts would have some property. This other property might be linguistic. But Naturalists must answer this question. We must be told what these Naturalists are claiming, and what our new belief would be if we accepted their view. We can then ask whether this new belief would be important, as these Naturalists claim it to be.

. . . These people might reply:

> For our view to be important, why do we need to make some claim about the relation between *different* properties? Why isn't it enough to learn that some acts would maximize happiness, and that this property is the same as that of being what we ought to do?

These properties could not, I believe, be the same. For this reason, . . . it is highly misleading to ask whether, *if* these properties *were* the same, that would be an important truth. But we are now trying to suppose that these properties are the same, and asking what would then follow.

If we learnt that there was only one property here, we would indeed be learning something. We would be learning that, when some act would maximize happiness, this act could not also have the different property of being what we ought to do. Since this information would be purely negative, however, it would not make this form of Naturalism a substantive moral view. If these Naturalists are not claiming that such acts would have some other property, they are not giving us any positive information. And if their claim gives us no such information, it could not be a positive substantive claim about what we ought to do.

Though this objection seems to me decisive, some Naturalists may still not be convinced. So I shall try to explain how Naturalism can seem so plausible. Many great philosophers have believed that normative facts are natural facts. Some examples are Hobbes, Locke, Hume, Bentham, and Mill.

As I have said, Naturalists might claim:

> To learn what we ought to do, it would be enough to learn that some acts have a certain natural property, which is the same as the property of being what we ought to do.

Even to me, after many years of thinking about and disbelieving Naturalism, this claim can seem plausible. When we consider such claims, however, we can be easily misled. Utilitarian Naturalists claim

> (C) The property of maximizing happiness is the same as the property of being what we ought to do.

This claim may seem to tell us what we ought to do. (C) may seem to be a longer way of saying

> (J) Maximizing happiness is what we ought to do.

If (J) were true, this claim would tell us what we ought to do. But (C) and (J) are quite different claims. Suppose that some rude person said

> Blowing your nose is what you ought to do.

This person would not mean

> The property of blowing your nose is the same as the property of being what you ought to do.

That claim would be absurd. This person would mean

> Blowing your nose is, or has the different property of being, what you ought to do.

In the same way, (J) means

> (K) Maximizing happiness is, or has the different property of being, what we ought to do.

Since (C) implies that there is no such different property, (C) could not be a positive substantive claim about what we ought to do.

There is another, more insidious way in which we can be misled by some of the claims that Naturalists make. I believe that, given the meaning of the phrases "being an act that would maximize happiness" and "being what we ought to do," it could not possibly be true that

(C) being an act that would maximize happiness is the same as being what we ought to do.

These two phrases could not refer to the same property. But this very fact can make (C) *seem* informative. We may think that, if (C) were true, (C) *would* be informative, since (C) would then tell us about the relation between two different properties. It may therefore seem that . . . Utilitarian Naturalism might both tell us what we ought to do, and explain why we ought to act in this way.

To illustrate this point, it may help to compare (C) with some other, less plausible claim. Our example can be

(L) Being square is the same as being blue.

This could not be an informative claim. Nor is it worth saying that, *if* (L) *were true,* (L) *would be informative.* If we were dreaming, or were only half awake, it might seem to us that (L) would be informative, because this claim would tell us about the relation between two different properties. But the fact that makes (L) seem informative also ensures that (L) is false. No claim could truly tell us that two quite different properties—such as being square and being blue—are one and the same property.

Similar remarks apply, though much less obviously, to (C). Utilitarian Naturalism may seem to be an important view, which might be informative. But what makes (C) seem informative also ensures that (C) is false.

As this comparison may also help to show, when some claim could not possibly be true, it can be misleading to suppose that this claim is true, and ask what would then follow. These Naturalists might claim:

If being an act that would maximize happiness were the same as being what we ought to do, this fact would explain why we ought to maximize happiness, since maximizing happiness would be our only way of doing what we ought to do.

As before, even to convinced Non-Naturalists like me, this claim can seem plausible. But we could similarly claim:

If being square were the same as being blue, this fact would explain why blue things were square, since being square would be the only way of being blue.

Such claims are not worth making. Naturalism can seem plausible because it can seem that

if having some natural property were the same as being what we ought to do, this claim would have great importance.

But this claim seems important only because it could not be true.

I shall now summarize some of these remarks. Normative properties, Naturalists believe, are the same as certain natural properties. To explain and defend this view, many Naturalists appeal to claims about the identity of certain other properties, such as the claim that heat is molecular kinetic energy. Claims about the identity of some property are of two kinds. Some of these claims are trivial, telling us only that a certain property is the same as itself. Other such claims, if they are true, also give us important information, by telling us how some property is related to one or more other properties. Most of these Naturalists ignore this distinction. . . .

This mistake is easy to make. Utilitarian Naturalists claim

(C) Being an act that would maximize happiness is the same as being what we ought to do.

This may seem to mean

Maximizing happiness is what we ought to do.

These may seem to be claims which are about a single property, but which also tell us what we ought to do. As I have said, however, for it to be true that

Maximizing happiness is what we ought to do,

it would have to be true that

Maximizing happiness is, or has the *different* property of being, what we ought to do.

Since (C) can easily *seem* informative, we can call this the *Single Property Illusion*.

There are some other ways in which these Naturalists might defend their view. I have claimed that, since (C) does not tell us about the relation between different properties, (C) could not give us substantive information. These Naturalists might reply that (C) might *indirectly* give us such information.

These people might first point out that, if (C) were true, [it] would be wrong to claim that, when some act would maximize happiness, this fact would make this act have the different property of being what we ought to do. There would be no such different property. But since this claim is purely negative, it does not make this form of Naturalism a positive substantive normative view. These Naturalists claim to be proposing such a view.

These people might next claim that (C) would also give us positive information. Some of these people argue that, though the concept *ought morally* does not have an explicit gap that is waiting to be filled, we can give an account of the role or function that this concept plays in our moral thinking. By appealing to this account, these Naturalists might say, we can show that, if (C) were true, this claim would indirectly give us important information. For example, we might learn that

(M) when some act would maximize happiness, that is the same as this act's being justifiable to others, praiseworthy, and something that we have strong reasons to do.

As before, I believe, this claim could not possibly be true. Being an act that would maximize happiness

could not be the *same* as being, or be *what it is* to be, an act that is justifiable to others, or praiseworthy, or something that we have strong reasons to do. But if we can somehow imagine or conceive that these phrases all refer to the same property, we should conclude that (M) would not then state a substantive normative fact. If *impossibly* these phrases all referred to the same property, (M) would not tell us how this property was related to any other property. So (M) could not give us important positive information.

These Naturalists might instead suggest:

(N) Given the role of the concept *ought* in our moral thinking, (C) would indirectly tell us that

(O) when some act would maximize happiness, this act would have certain other, normative properties.

Some examples might be the properties of being justifiable to others, praiseworthy, and something that we have strong reasons to do.

If, as I believe, (C) could not be true, it is misleading to *suppose* that (N) and (C) are true, and ask what would then follow. With that warning, we can add that (N) could not support Naturalism. (O) is a normative claim, and the facts stated by (O) might be irreducibly normative. To defend their Naturalism, these Naturalists would have to claim that these other normative properties are the same as certain natural properties. The Triviality Objection would apply to these new claims. This objection would not have been answered.

There is one other possibility. These Naturalists might suggest:

(P) given the role of the concept *ought* in our moral thinking, (C) would indirectly tell us that

(Q) when some act would maximize happiness, this act would have certain other, non-normative properties.

Some examples might be the properties of being widely believed to be justifiable to others, widely praised, and believed to be something that we have strong reasons to do.

But (P) could not support Naturalism. Naturalists believe that substantive normative facts are also natural facts. Since (Q) is not a normative claim, (Q) could not state a normative fact.

Similar remarks apply to other forms of Moral Naturalism. According to what we can call any

> *Standard Ought Claim*: When some act would have a certain natural property, this act would be what we ought to do.

There are two ways to understand such claims. According to Non-Naturalists, these claims imply that

> (R) when some act would have this natural property, this fact would make this act have the different property of being what we ought to do.

According to Naturalists, these claims imply that

> (S) when some act would have this natural property, this fact is the same as this act's being what we ought to do.

All such views face the Triviality Objection. We can argue:

> (1) Since (S) does not tell us how this natural property is related to some other, different, normative property, (S) is not a positive, substantive normative claim.

Therefore

> (2) If Naturalism were true, Standard Ought Claims would be trivial, and could not tell us positive substantive normative facts.

> (3) Such claims are not trivial, and might tell us such facts.

Therefore

Naturalism cannot be true.

I have, I believe, sufficiently defended (1) and (2) . . . And most Naturalists would accept (3).

In reply, Naturalists might claim:

> (T) Given the role of the concept *ought* in our moral thinking, (S) would not be trivial, since (S) would indirectly tell us that (U) when some act would have this natural property, this act would have certain other properties.

If, as I believe, (S) could not be true, it is misleading to suppose that (S) and (T) are true. With that warning, we can add that (T) would not support Naturalism. There are two possibilities. If these other properties were normative, Naturalists would have to claim that these properties were the same as certain natural properties. The Triviality Objection would apply to these claims, and would not have been answered. If these other properties were *not* normative, (T) would not show that (S) might indirectly tell us some substantive normative fact. So, on both possibilities, this reply fails. This argument, I believe, is sound, and shows that Naturalism cannot be true.

STUDY QUESTIONS

1. What are meant by "natural facts" and "normative facts"?
2. What does Parfit mean by "the normativity objection"?
3. According to Parfit, why are the analogies to scientific discoveries offered by Alan Gibbard (or Peter Railton) unconvincing?
4. According to Parfit, what is the "triviality objection"?

Realism

Michael Smith

Do moral judgments express beliefs, attempting to describe the way the world is? Or do moral judgments express desires, indicating how we want the world to be? Although both accounts look appealing, we appear to face a conflict between the objectivity and practicality of moral judgments. Michael Smith, Professor of Philosophy at Princeton University, argues that realists can adjudicate this conflict. According to Smith, although moral judgments are factual, they are nonetheless intimately linked to desire, expressing beliefs about what we would desire if we were fully informed and rational. This account reduces the normative to the natural and holds in virtue of the meaning of the terms involved. In other words, Smith defends a version of analytic naturalism.

It is a commonplace that we appraise each other's behavior and attitudes from the moral point of view. We say, for example, that we did the *wrong* thing when we refused to give to famine relief this year, though perhaps we did the *right* thing when we handed in the wallet we found on the street; that we would be *better* people if we displayed a greater sensitivity to the feelings of others, though perhaps *worse* if in doing so we lost the special concern we have for our family and friends.

Most of us take appraisal of this sort pretty much for granted. To the extent that we worry about moral appraisal, we simply worry about *getting it right*. Philosophers too have been concerned to get the answers to moral questions right. However, traditionally, they have also been worried about the whole business of moral appraisal itself. Their worry can be brought out by focusing on two of the more distinctive features of moral practice; for,

surprisingly, these features pull against each other, so threatening to make the very idea of a "moral" point of view altogether incoherent.

To begin, as we have already seen, it is distinctive of moral practice that we are concerned to get the answers to moral questions *right*. But this concern presupposes that there are correct answers to moral questions to be had. It thus seems to presuppose that there exists a domain of moral facts about which we can form beliefs and about which we may be mistaken. Moreover, these moral facts have a particular character. For we seem to think that the only relevant determinant of the rightness of an act is the circumstances in which the action takes place. Agents whose circumstances are identical face the same moral choice: if they did the same then either they both acted rightly or they both acted wrongly.

Indeed, something like this view of moral practice seems to explain our preoccupation with moral

From Michael Smith, "Realism," in *A Companion to Ethics*, ed. Peter Singer (Oxford: Blackwell Publishers, 1991). Reprinted by permission of the publisher.

argument. What seems to give moral argument its point and poignancy is the idea that, since we are all in the same boat, a careful mustering and assessment of the reasons for and against our moral opinions is the best way to discover what the moral facts really are. If the participants are open-minded and thinking correctly then, we seem to think, such an argument should result in a *convergence* in moral opinion—a convergence upon the truth. Individual reflection may serve the same purpose, but only when it simulates a real moral argument; for only then can we be certain that we are giving each side of the argument due consideration.

We may summarize this first feature of moral practice in the following terms: we seem to think moral questions have correct answers, that the correct answers are made correct by objective moral facts, that moral facts are determined by circumstances, and that, by moralizing, we can discover what these objective moral facts determined by the circumstances are. The term "objective" here simply signifies the possibility of a convergence in moral views of the kind just mentioned.

A second and rather different feature of moral practice concerns the practical implications of moral judgment, the way in which moral questions gain in their significance for us because of the special influence our moral opinions are supposed to have upon our actions. The idea is that when, say, we come to think that we did the wrong thing in refusing to give to famine relief, we come to think that we failed to do something for which there was a good reason. And this has motivational implications. For now imagine the situation if we refuse to give to famine relief when next the opportunity arises. Our refusal will occasion serious puzzlement, for we will have refused to do what we are known to think we have a good reason to do. Perhaps we will be able to explain ourselves. Perhaps we thought there was a better reason to do something else, or perhaps we were weak-willed. But, the point remains, an explanation of some sort will need to be forthcoming. An explanation will need to be forthcoming because, we seem to think, other things being equal, to have a moral opinion simply is to find yourself with a corresponding motivation to act.

These two distinctive features of moral practice—the *objectivity* and the *practicality* of moral judgment—are widely thought to have both metaphysical and psychological implications. However, and unfortunately, these implications are the exact opposite of each other. In order to see why this is thought to be so, we need to pause for a moment to reflect more generally on the nature of human psychology.

According to the standard picture of human psychology—a picture we owe to David Hume, the famous Scottish philosopher of the eighteenth century—there are two main kinds of psychological state. On the one hand there are beliefs, states that purport to represent the way the world is. Since our beliefs purport to represent the world, they are subject to rational criticism: specifically, they are assessable in terms of truth and falsehood according to whether or not they succeed in representing the world to be the way it really is.

On the other hand, however, there are also desires, states that represent how the world is to be. Desires are unlike beliefs in that they do not even purport to represent the way the world is. They are therefore not assessable in terms of truth and falsehood. Indeed, according to the standard picture, our desires are at bottom not subject to any sort of rational criticism at all. The fact that we have a certain desire is, with a proviso to be mentioned presently, simply a fact about ourselves to be acknowledged. It may be unfortunate that we have certain combinations of desires—perhaps our desires cannot all be satisfied together—but, *in themselves,* our desires are all on a par, rationally neutral.

This is important, for it suggests that though we may make discoveries about the world, and though these discoveries may rightly affect our beliefs, such discoveries should, again with one proviso to be mentioned presently, have no rational impact upon our desires. They may of course, have some *non-*rational impact. Seeing a spider I may be overcome with a morbid fear and desire never to be near one. However, this is not a change in my desires mandated by reason. It is a *non*-rational change in my desire.

Now for the proviso. Suppose, contrary to the example I just gave, that I acquire the desire never to be near a spider because I come to believe, falsely, that spiders give off an unpleasant odor. Then we would certainly ordinarily say that I have an "irrational desire." However, the reason we would say this clearly doesn't go against the spirit of what has been said so far. For my desire never to be near a spider is *based on* a further desire and belief: my desire not to smell that unpleasant odor and my belief that that odor is given off by spiders. Since I can be rationally criticized for having the belief, as it is false, I can be rationally criticized for having the desire it helps to produce.

The proviso is thus fairly minor: desires are subject to rational criticism, but only insofar as they are based on beliefs that are subject to rational criticism. Desires that are not related in some such way to beliefs that can be rationally criticized are not subject to rational criticism at all. We will return to this point presently.

According to the standard picture, then, there are two kinds of psychological state—beliefs and desires—utterly distinct and different from each other. The standard picture of human psychology is important because it provides us with a model for understanding human action. Human action is, according to this picture, produced by a combination of the two. Crudely, our beliefs tell us how the world is, and thus how it has to be changed, so as to make it the way our desires tell us it is to be. An action is thus the product of these two forces: a desire representing the way the world is to be and a belief telling us how the world has to be changed so as to make it that way.

Let's now return to consider the two features of moral judgment we discussed earlier. Consider first the objectivity of such judgment: the idea that moral questions have correct answers, that the correct answers are made correct by objective moral facts, that moral facts are determined by circumstances, and that, by moralizing, we can discover what these objective moral facts are. The metaphysical and psychological implications of this may now be summarized as follows. Metaphysically, the implication is that, amongst the various facts there are in the world, there aren't just facts about (say) the consequences of our actions on the well-being of our families and friends, there are also distinctively *moral* facts: facts about the rightness and wrongness of our actions having these consequences. And, psychologically, the implication is thus that when we make a moral judgment we thereby express our *beliefs* about the way these moral facts are. In forming moral opinions we acquire beliefs, representations of the way the world is morally.

Given the standard picture of human psychology, there is a further psychological implication. For whether or not people who have a certain moral belief desire to act accordingly must now be seen as a further and entirely separate question. They may happen to have a corresponding desire, they may not. However, either way, they cannot be rationally criticized. Having or failing to have a corresponding desire is simply a further fact about a person's psychology.

But now consider the second feature, the practicality of moral judgment. We saw earlier that to have a moral opinion simply is, contrary to what has just been said, to find ourselves with a corresponding motivation to act. If we think it right to give to famine relief then, other things being equal, we must be motivated to give to famine relief. The practicality of moral judgment thus seems to have a psychological and a metaphysical implication of its own. Psychologically, since making a moral judgment requires our having a certain desire, and no recognition of a fact about the world could rationally compel us to have one desire rather than another, our judgment must really simply *be* an expression of that desire. And this psychological implication has a metaphysical counterpart. For it seems to follow that, contrary to initial appearance, when we judge it right to give to famine relief we *are not* responding to any moral fact—the rightness of giving to famine relief. Indeed, moral facts are an idle postulate. In judging it right to give to famine relief we are really simply expressing our desire that people give to famine relief. It is as if we were yelling "Hooray for giving to famine relief!"—no mention of a moral fact there, in fact, no factual claim at all.

We are now in a position to see why philosophers have been worried about the whole business of moral appraisal. The problem is that the *objectivity* and the *practicality* of moral judgment pull in quite opposite directions from each other. The objectivity of moral judgment suggests that there are moral facts, determined by circumstances, and that our moral judgments express our beliefs about what these facts are. This enables us to make good sense of moral argument, and the like, but it leaves it entirely mysterious how or why having a moral view is supposed to have special links with what we are motivated to do. And the practicality of moral judgment suggests just the opposite, that our moral judgments express our desires. While this enables us to make good sense of the link between having a moral view and being motivated, it leaves it entirely mysterious what a moral argument is supposed to be an argument about.

The idea of a moral judgment thus looks like it may well be incoherent, for what is required to make sense of such a judgment is a queer sort of fact about the universe: a fact whose recognition necessarily impacts upon our desires. But the standard picture tells us that there are no such facts. Nothing could be everything a moral judgment purports to be—or so it may now seem.

At long last we are in a position to see what this essay is about. For *moral realism* is simply the metaphysical (or ontological) view that there exist moral facts. The psychological counterpart to realism is called "cognitivism," the view that moral judgments express our beliefs about what these moral facts are, and that we can come to discover what these facts are by engaging in moral argument and reflection.

Moral realism thus contrasts with two alternative metaphysical views about morality: *irrealism* (sometimes called "anti-realism") and *moral nihilism*. According to the irrealists, there are no moral facts, but neither are moral facts required to make sense of moral practice. We can happily acknowledge that our moral judgments simply express our desires about how people behave. This, the psychological counterpart to irrealism, is called "noncognitivism." . . .

By contrast, according to the moral nihilists, the irrealists are right that there are no moral facts, but wrong about what is required to make sense of moral practice. The nihilist thinks that without moral facts moral practice is all a sham, much like religious practice without belief in God.

I have taken some time before introducing the ideas of moral realism, irrealism, and nihilism because, as it seems to me, each has much to be said both in its favor and against it. In what follows I will explain in more detail some of the substantive views people have taken in this whole debate. However, I want to emphasize at the outset that nearly every substantive position is fraught with difficulty and controversy. The long introduction will hopefully have given some hint of why this is so. The very idea of moral practice may well be in deep trouble, much as the moral nihilist suggests.

Remember that, according to the irrealist, when we judge it right to give to famine relief we are expressing our desire that people give to famine relief; it is as if we were yelling "Hooray for giving to famine relief!" Irrealism is certainly an option to be considered. But it seems to me that it is ultimately an unattractive option.

To be sure, irrealists have a perfect explanation of the practicality of moral judgment. But it seems utterly implausible to suppose, as they therefore must, that moral judgments aren't truth-assessable at all. They must say this because they model a moral judgment on a yell of approval or disapproval. But when I yell "Hooray for giving to famine relief!," though my yell may be sincere or insincere, it can hardly be true or false. My yell reveals something about myself—that I have a certain desire—not about the world.

The problem here isn't just that we *say* that moral judgments can be true or false, though we certainly do do that. The problem is rather that the whole business of moral argument and moral reflection only makes sense on the assumption that moral judgments *are* truth-assessable. When we agonize over our moral opinions, we seem to be agonizing over whether our reasons for our beliefs are good enough reasons for believing what we believe to be true. And no irrealist surrogate seems up to the task of explaining this appearance away. For example, it seems utterly hopeless to suppose that we are agonizing over whether we *really* have the desires we have. Surely *this* question isn't so hard to answer!

Indeed, in this context, it is worthwhile asking what the irrealists' view of moral argument is supposed to be. They presumably imagine that what we are trying to do, when we engage in moral argument, is to get our opponent to have the same desires as we have. But, at bottom, they must also say that we are trying to do this *not* because the opponent rationally should have these desires—remember that, subject to the proviso mentioned, desires aren't supposed to be subject to rational criticism at all—but rather just because these are the desires *we* want him to have. But in that case moral argument begins to look massively self-obsessed, an imposition of *our* wants on others.

Irrealism isn't an attractive option. The irrealist's account of moral judgment as the expression of a desire simply fails to make sense of moral reflection. And the irrealist's account of moral argument makes moral persuasion look like it is itself immoral! What about the alternative, moral realism?

It might be thought that, since the moral realist admits the existence of moral facts, he has therefore no problem explaining the objectivity of moral judgment and the related phenomena of moral reflection and moral argument. It might be thought that the realist's only problem is that, if he is to eschew the existence of "queer" moral properties whose recognition connects necessarily with the will, then he cannot explain the practicality of moral judgment. But matters are in fact much more complicated.

Certainly the moral realist needs to face up to the fact that the practicality of moral judgment is problematic, from his point of view. But his problem is more than that. His problem is that, *because* he has no explanation of the practicality of moral judgment, he has no plausible story about what *kind* of fact a moral fact is. And if he has no plausible story about the kind of fact a moral fact is, then, despite initial appearance, he has no plausible story about what moral reflection and moral argument are all about.

In order to see this, remember what we said at the outset when we first introduced the idea of the practicality of moral judgment. We said then that the practicality of moral judgment is a consequence of the fact that judgments about right and wrong are

judgments about what we have reason to do and reason not to do. This is the subject matter of moral reflection and moral argument, *our reasons for action*. But the moral realist who admits an array of moral facts about which we may be motivationally neutral must reject such a conception of rightness and wrongness. After all, we could hardly remain motivationally neutral about what we think we have reason to do! The challenge such a realist faces is thus to provide us with some alternative account of what *kind* of fact a moral fact is; an alternative account of what moral reflection and moral argument are *about*.

Some moral realists do face up to this challenge. They have claimed, for example, that moral facts are facts that play a certain *explanatory role* in the social world: right acts are those that tend towards social stability, whereas wrong acts are those that tend towards social unrest. An Aristotelian version of this might be: right acts are those in accord with the "proper function" of human beings—a quasi-biological notion—wrong acts are those that are not in accord with this proper function. Moral reflection and moral argument are thus, they suggest, arguments about which features of actions feed this tendency towards unrest and stability. Or, in the Aristotelian version, they are arguments about which acts are in accord with the proper function of humans (and thus, ultimately, about what the proper function of a human being is). The word "tendency" is not idle here for such realists are quick to emphasize that other factors may mitigate the tendency towards stability and unrest, or may stop humans actually having their proper function.

Let's focus for a moment on the suggestion that a moral fact can be characterized in terms of a tendency towards social stability or unrest. This suggestion cannot be dismissed out of hand, for reflection of an armchair-sociological kind does suggest that the acts we are disposed to think of as right—those that provide for a more equitable satisfaction of different people's interests, say—do tend towards social stability, and that the acts we are disposed to think of as wrong—those that provide for a less equitable satisfaction of different people's interests, say—do tend towards social unrest. It is thus best to assume that we have here two *competing* conceptions of a moral fact. Which conception seems the more plausible?

On the one hand, we have the idea of a moral fact as a fact about what we have reason to do or not to do. On the other, we have the idea of a moral fact in terms of what tends towards social stability and unrest. If the question is "Which conception allows us to make the best sense of moral argument?" then the answer must surely be the former. For, to the extent that moral argument does focus on what tends towards social stability, it does so because social stability is deemed morally important, an outcome we have reason to produce.

Indeed, it seems to me that even this kind of moral realist's focus on *explanation* pushes us back in the direction of the idea of a moral fact as a fact about what we have reason to do. For, again, to the extent that we think of right acts as acts that tend towards social stability, we think that they have this tendency *because* they represent the reasonable thing for people to do. It is the tendency people have to do what is reasonable that is doing the explanatory work. But that, too, simply returns us to the original conception of a moral fact in terms of what we have reason to do. (We might say similar things about the idea that we can characterize a moral fact in terms of the proper function of human beings; for insofar as we understand the idea of the "proper function" of human beings, we think that their proper function is to be reasonable and rational.)

In the end, then, we might object that this kind of moral realist fails to provide us with a real *alternative* to our original conception of a moral fact. The real question, then, is whether the moral realist is forced to reject the idea that rightness and wrongness have to do with what we have reason to do and reason not to do. In the remainder of this essay I want to explore this question.

The devil of the piece is what I have been calling the "standard picture" of human psychology. For the standard picture gives us a model of what it is to have a reason in terms of a desire/belief pair. If the moral realist is to make headway in combining the objectivity and the practicality of moral judgment

without appealing to "queer" moral facts, he must challenge this standard picture.

The trouble is, however, that the standard picture looks substantially correct as an account of human motivation. After all, it is uncontroversial that the psychological states that motivate actions must be dispositions of some sort, dispositions to produce acts of the relevant kind. And it is also uncontroversial that actions are motivated by psychological states that have content: either they are produced by states that represent the way the world is (beliefs) or by states that represent the way the world is to be (desires), or, as the standard picture has it, they are produced by a pairing of the two (a desire and a belief).

But now reflect for a moment. A disposition to produce acts of some relevant kind, if it has content, must have, as its content, a representation of the way the world is to be, and so it must be a desire. For how else could the psychological state in question *target* the state of affairs to be produced? (And how could it produce what is to be produced without having targeted it?) Moreover, if this state is to produce the targeted state of affairs, it must also be paired with a representation of how the world is, and so it must be paired with a belief. For only so will the relevant *change* in the world be produced so as to bring about the targeted state of affairs.

It therefore seems that the standard picture is right in insisting that desires are required in order to motivate actions. The place to challenge the standard picture, then, is not in its account of what motivates action, but rather in its tacit conflation of *reasons* with *motives*. Seeing why this is a conflation also enables us to see why we may legitimately talk about our *beliefs* about the reasons we have, and why having such beliefs makes it rational to have corresponding desires.

Imagine that you are giving the baby a bath. As you do, it begins to scream uncontrollably. Nothing you do seems to help. As you watch it scream, you are overcome with a desire to drown the baby in the bathwater. Certainly you may now be *motivated* to drown the baby. (You may even actually drown it.) But does the mere fact that you have this desire, and are thus motivated, mean that you have a *reason* to drown the baby?

One commonsensical answer is that, since the desire is not *worth* satisfying, it does not provide you with such a reason; that, in this case, you are motivated to do something you have *no* reason to do. However, the standard picture seems utterly unable to accept this answer. After all, your desire to drown the baby need be based on no false belief. As such, it is entirely beyond rational criticism—or so that standard picture tells us.

The problem, here, is that the standard picture gives no special privilege to what we would want if we were "cool, calm and collected" (to use a flippant phrase). Yet we seem ordinarily to think that not being cool, calm and collected may lead to all sorts of irrational emotional outbursts. Having those desires that we would have if we were cool, calm and collected thus seems to be an independent rational ideal. When cool, calm and collected, you would wish for the baby not to be drowned, no matter how much it screams, and no matter how overcome you may be, in your uncool, uncalm and uncollected state, with a desire to drown it. This is why you have no reason to drown the baby.

Perhaps we have already said enough to reconcile the objectivity of moral judgment with its practicality. Judgments of right and wrong are judgments about what we have reason to do and reason not to do. But what sort of fact is a fact about what we have reason to do? The preceding discussion suggests an answer. It suggests that facts about what we have reason to do are not facts about what we *do* desire, as the standard picture would have it, but are rather facts about what we *would* desire if we were in certain idealized conditions of reflection: if, say, we were well-informed, cool, calm and collected. According to this account, then, I have a reason to give to famine relief in my particular circumstances just in case, if I were in such idealized conditions of reflection, I would desire that, even when in my particular circumstances, I give to famine relief. And this sort of fact may certainly be the object of a belief.

Moreover, this account of what it is to have a reason makes it plain why the standard picture of human psychology is wrong to insist that beliefs and desires are altogether distinct; why, on the contrary, having certain beliefs, beliefs about what we have

reason to do, does make it rational for us to have certain desires, desires to do what we believe we have reason to do.

In order to see this, suppose I believe that I would desire to give to famine relief if I were cool, calm and collected—i.e. more colloquially, I believe I have a reason to give to famine relief—but, being uncool, uncalm and uncollected, I don't desire to give to famine relief. Am I rationally criticizable for not having the desire? I surely am. After all, from my own point of view my beliefs and desires form a more coherent, and thus a rationally preferable, package if I do in fact desire to do what I believe I would desire to do if I were cool, calm and collected. This is because, since it is an independent rational ideal to have the desires I would have if I were cool, calm and collected, so, from my own point of view, if I believe that I would have a certain desire under such conditions and yet fail to have it, then my beliefs and desires fail to meet this ideal. To believe that I would desire to give to famine relief if I were cool, calm and collected, and yet to fail to desire to give to famine relief, is thus to manifest a commonly recognizable species of rational failure.

If this is right, then it follows that, contrary to the standard picture of human psychology, there is in fact no problem at all in supposing that I may have genuine *beliefs* about what I have reason to do, where having those beliefs makes it rational for me to have the corresponding *desires.* And if there is no problem at all in supposing that this may be so, then there is no problem in reconciling the practicality of moral judgment with the claim that moral judgments express our beliefs about the reasons we have.

However, this doesn't yet suffice to solve the problem facing the moral realist. For moral judgments aren't *just* judgments about the reasons we have. They are judgments about the reasons we have *where those reasons are supposed to be determined entirely by our circumstances.* As I put it earlier, people in the same circumstances face the same moral choice: if they did the same action then either they both acted rightly (they both did what they had reason to do) or they both acted wrongly (they both did what they had reason not to do). Does the account of what it is to have a reason just given entail that this is so?

Suppose our circumstances are identical, and let's ask whether it is right for each of us to give to famine relief: that is, whether we each have a reason to do so. According to the account on offer it is right that I give to famine relief just in case I have a reason to give to famine relief, and I have such a reason just in case, if I were in idealized conditions of reflection—well-informed, cool, calm and collected—I would desire to give to famine relief. And the same is true of you. If our circumstances are the same then, supposedly, we should both have such a reason or both lack such a reason. But do we?

The question is whether, if we were well-informed, cool, calm and collected, we would tend to *converge* in the desires we have. Would we converge or would there always be the possibility of some non-rationally-explicable difference in our desires *even under such conditions?* The standard picture of human psychology now returns to center-stage. For it tells us that there is *always* the possibility of some non-rationally-explicable difference in our desires even under such idealized conditions of reflection. This is the residue of the standard picture's conception of desire as a psychological state that is beyond rational criticism.

If this is right then the moral realist's attempt to combine the objectivity and the practicality of moral judgment must be deemed a failure. We are forced to accept that there is a *fundamental relativity* in the reasons we have. What we have reason to do is relative to what we would desire under certain idealized conditions of reflection, and this may differ from person to person. It is not wholly determined by our circumstances, as moral facts are supposed to be.

Many philosophers accept the standard picture's pronouncement on this point. But accepting there is such a fundamental relativity in our reasons seems altogether premature to me. It puts the cart before the horse. For surely moral practice is itself the forum in which we will *discover* whether there is a fundamental relativity in our reasons.

After all, in moral practice we attempt to change people's moral beliefs by engaging them in rational argument: i.e. by getting their beliefs to approximate those they would have under more idealized conditions of reflection. And sometimes we succeed. When we succeed, other things being equal, we succeed in changing their desires. But if we accept that there is a fundamental relativity in our reasons then we can say, in advance, that this procedure will never result in a massive *convergence* in moral beliefs; for we know in advance that there will never be a convergence in the desires we have under such idealized conditions of reflection. Or rather, and more accurately, if there is a fundamental relativity in our reasons then it follows that any convergence we find in our moral beliefs, and thus in our desires, must be entirely contingent. It could in no way be explained by, or suggestive of, the fact that the desires that emerge have some *privileged* rational status.

My question is: "Why accept this?" Why not think, instead, that if such a convergence emerged in moral practice then that would itself suggest that these particular moral beliefs, and the corresponding desires, *do* enjoy a privileged rational status? After all, something like such a convergence in mathematical practice lies behind our conviction that mathematical claims enjoy a privileged rational status. So why not think that a like convergence in moral practice would show that moral judgments enjoy the same privileged rational status? At this point, the standard picture's insistence that there is a fundamental relativity in our reasons begins to sound all too much like a hollow dogma.

The kind of moral realism described here endorses a conception of moral facts that is a far cry from the picture presented at the outset: moral facts as queer facts about the universe whose recognition necessarily impacts upon our desires. Instead, the realist has eschewed queer facts about the universe in favor of a more "subjectivist" conception of moral facts. This emerged in the realist's analysis of what it is to have a reason. . . . The realist's point, however, is that such a conception of moral facts may make them subjective only in the innocuous sense that they are facts about what we would *want* under certain idealized conditions of reflection, where wants are, admittedly, a kind of psychological state enjoyed by subjects. But moral facts remain objective insofar as they are facts about what *we,* not just *you* or *I*, would want under such conditions. The existence of a moral fact—say, the rightness of giving to famine relief in certain circumstances—requires that, under idealized conditions of reflection, rational creatures would *converge* upon a desire to give to famine relief in such circumstances.

Of course, it must be agreed on all sides that moral argument has not yet produced the sort of convergence in our desires that would make the idea of a moral fact—a fact about the reasons we have entirely determined by our circumstances—look plausible. But neither has moral argument had much of a history in times in which we have been able to engage in free reflection unhampered by a false biology (the Aristotelian tradition) or a false belief in God (the Judeo-Christian tradition). It remains to be seen whether sustained moral argument can elicit the requisite convergence in our moral beliefs, and corresponding desires, to make the idea of a moral fact look plausible. The kind of moral realism described here holds out the hope that it will. Only time will tell.

STUDY QUESTIONS

1. According to Smith, why have philosophers been worried about the business of moral appraisal?
2. How do desires differ from beliefs?
3. Can you make a moral judgment yet not be motivated to act accordingly?
4. If you care about friendship, family, and beauty, and I care exclusively about my collection of vintage cars, are my desires more rational than yours?

Moral Functionalism

Frank Jackson & Philip Pettit

Analytic naturalism maintains that the reduction of the normative to the natural holds in virtue of the meaning of the terms involved. But is this form of naturalism vulnerable to G. E. Moore's open question argument? After all, if good were identical with some natural property analytically, a competent speaker presumably would have no reason to wonder whether something with that natural property is good. Perhaps, however, not all analytic identities are obvious. So argues Frank Jackson, Professor of Philosophy at Australia National University, and Philip Pettit, Professor of Philosophy at Princeton University.

Their doctrine of moral functionalism takes its cue from functionalism in "Philosophy of Mind," which holds that mental states just are the causal relations between typical behavioral causes (inputs), behavioral effects (outputs), and the relations of both to other mental states. For example, what makes an inner state a pain is its being the type of state caused by a flame, resulting in avoidance, and leading to anxiety. A complete definition would require that the totality of such conditions be assembled, but together they would provide a satisfactory account of pain.

Moral functionalism operates similarly. Consider fairness. As Jackson and Pettit explain, the commonplaces about fairness in ordinary moral thinking—"folk moral theory," as they call it—when brought together exemplify a descriptive property that displays fairness-behavior. Thus an even distribution of goods is seen as appropriate (input), causes satisfaction (output), and leads to future efforts to seek arrangements of this sort. If the totality of such conditions were assembled, we could arrive at a complex, analytic definition of fairness in terms of functional roles. Thus Jackson and Pettit provide an option for an analytic reduction of the normative that does not evidently fall prey to the open-question argument.

I. THE CONTENT OF EVALUATIVE BELIEF

. . . [O]ur aim is to present the functionalist theory of evaluative content. The argument for the theory has two premises, one bearing on the supervenience of the evaluative on the descriptive, the other on the networked nature of moral terms. We shall present each of the premises, characterize the theory that they support, and then show why the sort of content in question counts as evaluative.

From Frank Jackson and Philip Pettit, "Moral Functionalism and Moral Motivation," *The Philosophical Quarterly* 45 (1995). Reprinted by permission of the publisher.

The Supervenience of the Evaluative on the Descriptive

One of the most striking features of moral beliefs, and evaluative beliefs generally, is that the evaluative facts they bear upon satisfy a certain supervenience condition relative to descriptive facts. It is usually urged that if two options are descriptively indiscernible in regard to universal features then they are morally indiscernible as well: supervenience is associated with universalizability. This supervenience of the evaluative on the descriptive is *a priori* knowable, because it is marked by a common feature of our practice in moral argument, and anyone party to that practice is in a position to recognize that the supervenience obtains. The feature is that you can justifiably make a moral difference between two options only so far as you can point to a descriptive difference between them. No evaluative discriminability without descriptive discriminability. If you say that that action is right, but this wrong, and you cannot point to some other, descriptive difference between them, then your status as a participant in evaluative discourse will be up for question.

The supervenience of the evaluative on the descriptive, as we have characterized it so far, means that for any possible world w, if x and y are descriptively exactly alike in w, then x and y are alike in moral respects too. But our practice in moral argument supports a somewhat stronger supervenience claim, and makes it *a priori* knowable too: for any two worlds that are descriptively exactly alike in other respects, in the attitudes that people have, in the effects to which actions lead, and so on, if x in one is descriptively exactly like y in the other, then x and y are exactly alike in moral respects. More globally, if two worlds, w and w', are exactly alike in descriptive respects, then w and w' are exactly alike in evaluative respects too. The fact that moral evaluation is answerable to descriptive considerations means that there is no room for a difference of value between two worlds that are exactly alike in descriptive regards.

The *a priori* supervenience of the moral on the descriptive gives sharp expression to the lesson taught by the answerability of evaluation to descriptive considerations. This is that there is no possibility that moral beliefs might partition descriptively indiscernible possible worlds in a manner additional to the partitioning introduced by descriptive beliefs. If two worlds are descriptively indiscernible, then there is no difference available to be captured in evaluative terms. Characterize a world or an option evaluatively and you assign it to a sort that is adequately identifiable in descriptive terms. Evaluation, to put an ironic twist on the lesson, is description by other means.

The Networked Character of Moral Terms

What, then, are we to say about the meaning of moral terms? The descriptive answerability of evaluation would be unsurprising, if evaluative terms were all descriptively definable, one by one. But we see no plausibility in the idea of providing such an atomistic reduction of evaluative terms. . . . Nor is the idea likely to appeal to many contemporary philosophers. By most accounts, moral terms are involved in a network of content-relevant connections, including connections with other moral and evaluative terms. No simple atomistic definition is going to yield an understanding of a moral term, because each such term is used in a way that presupposes a large network of connections with other terms, evaluative and descriptive. Take the example of fairness. That something is fair means that conditions of the kind registered in the following illustrative commonplaces are fulfilled.

(1) *Commonplaces about presentation.* In most contexts "I cut, you choose" is a fair sort of procedure: if anything is fair, then that is. And a similar exemplary status is enjoyed by equal division and by any procedure that departs from equal division only so far as independent claims require. Other arrangements are judged to be fair on the basis of similarity with such paradigms.

(2) *Commonplaces about truth-conditions.* There can be no difference in fairness without a descriptive difference: fairness is descriptively supervenient.

(3) *Commonplaces about justification.* If one alternative is fair, and if other things are equal, then that is the right option for the agent to desire and pursue. The agent may reasonably feel guilt, and others resentment, about failure to choose such an option, at any rate where the choice would not have been very difficult to make.

(4) *Commonplaces about justificatory power.* Fairness is potentially more important in the determination of rightness, and in the justification of choice, than being polite or diverting. But fairness is less important in general than saving innocent human lives: better be unfair than allow someone innocent to perish.

(5) *Commonplaces about motivation.* Anyone who believes that one option is fair will at least prefer that option, *ceteris paribus,* to alternatives. Not to do so is probably to be put down to a failure like weakness of will, a form of practical unreason . . .

(6) *Commonplaces about motivational power.* Believing one option to be fair is likely to motivate an agent more strongly than seeing another as polite or diverting, but less strongly than recognizing a further option as a means of saving innocent human life. If these asymmetries do not hold, that is probably due to some form of practical unreason.

(7) *Commonplaces about virtue.* The fact that something is fair, if it is a fact, is likely to be more salient to people the more they display the virtuous character traits of spontaneously choosing what is right.

Such commonplaces are candidates for *a priori* truths: they are putatively such that anyone who knows how to use the term "fair" is in a position to see that they hold. . . . Those that are *a priori* true will give us the conditions under which fairness is instantiated, though it should be noticed that they do not entail that the property ever is instantiated. As "Bachelors are unmarried males" is consistent with there being no bachelors, so the commonplaces for fairness are consistent with there being no such property realized in the actual world.

What is true of "fair" is true of any moral term. The term makes its particular contribution to evaluation just so far as it engages the commonplaces linking it with other terms. What is said or believed in characterizing an option as fair ties up with the fact that accepting the characterization means becoming disposed to draw the lessons articulated in the commonplaces. If I think that an option is fair then I expect people, myself included, to be able to see it as of a kind with certain paradigms of fairness; to be more impressed by that fact than by the fact that it is a somewhat embarrassing choice to make; to believe that, other things being equal, the option is right; and, if I am not the victim of some *malaise,* to be drawn towards the option. It is in virtue of making such connections, at least in part, that the characterization of the option as fair is contentful or informative.

The networked character of moral terms means that there is no plausibility in the idea of giving each term a separate descriptive definition, without regard to the definition of others. What it is to be fair, in descriptive terms, must tie up with what it is to be right, in descriptive terms, if a connection between those properties is assumed in the way we deploy the words. But if moral terms are not going to be definable, one by one, in descriptive terms, how are we to make sense of the answerability of evaluation to descriptive considerations? How are we to make sense of the *a priori* supervenience of the evaluative on the descriptive?

The Functionalist Theory of Moral Content

The most attractive possibility that we see is to view moral terms as . . . specified by their role in received moral theory—in "folk moral theory"—and while this theory has a purely descriptive content, so that we can understand the answerability of evaluation to descriptive considerations, the content of any one claim is fixed only so far as the contents of others are fixed simultaneously. Moral terms are reducible to descriptive terms, at least in principle, but the reduction involved is holistic, not atomistic.

. . . What property do I ascribe to an option in characterizing it as fair? I ascribe to it that property which fills the place marked out for fairness in ordinary moral thinking: it belongs to certain paradigms that we find saliently similar; it inclines us to judge that a bearer is right, i.e., has the descriptive property associated with the rightness-role; it inclines us to make this judgment more or less strongly than would certain other descriptive properties that are assigned otherwise similar roles within the theory; it tends to arouse a desire for the realization of the option; and so on. The term "fair" picks out a descriptive property, then, but it does so by virtue of the place that that property occupies in folk moral theory, and in a manner that requires other moral terms simultaneously to pick out complementary descriptive properties.

The approach characterized in these remarks amounts to what we call a functionalist theory of moral terms. The analogy with the familiar functionalist theory of psychological terms will be obvious. According to the psychological functionalist, to believe that *p* is to instantiate an as-it-happens physical state of displaying a belief-that-*p* profile: it is to exhibit the required connections. According to the moral functionalist, for an option to be fair is for it to instantiate a descriptive property such that the option displays fairness-behavior: it connects up with other things in the manner distinctive of fair alternatives.

But while the psychological parallel may be useful in introducing moral functionalism, we should stress the differences between the doctrines. First, it is neither necessary nor *a priori* knowable that physical properties are what ensure the fulfilment of the roles associated with psychological properties. It is, however, both necessary and *a priori* knowable that descriptive properties are what ensure the fulfilment of the roles associated with moral properties. Second, functionalism about the mind associates primarily causal roles with the various mental properties. By contrast, although the functionalist account of moral properties may include as part of the role definitive of fairness "Many acts are right because they are fair," the "because" is not a causal "because." The fairness of an action does not causally explain its rightness.

We think that a functionalist account of moral content is attractive for its ability to explain the supervenience of the evaluative on the descriptive, and the *a priori* status of that supervenience; in particular, it can explain these consistently with admitting the networked character of moral terms. If two worlds are descriptively indiscernible, then they will be indiscernible in regard to properties associated with roles that descriptive properties underpin: same underpinnings, same roles. And so the truth of moral functionalism would ensure the (*a priori*) supervenience of the evaluative on the descriptive.

There is more to be said, however, in favor of the functionalist view. It makes good sense of what goes on in moral thinking, both in everyday life and in philosophy. In moral thinking we try to form our opinions on new moral questions and to examine and, if necessary, revise our existing opinions on old. According to the functionalist view, the meaning of relevant moral terms will be fixed by roles which certain commonplaces give them, and so moral thinking is bound to involve the attempt to use commonplaces as a base, and holding on to as much of that base as possible, or at least to the parts considered most secure, to fix opinions on particular questions. The commonplaces that emerge in this process as those whose rejection cannot be countenanced will be taken to fix the relevant roles; they are the *a priori* compulsory propositions that anyone who knows how to use the terms is in a position to recognize as true. Other commonplaces—other putatively *a priori* propositions—will have to be dismissed as false or downgraded to the status of empirical, contingent truths.

This account of moral thinking fits with Rawls' (1971) influential argument that systematic moral thinking involves the attempt to equilibrate such general principles as we find we really cannot give up with considered judgments as to how various options should be morally characterized. Is such and such an arrangement to be regarded as fair? The issue turns, by his account, on whether judging that it is fair is consistent with general considerations like the following: that its fairness ought to put it in a salient family resemblance with certain paradigms (is it really on a par with equal division?); that its fairness ought to mean that we would desire it if unbiased (would parties in the original position prefer it?); that its fairness ought to make it desirable in a more powerful and important way than would the property of being, say, economically efficient (does it have the "primary" virtue of an institution?); that its fairness ought to make it look like the right arrangement to have (can we give it our considered approval?); and so on. This is exactly what we would expect, under a functionalist account of moral content.

The fact that moral thinking follows this pattern means, it should be noticed, that folk moral theory is always on the advance, as people look for the most consistent way of equilibrating their general principles and their particular judgments, not just about fair institutions, but also about whether abortion should be available on demand, whether the state should impose any moral views and whether the public water supply should be fluoridated. The drive for equilibrium or consistency may reflect back on general principles, as Rawls himself emphasizes: it may make for a shift in our shared folk theory.

The functionalist account also makes sense of the more comprehensive philosophical enterprise that attempts, not just to develop systematic moral opinion, but to identify a canonical method of moral thought. Different moral methods, as we see them from a functionalist viewpoint, start from different points in the moral network of putatively *a priori* commonplaces, and argue that their chosen starting-point offers the most advantageous platform for moral thinking, the platform from which it is easiest to advance moral opinion, while preserving as much as possible of the network. Utilitarians start from the commonplace connection of value with certain descriptively given paradigms, in particular with the realization of happiness, arguing that we can save most of the commonplaces of folk moral theory, and develop reliable moral opinions, by looking always for what promotes happiness. In a similar vein, subjectivists and dispositionalists, perhaps non-cognitivists too, start from the commonplace connection between value and what we desire or would desire in favored circumstances; contractarians start from the commonplace connection between the positive evaluation of something and its being found justifiable by others; virtue theorists start

from the commonplace connection between the perception or pursuit of value and the possession of certain character traits; and so on.

This view of existing moral philosophies is highly ecumenical in suggesting that they represent different but not necessarily inconsistent methods or strategies for moral thought. As a matter of fact, of course, most of the philosophies in question are given constitutive as well as methodological significance by their defenders; they are presented as rival, sectarian attempts, in T. M. Scanlon's words (1982: 106), to give "a philosophical explanation of the subject-matter of morality."

There are two different ways, from a functionalist perspective, to give constitutive significance to a sectarian philosophy. One may hold, consistently with functionalism, that a particular approach points us towards the descriptive properties that fill the moral roles. The role-fillers are all felicific properties, the utilitarian will say; they all relate to what people find unobjectionable, the contractarian will say; and so on. Alternatively, one may hold that a given sectarian philosophy tells us that only certain parts of the moral roles, only certain subsets of the commonplaces, matter to the strict understanding of the moral terms; the other commonplaces may be accepted or rejected, but in either case they will not be involved in the meaning of moral terms. This alternative will suggest that folk moral theory is excessively generous in the networks of commonplaces that it countenances: all that will allegedly matter for the meaning of this or that moral term is consistency with some fragment of the network—the part that specifies certain paradigms, or a motivational connection, or a justificatory capacity, or a linkage with virtue, or whatever.

In conclusion, there are three things it is important to notice about our functionalist account. First, it leaves open whether rightness, say, is the ground-level (descriptive) property that occupies the rightness-role, e.g., the property of maximizing happiness, or whether it is the higher-order property of having a property that occupies the rightness-role . . . On either approach, an action is right if and only if it has that role-filling property: the question left open does not bear on the conditions for being right but on the metaphysical matter of what rightness, the moral property, is. And on either approach, to believe that φ-ing is right is not to believe that φ-ing has the descriptive, role-filling property, e.g., that it maximizes happiness. It is, rather, to believe that φ-ing has the property that occupies the rightness-role, whatever that property is.

The second thing to notice is that the version of moral functionalism that identifies the moral properties with the ground-level, role-filling properties comes in two salient varieties. We can think of a role in folk moral theory as picking out a moral property in rigid or in non-rigid fashion. On the first construal, rightness is associated with the property that *actually* occupies the role of rightness; on the second, rightness is associated with a property that may vary from world to world, as now one property, now another, occupies the rightness-role *there*. Under either construal, however, it may be *a posteriori* which property rightness is associated with.

The third thing to notice is that the functionalist theory is not exposed to any simple version of the open question argument. Take, for instance, the argument that says it cannot be correct to hold that x is right if and only if x has some role-filling descriptive property, because with any descriptive property it is open to significant question whether or not it is right to pursue that property. This argument has no bite precisely because the biconditional linking rightness with a role-filling descriptive property may be *a posteriori* in character, according to the theory. The theory allows that it need not be a conceptual matter that x is right if and only if x is F, where F might be "maximizes happiness," "accords with such and such a list of *prima facie* duties," "is what a person with such and such virtues would do," or whatever. What has to be a conceptual matter is only that x is right just in case x has the property, whatever it is, that plays the rightness-role.

It is true that, according to the functionalist theory, the total body of descriptive information entails the evaluative way things are (Jackson 1992). For the network of connections posited in folk moral theory can be given in purely descriptive terms, and the information about which properties fill the roles can also be given in descriptive terms. But the entailment here will not be an obvious one, since the network postulated is complicated and in process of articulation, under the drive for reflective equilibrium; arguably, indeed, it is something we shall never reach but rather shall converge on over time. Besides, . . . our folk moral grasp of that network has features that undermine the open question argument. It is tacit in a way that makes claims about the descriptive connections less than immediately accessible. And it is practical in a way that links access to those connections with the presence of a presumptively defensible desire which it is hard to envisage having while at the same time regarding the relevant question of rightness as open.

Evaluative Content?

The principal mark of whether a given content has practical evaluative significance, i.e., of whether it is an evaluative as distinct from a purely descriptive content, is whether assenting to the content gives a person reason, however defeasible, to form the appropriate desire and choice: whether the truth of the claim in question offers inferential or quasi-inferential support—deliberative support, as it is usually described—for such a positive response. We think that our account of the content of practical evaluation explains why moral content has this decision-supporting significance.

We can distinguish direct from indirect information bearing on what we think we ought to do. Direct information tells us about, say, the incidence of caries after fluoridation, the costs and the possible risks of fluoridation, and so forth. Indirect information tells us about the attitudes of others to fluoridation, and about what we ourselves would feel if various circumstances were different, or if we knew more, and so forth. The indirect information is not so much information about the nature of the contemplated course of action itself as information relating to attitudes of ourselves and others to the course of action.

Indirect information can be very telling for our views as to what we ought to do. "You wouldn't take that attitude if you hadn't had that row with Jones last year," "People whose judgment you respect wouldn't approve," "If you knew what I know, you wouldn't go ahead," "An expert committee has recommended against it": there is something amiss about someone who accepts such claims but fails to see them as reasons, however defeasible, for acting accordingly. Suppose you believe that you would desire something if a certain irrelevant incident had not occurred, or if you were as wise as some people you admire, or if you had certain information or expertise. You are then going to believe that if you do not desire it now, that is because of some inappropriate factor. It should be no surprise if in these circumstances you see reason why you should desire the matter in question.

The functionalist account of the content of moral belief shows that it gives the subject the same sort of indirect information about the appeal of the option it recommends. We mentioned, in illustration of the connections that go with fairness, that to judge that an option is fair or right, other things being equal, is to tend to desire it. But this means that to judge that something is fair or right, and that other things are equal, is to have indirect information of the sort that we have been discussing, to believe, e.g., that if ideally situated in the relevant way, one would desire the option. And so one will have reason to think that one ought to desire and pursue the option now.

REFERENCES

Jackson, F. 1992. Critical Notice of Susan Hurley's *Natural Reasons, Australasian Journal of Philosophy* 70, pp. 475–87.

Rawls, J. 1971. *A Theory of Justice* (Harvard UP).

Scanlon, T.M. 1982. "Contractualism and Utilitarianism," in A. Sen and B. Williams (eds), *Utilitarianism and Beyond* (Cambridge UP).

STUDY QUESTIONS

1. What do Jackson and Pettit mean by the "networked character of moral terms"?
2. What is meant by "the supervenient of the evaluative on the descriptive"?
3. What do Jackson and Pettit mean by "folk morality"?
4. Why do Jackson and Pettit believe that moral functionalism is not exposed to any simple version of the open-question argument?

Does Analytical Moral Naturalism Rest on a Mistake?

Susana Nuccetelli & Gary Seay

Susana Nuccetelli, Professor of Philosophy at St. Cloud State University, and Gary Seay, Professor of Philosophy at Medgar Evers College, City University of New York, argue that a revised version of Moore's open-question argument can be marshaled against analytical naturalism. They challenge the contention that, without loss, natural predicates could be substituted for normative ones.

According to moral functionalists, a certain naturalistic predicate—the one that plays the relevant roles in folk morality—is equivalent to, for example, the normative predicate "right." But Nuccetelli and Seay maintain that this equivalence is subject to doubt. For one can always sensibly ask regarding any candidates for naturalistic replacement, "Are my uses of 'right' identical in content to my uses of the proposed naturalistic predicate?"

This revised formulation of the open-question argument differs from Moore's in two ways. First, since the questions are asked from the first-person perspective, the doubts raised are *a priori*. For, as Nuccetelli and Seay note, self-ascriptions of linguistic content are widely held to be independent of empirical examination. Second, unlike Moore's original version, the revised formulation seeks to show only the plausibility of believing that normative terms cannot be replaced by naturalistic terms.

In short, Nuccetelli and Seay conclude that their revised open-question argument puts the dialectical burden squarely on the shoulders of the analytical naturalist.

More than a century ago, G. E. Moore famously attempted to refute all versions of moral naturalism by offering an extended inference consisting of the open question argument followed by the charge that moral naturalism commits a "naturalistic fallacy." Although there is consensus that this extended inference fails to undermine *all* varieties of moral naturalism, the open question argument (OQA) is often vindicated as an argument against analytical moral naturalism. By contrast, the charge that analytical naturalism commits the naturalistic fallacy usually finds no takers at all. In this paper we argue that analytical naturalism of the sort recently proposed by Frank Jackson (1998, 2003) and Michael Smith (2000) does after all rest on a mistake—though perhaps not the one Moore had in mind when he made the naturalistic fallacy charge.

From Susana Nuccetelli and Gary Seay, "Does Analytical Moral Naturalism Rest on a Mistake?" in *Ethical Naturalism: Current Debates,* eds. Susana Nuccetelli and Gary Seay (Cambridge: Cambridge University Press, 2012). Reprinted by permission of the publisher.

Analytical moral naturalism is roughly the doctrine that some moral predicates and sentences are semantically equivalent to predicates and sentences framed in non-moral terms. One attraction of analytical naturalism is that it promises to deliver a naturalistic account of the content of moral judgment that leaves no ground for objections inspired by the OQA—which argues, in brief, that no matter how much purely descriptive information is available about an action, it's still an open question whether that action is right or its end good, or whether we ought to perform it. Analytical naturalism attempts to accomplish this by resorting to conceptual analysis for moral predicates and sentences. Given this doctrine, it is at least possible that there are some such a priori or conceptual equivalences. If so, it is at least possible that the moral reduces to the natural in an *a priori* or analytical way. But our version of the OQA challenges this claim by showing that the reductions envisaged by these analytical naturalists are open to doubt on a priori grounds. We further contend that, in the dialectical context created by a properly construed OQA, a "digging in the heels" defense of such reductionist strategy would in the end beg the question against the Moorean.

. . . For both Smith and Jackson, the most plausible version of ethical naturalism is analytical and has a realist gloss. It holds the conjunction of two theses:

(1) Some moral properties are identical to natural properties.

(2) Moral predicates and sentences could be replaced without significant loss by purely descriptive predicates and sentences.

. . . [E]ach of the analytical naturalists' theses entails the falsity of non-naturalism, according to which at least some moral predicates and sentences are not only *not* replaceable without significant loss by purely descriptive predicates and sentences, but express irreducible moral properties and facts.

Of concern here is a non-naturalist objection to analytical naturalism's thesis (2) standardly raised by arguments along the lines of Moore's OQA. If, as analytical naturalists contend, at least some moral predicates and sentences are conceptually equivalent to purely descriptive predicates and sentences, the possibility of replacing expressions in the moral vocabulary with purely descriptive expressions would be warranted a priori—although exactly *which* descriptive predicates and sentences might turn out to be the correct naturalistic replacements may well amount to an empirical matter of fact. . . . Jackson has it that there are a priori or conceptual entailments between moral and non-moral predicates and sentences, which follow a priori from the moral functionalist account of moral properties and facts. On his view, "[w]hat is a priori according to moral functionalism is not that rightness is such and such a descriptive property, but rather that *A* is right if and only if it has whatever property it is that plays the rightness role in mature folk morality, and it is an *a posteriori* matter what that property is" (1998: 151).

The first step in this analytical naturalist account, then, is a priori: namely, determining by analysis and reflection on our conception of certain moral predicates and sentences the conditions constraining the use of moral expressions, which would in turn constrain the naturalistic expressions that might qualify as replacements. But much of the remaining task facing the analytical naturalist is empirical, since it involves accounting for the content of moral judgment, which ultimately depends on being able to formulate correct statements of identity between expressions in both the moral and the descriptive vocabularies (Jackson 1998: 150; Smith 2000: 31). Since determining such semantic equivalences is likely to require empirical investigation and reasoned argument, there is logical space for the following reply to Moore's OQA: given that identifying the relevant semantic equivalences is not, for analytical naturalism, an obvious matter, why should we think that the question of whether a certain equivalence holds will "always and genuinely" be an open question? That is, in response to the OQA, the analytical naturalist maintains that the correct conceptual equivalences between moral and descriptive expressions need not be trivial or obvious, but could be quite complex, and in need of negotiation (Jackson 1998: 150)[1] or reasoned argument (Smith 2000: 31). Thus, if this reply is found compelling, the analytical naturalist program would appear beyond the reach of objections inspired by the OQA, none of which could therefore succeed against this version of naturalistic moral realism.

After all, Jackson seems to have a point in replying to the OQA by noticing that "it is true that a sufficiently rich descriptive story leads a priori to an act's being right; but *this will be a clear case of an unobvious a priori or conceptual entailment,* precisely because of the complexity of the moral functionalist story" (1998: 151). Likewise, according to Smith's response to the OQA, although it is an a posteriori matter *which* property plays a certain moral role, the constraints on the property that could play that role can be settled only a priori because they are to be determined either by stipulation in the act of reference-fixing itself, or by reflection on the meaning of the words (Smith 2000: 29). In many cases, coming up with the correct analysis of the relevant constraints on moral concepts would be open to "reasoned argument," and therefore might appear to be an open question. But that is simply because the task at hand is not obvious or trivial. If so, any such conceptual analysis may be correct yet open to reasoned argument. But this is only owing to the fact that its correctness does not depend on its being either open to reasoned argument or obvious. In fact, a conceptual analysis of moral concepts is likely to be open to reasoned argument about "what the complex set of constraints on the use of the word being analyzed is and whether or not this complex set is entailed by the proposed analysis" (Smith 2000: 31).

Thus there appear to be good reasons, argued independently by both Jackson and Smith, to think that the OQA has no intuitive force against the doctrine that some a priori or conceptual equivalences obtain between the building blocks of moral and purely descriptive language. Given this doctrine, other things being equal, some sentences ascribing moral predicates to actions, things, or states of affairs are content-equivalent to some sentences ascribing purely descriptive predicates instead.

Needless to say, if this is plausible, then given a common assumption about the parallel between linguistic and mental content, an analytical naturalist account of mental content along similar lines would also be plausible.

We turn now, for the remainder of this paper, to the analytical naturalist claim that some conceptual equivalences hold between *predicates* (not sentences) in the moral and non-moral vocabularies. On Smith and Jackson's account, since such equivalences are likely to be unobvious, the theory that countenances them is therefore unaffected by Moore's OQA. But we think that a modified inference, the OQA*, in fact raises a priori doubts about the analytical naturalist's claim that moral expressions such as "good," "ought," and "right" could be replaced without significant loss by predicates in a purely descriptive vocabulary. Our OQA* begins by supposing the truth of at least one such statement of equivalence. Let's suppose that the moral predicate "right" expresses a concept that is equivalent to that expressed by the purely descriptive predicate "*N,*" where "*N*" stands for whatever naturalistic predicate will turn out to denote the natural property that plays the rightness role in the ordinary conception of rightness. As far as our OQA* is concerned, what that predicate and the naturalistic property it denotes *are* could be currently under negotiation. Furthermore, these questions could end up being settled in mature folk morality, as Jackson predicts, by the convergence of our ordinary conceptions on the relevant predicates and properties.[2] Let's assume that now *N* stands for a complex (possibly infinite) disjunction where the moral predicate "right" is satisfied by action A just in case A is either utility-maximizing, or what we desire to desire, or conducive to maximal preference-satisfaction, etc.

The OQA* can now be deployed to raise a priori doubts about whether a moral predicate such as "right" is content-equivalent to a naturalistic predicate (of whatever sort). For, given this argument, the claim that "right" can be replaced without significant loss by a predicate or predicates falling within *N* seems open to doubt on a priori grounds. To support this, the OQA* first considers a certain naturalistic predicate (or predicates) that might be a candidate for replacing "right" without significant loss. It then contends that the sort of judgment involved in assessing that putative equivalence of predicates is based initially on a self-ascriptive comparative judgment of content. Judgments of that sort are plausibly regarded as a priori in the sense that their epistemic justification requires neither evidence nor inference from evidence. Clearly, if such are the grounds for doubting a proposed naturalistic replacement, that doubt would be a priori. Once OQA* makes it plausible that there are after all a priori grounds for doubting a purported naturalistic replacement for "right," the argument then maintains that its steps could be iterated for other suitable candidates for naturalistic replacement of "right"— or of "good," "ought," and the like. If this is correct, then it is open to a priori doubt whether any moral predicate could be replaced *without significant loss* by a naturalistic predicate or predicates.

Obviously, we should expect a great number of currently known and unknown candidates for naturalistic replacements of "right." Thus, perforce, the OQA*, if compelling, would render its conclusion plausible at best. To run this argument, we need not make comparative judgments of content about *every* candidate for naturalistic replacement of a moral predicate: as a plausibility argument, simply making them for a representative number of such candidates would suffice. In addition, there is plainly no need to make comparative judgments of content about a putative replacement of "right" with, say, "being a cabbage" (Parfit 2011). But we need to consider those candidates that have some chance of being naturalistic replacements of a moral predicate—for example:

Utilitarian
The moral predicate "right" can be replaced without significant loss by the purely descriptive predicate, "utility-maximizing."

An OQA* could now be deployed to raise a priori doubts about Utilitarian. For evaluating the alleged content-equivalence triggers the standard Moorean question, construed as. Is "maximizes utility" content-equivalent to "right"? To answer this

requires that one first make an a priori comparative judgment of content for both predicates, which starts out with self-ascriptive comparative judgments of content of the form: are my tokens of "M" content-equivalent to my tokens of "N"? The intuitions elicited in response to the Moorean question are initially first person, since they require that one compare one's conceptions of the content of the predicates involved. They are therefore epistemically privileged intuitions, for under normal circumstances and in the absence of evidence to the contrary, their epistemic warrant requires neither investigation of the environment nor inference from evidence—provided of course that one understands the moral and non-moral predicates involved, and has no reason to doubt that one is a competent user of them (or to think that one's intuitions about their contents are atypical and therefore irrelevant to the folk conception of them).

Similar Moorean questions could be deployed to generate parallel doubts about other putative content-equivalences. Adequate answers to such questions would, at least initially, require access only to the concepts in one's own mind, together with a priori generalizations of the resulting intuitions about sameness and difference in their content. There is now dialectical space to claim that the doubts about putative content-equivalences that such questions generate are warranted a priori: as argued above, they rely on intuitions that, under normal circumstances and in the absence of contrary evidence, require no empirical investigation (though they are defeasible by empirical evidence).[3] In addition, those intuitions seem generally true, provided there are no reasons to think that one is not competent with the concepts involved. Arguments along similar lines could be run to generate a priori doubts about other putative naturalistic equivalences of "right," "good," "ought," and the like. Since Moorean questions are likely to elicit a priori doubts for each proposed naturalistic equivalence of moral predicates, the burden is now on the analytical naturalists to produce reasons strong enough to overcome such doubts.

Construed in this way, the OQA is beyond the reach of the responses to it offered by Jackson and

Smith, given that the argument does not depend on the relevant question's being open when it is significant or not trivial (or, alternatively, closed when it is insignificant or trivial). A priori warranted claims need not be trivial: what characterizes them instead is that they can be settled without empirical investigation. The OQA* is therefore immune to Jackson and Smith's line of reply to Moorean arguments that starts out by observing something that Moore seems to have missed: namely, that a conceptual analysis could be correct but neither obvious nor trivial. In the case of the conceptual equivalences between moral and purely descriptive predicates countenanced by analytical naturalists, the Moorean question might appear open while being in fact closed. Does this challenge our argument? We think not, since we can concede the possibility that our self-ascriptive comparative judgments of content could on occasion be mistaken. Given resource limitations such as time and concentration-span, we could mistake for an open question one that is in fact closed. But the OQA* is not offered as a refutation of analytical naturalism: it's merely a plausibility argument against it, resting on well-known reasons in the literature on knowledge of content to the effect that, under normal circumstances and in the absence of evidence to the contrary, self-ascriptive comparative judgments of linguistic and mental contents depend on no empirical investigation and are generally not mistaken. We submit that there appear to be a priori grounds to doubt that purely descriptive candidates could replace moral predicates such as "right," "good," and "ought" without significant loss.

Again, our OQA* is a plausibility argument against the versions of analytical naturalism favored by Jackson and Smith, rather than a refutation of them. Although the idea of reconstructing the OQA as a plausibility argument against analytical naturalism is not new, we know of no previous attempt at grounding the openness of the Moorean question on the apriority of first-person, comparative judgments of content. Our argument may be summarized as follows:

(1) If "right" could be replaced (without significant loss) by "maximizes utility," then whether "maximizes utility" and "right" are content-equivalent is not open to doubt on a priori grounds.

(2) But whether "right" and "maximizes utility" are content-equivalent is open to doubt on a priori grounds.

Therefore,

(3) It is reasonable to believe that "right" cannot be replaced (without significant loss) by "utility-maximizing."

(4) Steps (1) through (3) can be iterated for a great number of purely descriptive replacements of "right."

Therefore,

(5) It is reasonable to believe that "right" cannot be replaced (without significant loss) by purely descriptive terms.

(6) Steps (1) through (5) can be iterated for a great number of purely descriptive replacements of "good," "ought," and other moral terms.

Therefore,

(7) It is reasonable to believe that "good," "ought," and other moral terms cannot be replaced (without significant loss) by purely descriptive terms.

We believe that the OQA* puts the burden of argument on analytical naturalism. What turns dialectical space this way is the appeal to an a priori warrant for Moorean intuitions about the failure of content-equivalence in candidates for replacement of moral terms such as Utilitarian. Given that warrant, the burden of reason rests with the analytical naturalists, who must not only make a compelling case for the possibility of their reductive analyses, but also explain away a priori doubts generated by the OQA*. Merely claiming that correct but non-trivial analyses are possible is not sufficient to overcome those doubts.

Whether moral predicates such as "right," "good," and "ought" are a priori or conceptually equivalent to some purely descriptive predicates, then, seems open to a priori doubt. We will now show that, in the dialectical context created by the OQA*, the claim that such conceptual equivalences hold amounts to a pattern of dialectical failure, which we shall call "the analytical naturalist mistake." The type of error we have in mind is a dialectical phenomenon of failure that Moore would perhaps have done better to point out rather than raise the naturalistic fallacy charge against. In fact, our account of what has gone wrong with the analytical naturalists' defense of their reductive program can make sense of Moore's confused remarks about the naturalistic fallacy in chapter 1 of *Principia Ethica* (1903: section 12). Although his claim to have found a special type of *fallacy* identifiable as "naturalistic" may well be unjustifiable, his skepticism about certain analyses of ethical naturalists—as well as of other analyses featuring only purely natural terms, or where one term is ethical and the other metaphysical—might be justified on different grounds. Surely we are entitled to be suspicious of any conceptual equivalence whose proponent is unable to overcome a priori doubts about that equivalence. Interpreted in this way, Moore was clearly right in criticizing *"Pleasant* is the sensation of red" and *"Goodness* is what's commanded by God." Likewise, we are entitled to reject attempted definitions which, in the context of a certain debate, are dialectically abusive in some sense—as in the rather obvious case where abortion is defined as "a form of infanticide," or "a killing of an unborn baby." Plainly, in the context of the debate over the moral status of abortion, the claim that "killing fetuses" and "killing babies" are conceptually equivalent could not overcome a priori doubts raised by an OQA-inspired objector.

On our view, the analytical naturalist commits a parallel dialectical mistake. For he maintains that, once all negotiations about the content and reference of moral predicates such as "right," "good," and "ought" are settled (allegedly by convergence of individual conceptions), those predicates will turn out

to be equivalent to certain purely descriptive predicates. By advocating such equivalences, he presupposes that he has some evidence or some reason to dismiss the a priori doubts arising from a properly construed OQA. As mentioned above, he dismisses Moore's OQA on the grounds that a conceptual equivalence could be correct but not trivial or in need of reasoned argument. But that is not an objection to OQA*, whose Moorean question suggests that, for all we can tell now, at least from the first-person perspective, moral predicates do not seem conceptually equivalent to purely descriptive predicates. Thus, the analytical dialectical mistake is simply that of begging the question against a great number of philosophers, from non-naturalists to moral nihilists, who have found some version of the OQA persuasive. In the end, analytical naturalism might turn out to be true, but analytical naturalists must first discharge the burden of reason—which involves producing evidence or reasons that have enough force to overcome OQA*—inspired a priori doubts about the possibility of the proposed reductive program. Until then, non-naturalists and moral nihilists . . . confronted with this sort of tactic in metaethical debate can dismiss the analytical naturalist proposal by simply showing that it begs the question against reasoning along the lines of OQA*.

On our view, this is what Moore should have said on the question of where analytical naturalism goes wrong. Recognizing occurrences of the analytical naturalist mistake has a more modest cash value than Moore's original naturalistic fallacy charge, since we do not claim to have thereby refuted even the analytical variety of moral naturalism. We merely think that such recognition puts the onus on those favoring analytical naturalism to provide independent reasons that are strong enough to explain away a priori doubts about the possibility of replacing moral predicates such as "right," "good," and "ought" with purely descriptive predicates without significant loss.

Our account has the consequence that, rather than its being Moore's argument that begs the question . . ., it is actually the reductive program of semantic naturalists that begs the question against the Moorean inference. But, then, why has that inference been thought by many to amount to nothing more than a *petitio*? For one thing, critics may have been misled by Moore's own inflationary view about the number of reductive programs that have committed what for him appears to be an actual fallacy. As we have seen, he did claim to have found the fallacy in the work of many philosophers and social scientists, including controversial cases such as that of J. S. Mill. In addition, he seems to have conflated analytical and non-analytical varieties of ethical naturalism, charging that they *all* committed the alleged fallacy.

On the other hand, it must be acknowledged that critics have not always given the most charitable reading to Moore's inference. They have notoriously evaluated the naturalistic fallacy charge in isolation from its dialectical context, which is an OQA properly construed as a plausibility argument against analytical versions of moral naturalism. Moreover, even if it makes no sense to charge that such theories commit a naturalistic fallacy, our contention has been that they do seem to rest on a mistake akin to the broader dialectical phenomenon of begging the question.

Let us now take stock of our version of Moore's extended inference. We have argued that OQA*, construed as a plausibility argument, is nonetheless strong enough to generate a priori doubts about the possibility of replacing moral predicates with purely descriptive predicates without significant loss. If we are right, then the reductive program of analytical naturalists such as Jackson and Smith does instantiate a pattern of dialectical mistake: one committed by any argumentative strategy that assumes the possibility of conceptual equivalences that are in fact open to doubt on a priori grounds. As a result, no such strategy could be cogent. A Moorean inference is thus shown to have some force against attempts to reduce the moral to the non-moral by means of taking some expressions in

the moral vocabulary to be conceptually equivalent to others in a purely descriptive vocabulary.

NOTES

1. In rejecting the OQA, Jackson writes, "[W]hat exactly is supposed to be always and genuinely an open question? Any and every identification of rightness, say, with some descriptive property? But this claim could be no objection to moral functionalist styles of analytical descriptivism. The identifications of ethical properties with descriptive properties offered by moral functionalism are one and all a posteriori" (1998: 150). See also Jackson (1998: 145, n. 10).

2. On the issue of how the alleged equivalences between moral and non-moral expressions are going to be settled, Jackson seems confident that this will be the outcome of a mature folk morality. Smith is similarly optimistic in holding that, at the end of the day, there will be convergence in reasoned argument about the a priori constraints that govern the ordinary conception of some moral terms. . . .

3. On our view, comparative judgments of content are a priori warranted, in the sense of being non-evidential. They might also be generally true, provided the thinker is a competent user of the concepts involved. . . .

REFERENCES

Jackson, F. 1998. *From Metaphysics to Ethics: A Defence of Conceptual Analysis.* Oxford: Clarendon Press.
——— 2003. "Cognitivism, A Priori Deduction, and Moore." Ethics 3:557–75.
Moore, G. E. 1903. *Principia Ethica.* Cambridge University Press.
Parfit, D. 2011. *On What Matters.* Oxford University Press.
Smith, M. 2000. "Moral Realism." In H. LaFollette (ed.), The Blackwell Guide to Ethical Theory. Oxford: Blackwell, 15–37.

STUDY QUESTIONS

1. Could "right" be replaced, without loss, by "maximizes utility"?
2. Could self-ascriptive judgments of linguistic content be mistaken?
3. In what ways does Nuccetelli and Seay's version of the open-question argument differ from Moore's?
4. According to Nuccetelli and Seay, what mistake is made by analytical naturalists?

Part IV

NON-COGNITIVISM

Language, Truth, and Logic

A. J. Ayer

A state of mind is cognitive if it involves beliefs. But perhaps our normative thoughts are not cognitive. Those who maintain this view, so-called non-cognitivists, argue that when we say "lying is wrong," we are not stating a belief but, instead, expressing a negative emotion about lying.

Alfred Jules Ayer (1910–1989) was Wykeham Professor of Logic at the University of Oxford. He argues that because ethical judgments are not empirically verifiable, they are neither true nor false. When we add a normative word to an utterance, we do not change what the utterance is about but, instead, add the equivalent of an exclamation point. Thus, according to Ayer, when we say that "lying is wrong," we are actually saying "lying—boo!"

There is still one objection to be met before we can claim to have justified our view that all synthetic propositions are empirical hypotheses. This objection is based on the common supposition that our speculative knowledge is of two distinct kinds—that which relates to questions of empirical fact, and that which relates to questions of value. It will be said that "statements of value" are genuine synthetic propositions, but that they cannot with any show of justice be represented as hypotheses, which are used to predict the course of our sensations; and, accordingly, that the existence of ethics and aesthetics as branches of speculative knowledge presents an insuperable objection to our radical empiricist thesis.

In face of this objection, it is our business to give an account of "judgments of value" which is both satisfactory in itself and consistent with our general empiricist principles. We shall set ourselves to show that in so far as statements of value are significant, they are ordinary "scientific" statements; and that in so far as they are not scientific, they are not in the literal sense significant, but are simply expressions of emotion which can be neither true nor false. In maintaining this view, we may confine ourselves for the present to the case of ethical statements. What is said about them will be found to apply, *mutatis mutandis,* to the case of aesthetic statements also.

The ordinary system of ethics, as elaborated in the works of ethical philosophers, is very far from being a homogeneous whole. Not only is it apt to contain pieces of metaphysics, and analyses of non-ethical concepts: its actual ethical contents are themselves of very different kinds. We may divide them, indeed, into four main classes. There are, first of all, propositions which express definitions of ethical terms, or judgments about the legitimacy or possibility of certain definitions. Secondly, there are

From A. J. Ayer, *Language, Truth, and Logic* (New York: Dover Publications, 1952). Reprinted by permission of the publisher.

propositions describing the phenomena of moral experience, and their causes. Thirdly, there are exhortations to moral virtue. And, lastly, there are actual ethical judgments. It is unfortunately the case that the distinction between these four classes, plain as it is, is commonly ignored by ethical philosophers; with the result that it is often very difficult to tell from their works what it is that they are seeking to discover or prove.

In fact, it is easy to see that only the first of our four classes, namely that which comprises the propositions relating to the definitions of ethical terms, can be said to constitute ethical philosophy. The propositions which describe the phenomena of moral experience, and their causes, must be assigned to the science of psychology, or sociology. The exhortations to moral virtue are not propositions at all, but ejaculations or commands which are designed to provoke the reader to action of a certain sort. Accordingly, they do not belong to any branch of philosophy or science. As for the expressions of ethical judgments, we have not yet determined how they should be classified. But inasmuch as they are certainly neither definitions nor comments upon definitions, nor quotations, we may say decisively that they do not belong to ethical philosophy. A strictly philosophical treatise on ethics should therefore make no ethical pronouncements. But it should, by giving an analysis of ethical terms, show what is the category to which all such pronouncements belong. And this is what we are now about to do.

A question which is often discussed by ethical philosophers is whether it is possible to find definitions which would reduce all ethical terms to one or two fundamental terms. But this question, though it undeniably belongs to ethical philosophy, is not relevant to our present enquiry. We are not now concerned to discover which term, within the sphere of ethical terms, is to be taken as fundamental; whether, for example, "good" can be defined in terms of "right" or "right" in terms of "good," or both in terms of "value." What we are interested in is the possibility of reducing the whole sphere of ethical terms to non-ethical terms. We are enquiring whether statements of ethical value can be translated into statements of empirical fact.

That they can be so translated is the contention of those ethical philosophers who are commonly called subjectivists, and of those who are known as utilitarians. For the utilitarian defines the rightness of actions, and the goodness of ends, in terms of the pleasure, or happiness, or satisfaction, to which they give rise; the subjectivist, in terms of the feelings of approval which a certain person, or group of people, has towards them. Each of these types of definition makes moral judgments into a sub-class of psychological or sociological judgments; and for this reason they are very attractive to us. For, if either was correct, it would follow that ethical assertions were not generically different from the factual assertions which are ordinarily contrasted with them; and the account which we have already given of empirical hypotheses would apply to them also.

Nevertheless we shall not adopt either a subjectivist or a utilitarian analysis of ethical terms. We reject the subjectivist view that to call an action right, or a thing good, is to say that it is generally approved of, because it is not self-contradictory to assert that some actions which are generally approved of are not right, or that some things which are generally approved of are not good. And we reject the alternative subjectivist view that a man who asserts that a certain action is right, or that a certain thing is good, is saying that he himself approves of it, on the ground that a man who confessed that he sometimes approved of what was bad or wrong would not be contradicting himself. And a similar argument is fatal to utilitarianism. We cannot agree that to call an action right is to say that of all the actions possible in the circumstances it would cause, or be likely to cause, the greatest happiness, or the greatest balance of pleasure over pain, or the greatest balance of satisfied over unsatisfied desire, because we find that it is not self-contradictory to say that it is sometimes wrong to perform the action which would actually or probably cause the greatest happiness, or the greatest balance of pleasure over pain, or of satisfied over unsatisfied desire. And since it is not self-contradictory to say that some pleasant things are not good, or that some bad things are desired, it cannot be the case that the sentence "x is good" is equivalent to "x is pleasant," or to "x is desired." And to every other variant of utilitarianism with which I am acquainted the same objection can be made. And therefore we should, I think, conclude that the validity of ethical judgments is not determined by the felicific tendencies of actions, any more than by the nature of people's feelings; but that it must be regarded as "absolute" or "intrinsic," and not empirically calculable.

If we say this, we are not, of course, denying that it is possible to invent a language in which all ethical symbols are definable in non-ethical terms, or even that it is desirable to invent such a language and adopt it in place of our own; what we are denying is that the suggested reduction of ethical to non-ethical statements is consistent with the conventions of our actual language. That is, we reject utilitarianism and subjectivism, not as proposals to replace our existing ethical notions by new ones, but as analyses of our existing ethical notions. Our contention is simply that, in our language, sentences which contain normative ethical symbols are not equivalent to sentences which express psychological propositions, or indeed empirical propositions of any kind.

It is advisable here to make it plain that it is only normative ethical symbols, and not descriptive ethical symbols, that are held by us to be indefinable in factual terms. There is a danger of confusing these two types of symbols, because they are commonly constituted by signs of the same sensible form. Thus a complex sign of the form "*x* is wrong" may constitute a sentence which expresses a moral judgment concerning a certain type of conduct, or it may constitute a sentence which states that a certain type of conduct is repugnant to the moral sense of a particular society. In the latter case, the symbol "wrong" is a descriptive ethical symbol, and the sentence in which it occurs expresses an ordinary sociological proposition; in the former case, the symbol "wrong" is a normative ethical symbol, and the sentence in which it occurs does not, we maintain, express an empirical proposition at all. It is only with normative ethics that we are at present concerned; so that whenever ethical symbols are used in the course of this argument without qualification, they are always to be interpreted as symbols of the normative type.

In admitting that normative ethical concepts are irreducible to empirical concepts, we seem to be leaving the way clear for the "absolutist" view of ethics—that is, the view that statements of value are not controlled by observation, as ordinary empirical propositions are, but only by a mysterious "intellectual intuition." A feature of this theory, which is seldom recognized by its advocates, is that it makes statements of value unverifiable. For it is notorious that what seems intuitively certain to one person may seem doubtful, or even false, to another. So that unless it is possible to provide some criterion by which one may decide between conflicting intuitions, a mere appeal to intuition is worthless as a test of a proposition's validity. But in the case of moral judgments, no such criterion can be given. Some moralists claim to settle the matter by saying that they "know" that their own moral judgments are correct. But such an assertion is of purely psychological interest, and has not the slightest tendency to prove the validity of any moral judgment. For dissentient moralists may equally well "know" that their ethical views are correct. And, as far as subjective certainty goes, there will be nothing to choose between them. When such differences of opinion arise in connection with an ordinary empirical proposition, one may attempt to resolve them by referring to, or actually carrying out, some relevant empirical test. But with regard to ethical statements, there is, on the "absolutist" or "intuitionist" theory, no relevant empirical test. We are therefore justified in saying that on this theory ethical statements are held to be unverifiable. They are, of course, also held to be genuine synthetic propositions.

Considering the use which we have made of the principle that a synthetic proposition is significant only if it is empirically verifiable, it is clear that the acceptance of an "absolutist" theory of ethics would undermine the whole of our main argument. And as we have already rejected the "naturalistic" theories which are commonly supposed to provide the only alternative to "absolutism" in ethics, we seem to have reached a difficult position. We shall meet the difficulty by showing that the correct treatment of ethical statements is afforded by a third theory, which is wholly compatible with our radical empiricism.

We begin by admitting that the fundamental ethical concepts are unanalyzable, inasmuch as there is no criterion by which one can test the validity of the judgments in which they occur. So far we are in agreement with the absolutists. But, unlike the absolutists, we are able to give an explanation of this fact about ethical concepts. We say that the reason why they are unanalyzable is that they are mere pseudo-concepts. The presence of an ethical symbol in a proposition adds nothing to its factual content. Thus if I say to someone, "You acted wrongly in stealing that money," I am not stating anything more than if I had simply said, "You stole that money." In adding that this action is wrong I am not making any further statement about it. I am simply evincing my moral disapproval of it. It is as if I had said, "You stole that money," in a peculiar tone of horror, or written it with the addition of some special exclamation marks. The tone, or the exclamation marks, adds nothing to the literal meaning of the sentence. It merely serves to show that the expression of it is attended by certain feelings in the speaker.

If now I generalize my previous statement and say, "Stealing money is wrong," I produce a sentence which has no factual meaning—that is, expresses no proposition which can be either true or false. It is as if I had written "Stealing money!!"—where the shape and thickness of the exclamation marks show, by a suitable convention, that a special sort of moral disapproval is the feeling which is being expressed. It is clear that there is nothing said here which can be true or false. Another man may disagree with me about the wrongness of stealing, in the sense that he may not have the same feelings about stealing as I have, and he may quarrel with me on account of my moral sentiments. But he cannot, strictly speaking, contradict me. For in saying that a certain type of action is right or wrong. I am not making any factual statement, not even a statement about my own state of mind, I am merely expressing certain moral sentiments. And the man who is ostensibly contradicting me is merely expressing his moral sentiments. So that there is plainly no sense in asking which of us is the right. For neither of us is asserting a genuine proposition.

What we have just been saying about the symbol "wrong" applies to all normative ethical symbols.

Sometimes they occur in sentences which record ordinary empirical facts besides expressing ethical feeling about those facts: sometimes they occur in sentences which simply express ethical feeling about a certain type of action, or situation, without making any statement of fact. But in every case in which one would commonly be said to be making an ethical judgment, the function of the relevant ethical word is purely "emotive." It is used to express feeling about certain objects, but not to make any assertion about them.

It is worth mentioning that ethical terms do not serve only to express feeling. They are calculated also to arouse feeling, and so to stimulate action. Indeed some of them are used in such a way as to give the sentences in which they occur the effect of commands. Thus the sentence "It is your duty to tell the truth" may be regarded both as the expression of a certain sort of ethical feeling about truthfulness and as the expression of the command "Tell the truth." The sentence "You ought to tell the truth" also involves the command "Tell the truth," but here the tone of the command is less emphatic. In the sentence "It is good to tell the truth" the command has become little more than a suggestion. And thus the "meaning" of the word "good," in its ethical usage, is differentiated from that of the word "duty" or the word "ought." In fact we may define the meaning of the various ethical words in terms both of the different feelings they are ordinarily taken to express, and also the different responses which they are calculated to provoke.

We can now see why it is impossible to find a criterion for determining the validity of ethical judgments. It is not because they have an "absolute" validity which is mysteriously independent of ordinary sense-experience, but because they have no objective validity whatsoever. If a sentence makes no statement at all, there is obviously no sense in asking whether what it says is true or false. And we have seen that sentences which simply express moral judgments do not say anything. They are pure expressions of feeling and as such do not come under the category of truth and falsehood. They are unverifiable for the same reason as a cry of pain or a word of command is unverifiable—because they do not express genuine propositions.

Thus, although our theory of ethics might fairly be said to be radically subjectivist, it differs in a very important respect from the orthodox subjectivist theory. For the orthodox subjectivist does not deny, as we do, that the sentences of a moralizer express genuine propositions. All he denies is that they express propositions of a unique non-empirical character. His own view is that they express propositions about the speaker's feelings. If this were so, ethical judgments clearly would be capable of being true or false. They would be true if the speaker had the relevant feelings, and false if he had not. And this is a matter which is, in principle, empirically verifiable. Furthermore they could be significantly contradicted. For if I say, "Tolerance is a virtue," and someone answers, "You don't approve of it," he would, on the ordinary subjectivist theory, be contradicting me. On our theory, he would not be contradicting me, because, in saying that tolerance was a virtue, I should not be making any statement about my own feelings or about anything else. I should simply be evincing my feelings, which is not at all the same thing as saying that I have them.

The distinction between the expression of feeling and the assertion of feeling is complicated by the fact that the assertion that one has a certain feeling often accompanies the expression of that feeling, and is then, indeed, a factor in the expression of that feeling. Thus I may simultaneously express boredom and say that I am bored, and in that case my utterance of the words, "I am bored," is one of the circumstances which make it true to say that I am expressing or evincing boredom. But I can express boredom without actually saying that I am bored. I can express it by my tone and gestures, while making a statement about something wholly unconnected with it, or by an ejaculation, or without uttering any words at all. So that even if the assertion that one has a certain feeling always involves the expression of that feeling, the expression of a feeling assuredly does not always involve the assertion that one has it. And this is the important point to grasp in considering the distinction between our theory and the ordinary subjectivist theory. For whereas the subjectivist holds that ethical statements actually assert the existence of certain feelings, we hold that ethical statements are expressions and excitants of feeling which do not necessarily involve any assertions.

We have already remarked that the main objection to the ordinary subjectivist theory is that the validity of ethical judgments is not determined by the nature of their author's feelings. And this is an objection which our theory escapes. For it does not imply that the existence of any feelings is a necessary and sufficient condition of the validity of an ethical judgment. It implies, on the contrary, that ethical judgments have no validity.

There is, however, a celebrated argument against subjectivist theories which our theory does not escape. It has been pointed out by Moore that if ethical statements were simply statements about the speaker's feelings, it would be impossible to argue about questions of value. To take a typical example: if a man said that thrift was a virtue, and another replied that it was a vice, they would not, on this theory, be disputing with one another. One would be saying that he approved of thrift, and the other that *he* didn't; and there is no reason why both these statements should not be true. Now Moore held it to be obvious that we do dispute about questions of value, and accordingly concluded that the particular form of subjectivism which he was discussing was false.

It is plain that the conclusion that it is impossible to dispute about questions of value follows from our theory also. For as we hold that such sentences as "Thrift is a virtue" and "Thrift is a vice" do not express propositions at all, we clearly cannot hold that they express incompatible propositions. We must therefore admit that if Moore's argument really refutes the ordinary subjectivist theory, it also refutes ours. But, in fact, we deny that it does refute even the ordinary subjectivist theory. For we hold that one really never does dispute about questions of value.

This may seem, at first sight, to be a very paradoxical assertion. For we certainly do engage in disputes which are ordinarily regarded as disputes about questions of value. But, in all such cases, we find, if we consider the matter closely, that the dispute is not really about a question of value, but about a question of fact. When someone disagrees with us about the moral value of a certain action or type of action, we do admittedly resort to argument in order to win him over to our way of thinking. But we do not attempt to show by our arguments that he has the "wrong" ethical feeling towards a situation whose nature he has correctly apprehended. What we attempt to show is that he is mistaken about the facts of the case. We argue that he has misconceived the agent's motive: or that he has misjudged the effects of the action, or its probable effects in view of the agent's knowledge; or that he has failed to take into account the special circumstances in which the agent was placed. Or else we employ more general arguments about the effects which actions of a certain type tend to produce, or the qualities which are usually manifested in their performance. We do this in the hope that we have only to get our opponent to agree with us about the nature of the empirical facts for him to adopt the same moral attitude towards them as we do. And as the people with whom we argue have generally received the same moral education as ourselves, and live in the same social order, our expectation is usually justified. But if our opponent happens to have undergone a different process of moral "conditioning" from ourselves, so that, even when he acknowledges all the facts, he still disagrees with us about the moral value of the actions under discussion, then we abandon the attempt to convince him by argument. We say that it is impossible to argue with him because he has a distorted or undeveloped moral sense; which signifies merely that he employs a different set of values from our own. We feel that our own system of values is superior, and therefore speak in such derogatory terms of his. But we cannot bring forward any arguments to show that our system is superior. For our judgment that it is so is itself a judgment of value, and accordingly outside the scope of argument. It is because argument fails us when we come to deal with pure questions of value, as distinct from questions of fact, that we finally resort to mere abuse.

In short, we find that argument is possible on moral questions only if some system of values is presupposed. If our opponent concurs with us in expressing moral disapproval of all actions of a given type *t,* then we may get him to condemn a particular action A, bringing forward arguments to show that A is of type *t.* For the question whether A does or does not belong to that type is a plain question of fact. Given that a man has certain moral principles, we argue that he must, in order to be consistent, react morally to certain things in a certain way. What we do not and cannot argue about is the validity of these moral principles. We merely praise or condemn them in the light of our own feelings.

If anyone doubts the accuracy of this account of moral disputes, let him try to construct even an imaginary argument on a question of value which does not reduce itself to an argument about a question of logic or about an empirical matter of fact. I am confident that he will not succeed in producing a single example. And if that is the case, he must allow that its involving the impossibility of purely ethical arguments is not, as Moore thought, a ground of objection to our theory, but rather a point in favor of it.

Having upheld our theory against the only criticism which appeared to threaten it, we may now use it to define the nature of all ethical enquiries. We find that ethical philosophy consists simply in saying that ethical concepts are pseudo-concepts and therefore unanalyzable. The further task of describing the different feelings that the different ethical terms are used to express, and the different reactions that they customarily provoke, is a task for the psychologist. There cannot be such a thing as ethical science, if by ethical science one means the elaboration of a "true" system of morals. For we have seen that, as ethical judgments are mere expressions of feeling, there can be no way of determining the validity of any ethical system, and, indeed, no sense in asking whether any such system is true. All that one may legitimately enquire in this connection is, What are the moral habits of a given person or group of people, and what causes them to have precisely those habits and feelings? And this enquiry falls wholly within the scope of the existing social sciences.

It appears, then, that ethics, as a branch of knowledge, is nothing more than a department of psychology and sociology. And in case anyone thinks that we are overlooking the existence of casuistry, we may remark that casuistry is not a science, but is a purely analytical investigation of the structure of a given moral system. In other words, it is an exercise in formal logic.

When one comes to pursue the psychological enquiries which constitute ethical science, one is immediately enabled to account for the Kantian and hedonistic theories of morals. For one finds that one of the chief causes of moral behavior is fear, both conscious and unconscious, of a god's displeasure, and fear of the enmity of society. And this, indeed, is the reason why moral precepts present themselves to some people as "categorical" commands. And one finds, also, that the moral code of a society is partly determined by the beliefs of that society concerning the conditions of its own happiness—or, in other words, that a society tends to encourage or discourage a given type of conduct by the use of moral sanctions according as it appears to promote or detract from the contentment of the society as a whole. And this is the reason why altruism is recommended in most moral codes and egotism condemned. It is from the observation of this connection between morality and happiness that hedonistic or eudaemonistic theories of morals ultimately spring, just as the moral theory of Kant is based on the fact, previously explained, that moral precepts have for some people the force of inexorable commands. As each of these theories ignores the fact which lies at the root of the other, both may be criticized as being one-sided; but this is not the main objection to either of them. Their essential defect is that they treat propositions which refer to the causes and attributes of our ethical feelings as if they were definitions of ethical concepts. And thus they fail to recognize that ethical concepts are pseudo-concepts and consequently indefinable. . . .

STUDY QUESTIONS

1. According to emotivism, do those who say stealing is wrong thereby say that they disapprove of stealing?
2. According to Ayer, why are moral judgments unanalyzable?
3. According to Ayer, is argument over moral issues possible?
4. Can emotivists believe your moral judgments are wrong?

The Emotive Meaning of Ethical Terms

C. L. Stevenson

Charles Leslie Stevenson (1908–1979) was Professor of Philosophy at the University of Michigan. He argues that disagreements about value, while often having a factual component, are fundamentally disagreements in attitude, with each individual seeking to persuade others to share an interest. Thus, for Stevenson, unlike Ayer, normative talk is about something. It has an emotive meaning expressing approval or disapproval and seeking to influence the feelings of others. In short, when we say "lying is bad," we are really saying "I disapprove of lying, and you should also."

I

Ethical questions first arise in the form "Is so and so good?", or "Is this alternative better than that?" These questions are difficult partly because we don't quite know what we are seeking. We are asking, "Is there a needle in that haystack?" without even knowing just what a needle is. So the first thing to do is to examine the questions themselves. We must try to make them clearer, either by defining the terms in which they are expressed, or by any other method that is available.

The present paper is concerned wholly with this preliminary step of making ethical questions clear. In order to help answer the question "Is X good?" we must *substitute* for it a question which is free from ambiguity and confusion.

It is obvious that in substituting a clearer question we must not introduce some utterly different kind of question. It won't do (to take an extreme instance of a prevalent fallacy) to substitute for "Is X good?" the question "Is X pink with yellow trimmings?" and then point out how easy the question really is. This would beg the original question, not help answer it. On the other hand, we must not expect the substituted question to be strictly "identical" with the original one. The original question may embody hypostatization, anthropomorphism, vagueness, and all the other ills to which our ordinary discourse is subject. If our substituted question is to be clearer, it must remove these ills. The questions will be identical only in the sense that a child is identical with the man he later becomes. Hence we must not demand that the substitution strike us, on immediate introspection, as making no change in meaning.

Just how, then, must the substituted question be related to the original? Let us assume (inaccurately) that it must result from replacing "good" by some set of terms which define it. The question then resolves itself to this: How must the defined meaning of "good" be related to its original meaning?

I answer that it must be *relevant*. A defined meaning will be called "relevant" to the original

From C. L. Stevenson, "The Emotive Meaning of Ethical Terms," *Mind* 46 (1937). Reprinted by permission of the publisher.

meaning under these circumstances: Those who have understood the definition must be able to say all that they then want to say by using the term in the defined way. They must never have occasion to use the term in the old, unclear sense. (If a person did have to go on using the word in the old sense, then to this extent his meaning would not be clarified, and the philosophical task would not be completed.) It frequently happens that a word is used so confusedly and ambiguously that we must give it *several* defined meanings, rather than one. In this case only the whole set of defined meanings will be called "relevant," and any one of them will be called "partially relevant." This is not a rigorous treatment of *relevance,* by any means; but it will serve for the present purposes.

Let us now turn to our particular task—that of giving a relevant definition of "good." Let us first examine some of the ways in which others have attempted to do this.

The word "good" has often been defined in terms of *approval,* or similar psychological attitudes. We may take as typical examples: "good" means *desired by me* (Hobbes); and "good" means *approved by most people* (Hume, in effect). It will be convenient to refer to definitions of this sort as "interest theories," following Mr. R. B. Perry, although neither "interest" nor "theory" is used in the most usual way.

Are definitions of this sort relevant?

It is idle to deny their *partial* relevance. The most superficial inquiry will reveal that "good" is exceedingly ambiguous. To maintain that "good" is *never* used in Hobbes's sense, and never in Hume's, is only to manifest an insensitivity to the complexities of language. We must recognize, perhaps, not only these senses, but a variety of similar ones, differing both with regard to the kind of interest in question, and with regard to the people who are said to have the interest.

But this is a minor matter. The essential question is not whether interest theories are *partially* relevant, but whether they are *wholly* relevant. This is the only point for intelligent dispute. Briefly; Granted that some senses of "good" may relevantly be defined in terms of interest, is there some *other*

sense which is not relevantly so defined? We must give this question careful attention. For it is quite possible that when philosophers (and many others) have found the question "Is X good?" so difficult, they have been grasping for this *other* sense of "good." and not any sense relevantly defined in terms of interest. If we insist on defining "good" in terms of interest, and answer the question when thus interpreted, we may be begging *their* question entirely. Of course this *other* sense of "good" may not exist, or it may be a complete confusion; but that is what we must discover.

Now many have maintained that interest theories are *far* from being completely relevant. They have argued that such theories neglect the very sense of "good" which is most vital. And certainly, their arguments are not without plausibility.

Only . . . what *is* this "vital" sense of "good"? The answers have been so vague, and so beset with difficulties, that one can scarcely determine.

There are certain requirements, however, with which this "vital" sense has been expected to comply—requirements which appeal strongly to our common sense. It will be helpful to summarize these, showing how they exclude the interest theories:

In the first place, we must be able sensibly to *disagree* about whether something is "good." This condition rules out Hobbes's definition. For consider the following argument: "This is good." "That isn't so; it's not good." As translated by Hobbes, this becomes: "I desire this." "That isn't so, for *I* don't." The speakers are not contradicting one another, and think they are, only because of an elementary confusion in the use of pronouns. The definition, "good" means *desired by my community,* is also excluded, for how could people from different communities disagree?[1]

In the second place, "goodness" must have, so to speak, a magnetism. A person who recognizes X to be "good" must *ipso facto* acquire a stronger tendency to act in its favor than he otherwise would have had. This rules out the Humean type of definition. For according to Hume, to recognize that something is "good" is simply to recognize that the majority approve of it. Clearly, a man may see that the majority approve of X without having, himself, a stronger tendency to favor it. This requirement excludes any attempt to define "good" in terms of the interest of people *other* than the speaker.[2]

In the third place, the "goodness" of anything must not be verifiable solely by use of the scientific method. "Ethics must not be psychology." This restriction rules out all of the traditional interest theories, without exception. It is so sweeping a restriction that we must examine its plausibility. What are the methodological implications of interest theories which are here rejected?

According to Hobbes's definition, a person can prove his ethical judgments, with finality, by showing that he is not making an introspective error about his desires. According to Hume's definition, one may prove ethical judgments (roughly speaking) by taking a vote. *This* use of the empirical method, at any rate, seems highly remote from what we usually accept as proof, and reflects on the complete relevance of the definitions which imply it.

But aren't there more complicated interest theories which are immune from such methodological implications? No, for the same factors appear; they are only put off for a while. Consider, for example, the definition: "X is good" means most *people would approve of X if they knew its nature and consequences.* How, according to this definition, could we prove that a certain X was good? We should first have to find out, empirically, just what X was like, and what its consequences would be. To this extent the empirical method, as required by the definition, seems beyond intelligent objection. But what remains? We should next have to discover whether most people would approve of the sort of thing we had discovered X to be. This couldn't be determined by popular vote—but only because it would be too difficult to explain to the voters, beforehand, what the nature and consequences of X really were. Apart from this, voting would be a pertinent method. We are again reduced to counting noses, as a *perfectly final* appeal.

Now we need not scorn voting entirely. A man who rejected interest theories as irrelevant might readily make the following statement: "If I believed that X would be approved by the majority, when they knew all about it. I should be strongly *led* to say that X was good." But he would continue: *"Need* I say that X was good, under the circumstances? Wouldn't my acceptance of the alleged 'final proof' result simply from my being democratic? What about the more aristocratic people? They would simply say that the approval of most people, even when they knew all about the object of their approval, simply had nothing to do with the goodness of anything, and they would probably add a few remarks about the low state of people's interests." It would indeed seem, from these considerations, that the definition we have been considering has presupposed democratic ideals from the start; it has dressed up democratic propaganda in the guise of a definition.

The omnipotence of the empirical method, as implied by interest theories and others, may be shown unacceptable in a somewhat different way. Mr. G. E. Moore's familiar objection about the open question is chiefly pertinent in this regard. No matter what set of scientifically knowable properties a thing may have (says Moore, in effect), you will find, on careful introspection, that it is an open question to ask whether anything having these properties is *good.* It is difficult to believe that this recurrent question is a totally confused one, or that it seems open only because of the ambiguity of "good." Rather, we must be using some sense of "good" which is not definable, relevantly, in terms of anything scientifically knowable. That is, the scientific method is not sufficient for ethics.[3]

These, then, are the requirements with which the "vital" sense of "good" is expected to comply: (1) goodness must be a topic for intelligent disagreement; (2) it must be "magnetic"; and (3) it must not be discoverable solely through the scientific method.

II

Let us now turn to my own analysis of ethical judgments. First let me present my position dogmatically, showing to what extent I vary from tradition.

I believe that the three requirements, given above, are perfectly sensible; that there is some *one* sense of "good" which satisfies all three requirements; and that no traditional interest theory satisfies them all. But this does not imply that "good" must be explained in terms of a Platonic Idea, or of a Categorical Imperative, or of an unique, unanalyzable property. On the contrary, the three requirements can be met by a *kind* of interest theory. *But we must give up a presupposition which all the traditional interest theories have made.*

Traditional interest theories hold that ethical statements are *descriptive* of the existing state of interests—that they simply *give information* about interests. (More accurately, ethical judgments are said to describe what the state of interests is, was, or will be, or to indicate what the state of interests *would* be under specified circumstances.) It is this emphasis on description, on information, which leads to their incomplete relevance. Doubtless there is always *some* elements of description in ethical judgments, but this is by no means all. Their major use is not to indicate facts, but to *create an influence.* Instead of merely describing people's interests, they *change* or *intensify* them. They *recommend* an interest in an object, rather than state that the interest already exists.

For instance: When you tell a man that he oughtn't to steal, your object isn't merely to let him know that people disapprove of stealing. You are attempting, rather, to get *him* to disapprove of it. Your ethical judgment has a quasi-imperative force which, operating through suggestion, and intensified by your tone of voice, readily permits you to begin to *influence,* to *modify,* his interests. If in the end you do not succeed in getting *him* to disapprove of stealing, you will feel that you've failed to convince him that stealing is wrong. You will continue to feel this, even though he fully acknowledges that you disapprove of it, and that almost everyone else does. When you point out to him the consequences of his actions—consequences which you suspect he already disapproves of—these *reasons* which support your ethical judgment are simply a means of facilitating your influence. If you think you can change his interests by making vivid to him how others will disapprove of him, you will do so; otherwise not. So the consideration about other people's interest is just an additional means you may employ, in order to

move him, and is not a part of the ethical judgment itself. Your ethical judgment doesn't merely describe interests to him, it directs his very interests. The difference between the traditional interest theories and my view is like the difference between describing a desert and irrigating it.

Another example: A munition maker declares that war is a good thing. If he merely meant that he approved of it, he would not have to insist so strongly, nor grow so excited in his argument. People would be quite easily convinced that he approved of it. If he merely meant that most people approved of war, or that most people would approve of it if they knew the consequences, he would have to yield his point if it were proved that this wasn't so. But he wouldn't do this, nor does consistency require it. He is not *describing* the state of people's approval; he is trying to *change* it by his influence. If he found that few people approved of war, he might insist all the more strongly that it was good, for there would be more changing to be done.

This example illustrates how "good" may be used for what most of us would call bad purposes. Such cases are as pertinent as any others. I am not indicating the *good* way of using "good." I am not influencing people, but am describing the way this influence sometimes goes on. If the reader wishes to say that the munition maker's influence is bad—that is, if the reader wishes to awaken people's disapproval of the man, and to make him disapprove of his own actions—I should at another time be willing to join in this undertaking. But this is not the present concern. I am not using ethical terms, but am indicating how they *are* used. The munition maker, in his use of "good," illustrates the persuasive character of the word just as well as does the unselfish man who, eager to encourage in each of us a desire for the happiness of all, contends that the supreme good is peace.

Thus ethical terms are *instruments* used in the complicated interplay and readjustment of human interests. This can be seen plainly from more general observations. People from widely separated communities have different moral attitudes. Why? To a great extent because they have been subject to different social influences. Now clearly this influence doesn't operate through sticks and stones alone; words play a great part. People praise one another, to encourage certain inclinations, and blame one another, to discourage others. Those of forceful personalities issue commands which weaker people, for complicated instinctive reasons, find it difficult to disobey, quite apart from fears of consequences. Further influence is brought to bear by writers and orators. Thus social influence is exerted, to an enormous extent, by means that have nothing to do with physical force or material reward. The ethical terms facilitate such influence. Being suited for use in *suggestion,* they are a means by which men's attitudes may be led this way or that. The reason, then, that we find a greater similarity in the moral attitudes of one community than in those of different communities is largely this: ethical judgments propagate themselves. One man says "This is good"; this may influence the approval of another person, who then makes the same ethical judgment, which in turn influences another person, and so on. In the end, by a process of mutual influence, people take up more or less the same attitudes. Between people of widely separated communities, of course, the influence is less strong; hence different communities have different attitudes.

These remarks will serve to give a general idea of my point of view. We must now go into more detail. There are several questions which must be answered: How does an ethical sentence acquire its power of influencing people—why is it suited to suggestion? Again, what has this influence to do with the *meaning* of ethical terms? And finally, do these considerations really lead us to a sense of "good" which meets the requirements mentioned in the preceding section?

Let us deal first with the question about *meaning.* This is far from an easy question, so we must enter into a preliminary inquiry about meaning in general. Although a seeming digression, this will prove indispensable.

III

Broadly speaking, there are two different *purposes* which lead us to use language. On the one hand we use words (as in science) to record, clarify, and communicate *beliefs.* On the other hand we use words to give vent to our feelings (interjections), or to create moods (poetry), or to incite people to actions or attitudes (oratory).

The first use of words I shall call "descriptive"; the second, "dynamic." Note that the distinction depends solely upon the *purpose* of the *speaker.*

When a person says "Hydrogen is the lightest known gas," his purpose *may* be simply to lead the hearer to believe this, or to believe that the speaker believes it. In that case the words are used descriptively. When a person cuts himself and says "Damn," his purpose is not ordinarily to record, clarify, or communicate any belief. The word is used dynamically. The two ways of using words, however, are by no means mutually exclusive. This is obvious from the fact that our purposes are often complex. Thus when one says "I want you to close the door," part of his purpose, ordinarily, is to lead the hearer to believe that he has this want. To that extent the words are used descriptively. But the major part of one's purpose is to lead the hearer to *satisfy* the want. To that extent the words are used dynamically.

It very frequently happens that the same sentence may have a dynamic use on one occasion, and may not have a dynamic use on another; and that it may have different dynamic uses on different occasions. For instance: A man says to a visiting neighbor, "I am loaded down with work." His purpose may be to let the neighbor know how life is going with him. This would *not* be a dynamic use of words. He may make the remark, however, in order to drop a hint. This *would* be dynamic usage (as well as descriptive). Again, he may make the remark to arouse the neighbor's sympathy. This would be a *different* dynamic usage from that of hinting.

Or again, when we say to a man. "Of course you won't make those mistakes any more," we *may* simply be making a prediction. But we are more likely to be using "suggestion," in order to encourage him and hence *keep* him from making mistakes. The first use would be descriptive; the second, mainly dynamic.

From these examples it will be clear that we can't determine whether words are used dynamically or not, merely by reading the dictionary—even assuming that everyone is faithful to dictionary meanings. Indeed, to know whether a person is using a word dynamically, we must note his tone of voice, his gestures, the general circumstances under which he is speaking, and so on.

We must now proceed to an important question: What has the dynamic use of words to do with their *meaning*? One thing is clear—we must not define "meaning" in a way that would make meaning vary with dynamic usage. If we did, we should have no use for the term. All that we could say about such "meaning" would be that it is very complicated, and subject to constant change. So we must certainly distinguish between the dynamic use of words and their meaning.

It doesn't follow, however, that we must define "meaning" in some psychological fashion. We must simply restrict the psychological field. Instead of identifying meaning with *all* the psychological causes and effects that attend a word's utterance, we must identify it with those that it has a *tendency* (causal property, dispositional property) to be connected with. The tendency must be of a particular kind, moreover. It must exist for all who speak the language; it must be persistent; and must be realizable more or less independently of determinate circumstances attending the word's utterance. There will be further restrictions dealing with the interrelation of words in different contexts. Moreover, we must include, under the psychological responses which the words tend to produce, not only immediately introspectable experiences, but *dispositions* to react in a given way with appropriate stimuli. . . . Suffice it now to say that I think "meaning" may be thus defined in a way to include "propositional" meaning as an important kind. Now a word may *tend* to have causal relations which in fact it sometimes doesn't; and it may sometimes have causal relations which it *doesn't tend* to have. And since the tendency of words which constitutes their meaning must be of a particular kind, and may include, as responses, dispositions to reactions, of which any of *several* immediate experiences may be a sign, then there is nothing surprising in the fact that words have a permanent meaning, in spite

of the fact that the immediately introspectable experiences which attend their usage are so highly varied.

When "meaning" is defined in this way, meaning will not include dynamic use. For although words are sometimes accompanied by dynamic purposes, they do not *tend* to be accompanied by them in the way above mentioned. *E.g.,* there is no tendency realizable independently of the determinate circumstances under which the words are uttered.

There will be a kind of meaning, however, in the sense above defined, which has an intimate relation to dynamic usage. I refer to "emotive" meaning (in a sense roughly like that employed by Ogden and Richards).[4] The emotive meaning of a word is a tendency of a word, arising through the history of its usage, to produce (result from) *affective* responses in people. It is the immediate aura of feeling which hovers about a word. Such tendencies to produce affective responses cling to words very tenaciously. It would be difficult, for instance, to express merriment by using the interjection "alas." Because of the persistence of such affective tendencies (among other reasons) it becomes feasible to classify them as "meanings."

Just *what* is the relation between emotive meaning and the dynamic use of words? Let us take an example. Suppose that a man is talking with a group of people which includes Miss Jones, aged 59. He refers to her, without thinking, as an "old maid." Now even if his purposes are perfectly innocent—even if he is using the words purely descriptively—Miss Jones won't think so. She will think he is encouraging the others to have contempt for her, and will draw in her skirts, defensively. The man might have done better if instead of saying "old maid" he had said "elderly spinster." The latter words could have been put to the same descriptive use, and would not so readily have caused suspicions about the dynamic use.

"Old maid" and "elderly spinster" differ, to be sure, only in emotive meaning. From the example it will be clear that certain words, because of their emotive meaning, are suited to a certain kind of dynamic use—so well suited, in fact, that the hearer is likely to be misled when we use them in any other way. The more pronounced a word's emotive meaning is, the less likely people are to use it purely descriptively. Some words are suited to encourage people, some to discourage them, some to quiet them, and so on.

Even in these cases, of course, the dynamic purposes are not to be identified with any sort of meaning; for the emotive meaning accompanies a word much more persistently than do the dynamic purposes. But there is an important contingent relation between emotive meaning and dynamic purpose: the former assists the latter. Hence if we define emotively laden terms in a way that neglects their emotive meaning, we are likely to be confusing. *We lead people to think that the terms defined are used dynamically less often than they are.*

IV

Let us now apply these remarks in defining "good." This word may be used morally or non-morally. I shall deal with the non-moral usage almost entirely, but only because it is simpler. The main points of the analysis will apply equally well to either usage.

As a preliminary definition, let us take an inaccurate approximation. It may be more misleading than helpful, but will do to begin with. Roughly, then, the sentence "X is good" means *We like X*. ("We" includes the hearer or hearers.)

At first glance this definition sounds absurd. If used, we should expect to find the following sort of conversation: A. "This is good." B. "But I *don't* like it. What led you to believe that I did?" The unnaturalness of B's reply, judged by ordinary word-usage, would seem to cast doubt on the relevance of my definition.

B's unnaturalness, however, lies simply in this: he is assuming that "We like it" (as would occur implicitly in the use of "good") is being used descriptively. This won't do. When "We like it" is to take the place of "This is good," the former sentence must be used not purely descriptively, but dynamically. More specifically, it must be used to promote a very subtle (and for the non-moral sense in question, a very easily resisted) kind of *suggestion.* To the

extent that "we" refers to the hearer, it must have the dynamic use, essential to suggestion, of leading the hearer to *make* true what is said, rather than merely to believe it. And to the extent that "we" refers to the speaker, the sentence must have not only the descriptive use of indicating belief about the speaker's interest, but the quasi-interjectory, dynamic function of giving direct expression to the interest. (This immediate expression of feelings assists in the process of suggestion. It is difficult to disapprove in the face of another's enthusiasm.)

For an example of a case where "We like this" is used in the dynamic way that "This is good" is used, consider the case of a mother who says to her several children, "One thing is certain, *we all like to be neat*." If she really believed this, she wouldn't bother to say so. But she is not using the words descriptively. She is *encouraging* the children to like neatness. By telling them that they like neatness, she will lead them to *make* her statement true, so to speak. If, instead of saying "We all like to be neat" in this way, she had said "It's a good thing to be neat," the effect would have been approximately the same.

But these remarks are still misleading. Even when "We like it" is used for suggestion, it isn't quite like "This is good." The latter is more subtle. With such a sentence as "This is a good book," for example, it would be practically impossible to use instead "We like this book." When the latter is used, it must be accompanied by so exaggerated an intonation, to prevent its becoming confused with a descriptive statement, that the force of suggestion becomes stronger, and ludicrously more overt, than when "good" is used.

The definition is inadequate, further, in that the definiens has been restricted to dynamic usage. Having said that dynamic usage was different from meaning, I should not have to mention it in giving the *meaning* of "good."

It is in connection with this last point that we must return to emotive meaning. The word "good" has a pleasing emotive meaning which fits it especially for the dynamic use of suggesting favorable interest. But the sentence "We like it" has no such emotive meaning. Hence my definition has neglected emotive meaning entirely. Now to neglect emotive meaning is likely to lead to endless confusions, as we shall presently see; so I have sought to make up for the inadequacy of the definition by letting the restriction about dynamic usage take the place of emotive meaning. What I should do, of course, is to find a definiens whose emotive meaning, like that of "good," simply does *lead* to dynamic usage.

Why didn't I do this? I answer that it isn't possible, if the definition is to afford us increased clarity. No two words, in the first place, have quite the same emotive meaning. The most we can hope for is a rough approximation. But if we seek for such an approximation for "good," we shall find nothing more than synonyms, such as "desirable" or "valuable"; and these are profitless because they do not clear up the connection between "good" and favorable interest. If we reject such synonyms, in favor of non-ethical terms, we shall be highly misleading. For instance: "This is good" has something like the meaning of "I *do* like this; do so as well." But this is certainly not accurate. For the imperative makes an appeal to the conscious efforts of the hearer. Of course he can't like something just by trying. He must be led to like it through suggestion. Hence an ethical sentence differs from an imperative in that it enables one to make changes in a much more subtle, less fully conscious way. Note that the ethical sentence centers the hearer's attention not on his interests, but on the object of interest, and thereby facilitates suggestion. Because of its subtlety, moreover, an ethical sentence readily permits counter-suggestion, and leads to the give and take situation which is so characteristic of arguments about values.

Strictly speaking, then, it is impossible to define "good" in terms of favorable interest if emotive meaning is not to be distorted. Yet it is possible to say that "This is good" is *about* the favorable interest of the speaker and the hearer or hearers, and that it has a pleasing emotive meaning which fits the words for use in suggestion. This is a rough description of meaning, not a definition. But it serves the same clarifying function that a definition ordinarily does; and that, after all, is enough.

A word must be added about the moral use of "good." This differs from the above in that it is about a different kind of interest. Instead of being about what the hearer and speaker *like,* it is about a stronger sort of approval. When a person *likes* something, he is pleased when it prospers, and disappointed when it doesn't. When a person *morally approves* of something, he experiences a rich feeling of security when it prospers, and is indignant, or "shocked" when it doesn't. These are rough and inaccurate examples of the many factors which one would have to mention in distinguishing the two kinds of interest. In the moral usage, as well as in the non-moral, "good" has an emotive meaning which adapts it to suggestion.

And now, are these considerations of any importance? Why do I stress emotive meanings in this fashion? Does the omission of them really lead people into errors? I think, indeed, that the errors resulting from such omissions are enormous. In order to see this, however, we must return to the restrictions, mentioned in section I, with which the "vital" sense of "good" has been expected to comply.

V

The first restriction, it will be remembered, had to do with disagreement. Now there is clearly some sense in which people disagree on ethical points; but we must not rashly assume that all disagreement is modelled after the sort that occurs in the natural sciences. We must distinguish between "disagreement in belief" (typical of the sciences) and "disagreement in interest." Disagreement in belief occurs when A believes *p* and B disbelieves it. Disagreement in interest occurs when A has a favorable interest in X, when B has an unfavorable one in it, and when neither is content to let the other's interest remain unchanged.

Let me give an example of disagreement in interest. A. "Let's go to a cinema tonight." B. "I don't want to do that. Let's go to the symphony." A continues to insist on the cinema, B on the symphony. This is disagreement in a perfectly conventional sense. They can't agree on where they want to go, and each is trying to redirect the other's interest. (Note that imperatives are used in the example.)

It is disagreement in *interest* which takes places in ethics. When C says "This is good," and D says "No, it's bad," we have a case of suggestion and counter-suggestion. Each man is trying to redirect the other's interest. There obviously need be no domineering, since each may be willing to give ear to the other's influence; but each is trying to move the other none the less. It is in this sense that they disagree. Those who argue that certain interest theories make no provision for disagreement have been misled, I believe, simply because the traditional theories, in leaving out emotive meaning, give the impression that ethical judgments are used descriptively only; and of course when judgments are used purely descriptively, the only disagreement that can arise is disagreement *in belief.* Such disagreement may be disagreement in belief *about* interests; but this is not the same as disagreement *in* interest. My definition doesn't provide for disagreement in belief about interests, any more than does Hobbes's; but that is no matter, for there is no reason to believe, at least on commonsense grounds, that this kind of disagreement exists. There is only disagreement *in* interest. (We shall see in a moment that disagreement in interest does not remove ethics from sober argument—that this kind of disagreement may often be resolved through empirical means.)

The second restriction, about "magnetism," or the connection between goodness and actions, requires only a word. This rules out *only* those interest theories which do *not* include the interest of the speaker, in defining "good." My account does include the speaker's interest; hence is immune.

The third restriction, about the empirical method, may be met in a way that springs naturally from the above account of disagreement. Let us put the question in this way: When two people disagree over an ethical matter, can they completely resolve the disagreement through empirical considerations, assuming that each applies the empirical method exhaustively, consistently, and without error?

I answer that sometimes they can, and sometimes they cannot; and that at any rate, even when they can, the relation between empirical knowledge and ethical judgments is quite different from the one which traditional interest theories seem to imply.

This can best be seen from an analogy. Let's return to the example where A and B couldn't agree on a cinema or a symphony. The example differed from an ethical argument in that imperatives were used, rather than ethical judgments; but was analogous to the extent that each person was endeavoring to modify the other's interest. Now how would these people argue the case, assuming that they were too intelligent just to shout at one another?

Clearly, they would give "reasons" to support their imperatives. A might say, "But you know, Garbo is at the Bijou." His hope is that B, who admires Garbo, will acquire a desire to go to the cinema when he knows what play will be there. B may counter, "But Toscanini is guest conductor tonight, in an all-Beethoven programme." And so on. Each supports his imperative (*"Let's* do so and so") by reasons which may be empirically established.

To generalize from this: disagreement in interest may be rooted in disagreement in belief. That is to say, people who disagree in interest would often cease to do so if they knew the precise nature and consequences of the object of their interest. To this extent disagreement in interest may be resolved by securing agreement in belief, which in turn may be secured empirically.

This generalization holds for ethics. If A and B, instead of using imperatives, had said, respectively. "It would be *better* to go to the cinema," and "It would be better to go to the symphony," the reasons which they would advance would be roughly the same. They would each give a more thorough account of the object of interest, with the purpose of completing the redirection of interest which was begun by the suggestive force of the ethical sentence. On the whole, of course, the suggestive force of the ethical statement merely exerts enough pressure to start such trains of reasons, since the reasons are much more essential in resolving disagreement in interest than the persuasive effect of the ethical judgment itself.

Thus the empirical method is relevant to ethics simply because our knowledge of the world is a determining factor to our interests. But note that empirical facts are not inductive grounds from which the ethical judgment problematically follows.

(This is what traditional interest theories imply.) If someone said "Close the door," and added the reason "We'll catch cold," the latter would scarcely be called an inductive ground of the former. Now imperatives are related to the reasons which support them in the same way that ethical judgments are related to reasons.

Is the empirical method *sufficient* for attaining ethical agreement? Clearly not. For empirical knowledge resolves disagreement in interest only to the extent that such disagreement is rooted in disagreement in belief. Not all disagreement in interest is of this sort. For instance: A is of a sympathetic nature, and B isn't. They are arguing about whether a public dole would be good. Suppose that they discovered all the consequences of the dole. Isn't it possible, even so, that A will say that it's good, and B that it's bad? The disagreement in interest may arise not from limited factual knowledge, but simply from A's sympathy and B's coldness. Or again, suppose, in the above argument, that A was poor and unemployed, and that B was rich. Here again the disagreement might not be due to different factual knowledge. It would be due to the different social positions of the men, together with their predominant self-interest.

When ethical disagreement is not rooted in disagreement in belief, is there *any* method by which it may be settled? If one means by "method" a *rational* method, then there is no method. But in any case there is a "way." Let's consider the above example, again, where disagreement was due to A's sympathy and B's coldness. Must they end by saying. "Well, it's just a matter of our having different temperaments"? Not necessarily. A, for instance, may try to *change* the temperament of his opponent. He may pour out his enthusiasms in such a moving way— present the sufferings of the poor with such appeal— that he will lead his opponent to see life through different eyes. He may build up, by the contagion of his feelings, an influence which will modify B's temperament, and create in him a sympathy for the poor which didn't previously exist. This is often the only way to obtain ethical agreement, if there is any way at all. It is persuasive, not empirical or rational; but that is no reason for neglecting it. There is no reason to scorn it, either, for it is only by such means

that our personalities are able to grow, through our contact with others.

The point I wish to stress, however, is simply that the empirical method is instrumental to ethical agreement only to the extent that disagreement in interest is rooted in disagreement in belief. There is little reason to believe that all disagreement is of this sort. Hence the empirical method is not sufficient for ethics. In any case, ethics is not psychology, since psychology doesn't endeavor to *direct* our interests; it discovers facts about the ways in which interests are or can be directed, but that's quite another matter.

To summarize this section: my analysis of ethical judgments meets the three requirements for the "vital" sense of "good" that were mentioned in section I. The traditional interest theories fail to meet these requirements simply because they neglect emotive meaning. This neglect leads them to neglect dynamic usage, and the sort of disagreement that results from such usage, together with the method of resolving the disagreement. I may add that my analysis answers Moore's objection about the open question. Whatever scientifically knowable properties a thing may have, it *is* always open to question whether a thing having these (enumerated) qualities is good. For to ask whether it is good is to ask for *influence*. And whatever I may know about an object, I can still ask, quite pertinently, to be influenced with regard to my interest in it.

VI

And now, have I really pointed out the "vital" sense of "good"?

I suppose that many still will say "No," claiming that I have simply failed to set down *enough* requirements which this sense must meet, and that my analysis, like all others given in terms of interest, is a way of begging the issue. They will say: "When we ask 'Is X good?' we don't want mere influence, mere advice. We decidedly don't want to be influenced through persuasion, nor are we fully content when the influence is supported by a wide scientific knowledge of X. The answer to our question will, of course, modify our interests. But this is only because an unique sort of *truth* will be revealed to us—a truth which must be apprehended *a priori*. We want our interests to be guided by this truth, and by nothing else. To substitute for such a truth mere emotive meaning and suggestion is to conceal from us the very object of our search."

I can only answer that I do not understand. What is this truth to be *about*? For I recollect no Platonic Idea, nor do I know what to *try* to recollect. I find no indefinable property, nor do I know what to look for. And the "self-evident" deliverances of reason, which so many philosophers have claimed, seem, on examination, to be deliverances of their respective reasons only (if of anyone's) and not of mine.

I strongly suspect, indeed, that any sense of "good" which is expected both to unite itself in synthetic *a priori* fashion with other concepts, and to influence interests as well, is really a great confusion. I extract from this meaning the power of influence alone, which I find the only intelligible part. If the rest is confusion, however, then it certainly deserves more than the shrug of one's shoulders. What I should like to do is to *account* for the confusion—to examine the psychological needs which have given rise to it, and to show how these needs may be satisfied in another way. This is *the* problem, if

confusion is to be stopped at its source. But it is an enormous problem, and my reflections on it, which are at present worked out only roughly, must be reserved until some later time.

I may add that if "X is good" is essentially a vehicle for suggestion, it is scarcely a statement which philosophers, any more than many other men, are called upon to make. To the extent that ethics predicates the ethical terms of anything, rather than explains their meaning, it ceases to be a reflective study. Ethical statements are social instruments. They are used in a cooperative enterprise in which we are mutually adjusting ourselves to the interests of others. Philosophers have a part in this, as do all men, but not the major part.

NOTES

1. See G. E. Moore's *Philosophical Studies,* pp. 332–334.
2. See G. C. Field's *Moral Theory,* pp. 52, 56–57.
3. See G. E. Moore's *Principia Ethica,* chap i. I am simply trying to preserve the spirit of Moore's objection, and not the exact form of it.
4. See *The Meaning of Meaning,* by C. K. Ogden and I. A. Richards. On p. 125, second edition, there is a passage on ethics which was the source of the ideas embodied in this paper.

STUDY QUESTIONS

1. How do disagreements in belief differ from disagreements in attitude?
2. Can science ever help resolve a non-moral value disagreement?
3. Can science ever help resolve a moral disagreement?
4. How does Stevenson respond to the claim that moral truths are self-evident?

The Language of Morals

R. M. Hare

Richard M. Hare (1919–2002) was White's Professor of Moral Philosophy at the University of Oxford. He maintains that normative utterances are prescriptive in that they aim to direct, not describe, action. For example, to say "lying is wrong" is to say "Don't lie!" Thus normative terms, like other terms that indicate grammatical mood, convey what sort of statements are being uttered. Those in the imperative mood do not make any claims to truth. The reply to "Shut the door!" is not "That's false." This approach puts Hare in the non-cognitivist camp. He argues, however, that the function of normative talk is not to express the speaker's mind. Just as instructions for cooking omelets are about eggs, not the psyche of the cook, "Don't lie" is about lying, not about the emotions of the speaker. Against Stevenson, he notes that telling people not to lie is different than seeking to persuade them not to lie.

1 PRESCRIPTIVE LANGUAGE

1.1.

If we were to ask of a person "What are his moral principles?" the way in which we could be most sure of a true answer would be by studying what he *did*. He might, to be sure, profess in his conversation all sorts of principles, which in his actions he completely disregarded; but it would be when, knowing all the relevant facts of a situation, he was faced with choices or decisions between alternative courses of action, between alternative answers to the question "What shall I do?", that he would reveal in what principles of conduct he really believed. The reason why actions are in a peculiar way revelatory of moral principles is that the function of moral principles is to guide conduct. The language of morals is one sort of prescriptive language. And this is what makes ethics worth studying: for the question "What shall I do?" is one that we cannot for long evade; the problems of conduct, though sometimes less diverting than crossword puzzles, *have to be solved* in a way that crossword puzzles do not. We cannot wait to see the solution in the next issue, because on the solution of the problems depends what happens in the next issue. Thus, in a world in which the problems of conduct become every day more complex and tormenting, there is a great need for an understanding of the language in which these problems are posed and answered. For confusion about our moral language leads, not merely to theoretical muddles, but to needless practical perplexities.

An old-fashioned, but still useful, way of studying anything is *per genus et differentiam*; if moral language belongs to the genus "prescriptive

From R. M. Hare, *The Language of Morals* (New York: Oxford, 1952).

language," we shall most easily understand its nature if we compare and contrast first of all prescriptive language with other sorts of language, and then moral language with other sorts of prescriptive language. . . .

1.2.

The writers of elementary grammar books sometimes classify sentences according as they express statements, commands, or questions. This classification is not exhaustive or rigorous enough for the logician. For example, logicians have devoted much labor to showing that sentences in the indicative mood may be of very various logical characters, and that the classification of them all under the one name "statements" may lead to serious error if it makes us ignore the important differences between them. . . .

Imperatives, likewise, are a mixed bunch. Even if we exclude sentences like "Would I were in Grantchester!" which are dealt with by some grammarians in the same division of their books as imperatives, we still have, among sentences that are in the imperative mood proper, many different kinds of utterance. We have military orders (parade-ground and otherwise), architects' specifications, instructions for cooking omclcts or operating vacuum cleaners, pieces of advice, requests, entreaties, and countless other sorts of sentence, many of whose functions shade into one another. . . . I shall . . . follow the grammarians and use the single term "command" to cover all these sorts of thing that sentences in the imperative mood express, and within the class of commands make only some very broad distinctions. The justification for this procedure is that I hope to interest the reader in features that are common to all, or nearly all, these types of sentence; with their differences he is no doubt familiar enough. For the same reason I shall use the word "statement" to cover whatever is expressed by typical indicative sentences, if there be such. I shall be drawing a contrast, that is to say, between sentences like "Shut the door" and sentences like "You are going to shut the door."

It is difficult to deny that there is a difference between statements and commands; but it is far harder to say just what the difference is. It is not merely one of grammatical form; for if we had to study a newly discovered language we should be able to identify those grammatical forms which were used for expressing statements and commands respectively, and should call these forms "indicative" and "imperative" (if the language were constructed in such a way as to make this distinction useful). The distinction lies between the meanings which the different grammatical forms convey. Both are used for talking about a subject-matter, but they are used for talking about it in different ways. The two sentences "You are going to shut the door" and "Shut the door" are both about your shutting the door in the immediate future; but what they say about it is quite different. An indicative sentence is used for telling someone that something is the case; an imperative is not—it is used for telling someone to make something the case.

1.3.

It is well worth the moral philosopher's while examining some of the theories which have been, or which might be, held about the way in which imperatives have meaning. They offer a most arresting parallel to similar theories about moral judgments, and this parallel indicates that there may be some important logical similarity between the two. Let us first consider . . . theories, similar to the type of ethical theory to which I shall later give the name "naturalist." Both are attempts to "reduce" imperatives to indicatives. The first does this by representing them as expressing statements about the mind of the speaker. Just as it has been held that "A is right" means "I approve of A," so it might be held that "Shut the door" means "I want you to shut the door." There is on the colloquial plane no harm in saying this; but it may be very misleading philosophically. It has the consequence that if I say "Shut the door" and you say (to the same person) "Do not shut the door," we are not contradicting one another; and this is odd. The upholder of the theory may reply that although there is no contradiction, there is a disagreement in wishes, and that this is sufficient to account for the feeling we have that the two sentences are somehow incompatible with one another (that "not" has the same function as in the sentence "You are not going to shut the door"). But there remains the difficulty that the sentence "Shut the door" seems to be about shutting the door, and not about the speaker's frame of mind, just as instructions for cooking omelets ("Take four eggs, etc.") are instructions about eggs, not introspective analyses of the psyche of Mrs. Becton. To say that "Shut the door" means the same as "I want you to shut the door" is like saying that "You are going to shut the door" means the same as "I believe that you are going to shut the door." In both cases it seems strange to represent a remark about shutting the door as a remark about what is going on in my mind. But in fact neither the word "believe" nor the word "want" will bear this interpretation. "I believe that you are going to shut the door" is not (except in a highly figurative way) a statement about my mind; it is a tentative statement about your shutting the door, a more hesitant version of "You are going to shut the door"; and similarly, "I want you to shut the door" is not a statement about my mind but a polite way of saying the imperative "Shut the door." Unless we understand the logic of "You are going to shut the door," we cannot understand the logic of "I believe that you are going to shut the door"; and similarly unless we understand "Shut the door" we are unlikely to understand "I want you to shut the door." The theory, therefore, explains nothing; and the parallel ethical theory is in the same case; for "I approve of A" is merely a more complicated and circumlocutory way of saying "A is right." It is not a statement, verifiable by observation, that I have a recognizable feeling or recurrent frame of mind; it is a value-judgment; if I ask "Do I approve of A?" my answer is a moral decision, not an observation of introspectible fact. "I approve of A" would be unintelligible to someone who did not understand "A is right," and the explanation is a case of *obscurum per obscurius*. . . .

1.5.

The feeling, that only "proper indicatives" are above suspicion, can survive (surprisingly) the discovery that there are perfectly good significant sentences of our ordinary speech which are not reducible to indicatives. It survives in the assumption that any meaning which is discovered for these sentences must necessarily be of some logically inferior status to that of indicatives. This assumption has led philosophers such as Professor A. J. Ayer, in the course of expounding their most valuable research into the logical nature of moral judgments, to make incidental remarks which have raised needless storms of protest.[1] The substance of Ayer's theory is that moral judgments do not ordinarily function in the same way as the class of indicative sentences marked out by his verification-criterion. But by his way of stating his view, and his assimilation of moral judgments to other (quite distinct) types of sentence which are also marked off from typical indicatives by this criterion, he stirred up dust which has not yet subsided. All this might be closely paralleled by a similar treatment of imperatives—and it seems that writers of the same general line of thought as Ayer would have said the same sort of thing about imperatives as they did about moral judgments. Suppose that we recognize the obvious fact that imperatives are not like typical indicatives. Suppose, further, that we regard only typical indicatives as above suspicion. It will be natural then to say "Imperatives do not state anything, they only express wishes." Now to say that imperatives express wishes is, like the first theory which we considered, unexceptionable on the colloquial plane; we would indeed say, if someone said "Keep my name out of this," that he had expressed a wish to have his name kept out of it. But nevertheless the extreme ambiguity of the word "express" may generate philosophical confusion. We speak of expressing statements, opinions, beliefs, mathematical relations, and so on; and if it is in one of these senses that the word is used, the theory, though it tells us little, is harmless. But unfortunately it is also used in ways which are unlike these; and Ayer's use (in speaking of moral judgments) of the word "evince" as its rough synonym was dangerous. Artists and composers and poets are said to express their own and our feelings; oaths are said to express anger; and dancing upon the table may express joy. Thus to say that imperatives express wishes may lead the unwary to suppose that what happens when we use one, is this: we have welling up inside us a kind of longing, to which, when the pressure gets too great for us to bear, we give vent by saying an imperative sentence. Such an interpretation, when applied to such sentences as "Supply and fit to door mortise dead latch and plastic knob furniture." is unplausible. And it would seem that value-judgments also may fail to satisfy the verification-criterion, and indeed be in some sense, like imperatives, prescriptive, without having this sort of thing said about them. It is perfectly unexceptionable, on the colloquial plane, to say that the sentence "A is good" is used to express approval of A . . . but it is philosophically misleading if we think that the approval which is expressed is a peculiar warm feeling inside us. If the Minister of Local Government expresses approval of my town plan by getting his underlings to write to me saying "The Minister approves of your plan" or "The Minister thinks your plan is the best one," I shall in no circumstances confirm the letter by getting a private detective to observe the Minister for signs of emotion. In this case, to have such a letter sent *is* to approve.

1.6.

There could be no analogue, in the case of singular imperatives, of the "attitude" variety of the approval theory of value-judgments;[2] but it is possible to construct such a theory about *universal* imperative sentences. If someone said "Never hit a man when he is down," it would be natural to say that he had expressed a certain attitude towards such conduct. It is extremely hard to define exactly this attitude or give criteria for recognizing it, just as it is difficult to say exactly what *moral* approval is as opposed to other sorts of approval. The only safe way of characterizing the attitude which is expressed by a universal imperative is to say "The attitude that one should not (or should) do so and so"; and the only safe way of characterizing the attitude which is expressed by a moral judgment is to say "The attitude that it is wrong (or right) to do so and so." To maintain an attitude of "moral approval" towards a certain practice is to have a disposition to think, on the appropriate occasions, that it is right; or, if "think" itself is a dispositional word, it is simply to think that it is right; and our thinking that it is right may be betrayed or exhibited . . . by our acting in certain ways (above all, doing acts of the sort in question when the occasion arises; next, saying that they are right; applauding them in other ways, and so on). But there is in all this nothing to explain just *what* one thinks when one thinks that a certain sort of act is right. And similarly, if we said that "Never hit a man when he is down" expressed an attitude that one should not hit, etc. (or an attitude of aversion from hitting, or a "contra-attitude" towards hitting), we should not have said anything that would be intelligible to someone who did not understand the sentence which we were trying to explain.

I wish to emphasize that I am not seeking to refute any of these theories. They have all of them the characteristic that, if put in everyday terms, they say nothing exceptionable so far as their main contentions go; but when we seek to understand how they explain the philosophical perplexities which generated them, we are either forced to interpret them in such a way as to render them unplausible, or else find that they merely set the same problems in a more complicated way. Sentences containing the word "approve" are so difficult of analysis that it seems perverse to use this notion to explain the meaning of moral judgments which we learn to make years before we learn the word "approve"; and similarly, it would be perverse to explain the meaning of the imperative mood in terms of wishing or any other feeling or attitude; for we learn how to respond to and use commands long before we learn the comparatively complex notions of "wish," "desire," "aversion," etc.

1.7.

We must now consider another group of theories which have often been held concurrently with the group just considered. These hold that the function in language of either moral judgments or imperatives (which the theories often equate) is to affect causally the behavior or emotions of the hearer. . . . Professor Ayer writes:

Ethical terms do not serve only to express feeling. They are calculated also to arouse feeling, and so to stimulate action. Indeed some of them are used in such a way as to give the sentences in which they occur the effect of commands.[3]

More recently this sort of view has been elaborated by Professor Stevenson.[4] Here again we have a type of theory which may be on the colloquial plane harmless, but which suggests philosophical errors by seeming to assimilate the processes of using a command or a moral judgment to other processes which are in fact markedly dissimilar.

It is indeed true of imperative sentences that if anyone, in using them, is being sincere or honest, he intends that the person referred to should *do* something (namely, what is commanded). This is indeed a test of sincerity in the case of commands, just as a statement is held to be sincere only if the speaker believes it. And there are similar criteria, as we shall later see, for sincerely assenting to commands and statements that have been given or made by someone else. But this is not quite what the theories suggest. They suggest, rather, that the function of a command is to affect the hearer causally, or get him to do something; and to say this may be misleading. In ordinary parlance there is no harm in saying that in using a command our intention is to get someone to do something; but for philosophical purposes an important distinction has to be made. The processes of *telling* someone to do something, and *getting* him to do it, are quite distinct, logically, from each other. The distinction may be elucidated by considering a parallel one in the case of statements. To tell someone that something is the case is logically distinct from getting (or trying to get) him to believe it. Having told someone that something is the case we may, if he is not disposed to believe what we say, start on a quite different process of trying to get him to believe it (trying to persuade or convince him that what we have said is true). No one, in seeking to explain the function of indicative sentences, would say that they were attempts to persuade someone that something is the case. And there is no more reason for saying that commands are attempts to persuade or get someone to do something; here, too,

we first tell someone what he is to do, and then, if he is not disposed to do what we say, we may start on the wholly different process of trying to get him to do it. Thus the instruction already quoted "Supply and fit to door mortise dead latch and plastic knob furniture" is not intended to *galvanize* joiners into activity; for such a purpose other means are employed.

This distinction is important for moral philosophy; for in fact the suggestion, that the function of moral judgments was to persuade, led to a difficulty in distinguishing their function from that of propaganda.[5] . . . We have here, as often in philosophy, a mixture of two distinctions. The first is that between the language of statements and prescriptive language. The second is that between telling someone something and getting him to believe or do what one has told him. That these two distinctions are quite different, and overlap each other, should be clear after a moment's consideration. For we may tell someone, either that something is the case, or to do something; here there is no attempt at persuasion (or influencing or inducing or getting to). If the person is not disposed to assent to what we tell him, we may then resort to rhetoric, propaganda, marshalling of additional facts, psychological tricks, threats, bribes, torture, mockery, promises of protection, and a variety of other expedients. All of these are ways of inducing him or getting him to do something; the first four are also ways of getting him to believe something; none of them are ways of telling him something, though those of them which involve the employment of language may include telling him all sorts of things. Regarded as inducements or expedients for persuasion, their success is judged solely by their effects—by whether the person believes or does what we are trying to get him to believe or do. It does not matter whether the means used to persuade him are fair or foul, so long as they do persuade him. And therefore the natural reaction to the realization that someone is trying to persuade us is "He's trying to get at me; I must be on my guard; I mustn't let him bias my decision unfairly; I must be careful to make up my own mind in the matter and remain a free responsible agent." Such a reaction to moral judgments should not be encouraged by philosophers. On the other hand, these are not natural reactions either to someone's telling us that something is the case, or to his telling us to do something (for example, to fit a latch to the door). Telling someone to do something, or that something is the case, is answering the question "What shall I do?" or "What are the facts?" When we have answered these questions the hearer knows what to do or what the facts are—if what we have told him is right. He is not necessarily thereby *influenced* one way or the other, nor have we failed if he is not; for he may decide to disbelieve or disobey us, and the mere telling him does nothing—and seeks to do nothing—to prevent him doing this. But persuasion is not directed to a person as a rational agent, who is asking himself (or us) "What shall I do?"; it is not an answer to this or to any other question; it is an attempt to *make* him answer it in a particular way.

It is easy to see, therefore, why the so-called "imperative theory" of moral judgments raised the protests that it did. Because based on a misconception of the function, not only of moral judgments but also of the commands to which they were being assimilated, it seemed to impugn the rationality of moral discourse. But if we realize that commands, however much they may differ from statements, are like them in this, that they consist in telling someone something, not in seeking to influence him, it does no harm to draw attention to the similarities between commands and moral judgments. For, as I shall show, commands, because they, like statements, are essentially intended for answering questions asked by rational agents, are governed by logical rules just as statements are. And this means that moral judgments may also be so governed. We remember that the greatest of all rationalists, Kant, referred to moral judgments as imperatives; though we must remember also that he was using the latter term in an extended sense, and that moral judgments, though they are like imperatives in some respects, are unlike them in others. . . .

9.4.

That the descriptive meaning of the word "good" is in morals, as elsewhere, secondary to the evaluative, may be seen in the following example. Let us suppose that a missionary, armed with a grammar book, lands on a cannibal island. The vocabulary of his grammar book gives him the equivalent, in the cannibals' language, of the English word "good." Let us suppose that, by a queer coincidence, the word is "good." And let us suppose, also, that it really is the equivalent—that it is, as the Oxford English Dictionary puts it, "the most general adjective of commendation" in their language. If the missionary has mastered his vocabulary, he can, so long as he uses the word evaluatively and not descriptively, communicate with them about morals quite happily. They know that when he uses the word he is commending the person or object that he applies it to. The only thing they will find odd is that he applies it to such unexpected people, people who are meek and gentle and do not collect large quantities of scalps; whereas they themselves are accustomed to commend people who are bold and burly and collect more scalps than the average. But they and the missionary are under no misapprehension about the meaning, in the evaluative sense, of the word "good"; it is the word one uses for commending. If they were under such a misapprehension, moral communication between them would be impossible.

We thus have a situation which would appear paradoxical to someone who thought that "good" (either in English or in the cannibals' language) was a quality-word like 'red.' Even if the qualities in people which the missionary commended had nothing in common with the qualities which the cannibals commended, yet they would both know what the word "good" meant. If "good" were like "red," this would be impossible; for then the cannibals' word and the English word would not be synonymous. If this were so, then when the missionary said that people who collected no scalps were good (English), and the cannibals said that people who collected a lot of scalps were good (cannibal), they would not be disagreeing, because in English (at any rate missionary English), "good" would mean among other things "doing no murder," whereas in the cannibals' language "good" would mean something quite different, among other things "productive of maximum scalps." It is because in its primary evaluative meaning "good" means neither of these things, but is in both languages the most general adjective of commendation, that the missionary can use it to teach the cannibals Christian morals.

Suppose, however, that the missionary's mission is successful. Then, the former cannibals will come to commend the same qualities in people as the missionary, and the words "good man" will come to have a more or less common descriptive meaning. The danger will then be that the cannibals may, after a generation or two, think that that is the only sort of meaning they have. "Good" will in that case mean for them simply "doing what it says in the Sermon on the Mount"; and they may come to forget that it is a word of commendation; they will not realize that opinions about moral goodness have a bearing on what they themselves are to do. Their standards will then be in mortal danger. A Communist, landing on the island to convert the people to his way of life, may even take advantage of the ossification of their standards. He may say "All these 'good' Christians—missionaries and colonial servants and the rest—are just deceiving you to their own profit." This would be to use the word descriptively with a dash of irony; and he could not do this plausibly unless the standards of the Christians had become considerably ossified. . . .

Moral principles or standards are first established; then they get too rigid, and the words used in referring to them become too dominantly descriptive; their evaluative force has to be painfully revived before the standards are out of danger. In the course of revival, the standards get adapted to changed circumstances; moral reform takes place, and its instrument is the evaluative use of value-language. The remedy, in fact, for moral stagnation and decay is to learn to use our value-language for the purpose for which it is designed; and this involves not merely a lesson in talking, but a lesson in doing that which we commend; for unless we are prepared to do this we are doing no more than pay lip-service to a conventional standard.

NOTES

1. See especially *Language, Truth and Logic,* 2nd ed., pp. 108–9. For a later and more balanced statement, see "On the Analysis of Moral Judgments," *Philosophical Essays,* pp. 231 ff.
2. See, for example, C. L. Stevenson, *Ethics and Language.*
3. *Language, Truth and Logic,* 2nd ed., p. 108.
4. *Ethics and Language,* especially p. 21.
5. Cf. Stevenson, *Ethics and Language,* ch. xi.

STUDY QUESTIONS

1. How do imperatives acquire their meaning?
2. According to Hare, what is the difference between prescribing and convincing?
3. Do normative judgments have functions other than prescribing?
4. What points does Hare believe are established by the case of the missionaries and cannibals?

Antirealist Expressivism and Quasi-Realism

Simon Blackburn

Simon Blackburn is a Fellow of Trinity College, Cambridge. He defends a particular version of non-cognitivism known as expressivism. Unlike the emotivism of Ayer and Stevenson, which attempts to tell us what normative words mean by looking to the functions they perform, expressivism holds that the meaning of normative words is determined by the states of mind they express. As Blackburn emphasizes, expressivism is not subjectivism. Rather, according to the expressivist, when speakers make normative utterances they are not describing their minds but, instead, are voicing their minds, indicating their view of how the world should be. Thus expressivism accounts for why an individual who judges that "lying is wrong" is at least somewhat motivated not to lie. For making this assessment does not involve forming a belief but, rather, being in a negative state of mind concerning lying.

But does supporting expressivism require relinquishing the appearance of realism? Blackburn thinks not, arguing in favor of quasi-realism. This program sheds the metaphysical commitments of realism while seeking to retain those features that are widely accepted. If successful, a quasi-realist version of expressivism procures the advantages of emotivism and realism while avoiding the disadvantages of each.

1. SOME BACKGROUND

Positions known as 'expressivist' in contemporary moral philosophy have an ancestry in the sentimentalists' opposition to rationalism in the eighteenth century, and particularly in the moral theory of David Hume (1888). In his *Treatise,* Hume undertakes to show that morality is "more properly felt than judged of," and firmly locates it as a delivery of our passions or sentiments. It is not the result of any kind of algebra or geometry of reason, and neither is it a matter of observation. Hume had many objections to these rival views, but most forcefully he argued that ethics is essentially a practical subject, and in order to control our practice it needs a motivational aspect that neither of these sources could supply. Moral commitments exist purely in order to determine preference and practice, whereas other commitments exist at the service of any desire that happens to come along and pick them up. This is not, of course, to say that we always do what we think we ought to do, for attitudes can have the most surprising expression, depending on what else is in the agent's psychological mix. It is at best to say that

From Simon Blackburn, "Antirealist Expressivism and Quasi-Realism," in *The Oxford Handbook of Ethical Theory*, ed. David Copp (Oxford: Oxford University Press, 2006). Reprinted by permission of the publisher.

we do what we think we ought to do, or love what we admire, other things being equal. Other things are not always equal, and all that should be claimed is that when people knowingly succumb to temptation, or are attracted by what they know to be wrong, something is out of joint. The natural expressions of love are concern and kindness, but when things are out of joint, love leads people to kill that which they love.

Hume's view attracted few other philosophers, until in the twentieth century the objections to a rival, 'realist' theory, making ethics a matter of knowledge and truth, became sufficiently pressing to motivate philosophers to revisit the eighteenth-century tradition.

Shortly after the beginning of the twentieth century, G. E. Moore delivered what became known as the Open Question Argument against ethical naturalism. This argument purported to show that any adequate philosophy of ethics needed to put a distance between moral and ethical judgment, on the one hand, and judgment about empirical matters, or about the kind of things talked of in natural science, on the other hand. Moore's argument purported to separate strictly moral or ethical judgments, or what he called judgments of Goodness, from the whole field of empirical and scientific judgment. Judgments of Goodness give us the field of normative judgment, whereby we endorse some things and condemn others, or insist on some things and permit others. By Moore's argument, they are to be separated from judgments about how things stand, including how they stand psychologically. Judgments of health and happiness, what is actually desired or avoided, fall on the 'natural' side. Judgments of what ought to be the case, or what is good or desirable, fall on the normative side.

Of course, people will make normative judgments in the light of what they take the empirical and scientific facts to be. But the Open Question Argument asserts that people might take all the empirical and scientific facts as settled, but still have room to doubt whether a particular moral judgment, or judgment of Goodness, is the one to make in the light of those facts. In particular, people making a bizarre evaluation in the light of agreed facts might

convict themselves of being unpleasant or idiosyncratic, but they do not disqualify themselves as not knowing the meaning of moral terms.

Similarly, those who look to rather different facts in the light of which to make judgments of Goodness do not thereby talk past each other. They are to be seen as disagreeing. But disagreement involves shared content of judgment, a content that one side judges true and the other side judges false. Hence, again, there is a space between the proposition or content judged and the underlying standards in virtue of which it is judged. Different standards may still result in the same verdict, and a dissident giving a different verdict can still be in the business of making valuations.

Moore himself took the argument to compel ethical intuitionism. This is the view that moral judgments have a distinct identity, and that these distinct, sui generis propositions are judged only by an equally distinct faculty of intuition, specially adapted to deliver them. Thinking of truth, the view would be that these propositions are made true or false by their own kinds of fact, facts about the normative order of things. It seems as though Plato was right, that there is a world of Forms, or Norms—a kind of cosmic determination of what is right or wrong, rational or unacceptable. Something above and beyond Nature, something non-natural, includes haloes on some kinds of conduct, and razor wire forbidding others. These norms are, fortunately, accessible to human beings, but only through a strange, tailor-made faculty known as intuition.

It is easy to see that this yields no very satisfactory philosophy of value. Among other problems, it gives no account of why we should be interested in the propositions that, on the theory, form the subject matter of ethics. Just as colors seem to be entirely optional objects of concern, so norms, values, duties, rights, and indeed other things that float free of the natural world must surely be optional objects of interest. For those of us mired in practical matters, such as human pleasures and pains, desires and needs, the world of ethics would seem to be something of a distraction. If the normative nature of things is so distinct from their ordinary nature, it is not only difficult to see how it has to be an object of interest, but even difficult to see how it is possible for it to engage us. The 'magnetism' of Goodness seems quite inexplicable. Yet Moore's argument against naturalism seemed to block any return to saying that the subject matter of ethics is just underlying human pleasures and pains, desires and needs.

After Moore, philosophers fixing their gaze on judgments of Goodness eventually confronted the dilemma that either their content was equivalent to that of empirical or scientific propositions or it was not. If the former, the account conflates 'is' with 'ought' and falls to the Open Question Argument. If the latter, the account fails because of the nebulous subject matter with which it purports to deal. This impasse opened the way toward an entirely different approach. This did not stare at the judgment of Goodness, asking what was being judged true or false. Instead it asked what was being done by human beings when they go in for ethics. And there seemed to be an obvious answer: when people express themselves in the normative terms of ethics and morals, they are voicing practical attitudes and emotions. They may be doing other things as well: inviting or insisting on others sharing those attitudes or emotions, or prescribing ways to behave, or demanding conformity to ways of behaving. These practical functions seem to give ethics its identity. In that case, the function of normative sentences is not to represent either peculiar Moorean facts about the world or more mundane empirical facts about the world. It is to avow attitudes, to persuade others, to insist on conformities and prescribe behavior. So was born the 'emotivism' of A. J. Ayer and Charles Stevenson (Ayer, 1936; Stevenson, 1944). In Ayer's famous words:

> The presence of an ethical symbol in a proposition adds nothing to its factual content. Thus if I say to someone, "You acted wrongly in stealing that money," I am not stating anything more than if I had simply said, "You stole that money." In adding that this action is wrong I am not making any further statement about it. I am simply evincing my moral disapproval of it. It is as if I had said "You stole that money" in a peculiar tone of horror, or written it with the addition of some special exclamation marks.

2. REFINING THE THEORY

This practical approach to the function of moral language and moral thought allows for a number of refinements. Although Ayer and Stevenson concentrated upon the practical function of expressing emotion, it was easy to see that in many cases, ethical thinking can be relatively unemotional. The eighteenth century worked in terms of sentiments and passions. A better term may be 'attitude' or 'stance.' R. M. Hare influentially put the issuing of prescriptions at the heart of his account (1952). In more modern writings, the approach is generically called 'expressivism,' leaving some latitude in identifying exactly what is expressed. This latitude is not a weakness of the approach, but simply reflects the fact that our ethical reactions can be more or less emotional, more or less demanding, and more or less prescriptive. Different cultures may exhibit different ethical 'styles.' One may work in terms of sin, bringing in attitudes like disgust and fear of pollution. Another may work in terms of shame, with social sanctions expressed in terms of contempt and designed to arouse corresponding embarrassment or shame on the part of the wrongdoer. And a third may work in terms of guilt, with social sanctions expressed in terms of anger and resentment, and designed to arouse corresponding guilt on the part of the wrongdoer. In other words, the ethic of a culture can be 'variably realized' in the emotional tone that accompanies the practical pressures people put on themselves and others.

There is a need to give some further description of the territory, however. For if nothing more is said, expressivism would face the objection that the state of mind expressed may just be the state of mind of believing that something is Good, and no advance has been made. The most influential metaphor directing this part of the area has been that of Elizabeth Anscombe (1957). Anscombe contrasted two different ways of using a shopping list. In the first, the list directs the subject's purchases. It tells the subject what to do. In the second, the list records the subject's purchases. It records what the subject has bought. In the first use, the list is prescriptive or directive, whereas in the second, it is descriptive or representational. A philosopher like Moore conceives of normative propositions as representational, but then flounders on the question of what they represent. The expressivist approach conceives them as prescriptive or directive. In the best known way of explaining the metaphor, it is said that normative language has a different 'direction of fit' to the world. It exists in order to direct action and change the world. It does not exist in order to represent any natural part of it, and still less some occult part of it (Smith, 1988).

This makes it sound as though normative expressions are more like expressions of desire—which also have the different direction of fit with the world—than like expressions of representational states such as belief. So a direct approach to identifying the relevant attitudes would be to seek an outright reduction of moral attitude, for example, in terms of what we desire, or what we desire to desire. But such reductions are usually uncomfortable. Simple desire or liking scarcely gets us into the territory of ethics at all, not least since there need be no disagreement between two people, one of whom likes X and one of whom does not. At the least, ethics seems to concern desires that in some sense we insist upon, or which we demand from other people.

Desire to desire does not do either. For I may desire to desire X because I regret my feeble appetite for X and am aware that people who do desire X get more fun out of life. But that is different both from admiring X and admiring the desire for X. A better general description might locate the ethical in terms of those springs of action with which an agent is most identified, and this in turn would be manifested by things like reluctance to change or reluctance to tolerate variation. Ethics is about our practical insistences, including centrally those with which we set ourselves to comply, or hope ourselves to comply (Blackburn, 1998; Tiberius, 2000).

The obvious advantage of expressivism is that it has no difficulty accounting for the motivational nature of moral commitment. Moral commitment is described and identified in terms of its motivational function. Attitudes, for or against things, are unproblematically motivating. But then a difficulty opens up on the other side, falling into danger of making

the connection too close, which means closing any space for the phenomena of weakness of will. We want to leave it open that an agent should judge, with certainty, that succumbing to some temptation is not the thing to do, but go ahead and do it anyhow. We do not always live up to our better selves. We may fail to do so when we are listless or peevish, or simply perverse or weak. The expressivist (like anybody else) should acknowledge such phenomena.

In order to accommodate them to an attitudinal account of ethical commitment, they should be diagnosed as cases of the house divided against itself. With weakness of will part of us pulls one way, but part of us pulls the other way, and on the particular occasion this is the part that wins. An attitude can be compared with a disposition, and dispositions do not always manifest themselves when you might expect them to do so. A fragile glass might unexpectedly bounce on being dropped instead of shattering. If it bounces too often, the view that it is fragile starts to lose ground. Similarly, if temptation wins too often, we begin to doubt the strength of the alleged moral commitment, and diagnoses of hypocrisy or mere lip-service to an ideal start to gain ground. But in honest-to-God weakness of will, the moral vector is still operating, and this can be shown by subsequent remorse, or embarrassment at being caught, or a variety of discomforts. Weakness of will is typically uncomfortable, just because our inclinations are out of line with what we would wish to insist on, from ourselves or others. If we consider an attitude such as disapproval of an action, the right thing for an expressivist to say is that such an attitude is (necessarily) such as to result in condemnation of the action or avoidance of the action, other things being equal. But this does not mean that in our actual psychologies, the attitude inevitably trumps whatever other desires or tendencies pull us toward the action. For other things are not always equal.

It is also plain that expressing an attitude should not be thought of simply in terms of letting other people know that you have the attitude. Rather, an attitude is put forward as something to be adopted. The notion is one of attempting public coordination or sharing of the attitude. Similarly, the speaker's own state of mind is not the topic. Not only can one express attitudes one does not oneself hold, but one can sincerely express attitudes one falsely believes oneself to hold, and it can be one's subsequent behavior that informs someone of the mistake. This is no more than parallel to cases where in describing things one can say things one does not oneself believe, or which one sincerely but mistakenly supposes oneself to believe.

Expressivism thus distinguished itself from the position sometimes called naive or vulgar subjectivism, in which a speaker is interpreted as simply describing what he or she feels about an issue. For the naive subjectivist, ethical judgments are true or false according to whether the speaker is sincere. The truth-condition of a speaker's utterance "Hitler was abominable" is just that the speaker holds or feels that Hitler is abominable. This account is just wrong. It is not our practice to allow the truth of such a claim simply on the grounds that the speaker feels one way or another (the theory is also regressive, in that it still needs an account of what it is that the speaker feels, the content of the "that" clause). Expressivism avoids these problems by denying that the speaker is describing his own mind. He is voicing his mind, that is, putting forward an attitude or stance as the attitude or stance that is to be held.

An expressivist theory will also want to say something about strength of attitude. There is a difference, intuitively, between believing with not too much confidence that Saddam Hussein is very bad indeed and believing with a lot of confidence or certainty that he is at least rather bad. If expressivism is to cope with this kind of subtle difference, it will need a parallel difference in attitude. But since attitudes do not seem to be more or less probable, this may prove difficult to do. We might imagine an attitude of 'loathing,' corresponding to the view that Saddam is very bad indeed, and an attitude of 'disliking,' corresponding to the view that he is rather bad. This gives us one dimension of variation. Then the problem is that our moral beliefs seem to permit two dimensions: the very bad/rather bad dimension, and the probable/certain dimension. Here the solution will be to come up with a difference that plays the same function as the probable/certain dimension. We might suggest a difference in the 'robustness'

with which an attitude is held, measured by the amount of evidence or persuasion it would take to shift it. Loathing of Saddam combined with a tincture of uncertainty about a lot of the evidence might succumb quite quickly to propaganda on his behalf, whereas dislike of him that is strongly founded would survive all but the most revisionary of stories about recent history.

At first sight, disagreement in attitude is easy to understand. If I am for something, and you are against it, then we disagree. If it is the time for our attitudes to issue in a choice, then, other things being equal, I will choose it and you will not, or I will require it and you will require its absence. But, as with confidence, there are subtleties here as well. I may admire something, but you simply have no opinion about it. Is this to count as disagreement? We might so count it: zealots reject anything other than precise conformity of attitude. This is the idea that if you are not with us you are against us, as when a true believer counts agnosticism as a heresy just as much as overt atheism. But in principle, having no attitude either way is to be distinguished from having thought about it and decided that there is equal merit on both sides. Again, the expressivist can point to the relative robustness of the different states. In probability theory, a gambler who has no opinion either way about whether a coin is biased may bet at the same rate as someone who has done exhaustive experiments and convinced herself that the coin is unbiased. The difference between them is that it would take more evidence to shift the betting rate of the second person than the first. Her betting rate is robust. Similarly, if someone has no attitude either way, they should be relatively quickly responsive to incoming evidence in favor of one side or the other. Whereas if someone has thought about it and arrived at the view that there are equal merits on each side, it will take more to persuade her of an asymmetry.

3. EXPRESSIVISM AND ERROR

Even if it provides a satisfactory account of the states of mind, the 'attitudes' associated with normativity, expressivism still faces problems. To many philosophers, it seems to take away too much. It seems to take away any notion of real normative truth. Indeed, that was one of its motivations, since it was difficulty with the nature of normative facts and our access to them that led to the flight from Moore. But then the fear arises that we are left with too little. The fear crystallizes around the idea that our language, thought, and practice are premised on the idea that there is a normative order, a way things ought to be. But expressivism tries to get by without saying this, and so in the eyes of critics it falls short of giving an adequate account of ethical language, thought, and practice. These are premised on allegiance to a moral 'reality.' But expressivism regards moral reality as a myth, and allegiance to it as self-deception.

This kind of unease can be expressed in many ways. When we moralize (using this is a catch-all term for any way of expressing evaluative or normative opinion), we think we are getting things right. We think some opinions are certain, and others less so. If we are of undogmatic temper, we may indeed worry whether our cherished moral opinion may, in fact, be mistaken. We certainly think others are often mistaken. We also go in for working out the implications of our views, sometimes getting ourselves into quite complex chains of moral reasonings. We do not automatically suppose that our first thoughts are our best thoughts. We go cautiously, acknowledge fallibility, and sometimes recognize that we were wrong. But sometimes we think we know the answer, and we think we know of methods for getting the answer. We prize our rationality, in this area as others, and our objectivity when we follow the argument wherever it leads. We also recognize that moral truth is often 'mind-independent.' Our thinking something is right or wrong does not make it so. Our responses have to answer to the moral truth. They do not create it.

All these thoughts and activities make up what we can call the realist surface of everyday moralizing. They seem to suggest that we take ourselves to be beholden to a moral reality, which we are attempting to represent correctly. . . .

If ordinary moralizing with its realist surface is indefensible, what does the defensible

substitute look like, and how is it different? Perhaps it would look very different. For example, it might deal only in overt prescriptions like the Ten Commandments: thou shalt do this, thou shalt not do that. Or it might confine itself to overt expressions of being for something (Hooray!) or against it (Boo!). Such simple language would have no room for expressing thoughts of fallibility, or mistake, or improvement, or getting things right, nor any other thoughts that essentially involve some idea of moral truth or falsity.

But perhaps the defensible substitute would not look nearly as different as this, or even very different at all. This opens the door to the persona christened the "quasi-realist" (Blackburn, 1984, p. 171). Quasi-realism was explained as trying to earn, on an expressivist basis, the features that tempt people to realism. In other words, it suggests that the realistic surface of the discourse does not have to be jettisoned. It can be explained and defended even by expressivists. Perhaps surprisingly, thoughts about fallibility, objectivity, independence, knowledge, and rationality, as well as truth and falsity themselves, would be available even to people thinking of themselves as antirealists.

Quasi-realism is different from expressivism itself. . . . And one might hold that the program of reconciling the realistic surface with the expressivist account is successful, but have other reasons for rejecting the expressivist account. But to the extent that quasi realism is successful, the doubts arising from the realistic surface of moralizing disappear. So quasi-realism . . . attempts to show that ordinary moral thought is not infected root and branch with philosophical myth.

Quasi-realism works to explain why things that steer philosophers toward realism need not do so. Suppose, for example, a realist trumpets the mind-independence of ethics. A person or a culture may think something right without that making it right. Denying women the vote is wrong, whatever you or I or anyone else thinks. Can an expressivist say as much? This is to be assessed in the standard way, of imagining scenarios or possible worlds in which you or I or others think that women should not have a vote, and passing a verdict on them. Naturally, these scenarios or possibilities excite condemnation, and so the answer is that denying women the vote is wrong, whatever you or I or anyone else thinks about it. In giving that answer one is, of course, standing *within* one's own moral view. One is assessing the scenario in the light of things one thinks and feels about such matters. But that is no objection, since there is no other mode of assessment possible. One cannot pass a verdict without using those parts of one's mind that enable one to pass a verdict.

Again, consider the idea that on some moral matter we may not know the truth. For example, imagine us wondering what to think about someone's conduct. Was he selfish and despicable, or prudently protecting himself in an unfortunate situation? Things are factored in; the matter is turned in different lights; things we do not know about may be suggested. Any verdict may be provisional and liable to reassessment in the light of further information, or a more imaginative understanding of information we already have. We may incline one way, but admit that we do not really know, just because we have a lively awareness of further evidence, further factors, possible improvements in our understanding of what happened or our reactions to what we know happened. Such things might dispose us to incline a different way. Again, the phenomenon seems entirely consistent with, and indeed explicable by, the expressivist.

For a final example, consider the idea that on any moral issue, there is just one right answer. Rather than seeing this as a metaphysical thesis, testifying to the completeness of Moore's world of Norms and Forms, the quasi-realist will encourage a pragmatic or practical construal. The doctrine can be seen as a strenuous piece of practical advice: when there are still two things to think, keep on worrying. Beaver away, and eventually, it is promised, one opinion will deserve to prevail. This is itself the expression of an attitude to practical reasoning (and by no means a compulsory one). Accepting such an attitude is not, however, the badge of realism, but simply the optimism that our best efforts can, in the end, close any issue, provided we keep at it long enough. . . .

REFERENCES

Anscombe, Elizabeth. 1957. *Intention.* Oxford: Blackwell.
Ayer, A. J. 1936. *Language, Truth, and Logic.* London: Victor Gollancz.
Blackburn, Simon. 1984. *Spreading the Word.* Oxford: Oxford University Press.
———. 1998. "Trust, Cooperation, and Human Psychology." In *Trust and Governance,* ed. Margaret Levi and Valerie Braithwaite, 28–45. New York: Russell Sage Foundation.
Hare, R. M. 1952. *The Language of Morals.* Oxford: Oxford University Press.
Hume, David. [1739]. 1888. *Treatise of Human Nature.* Ed. L. A. Selby-Bigge. Oxford: Oxford University Press.
Smith, Michael. 1988. "Reason and Desire." *Proceedings of the Aristotelian Society* 88: 243–258.
Stevenson, Charles. 1944. *Ethics and Language.* New Haven, Conn.: Yale University Press.
Tiberius, Valerie. 2000. "Humean Heroism: Value Commitments and the Source of Normativity." *Pacific Philosophical Quarterly* 81: 426–446.

STUDY QUESTIONS

1. Why does Blackburn think that non-cognitivists were the real beneficiaries of Moore's open-question argument?
2. What is the main difference between expressivism and emotivism?
3. According to Blackburn, why is expressivism not a form of subjectivism?
4. What is quasi-realism?

What Is the Frege-Geach Problem?

Mark Schroeder

Mark Schroeder, Professor of Philosophy at the University of Southern California, provides an overview of the so-called Frege-Geach problem for non-cognitivism. The reason for its name is that the issue was presented by Peter Geach (1916–2013), Professor of Logic at the University of Leeds, who attributed the concern to Gottlob Frege (1848–1925), the eminent German mathematician and philosopher. Recall that the unifying idea behind non-cognitivism is that normative and descriptive utterances are fundamentally different. Yet no linguistic evidence demonstrates that normative terms operate differently from descriptive terms. Consider the following set of sentences, paying close attention to the italicized uses of "wrong":

1. Lying is *wrong*.
2. If lying is *wrong*, then getting someone to lie is wrong.
3. Hence, getting someone to lie is wrong.

This argument appears valid—that is, the premises imply the conclusion. The use of "wrong" in the first sentence, however, is understood in a non-cognitive sense, while the initial use of "wrong" in the second sentence does not emote, prescribe, or express an attitude. Hence, non-cognitivists are committed to assigning different meanings to these two uses of "wrong." Thus it appears that the argument is not valid after all, which is a troubling result, and one that can be found in any context that involves complex sentences with simpler normative sentences embedded within them. Schroeder considers various attempts to defuse this difficulty for non-cognitivism but finds no proposed solution satisfactory.

WHAT IS NONCOGNITIVISM?

Classificatory labels like "emotivism," "noncognitivism," and "expressivism" have been used in a variety of ways. For the purposes of this article, I will use "noncognitivism" as a catch-all label for the wide and heterogeneous class of views which includes Ayer, . . . Stevenson, Hare, Blackburn, and Gibbard as primary exemplars. These authors differ widely over how they believe moral language to work, but they all agree that the *kind* of meaning that moral terms (like "wrong") have is importantly

From Mark Schroeder, "What Is the Frege-Geach Problem?" *Philosophy Compass* 3/4 (2008). Reprinted by permission of the publisher.

different from the *kind* of meaning that descriptive terms (like "green") have.

Among emotivist views, which were the first kind of noncognitivist views defended, though all shared the view that moral terms have a different kind of meaning than descriptive terms, and all agreed that moral terms had something to do with the emotions, there was a fair bit of disagreement over just what moral terms did have to do with the emotions. According to some views, for example, moral sentences are used to *create an effect*—to elicit an emotion on the part of the audience. While according to other views, moral sentences are used to *express* or *give voice to* the emotions of the *speaker.* Sometimes these views were put together, either explicitly or without discussion, and sometimes they were put together with other views about the use of moral language, which didn't directly relate to the emotions, strictly speaking. For example, some theorists said that moral sentences are disguised imperatives, or even that they are disguised commands.

When R. M. Hare published *The Language of Morals* in 1952, he was highly critical of earlier noncognitivists for assimilating moral language to other kinds of language. Moral language, Hare held, is [not] *just like* exclamations, as Ayer's colorful prose suggests . . . Instead, Hare held, what was right about the noncognitivist family of views was that moral language belongs to a broad family of language, *prescriptive* language, of which imperatives are another and more familiar instance. Moral sentences are not disguised imperatives, on Hare's view, but they do have a meaning of broadly the same kind as imperatives, contrasting with the kind of meaning that ordinary descriptive sentences like "grass is green" have.

Contemporary versions of noncognitivism differ from each of these previous classes of views in yet another way. Over the last quarter century, [noncognitivists] have developed views which fit into the tradition descending from Ayer and Stevenson, but which have a more detailed flavor that has come to be known as *expressivism.* The basic idea of expressivism is that it is the job of a semantic theory to explain what a sentence, "P," means, by saying what it is to think that P. Whatever a given theory says it is to think that P, that is the mental state that the theory counts as being *expressed* by "P." So a complete expressivist theory would assign each sentence of the language to a mental state which it expresses, and this would constitute, according to expressivists, a semantic theory for the language. Metaethical expressivists like Blackburn . . . go on, further, to explain that moral sentences differ in the kind of meaning that they have from ordinary descriptive sentences, because the kind of mental state that they express differs from the kind of mental state expressed by ordinary descriptive sentences.

So noncognitivist views differ widely both in their commitments and in their theoretical framework. The safest way to characterize what all of these views have in common is that they reject the idea that moral terms have the same kind of meaning as ordinary descriptive terms. Once we characterize noncognitivist views in this way, moreover, it is easy to characterize the crux of the Frege-Geach Problem. It is that there is no linguistic evidence whatsoever that the meaning of moral terms works differently than that of ordinary descriptive terms. On the contrary, everything that you can do syntactically with a descriptive predicate like "green," you can do with a moral predicate like "wrong," and when you do those things, they have the *same semantic effects.*

So the Frege-Geach Problem is at bottom the problem of how it could be that moral and descriptive terms have exactly the same sort of semantic properties in complex sentences, even though they have different kinds of meaning. In the following sections I'll trace the historical development of this very general problem, of which a relatively narrow set of issues has occupied philosophers' attention.

GEACH['S] ORIGINAL OBJECTION

Geach['s] objections were originally formulated against noncognitivist views which they understood to involve a certain kind of claim about the *speech acts* involved in asserting moral sentences. Hare had said that to call something "good" is to *commend* it, and took this to tell us something about the *meaning* of "good"—not just a fact about what people in general happen to use the word "good" in order to do. So Geach took Hare to be committed to the view that a given appearance of the word "good" means *good* just in case it is being used to commend. That is why he chose examples in which it is clear that the word "good" is *not* being used to commend. Some of the best examples of this were questions, negations, and the antecedents of conditionals: in ordinary cases, people do not say "is this good?" in order to commend it, nor do they say, "this is not good" or "if this is good, then that is good" to commend it. So, Geach inferred, it follows from Hare's commitments that "good" must mean something else when it appears in these sentences, because it is not being used to commend.

Geach's argument did not end there, however; instead, he argued that "good" *must* mean the same thing in these sentences as it does in "this is good." That is because "this is good" is the *answer* to "is this good?", because "this is good" *contradicts* "this is not good," and because "that is good" follows logically, by *modus ponens,* from "this is good" and "if this is good, then that is good." What Geach was doing, in offering this argument, was showing that these *semantic properties* of questions, negations, and conditionals—of what their answers are, of what contradicts them, and of what logically valid arguments they figure in—are explained by the fact that the terms involved *mean the same thing* as they do in the unembedded sentence, "this is good." So Geach concluded that Hare's view was in a very bad way. It was committed to denying exactly what was necessary in order to explain the semantic properties of these complex sentences. . . .

. . . Geach . . . [was, in short,] pressing the objection that noncognitivists are committed to denying that "good" or "wrong" mean the same thing in at least certain kinds of embedded contexts as they do in simple atomic sentences, and that this is bad, because we *need* to assume that they mean the same thing in both places, in order to explain the semantic properties of the complex sentences.

HARE'S ANSWER: COMPOSITIONAL SEMANTICS

Hare replied . . . in 1970, and gave the answer to this objection that has informed essentially all substantive approaches to the Frege-Geach Problem since then. Hare argued that the problem noncognitivists face in accounting for the meaning of complex sentences is essentially no different from the problem that everyone faces in accounting for the meaning of complex ordinary descriptive sentences. For example, "this is not green" does not have the same truth-conditions as "this is green," but that doesn't stop ordinary truth-conditional semanticists from holding that "green" means the same thing in both sentences. So why should the fact that "this is not good" is not used to perform the same speech act as "this is good" mean that noncognitivists are forced to hold that "good" doesn't mean the same thing in both sentences?

The answer offered by ordinary truth-conditional semanticists, as Hare understood it, is to say that though the truth-conditions of "this is not green" are not the *same* as those for "this is green," they are still a *function* of those truth-conditions—a function given by the meaning of the word "not." So "this is green" means the same thing in both sentences, because it makes the same *contribution* toward the truth-conditions of the whole sentence. So similarly, Hare held, all that the noncognitivist needs in order to be able to say the same thing, is to hold that the speech act performed by "this is not good"—which is, of course, something other than commendation of the referent of "this"—is a *function* of the speech act performed by "this is good"—a function given by the meaning of "not." Then, Hare will say, "good" means the same thing in both sentences, because it makes the same contribution to the speech act performed by the whole sentence.

There is an important hitch for Hare's answer to Geach . . . , which it is important to appreciate before we go on. Strictly speaking, the reason why ordinary truth-conditional semanticists can say that the truth-conditions of "this is not green" are a function of the truth-conditions of "this is green," is that they think that "this is green" *really has* truth-conditions, even when it is embedded in the larger sentence, "this is not green." But Geach's point was not just that someone who says "this is not good" does not use the *whole sentence* to commend the referent of "this"; it was that in ordinary cases someone who says "this is not good" does not engage in any speech act of commendation *at all*—even by a proper *part* of the sentence.

If Hare wants to solve this problem, he needs to associate the meaning of a moral sentence with a speech act that it is *suited for*—not with one that is actually performed by each occurrence of a sentence with that meaning. This should not be a surprise; just as speakers can utter complex sentences which contain "this is good" as parts without commending the referent of "this," they can also utter "this is good" sarcastically or in other ways that do not involve commending the referent of "this," either. Similarly, however, speakers can utter imperatives without issuing commands. For example, they can be uttered in jest, or to convey information. So Hare should say that the relationship between "this is good" and commendation is like the relationship between "do this" and commanding, and say that it is the job of a semantic theory to assign each sentence to the speech act that it is in this sense *suited* to perform, assigning suitable speech acts to complex sentences as a function of the speech acts assigned to their parts that is given by the meaning of the words—like "not" and "if . . . then" that are used to construct the complex sentence.

Hare's answer . . . therefore meets the terms of Geach['s] . . . original challenge: it explains how moral terms like "good" could have the same meaning in both places in which they appear. But importantly, it doesn't yet solve the problem raised by their arguments, because not just any function assigning a speech act to be used by "this is not good" will suffice to explain why it has the semantic properties that it does. Just to take two obvious examples, neither the identity function nor the function which maps every speech act to the speech act of promising to get married before July would yield an adequate semantic account of the meaning of "not."

THE NEW SHAPE OF THE PROBLEM

So if noncognitivists take Hare's answer . . . seriously, they still owe us, for every complex-sentence-forming construction in natural languages, an account of just *what* gets assigned to the complex sentence as a function of the assignment to its parts, and an explanation of why this semantic theory yields the right predictions about the semantic properties of questions, negations, conditionals, and so on. Speech-act theories like Hare's will need a compositional semantics which assigns to every sentence the speech act that it is suited for performing, and contemporary expressivist views will need a compositional semantics which assigns to every sentence the mental state that it expresses. So for different kinds of noncognitivist view[s], their semantic theory will take different forms, but these views can still follow the broad outlines of Hare's suggestion.

This is what "solutions" to the Frege-Geach Problem are really trying to do. They are trying to fulfill Hare's promise that a noncognitivist view can do the same thing as an ordinary truth-conditional view, and provide a compositional semantics for at least certain linguistic constructions which tells us the meaning of complex sentences of a certain kind in terms of the meanings of the parts of that sentence—either in terms of speech acts or more commonly, in terms of mental states expressed—and then tries to show that this is an adequate semantics for the sentence, because it can predict and explain the sentence's semantic properties. For example, an adequate semantics for "not" must explain why negated sentences contradict the sentences they negate, and an adequate semantics for conditionals must explain why they license *modus ponens*.

The problem is *very big*, because for every complex-sentence-forming construction in natural languages, sentences formed using that construction using moral terms like "good" have the same sort of semantic properties as sentences formed using that construction using ordinary descriptive terms like "green." This is true not only for questions, negations, and conditionals, but also for quantifiers, modals, tense, attitude-verbs, generics, adverbs of quantification, intensifying adverbs like "very," and so on. Noncognitivists believe that moral terms have a different kind of semantics than ordinary descriptive terms, but somehow every complex-sentence-forming construction manages to do exactly the same sort of things with them that it does with ordinary descriptive terms.

This is the new shape of the Frege-Geach Problem . . . The problem is to construct a compositional semantics for natural languages which makes complex moral sentences and complex descriptive sentences turn out to have the same kinds of semantic properties—and the *right* kind of semantic properties—even though moral and descriptive terms really have two quite different kinds of meaning.

EARLY APPROACHES TO CONDITIONALS: HIGHER-ORDER ATTITUDES

Despite the broad scope of the Frege-Geach Problem, most research devoted to it during the 1980s and 1990s focused on the case of conditionals, and specifically of explaining why *modus ponens* is a valid rule of inference. . . . Expressivist treatments of "wrong" generally hold that atomic "wrong" sentences express some negative attitude toward their subjects. Without loss of generality, I'll call this negative attitude *disapproval,* even though different expressivist views will have different theories about precisely what this attitude involves and what it should be called. Schematically, then, such expressivist views hold that for any value of "X," "X is wrong" expresses a negative attitude called *disapproval* toward the referent of "X."

An important early category of expressivist approaches to conditionals treated them as expressing *higher-order attitudes* toward the attitudes expressed by their parts. So, for example, Simon Blackburn (*Spreading the Word*) proposed . . . that "if stealing is wrong, then murder is wrong" expresses disapproval of the state of both disapproving of stealing and not disapproving of murder. So it

expresses a higher-order attitude toward the mental states expressed by the parts of the sentence.

Blackburn's approach is designed to explain why someone who accepts "stealing is wrong" and "if stealing is wrong, then murder is wrong" is under a kind of rational pressure to accept "murder is wrong"—or at least to give up on one of the other two.[1] This is because so long as she accepts "stealing is wrong" and *doesn't* accept "murder is wrong," she is in the very state that she disapproves of, in virtue of accepting the conditional. So Blackburn held that there is a kind of "incoherence" in her attitudes—an incoherence that can be resolved by going on to accept the conclusion, or by giving up on one of the premises.

. . . But . . . compare the following two arguments:

1a Stealing is wrong.
2a If stealing is wrong, then murder is wrong.
3a Murder is wrong.

1b Stealing is wrong.
2b It is wrong to both disapprove of stealing and not disapprove of murder.
3b Murder is wrong.

The problem is that on Blackburn's account, sentences 2a and 2b express the very same attitude—disapproval of the state of both disapproving of stealing and not disapproving of murder. So if his account *does* suffice to explain why the former argument is valid, then it also suffices to explain why the latter argument is valid. But the latter argument is not, intuitively, valid. So Blackburn's higher-order attitudes approach overgenerates validity.

The problem . . . is that the *kind* of rational incoherence that is generated by Blackburn's explanation is not the incoherence of having inconsistent beliefs or of having a belief and failing to draw one of its consequences. It is the kind of incoherence involved in thinking that murder is wrong and murdering anyway. . . . The . . . main lesson we have learned from higher-order attitude accounts [is that] if expressivists are to be able to explain validity, they are going to need to appeal to a kind of incoherence among attitudes that is of a more specific type than the broad kind of incoherence to which Blackburn initially appealed. They are going to have to appeal to incoherence among attitudes that is of the very same type as the incoherence involved in both believing that *p* and also believing that ~*p*. . . .

THE NEGATION PROBLEM

Since the mid-1990s, conditionals have attracted much less direct attention, and more attention has been paid to the case of negation. The reason for this is simple; at a minimum, explaining why conditionals validate *modus ponens* requires explaining why {"P," "P→Q," "~Q"} is an inconsistent set of sentences. But this problem has many moving pieces: it requires having in hand an expressivist account not only of the semantics of the conditional, but of negation, and an expressivist account of the inconsistency of sentences, besides.[2] So much investigation has adopted a more conservative strategy, and focused on trying to acquire an adequate expressivist semantics for negation first, so that it can be used as a *fixed point* in developing an expressivist semantics for conditionals. The most important semantic property of negation, after all, is that negated sentences should turn out to be inconsistent with the sentences they negate, and to explain why {"P," "~P"} is an inconsistent set, we need only know the semantics for negation and how inconsistency works—we don't need to know anything about conditionals.

Moreover, . . . not just any old kind of mental incoherence or rational tension between two mental states will suffice in order to explain inconsistency between the sentences that express them. The way that beliefs with inconsistent contents clash with one another is fine, but the way that having an attitude and disapproving of oneself for having that attitude clash is not fine. . . .

If ordinary descriptive beliefs were the only kinds of mental state that could disagree with one another, then it would follow immediately that the only way "murder is wrong" and "murder is not wrong" could be inconsistent, would be if they both express ordinary descriptive beliefs. But this is

precisely what expressivists . . . deny. But fortunately, . . . beliefs are not the only kinds of mental states which appear to conflict with one another. As has received a great deal of attention in the philosophy of action, there is a very similar kind of rational conflict between *intending* inconsistent things as between *believing* inconsistent things.

So if intentions—or other noncognitive attitudes like *disapproval*—share with beliefs the property that they disagree with each other just in case they are toward inconsistent contents, then expressivists can hope to explain inconsistency between moral sentences and their negations, by assigning "stealing is wrong" and "stealing is not wrong" to states of disapproval of inconsistent things. For example, if "stealing is wrong" expresses disapproval of stealing, and "stealing is not wrong" expresses disapproval of not stealing, then we could use the fact that these two states disagree with one another in order to explain why "stealing is wrong" and "stealing is not wrong" are inconsistent.

But this approach meets an important obstacle. The obstacle is that even if disapproval of stealing and disapproval of not stealing disagree, the latter is not, in fact, the attitude expressed by "stealing is not wrong," but rather that expressed by "not stealing is wrong." This means not only that we have failed to give an account of what mental state is expressed by "stealing is not wrong," but also that there is no state that we can assign to it, such that we can explain all of the inconsistencies that we need to explain as cases of disapproving of inconsistent contents— which disagree in the same . . . [way] as beliefs with inconsistent contents do: by being cases of the same attitude with inconsistent contents.

This is easy to prove. Compare the following four sentences:

1c Stealing is wrong.	→ DIS(stealing)
2c Stealing is not wrong.	→ DIS(*x*)
3c Not stealing is wrong.	→ DIS(not stealing)
4c Not stealing is not wrong.	→ DIS(*y*)

Both 1c and 2c are inconsistent sentences, as are 3c and 4c. So if their inconsistency is to be explained in terms of . . . the mental states that they express—states which rationally conflict with each other in just the same way that beliefs with inconsistent contents do—and this is to be explained by the fact that disapproval, like belief and intention, is the sort of attitude that it rationally conflicts in this way to hold toward inconsistent contents, then 2b and 4c must express some states of disapproval. 2c must express disapproval of something inconsistent with stealing, in order to explain why 1c and 2c are inconsistent, and 4c must express disapproval of something inconsistent with not stealing, in order to explain why 3c and 4c are inconsistent. But if *x* is inconsistent with stealing, and *y* is inconsistent with not stealing, then it follows that *x* and *y* must be inconsistent with each other. But this yields the prediction that the states of mind expressed by 2c and 4c rationally conflict in exactly the way required in order to explain the inconsistency of 2c and 4c. But 2c and 4c are not inconsistent sentences!

THE HIERARCHY OF ATTITUDES

Faced with this problem, . . . contemporary expressivist views have granted that "stealing is not wrong" cannot express the same kind of attitude as "stealing is wrong" expresses toward stealing. And this has led most theorists . . . to postulate that "stealing is not wrong" expresses a new and *different* attitude toward stealing, which is nevertheless assumed to disagree with disapproval of stealing. So rather than being inconsistent because they express the same attitude toward inconsistent contents, as "grass is green" and "grass is not green" are, these views hold that "stealing is wrong" and "stealing is not wrong" are inconsistent because they express different attitudes toward the *same* content—attitudes which just happen to disagree with one another.

This is the first step on the expressivist trip toward the postulation of an entire hierarchy of distinct noncognitive attitudes that can be expressed by moral sentences. . . . [A] simple example . . . illustrate[s] where the pressure to postulate a new and distinct attitude expressed by the negations of atomic sentences comes from:

w Jon thinks that stealing is wrong.
n1 Jon doesn't think that stealing is wrong.
n2 Jon thinks that stealing is not wrong.
n3 Jon thinks that not stealing is wrong.

The task of providing an expressivist semantics for "not" is the task of giving content to n2—for expressivism is the view that you give the meaning of "P" by saying what it is to think that P. But the trouble is that we can't just read this off of the expressivist account of the meaning of "stealing is wrong," because w lacks sufficient structure. As n1 to n3 illustrate, there are three places in which a "not" can be inserted in w. But as n1* to n3* below illustrate, there are *not* three places in which a "not" can be inserted in the schematic expressivist account of w:

w* Jon disapproves of stealing.
n1* Jon doesn't disapprove of stealing.
n2* ???
n3* Jon disapproves of not stealing.

. . . [T]he reason why expressivists have needed to resort to an attitude *distinct* from disapproval to be expressed by the negations of atomic "wrong" sentences, is in order to make up for the lack of structure in their account of the attitude expressed by the atomic sentences. But this also suffices to show that the problem exists not only for negation, but for *every* complex-sentence-forming construction, as the following examples illustrate:

&1 Jon thinks that stealing is wrong and thinks that murdering is wrong.
&2 Jon thinks that stealing is wrong and murdering is wrong.
&3 Jon thinks that stealing and murdering is wrong.

∀1 Everything is such that Jon thinks that it is wrong.
∀2 Jon thinks that everything is wrong.
∀3 Jon thinks that (doing everything) is wrong.

P1 Jon thought that stealing is wrong.
P2 Jon thinks that stealing was wrong.
P3 Jon thinks that having stolen is wrong.

◊1 It is possible that Jon thinks stealing is wrong.

◊2 Jon thinks that it is possible that stealing is wrong.

◊3 Jon thinks that (possibly stealing) is wrong.

And it is easy to extend such examples indefinitely. For each case, all three sentences need to be distinguished. For each case, providing an expressivist semantics for that complex-sentence-forming construction is a matter of giving content to the second sentence. And for each case, there is one too few places in the structure of sentence w, for any account of the second sentence to fall out. So for each such construction, expressivists need to postulate a new attitude to be expressed by sentences formed by that construction, in order to make up for this lack of structure.

Moreover, things don't end there; for the same reasons that conjunctions of atomic sentences require a new attitude, conjunctions of negations of atomic sentences require a new attitude, as do conjunctions of conjunctions. Similarly, for the same reasons that negations of atomic sentences require a new attitude, so do negations of conjunctions. So explicit advocates of the hierarchy of attitudes . . . rapidly commit to thousands and thousands of distinct kinds of attitudes to be expressed by even relatively simple moral sentences. . . .

COMBINING WITH DESCRIPTIVE LANGUAGE

In addition to the obstacles so far encountered, expressivists face a special problem in trying to provide a unified semantics for both moral and descriptive language. The problem, at bottom, is that in order to provide a semantics for "not," "if . . . then," and other constructions as they apply to *moral* sentences, expressivists acquire commitments which act as a *constraint* on their semantics for complex ordinary descriptive sentences like "grass is not green."

. . . The problem is that two-place connectives like "and," "or," and binary quantifiers can take two moral arguments, but they can also take one moral and one descriptive argument, or two descriptive arguments, as these examples illustrate:

1d Stealing is wrong or murder is wrong.

2d Stealing is wrong or grass is green.

3d Snow is white or grass is green.

If "or" is to have the same meaning in all three of these sentences, therefore, then its meaning in 3d will be constrained by the commitments that expressivists need to adopt in order to get it to work in 1d and 2d. And the same goes, in principle, for one-place connectives, as well—if they are to have the same meaning in both moral and descriptive sentences, then their meaning in purely descriptive sentences will be constrained by the expressivist's commitments about how they need to work in moral sentences. . . .

In general it is fair to say that dealing with the extra constraint that an expressivist treatment of moral language poses on how expressivists are to account for the meaning of ordinary complex descriptive sentences is one of the most central and difficult aspects of the Frege-Geach Problem. It is hard enough to give an adequate semantic account for a wide range of difficult-to-understand natural language constructions, from indicative conditionals to generics to epistemic modals. It's only harder to approach these problems under the kinds of extra constraints imposed by expressivism.

IS THE PROBLEM REALLY ONE ABOUT TRUTH OR LOGIC?

Notice that the essence of the Frege-Geach Problem has nothing especially to do with truth, nor with logic, nor with reasoning. And it is certainly not simply a problem about explaining moral *modus ponens* arguments. Many authors *have* claimed that the Frege-Geach Problem is about accounting for logic, but we've seen here that that is far from the case. The problem has often been thought to be specifically about logic primarily because of the effectiveness of Geach's example of a *modus ponens* argument (which he used in order to argue that "good" must mean the same thing when it appears inside the antecedent of a conditional as outside it) and because most discussions of the problem over the last twenty years have been heavily influenced by Blackburn's formulations, and he strongly emphasized this aspect of the problem.

But in fact the problem is much more general. Consider, for example, the case of attitude-ascriptions. "Max hopes that this is good," "Max wonders whether this is good," and "Max is ecstatic that this is good" are just a small sampling of the very wide range of attitude-ascriptions. Each of these constructions works just like their counterparts with ordinary descriptive complements: "Max hopes that this is green," "Max wonders whether this is green," and "Max is ecstatic that this is green." Whereas the primary semantic properties of words like "not," "and," and "if . . . then" might be characterized as *logical* properties, the primary semantic properties of "hopes that," "wonders whether," and "is ecstatic that" wouldn't be so characterized. Yet noncognitivists owe an account of the meaning of each and every attitude verb, just as much as they owe an account of "not," "and," and "if . . . then." Very little progress has yet been made on how noncognitivists can treat attitude verbs, and the prospects for further progress look dim. . . .

SUMMARY

At bottom, the essence of the Frege-Geach Problem is that moral and descriptive terms play exactly the same kind of semantic role in every kind of complex linguistic construction in natural languages. Since noncognitivist views consist centrally in the idea that moral terms like "wrong" have a *different* kind of meaning from ordinary descriptive terms like "green," that makes noncognitivism look like a very unpromising hypothesis about natural language semantics. At the very least, if noncognitivism is going to get off of the ground, noncognitivists have their work cut out for them—not only to explain the meaning of complex moral sentences, but to offer a

compositional semantics for English that predicts and explains why despite their differences, moral and descriptive terms function in all of the same kinds of ways. That is the Frege-Geach Problem for noncognitivist metaethical theories.

NOTES

1. Here I use "accept" as a shorthand for "is in the mental state expressed by."
2. Expressivists can't appeal directly to truth or satisfaction in their account of inconsistency of sentences, because their semantics doesn't generate truth-conditions; only mental states.

WORKS CITED

Ayer, A. J. *Language, Truth, and Logic.* New York, NY: Dover, 1936.

Blackburn, Simon. "Attitudes and Contents". *Ethics* 98.3 (1988): 501–17.

———. *Essays in Quasi-Realism.* Oxford: Oxford UP, 1993.

———. "Moral Realism" (1973). Reprinted in Simon Blackburn. *Essays in Quasi-Realism.* Oxford: Oxford UP, 1993. 111–29.

———. *Ruling Passions.* Oxford: Oxford UP, 1998.

———. *Spreading the Word.* Oxford: Oxford UP, 1984.

Geach, P. T. "Ascriptivism". *Philosophical Review* 69 (1960): 221–5.

———. "Assertion". *Philosophical Review* 74 (1965): 449–65.

———. "Imperative and Deontic Logic". *Analysis* 18 (1958): 49–56.

Gibbard, Allan. *Thinking How to Live.* Cambridge, MA: Harvard UP, 2003.

———. *Wise Choices, Apt Feelings.* Cambridge, MA: Harvard UP, 1990.

Hare, R. M. *The Language of Morals.* Oxford: Oxford UP, 1952.

———. "Meaning and Speech Acts". *The Philosophical Review* 79.1 (1970): 3–24.

Stevenson, C. L. "The Emotive Meaning of Ethical Terms" (1937). Reprinted in C. L. Stevenson. *Facts and Values.* Westport, CT: Greenwood Press, 1963, 10–31

———. *Ethics and Language.* Oxford: Oxford UP, 1944.

———. *Facts and Values.* Westport, CT: Greenwood Press, 1963.

STUDY QUESTIONS

1. According to Schroder, what is the "basic idea" of expressivism?
2. According to Schroder, what is the essence of the Frege-Geach problem?
3. According to Schroder, why do accounts of higher-order attitudes fail to solve the Frege-Geach problem?
4. What is the negation problem?

The Reasons of a Living Being

Allan Gibbard

Allan Gibbard, Professor of Philosophy at the University of Michigan, offers an account of normative judgments that proposes a solution to the Frege-Geach problem. Gibbard's basic idea is that when we think about what we ought to do, we engage in hypothetical contingency planning. Furthermore, when we think about what another person ought to do, we engage in hypothetical contingency planning, deliberating as if on another's behalf.

Consider the following set of sentences:

1. Lying is wrong.
2. If lying is wrong, then getting someone to lie is wrong.
3. Hence, getting someone to lie is wrong.

By asserting (1), that lying is wrong, we express the decision to rule out any plan that includes lying. Furthermore, we rule out any plan that involves lying in every possible circumstance, thereby constructing what Gibbard calls a "hyperplan." By asserting (2), we assume lying is wrong and consequently express the decision to rule out any plan that involves getting someone to lie. Taking (1) and (2) together, we are forced, as in any valid argument, to accept (3)—that is, that getting someone to lie is wrong. To be in the states of planning captured by (1) and (2) but not (3) would result in a disagreement in plans.

In short, by thinking of normative judgments as expressing decisions about what the speaker plans, Gibbard concludes that he has found a solution to the Frege-Geach problem.

. . . Moore argued that moral questions concern a non-natural property. When we try to settle a moral question, he maintained, we're not in the same line of inquiry as when we use empirical, scientific methods to inquire into the natural world. Notoriously, Moore had an "open question" argument which seems in retrospect to be dubious, and a "naturalistic fallacy" which he put in many different ways, all of which seem to beg the question. Later on he saw his first book as terribly confused. But he had another line of argument which, it seems to me, just won't go away; I call it the "What's at issue?" argument.

From Allan Gibbard, "The Reasons of a Living Being," *Proceedings and Addresses of the American Philosophical Association* 76 (2002). Reprinted by permission of the publisher.

Jack, imagine, claims that all pleasure is good in itself, but Jill says that guilty pleasures are not in themselves good. So Jack says that all pleasure is intrinsically good, and Jill disagrees. What's at issue in all this? The two disagree about something, sure enough—but what? Jack, imagine, adds that after all, 'good' just *means* pleasant. But if he is right about what 'good' means, then they can't be disputing whether all pleasure is good, for they both agree that all pleasure is pleasant. Take any proffered definition of 'good,' Moore argued, and we can construct a similar puzzle for it. Now whether any Moore-like argument can be made to work is still a matter of controversy, but Moore does, with this argument, offer us a broad test for any account of what moral claims consist in: ask what's at issue. What, according to the account, is at issue in moral disputes? What does the disagreement consist in? Some accounts, even today, fail to offer plausible answers to this question.

Charles Stevenson thought that Moore's arguments on this score worked, or at least that he could find arguments like Moore's that worked. And Stevenson had an answer to the "What's at issue?" challenge: Jack's for and Jill's not. What's at issue is what pleasures to aim for. Jack intrinsically favors all pleasure, whereas Jill withholds intrinsic favor from guilty pleasures. The two disagree not in belief about some special property; instead, they disagree in attitude. . . .

We can broaden the puzzle the great non-naturalists and emotivists addressed, to one of rationality, or to something grandiose like "the place of reasons in a natural world." Reasons are what weigh toward something's being rational. What's puzzling in moral disputes, then, may boil down to what's puzzling about reasons—reasons to do things, reasons to believe things, and the like. What reasons do you have to help others? Do you have reason to care if they suffer, apart from how their suffering comes to affect you? How do you have reason to feel about someone who preys on others? Is the pleasure something brings you always reason to favor it?

Reasons are puzzling, and one of the puzzles is this: We are living beings, and as such, we are parts of the world of nature. In the natural world, though,

clearly we are exceptional. Our species has developed refined and ingenious ways of studying the natural world, and these methods tell us of many ways in which we are exceptional. For one thing, of course, we are living, and life is so unlike anything else in the universe that it long seemed that the only possible explanation was a special vital principle. Since Darwin, though, we begin to see how aeons of natural selection can account for why life, viewed as part of nature, is so different from non-life. Even among living organisms we are exceptional, and the human brain is vastly more complex than anything else we know about. Human history, politics, social life, learning, and the arts are far more complex than anything even in the life of chimpanzees, though the genetic equipment that allows a human child to grow up to participate in all this is just a last minute evolutionary tinkering, over the past couple of hundred thousand generations, with a tiny proportion of chimp DNA. Biological thinking may give some hints as to how natural selection worked to shape the potentialities of a human infant. We can get some idea of how babies equipped with these potentialities grow up, in interaction with older people who all started out as babies, to become the human adults we know. Lore, literature, and common sense tell us much, and psychology and social sciences at their best can extend this knowledge and help us integrate it into what we know of the workings of the natural world.

We are exceptional, though, in ways that seem to resist incorporation into any such scientific picture. We have thoughts and opinions and we make assertions to each other. We are conscious of colors and feelings. And crucially, we have reasons to do things. Imagine a science of humanity so successful that it could explain, in terms of levels of complexity built on fundamental physics, the sound waves that come from my mouth, all the neuronal patterns in your heads as a result, and all the movements of our limbs and fingers for the next week. Such a science would have to show us as exceptional indeed in the universe. But throughout the era of modern natural science, at least since Galileo and Descartes and Hobbes, crucial parts of philosophy have tackled what's exceptional about us and seems to be left out of the picture. Philosophy is always dealing with how to make sense of new findings in science, thinking how they might transform our visions of ourselves and our surroundings, or how they might fit in with things we always thought we knew. That is by no means all that philosophy does, but questions of what to make of the scientific image form a significant part of our job. And so we ask where in a naturalistic picture of ourselves are beliefs, consciousness, and reasons.

Moore thought that moral facts somehow lie outside the world that empirical science can study. We can broaden this to a claim about the space of reasons as a whole, which, we can say, lies outside the space of causes. The "space of reasons" is the whole realm of normativity, to use a less picturesque, more technical term in the philosopher's lexicon. This is the realm of *oughts,* we might say, for what I ought to do is what the reasons that pertain weigh all told toward doing. The reasons to do something, as T. M. Scanlon puts it, are considerations that count in favor of doing it.

Now Stevenson and Ayer devised a cluster of strategies which I want to broaden. . . . Moral claims, they agreed with Moore, aren't claims that can form part of the empirical sciences. But still, we can understand what we are doing when we make moral claims: according to Ayer, we are expressing emotions or attitudes. There is a broad strategy at work here, a strategy that has come to be known as *expressivism*. . . . To explain the meaning of a term, to explain the concept that the term conveys, don't offer a straight definition. For normative terms, Moore and the non-naturalists are right that no definition in non-normative terms will capture the meaning. Instead, explain the states of mind that the uses of the term *express*—and don't just explain it as the "belief" that so-and-so. Trivially, normative statements express normative beliefs or judgments. Ayer and Stevenson proposed that moral judgments are feelings or attitudes. I have said that we can broaden the question of meanings to cover normative terms in general. Suppose, then, we try the expressivist twist on oughts in general. What kind of state of mind do *ought* claims express?

Ayer stressed the difference between expressing an attitude and saying that one has it. It is, as our

pedagogical lore has it, the difference between saying "Boo for lying" and saying "I'm against it." This difference is subtle, since either one of these speech act gets the hearer to think the speaker is against lying. Stevenson's talk of disagreement, though, lets us get at the difference. If you say "I'm against it," then literally, I disagree if I think you're not against it. If you say "Boo for lying," I disagree only if I disagree with your opposition to lying. What's at issue in the two cases, then, is different: With "I'm against it," what's literally at issue is your state of mind, whereas if you say "Boo!" what's at issue are feelings.

What's at issue with *ought*s in general, then? Jack and Jill need water, imagine, but the hill is slippery. I say that Jack ought now to go up the hill, but you disagree. What's at issue between us? Isn't the issue what to do? It's not an issue of what to do in your case or in mine, but somehow in Jack's, in Jack's shoes. When we explore together what Jack ought to do, we engage in a kind of hypothetical contingency planning. We put our heads together and think the problem through as if on Jack's behalf. Jack himself thinks fleetingly what to do, and decides to follow Jill up the hill. When he falls and breaks his crown and the dangers become more vivid to him, he may come to disagree with that earlier decision. You and I address the same problem as Jack himself rethinks: what to do in his original situation. You disagree, perhaps, with Jack's decision to go up the hill, whereas I agree with it. Switching to normative language, we can describe our states of mind like this: you and Jack both think he ought not to have gone up the hill, whereas I disagree: given the need for water, I conclude, getting the water was, in prospect, worth the danger.

Why should you or I plan, though, for such a fantastic contingency? Why, for that matter, should Jack rethink his decision, when the moving finger has writ and he can't unbreak his crown? It's clear enough why to plan for some contingencies you might face—a traffic jam on the Dan Ryan Expressway, say, when you want to drive south. Why, though, plan for contingencies you know you won't face—such as Jack's choice of whether to go up the hill? Well of course, mostly we don't. Even if I am right that *ought* thoughts are plans, we don't usually worry ourselves with whether, in light of the needs and the dangers, Jack ought to have gone up the hill. But we do do considerable planning for how to cope with needs and dangers; that is a crucial part of life to plan for. Jack reconsiders after the fact because he will face such choices again; he is engaged in a kind of rehearsal for further such choices. You and I might join him in this, considering Jack's plight as an exercise in planning for life. Just as Jack might disagree with his earlier decision and so emerge wiser from the calamity, so might you or I. Of course mostly, when we engage scenarios and the places one might hypothetically occupy in them, we aren't thinking to some aforethought purpose—any more than children play to develop their skills and social knowledge, or you read a novel to sharpen your powers of social apprehension. We humans are just built to engage in such activities, and it's a good thing we are, since doing so functions as rehearsal for later eventualities. We are curious about *ought*s as well as *is*s.

There is a place in our lives, then, for planning even for the wildest of contingencies. Still, does this really vindicate disagreement in plan? Why treat your plans and mine for Jack's plight as anything on which we could disagree with each other? You have your plans and I have mine; why isn't that just a difference between us as with age, height, or tastes? You have a flatter head than I do, suppose: that's not a disagreement between us; it's just a difference in how we are. You plan, for the contingency of Jack's plight, to stay safe and waterless at the foot of the hill, whereas I plan, as did Jack, to go up the hill with Jill. Isn't this just another difference in our biographies? How is it a disagreement?

What you are to do in Jack's plight and what I am to do are not separate questions: Jack's exact circumstances include everything about him, and our question is what to do if one is *he*—and thus exactly like him in every respect in which we differ. Still, why treat that as something you and I can discuss and agree on or disagree on? That, I say, is because we need to be able to put our heads together. Often we need to think cooperatively, treating each other's thoughts like thoughts that occur to oneself,

to be considered and supported or refuted, to be accepted or rejected. It is not always good for a person to think alone.

So let's extend Stevenson to say that there is such a thing as disagreement in plan. You and I can disagree on what to do if in Jack's situation, with all his characteristics. This, note, isn't the same thing as "disagreement in attitude" as Stevenson used the phrase. His disagreement in attitude is disagreement as to what shall happen. Imagine a pacifist who is meek on principle and a bully who takes advantage of this and slaps the pacifist's cheek. When it comes to what shall happen, the two might both favor the same thing: that the pacifist turn the other cheek. On this one point, the two agree in Stevensonian attitude: they both favor the same thing's happening. But they disagree in plan; they disagree on what to do if in the shoes of the pacifist. The bully plans to strike back in such cases, but the pacifist instead turns the other cheek. The bully is planning, to be sure, for the contingency of being someone who is meek on principle, someone who is going, as it happens, to turn the other cheek. But the bully disagrees with the pacifist's plan. The bully's hypothetical preference for the pacifist's situation is to snap out of his pacifism and strike back. The two disagree in plan, then, for the contingency of being the stricken pacifist.

Now the possibility of such disagreement in plan, I claim, has far-reaching consequences. . . . One chief consequence is that we can deal with complex normative claims. We get an answer to the Frege-Geach challenge to expressivism. The mother admonishes, "If lying is wrong, then getting your brother to lie is wrong too." Starting with the notion of disagreement, we can say canonically what the content of such a plan-laden claim is. The mother has come out in disagreement with any plan to shun lying but get one's brother to lie. In general, to get the content of a plan-laden claim, we map all the combinations of pure plans and pure factual beliefs with which the claim is in disagreement. Disagreement is the key to content; content is what there is to agree or disagree with. So allowing for disagreement in plan gives us plan-laden content—normative content.

A second chief consequence will sound surprising, coming from an expressivist. In a sense, it follows, normative terms like 'ought' refer to properties and relations—indeed to properties and relations that are natural, that can figure in an empirical science of humanity. My argument for this is transcendental: As planners, capable of agreement or disagreement in plan, we are each committed to this naturalistic-sounding thesis. Once we establish this thesis as one to which we are all committed, this thesis of natural constitution, we can proceed to assert it: There is a natural property that constitutes being what one ought to do. Thus we are all committed to agreeing, in a way, with normative naturalists: the term 'ought' refers, in a sense, to a natural property.

And what property is this? The question is not linguistic; rather, it's the grand, basic question in ethics, the question of how to live. You accept an answer to this question if you have fully thought out what to live for and have come to a conclusion. Consider a view that fits some aspects of Henry Sidgwick's doctrines: A universal hedonist whom I'll call Henry plans always, in every conceivable contingency, to do whatever holds out maximal prospects for net pleasure in the universe. Henry, then, has a view about the property that constitutes being what one ought to do. It is, he says, the property of being *unihedonic,* as we might call it: the property of holding out maximal prospects for net pleasure in the universe.

Henry, then, accepts this thesis of natural constitution. Indeed not only does he think that there's a natural property that constitutes being what one ought to do; he has a view on what it is. Many of us, though, don't have anything like a complete contingency plan for what to pursue in life, or a formula for constructing such a plan. Still, I claim, we are each committed to the thesis of natural constitution. For suppose you are at least consistent. Then the thesis is something you'd accept if, fantastically, you completely filled out your views on how to live, and did so without changing your mind about anything. Any way of filling out your plans, becoming hyperdecided on how to live, brings with it accepting the thesis of natural constitution. So it's something you

are already committed to as you think your way toward a fuller view of how to live. It's something that obtains, you can say, no matter what turns out to be the way to live.

Now I don't mean you to be convinced by this cryptic sketch of an argument. Even if I had succeeded in making the argument clear, it would raise many issues I can't quickly resolve. I want to sketch the possibility, though, of a view of normative concepts that has us sounding like expressivists, like non-naturalists, and like naturalistic realists in important respects—all at the same time. We start out with devices of the classic emotivists: with disagreement in plan reminiscent of Stevenson, and with Ayer's talk of expressing a state of mind. We let the state of mind in question be a kind of contingency planning for living. As Ayer and Stevenson saw, we derive Moore's conclusion that normative concepts aren't naturalistic. Two people might agree, in naturalistic terms, on all the natural facts and still disagree basically in plan. Something is at issue between them, but not something we can put in naturalistic terms. It's a question of *how to live.* Still, as naturalistic realists insist, normative terms like 'ought' do signify natural properties. That's something that Ayer and Stevenson didn't say, but it falls out as a consequence of some of their ways of thinking.

Simon Blackburn coined the term 'quasi-realism' for a program like this one. We start out without helping ourselves to ethical and other normative properties. Then, we earn the right to speak as realists do. Indeed we may be hard pressed to identify any real differences between naturalistic realism, non-naturalistic realism, and expressivism, once these positions are suitably refined. We may have a happy convergence of different approaches to metanormative theory. . . .

Everything I have been saying depends on a distinction that has been in the air in recent decades but which wasn't much around when Ayer and Stevenson were doing most of their work. It's the distinction between properties and concepts. The property of being water, we can say, turns out to be the property of being H_2O, of consisting in molecules of a certain kind. Still, the concepts are different: the pre-scientific concept of being water isn't the scientific concept of being H_2O. It was a live question at one time whether water was H_2O, a question on which people could coherently disagree. People disagreed as to whether water is H_2O; they didn't disagree as to whether water is water. We can ask what was at issue. Disagreement, then, is a matter of concepts, not properties: it isn't always preserved when we substitute distinct concepts of the same property.

Once we have this distinction, we can say this: All properties are natural, but some concepts of properties aren't descriptive and naturalistic. Some concepts find their place not in naturalistic description but in planning. Suppose, then, that Henry the universal hedonist is right on how to live: the thing to promote in life is the happiness of all. Then the property of being what one ought to do just *is* the property of being unihedonic, of holding out maximal prospects for total net pleasure in the universe. But the concept of ought is distinct from the concept of being unihedonic. For a perfectionist Percella can dispute with Henry: Percella says that the unihedonic thing isn't always what one ought to do. Henry understands her—and nothing about logic or our linguistic conventions by itself settles who is right. Percella and Henry have the same concepts; that's why they can engage each other's claims and not just talk past each other. Henry is right, we are supposing, and so the terms 'ought' and 'unihedonic' refer to the same natural property. But conceptually, Percella is coherent. Once she explains what perfection consists in, on her view, we know what's at issue between her and Henry. It's whether to live for universal happiness or to attain that kind of perfection.

This scheme, as I've been saying, has attractive features. Some tenets of Sidgwick's and Moore's ethical intuitionism seem hard to escape, and the scheme delivers these tenets. The inescapable tenets consist, it turns out, just in what we have to accept if we are to plan our lives coherently and intelligibly. We don't need non-natural properties, just the kinds of non-descriptive, non-naturalistic concepts that would have to figure in planning. Normative concepts do signify natural properties, we can say, but they have their own special way of doing so. The

scheme respects normative thinking: it avoids any blanket debunking of it—though we should still debunk certain theories of what normative thinking consists in. And it's a good thing that we can see normative thinking as inescapable in intelligent living. For normative thinking figures in a wide range of areas that we couldn't give up as nonsense. Normative epistemology, for instance, we can now say, consists in contingency plans for forming beliefs. It's a serious question, for instance, whether the evidence supports a Darwinian theory of natural selection, and more broadly, what the canons of scientific evidence are. I take these to be planning questions, questions of how much credence to put in theories given various epistemic contingencies. They are questions of what we ought to believe. Oughts are to be found even in places far from ethics.

Is this picture I have given, though, a naturalistic one? Does it really let us dispense with all mumbo jumbo of a non-natural realm? Not exactly: We can view ourselves as complex products of natural selection and the kind of cultural history that natural selection could make possible. We can see, in these terms, why beings like us might be interpretable as planners who share our planning thoughts. Suppose we view ourselves this way, and suppose furthermore, we interpret such natural beings as keeping track of what disagrees with what. Then we are interpreting ourselves as having normative thoughts. We can see, in short, why natural beings like us would be plausibly interpretable as having normative thoughts.

The scheme I have been sketching has a further happy consequence: If you start out as a nonnaturalist, you have to accept certain features of the space of reasons as just brute normative facts: for instance, that the normative supervenes on the natural. Once we see normative facts as plans, we see why this supervenience is something that any planner is committed to. Plans must be couched in empirical, naturalistic terms because we have to be able to recognize the situations the plans address. A plan to do whatever there's most reason to do, for instance, is no plan at all, until it's supplemented by an account of how to recognize what there's most reason to do. With this supplement, the plan is in effect couched in empirical terms.

On the other hand, the scheme in no way lets us substitute naturalistic thinking for normative thinking. Instead it follows Moore in concluding that there's just no substitute for normative thinking. And moreover, it doesn't tell us how to translate, in strictly naturalistic terms, claims about people's normative states of mind. Take the claim, "Jack is convinced that he ought to go up the hill." I haven't indicated how to translate such a psychological claim into terms that fit a broadly Galilean picture of the universe. Imagine we understood Jack completely as a physical system. Imagine we understood him, at many different levels of explanation, as a product of natural selection and a vastly complex human ecology. This would include grasping the explanatory patterns of his neurophysiology, understanding how evolutionary signaling theory applies to his patterns of neural firings and the sound waves that come out of his mouth, and all sorts of things like that. My hope is that the expressivistic scheme I've sketched would then let us see why Jack, so viewed, is conveniently interpretable as thinking that he ought to go up the hill.

He'd be conveniently interpretable that way, I'm saying. For Jack, viewed as a natural system, is conveniently interpretable as keeping track of his surroundings. (We have some naturalistic idea, for instance, how rats keep track of their position in a maze.) He'll be conveniently interpretable as planning, and we can conveniently interpret him as agreeing and disagreeing with combinations of plan and mundane fact. And that, I'm saying, is all we need if we are to interpret him as having normative thoughts.

I'm speaking of convenient interpretation, how a natural being, viewed naturalistically, might be conveniently interpreted. But how much does this establish if true? For anything I've claimed, a convenient interpretation might be no more than a convenient fiction—like the stupidities we attribute to the computers on our desks. When Jack is conveniently interpretable as thinking he ought to go up the hill, is that what he's really convinced of? Is he really thinking he ought to go up the hill?

That, I have implied, is a question of agreement and disagreement: for issues of meaning and interpretation, as I've been harping, agreement and disagreement are the key. What Jack accepts by way of *ought*s and *is*s, I've been saying, is a question of which possible states of mind he disagrees with and which he doesn't. Now I haven't offered any naturalistic translation of claims about disagreement. And if I did, my translation might be subject to Moore-like challenges. Do Jack and Jill really disagree with each other on whether he ought to go up the hill? Suppose you and I disagree on this question of how to interpret the two. What's then at issue between us? That is Moore's challenge, transferred from ethics to the theory of meaning itself. It's a question about the meaning of meaning, or the meaning of claims about mental content, claims about what people are thinking. And I have not said, or even sketched, how to respond.

Issues of meaning and mental content may in part themselves be normative issues. A number of leading philosophers have asserted that they are, and whether meaning is in some sense "normative" is a daunting question. The question has received intensive scrutiny over the past decade or two, and the issues still aren't entirely clarified. Perhaps to understand claims about what Jack really is thinking, you have to understand about commitments, or about correctness—and the concepts of commitment and correctness seem to be normative ones. Take two claims that contradict each other: Jack thinks, imagine, that snow is white whereas Jill thinks that nothing is white. Jack and Jill disagree—and this implies, among other things, that we ought not to accept both these claims at once. We ought not both to accept that snow is white and to accept that nothing is white—that's a normative claim. Claims about states of mind and their content seem themselves, then, to be fraught with ought. Some philosophers argue that this appearance dissolves on close scrutiny, and I'm not claiming to establish this "normativity of meaning" thesis or even urging us to accept it. But I'm not denying it either. Perhaps the right theory of normative thinking must itself be a normative theory. . . .

If so, then the account we end up with won't be strictly expressivistic or strictly quasi-realistic, by a stringent standard of what qualifies under these terms. That is to say, it won't fit the following pattern: that it starts out helping itself to a purely non-normative reality, and ends up, all on its own, earning our right to realistic ways of talking about oughts.

Still, the account is expressivistic in a weaker sense. It draws on central philosophical devices of Ayer and Stevenson. And if it succeeds in its ambition, it makes clear how natural beings like us would be conveniently interpretable as having *ought* thoughts. As for whether this interpretation would really get things right, perhaps we should take this question with a grain of salt. Suppose none of our uncertainties were scientific: we understood Jack completely in purely naturalistic terms, insofar as beings like him or us can be understood in naturalistic terms. Suppose you and I none the less have competing interpretations of Jack, and that these interpretations both are as convenient as can be. As Moore might ask, what's then at issue between us? Perhaps nothing real at all is at issue. . . .

We can perhaps be skeptics about picky questions of meaning that go beyond questions of convenient interpretability.

With normative questions, in contrast, it is hard to be a skeptic; it's hard to take the questions with too many grains of salt. The question of what to do is inescapable. Sartre's man who asks himself whether to join the resistance or take care of his mother can't dismiss the question as nonsense. When he comes to a decision, he has accepted an answer to a normative question, the question of what he ought to do in the circumstance.

Or at least, he has come to a normative view *if* a big if is satisfied. He has reached an ought conclusion *if* there is such a thing as agreement and disagreement in plan, if we can come to agree or disagree with his conclusion. Whether there is such a thing as disagreement in plan, though, is a deep question—as I have indicated. You and I can certainly think what to do if in this Frenchman's exact circumstances, and form a different plan from his. The deep question is why to treat this as any sort of disagreement. Why think there is such a thing as disagreement in plan? My answer has gone in two stages. First, in planning I have to be able to change

my mind, and this amounts to disagreeing with things I had concluded earlier. Second, in thinking how to live, we need each other's help.

Disagreement in plan, I have been saying, is the key to explaining normative concepts—that along with Ayer's distinction between expressing a state of mind and saying that one is in it. The concepts we explain with these devices act much as the classic non-naturalists recount. Explanatory devices we get from the classic emotivists Ayer and Stevenson, then, lead us to crucial aspects of Sidgwick, Moore, Ross, and Ewing. Now if we really get this much convergence, that should be grounds for celebration: perhaps we're really getting at what's going on with *is* and *ought*. Of course, whether we do achieve this convergence is bound to go on being controversial— and legitimately so, as we work to understand better the tangle of issues in play. The convergence also leaves the question, though, whether an expressivism that draws on Ayer and Stevenson tells non-naturalistic normative realists anything they didn't know before.

Let me review, then, some of the ways that Ayer's and Stevenson's devices lead to illumination, if I am right. First of all, Ayer's and Stevenson's devices let us take what comes across a mystery, as Moore presents it, and see it in terms of something familiar and fairly comprehensible. We can explain ought convictions as plans, oughts as deliverances of planning. Second, the brute features of Moore's non-natural realm fall out as things a coherent planner would have to believe in. We get supervenience of the normative on the natural, and get something that fits Moore's talk of "*the* good" as something natural: there's a natural property, I've been saying, that constitutes being what one ought to do.

So do we eliminate the mumbo jumbo of a non-natural realm we can intuit? Not exactly, but we see why a being like you or me would have to be interpretable as committed to this mumbo jumbo. We work toward a naturalistic view of why we'd have to be so interpretable. All this is in a world where all properties are natural—though non-naturalistic concepts apply to it, and we can see why.

We ourselves are parts of the natural world we study, and the moral, perhaps, is that this makes for concepts that aren't just naturalistic classifications of nature. I have been exploring some ways all this might happen—but mostly, I have been musing over the consequences of a philosophical approach, a theory of normative concepts. I went in haste over a number of theses and issues, sketching this approach not so much with an eye to laying out "What does it mean and how do we know?" but to the question "So what?" In particular, what does all this say about whether we live as purely natural parts of a purely natural world? Is what I've been sketching, then, naturalism, non-naturalism, or something else? It's a view that's all three, I answer, in ways we need to distinguish. It's not the classic emotivism of Ayer and Stevenson, but still, devices those thinkers invented help us construct a view that takes in crucial aspects of all three of these classic positions.

STUDY QUESTIONS

1. According to Gibbard, what states of mind are expressed when we make a normative judgment?
2. According to Gibbard, what is a normative disagreement?
3. According to Gibbard, what is it to hyperdecide?
4. Has Gibbard's analysis solved the Frege-Geach problem?

Ecumenical Expressivism

Michael Ridge

According to expressivism, the meaning of a term is determined by the mental state it expresses, and furthermore, the mental states expressed by normative terms are non-cognitive. But might normative utterances possess a cognitive as well as a non-cognitive aspect? Michael Ridge, Professor of Philosophy at the University of Edinburgh, explores this possibility, which has come to be known as "hybrid expressivism." Ridge argues that when we state that "lying is wrong," we express an attitude of disapproval toward lying, perhaps because it's hurtful, as well as a belief, in this case that lies are hurtful. Ridge concludes that because normative utterances express both cognitive and non-cognitive states, the Frege-Geach problem is no more troubling for expressivism than for any purely cognitivist view.

Metaethical expressivism has many virtues. It can explain the depth of moral disagreement, fits easily into a naturalistic world view, and can explain how moral judgment guides action. Moreover, so-called quasi-realist forms of expressivism can accommodate many of the realist-sounding things we say.[1] However, expressivism seems to have trouble making sense of utterances in which moral predicates occur in unasserted contexts. While we might be able to make sense of "torture is wrong" roughly along the lines of "Boo for torture!" it is hard to see how an account of this sort could deal with utterances like "If torture is wrong then Camp X-Ray should be abolished." A speaker can accept the latter without disapproving of torture or Camp X-Ray. Moreover, any extension of expressivism to deal with such utterances must accommodate the validity of arguments in which they are premises. Since this problem comes to us through the work of P. T. Geach

and is analogous to a problem Frege once posed for certain theories of negation, it is usually referred to as the "Frege-Geach problem." In this article I articulate a new version of expressivism called "Ecumenical Expressivism," which can avoid the Frege-Geach problem altogether. A crucial idea is that expressivism can and should embrace the thesis that moral utterances express both desires and beliefs. Before turning to the Frege-Geach problem, we must first do some philosophical spadework to uncover the logical space Ecumenical Expressivism occupies.

I. A TALE OF A FALSE DICHOTOMY

Philosophical folklore tells a tale of a fundamental dichotomy in moral semantics, according to which

---

From Michael Ridge, "Ecumenical Expressivism: Finessing Frege," *Ethics* 116 (2006). Reprinted by permission of the publisher.

moral utterances either (*a*) express beliefs but not desires or (*b*) express desires but not beliefs. This tale is a chapter of a larger narrative in the philosophy of language. This larger narrative depicts the meanings of words and sentences quite generally in terms of how they conventionally express states of mind. Perhaps the most famous rendition of this story comes from John Locke.[2] On any version of this story worth telling, we must distinguish the meaning of a word or sentence from what a particular speaker means by that word or sentence, a distinction famously drawn by Paul Grice.[3] For example, suppose someone answers the question "Is Tony Blair an honest person?" by saying "Blair is a typical politician." In this context, it will be clear that the speaker means that Blair is not very honest. Nonetheless, his sentence does not mean that Blair is not very honest. In Grice's famous terms, the idea that Blair is not very honest is a conversational implicature of the utterance rather than part of its strict and literal meaning. . . .

The Lockean framework suggests that moral semantics should be understood in terms of the question "What states of mind do moral words and sentences conventionally express?" No plausible Lockean story will hold that all sentences express beliefs and only beliefs. Many nonassertoric utterances express nonbelief states. Utterances of sentences like "Hooray for Hollywood!" and "Boo for Bollywood!" express attitudes of approval and disapproval rather than beliefs. What sorts of states of mind are moral sentences conventionally used to express? A philosophically innocent answer is that they express moral judgments. This is fine as far as it goes, but we must now ask the question "What is a moral judgment?" On the one hand, we assess people's moral judgments as true or false, we subject them to epistemic norms, and they can figure in rational inferences. These features suggest that moral judgments are beliefs. On the other hand, moral judgments can guide action without the help of an independently existing desire. Furthermore, intelligible moral disagreement can persist beyond agreement on the relevant facts. These considerations suggest that moral judgments are desires.

These competing considerations have generated two diametrically opposed philosophical camps.

Cognitivists insist that moral utterances express beliefs rather than desires, while expressivists hold that moral utterances express desires rather than beliefs. . . . This story seems unlikely to have a happy ending. Two camps of theory builders emerge, with the members of each camp developing increasingly sophisticated theories designed to accommodate the features so easily accommodated by the opposition. Cognitivists try to show how beliefs can play the motivational role more naturally associated with desire. Expressivists argue that noncognitive attitudes of the right sort can play the intellectual roles more naturally associated with belief. Not surprisingly, these efforts can seem like attempts to fit a square peg in a round hole. Our story begins to look like a tragedy or a dark comedy.

Fortunately, our choices are not limited to (*a*) the thesis that moral utterances express beliefs but not desires and (*b*) the thesis that they instead express desires but not beliefs. That is indeed a false dichotomy. For we can instead hold that moral utterances express both beliefs and desires. An approach based on this idea would have certain obvious advantages. After all, if moral utterances express both beliefs and desires then it should be much easier to accommodate both the desire-like and belief-like aspects of moral judgment. Call any view according to which moral utterances express beliefs and desires "ecumenical" to mark the inclusiveness of such views. . . .

II. TRANSFORMING THE DEBATE

The Ecumenical View suggests that if there is real dispute between cognitivists and expressivists then it cannot simply be about the action-guiding features of moral judgment. Perhaps we should focus instead on the possibility of apparently intelligible moral disagreement in spite of agreement on all the relevant facts. G. E. Moore's famous . . . open question argument is relevant here.[4] Take any proposed naturalistic analysis N of a moral predicate M. Moore's open question argument maintains that it will always be possible for someone without conceptual confusion to grant that something is N but still wonder whether it is really M. If, however, N really was an accurate analysis of M then the question "I know it is N but is it M?" would not be conceptually open. Prima facie, the open question argument seems to beg the question. For if the naturalist maintains that a given moral predicate M is equivalent in meaning to some naturalistic definition N then the fact that these questions are not conceptually open is a direct and obvious consequence of her view. However, the open question argument can be understood in a non-question-begging way. . . . The crucial move is to understand the argument as an inference to the best explanation. On this interpretation, the main premise of the argument is not that the relevant questions really are open but the more modest premise that they seem open to competent users of the terms. This argument does not beg the question insofar as the naturalist can consistently grant that the relevant questions do at least seem open to competent speakers. The issue is how best to explain this appearance. The argument maintains that the best explanation is that these questions really are open. That is, after all, a relatively simple and direct explanation of the sort that we would accept by default in other contexts. For example, we would accept such an answer when considering why the question "I know he is popular, but is he intelligent?" seems open to competent speakers. The fact that competent speakers persist in finding such questions open even when presented with a wide variety of proposed analyses bolsters this explanation's plausibility.

Generations of expressivists have argued that they are the real beneficiaries of Moore's argument. For Moore's nonnaturalism encounters several notoriously difficult problems shared by any antireductionist account of moral properties. For example, antireductionist accounts have trouble explaining why moral properties supervene on nonmoral properties. For if moral properties really are irreducible then moral and nonmoral properties are in Hume's terminology "distinct existences," which makes it puzzling why a difference in the former must always supervene on a difference in the latter. By contrast, expressivism offers a straightforward explanation of why our practices include a supervenience constraint. Whereas antireductionist realists must explain a metaphysical relationship between distinct properties, the expressivist needs only to explain the sensibility of adopting a supervenience constraint. Since the point of moral discourse is to recommend options on the basis of their natural properties, it is easy to see why such a constraint is sensible. Without such a constraint then it would be hard to see in what sense options were recommended on the basis of their natural properties.

. . . [T]he point here is . . . to see how we should define cognitivism and expressivism if these arguments provide the main motivations for expressivism. This suggests that expressivists must insist that moral utterances do not express beliefs which are such that the utterance is true just in case the belief is true. For the open question argument is meant to show that no representation of the facts can commit someone to a moral stance. So perhaps we should understand cognitivism and expressivism as follows:

> Cognitivism: For any moral sentence M, M is conventionally used to express a belief such that M is true if and only if the belief is true.
> Expressivism: For any moral sentence M, M is not conventionally used to express a belief such that M is true if and only if the belief is true.

This distinction is exclusive but not exhaustive. For there is logical space for a hybrid view according to which some but not all moral utterances express beliefs which provide their truth-conditions.[5] For present purposes I put such hybrid views to one side, except to note that classifying them as hybrid views is plausible. More important, expressivism as defined above is a negative thesis, but expressivists historically also embrace the positive thesis that moral utterances express attitudes of approval and disapproval. Since part of my point is that this positive thesis can be understood as common ground between expressivists and cognitivists, I have not included it as a defining feature of expressivism.

On this taxonomy there will be cognitivist and expressivist versions of the Ecumenical View.

Ecumenical Cognitivism allows that moral utterances express both beliefs and desires and insists that the utterances are true if and only if one of the beliefs expressed is true. Ecumenical Expressivism also allows that moral utterances express both beliefs and desires but denies that a moral utterance is guaranteed to be true just in case the belief(s) it expresses is (are) true. . . .

. . . [T]he possibility of Ecumenical Expressivism has, as far as I know, been entirely neglected. The contrast between Ecumenical Expressivism and Ecumenical Cognitivism can seem subtle, but the differences are precisely the ones that are relevant from the point of view of Moorean open question intuitions and worries about explaining supervenience. For the Ecumenical Cognitivist, belief has a kind of priority, in that which beliefs are candidates for counting as moral is fixed by their content. Either this privileged content is about some irreducible moral property or not. If it is then worries about explaining supervenience arise; if not then Moorean worries are germane. Ecumenical Expressivism instead gives logical priority to desire. The belief that a given moralizer must have to count as judging that X is morally right is a function of that speaker's potentially idiosyncratic proattitudes rather than vice versa. So someone who approves of actions insofar as they maximize utility will count as thinking charity is morally right only if she believes that charity maximizes utility. However, this is the relevant content only because of the person's attitudes. Since making a moral judgment does not on this account require a belief with any particular content, Ecumenical Expressivism avoids the open question argument. Moreover, Ecumenical Expressivism can embrace the standard expressivist explanation of supervenience canvassed above.

Ecumenical Expressivism is a sort of dialectical mirror image of Ecumenical Cognitivism. Just as Ecumenical Cognitivism can steal the thunder of traditional expressivists by accommodating the motivating power of moral judgment "on the cheap," Ecumenical Expressivism can steal the thunder of traditional cognitivists by accommodating the logical features of moral judgment on the cheap. The real issue between cognitivists and expressivists

may therefore have little or nothing to do with judgment internalism or the Frege-Geach problem. Instead, the dispute may hinge on more old-fashioned (and unfashionable) Moorean open questions and supervenience.

In a way, the suggestion that expressivists can make room for the expression of beliefs should not be surprising. In light of so-called thick moral predicates like "cowardly" it has long been clear that expressivists cannot plausibly insist that moral utterances never express beliefs. To say someone is cowardly is at least in part to express the belief that the person is easily motivated by fear, and expressivists have admitted this much. . . .

. . . [E]xpressivists can provide a thorough and systematic account of the role of belief in moral judgment for both thin and thick moral predicates, and that doing so provides crucial resources with which to disarm the Frege-Geach problem. The role of belief in Ayer's account is too limited to achieve this goal. Atomic moral utterances will on his view often simply be the expressions of a suitable noncognitive attitude. Saying "stealing is wrong," for example, is on Ayer's view not to express a belief at all but simply to express a suitable attitude against stealing. Utterances like "Your stealing that money was wrong" express a belief (if they do at all; even this is controversial) only because of the particular presupposition which happens to be involved in that utterance. Many atomic moral utterances will involve no such presuppositions. . . .

III. THE FREGE-GEACH PROBLEM

It is a platitude that moral predicates can be embedded in unasserted contexts and valid arguments. The following simple argument is often used to illustrate the point:

(1) Lying is wrong.
(2) If lying is wrong then getting one's little brother to lie is wrong.
Therefore, (3) getting one's little brother to lie is wrong.

If 'wrong' in premise 1 expresses disapproval of lying, while 'wrong' in premise 2 does not express disapproval[,] then 'wrong' is used with different meanings in premises 1 and 2. In that case, there is a fallacy of equivocation. However, the idea that arguments of this form must involve such equivocation is absurd. Giving an account of the meanings of moral predicates in unasserted contexts which can explain the validity of such arguments is the heart of the Frege-Geach problem. . . .

. . . [W]e . . . need some account of what states of mind are expressed by utterances with moral predicates in unasserted contexts and an account of what constitutes the acceptance of such utterances. Furthermore, this account must meet certain constraints. First, it must explain why anyone who accepts the premises but denies the conclusion of a valid argument is making a logical mistake. This inconsistency must be distinguished from the pragmatic inconsistency found in the kinds of sentences famously discussed by Moore (e.g., "I believe that p but not-p.") since those so-called paradoxes do not involve outright contradiction. Call this the "inconsistency constraint."[6] Finally, expressivism must also explain how it can sometimes be rational to infer the conclusion of a valid argument using moral predicates. Call this the "rational inference constraint." . . .

IV. ECUMENICAL EXPRESSIVISM

Consider the sentence "There is moral reason not to eat meat." On the Ecumenical Expressivist account, an utterance of this sentence will express both an attitude in favor of certain kinds of actions and omissions and a belief that refraining from eating meat is an omission of the relevant kind. Perhaps I am a utilitarian and approve of actions and omissions just insofar as they promote happiness. However, on an expressivist account maximizing utility cannot be part of the meaning of my sentence. Perhaps we should therefore understand moral predicates as expressing both a speaker's attitude in favor of actions in general insofar as they have a certain property (whatever property guides the speaker's approval of actions quite generally) and a belief which makes anaphoric reference to that property. The speaker may or may not have a very clear idea of what the relevant property is. The crucial idea here would be one of anaphoric pronominal back reference to the relevant property. An utterance of the sentence "There is moral reason not to eat meat" would on this account express a speaker's attitudes in favor of actions insofar as they have a certain property and the belief that refraining from eating meat has that property. Returning to our analogy with uses of 'hooray,' consider the following sentence (call it "MP"): "Hooray for teams that have a certain property such that Manchester United has that property just in case the Packers have it." Again, this is a very odd sentence; cheers tend to be much less verbose and more catchy. Nonetheless it is good English and provides a useful albeit imperfect analogy. An utterance of MP expresses an attitude of approval keyed to a certain property and expresses a belief involving anaphoric reference to that property—the belief that Manchester has the property just in case the Packers have it. Moreover, the utterance manages to do all of this without inheriting the truth-conditions of the belief it expresses.

One advantage of this approach is that it accommodates the plausible idea that a competent user of a predicate must be committed to applying the predicate to all and only things with certain features. In other words, competence with a predicate presupposes a rough-and-ready conception of necessary and sufficient conditions for the predicate's application. The speaker's appreciation of these conditions may be vague and indeterminate. This requirement for competence with a predicate can sound very demanding, but it is actually rather lax. To emphasize how relaxed this constraint is, note that one could be competent with a predicate on this account simply by supposing that a predicate applies to something just in case it is sufficiently similar to a particular paradigm, where "sufficient similarity" is left completely vague and open-ended. Cognitive science models of how people make moral judgments which emphasize the idea of prototypes are compatible with Ecumenical Expressivism.

Once again, the idea is not that a competent speaker necessarily could articulate the property in virtue of which she approves of actions. This is why the device of anaphora is essential. The suggestion that someone has a certain je ne sais quoi provides a helpful analogy, since that suggestion implies both a proattitude toward someone in virtue of some of her properties and an explicit recognition that one is not sure just what those properties are. Of course, the analogy is not perfect; a moral speaker may well know exactly what properties she has in mind. The point here is simply that one need not know this to be a sincere and competent user of moral predicates. Another analogy can be found in an utterance of a sentence like "There's something about Mary." Sentences of the form "There's something about X" have become idiomatic and express an attitude of approval toward X in virtue of certain of X's properties even though the speaker may be unsure exactly what those properties are. Note that while we might treat an utterance of "There is something about Mary" as truth-apt, it would be a mistake for a speaker to endorse it as true simply because she agrees that Mary does in fact have some properties (doesn't everything?!). Rather, anyone who endorsed such an idiomatic utterance as true would thereby express suitable proattitudes with respect to Mary in virtue of some of her properties.

A similar case, but with the opposite conative valence, is the idiomatic remark that "Something is rotten in the state of Denmark," which is almost never taken to have what a naive compositional analysis would suggest to be its literal meaning. Normally, such an utterance serves to express the speaker's sense of unease with some feature of a contextually relevant situation even though the speaker may be unsure just what the relevant feature is. . . .

So perhaps we should understand atomic uses of moral predicates as follows:

"There is moral reason to X" expresses (a) an attitude of approval of a certain kind toward actions insofar as they have a certain property and (b) a belief that X has that property.

"Morally, there is most reason to X" ("Morally, one ought to X") expresses (a) an attitude of approval of a certain kind toward actions insofar as they have a certain property and (b) a belief that X has that property to a greater extent than any of the available alternatives.

"The fact that X would be P is a moral reason to X" expresses (a) an attitude of approval of a certain kind toward actions insofar as they have a certain property and (b) a belief that being P constitutes that property with respect to X.

A number of points need to be made to clarify this proposal.

First, the beliefs expressed by moral utterances must be understood as not thereby guaranteed to provide their truth-conditions. Otherwise the resulting position would not be an expressivist one. . . .

Second, the version of Ecumenical Expressivism developed here makes heavy use of the idea of anaphoric beliefs. One interesting objection explores how it might deal with anaphoric utterances. Suppose, for example, that you say "Sacrificing the happiness of a few for the greater happiness of the many is right." I, no utilitarian, reply by saying "Sacrificing the happiness of a few for the greater happiness of the many sometimes has that property, but sometimes it does not." On a natural understanding of anaphora, my use of 'that property' refers back to the property to which you referred. By hypothesis, I am no utilitarian, so my utterance should not suggest that I share your tendency to evaluate actions simply in terms of whether they maximize happiness. What should expressivists say about such utterances?

Contemporary expressivists maintain that . . . moral predicates refer to moral properties. On Allan Gibbard's view, for example, normative utterances express a speaker's plans. More generally, judgments in which normative predicates figure are in his terms 'plan-laden,' which is to say that such judgments essentially involve deciding how to act and in this sense are not purely descriptive. Crucially, claims about the reference of moral predicates are plan-laden on Gibbard's view. As Gibbard puts the point, "Any planner is committed to a Claim of *Factual Constitution*: that there is a factual property that *constitutes* being okay to do. This too will be a plan-laden truth, not a truth of prosaic fact."[7] . . .

We are now in a position to return to utterances involving anaphoric reference to moral properties. When my interlocutor says that sacrificing the happiness of the few is right, his use of 'right' quasi-signifies the property of being right, but just which property that is remains a substantive moral (plan-laden, in Gibbard's framework) question. When I respond by remarking that "sometimes sacrificing the few has that property, but sometimes it does not," my use of 'that property' makes anaphoric reference to whatever property his use of 'right' signifies or (as in this case) quasi-signifies. So my use of 'that property' quasi-signifies the property of being right, which in my view may well not be the same property my interlocutor takes it to be. So such anaphoric reference will in effect involve substantive first-order judgment and hence will involve the expression of a suitable noncognitive attitude. The Ecumenical Expressivist should join with Non-Ecumenical Expressivists like Gibbard in holding that this is a first-order moral judgment. . . .

V. AVOIDING THE FREGE-GEACH PROBLEM "ON THE CHEAP"

How might Ecumenical Expressivism deal with logically complex sentences? First, consider negation. Just as with atomic moral judgments, negation is best understood in terms of a belief whose content is a function of the agent's proattitudes:

> "There is no moral reason to X" expresses (*a*) an attitude of approval toward actions insofar as they have a certain property and (*b*) the belief that X lacks that property.

One virtue of this account is that it can easily accommodate scope distinctions that have caused problems for traditional Non-Ecumenical versions of expressivism. In particular, we must distinguish

someone's thinking that there is no moral reason to X from thinking that there is moral reason not to X. Non-Ecumenical forms of expressivism have had trouble with this distinction because they work only with desires. For Non-Ecumenical Expressivists seem stuck explaining what it is to think that there is no moral reason to perform a given action in terms of indifference to the performance of that action. However, indifference also is the Non-Ecumenical Expressivist's best shot at explaining what it is for a speaker to suspend judgment as to whether there is any moral reason to perform a given action. Non-Ecumenical Expressivism therefore runs a serious risk of blurring the distinction between thinking that there is no reason to X and having no view as to whether there is reason to X. For Ecumenical Expressivism, this distinction is easy. To think that there is no moral reason to X is to approve of actions in virtue of their having a certain property and to believe that Xing does not have that property. Whereas not to have a view as to whether there is moral reason to X would be to approve of actions in virtue of their having a certain property but to suspend judgment as to whether X has that property. . . .

The final ingredient in the proposed solution to the Frege-Geach problem is a suitable definition of validity. Standard accounts hold that an argument is valid just in case it is impossible for its premises to be true while its conclusion is false. Since some versions of Ecumenical Expressivism hold that moral utterances are not truth-apt, we cannot take this account over as it stands. We can, however, adopt a close cousin:

> An argument is valid just in case any possible believer who accepts all of the premises but at one and the same time denies the conclusion would thereby be guaranteed to have inconsistent beliefs.[8]

It is crucial to the tenability of this definition that it ranges over all possible believers. Suppose I am a utilitarian, so I approve of actions insofar as they maximize utility. In that case it would be contradictory for me to think that an action maximizes utility yet is not morally right. However, the inference

"X maximizes utility, therefore X is morally right" had better not be valid, on pain of contradicting Moorean open question intuitions. Fortunately, on the account offered here this argument is invalid. For while it is true that a utilitarian who believes both that an action maximizes utility and that the action is not morally right is thereby caught in an inconsistency, it is not true that any possible believer who believes that a given action maximizes utility and that the action is not morally right is thereby guaranteed to be caught in an inconsistency. Anyone not committed to utilitarianism can accept the premise and reject the conclusion without inconsistency. . . .

. . . [H]ow might the proposed account of validity help us deal with the Frege-Geach problem? Consider how this account of validity applies to arguments employing moral predicates. Begin with the simplest form of argument, reiteration—"p, therefore p." Let 'p' be an atomic moral utterance such as "There is moral reason not to have abortions." On the proposed conception of validity, the argument is valid just in case any agent who accepts the premise but denies the conclusion would thereby be guaranteed to be caught in an inconsistency in belief. Since the denial of the conclusion would simply be "There is no moral reason not to have abortions" the question is whether anyone who accepts A, "There is moral reason not to have abortions," and who accepts not-A, "There is no moral reason not to have abortions," is thereby caught in an inconsistency. On the model proposed here, any possible agent who accepts A and accepts not-A both thinks that refraining from having abortion has a certain property and thinks that abortion does not have that property. This clearly is an inconsistency of a familiar kind—inconsistency in belief.

It is straightforward to see how this account can be extended to deal with other logically complex sentences. The general scheme for any logically complex sentence in which 'moral reason' appears is as follows. Let 'p' stand for a logically complex sentence in which "there is a moral reason to X" (but no other moral predicates) appears. An utterance of 'p' expresses (a) the agent's approval of actions insofar as they have a certain property and (b) the agent's belief that p*, where p* is identical to p save that all

occurrences of the form "there is a moral reason to X" are replaced by "Xing has that property," where 'that property' is to be understood as making anaphoric reference to the property mentioned in a. The same strategy can be extended to other sentences in which 'moral reason' is used in fairly obvious ways. For example, consider a logically complex utterance 'q' in which a phrase of the form "the fact that X is p is a moral reason to X" occurs. Any such utterance expresses (a) the agent's approval of actions insofar as they have a certain property and (b) the agent's belief that q*, where q* is identical to q save that all occurrences of the form "the fact that X is p is a moral reason to X" are replaced by "the fact that Xing has that property," where 'that property' once again is to be understood as making anaphoric reference to the property mentioned in a.

It should be clear by now how this account can explain the validity of arguments with moral predicates quite generally. Consider the standard case of modus ponens:

(1) There is moral reason not to lie.
(2) If there is moral reason not to lie, then there is moral reason not to encourage your little brother to lie.
(3) Therefore, there is moral reason not to encourage your little brother to lie.

On the proposed account, the acceptance of premise 1 requires the belief that there is some not lying that has "that property," where the use of 'that property' denotes the property in virtue of which the speaker disapproves of actions quite generally. The acceptance of premise 2 involves the belief that if refraining from lying has that property then refraining from getting your little brother to lie also has it. To deny premise 3, though, would be to believe that not encouraging little brother to lie does not have that very property. This is an inconsistent set of beliefs, and so the argument is logically valid on the proposed account. The general strategy works across the board in an elegant way, no matter how complicated the judgments. In contrast with a "logic of attitudes" approach, there is no pressure to generate increasingly sophisticated higher-order attitudes to model increasingly complex sentences. The Frege-Geach problem simply does not arise in the first place.

VI. MEETING THE TWO CONSTRAINTS

We should now see whether Ecumenical Expressivism does better than its rivals in meeting the two constraints canvassed at the end of Section III (the inconsistency constraint and the rational inference constraint). Expressivists have often held that we must broaden our conception of inconsistency and rely on a logic of attitudes to make sense of the validity of moral arguments. Critics have argued that such accounts inevitably confuse moral mistakes with logical mistakes. Furthermore, such accounts arguably conflate the kind of inconsistency involved in sentences associated with Moore's paradox (e.g., "p but I don't believe it" and "I believe that p but not p") with logical inconsistency. Moorean sentences do not involve logical inconsistency—they could be true. If, however, we analyze moral arguments in terms of a logic of attitudes then this distinction becomes problematic. . . . The general idea of the logic of attitudes approach is that it is inconsistent to have a higher-order attitude toward an attitude while nonetheless having that attitude. The following sentence is inconsistent in just that sense: "It is wrong for me to believe that my father is unfaithful to my mother but my father is unfaithful to my mother." Clearly this sentence is not logically inconsistent, but it expresses both an attitude of disapproval toward another attitude and that very attitude (the infidelity belief) and so comes out as inconsistent on a logic of attitudes approach.

The same basic problem infects the more recent "commitment-based" approaches to the Frege-Geach problem. For if to say "Believing that p is bad" is to express one's commitment to avoiding the belief that p, then avowing "Believing that p is bad" will wrongly come out as inconsistent in the relevant sense with p, which in turn implies that "The belief that p is bad, so not-p" is valid. Gibbard's version of the commitment-based approach holds that an

argument is valid when accepting the premises and rejecting the conclusion is incompatible with becoming fully decided on all matters (factual and normative) without flouting one's own commitments. The point is that on Gibbard's own account, "Believing that p is bad" expresses a commitment to avoid believing that p.[9] Clearly, that commitment can never be fulfilled so long as the agent believes that p. So anyone who accepts that believing that p is bad in Gibbard's sense yet believes that p cannot live up to her commitment not to believe that p without changing her mind. So Gibbard's account implies that "believing that p is bad" is logically inconsistent with "p," which in turn incorrectly implies that "believing that p is bad, so not-p" is valid.

By contrast, Ecumenical Expressivism avoids these problems from the outset. Ecumenical Expressivism does not require a separate logic of attitudes and does not conflate logical inconsistency with Moorean paradox. For those problem cases arose only because inconsistency was being understood in terms of disapproving of one's own attitudes or failing to live up to one's commitments. Ecumenical Expressivism eschews these approaches and understands the relevant inconsistency as ordinary inconsistency in belief. Moreover, unlike its rivals, Ecumenical Expressivism can meet what I earlier called the "rational inference constraint." Consider the following argument:

(1) Lying is bad.
(2) If lying is bad then God did not lie.
(3) Therefore, God did not lie.

The argument's validity is straightforward. Accepting premise 1 commits a speaker to believing that refraining from lying has a certain property (the one to which his approval is keyed), accepting premise 2 commits a speaker to believing that if refraining from lying has that property then God did not lie, while denying premise 3 commits a speaker to believing that God did lie. These three beliefs are inconsistent in a perfectly familiar sense. Moreover, we can imagine circumstances in which it might be reasonable to infer premise 3 from premises 1 and 2. This is an important advantage of Ecumenical

Expressivism over traditional forms of expressivism. On Blackburn's most recent account and the sort of account favored by . . . Gibbard, embedded contexts express the speaker's "commitments."[10] For example, accepting a disjunction is being committed to accepting the attitude expressed by one of the disjuncts if the attitude expressed by the other disjunct becomes "untenable." These commitments underwrite the making of various inferences. Gibbard offers a similar account. Gibbard suggests that deciding what to do and deciding what one ought to do are really one and the same thing. In light of this identification he constructs the idea of a "hyperplan," in which one has a universal plan of life, a plan that "covers any occasion of choice one might conceivably be in, and for each alternative open on such an occasion, to adopt the plan involves either rejecting that alternative or rejecting rejecting it."[11] He then suggests that logically complex evaluative and normative utterances express one's commitment to rejecting certain universal plans of life. For example, to say that I ought to X or Y is to express my commitment to rejecting universal plans of life in which I neither X nor Y. Gibbard explains logically complex contexts in terms of commitments to rejecting certain combinations of attitudes.

The idea is that the inconsistency that underwrites the validity of moral arguments is the inconsistency of accepting a commitment not to have certain combinations of attitudes but having them anyway. Now consider again this argument:

(1) Lying is bad.
(2) If lying is bad then God did not lie.
(3) Therefore, God did not lie.

Suppose for the sake of argument that the commitment-based approach can explain the validity of such arguments. . . . [A] further problem remains. Suppose I accept premise 2 and suspend judgment with regard to premise 1. I then come to accept premise 1 in a way that is not irrational. I then infer premise 3 from premises 1 and 2. It seems like this could be a perfectly rational inference. However, the reason that the inference would go through would seem to be because I have adopted a noncognitive

attitude that gives me a practical reason to accept the conclusion. For on Non-Ecumenical accounts, the acceptance of an atomic moral sentence like premise 1 just is the adoption of a suitable noncognitive attitude—roughly, a desire that people not lie or a preference that people internalize norms forbidding lying or something along these lines. The inference would have to go from an attitude of disapproval of lying and a commitment not to combine that attitude with a belief that God lied to the conclusion that God did not lie. It is hard to see how this inference could be epistemologically faultless. For the fact that I have committed myself not to accept that God lied while disapproving of lying and the fact that I disapprove of lying do not provide me with any epistemically respectable reason to infer that God did not lie. Beliefs that are motivated by one's attitudes and commitments as to what attitudes and beliefs one is willing to hold are paradigm cases of wishful thinking. Epistemologically, beliefs should be based on perceptual evidence or other beliefs, not the result of attitudes or commitments. Nor is this problem a minor or localized one; it seems that on the commitment-based account any inference of the logical form "p, if p then q, so q," where 'p' is an evaluative thesis and 'q' is a descriptive one, will be such that anyone who makes such inferences is guilty of wishful thinking. Ecumenical Expressivism simply does not face this problem. For on an Ecumenical Expressivist account the conclusions of such arguments are inferred from other beliefs.

VII. CONCLUSION

Metaethical debates have become mired in disputes about the extent to which moral judgments are belief-like and the extent to which they are desire-like. This debate rests on a false dichotomy. Ecumenical Views insist that moral utterances express both beliefs and desires. . . . Ecumenical Expressivists can and should agree with cognitivists that belief is "internal" to moral judgment. Doing so immunizes expressivism against the Frege-Geach problem without provoking any further unfortunate side effects.

NOTES

1. See Simon Blackburn, *Essays in Quasi-Realism* (Oxford: Oxford University Press, 1993).
2. In book 3 of *An Essay concerning Human Understanding*. See http://www.ilt.columbia.edu/publications/Projects/digitexts/locke/understanding/chapter0301.html
3. See H. P. Grice, "Utterer's Meaning, Sentence Meaning, and Word Meaning," *Foundations of Language* 4 (1968): 225–42. . . .
4. G. E. Moore, *Principia Ethica* (Cambridge: Cambridge University Press, 1903).
5. . . . See Paul Edwards, *The Logic of Moral Discourse* (Glencoe, IL: Free Press, 1955). . . .
6. Here my discussion dovetails with Gibbard's, which itself picks up on some nice points developed by James Dreier. See Allan Gibbard, *Thinking How to Live* (Cambridge, MA: Harvard University Press, 2003), 61–68; and James Dreier, "Expressivist Embeddings and Deflationist Truth," *Philosophical Studies* 83 (1996): 29–51.
7. Gibbard, *Thinking How to Live*, 94.
8. The 'thereby' in this definition can be read in stronger or weaker ways. On a strong reading, both the premises and the denial of the conclusion must figure in the explanation of why the person has beliefs with inconsistent contents. This reading of the 'thereby' yields a logic closer to traditional relevance logics than classical logic, since it will not entail that a contradiction entails absolutely everything. On a weaker reading, it is enough that accepting the premises and denying the conclusion are sufficient for having beliefs with inconsistent contents. This reading of 'thereby' yields something much more like classical logic. . . .
9. In his more recent work, Gibbard holds that atomic normative judgments like "believing that p is bad" express plans, but it seems reasonable enough to suppose that a plan not to believe that p amounts to a commitment to avoid believing that p.
10. For Blackburn's earliest account, see Simon Blackburn, *Spreading the Word* (Oxford: Oxford University Press, 1984). He later switches from talk of what one attitude "involves" to a theory employing higher-order attitudes in *Essays in Quasi-Realism*. For his most recent account, see Simon Blackburn, *Ruling Passions* (Oxford: Oxford University Press, 1998). . . .
11. Gibbard, *Thinking How to Live*, 56.

STUDY QUESTIONS

1. Might an utterance express both a desire and a belief?
2. According to Ridge, what is the contrast between ecumenical expressivism and ecumenical cognitivism?
3. According to Ridge, how does ecumenical expressivism avoid Moore's open-question argument?
4. According to Ridge, how does ecumenical expressivism avoid the Frege-Geach problem?

The Logic of Moral Discourse

Paul Edwards

In the previous essay, Ridge refers to the existence of "a logical space for the hybrid view according to which some but not all moral utterances express beliefs which provide their truth-conditions." In a footnote, he adds that Paul Edwards (1923–2004), who was Professor of Philosophy at Brooklyn College of the City University of New York, defends such a view.

Edwards argues that judgments of moral value be analyzed along the same lines as judgments of non-moral value. Consider, for example, the assertion that "The steak at Barney's is rather nice." The statement expresses the speaker's favorable attitude toward the qualities of the steak. But if the steak doesn't have those qualities, then the statement is false. Niceness thus lies with the steak, not the speaker's feelings or any special quality apart from the steak. The assertion is descriptive, not autobiographical. Edwards argues that we should treat goodness along similar lines. Hence the assertion that "you are a good person" expresses the speaker's favorable attitude toward your qualities. But if you don't have those qualities, the statement is false. Thus goodness is properly attributed to you on account of your qualities, not the speaker's feelings or any special quality apart from you. In short, though attitudes are what cause speakers to make moral judgments, what is referred to is not those attitudes but the properties of people, actions, or situations.

. . . The topic I am about to discuss has hardly been treated at all by philosophers. This is a great misfortune since, as I hope to show, a thorough discussion of it throws very much light on the nature of moral judgments, making some famous theories quite incredible. . . .

MR. HORN AND THE STEAK AT BARNEY'S

Let us consider the following situation (Situation I): Horn, a friend of mine who lives in Oklahoma, has arrived in New York for a visit. Before deciding where to eat, he asks me the following question: "What is the steak like at Barney's, the place we passed on the way from the station?" It should be added that both Horn and I are, at any rate as regards food, persons of very average (Western) taste. Both of us, furthermore, know this about each other. Now, each of the following three answers would, in the circumstances, give useful information to Horn—the information or at least the sort of information he wants to obtain:

> Answer A: "The steak at Barney's is always tender, made of very fresh meat, fairly thick

From Paul Edwards, *The Logic of Moral Discourse* (Glencoe, IL: The Free Press, 1955). Reprinted by permission of the publisher.

but rather small in size, and it is done to the exact degree of rareness or otherwise that the customer desires."

Answer B: "The steak at Barney's is always rather nice."

Answer C: "I rather like the steak at Barney's."

It is important to be clear about the likenesses and differences between answers A and B. If the steak at Barney's is really always tender, made of the freshest meat, fairly thick but rather small, and done to the exact degree of rareness that the customer desires, then answer A would of course be a true statement. If on the other hand the steak at Barney's is not always both tender and made of the freshest meat, and fairly thick but rather small, and done to the exact degree of rareness the customer desires, then answer A is false, though if it only lacks one of these features we would still say it came pretty close to the truth or that it was "nearly" or "pretty" true.

The facts which would make answer A a true statement would equally make answer B a true statement: if Horn were to eat steaks regularly at Barney's and if he invariably found them to be tender, made of the freshest meat, and so on, then he would undoubtedly be willing to say that I had spoken the truth, that the steak at Barney's is really rather nice. However, not all the sets of facts which serve to falsify answer A would ipso facto falsify answer B. Some would, others would not. In all the following sets of circumstances, answer A would be false.

(1) The steak at Barney's is always stale, peppery, thin, rather small, and never done to the exact degree of rareness or otherwise desired.

(2) It is always tough, stale, thick, large and done to the exact degree of rareness desired.

(3) It is always tender, fresh, thin but large, and done pretty much to the degree of rareness the customer desires.

(4) It is always tender, fairly fresh, middle thick and large and done to the exact degree of rareness desired.

Answer B on the other hand, would be false only in cases (1) and (2), but not in cases (3) and (4).

A person with average taste calls a steak nice when it is tender, fresh, thin but large, and done pretty much to the degree of rareness desired as readily as when it is tender, made of the freshest meat, fairly thick but rather small in size and done to the exact degree of rareness the customer desires.

The relation between answer A and answer B is somewhat like the relation between the statement, "I shall get to the office not earlier than 3:59 and not later than 4:01" and the statement, "I shall get to the office around 4." The facts which would make the former statement true would ipso facto make the latter statement true: if, e.g., I came to the office at 3:59 sharp both statements would be true. Some of the facts, furthermore, which would make the former statement false would also make the latter statement false. Thus if I got to the office at 6:05 this would make both statements false. However some of the facts which would falsify the first statement would not falsify the second. For instance, if I got to the office at 4:04 this would make the first statement false but it would make the second statement true.

We may sum up the relations between these two statements by saying "I shall get to the office around 4" says, in an indefinite or less definite way, the same sort of thing as "I shall get to the office not earlier than 3:49 and not later than 4:01." Similarly, answer B says, in a vague way, the same sort of thing as answer A. "I shall get to the office around 4" is in most contexts equivalent to "I shall get to the office at 4 or at 3:59 or at 3:58 or at 3:57 or at 3:56 or at 4:01 or at 4:03, etc." Similarly, in the above context, answer B is equivalent to "The steak at Barney's is either tender, fresh, fairly thick but rather small, and done to the exact degree of rareness desired, or tender, fresh, thin but rather large, and done pretty much to the degree of rareness desired or tender, fresh, middle thick and large, and done more or less to the degree of rareness desired, etc."

This conclusion that "The steak at Barney's is nice" is a vague statement must not be misinterpreted in either of two ways: firstly, this in no way implies that it is a "subjective claim." On the contrary, it is clearly an objective claim[1] . . . It is not a statement *about* my feelings or attitude, but about the features of the steak at Barney's. If I suddenly came to dislike steaks which are tender, fresh, fairly thick but rather small, and done to the exact degree of rareness desired, or which are tender, fresh, fairly thin but rather large and more or less done to the degree of rareness desired, this would not falsify my statement "The steak at Barney's is nice," as meant at the time at which I made it, though presumably I would, from then on, start using the word "nice" in a different sense. In fact even if at the time at which I made the statement I really, contrary to Horn's belief, disliked steaks which are tender, fresh, and so on, my answer B would still not be false. For I might have deliberately adjusted by usage of "nice" to that of the person of average taste.

The following parallel may help to make this clear: on a midsummer day my friend Riker pays me a visit. Both of us are accustomed to living in what geographers call the temperate zones—in climate such as prevails in New York City. Both of us are people with a fairly average constitution and we know this about each other. As he enters my apartment, I ask Riker: "What is it like outside?" He answers: "It's terribly hot." This statement of his is obviously an objective claim meaning something like "The temperature is well above 85 degrees." If the temperature were in fact 45 degrees the statement would clearly be false. I also have a friend by the name of Mittelmann who, until very recently, spent his life near the equator, i.e., in what is called the torrid zone. He never feels hot unless the temperature is well over 105 degrees. Supposing now Mittelmann visits me one day when the temperature is in fact 95 degrees, but he does not feel hot at all and to my question, "What is it like outside?" he replies, "It's warm, but no more." His statement, too, is obviously an objective claim having more or less the same referent as Riker's statement "It's terribly hot." However, Mittelman might very well have discovered by the time he visits me that locals like myself refer to temperatures which he calls "warm" as "terribly hot" and then he might well answer my question in the same way as Riker answered it—by saying "It's terribly hot outside." He would then be using the word "terribly hot" in a sense different from that in which he used it while living in equatorial regions, but his statement would, as before, be an objective claim.

The fact that answer B, as given in a situation like Situation I, is an objective claim can also be made apparent in the following way: supposing Horn and I—both of us, it will be remembered, are persons of average Western taste—stand outside the Red Coach Grill debating whether we should go inside and order a steak. Neither of us has ever before had a meal at the Red Coach Grill. Horn says, "I venture the guess that the steak is rather nice here" to which I retort, "I venture to guess that it is absolutely awful." Now, supposing the steak at the Red Coach Grill is always tough, stale, thin, small and done to a degree of rareness which was not desired, then undoubtedly my statement will be true, and Horn's will be false. On the other hand, if the steak at the Red Coach Grill is always either tender, fresh, thin but large and done to the exact degree of rareness desired, or else tender, fresh, thick but not large, and more or less done to the degree of rareness desired, his statement would be true and mine would be false. Of course both of us might be wrong, but at least one of us must be wrong. Our statements are *logically* incompatible. Thus we cannot both be making autobiographical or subjective claims.

I hope I have made it clear that in saying answer B is indefinite or vague one does not imply that it is a subjective claim. I now have to make it clear also that to say answer B is indefinite in no way implies that it is useless. If the steak at Barney's is in fact tender, fresh, fairly thick but rather small and done to the exact degree of rareness desired, then undoubtedly answer A would provide Horn with more information than answer B. But even then answer B would not be useless. It would give him a general, rough idea of what the steak is like—all that he might need in order to decide whether to try Barney's or not. Supposing however that sometimes at Barney's the steak is tender, fresh, thick but small and done to the exact degree of rareness desired and at other times it is tender, fairly fresh, thin but large and done to the exact degree of rareness desired and that on many occasions it is tender, fresh, fairly thick and large, but done only very approximately to the degree of rareness desired. Under those circumstances, answer A would mislead Horn while answer B would not mislead him. Under those circumstances answer B would be the only reasonably brief way of giving him the information he is seeking.

Answer B differs from answer A not only in saying the same sort of thing more indefinitely. Answer A *expresses* only the speaker's belief that the steak has the features mentioned without also expressing a favorable or unfavorable attitude on his part towards the steak. Answer B on the other hand expresses not only a belief of this sort but also a favorable attitude. Of course together with a certain tone or in a certain contest, answer A may express this attitude also, but answer B does it simply in virtue of the use of the word "nice."

It is necessary to insist on the following point with the greatest possible emphasis: although it is our taste, our likes and dislikes which determine what features we refer to when we call a steak (or some other dish) nice, a statement like answer B is an objective claim. It asserts that these features belong to the steak at Barney's. It does not *assert* that we like steaks having these features.

One further remark concerning answer B must here be added. Although many features of the steak are relevant to its niceness or otherwise, some certainly are not. Thus, for instance, its shape is not relevant. If it is tender and fresh and done to the exact degree of rareness desired then it is nice whether it has an elliptical, a rectangular, or a rhomboid shape. If it is tough, stale and not done to the degree of rareness desired then it is not nice, no matter what its shape may be. Supposing people started liking steaks only if among other things, they had a rectangular shape. Then their shape would become relevant to their niceness. At the same time, however, the meaning of "nice" would have changed. As "nice" is used now by members of the Western taste-community, the shape of a steak is irrelevant to its niceness. . . .

Let $F_1 \ldots F_x$ be the features to one or other set of which answer B refers—i.e., the steak's tenderness, its freshness, etc. Now, it is very interesting to observe that if somebody were to ask, "What *reasons* are there for saying that the steak at Barney's is nice?" one perfectly appropriate answer would be an enumeration of one or other set of $F_1 \ldots F_x$. It is interesting to notice this because unless one keeps in mind two facts, one may here easily be tempted into the view that the steak's niceness is some special quality over and above $F_1 \ldots F_x$. Not to fall into this temptation all we have to do is to remember firstly that answer B, in addition to referring to $F_1 \ldots F_x$, also expresses the speaker's pro-attitude towards the steak at Barney's, and secondly that . . . there is such a thing as a reason for an attitude or an emotion.

The question, "What reasons are there for saying that the steak at Barney's is nice?" may then either mean (i) "What reasons are there for supposing that the steak really has the features referred to in answer B?" or (ii) "What are the features of the steak which are the reasons for your favorable attitude expressed by answer B?" If the features have not yet been enumerated the question can only mean (ii). The fact then that $F_1 \ldots F_x$ can be the reason for the steak's niceness does not show that the referent of answer B is something other than these features. What it shows is that the same features which are the referent of answer B are also the reasons of the attitude which the sentence expresses.

I next wish to return to a discussion of answer C—i.e., the statement, "I rather like the steak at Barney's," made in reply to Horn's question, "What is the steak like at Barney's?" I wish to throw light on the "logic" of this type of statement and its relation to answer B.

The main point to be observed here is that while in a somewhat narrow sense the two statements are not synonymous, in a broader sense, which it is not difficult to describe, they do mean the same. Answers B and C do not mean the same in the sense that their referents are not identical. "I like the steak at Barney's" is not false even if the steak there is always tough and stale and small and is never done to the degree of rareness desired. It *is* false if I don't really like the steak there, even though it always is tender, and fresh and thick and done to the exact degree of rareness desired.

However, the two statements do mean the same in the sense that they have *the same force or do the same work*: they both, if true, equally give Horn the information he wants *concerning the steak at Barney's* and they both, if false, equally mislead him concerning the steak there. The reason for this is, of course, the fact that answer C . . . implies answer B. Being a member of the Western taste-community, I would not like a steak unless it is either tender, made of fresh meat, thick but rather small, and done to the exact degree of rareness desired, or unless it is tender, fresh, thin but large and done pretty much to the degree of rareness desired or . . .

That answers B and C are in this way synonymous is also apparent from the fact that Horn might instead of using the words, "What is the steak like at Barney's?" just as appropriately have framed his question as, "How do you like the steak at Barney's?" In contexts like Situation I we use these two forms of speech quite interchangeably to express our desire for information concerning certain events or objects: "How was last night's concert?" and "How did you like the concert last night?" or "How was Truman's speech?" and "How did you like Truman's speech?", and so forth.

Observing this synonymity between statements like "The steak at Barney's is nice" and "I like the steak at Barney's," many people have inferred that statements of the former type are "merely subjective," that they are merely assertions about or expressions of the speaker's taste. . . . It is not difficult to see, however, that what the synonymity between statements like answer B and statements like answer C proves is not that statements of the B-type are "merely subjective." It proves that, contrary to linguistic appearances, statements of the C-type are *not* merely subjective. . . .

In the light of our discussion, I wish to insist on the following points:

(i) the niceness belongs to, is "located" in the steak, not in me or my feelings;

(ii) the niceness of the steak is *not* identical with any one or any one set of nice-making characteristics;

(iii) although niceness is objective there is no feature or set of features to which one can point and say, "This is niceness";

(iv) nevertheless niceness is not something distinct from or over and above these features—it *disjunctively* refers to an indefinite set of them.

GOOD AND NICE

. . . [T]he usage of "good" resembles that of "nice" in the following respects: (i) the sentences in which it is used as predicate are, frequently at any rate, objective claims and (ii) their meaning tends to vary with the person or group of the person who employs them.

Some further resemblances can be brought out by contrasting the two statements, made by me:

"X.Y. is gentle, loving, does not lie, and is free from envy and malice," and,
"X.Y. is a good person"

. . . [T]he second statement, which is in our sense a moral judgment, says the *same sort* of thing as the first, but more indefinitely. In both cases, too, the second statement expresses the speaker's attitude of approval or admiration while the first does not or not so definitely. It is true that words like "gentle" and "kind" and "truthful" are very generally accompanied by approval, but not nearly as generally as "good." We may express the difference by saying that while "good" expresses the speaker's approval, "kind" and "gentle" and "truthful" only *tend to* express his approval. . . .

It is worth our while now to recall . . . that when, in circumstances like Situation I, I say, "the steak at Barney's is nice" my taste determines what features in a steak I refer to by "nice," but the statement itself refers to the features and not to my taste.

Similarly, what causes me to call X.Y. a good person is my favorable attitude to gentleness and truthfulness and freedom from envy. But what I refer to when I say, "X.Y. is a good person" are these features in X.Y. and not my approval. . . . [W]hat determines one to regard a person or an action as good is one's approval of certain of the qualities of that person or action, but in saying that the person or the action is good one refers to the qualities and not to the approval. This is the most important point of my whole treatise. I shall therefore state it once more in slightly different language. *the referent of the moral judgment is determined by the speaker's attitude, but it is not that attitude.*

. . . When a person makes such statements as, "It is going to rain tomorrow" or "the pressure exerted by a liquid is exactly proportional to its density," it is quite unnecessary to know anything about his emotion or attitude in order to know what he is asserting. On the other hand, in the case of moral judgments it is necessary to know this. "It will rain tomorrow" and "X.Y. is a profoundly good person" are both objective statements. But to know what the first refers to one needs to make no investigation concerning the author's approvals and disapprovals. To know what the second refers to one must know something about the author's approvals and disapprovals.

NOTE

1. [Edwards uses the term "objective" to refer to "statements or claims" whose "subject matter is something other than a mental event in somebody's mind."—Eds.]

STUDY QUESTIONS

1. When we praise the quality of a steak, are we making an objective claim?
2. To know the meaning of the assertion "The steak at Barney's is rather nice," do we need to know anything about the attitudes of the speaker?
3. To know the meaning of the assertion "Jill is a good person," do we need to know anything about the attitudes of the speaker?
4. Are judgments of moral value structurally similar to judgments of non-moral value?

Part V

ERROR THEORY

Ethics: Inventing Right and Wrong

J. L. Mackie

J. L. Mackie (1917–1981) was an Australian philosopher who was elected a fellow at University College, Oxford. He argues that moral judgments are objectively prescriptive—that is, they apply independently of an agent's desires or purposes. But no such objectively prescriptive properties exist. Hence ethical claims are systematically in error. For this reason, Mackie refers to his view as an "error theory." People may believe they are apprehending moral values in the world, but such strange entities do not exist, and even if they did, we would lack any special faculty that would enable us to perceive them.

THE SUBJECTIVITY OF VALUES

1. Moral Skepticism

There are no objective values. This is a bald statement of the thesis of this chapter, but before arguing for it I shall try to clarify and restrict it in ways that may meet some objections and prevent some misunderstanding.

The statement of this thesis is liable to provoke one of three very different reactions. Some will think it not merely false but pernicious; they will see it as a threat to morality and to everything else that is worthwhile, and they will find the presenting of such a thesis in what purports to be a [chapter] on ethics paradoxical or even outrageous. Others will regard it as a trivial truth, almost too obvious to be worth mentioning, and certainly too plain to be worth much argument. Others again will say that it is meaningless or empty, that no real issue is raised by the question whether values are or are not part of the fabric of the world. But, precisely because there can be these three different reactions, much more needs to be said.

The claim that values are not objective, are not part of the fabric of the world, is meant to include not only moral goodness, which might be most naturally equated with moral value, but also other things that could be more loosely called moral values or disvalues—rightness and wrongness, duty, obligation, an action's being rotten and contemptible, and so on. It also includes non-moral values, notably aesthetic ones, beauty and various kinds of artistic merit. I shall not discuss these explicitly, but clearly much the same considerations apply to aesthetic and to moral values, and there would be at least some initial implausibility in a view that gave the one a different status from the other.

Since it is with moral values that I am primarily concerned, the view I am adopting may be called moral skepticism. But this name is likely to be misunderstood: "moral skepticism" might also be used

From J. L. Mackie, *Ethics: Inventing Right and Wrong* (Harmondsworth: Penguin, 1977). Reprinted by permission of the publisher.

as a name for either of two first order views, or perhaps for an incoherent mixture of the two. A moral skeptic might be the sort of person who says "All this talk of morality is tripe," who rejects morality and will take no notice of it. Such a person may be literally rejecting all moral judgments: he is more likely to be making moral judgments of his own, expressing a positive moral condemnation of all that conventionally passes for morality: or he may be confusing these two logically incompatible views, and saying that he rejects all morality, while he is in fact rejecting only a particular morality that is current in the society in which he has grown up. But I am not at present concerned with the merits or faults of such a position. These are first order moral views, positive or negative: the person who adopts either of them is taking a certain practical, normative, stand. By contrast, what I am discussing is a second order view, a view about the status of moral values and the nature of moral valuing, about where and how they fit into the world. These first and second order views are not merely distinct but completely independent: one could be a second order moral skeptic without being a first order one, or again the other way round. A man could hold strong moral views, and indeed ones whose content was thoroughly conventional, while believing that they were simply attitudes and policies with regard to conduct that he and other people held. Conversely, a man could reject all established morality while believing it to be an objective truth that it was evil or corrupt.

With another sort of misunderstanding moral skepticism would seem not so much pernicious as absurd. How could anyone deny that there is a difference between a kind action and a cruel one, or that a coward and a brave man behave differently in the face of danger? Of course, this is undeniable, but it is not to the point. The kinds of behavior to which moral values and disvalues are ascribed are indeed part of the furniture of the world, and so are the natural, descriptive, differences between them, but not, perhaps, their differences in value. It is a hard fact that cruel actions differ from kind ones, and hence that we can learn, as in fact we all do, to distinguish them fairly well in practice, and to use the words "cruel" and "kind" with fairly clear descriptive

meanings: but is it an equally hard fact that actions which are cruel in such a descriptive sense are to be condemned? The present issue is with regard to the objectivity specifically of value, not with regard to the objectivity of those natural, factual, differences on the basis of which differing values are assigned.

2. Subjectivism

Another name often used, as an alternative to "moral skepticism," for the view I am discussing is "subjectivism." But this too has more than one meaning. Moral subjectivism too could be a first order, normative, view, namely that everyone really ought to do whatever he thinks he should. This plainly is a (systematic) first order view, on examination it soon ceases to be plausible, but that is beside the point, for it is quite independent of the second order thesis at present under consideration. What is more confusing is that different second order views compete for the name "subjectivism." Several of these are doctrines about the meaning of moral terms and moral statements. What is often called moral subjectivism is the doctrine that, for example, "This action is right" *means* "I approve of this action," or more generally that moral judgments are equivalent to reports of the speaker's own feelings or attitudes. But the view I am now discussing is to be distinguished in two vital respects from any such doctrine as this. First, what I have called moral skepticism is a negative doctrine, not a positive one: it says what there isn't, not what there is. It says that there do not exist entities or relations of a certain kind, objective values or requirements, which many people have believed to exist. Of course, the moral skeptic cannot leave it at that. If his position is to be at all plausible, he must give some account of how other people have fallen into what he regards as an error, and this account will have to include some positive suggestions about how values fail to be objective, about what has been mistaken for, or has led to false beliefs about, objective values. But this will be a development of this theory, not its core: its core is the negation. Secondly, what I have called moral skepticism is an ontological thesis, not a linguistic or conceptual one. It is not, like the other doctrine often called moral subjectivism, a view about the meanings of moral statements. Again, no doubt, if it is to be at all plausible, it will have to give some account of their meanings, and I shall say something about this in Section 7 . . . But this too will be a development of the theory, not its core.

It is true that those who have accepted the moral subjectivism which is the doctrine that moral judgments are equivalent to reports of the speaker's own feelings or attitudes have usually presupposed what I am calling moral skepticism. It is because they have assumed that there are no objective values that they have looked elsewhere for an analysis of what moral statements might mean, and have settled upon subjective reports. Indeed, if all our moral statements were such subjective reports, it would follow that, at least so far as we are aware, there are no objective moral values. If we were aware of them, we would say something about them. In this sense this sort of subjectivism entails moral skepticism. But the converse entailment does not hold. The denial that there are objective values does not commit one to any particular view about what moral statements mean, and certainly not to the view that they are equivalent to subjective reports. No doubt if moral values are not objective they are in some very broad sense subjective, and for this reason I would accept "moral subjectivism" as an alternative name to "moral skepticism." But subjectivism in this broad sense must be distinguished from the specific doctrine about meaning referred to above. Neither name is altogether satisfactory: we simply have to guard against the (different) misinterpretations which each may suggest. . . .

7. The Claim to Objectivity

If I have succeeded in specifying precisely enough the moral values whose objectivity I am denying, my thesis may now seem to be trivially true. Of course, some will say, valuing, preferring, choosing, recommending, rejecting, condemning, and so on, are human activities, and there is no need to look for values that are prior to and logically independent of all such activities. There may be widespread agreement in valuing, and particular value-judgments are not in general arbitrary or isolated: they typically cohere with others, or can be criticized if they do not, reasons can be given for them, and so on: but if all that the subjectivist is maintaining is that desires, ends, purposes, and the like figure somewhere in the system of reasons, and that no ends or purposes are objective as opposed to being merely intersubjective, then this may be conceded without much fuss.

But I do not think that this should be conceded so easily. . . . [T]he main tradition of European moral philosophy includes the contrary claim, that there are objective values of just the sort I have denied. I [here] refer . . . to Plato, Kant, and Sidgwick. Kant in particular holds that the categorical imperative is not only categorical and imperative but objectively so: though a rational being gives the moral law to himself, the law that he thus makes is determinate and necessary. Aristotle begins the *Nicomachean Ethics* by saying that the good is that at which all things aim, and that ethics is part of a science which he calls "politics," whose goal is not knowledge but practice: yet he does not doubt that there can be *knowledge* of what is the good for man, nor, once he has identified this as well-being or happiness, *eudaimonia,* that it can be known, rationally determined, in what happiness consists; and it is plain that he thinks that this happiness is intrinsically desirable, not good simply because it is desired. The rationalist Samuel Clarke holds that

> these eternal and necessary differences of things make it *fit and reasonable* for creatures so to act . . . even separate from the consideration of these rules being the *positive will* or *command of God*; and also antecedent to any respect or regard, expectation or apprehension, of any *particular private and personal advantage or disadvantage, reward or punishment,* either present or future. . . .

Even the sentimentalist Hutcheson defines moral goodness as "some quality apprehended in actions, which procures approbation . . . ," while saying that the moral sense by which we perceive virtue and vice has been given to us (by the Author of nature) to direct our actions. Hume indeed was on the other side, but he is still a witness to the dominance of the objectivist tradition, since he claims that when we "see that the distinction of vice and virtue is not founded merely on the relations of objects, nor is perceiv'd by reason," this "wou'd subvert all the vulgar systems of morality." And Richard Price insists that right and wrong are "real characters of actions," not "qualities of our minds," and are perceived by the understanding; he criticizes the notion of moral sense on the ground that it would make virtue an affair of taste, and moral right and wrong "nothing in the objects themselves"; he rejects Hutcheson's view because (perhaps mistakenly) he sees it as collapsing into Hume's.

But this objectivism about values is not only a feature of the philosophical tradition. It has also a firm basis in ordinary thought, and even in the meanings of moral terms. No doubt it was an extravagance for Moore to say that "good" is the name of a non-natural quality, but it would not be so far wrong to say that in moral contexts it is used as if it were the name of a supposed non-natural quality, where the description "non-natural" leaves room for the peculiar evaluative, prescriptive, intrinsically action-guiding aspects of this supposed quality. This point can be illustrated by reflection on the conflicts and swings of opinion in recent years between non-cognitivist and naturalist views about the central, basic, meanings of ethical terms. If we reject the view that it is the function of such terms to introduce objective values into discourse about conduct and choices of action, there seem to be two main alternative types of account. One (which has importantly different subdivisions) is that they conventionally express either attitudes which the speaker purports to adopt towards whatever it is that he characterizes morally, or prescriptions or recommendations, subject perhaps to the logical constraint of universalizability. Different views of this type share the central thesis that ethical terms have, at least partly and primarily, some sort of non-cognitive, non-descriptive, meaning. Views of the other type hold that they are descriptive in meaning, but descriptive of natural features, partly of such features as everyone, even the non-cognitivist, would recognize as distinguishing kind actions from cruel ones,

courage from cowardice, politeness from rudeness, and so on, and partly (though these two overlap) of relations between the actions and some human wants, satisfactions, and the like. I believe that views of both these types capture part of the truth. Each approach can account for the fact that moral judgments are action-guiding or practical. Yet each gains much of its plausibility from the felt inadequacy of the other. It is a very natural reaction to any non-cognitive analysis of ethical terms to protest that there is more to ethics than this, something more external to the maker of moral judgments, more authoritative over both him and those of or to whom he speaks, and this reaction is likely to persist even when full allowance has been made for the logical, formal, constraints of full-blooded prescriptivity and universalizability. Ethics, we are inclined to believe, is more a matter of knowledge and less a matter of decision than any non-cognitive analysis allows. And of course naturalism satisfies this demand. It will not be a matter of choice or decision whether an action is cruel or unjust or imprudent or whether it is likely to produce more distress than pleasure. But in satisfying this demand, it introduces a converse deficiency. On a naturalist analysis, moral judgments can be practical, but their practicality is wholly relative to desires or possible satisfactions of the person or persons whose actions are to be guided; but moral judgments seem to say more than this. This view leaves out the categorical quality of moral requirements. In fact both naturalist and non-cognitive analyses leave out the apparent authority of ethics, the one by excluding the categorically imperative aspect, the other the claim to objective validity or truth. The ordinary user of moral language means to say something about whatever it is that he characterizes morally, for example a possible action, as it is in itself, or would be if it were realized, and not about, or even simply expressive of, his, or anyone else's, attitude or relation to it. But the something he wants to say is not purely descriptive, certainly not inert, but something that involves a call for action or for the refraining from action, and one that is absolute, not contingent upon any desire or preference or policy or choice, his own or anyone else's. Someone in a state of moral perplexity, wondering whether it would be wrong for him to engage, say, in research related to bacteriological warfare, wants to arrive at some judgment about this concrete case, his doing this work at this time in these actual circumstances; his relevant characteristics will be part of the subject of the judgment, but no relation between him and the proposed action will be part of the predicate. The question is not, for example, whether he really wants to do this work, whether it will satisfy or dissatisfy him, whether he will in the long run have a pro-attitude towards it, or even whether this is an action of a sort that he can happily and sincerely recommend in all relevantly similar cases. Nor is he even wondering just whether to recommend such action in all relevantly similar cases. He wants to know whether this course of action would be wrong in itself. Something like this is the everyday objectivist concept of which talk about non-natural qualities is a philosopher's reconstruction.

The prevalence of this tendency to objectify values—and not only moral ones—is confirmed by a pattern of thinking that we find in existentialists and those influenced by them. The denial of objective values can carry with it an extreme emotional reaction, a feeling that nothing matters at all, that life has lost its purpose. Of course this does not follow; the lack of objective values is not a good reason for abandoning subjective concern or for ceasing to want anything. But the abandonment of a belief in objective values can cause, at least temporarily, a decay of subjective concern and sense of purpose. That it does so is evidence that the people in whom this reaction occurs have been tending to objectify their concerns and purposes, have been giving them a fictitious external authority. A claim to objectivity has been so strongly associated with their subjective concerns and purposes that the collapse of the former seems to undermine the latter as well.

This view, that conceptual analysis would reveal a claim to objectivity, is sometimes dramatically confirmed by philosophers who are officially on the other side. Bertrand Russell, for example, says that "ethical propositions should be expressed in the optative mood, not in the indicative"; he defends himself effectively against the charge of inconsistency in both holding ultimate ethical valuations to

be subjective and expressing emphatic opinions on ethical questions. Yet at the end he admits:

> Certainly there *seems* to be something more. Suppose, for example, that some one were to advocate the introduction of bullfighting in this country. In opposing the proposal, I should *feel,* not only that I was expressing my desires, but that my desires in the matter are *right,* whatever that may mean. As a matter of argument, I can, I think, show that I am not guilty of any logical inconsistency in holding to the above interpretation of ethics and at the same time expressing strong ethical preferences. But in feeling I am not satisfied.

But he concludes, reasonably enough, with the remark: "I can only say that, while my own opinions as to ethics do not satisfy me, other people's satisfy me still less."

I conclude, then, that ordinary moral judgments include a claim to objectivity, an assumption that there are objective values in just the sense in which I am concerned to deny this. And I do not think it is going too far to say that this assumption has been incorporated in the basic, conventional, meanings of moral terms. Any analysis of the meanings of moral terms which omits this claim to objective, intrinsic, prescriptivity is to that extent incomplete; and this is true of any non-cognitive analysis, any naturalist one, and any combination of the two.

If second order ethics were confined, then, to linguistic and conceptual analysis, it ought to conclude that moral values at least are objective: that they are so is part of what our ordinary moral statements mean: the traditional moral concepts of the ordinary man as well as of the main line of Western philosophers are concepts of objective value. But it is precisely for this reason that linguistic and conceptual analysis is not enough. The claim to objectivity, however ingrained in our language and thought, is not self-validating. It can and should be questioned. But the denial of objective values will have to be put forward not as the result of an analytic approach, but as an "error theory," a theory that although most people in making moral judgments implicitly claim, among other things, to be pointing to something objectively prescriptive, these claims are all false. It is this that makes the name "moral skepticism" appropriate.

But since this is an error theory, since it goes against assumptions ingrained in our thought and built into some of the ways in which language is used, since it conflicts with what is sometimes called common sense, it needs very solid support. It is not something we can accept lightly or casually and then quietly pass on. If we are to adopt this view, we must argue explicitly for it. Traditionally it has been supported by arguments of two main kinds, which I shall call the argument from relativity and the argument from queerness, but these can, as I shall show, be supplemented in several ways.

8. The Argument from Relativity

The argument from relativity has as its premise the well-known variation in moral codes from one society to another and from one period to another, and also the differences in moral belief between different groups and classes within a complex community. Such variation is in itself merely a truth of descriptive morality, a fact of anthropology which entails neither first order nor second order ethical views. Yet it may indirectly support second order subjectivism: radical differences between first order moral judgments make it difficult to treat those judgments as apprehensions of objective truths. But it is not the mere occurrence of disagreements that tells against the objectivity of values. Disagreement on questions in history or biology or cosmology does not show that there are no objective issues in these fields for investigation to disagree about. But such scientific disagreement results from speculative inferences or explanatory hypotheses based on inadequate evidence, and it is hardly plausible to interpret moral disagreement in the same way. Disagreement about moral codes seems to reflect people's adherence to and participation in different ways of life. The causal connection seems to be mainly that way round: it is that people approve of monogamy because they participate in a monogamous way of life rather than that they participate in a monogamous way of life

because they approve of monogamy. Of course, the standards may be an idealization of the way of life from which they arise: the monogamy in which people participate may be less complete, less rigid, than that of which it leads them to approve. This is not to say that moral judgments are purely conventional. Of course there have been and are moral heretics and moral reformers, people who have turned against the established rules and practices of their own communities for moral reasons, and often for moral reasons that we would endorse. But this can usually be understood as the extension, in ways which, though new and unconventional, seemed to them to be required for consistency, of rules to which they already adhered as arising out of an existing way of life. In short, the argument from relativity has some force simply because the actual variations in the moral codes are more readily explained by the hypothesis that they reflect ways of life than by the hypothesis that they express perceptions, most of them seriously inadequate and badly distorted, of objective values.

But there is a well-known counter to this argument from relativity, namely to say that the items for which objective validity is in the first place to be claimed are not specific moral rules or codes but very general basic principles which are recognized at least implicitly to some extent in all society—such principles as provide the foundations of what Sidgwick has called different methods of ethics, the principle of universalizability, perhaps, or the rule that one ought to conform to the specific rules of any way of life in which one takes part, from which one profits, and on which one relies, or some utilitarian principle of doing what tends, or seems likely, to promote the general happiness. It is easy to show that such general principles, married with differing concrete circumstances, different existing social patterns or different preferences, will beget different specific moral rules, and there is some plausibility in the claim that the specific rules thus generated will vary from community to community or from group to group in close agreement with the actual variations in accepted codes.

The argument from relativity can be only partly countered in this way. To take this line the moral objectivist has to say that it is only in these principles that the objective moral character attaches immediately to its descriptively specified ground or subject: other moral judgments are objectively valid or true, but only derivatively and contingently—if things had been otherwise, quite different sorts of actions would have been right. And despite the prominence in recent philosophical ethics of universalization, utilitarian principles, and the like, these are very far from constituting the whole of what is actually affirmed as basic in ordinary moral thought. Much of this is concerned rather with what Hare calls "ideals" or, less kindly, "fanaticism." That is, people judge that some things are good or right, and others are bad or wrong, not because—or at any rate not only because—they exemplify some general principle for which widespread implicit acceptance could be claimed, but because something about those things arouses certain responses immediately in them, though they would arouse radically and irresolvably different responses in others. "Moral sense" or "intuition" is an initially more plausible description of what supplies many of our basic moral judgments than "reason." With regard to all these starting points of moral thinking the argument from relativity remains in full force.

9. The Argument from Queerness

Even more important, however, and certainly more generally applicable, is the argument from queerness. This has two parts, one metaphysical, the other epistemological. If there were objective values, then they would be entities or qualities or relations of a very strange sort, utterly different from anything else in the universe. Correspondingly, if we were aware of them, it would have to be by some special faculty of moral perception or intuition, utterly different from our ordinary ways of knowing everything else. These points were recognized by Moore when he spoke of non-natural qualities, and by the intuitionists in their talk about a "faculty of moral intuition." Intuitionism has long been out of favor, and it is indeed easy to point out its implausibilities. What is not so often stressed, but is more important, is that the central thesis of intuitionism is one to

which any objectivist view of values is in the end committed: intuitionism merely makes unpalatably plain what other forms of objectivism wrap up. Of course the suggestion that moral judgments are made or moral problems solved by just sitting down and having an ethical intuition is a travesty of actual moral thinking. But, however complex the real process, it will require (if it is to yield authoritatively prescriptive conclusions) some input of this distinctive sort, either premises or forms of argument or both. When we ask the awkward question, how we can be aware of this authoritative prescriptivity, of the truth of these distinctively ethical premises or of the cogency of this distinctively ethical pattern of reasoning, none of our ordinary accounts of sensory perception or introspection or the framing and confirming of explanatory hypotheses or inference or logical construction or conceptual analysis, or any combination of these, will provide a satisfactory answer; "a special sort of intuition" is a lame answer, but it is the one to which the clearheaded objectivist is compelled to resort.

Indeed, the best move for the moral objectivist is not to evade this issue, but to look for companions in guilt. For example, Richard Price argues that it is not moral knowledge alone that such an empiricism as those of Locke and Hume is unable to account for, but also our knowledge and even our ideas of essence, number, identity, diversity, solidity, inertia, substance, the necessary existence and infinite extension of time and space, necessity and possibility in general, power, and causation. If the understanding, which Price defines as the faculty within us that discerns truth, is also a source of new simple ideas of so many other sorts, may it not also be a power of immediately perceiving right and wrong, which yet are real characters of actions?

This is an important counter to the argument from queerness. The only adequate reply to it would be to show how, on empiricist foundations, we can construct an account of the ideas and beliefs and knowledge that we have of all these matters. I cannot even begin to do that here, though I have undertaken some parts of the task elsewhere. I can only state my belief that satisfactory accounts of most of these can be given in empirical terms. If some supposed metaphysical necessities or essences resist such treatment, then they too should be included, along with objective values, among the targets of the argument from queerness.

This queerness does not consist simply in the fact that ethical statements are "unverifiable." Although logical positivism with its verifiability theory of descriptive meaning gave an impetus to non-cognitive accounts of ethics, it is not only logical positivists but also empiricists of a much more liberal sort who should find objective values hard to accommodate. Indeed. I would not only reject the verifiability principle but also deny the conclusion commonly drawn from it, that moral judgments lack descriptive meaning. The assertion that there are objective values or intrinsically prescriptive entities or features of some kind, which ordinary moral judgments presuppose, is, I hold, not meaningless but false.

Plato's Forms give a dramatic picture of what objective values would have to be. The Form of the Good is such that knowledge of it provides the knower with both a direction and an overriding motive; something's being good both tells the person who knows this to pursue it and makes him pursue it. An objective good would be sought by anyone who was acquainted with it, not because of any contingent fact that this person, or every person, is so constituted that he desires this end, but just because the end has to-be-pursuedness somehow built into it. Similarly, if there were objective principles of right and wrong, any wrong (possible) course of action would have not-to-be-doneness somehow built into it. Or we should have something like Clarke's necessary relations of fitness between situations and actions, so that a situation would have a demand for such-and-such an action somehow built into it.

The need for an argument of this sort can be brought out by reflection on Hume's argument that "reason"—in which at this stage he includes all sorts of knowing as well as reasoning—can never be an "influencing motive of the will." Someone might object that Hume has argued unfairly from the lack of influencing power (not contingent upon desires) in ordinary objects of knowledge and ordinary reasoning, and might maintain that values differ from natural objects precisely in their power, when known, automatically to influence the will. To this Hume could, and would need to, reply that this objection involves the postulating of value-entities or value-features of quite a different order from anything else with which we are acquainted, and of a corresponding faculty with which to detect them. That is, he would have to supplement his explicit argument with what I have called the argument from queerness.

Another way of bringing out this queerness is to ask, about anything that is supposed to have some objective moral quality, how this is linked with its natural features. What is the connection between the natural fact that an action is a piece of deliberate cruelty—say, causing pain just for fun—and the moral fact that it is wrong? It cannot be an entailment, a logical or semantic necessity. Yet it is not merely that the two features occur together. The wrongness must somehow be "consequential" or "supervenient"; it is wrong because it is a piece of deliberate cruelty. But just what *in the world* is signified by this "because"? And how do we know the relation that it signifies, if this is something more than such actions being socially condemned, and condemned by us too, perhaps through our having absorbed attitudes from our social environment? It is not even sufficient to postulate a faculty which "sees" the wrongness: something must be postulated which can see at once the natural features that constitute the cruelty, and the wrongness, and the mysterious consequential link between the two. Alternatively, the intuition required might be the perception that wrongness is a higher order property belonging to certain natural properties; but what is this belonging of properties to other properties, and how can we discern it? How much simpler and more comprehensible the situation would be if we could replace the moral quality with some sort of subjective response which could be causally related to the detection of the natural features on which the supposed quality is said to be consequential.

It may be thought that the argument from queerness is given an unfair start if we thus relate it to what are admittedly among the wilder products of philosophical fancy—Platonic Forms, non-natural qualities, self-evident relations of fitness, faculties of intuition, and the like. Is it equally forceful if applied to the terms in which everyday moral judgments are more likely to be expressed—though still, as has been argued in Section 7, with a claim to objectivity—"you must do this," "you can't do that," "obligation," "unjust," "rotten," "disgraceful," "mean," or talk about good reasons for or against possible actions? Admittedly not; but that is because the objective prescriptivity, the element a claim for whose authoritativeness is embedded in ordinary moral thought and language, is not yet isolated in these forms of speech, but is presented along with relations to desires and feelings, reasoning about the means to desired ends, interpersonal demands, the injustice which consists in the violation of what are in the context the accepted standards of merit, the psychological constituents of meanness, and so on. There is nothing queer about any of these, and under cover of them the claim for moral authority may pass unnoticed. But if I am right in arguing that it is ordinarily there, and is therefore very likely to be incorporated almost automatically in philosophical accounts of ethics which systematize our ordinary thought even in such apparently innocent terms as these, it needs to be examined, and for this purpose it needs to be isolated and exposed as it is by the less cautious philosophical reconstructions.

10. Patterns of Objectification

Considerations of these kinds suggest that it is in the end less paradoxical to reject than to retain the common-sense belief in the objectivity of moral values, provided that we can explain how this belief, if it is false, has become established and is so resistant to criticisms. This proviso is not difficult to satisfy.

On a subjectivist view, the supposedly objective values will be based in fact upon attitudes which the person has who takes himself to be recognizing and responding to those values. If we admit what Hume calls the mind's "propensity to spread itself on external objects," we can understand the supposed objectivity of moral qualities as arising from what we can call the projection or objectification of moral

attitudes. This would be analogous to what is called the "pathetic fallacy," the tendency to read our feelings into their objects. If a fungus, say, fills us with disgust, we may be inclined to ascribe to the fungus itself a non-natural quality of foulness. But in moral contexts there is more than this propensity at work. Moral attitudes themselves are at least partly social in origin: socially established—and socially necessary—patterns of behavior put pressure on individuals, and each individual tends to internalize these pressures and to join in requiring these patterns of behavior of himself and of others. The attitudes that are objectified into moral values have indeed an external source, though not the one assigned to them by the belief in their absolute authority. Moreover, there are motives that would support objectification. We need morality to regulate interpersonal relations, to control some of the ways in which people behave towards one another, often in opposition to contrary inclinations. We therefore want our moral judgments to be authoritative for other agents as well as for ourselves: objective validity would give them the authority required. Aesthetic values are logically in the same position as moral ones; much the same metaphysical and epistemological considerations apply to them. But aesthetic values are less strongly objectified than moral ones; their subjective status, and an "error theory" with regard to such claims to objectivity as are incorporated in aesthetic judgments, will be more readily accepted, just because the motives for their objectification are less compelling.

But it would be misleading to think of the objectification of moral values as primarily the projection of feelings, as in the pathetic fallacy. More important are wants and demands. As Hobbes says, "whatsoever is the object of any man's Appetite or Desire, that is it, which he for his part calleth *Good*"; and certainly both the adjective "good" and the noun "goods" are used in non-moral contexts of things because they are such as to satisfy desires. We get the notion of something's being objectively good, or having intrinsic value, by reversing the direction of dependence here, by making the desire depend upon the goodness, instead of the goodness on the desire. And this is aided by the fact that the desired thing will indeed have features that make it desired, that enable it to arouse a desire or that make it such as to satisfy some desire that is already there. It is fairly easy to confuse the way in which a thing's desirability is indeed objective with its having in our sense objective value. The fact that the word "good" serves as one of our main moral terms is a trace of this pattern of objectification.

Similarly related uses of words are covered by the distinction between hypothetical and categorical imperatives. The statement that someone "ought to" or, more strongly, "must" do such-and-such may be backed up explicitly or implicitly by reference to what he wants or to what his purposes and objects are. Again, there may be a reference to the purposes of someone else, perhaps the speaker: "You must do this"—"Why?"—"Because I want such-and-such." The moral categorical imperative which could be expressed in the same words can be seen as resulting from the suppression of the conditional clause in a hypothetical imperative without its being replaced by any such reference to the speaker's wants. The action in question is still required in something like the way in which it would be if it were appropriately related to a want, but it is no longer admitted that there is any contingent want upon which its being required depends. Again this move can be understood when we remember that at least our central and basic moral judgments represent social demands, where the source of the demand is indeterminate and diffuse. Whose demands or wants are in question, the agent's, or the speaker's, or those of an indefinite multitude of other people? All of these in a way, but there are advantages in not specifying them precisely. The speaker is expressing demands which he makes as a member of a community, which he has developed in and by participation in a joint way of life; also, what is required of this particular agent would be required of any other in a relevantly similar situation; but the agent too is expected to have internalized the relevant demands, to act as if the ends for which the action is required were his own. By suppressing any explicit reference to demands and making the imperatives categorical we facilitate conceptual moves from one such demand relation to another. The moral uses of such words as

"must" and "ought" and "should," all of which are used also to express hypothetical imperatives, are traces of this pattern of objectification.

It may be objected that this explanation links normative ethics too closely with descriptive morality, with the mores or socially enforced patterns of behavior that anthropologists record. But it can hardly be denied that moral thinking starts from the enforcement of social codes. Of course it is not confined to that. But even when moral judgments are detached from the mores of any actual society they are liable to be framed with reference to an ideal community of moral agents, such as Kant's kingdom of ends, which but for the need to give God a special place in it would have been better called a commonwealth of ends.

Another way of explaining the objectification of moral values is to say that ethics is a system of law from which the legislator has been removed. This might have been derived either from the positive law of a state or from a supposed system of divine law. There can be no doubt that some features of modern European moral concepts are traceable to the theological ethics of Christianity. The stress on quasi-imperative notions, on what ought to be done or on what is wrong in a sense that is close to that of "forbidden," are surely relics of divine commands. Admittedly, the central ethical concepts for Plato and Aristotle also are in a broad sense prescriptive or intrinsically action-guiding, but in concentrating rather on "good" than on "ought" they show that their moral thought is an objectification of the desired and the satisfying rather than of the commanded. Elizabeth Anscombe has argued that modern, non-Aristotelian, concepts of *moral* obligation, *moral* duty, of what is *morally* right and wrong, and of the *moral* sense of "ought" are survivals outside the framework of thought that made them really intelligible, namely the belief in divine law. She infers that "ought" has "become a word of mere mesmeric force," with only a "delusive appearance of content," and that we would do better to discard such terms and concepts altogether, and go back to Aristotelian ones.

There is much to be said for this view. But while we can explain some distinctive features of modern moral philosophy in this way, it would be a mistake to see the whole problem of the claim to objective prescriptivity as merely local and unnecessary, as a post-operative complication of a society from which a dominant system of theistic belief has recently been rather hastily excised. As Cudworth and Clarke and Price, for example, show, even those who still admit divine commands, or the positive law of God, may believe moral values to have an independent objective but still action-guiding authority. Responding to Plato's *Euthyphro* dilemma, they believe that God commands what he commands because it is in itself good or right, not that it is good or right merely because and in that he commands it. Otherwise God himself could not be called good. Price asks, "What can be more preposterous, than to make the Deity nothing but will; and to exalt this on the ruins of all his attributes?" The apparent objectivity of moral value is a widespread phenomenon which has more than one source: the persistence of a belief in something like divine law when the belief in the divine legislator has faded out is only one factor among others. There are several different patterns of objectification, all of which have left characteristic traces in our actual moral concepts and moral language. . . .

12. Conclusion

I have maintained that there is a real issue about the status of values, including moral values. Moral skepticism, the denial of objective moral values, is not to be confused with any one of several first order normative views, or with any linguistic or conceptual analysis. Indeed, ordinary moral judgements involve a claim to objectivity which both non-cognitive and naturalist analyses fail to capture. Moral skepticism must, therefore, take the form of an error theory, admitting that a belief in objective values is built into ordinary moral thought and language, but holding that this ingrained belief is false. As such, it needs arguments to support it against "common sense." But solid arguments can be found. The considerations that favor moral skepticism are: first, the relativity or variability of some important starting points of moral thinking and their apparent dependence on actual ways of life; secondly, the metaphysical peculiarity of the supposed objective values, in that they would have to be intrinsically action-guiding and motivating; thirdly, the problem of how such values could be consequential or supervenient upon natural features; fourthly, the corresponding epistemological difficulty of accounting for our knowledge of value entities or features and of their links with the features on which they would be consequential; fifthly, the possibility of explaining, in terms of several different patterns of objectification, traces of which remain in moral language and moral concepts, how even if there were no such objective values people not only might have come to suppose that there are but also might persist firmly in that belief. These five points sum up the case for moral skepticism; but of almost equal importance are the preliminary removal of misunderstandings that often prevent this thesis from being considered fairly and explicitly, and the isolation of those items about which the moral skeptic is skeptical from many associated qualities and relations whose objective status is not in dispute.

STUDY QUESTIONS

1. Why does Mackie label his view an "error theory"?
2. To recognize moral values, do you need a special faculty of moral perception?
3. Does the variation in moral codes from one society to another provide evidence in favor of Mackie's view?
4. Is Mackie's theory supposed to apply to non-moral value judgments?

Against External Skepticism

Ronald Dworkin

Ronald Dworkin (1931–2013) was Professor of Philosophy and of Law at New York University. He argues that error theorists, such as Mackie, hold that all moral statements are false. But consider the claim that "lying is impermissible." To say that this statement is false, Dworkin claims, is equivalent to asserting that it is not the case that lying is impermissible. And this statement is an ordinary moral claim about lying. Hence the error theorist is committed to the truth of certain moral claims. Dworkin thus concludes that the Error Theory turns out to be a moral theory in disguise.

TWO IMPORTANT DISTINCTIONS

Internal and External Skepticism

. . . Internal skepticism about morality is a first-order, substantive moral judgment. It appeals to more abstract judgments about morality in order to deny that certain more concrete or applied judgments are true. External skepticism, on the contrary, purports to rely entirely on second-order, external statements about morality. Some external skeptics rely on social facts . . . : they say that the historical and geographical diversity of moral opinions shows that no such opinion can be objectively true, for example. But the most sophisticated external skeptics rely . . . on metaphysical theses about the kind of entities the universe contains. They assume that these metaphysical theses are external statements about morality rather than internal judgments of morality. So, as the metaphor suggests, internal skepticism stands within first-order, substantive morality while external skepticism is supposedly Archimedean: it stands above morality and judges it from outside. Internal skeptics cannot be skeptical about morality all the way down, because they must assume the truth of some very general moral claim in order to establish their skepticism about other moral claims. They rely on morality to denigrate morality. External skeptics do claim to be skeptical about morality all the way down. They are able to denigrate moral truth, they say, without relying on it.

Error and Status Skepticism

We need a further distinction within external skepticism: between error and status skepticism. Error skeptics hold that all moral judgments are false. An error skeptic might read the ordinary view as assuming that moral entities exist: that the universe contains not only quarks, mesons, and other very small physical particles but also what I [call] morons,

From Ronald Dworkin, *Justice for Hedgehogs* (Cambridge, MA: Harvard University Press, 2011). Reprinted by permission of the publisher.

special particles whose configuration might make it true that people should not torture babies and that optional military invasions seeking regime change are immoral. He might then declare that because there are no moral particles, it is a mistake to say that torturing babies is wrong . . . This is not internal skepticism, because it does not purport to rely on even counterfactual moral judgments for its authority. It is external skepticism because it purports to rely only on value-neutral metaphysics: it relies only on the metaphysical claim that there are no moral particles.

Status skeptics disagree: they are skeptical of the ordinary view in a different way. The ordinary view treats moral judgments as descriptions of how things actually are: they are claims of moral fact. Status skeptics deny moral judgment that status: they believe it is a mistake to treat them as descriptions of anything. They distinguish between description and other activities like coughing, expressing emotion, issuing a command, or embracing a commitment, and they hold that expressing a moral opinion is not describing but something that belongs in the latter group of activities. Status skeptics therefore do not say, as error skeptics do, that morality is a misconceived enterprise. They say it is a misunderstood enterprise.

Status skepticism evolved rapidly during the twentieth century. Initial forms were crude: A. J. Ayer, for example, in . . . *Language, Truth, and Logic,* insisted that moral judgments are no different from other vehicles for venting emotions. Someone who declares that tax cheating is wrong is only, in effect, shouting "Boo tax cheating." Later versions of status skepticism became more sophisticated. Richard Hare, for instance, whose work was very influential, treated moral judgments as disguised and generalized commands. "Cheating is wrong" should be understood as "Don't cheat." For Hare, however, the preference expressed by a moral judgment is very special: it is universal in its content so that it embraces everyone who is situated in the way it assumes, including the speaker. Hare's analysis is still status-skeptical, however, because, like Ayer's puffs of emotion, his preference expressions are not candidates for truth or falsity.

These early versions wore their skepticism on the sleeve. Hare said that a Nazi who would apply his strictures to himself, should he turn out to be a Jew, has not made a moral mistake. Later in the century external skepticism became more ambiguous. Allan Gibbard and Simon Blackburn, for example, have called themselves, variously, "noncognitivists," "expressivists," "projectivists," and "quasi-realists," which suggests sharp disagreement with the ordinary view. Gibbard says that moral judgments should be understood as expressing acceptance of a plan for living: not "as beliefs with such and such content" but rather as "sentiments or attitudes, perhaps, or as universal preferences, states of norm acceptance—or states of planning."[1] But Blackburn and Gibbard both labor to show how, on their view, an expressivist who takes this view of moral judgment can nevertheless sensibly speak of moral judgments as true or false, and that he can also mimic in other, more complex, ways how people who hold the ordinary view speak about moral issues. But they treat these claims of truth as part of an activity that is nevertheless, they insist, different from describing how things are.

INTERNAL SKEPTICISM

Because internal skeptics rely on the truth of substantive moral claims, they can only be partial error skeptics. There is no internal status skepticism. Internal skeptics differ from one another in the scope of their skepticism. Some internal skepticism is quite circumscribed and topical. Many people think, for instance, that the choices that adult partners make about the mechanics of sex raise no moral issues: they think that all judgments that condemn certain sexual choices are false. They ground this limited skepticism in positive opinions about what makes acts right or wrong; they do not believe that the details of adult consensual sex, whether heterosexual or homosexual, have any right- or wrong-making features. . . .

Other versions of internal error skepticism are much broader, and some are near global because they reject all moral judgments except counterfactual ones. . . . [T]hat because there is no god, nothing is right or wrong . . . is a piece of global internal skepticism; it is based on the moral conviction that a supernatural will is the only possible basis for positive morality. . . . Another now popular opinion holds that no universal moral claim is sound because morality is relative to culture; this view, too, is internally skeptical because it relies on the conviction that morality rises only out of the practices of particular communities. Yet another form of global internal skepticism notices that human beings are incredibly small and evaporating parts of an inconceivably vast and durable universe and concludes that nothing we do can matter—morally or otherwise—anyway.[2] True, the moral convictions on which these examples of global internal skepticism rely are counterfactual convictions: they assume that the positive moral claims they reject would be valid if certain conditions were satisfied—if a god did exist or moral conventions were uniform across cultures or the universe was much smaller. Still, even these counterfactual convictions are substantive moral judgments.

. . . Internal skepticism does not deny what I wish to establish: that philosophical challenges to the truth of moral judgments are themselves substantive moral theories. It does not deny—on the contrary it assumes—that moral judgments are capable of truth. . . .

THE APPEAL OF STATUS SKEPTICISM

Both forms of external skepticism—error and status skepticism—are different from . . . biological and social-scientific theories. . . . Neo-Darwinian theories about the development of moral beliefs and institutions, for instance, are external but in no way skeptical. There is no inconsistency in holding the following set of opinions: (1) that a wired-in condemnation of murder had survival value in the ancestral savannahs, (2) that this fact figures in the best explanation why moral condemnation of murder is so widespread across history and cultures, and (3) that it is objectively true that murder is morally wrong. The first two of these claims are anthropological and

the third is moral; there can be no conflict in combining the moral with the anthropological in this way. So external skeptics cannot rely only on anthropology or any other biological or social science. They rely on a very different kind of putatively external theory: they rely on philosophical theories about what there is in the universe or about the conditions under which people can be thought to acquire responsible belief.

In one way internal and external skepticism are in sharp contrast. Internal skepticism would be self-defeating if it denied that moral judgments are candidates for truth; it cannot rely on any coruscating metaphysics that has that consequence. External skepticism, on the other hand, cannot leave any moral judgments standing as candidates for truth: it must show them all to be error or all to have some status that rules out their being true. External skepticism would be immediately self-defeating if it exempted any substantive moral judgment from its skeptical scope.

In another way, however, internal skepticism and external error skepticism are alike. Internal skepticism plays for keeps. It has direct implications for action: if someone is internally skeptical about sexual morality, he cannot consistently censure people for their sexual choices or lobby for outlawing homosexuality on moral grounds. If he believes that morality is dead because there is no god, then he must not ostracize others because they have behaved badly. External error skepticism also plays for keeps: an error skeptic may dislike the war in Iraq, but he cannot claim that the American invasion was immoral. External status skeptics, on the contrary, insist that their form of skepticism is neutral about moral claims and controversies and permits them to engage in moral condemnation with as much fervor as anyone else. Suppose we conclude, with the status skeptic, that moral claims are only projections of emotion onto a morally barren world. We will have changed our minds about the status of our moral convictions, but not about the content of those convictions. We can continue to insist that terrorism is always wrong, or that it is sometimes justified, or to offer or deny any other moral opinion we may entertain. The later status skeptics (assuming they are skeptics) even allow us to insist that our convictions are objectively true. We only say to ourselves (silently in order not to blunt the impact of what we say out loud) that in so insisting we are only projecting more complex attitudes.

This apparent neutrality gives status skepticism a seductive appeal. I said earlier that some of us are troubled by the philosophical challenges I described. We cannot believe in morons. And we have other reasons for shrinking from bold assertion that our moral beliefs are true: it seems arrogant, in the face of great cultural diversity, to claim that everyone who disagrees with us is in error. But any form of error skepticism seems out of the question. We can't really believe that there is nothing morally objectionable about suicide bombers or genocide or racial discrimination or forced clitoridectomy. External status skepticism offers people torn in that way exactly what they want. It is agreeably ecumenical. It allows its partisans to be as metaphysically and culturally modest as anyone might wish, to abandon all claims as to their own morality's ultimate truth or even superiority to other moralities. But it allows them to do this while still embracing their convictions as enthusiastically as ever, denouncing genocide or abortion or slavery or gender discrimination or welfare cheats with all their former vigor. They need only say that they have revised their view, not about the substance, but about the status, of their convictions. They no longer claim that their convictions mirror an external reality. But they still hold these convictions with the same intensity. They can be as willing to fight or even die for their beliefs as they ever were, but now with a difference. They can have their moral convictions and lose them too. . . .

External status skepticism is therefore much more popular among academic philosophers now than global internal skepticism or external error skepticism has ever been, and it is status skepticism that has infected contemporary intellectual life. . . . Philosophy can neither impeach nor validate any value judgment while standing wholly outside that judgment's domain. Internal skepticism is the only skeptical game in town. Perhaps it is neither true nor false that abortion is wicked or that the American

Constitution condemns all racial preference or that Beethoven was a greater creative artist than Picasso. But if so, this is not because there can be no right answer to such questions for reasons prior or external to value, but because that *is* the right answer internally, as a matter of sound moral or legal or aesthetic judgment. . . . We can't be skeptical about any domain of value all the way down. . . .

EXTERNAL SKEPTICISM

An Important Claim

. . . [M]oral skepticism is itself a moral position. That is an important claim that has been and will be severely challenged. If it is true, then external skepticism defeats itself. An external error skeptic holds that all moral judgments are objectively false, and an external status skeptic that moral judgments do not even purport to be true. Each contradicts himself if his own skeptical judgment is itself a moral judgment; surely he must claim truth for his own philosophical position. . . .

You might think it Pickwickean to insist that a philosophical statement that denies the existence of moral properties itself makes a moral claim. You might offer these analogies: the observation that astrology is bunk is not itself an astrological claim, and atheism is not a religious stance. That depends, however, on how we choose to define these categories. If we define an astrological judgment as one that asserts or presupposes some planetary influence on human lives, then the proposition that astrology is bunk, which denies any such influence, is not an astrological judgment. However, if we define an astrological judgment as one that describes the character and extent of planetary influence, then the statement that there is no such influence is indeed an astrological judgment. If we define a religious position as one that presupposes the existence of one or more divine beings, then atheism is not a religious position. But if we define it as one that offers an opinion about the existence or properties of divine beings, then atheism certainly is a religious position.

Cosmology is a domain of thought: it is a part of science more broadly understood. We can ask: What is true and false in that domain? What is true or false, that is, cosmologically speaking? Skepticism about astrology and God stake out answers to that question: they speak to the issue of what there is among the forces of our universe. We could hardly say, "Since we are atheists, we insist that nothing is true, cosmologically speaking." We have offered, in our atheism, an opinion about what is true in that domain. Morality is also a domain. Its topics, we might say, include these questions: Do people have any categorical responsibilities to other people—responsibilities, that is, that do not depend on what they want or think? If so, what categorical responsibilities do they have? Someone takes a position on these issues when he declares that the rich have a duty to help the poor. Someone else takes a contrary position when he denies that the rich have any such obligation because, he says, the poor have brought their poverty on themselves. A third person takes a broader form of that second position if he declares that no one ever has a moral obligation because moral obligations could be created only by a god and there is no god. A fourth person argues that no one ever has a moral obligation because there are no queer entities that could constitute a moral obligation. The latter two skeptics offer different kinds of reasons, but the state of affairs each claims to hold is the same. The *content* of the two claims—what the different skeptics claim to be the case, morally speaking—is the same. Both of them, not just the third, make a moral claim and so cannot consistently declare that no moral claim is true. Compare: we may say that no claim anyone makes about the shape or color of unicorns is true because there are no unicorns. But we can't then declare that no proposition of unicorn zoology can be true. . . .

Some philosophers have found what they take to be a mistake in my argument: I suffer from a mental block, they believe, about the possibilities of negation.[3] An external skeptic, on their view, declares that acts are neither morally required nor forbidden *nor* permitted. Surely that does not stake out a moral position but instead refuses to make any moral claim at all. So I am wrong, they say, to suppose that external skepticism is itself a moral position.

Consider this conversation:

A: Abortion is morally wicked: we always in all circumstances have a categorical reason—a reason that does not depend on what anyone wants or thinks—to prevent and condemn it.

B: On the contrary. In some circumstances abortion is morally required. Single teenage mothers with no resources have a categorical reason to abort.

C: You are both wrong. Abortion is never either morally required or morally forbidden. No one has a categorical reason either way. It is always permissible and never mandatory, like cutting your fingernails.

D: You are all three wrong. Abortion is never either morally forbidden or morally required *or* morally permissible.

A, B, and C make moral claims. Does D? Because it is unclear what he could mean by his mysterious claim, we ask him to elaborate.

He might say, first, "Any proposition that assumes the existence of something that does not exist is false. Or (as I sometimes think) neither true nor false. A, B, and C are all assuming that moral duties exist. But no such thing exists, so none of them is making a true statement." D has fallen victim to morons—or rather the lack of them. If there are morons, and morons make moral claims true or false, then we might imagine that morons, like quarks, have colors. An act is forbidden only if there are red morons in the neighborhood, required only if there are green ones, and permissible only if there are yellow ones. So D declares that, because there are no morons at all, abortion is neither forbidden, nor required, nor permissible. His assumption that there are no morons, he insists, is not itself a moral claim. It is a claim of physics or metaphysics. But he has seriously misunderstood the conversational situation. A, B, and C have each made a claim about what reasons of a certain kind—categorical reasons—people do or do not have. D's claim that no duties exist means that no one ever has a reason of that kind. So perforce he expresses a moral position; he agrees with C and cannot say, without contradiction, that what C says is false (or neither true nor false).

D might say: "A, B, and C are each relying on the existence of morons to sustain their claim." But they are doing no such thing. Even if A thinks there are morons, he would not cite their existence and color as arguments in his favor. He has very different kinds of arguments: that abortion insults the dignity of human life, for instance. But once again, to be generous to D, let us assume that A, B, and C are unusual and would cite morons as arguments. That doesn't help D's case. What matters is not the arguments that the trio make but what they take to be the conclusion of those arguments. To repeat: each makes a claim about the categorical reasons people do or do not have with respect to abortion. The upshot of D's various arguments, whatever they are, is a claim of the same kind. He thinks there are no such reasons and therefore disagrees with A and B and agrees with C. He makes a much more general claim than C does, but his claim includes C's. He has taken a position on a moral issue: he has taken a substantive, first-order, moral stance.

Now D corrects himself. "I should not have said that the claims of A, B, and C are false, or that they are neither true nor false. I should have said that they make no sense at all: I cannot understand what they could mean by claiming or denying categorical reasons. It's all gibberish to me." People often say that some proposition makes no sense when they mean only that it is silly or obviously wrong. If that is what D now means, he has not changed his approach; he has just added emphasis. What else might he mean? He might mean that he believes the others contradict themselves, claiming something impossible, as if they claimed to see a square circle on a park bench. That changes his argument but not his conclusion. If he thinks that categorical reasons are impossible, then once again he thinks that no one has a categorical reason for anything. He still takes a moral stand. One more try. Perhaps he means that he finds what the others say literally incomprehensible. He concedes that they seem to have a concept he lacks; he can't translate what they say into a language he understands. Of course that is preposterous: he knows very well what A, B, and C mean to

say about people's moral responsibilities. But if he insists that he doesn't understand, he ceases to be a skeptic of any kind. I can't be a skeptic in a language I can't understand.

The message of all this seems clear. When you make a statement about what moral responsibilities people have, you are declaring how things stand—morally speaking. There is no way out of or around the independence of value. Now, however, suppose that D replies in a very different way. "I mean that the arguments on both sides of the abortion issue are so evenly balanced that there is no right answer to the question whether abortion is forbidden or required or permissible. Any such claim assumes that the arguments for its position are stronger than those for the other, and that is false." . . . D, in this new elaboration, has indeterminacy in mind: that is why he says that all the other positions are false, not just unpersuasive. His position is now obviously a substantive moral claim. He does disagree, finally, with C as well as A and B, but he disagrees with them all because he holds a fourth moral opinion. He assesses the strength of the three moral opinions and finds none of them stronger than either of the others. That is a form of skepticism, but it is internal skepticism.

Hume's Principle

If, as I argue, any moral skepticism is itself a substantive moral claim, then external moral skepticism contradicts itself in the way I said. It also violates the principle of moral epistemology I [call] Hume's principle. This holds that no series of propositions about how the world is, as a matter of scientific or metaphysical fact, can provide a successful case on its own—without some value judgment hidden in the interstices—for any conclusion about what ought to be the case. Hume's principle seems to me obviously true. Consider this attempt to violate it. "Jack is in great pain and you could easily help him. Therefore, just for that reason, you have a moral duty to help him." If this is a good argument, just as it stands, then some principle about what makes an argument a good one must be at work. What is that principle? It cannot be any form of induction or generalization, because these would assume that you have had a moral duty in the past, which is a moral assumption. It cannot be a principle of deduction or semantic entailment. It needs something more, and that must be something—a hidden premise or an assumption about the nature of good moral reasoning—that is infused with moral force.

Yes, the fact that someone standing before you is evidently in great pain does seem by itself a reason why you ought to help him if you can. Nothing more needs to be said. But I assume you think this because you unselfconsciously accept, as something that goes without saying, a general responsibility to help people in grave need when you easily can. Suppose you make it explicit that you are not relying on any such background moral assumption. You declare that you have no view one way or the other about any general responsibility to help people in pain in circumstances just like these. You simply insist that in this particular case the pain before you, on its own, without any further assumption of that kind, imposes a moral responsibility on you. Your point then becomes not obvious but opaque.

Some philosophers have offered a different objection.[4] Hume's principle, they agree, does show that a set of nonmoral facts cannot, on their own, establish a moral claim. But it doesn't follow that nonmoral facts cannot, on their own, undermine a moral claim. So external skepticism, which seeks only to undermine, may succeed in spite of Hume's principle. But this rescue fails if, as I claim, skepticism is itself a moral position. Undermining the moral claim that people have a duty not to cheat is the same as establishing the moral claim that it isn't true that they have that duty. Hume's principle has been challenged in other ways; I find these challenges all unsuccessful.

Of course, Hume's principle does not outlaw the many disciplines—sociology, psychology, primatology, genetics, political science, and common sense—that study morality as a social and psychological phenomenon. Nor does it outlaw what I take to be at least part of Hume's own project: the natural history of moral sentiment and conviction. We can learn a great deal about morality and ourselves by attending to facts about what is and has been. We can speculate about why certain moral convictions are popular in some cultures and communities though not in others, about the varied forms of influence and pressure that have proved effective in perpetuating these convictions as social norms, about when and how children become sensitive to moral claim and censure, about why certain moral opinions are near universal among human beings, and about how the economic circumstances of a community, among other factors, correlate with the content of moral convictions current there.

These are all important and fascinating questions, and they have of course been set out much more precisely than I have just done. I distinguish them all, however, from the question before us now, the question that is usually of much greater interest to most of us: Which moral opinions are true? Hume's principle applies only to this latter question. This crucial distinction between moral judgments and descriptive studies about morality is sometimes obscured by an ambiguity in the idea of explanation. People ask: How can we explain morality? That might be understood as calling for the kind of factual explanation I just described. It might invite, for example, a neo-Darwinian account of the rise of certain practices among higher primates and early human beings. On the other hand it might call for a justification of moral practices and institutions. Justification is what someone has in mind who demands, in an angry tone, "Explain yourself!"

Error Skepticism

If external skepticism is itself a moral position, then it contradicts itself. External error skepticism seems most immediately vulnerable because it holds that all moral claims are false. Error skeptics might revise their view, however, to hold only that all positive moral judgments are false. Positive moral judgments, they might say, are those that offer guidance for action or approval: these include judgments that some action is morally required or forbidden, that some situation or person is morally good or bad, that someone has a moral virtue or vice, and so forth. They might call the alternatives to such claims—that some situation is neither good nor bad but morally neutral, or that some person is to be neither praised nor criticized for some trait of his character—negative moral judgments. But, as I said earlier, these are still moral judgments. They are as much moral judgments as the proposition that the law neither requires nor forbids drinking wine is a legal judgment. Error skepticism so revised would therefore be an example of global internal skepticism. It would have the same content, for instance, as the theory that God is the only possible author of moral duty and that he does not exist. An error skeptic might hope to rely on some argument parallel to that one: that only queer entities can impose moral duties and that there are no queer entities. . . .

Diversity

John Mackie, the most prominent recent error skeptic, argued that positive moral claims must be false because people disagree about which of them are true.[5] His sociological assumptions are largely correct. Moral diversity is sometimes exaggerated: the degree of convergence over basic moral matters throughout history is both striking and predictable. But people do disagree about important matters, like affirmative action, abortion, and social justice, even within particular cultures. Does that show that we actually have no moral duties or responsibilities at all?

Of course it should give us pause that others disagree with what we find so plain. How can I be sure that I am right when others, who seem just as intelligent and sensitive, deny that I am? But we cannot take the fact of disagreement itself to count as an argument that our moral convictions are mistaken. We would not count the popularity of any of our other convictions as evidence for their truth. The fact that almost everyone thinks that lying is sometimes permissible doesn't provide any reason at all for thinking that it is. Why then should we count disagreement about some opinion as evidence against its truth? Mackie and other skeptics have only one response to that sensible question. They take diversity to prove that moral conviction is not caused by moral truth. If it were, we would expect less disagreement. Suppose millions of people claimed to have seen unicorns but disagreed wildly about their color, size, and shape. We would discount their evidence. If there were

unicorns, and people had seen them, the actual properties of the beast would have caused more uniform reports.

. . . [E]rror skeptics are right to deny that moral truth causes moral conviction. People's personal histories, rather than any encounters with moral truth, cause their convictions. If so, some combination of convergence and diversity is exactly what we should expect. People's personal histories have a very great deal in common, starting with the human genome. Their situation, everywhere and always, is such that they are very likely to think that murder for private gain is wrong, for instance. But these histories also have a great deal not in common: the habitats, economies, and religions of people differ in ways that also make it predictable that they will disagree about morality too. In any case, because diversity is just a matter of anthropological fact, it cannot on its own show that all positive moral judgments are false. People, in their diversity, must still decide what is true, and this is a matter of the justification of conviction, not the best explanation of either convergence or divergence.

Morals and Motives

Mackie also said that positive moral judgments presuppose, as part of what they mean, an extraordinary claim: that when people come to hold a true positive moral opinion, they are just for that reason motivated to act in whatever way it commands. So if it is true that you ought not to cheat on your income tax, your coming to accept that truth must have the consequence that you feel drawn as by a magnet to report your income and deductions accurately. But that is, as Mackie put it, a "queer" consequence. In other domains, just accepting a fact doesn't automatically carry any motivating force: even if I accept that there is poison in a glass in front of me, I might, in certain circumstances, feel no reluctance to drink it. If moral propositions are different in this striking way—if belief about a moral fact carries an automatic motivational charge—then this must be because moral entities have a special and unique kind of magnetic force. The idea of an "objective good," Mackie said, is queer because it supposes that "objective good would be sought by anyone who was acquainted with it, not because of any contingent fact that this person, or every person, is so constituted that he desires this end, but just because the end has to-be-pursuedness somehow built into it. Similarly, if there were objective principles of right and wrong, any wrong (possible) course of action would have not-to-be-doneness somehow built into it."[6]

It is unclear how we should understand these supposedly lethal metaphors. We should certainly agree that there are no morons with automatic coercive moral force. But why should we think it follows that torture is not morally wrong? We might be driven to that conclusion if we held the theory of moral responsibility I just mentioned: that no positive moral opinion is justified unless that opinion has been produced by direct contact with some moral— and motivating—truth. . . . [H]owever, it seems that Mackie misunderstood the connection that people think holds between morality and motivation. He thought that people suppose that *true* positive moral judgments move them to act as the judgment directs. If they did think that, then they would indeed be presupposing a strange kind of moral force. In fact, however, people who find some automatic connection between moral conviction and motivation think this connection holds for false as well as true convictions. They think that anyone who really believes that he is morally required not to walk under ladders will feel constrained not to walk under them. It is conviction, not truth, that supposedly carries the motivational surge. So it cannot be a matter of queer entities.

NOTES

1. [Allan] Gibbard, *Thinking How to Live* (Cambridge, Mass.: Harvard University Press, 2003), 181.

2. Thomas Nagel quotes Conrad's wonderful description of this form of internal skepticism. "It was one of those dewy, clear, starry nights, oppressing our spirit, crushing our pride, by the brilliant evidence of the awful loneliness, of the hopeless obscure insignificance of our globe lost in the splendid revelation of a glittering, soulless universe. I hate such skies." See Joseph Conrad, *Chance,* Oxford World Classics edition (Oxford: Oxford University Press, 2002), 41; Nagel, *Secular Philosophy and the Religious Temperament* (Oxford: Oxford University Press, 2010), 9.

3. Michael Smith and Daniel Star suggest this mistake. Smith, "Dworkin on External Skepticism," *Boston University Law Review,* 90 (2010): 509–520; Star, "Moral Skepticism for Foxes," *Boston University Law Review,* 90 (2010): 497–508.

4. See [Russ] Shafer-Landau, "The Possibility of Metaethics," [*Boston University Law Review,* 90 (2010): 479–495,] and Star, "Moral Skepticism for Foxes." Star assumes, in the course of his discussion of the point, that the thesis that ought implies can is not a moral principle. But it certainly seems to be. It contradicts some plainly moral positions, including a view some commentators attribute to Nietzsche—that it is a tragedy that though every human being ought to live greatly, only very few can manage it. Star says, however, that it does not follow from the fact that people may reject that principle on moral grounds in some circumstances that it is "always" a moral principle. But since it has the same meaning when denied as it has when asserted, how can this not follow? In any case, what else could "ought implies can" be *but* a moral principle? It is not a factual generalization. Or a natural law. It is not a logical or semantic principle. Does it belong to some as yet unnamed class of non-normative ideas?

5. John Mackie, *Ethics: Inventing Right and Wrong* (New York: Penguin Books, 1977), 36–38.

6. Ibid., 38–42, 40.

STUDY QUESTIONS

1. What is the difference between internal and external skepticism?
2. What is the difference between error and status skepticism?
3. According to Dworkin, what is "Hume's Principle"?
4. Is the Error Theory itself a moral theory?

In Defense of Moral Error Theory

Jonas Olson

Jonas Olson is Reader in Practical Philosophy at Stockholm University, Sweden. According to Olson, the Error Theory maintains that moral claims are about categorical reasons, those that are inescapable because they are not dependent on the wants, desires, or ends of the agents to whom they apply. But there are no categorical reasons. Hence moral claims are systematically in error.

In reply to Dworkin's challenge that the Error Theory is simply a moral theory in disguise, Olson argues that "not wrong" does not imply "permissible." Granted, when we say something is "not wrong," we conversationally suggest that it is permissible, but this implicature can be canceled. For example, usually when we assert that something does not have horns, we conversationally suggest it does have horns. But when we assert that unicorns do not have horns, we cancel the implication that they do have horns by noting that unicorns do not exist. The error theorist talks about morality in the same way we talk about unicorns. Hence Olson concludes that Dworkin's challenge to the Error Theory fails.

1. INTRODUCTION

. . . Moral error theorists typically accept two claims—one conceptual and one ontological— about moral facts. The *conceptual claim* is that moral facts are or entail facts about categorical reasons (and correspondingly that moral claims are or entail claims about categorical reasons); the *ontological* claim is that there are no categorical reasons— and consequently no moral facts—in reality. I accept this version of moral error theory and I try to unpack what it amounts to in Section 2. In the course of doing so I consider two preliminary objections: that moral error theory is (probably) false because its implications are intuitively unacceptable (what I call

the Moorean objection) and that the general motivation for moral error theory is self-undermining in that it rests on a hidden appeal to norms.

The above characterization seems to entail the standard formulation of moral error theory, according to which first-order moral claims are uniformly false. Critics have argued that the standard formulation is incoherent since—by the law of excluded middle—the negation of a false claim is true. Hence if "Torture is wrong" is false, "Torture is not wrong" is true. Contrary to what moral error theorists contend, then, moral error theory seems to carry first-order moral implications that by the theory's own lights are uniformly false. In Section 3 I suggest a formulation that is consistent with the

From Jonas Olson, "In Defense of Moral Error Theory," in *New Waves in Metaethics,* ed. Michael Brady (New York: Palgrave Macmillan, 2011). Reprinted by permission of the publisher.

standard formulation of moral error theory, free of first-order moral implications, and subject to no logical difficulties. . . .

2. MOTIVATING MORAL ERROR THEORY

Ever since John Mackie's seminal discussion, standard arguments for moral error theory are routinely lumped together under the label "arguments from queerness" (Mackie, 1977: ch. 1). . . .

. . . [T]he most acute of Mackie's queerness worries is . . . that moral facts would have to be, as Mackie said, *objectively prescriptive*. What makes moral facts queer is that they make demands from which we cannot escape. . . .

As Mackie and other error theorists have noted, there is a sense in which we are all familiar with objective prescriptivity as instantiated in the real world. For instance, it is a familiar fact that chess players ought not to move the rook diagonally and that there are reasons for soccer players not to play the ball to their own goalkeeper when under pressure. But these are not examples of the kind of objective prescriptivity Mackie objected to. Mackie did not deny that there are rules and standards according to which certain agents in certain situations ought or have reason to behave in certain ways (Mackie, 1977, pp. 25–7).

The kind of objective prescriptivity Mackie did object to is one that involves *categorical* reasons. To say that there are categorical reasons for some agent, A, to behave in some way, Φ, is to say that there is reason for A to Φ irrespective of whether A's Φing would promote satisfaction or realization of some of A's desires or aims, or promote fulfillment of some role A occupies, or comply with the rules of some activity A is engaged in. Suppose, for instance, that torturing animals for fun is morally wrong and that donating 20 percent of one's income to charity is morally required. It seems commonsensical that there would then be reasons for any agent not to torture animals for fun and to donate 20 percent of her income to charity, even if doing so would not satisfy or realize one of her desires or aims, or promote fulfillment of some role she occupies, or comply with the rules

of some activity she is engaged in. In other words, moral facts entail facts about categorical reasons and moral claims entail claims about categorical reasons.

Elsewhere I have distinguished between *transcendent* and *immanent norms* (Olson, forthcoming). The former apply to agents categorically; their reason-giving force transcends particular aims, activities, or roles. Immanent norms, by contrast, are those whose reason-giving force depends on agents' engagement in certain goal-oriented or rule-governed activities or their occupation of certain roles, such as institutional or professional roles; the reason-giving force of immanent norms does not transcend goal-oriented or rule-governed activities or roles, which is why immanent norms imply merely *non-categorical* reasons.[1] Another way of putting it is to say that, while immanent norms determine correct behavior according to rules or fixed standards, it does not follow that there are *categorical reasons* to comply with these norms. For transcendent norms, it does follow that there are categorical reasons for compliance.

As mentioned above, it is a plausible conjecture that on the commonsense conception of moral norms these are examples of transcendent norms, whereas the norms of, for instance, chess, soccer, grammar, and etiquette are prime examples of immanent norms. To say that a norm is a moral norm is to say that there are reasons for any agent to comply with that norm, irrespective of her desires, ends, or roles. To say that some norm is a norm of etiquette or grammar, by contrast, is not to say that there are categorical reasons to comply with it, but rather to say that some sort of behavior would be incorrect relative to a certain standard of etiquette or relative to the rules of grammar. In my terminology, *norms* are transcendent or immanent and *reasons* are categorical or non-categorical.

Error theorists do not object to the existence of immanent norms and non-categorical reasons. There is nothing metaphysically queer about the fact that there is (conclusive) non-categorical reason for chess players not to move the rook diagonally, since this is just the fact that moving the rook diagonally is incorrect according to the rules of chess; there is nothing metaphysically queer about the fact that there is (non-conclusive) reason for soccer players not to play the ball to their own goalkeeper when under pressure, since this is just the fact that such play tends to give the opposing team opportunities to score (and preventing the opposing team from scoring is one of the goals in soccer). Similarly, there is nothing metaphysically queer about the fact that there is non-categorical reason for a soldier to comply with the orders of a general, since this is just the fact that complying with the orders of those superior in military rank is part of the role of being a soldier. Note that a soldier might not *desire* to comply with the general's order, and he might have no ends that would be served by his compliance. The same goes for chess players and soccer players; they might not desire to play by the rules and they need not even desire to win. That is why I add that error theorists can recognize non-categorical reasons that depend on agents' *roles* and goal-oriented or rule-governed *activities*. Agents can occupy roles they have no desire to fulfill and engage in activities they have no desire to succeed in.

Moral norms and moral reasons, as we have seen, are a different matter. The reason-giving force of moral norms transcends agents' desires, aims, and roles. One way of unpacking the popular view that moral facts are *non-natural* is in terms of categorical reasons. On this interpretation, what non-naturalist realists mean to capture in claiming that moral facts are non-natural is precisely that these facts are or entail categorical reasons. By contrast, facts about, for example, etiquette and rules of grammar are natural since they do not entail categorical reasons.

. . . [W]e can call the claim that moral facts are or entail categorical reasons (and correspondingly that moral claims are or entail claims about categorical reasons) *the conceptual claim*. Moral error theorists accept the conceptual claim, but they also accept *the ontological claim* that there are no such reasons in reality. . . .

2.1. Two Initial Objections: The Moorean Argument and the Hidden Appeal to Norms

At this point one might object that metaphysical doubts about transcendent norms and categorical

reasons are based on pretty advanced, or at least controversial, philosophical theorizing. And are we not comparatively more certain that some actions—for example, torturing animals or children for fun—really are morally wrong than we are that reality harbors no categorical reasons and consequently no moral truths? Since it marshals commonsense against philosophical theorizing, let us call this argument *the Moorean argument* against moral error theory.

But metaphysical qualms about categorical reasons are not the sole cornerstone of the case for moral error theory. Moral error theorists often give debunking explanations of why we humans tend to believe that there are moral facts (. . . Mackie, 1977, pp. 105–24). One important ingredient in these debunking explanations is the evolutionary advantages of moral beliefs. For instance, moral norms against stealing, harming, cheating, and so on tend to promote senses of trust and security, which facilitate cooperation, which in turn raise prospects of survival. As Mackie said, in human evolutionary history morality serves as a "device for counteracting limited sympathies" (1977, p. 107).

Belief in transcendent norms and correlative categorical reasons is useful in other respects too: it puts pressure on individual agents and makes them less likely to succumb to temptations to maximize expected short-term egoistic or parochial benefits. In short, morality persists in the world of human thinking partly because of its socially useful coordinating and regulative functions. . . .

. . . [T]hese elaborations have enough plausibility to undermine the Moorean argument. For, once we take these debunking explanations into consideration, it is far from clear that we are more certain that some actions—such as torturing animals or children for fun—really are morally wrong than we are that there are no categorical reasons and consequently no moral truths (. . . Mackie, 1977, p. 42). Proponents of the Moorean argument might protest that we *are* comparatively more certain that certain actions really are morally wrong than we are about the correctness of debunking explanations of these beliefs. But proponents of debunking theories . . . have the upper hand here, since these theories predict that certain moral beliefs will be held with a high degree of certainty, and also explain why this is so. The explanation is simply that the regulative and coordinating functions they facilitate are of such vital importance to us.

It is fairly obvious that the argument against categorical reasons that proceeds via Mackie's queerness worry and debunking explanations of moral beliefs is based on an appeal to Occam's Razor. The gist of the argument, after all, is that error theory offers a *theoretically simpler* and hence *preferable* explanation of the phenomena to be explained (i.e. moral thought and talk) than do competing realist explanations. But appeals to Occam's Razor and considerations of theoretical simplicity seem to be appeals to *norms*. And consequently the moral error theorist's argument against the existence of some norms, such as moral norms, seems to involve a hidden appeal to other norms, which makes it smack of self-defeat . . .

In response, the moral error theorist should concede that appeals to Occam's Razor and considerations of theoretical simplicity are indeed appeals to norms. But these are immanent rather than transcendent norms. To say that a theory T offers a theoretically simpler explanation of some phenomenon than a distinct theory T′ is not to say that the comparative simplicity of T is a *categorical* reason to prefer T to T′. It is just to say that T is in one respect preferable to T′ according to a standard of theory assessment commonly accepted by many philosophers, naturalists and non-naturalists alike, and commonly adopted in many natural and social sciences, to wit, that T is preferable to T′ if T makes fewer problematic assumptions without loss of explanatory power. This is the case with moral error theory as compared with realism. The greater theoretical simplicity of the former as compared with the latter is therefore a non-categorical reason to prefer moral error theory to realism. Appeals to norms such as Occam's Razor are hence unproblematic from the moral error theorist's naturalist perspective.

I hope that what has been said so far makes moral error theory seem, if not a promising theory, then at least not a dead end in metaethics. . . .

3. FORMULATING MORAL ERROR THEORY

It is routinely said that, according to moral error theory, first-order moral claims are uniformly false. A first-order moral claim is a claim that entails that some agent morally ought to do or not to do some action; that there are moral reasons for some agent to do or not to do some action; that some action is morally permissible; that some institution, character trait, or what have you, is morally good or bad; and the like. But this raises the question of what to say about the truth-values of negated first-order moral claims, which leads to two worries: Is the standard formulation of moral error theory coherent? Can it be maintained that moral error theory lacks first-order moral implications?

Mackie insisted that his error theory is purely a second-order view and as such logically independent of any first-order moral view (1977, pp. 15–17). But this can be doubted. According to the standard interpretation of Mackie's error theory, a first-order moral claim like "Torture is morally wrong" is false. According to the law of excluded middle it follows that its negation, "Torture is not morally wrong," is true. That torture is not morally wrong would seem to imply that torture is morally permissible. More generally, then, the apparent upshot is that, contrary to Mackie's contention, moral error theory does have first-order moral implications. And rather vulgar ones at that; if moral error theory is true, any action turns out to be morally permissible!

But it seems that we can also derive an opposite conclusion. According to moral error theory, "Torture is morally permissible" is false. According to the law of excluded middle it follows that torture is not morally permissible, which seems to entail that torture is morally impermissible. More generally, then, the apparent upshot is that any action is morally impermissible! This may not be a vulgar first-order moral implication, but it is surely absurd. It also transpires that the standard formulation of moral error theory leads to a straightforward logical contradiction, since we have derived that it is true that, for instance, torture is morally permissible (since any action is morally permissible) and that it is false that torture is morally permissible (since any action is morally impermissible). Ronald Dworkin has argued that this demonstrates the impossibility, indeed the incoherence, of being "sceptical about value [. . .] all the way down" (1996, p. 91). . . .

A . . . way out is to deny that the implications from "not wrong" to "permissible" and from "not permissible" to "wrong" are conceptual, and maintain instead that they are instances of conversational implicature. To illustrate, "not wrong" conversationally implicates "permissible," because normally when we claim that something is not wrong we speak from within a system of moral norms, or moral standards for short. According to most moral standards, any action that is not wrong according to that standard is permissible according to that standard. General compliance with Gricean maxims that bid us to make our statements relevant and not overly informative (Grice, 1989, p. 26ff.) ensures that we do not normally state explicitly that we speak from within some moral standard when we claim that something is not wrong. But the implicature from "not wrong" to "permissible" is cancellable. The error theorist can declare that torture is not wrong and go on to signal that she is not speaking from within a moral standard. She might say something like the following: "Torture is not wrong. But neither is it permissible. There are no moral properties and facts and consequently no action has moral status." This would cancel the implicature from "not wrong" to "permissible." (Analogous reasoning, of course, demonstrates why the error theorist's claim that torture is not morally permissible does not commit him to the view that torture is morally impermissible and hence morally wrong.) On this view, error theory has neither the vulgar implication that anything is permissible nor the absurd implication that anything is impermissible.

But one might object that the problems remain. The law of excluded middle entails that if "Torture is wrong" is false, then "Torture is not wrong" is true. If the latter claim is a first-order moral claim, the standard formulation of moral error theory still has first-order moral implications, that is, implications that by its own lights are false.

In response, recall that, according to our above definition, first-order moral claims are claims that entail that some agent morally ought to do or not to do some action; that some action is morally permissible; that some institution, character trait, or what have you, is morally good or bad; and so on. Now, according to the view on offer, a negated claim like "Torture is not wrong" does not *entail* that torture is permissible; it merely conversationally implicates that it is, since the implicature from "not wrong" to "permissible" is cancellable. Likewise, "Torture is not morally permissible" does not entail that torture is impermissible and hence wrong; it merely conversationally implicates that torture is impermissible and hence wrong. Thus negated atomic claims involving moral terms are not strictly speaking first-order moral claims, but some such claims conversationally implicate first-order moral claims. Since claims like "Torture is not wrong" are true, we cannot derive that their negations (such as "Torture is wrong") are true. This saves the standard formulation of moral error theory from the threat of incoherence and from implausible first-order moral implications. . . .

NOTE

1. To clarify: I take *norms* to be facts expressible by universally quantified sentences that imply that there are, for some class of agents in some set of circumstances, reasons to behave in a certain way, or that, for some class of agents in some set of circumstances, some form of behavior would be (in)correct or (im)permissible. *Reasons* I take to be facts that explain why some agent ought (*pro tanto*) to behave in certain ways, or why some form of behavior would be (in)correct or (im)permissible. I allow for the possibility that some norms are self-explaining—that some norm holds might itself be a reason to behave in certain ways. . . .

REFERENCES

Dworkin, R. (1996) "Objectivity and Truth: You'd Better Believe It," *Philosophy & Public Affairs* 25, 87–139.

Grice, H.P. (1989) *Studies in the Way of Words* (Cambridge, Mass.: Harvard University Press).

Mackie, J.L. (1977) *Ethics: Inventing Right and Wrong* (Harmondsworth: Penguin).

Olson, J. (forthcoming) "Error Theory and Reasons for Belief," in A. Reisner and A. Steglich-Petersen (eds) *Reasons for Belief* (Cambridge: Cambridge University Press).

STUDY QUESTIONS

1. What are categorical reasons?
2. What is the difference between transcendent and immanent norms?
3. Do error theorists deny the existence of immanent norms?
4. Might morality be understood exclusively in terms of immanent norms?

Moral Fictionalism

Richard Joyce

If the Error Theory is true, then what are its implications for action? Richard Joyce, Professor of Philosophy at Victoria University of Wellington, New Zealand, argues that we should treat morality as a fiction. On this view, when we assert "lying is wrong," we do not literally believe that lying is wrong but assert it as a useful make-believe. According to Joyce, doing so would serve to enhance one's self-control, minimizing the possibility of falling victim to weakness of will—that is, knowing what is best to do but nevertheless doing something else. Another advantage of maintaining the pretense of morality is that it provides protection against free-riders, those who benefit from a cooperative enterprise without contributing to it. Joyce concludes that we would be robbing ourselves of a valuable resource if we ceased thinking in moral terms.

IF THERE'S NOTHING THAT WE MORALLY OUGHT TO DO, THEN WHAT OUGHT WE TO DO?

On the very last page of his book *Ethics: Inventing Right and Wrong,* John Mackie (1977) suggests that moral discourse—which he has argued is deeply error-laden—can continue with the status of a "useful fiction." I presume that most people will agree, for a variety of reasons, that morality is in some manner useful. The problem, though, is that its usefulness may depend upon its being *believed,* but if we have read the earlier stages of Mackie's book and have been convinced by his arguments, then surely the possibility of believing in morality is no longer an option. Even if we somehow *could* carry on believing in it, surely we should not, for any recommendation in favor of having false beliefs while, at some level, knowing that they are false, is unlikely to be good advice. So how useful can morality be if we don't believe any of it?

This chapter will assume without discussion that Mackie's arguments for a moral error theory are cogent (or, at least, that their conclusion is true). This amounts to assuming two things: first, that moral discourse typically is assertoric (that is, moral judgments express belief states); second, that moral assertions typically are untrue. Mackie's particular argument holds that the problems of morality revolve around its commitment to Kantian categorical imperatives: morality requires that there are actions that persons ought to perform regardless of their ends. But, Mackie argues, such imperatives are indefensible, and therefore morality is flawed. A moral error

From Richard Joyce, "Moral Fictionalism," in *Fictionalism in Metaphysics,* ed. Mark Kalderon (New York: Oxford University Press, 2005). Reprinted by permission of the publisher.

theorist must hold that the problematic element of morality (categorical imperatives, in Mackie's opinion) is *central* to the discourse, such that any "tidied up" discourse, one with the defective elements extirpated, simply wouldn't count as a *moral* system at all. . . . The question that this chapter addresses is "What, then, ought we to do?" Mackie's answer appears to be "Carry on with morality as a fiction," and it is this possibility that I wish to examine closely. The aim is to understand what such an answer may mean, and to attempt a defense of it. I will call the view to be defended "moral fictionalism." . . . Note that fictionalism is not being suggested as something that is true of our actual moral discourse; rather, it is presented as a stance that we could take towards a subject matter—morality, in this case—if we have become convinced that the subject is hopelessly flawed in some respect, such that we cannot in good conscience carry on as before. . . .

One might think that the question "If a moral error theory is the case, what should we do?" is self-undermining. And so it would be, if it were asking what we *morally* ought to do, but that is not what is being asked. It is just a straightforward, common-or-garden, *practical* "ought." The answer that the question invites will be a hypothetical imperative, and we will assume that whatever arguments have led us to a moral error theory have not threatened hypothetical imperatives. (In other words, to hold a moral error theory is not to hold an error theory for practical normativity in general.) I do not want this issue to depend on any particular view of how we make such practical decisions. Let us just say that when morality is removed from the picture, what is practically called for is a matter of a cost-benefit analysis, where the costs and benefits can be understood liberally as preference satisfactions. By asking what *we* ought to do I am asking how a *group* of persons, who share a variety of broad interests, projects, ends—and who have come to the realization that morality is a bankrupt theory—might best carry on. . . .

I will begin by discussing fictionalism in general, outlining how it might be that a person might carry on using a discourse that she has come to see as flawed. It will be useful if initially we avoid the

distractions that the particular case of *moral* fictionalism might bring, and so I will begin by discussing an example that in some ways is less controversial: color fictionalism.

CRITICAL CONTEXTS

Suppose that after reading some eighteenth-century philosophers David comes to endorse an error theory about color. We needn't go into the arguments that might lead him to this conclusion, but they probably have something to do with the thought that one of the central platitudes about color is that it is a type of surface property of objects with which humans can have direct acquaintance (e.g., with normal eyesight on a sunny day), coupled with the thought that there simply aren't any properties like *that*. In other words, for philosophical reasons he ceases to believe that the world is colored in the way that it appears to be colored, which (further philosophical reasons lead him to think) implies that it is not colored at all. Maybe he is confused in coming to such a conclusion, but that is not the issue.

The issue is: given that he has come to have this philosophical belief (however confusedly) what happens to all his color discourse? Does he stop saying things like "The grass is green"? If someone asks him what color his mother's eyes are, does he reply that they are no color at all? Does he cease to appreciate sunsets or Impressionist paintings? Does he wear clashing clothes (while denying that anything really clashes with anything)? Of course not. In 99 percent of his life he carries on the same as everyone else. His vision is the same, his utterances about the world are the same, and even what he is thinking while making these utterances is the same. It is only in the philosophy classroom—moreover, only when discussing sensory perception—that when pressed on the question of whether the grass is green David might look uncomfortable, squirm, and say "Well, it's not *really* green—nothing is *really* green." This may seem like an uneasy position for him to be in. Sometimes—99 percent of the time, let's say—he is willing to utter "The grass is green," "The sky is blue," etc., while at other times—one percent of the time—he is inclined to deny these very same propositions. Which does he believe?

It seems to me that in this case what he affirms one percent of the time determines his beliefs. Why? Because the circumstance in which he denies that the world is colored—the philosophy classroom—is the context within which he is at his most undistracted, reflective, and critical. When one thinks critically, one subjects one's attitudes to careful scrutiny ("Is my acceptance of *p* really justified?"); robust forms of skepticism are given serious consideration; one looks for connections and incoherencies amongst one's attitudes; one forms higher order attitudes towards one's first-order judgments. It is important to see that this distinction between more critical and less critical contexts is asymmetric. It's not merely that a person attends to *different* beliefs when doing philosophy than when, say, shopping; nor that she questions everyday thinking when doing philosophy, but equally questions philosophy when shopping. Critical thinking investigates and challenges the presuppositions of ordinary thinking in a way that ordinary thinking does not investigate and challenge the presuppositions of critical thinking. Critical thinking is characterized by a tendency to ask oneself questions like "Am I really justified in accepting that things like shops exist?"—whereas the frame of mind one is in when shopping is *not* characterized by asking "Am I justified in accepting that there is some doubt as to whether shops exist?"

. . . In David's case, his most critical context is philosophical thought—thus, though he occupies this position only one percent of the time, we're supposing, it is his pronouncements therein that reveal his beliefs. The rest of the time he still *has* this skeptical belief, but he is not attending to it. Nevertheless, *all* the time David remains disposed to deny that the world is colored if placed in his most undistracted, reflective, and critical context, thus *all* the time this is what he believes.

FICTIVE JUDGMENTS

This leaves us with the question of how we should describe David's color claims in that 99 percent of

his life where he utters propositions (e.g., "The grass is green") that he disbelieves. We can begin by reminding ourselves of a more familiar circumstance in which people utter propositions that they disbelieve: story-telling. When I utter the sentence "There once was a goblin who liked jam" as part of telling a story, I am not expressing something that I really believe. If pressed in the appropriately serious way ("You don't *really* believe that there once was a goblin who liked jam, do you?") then I will "step out" of the fiction and deny those very propositions that a moment ago I was apparently affirming.

Some people have argued that sentences concerning fiction ought to be interpreted as containing a tacit story operator, such that they may be treated as true assertions; thus the sentence "There once was a goblin who liked jam" may be used to express the true proposition "According to Hans Christian Andersen's story, there once was a goblin who liked jam." (See, for example, Lewis, 1978.) This is inadequate as a general claim, for it fails to distinguish two different things that we can do with a story: describing the story versus telling the story. When we tell a story we are pretending something: that we are a person who has access to a realm of facts that we are reporting. (We might also partially pretend to be characters in the story, which is why we will speak their parts in a gruff or squeaky voice.) But if every sentence of the story uttered contained an unpronounced fiction operator, then there is no sense to be made of the claim that the storyteller is pretending. (How would one *pretend* that according to Hans Christian Andersen's story, there once was a goblin who liked jam?) This is not to deny that on occasions the proposition "According to Hans Christian Andersen's story, there once was a goblin who liked jam" might be expressed elliptically, minus the prefix, but this is not what we are doing when we *tell* the story. On such occasions we are not asserting anything, but *pretending* to assert.

The same distinction can be made regarding skeptical David's color claims. When, in ordinary conversation, he utters the sentence "The grass is green," we could interpret this as a kind of shorthand way of asserting something like "According to the fiction of a colored world, the grass is green" *or* we could interpret him as not asserting anything at all, but rather doing something rather like engaging in a make-believe: pretending to assert that the grass is green. I prefer the latter interpretation. It is true that at the moment of making the utterance it doesn't *seem* to David as if he is participating in an act of pretense, but nor does it seem to him as if he's making an implicit reference to the content of a well-known fiction. The matter won't be settled by asking David what he takes himself to be doing. Unless we force him into the philosophical context where he denies the existence of colors altogether, then asking him in an ordinary context whether he is asserting that the grass is green is likely to meet with an affirmative answer. But *that* claim—"Yes, I am asserting that the grass is green"—may be just another part of the fiction. . . . The issue of whether David's everyday utterance "The grass is green" is an assertion about a fiction or a fictional assertion is not an issue about how things feel to him—it is to be settled by philosophers providing an interpretation that construes David's linguistic practices most charitably.

The former interpretation—the "tacit story operator view"—does him no favors. One problem is that it cannot account for the fact that when in a more critical context David will explicitly *overturn* what he earlier claimed—he might say "What I said earlier was, strictly speaking, false." But if what he said earlier concerned the content of the fiction of a colored world, then he does not think it was false at all. A second problem with this interpretation is that it fails to make sense of the ways David might employ a color claim in a logically complex context (see Vision, 1994). For example, he might endorse the following argument:

P1 Fresh grass is green.
P2 My lawn is made of fresh grass.
C   Therefore, my lawn is green.

But if the first premise is elliptical for "According to the fiction of a colored world, fresh grass is green," then the argument is not valid at all. There is room for maintaining that the argument would be valid if all three claims were so prefixed, but the problem then would be that the revised second premise ("According to the fiction of a colored world, my lawn is made of fresh grass") seems so obviously false that it is surely not what David asserts when he utters P2. The fiction of a colored world, in so far as it has a determinate content at all, does not include claims about what anybody's lawn is made of (see comments by Lewis, 1978: 38–9).

To this it might be objected that the operator is being interpreted incorrectly. If "according to . . ." means not "it is claimed by . . ." but something more like "it is true in the fiction of . . . ," then perhaps we might after all allow that according to the fiction of a colored world that my lawn is made of fresh grass. In much the same way we might allow (indeed, insist) that it is true in the fiction of the Conan Doyle stories that humans do not have long hairy tails, that $6 + 5 = 11$, that Ireland is to the west of Britain, and so on, despite the fact that one will not find such things *claimed* by the stories (nor even—with, perhaps, the exception of the arithmetical truth—*implied* by anything claimed by the stories).

But this objection leads to unsightly consequences. Suppose David just casually asserts "My lawn is made of fresh grass." Since this assertion may at any time be pressed into service as the premise of an argument (the other premises of which include color claims), if the resulting argument is to be valid we will have to interpret him as *really* having asserted "It is true in the fiction of a colored world that my lawn is made of fresh grass." But the very same assertion may be employed by David as a premise in another argument that involves no color claims and no obvious fictionalizing: he may combine it with "Fresh grass is a type of vegetation," for example, to get the conclusion "My lawn is made up of a type of vegetation." In order for this new argument to be valid we had better interpret this new premise (and the new conclusion) as also bearing the prefix. In fact, any assertion that David makes might be combined with color claims as a premise of an apparently valid argument, and so if we're to maintain that apparent validity is real validity, we're going to have to interpret everything that he asserts about anything as having this unpronounced prefix. Things get worse still if we remind ourselves that color may not be the only fiction that David participates in. Eighteenth-century philosophy may also lead him to endorse an error theory for sound and smell, for causation, for virtue and vice, and thus in order for all his apparently unremarkable, apparently valid argumentative moves to be genuinely valid, we will have to interpret every claim issuing from his mouth as brimming with unspoken prefixes.

All such unpleasantness is avoided if we do away with tacit operators, and simply interpret David's utterance "Fresh grass is green" as a kind of make-believe assertion. The content of the proposition doesn't change, any more than when I say (as part of telling a story) "There once was a goblin who liked jam" I am using "jam" with some special meaning. The sentence "There once was a goblin who liked jam" has exactly the same content whether it is used as part of a fairy tale or to foolishly assert something false. What changes is the "force" with which it is uttered. When asserting it I am presenting it as something that I believe, and putting it forward as something that my audience should believe. Linguistic conventions decree that when it has been preceded by "Once upon a time . . . ," all such expectations are lifted.

What are we to make of an argument when some of the premises are uttered as an act of make-believe (e.g., as lines in a play) while others are straightforward assertions? Since the presence or absence of assertoric force doesn't affect the content of the premises, then if the argument was valid with its components asserted, it will be valid with them unasserted, and remain valid if some of the components are asserted and some of them are not. For example, the following is a valid argument:

P1 It is cold tonight.
P2 It is the height of summer.
P3 A cold night in the height of summer is unusual weather.
C   Tonight is unusual weather.

If a logic teacher recited this argument to a group of incoming undergraduates as an example of validity, she would not be asserting any of the premises or the conclusion—but it would be no less valid for that.

Alternatively, suppose that P1 is the line of a play, and the actor duly utters it while on stage, during a performance given on a hot summer's night. After the play, when pressed on climatic issues (curiously), he assents in all seriousness to P2 and P3. Clearly this person has not committed himself to the conclusion (which he may believe to be completely false), for the reason that he did not commit himself to P1. On the other hand, there is nothing to prevent him from "going along" with the pretense if for some reason he wants to, combining P2 and P3 with the make-believe P1, and endorsing the conclusion as part of a fictional act. If he does so, there will be no need to reinterpret his attitude to P2 and P3. These were asserted, and in asserting them he has committed himself to certain other conclusions (e.g., "If it were cold tonight, that would be unusual weather"), and may combine them with further asserted premises to yet further conclusions. In other words, unlike with the tacit operator account, we do not have to interpret David's ordinary claim "My lawn is made of fresh grass" as anything other than it appears to be, let alone extravagantly reinterpreting all his other ordinary assertions that are not color claims.

Let us say, then, that David is not only an error theorist about color, but also a fictionalist. He does not believe in color, but he continues to employ color discourse. His color claims are fictive judgments, which we may think of as a kind of "make-believe"— though one should be wary of the term, since the paradigm examples that it tends to bring to mind are of rather trivial activities (pretending that the puppet is talking, make-believing that the sofa is a boat, etc.). But there is no obvious reason to assume that make-believe is always a trivial business; indeed, an important objective of this chapter is to convince you otherwise. We have not specified David's reasons for making these fictive color judgments—let us just say that he finds it convenient to do so. This practical value need be nothing more than the convenience of carrying on in the manner to which he has grown accustomed.

Since David is capable of overturning his everyday color discourse whenever he enters a more critical frame of mind, we should hardly describe him as suffering from self-deception. He is no more self-deceived than is someone caught up in a good novel. I suppose that the term "self-deception" *could* be applied to an ordinary person engaged in a novel, but (A) it would be an uncomfortable stretch, and (B) it would merely show that self-deception need not be in the least pernicious. It is much better, I think, to distinguish being "caught up" in a fiction from being "deceived" by a fiction. A person deceived by a fiction is someone who might walk up and down Baker Street wondering where Holmes lived, or who tries to research Madame Bovary's ancestry, or who rushes on to the stage to save the princess. Fans of Sherlock Holmes do travel to Baker Street, of course, and they may well picture their hero there in the nineteenth century, but they know very well (most of them, I hope) what they're doing. At any time, if asked in all seriousness whether Holmes walked these streets, they will answer "No." They are not deceived and therefore not self-deceived; they are merely caught up in a fiction. It is the person who is incapable of dropping the fiction, who continues to speak of Holmes as a historical character even when in her most critical context, who is deceived. . . .

THE VALUE OF MORALITY

With a basic theory of fictionalism now on the table, we can turn, finally, to *moral* fictionalism. Suppose that a moral error theory is the case—or at least suppose that a group of people has become convinced of this—what should they do with their faulty moral talk? The conclusion that they should just abolish it, that it should go the way of witch discourse and phlogiston discourse, is certainly a tempting possibility, and may, for all I say here, turn out to be the correct response. But fictionalism shows us that it is not the *only* response; it is at least possible that they may reasonably elect to maintain moral discourse as a fiction. What they need to perform is a cost-benefit analysis. Let us suppose, firstly, that the option of carrying on *believing* in morality is closed to them. They have seen the cat out of the bag and they cannot believe otherwise. Even if they *could* somehow bring themselves sincerely to "forget" that they ever read Mackie's book

(for example), surely to embark on such a course is likely to bring negative consequences. . . .

Two options remain as contenders in the cost-benefit analysis: abolitionism (or we may call it "eliminativism") and fictionalism. For moral fictionalism to be viable it must win this pragmatic comparison. It is not required that taking a fictional stance towards moral discourse will supply *all* the benefits that came with sincere moral belief. It can be conceded up front that the pragmatically optimal situation for a group of people to be in is to have the attitude of sincere belief towards moral matters. But it must also be grasped that having a doxastic policy concordant with *critical inquiry* is almost guaranteed to serve better in practical terms for a group than any other policy. We are imagining a group of people whose careful pursuit of truth has overthrown their moral beliefs. Perhaps such people correctly recognize that they were happier and better off before the pursuit brought them so far, but there is now no going back, and to sacrifice the value of critical inquiry would be disastrous.

In order to assess who might win this two horse race, we must ask the question "What is the value of morality?" Unless we roughly know the answer we can have no idea of what costs its abolition may incur. Let us at first put fictionalism aside, and address the question of the value of morality *when it is believed.* We may then assume that this is a benefit that, *ceteris paribus,* will be lost if a group were to abolish morality, which puts us in a position to ask . . . whether their adopting a fictionalist stance would allow them to avoid some of those losses.

The popular thought that without morality all hell would break loose in human society is a naive one. Across a vast range of situations we all have perfectly good *prudential* reasons for continuing to act in cooperative ways with our fellow humans. In many situations reciprocal and cooperative relationships bring ongoing rewards to all parties, and do so *a fortiori* when defective behaviors are punished. When, in addition, we factor in the benefits of having a good reputation—a reputation that is based on past performance—then cooperative dispositions can easily out-compete hurtful dispositions on purely egoistic grounds.

To an individual who asks why she should not cheat her fellows if she thinks that she can get away with it, Hobbes long ago provided one kind of answer: because the punishment-enforcing power is very powerful indeed. This answer is developed and supplemented by Hume, who speaks of knaves "betrayed by their own maxims; and while they purpose to cheat with moderation and secrecy, a tempting incident occurs, nature is frail, and they give into the snare; whence they can never extricate themselves, without a total loss of reputation, and the forfeiture of all trust and confidence with mankind" (Hume, 1751/1983: 82). First, the knave misses out on benefits that by their very nature cannot be gained through defection: "Inward peace of mind, consciousness of integrity, a satisfactory review of [her] own conduct" (Hume, 1751/1983: 82)—advantages that are constituted by a disposition not to cheat one's fellows. Moreover, the knave will lose these benefits for comparatively trivial gains ("the feverish, empty amusements of luxury and expense"). Third, knaves will be epistemically fallible, and might think that they can get away with something when in fact they will be caught and punished. Fourth, since knaves have on their minds the possibility of cheating whenever they are confident of evading detection, they are likely to be tempted to cheat in situations where the chances of evading detection are less than certain, thus, again, risking severe punishment.

One result we can draw from Hobbes and Hume is that a person may have many reasons for acting in accordance with a moral requirement: the fear of punishment, the desire for an ongoing beneficial relationship, the motivation to maintain a good reputation, the simple fact that one on the whole *likes* one's fellows, that one has been brought up such that acting otherwise makes one feel rotten—all these being solid prudential reasons—plus the moral requirement to act. To subtract the last one leaves the others still very much in play. But if this is so, then what useful role does the last kind of consideration play at all? To answer this it is worth underlining the reference to *temptation* in Hume's answer to the sensible knave. Merely to believe of some action "This is the one that is in my long-term best interests" simply doesn't do the job. . . . Because short-term profit is tangible and present whereas long-term profit is distant and faint, the lure of the immediate may subvert the agent's ability to deliberate properly so as to obtain a valuable delayed benefit, leading him to "rationalize" a poor choice. Hobbes lamented this "perverse desire for present profit" (Hobbes, 1642/1983: 72)—something which Hume blamed for "all dissoluteness and disorder, repentance and misery" (Hume, 1751/1983: 55), adding that a person should embrace "any expedient, by which he may impose a restraint upon himself, and guard against this weakness" (Hume, 1739/1978: 536–7).[1] Let me hypothesize that an important value of moral beliefs is that they function as just such an expedient: supplementing and reinforcing the outputs of prudential reasoning. When a person believes that the valued action is *morally* required—that it *must* be performed whether he likes it or not—then the possibilities for rationalization diminish. If a person believes the action to be required by an authority from which he cannot escape, if he imbues it with a "must-be-doneness" (the categorical element of morality that Mackie found so troublesome), if he believes that in not performing he will not merely frustrate himself, but will become reprehensible and deserving of disapprobation—then he is more likely to perform the action. The distinctive value of categorical imperatives is that they silence calculation, which is a valuable thing when interfering forces can so easily hijack our prudential calculations. In this manner, moral beliefs function to bolster self-control against practical irrationality.

. . . This suffices to show why a moral error theorist should hesitate before embracing abolitionism, for it reveals a practical cost that would be incurred on that path. (If there are other sources of practical benefit brought by moral beliefs, then the costs of abolitionism are even higher.) The crucial question, then, is whether some of the costs may be avoided by taking a fictionalist stance towards morality—whether the practical benefits of moral belief may still be gained by an attitude that falls short of belief. On the face of it, it seems unlikely. How can a fiction have the kind of practical impact—moreover, the kind of practical *authority*—that confers on moral belief its instrumental value?

This is the major reason that moral fictionalism seems troubling in a way that color fictionalism does not: It seems implausible that a mere fiction could or should have such practical influence on important real-life decisions. In what remains of this chapter let me try to assuage this reasonable doubt.

MORAL FICTIONALISM

. . . In the previous section I argued that an important practical benefit to the individual of having moral beliefs is that they will serve as a bulwark against weakness of will—silencing certain kinds of vulnerable calculation, and thus blocking the temporary re-evaluation of outcomes that is characteristic of short-sighted rationalization. So our task is limited to addressing the question of whether a "mere fiction" could also provide a similar benefit.

A quick argument to show that a positive answer is within reach begins by noting that engagement with fiction can affect our emotional states. . . . All the empirical evidence supports commonsense on this matter: watching movies, reading novels, or simply engaging one's imagination can produce real episodes of fear, sadness, disgust, anger, and so on. . . . To this premise we can add the truism that emotional states can affect motivations, and thus behavior. Of course, the emotions arising from fictions do not necessarily affect behavior in the same manner as emotions arising in response to beliefs: the fear of fictional vampires is consistent with my sitting eating popcorn, whereas fear of vampires in which I *believed* would result in purchasing wooden stakes and a lot of garlic. But it does not follow that the emotions arising from engagement with fiction are "motivationally inert." Reading *Anna Karenina* may encourage a person to abandon a doomed love affair; watching *The Blair Witch Project* may lead one to cancel the planned camping trip in the woods. Needless to say, these aren't the kind of beneficial behavioral responses that the moral fictionalist is seeking, but they at least show that the causal links between involvement with a fiction and action are undeniably in place.

Let us turn our sights more directly on the question of how a person combats weakness of will.

Suppose I am determined to exercise regularly, after a lifetime of lethargy, but find myself succumbing to temptation. An effective strategy will be for me to lay down a strong and authoritative rule: *I must do fifty sit-ups every day, no less.* I am attempting to form a habit, and habits are formed—and, for the doggedly weak of will, maintained—by strictness and overcompensation. Perhaps in truth it doesn't much matter that I do fifty sit-ups every day, so long as I do more-or-less fifty on most days. But by allowing myself the occasional lapse, by giving myself permission *sometimes* to stray from the routine, I pave the way for akratic sabotage of my calculations—I threaten even my doing more-or-less fifty sit-ups on most days. I do better if I encourage myself to think in terms of fifty daily sit-ups as a non-negotiable value, as something I *must* do if I am ever to get fit.

However, to believe sincerely that fifty daily sit-ups are needed in order for me to achieve fitness is to have a false belief (we'll assume), the holding of which will require other compensating false beliefs. If it is true that *more-or-less* fifty sit-ups *nearly* every day is sufficient for health, then that is what I ought to believe. On the other hand, to *pay attention* to this belief exposes me to self-subversion—a slippery slope to inactivity. This is precisely a case where my best interests are served by rehearsing thoughts that are false, and that I know are false, in order to fend off my own weaknesses. But in order to get the benefit from this strategy there is no necessity that I *believe* the thoughts, or attempt to justify them as true when placed in a philosophically critical context. While doing my sit-ups I think to myself "Must . . . do . . . fifty!" but if, on some other occasion, you ask me whether I really *must* do fifty, then I will say "No, sometimes forty would suffice."

Human motivation is often aroused more effectively by mental images than by careful calculation. Hume uses the example of a drunkard "who has seen his companion die of a debauch, and dreads a like accident for himself: but as the memory of it decays away by degrees, his former security returns, and the danger seems less certain and real" (Hume, 1739/1978: 144). Hume's point is that humans put weight on near, recent, and concrete evidence, though there is no rational justification for our doing so.

We can imagine the drunkard being presented with impressive statistics on the probabilities of alcoholics suffering an unpleasant end, but remaining quite unmoved; yet one friend dies and he becomes a teetotaler (at least for a while). It's not that he disbelieved the statistics, and the death of the friend need not alter his beliefs about how likely he is to suffer a similar fate, but the "tangibility" of the one death has, in Hume's words, "a superior influence on the judgment, as well as on the passions" (Hume, 1739/1978: 143–4).

If the drunkard has decided that his long-term interests are best served by abstinence, what strategy should he pursue to that end? He should read the statistics, yes, but—perhaps even more importantly—he should attempt to keep the image of his dying friend vivid. He does still better if he can relate that image to his own plight, if he thinks: "If I drink, that's what will happen to me." Now that proposition is false. What is true is something like "If I drink, there's a 10 percent chance [say] of that happening to me." But *that* thought looks dangerous. He does better with the stronger: "If I drink, that's what *will* happen to me." Yet does he, need he, *believe* this? No: he need not believe it in order for it to affect his actions in the desirable way, and, moreover, he *ought not* to believe it because it is false. . . .

MORAL FICTIONALISM AS A PRECOMMITMENT

Sometimes, when on a long airplane flight, I succumb to weakness of will and eat all the awful in-flight food that I had promised myself I wouldn't eat. It happens because I am trapped and bored with the food right in front of me for a long time. In order to avoid this I have developed a strategy for resisting my own imprudence. If I have decided that I really don't want to eat that slice of cheesecake, but suspect that I won't be able to resist picking at it until it's all gone (despite its tasting of plastic), I smear some gravy on top of it. (It raises the eyebrows of the person sitting next to me, but certainly ensures that I won't eat the cheesecake.) In doing this I am, in a very unglamorous way, following the example of

Odysseus when he had himself bound to the mast of his ship so as not to give in to the song of the sirens. The circumstance in which he made that decision was one in which he was free of temptation, but he was shrewd enough to anticipate the overthrow of control. Such strategies for combating weakness of will John Elster calls "precommitments" (Elster, 1984: 37ff).

The decision to adopt morality as a fiction is best thought of as a kind of precommitment. It is not being suggested that someone enters a shop, is tempted to steal, decides to adopt morality as a fiction, and thus sustains her prudent though faltering decision not to steal. Rather, the resolution to accept the moral point of view is something that occurred in the person's past, and is now an accustomed way of thinking. Its role is that when entering a shop the possibility of stealing doesn't even enter her mind. If a knave were to say to her "Why not steal?" she would answer without hesitation "No!—Stealing is wrong." What goes through her mind may be exactly the same as what goes through the mind of the sincere moral believer—it need not "feel" like make-believe at all (and thus it may have the same influence on behavior as a belief). The difference between the two need only be a *disposition* that the fictionalist has (though is not paying attention to): the disposition to deny that anything is really morally wrong, when placed in her most critical context.

But what if the knave carries on: "But in all seriousness, taking into account philosophical issues, bearing in mind John Mackie's arguments—*why not steal*?" Then, *ex hypothesi,* our fictionalist will "step out" and admit that there is nothing morally wrong with stealing. So does she then stuff her pockets? No! For she still has all those Hobbesian and Humean reasons to refrain from stealing. . . . If (as seems correct) an individual's believing that some available action is morally required increases the probability of his performing that action, then it seems plausible to assume that the usefulness to an individual of moral belief lies at least in part in its increasing the probability of his performing those actions that he judges he morally ought. From these assumptions it follows that such actions were useful to him anyway—i.e., that he had a non-moral reason for performing them.

The idea of the precommitment to the moral fiction being a conscious choice that someone makes is an artificial idealization. (In this it differs from pouring gravy on cheesecake.) It is more likely that a person is simply brought up to think in moral terms; the precommitment is put in place by parents. In childhood such prescriptions may be presented and accepted as items of belief (it is not implausible to hold that the best way to encourage prudent habits is to tell children a few white lies); thus thinking of certain types of action as "morally right" and others as "morally wrong" becomes natural and ingrained. Later, when a broader and more sophisticated understanding is possible, the person may come to see how philosophically troubling is the idea that there really are actions that people *must* perform, irrespective of whether they wish to, regardless of whether it suits their ends—and if convinced by such arguments she becomes a moral error theorist. But these patterns of thought might be now so deeply embedded that in everyday life she carries on employing them—she finds it convenient and effective to do so, and finds that dropping them leaves her feeling vulnerable to temptations which, if pursued, she judges likely to lead to regret. There is, besides, a practical value to be gained simply from the convenience of carrying on in the manner to which she has grown accustomed. She doesn't cease to be a moral error theorist, but she becomes, in addition, a moral fictionalist. . . .

NOTE

1. I have altered Hume's text from the first person to the second person singular.

REFERENCES

Elster, Jon (1984). *Ulysses and the Sirens.* Cambridge: Cambridge University Press.

Hobbes, Thomas (1642/1983). *De Cive.* Oxford: Clarendon Press.

Hume, David (1739/1978). *A Treatise of Human Nature.* Oxford: Clarendon Press.

———— (1751/1983). *Enquiry Concerning the Principles of Morals.* Cambridge, MA: Hackett Publishing Company.

Lewis, David (1978). "Truth in Fiction." *American Philosophical Quarterly,* 15: 37–46.

Mackie, John (1977). *Ethics: Inventing Right and Wrong.* New York: Penguin Books.

Vision, Gerald (1994). "Fiction and Fictionalist Reductions." *Pacific Philosophical Quarterly,* 74: 150–74.

STUDY QUESTIONS

1. According to Joyce, what is "moral fictionalism"?
2. Is it possible to believe in morality while considering it a fiction?
3. What practical benefits does morality afford?
4. Would moral fictionalism retain the practical benefits usually associated with morality?

Part VI

RELATIVISM

Moral Isolationism

Mary Midgley

Some claim that the search for universal answers to moral questions is futile because morality differs from one culture to another. This view, sometimes referred to as "cultural relativism," maintains that while we can seek understanding of a particular culture's moral system, we have no basis for judging it, for morality is only a matter of custom. Mary Midgley, formerly Senior Lecturer in Philosophy at Newcastle University in England, argues against cultural relativism, maintaining that moral reasoning requires the possibility of judging the practices of other cultures.

All of us are, more or less, in trouble today about trying to understand cultures strange to us. We hear constantly of alien customs. We see changes in our lifetime which would have astonished our parents. I want to discuss here one very short way of dealing with this difficulty, a drastic way which many people now theoretically favor. It consists in simply denying that we can ever understand any culture except our own well enough to make judgments about it. Those who recommend this hold that the world is sharply divided into separate societies, sealed units, each with its own system of thought. They feel that the respect and tolerance due from one system to another forbids us ever to take up a critical position to any other culture. Moral judgment, they suggest, is a kind of coinage valid only in its country of origin.

I shall call this position "moral isolationism." I shall suggest that it is certainly not forced upon us, and indeed that it makes no sense at all. People usually take it up because they think it is a respectful attitude to other cultures. In fact, however, it is not respectful. Nobody can respect what is entirely unintelligible to them. To respect someone, we have to know enough about him to make a *favorable* judgment, however general and tentative. And we do understand people in other cultures to this extent. Otherwise a great mass of our most valuable thinking would be paralyzed.

To show this, I shall take a remote example, because we shall probably find it easier to think calmly about it than we should with a contemporary one, such as female circumcision in Africa or the Chinese Cultural Revolution. The principles involved will still be the same. My example is this. There is, it seems, a verb in classical Japanese which means "to try out one's new sword on a chance wayfarer." (The word is *tsujigiri,* literally "crossroads-cut.") A samurai sword had to be tried out because, if it was to work properly, it had to slice through someone at a single blow, from the shoulder to the opposite flank. Otherwise, the warrior bungled his stroke. This could injure his honor, offend his ancestors, and even let down his emperor. So tests were needed, and wayfarers had to be expended. Any wayfarer would

From Mary Midgley, *Heart and Mind: The Varieties of Moral Experience* (London: Routledge, 2003). Reprinted by permission of the publisher.

do—provided, of course, that he was not another Samurai. Scientists will recognize a familiar problem about the rights of experimental subjects.

Now when we hear of a custom like this, we may well reflect that we simply do not understand it; and therefore are not qualified to criticize it at all, because we are not members of that culture. But we are not members of any other culture either, except our own. So we extend the principle to cover all extraneous cultures, and we seem therefore to be moral isolationists. But this is, as we shall see, an impossible position. Let us ask what it would involve.

① We must ask first: Does the isolating barrier work both ways? Are people in other cultures equally unable to criticize *us*? This question struck me sharply when I read a remark in *The Guardian* by an anthropologist about a South American Indian who had been taken into a Brazilian town for an operation, which saved his life. When he came back to his village, he made several highly critical remarks about the white Brazilians' way of life. They may very well have been justified. But the interesting point was that the anthropologist called these remarks "a damning indictment of Western civilization." Now the Indian had been in that town about two weeks. Was he in a position to deliver a damning indictment? Would we ourselves be qualified to deliver such an indictment on the Samurai, provided we could spend two weeks in ancient Japan? What do we really think about this?

My own impression is that we believe that outsiders can, in principle, deliver perfectly good indictments—only, it usually takes more than two weeks to make them damning. Understanding has degrees. It is not a slapdash yes-or-no matter. Intelligent outsiders can progress in it, and in some ways will be at an advantage over the locals. But if this is so, it must clearly apply to ourselves as much as anybody else.

② Our next question is this: Does the isolating barrier between cultures block praise as well as blame? If I want to say that the Samurai culture has many virtues, or to praise the South American Indians, am I prevented from doing *that* by my outside status? Now, we certainly do need to praise other societies in this way. But it is hardly possible that we could praise

them effectively if we could not, in principle, criticize them. Our praise would be worthless if it rested on no definite grounds, if it did not flow from some understanding. Certainly we may need to praise things which we do not *fully* understand. We say "there's something very good here, but I can't quite make out what it is yet." This happens when we want to learn from strangers. And we can learn from strangers. But to do this we have to distinguish between those strangers who are worth learning from and those who are not. Can we then judge which is which?

③ This brings us to our third question: What is involved in judging? Now plainly there is no question here of sitting on a bench in a red robe and sentencing people. Judging simply means forming an opinion, and expressing it if it is called for. Is there anything wrong about this? Naturally, we ought to avoid forming—and expressing—*crude* opinions, like that of a simple-minded missionary, who might dismiss the whole Samurai culture as entirely bad, because non-Christian. But this is a different objection. The trouble with crude opinions is that they are crude, whoever forms them, not that they are formed by the wrong people. Anthropologists, after all, are outsiders quite as much as missionaries. Moral isolationism forbids us to form *any* opinions on these matters. Its ground for doing so is that we don't understand them. But there is much that we don't understand in our own culture too. This brings us to our last question: If we can't judge other cultures, can we really judge our own? Our efforts to do so will be much damaged if we are really deprived of our opinions about other societies, because these provide the range of comparison, the spectrum of alternatives against which we set what we want to understand. We would have to stop using the mirror which anthropology so helpfully holds up to us.

In short, moral isolationism would lay down a general ban on moral reasoning. Essentially, this is the program of immoralism, and it carries a distressing logical difficulty. Immoralists like Nietzsche are actually just a rather specialized sect of moralists. They can no more afford to put moralizing out of business than smugglers can afford to abolish customs regulations. The power of moral judgment is, in fact, not a luxury, not a perverse indulgence of the self-righteous. It is a necessity. When we judge something to be bad or good, better or worse than something else, we are taking it as an example to aim at or avoid. Without opinions of this sort, we would have no framework of comparison for our own policy, no chance of profiting by other people's insights or mistakes. In this vacuum, we could form no judgments on our own actions.

Now it would be odd if *Homo sapiens* had really got himself into a position as bad as this—a position where his main evolutionary asset, his brain, was so little use to him. None of us is going to accept this skeptical diagnosis. We cannot do so, because our involvement in moral isolationism does not flow from apathy, but from a rather acute concern about human hypocrisy and other forms of wickedness. But we polarize that concern around a few selected moral truths. We are rightly angry with those who despise, oppress or steamroll other cultures. We think that doing these things is actually *wrong*. But this is itself a moral judgment. We could not condemn oppression and insolence if we thought that all our condemnation were just a trivial local quirk of our own culture. We could still less do it if we tried to stop judging altogether.

Real moral skepticism, in fact, could lead only to inaction, to our losing all interest in moral questions, most of all in those which concern other societies. When we discuss these things, it becomes instantly clear how far we are from doing this. Suppose, for instance, that I criticize the bisecting Samurai, that I say his behavior is brutal. What will usually happen next is that someone will protest, will say that I have no right to make criticisms like that of another culture. But it is most unlikely that he will use this move to end the discussion of the subject. Instead, he will justify the Samurai. He will try to fill in the background, to make me understand the custom, by explaining the exalted ideals of discipline and devotion which produced it. He will probably talk of the lower value which the ancient Japanese placed on individual life generally. He may well suggest that this is a healthier attitude than our own obsession with security. He may add, too, that the wayfarers did not seriously mind being bisected, that in principle they accepted the whole arrangement.

Now an objector who talks like this is implying that it *is* possible to understand alien customs. That is just what he is trying to make me do. And he implies, too, that if I do succeed in understanding them, I shall do something better than giving up judging them. He expects me to change my present judgment to a truer one—namely, one that is favorable. And the standards I must use to do this cannot just be Samurai standards. They have to be ones current in my own culture. Ideals like discipline and devotion will not move anybody unless he himself accepts them. As it happens, neither discipline nor devotion is very popular in the West at present. Anyone who appeals to them may well have to do some more arguing to make *them* acceptable, before he can use them to explain the Samurai. But if he does succeed here, he will have persuaded us, not just that there was something to be said for them in ancient Japan, but that there would be here as well.

Isolating barriers simply cannot arise here. If we accept something as a serious moral truth about one culture, we can't refuse to apply it—in however different an outward form—to other cultures as well, wherever circumstances admit it. If we refuse to do this, we just are not taking the other culture seriously. This becomes clear if we look at the last argument used by my objector—that of justification by consent of the victim. It is suggested that sudden bisection is quite in order, *provided* that it takes place between consenting adults. I cannot now discuss how conclusive this justification is. What I am pointing out is simply that it can only work if we believe that *consent* can make such a transaction respectable—and this is a thoroughly modern and Western idea. It would probably never occur to a Samurai; if it did, it would surprise him very much. It is *our* standard. In applying it, too, we are likely to make another typically Western demand. We shall ask for good factual evidence that the wayfarers actually do have this rather surprising taste—that they are really willing to be bisected. In applying Western standards in this way, we are not being confused or irrelevant. We are asking the questions which arise *from where we stand,* questions which we can see the sense of. We do this because asking questions which you can't see the sense of is humbug. Certainly we can extend our questioning by imaginative effort. We can come to understand other societies better. By doing so, we may make their questions our own, or we may see that they are really forms of the questions which we are asking already. This is not impossible. It is just very hard work. The obstacles which often prevent it are simply those of ordinary ignorance, laziness and prejudice.

If there were really an isolating barrier, of course, our own culture could never have been formed. It is no sealed box, but a fertile jungle of different influences—Greek, Jewish, Roman, Norse, Celtic and so forth, into which further influences are still pouring—American, Indian, Japanese, Jamaican, you name it. The moral isolationist's picture of separate unmixable cultures is quite unreal. People who talk about British history usually stress the value of this fertilizing mix, no doubt rightly. But this is not just an odd fact about Britain. Except for the very smallest and most remote, all cultures are formed out of many streams. All have the problem of digesting and assimilating things which, at the start, they do not understand. All have the choice of learning something from this challenge, or, alternatively, of refusing to learn, and fighting it mindlessly instead.

This universal predicament has been obscured by the fact that anthropologists used to concentrate largely on very small and remote cultures, which did not seem to have this problem. These tiny societies, which had often forgotten their own history, made neat, self-contained subjects for study. No doubt it was valuable to emphasize their remoteness, their extreme strangeness, their independence of our cultural tradition. This emphasis was, I think, the root of moral isolationism. But, as the tribal studies themselves showed, even there the anthropologists were able to interpret what they saw and make judgments—often favorable—about the tribesmen. And the tribesmen, too, were quite equal to making judgments about the anthropologists—and about the tourists and Coca-Cola salesmen who followed them. Both sets of judgments, no doubt, were somewhat hasty, both have been refined in the light of further experience. A similar transaction between us and the Samurai might take even longer. But that is no reason at all for deeming it impossible. Morally as well as physically, there is only one world, and we all have to live in it.

STUDY QUESTIONS

1. What does Midgley mean by "moral isolationism"?
2. Are those opposed to our judging other cultures equally opposed to other cultures judging ours?
3. Do those who live in a culture necessarily understand it better than those who don't live in that culture?
4. If criticisms of other cultures are always inappropriate, can praise of other cultures ever be appropriate?

Moral Relativism Defended

Gilbert Harman

Moral relativism denies the existence of universal moral principles yet asserts the moral principle that one ought to act in conformity with the norms of one's own group. Is this position coherent? It is, according to Gilbert Harman, Professor of Philosophy at Princeton University. He defends a form of moral relativism that he maintains can escape the charge of inconsistency. Indeed, he believes that relativism is built into the form of a moral judgment. When we claim that someone ought to perform an action, we imply that the person is motivated to do so; otherwise, our judgment misfires. What accounts for the motivation? Harman answers that it is an implicit agreement in intentions shared by the speaker and audience. Because genuine moral judgments presuppose this agreement, different groups with different agreements yield different moralities.

My thesis is that morality arises when a group of people reach an implicit agreement or come to a tacit understanding about their relations with one another. Part of what I mean by this is that moral judgments—or, rather, an important class of them—make sense only in relation to and with reference to one or another such agreement or understanding. This is vague, and I shall try to make it more precise in what follows. But it should be clear that I intend to argue for a version of what has been called moral relativism. . . .

Most arguments against relativism make use of a strategy of dissuasive definition; they define moral relativism as an inconsistent thesis. For example, they define it as the assertion that (*a*) there are no universal moral principles and (*b*) one ought to act in accordance with the principles of one's own group, where this latter principle, (*b*), *is* supposed to be a universal moral principle.[1] It is easy enough to show that this version of moral relativism will not do, but that is no reason to think that a defender of moral relativism cannot find a better definition.

My moral relativism is a soberly logical thesis—a thesis about logical form, if you like. Just as the judgment that something is large makes sense only in relation to one or another comparison class, so too, I will argue, the judgment that it is wrong of someone to do something makes sense only in relation to an agreement or understanding. A dog may be large in relation to chihuahuas but not large in relation to dogs in general. Similarly, I will argue, an action may be wrong in relation to one agreement but not in relation to another. Just as it makes no sense to ask whether a dog is large, period, apart from any relation to a comparison class, so too, I will argue, it makes no sense to ask whether an

From Gilbert Harman, "Moral Relativism Defended," *The Philosophical Review* 84 (1975). Reprinted by permission of the publisher.

action is wrong, period, apart from any relation to an agreement.

There is an agreement, in the relevant sense, if each of a number of people intends to adhere to some schedule, plan, or set of principles, intending to do this on the understanding that the others similarly intend. The agreement or understanding need not be conscious or explicit; and I will not here try to say what distinguishes moral agreements from, for example, conventions of the road or conventions of etiquette, since these distinctions will not be important as regards the purely logical thesis that I will be defending.

Although I want to say that certain moral judgments are made in relation to an agreement, I do not want to say this about all moral judgments. Perhaps it is true that all moral judgments are made in relation to an agreement; nevertheless, that is not what I will be arguing. For I want to say that there is a way in which certain moral judgments are relative to an agreement but other moral judgments are not. My relativism is a thesis only about what I will call "inner judgments," such as the judgment that someone ought or ought not to have acted in a certain way or the judgment that it was right or wrong of him to have done so. My relativism is not meant to apply, for example, to the judgment that someone is evil or the judgment that a given institution is unjust.

In particular, I am not denying (nor am I asserting) that some moralities are "objectively" better than others or that there are objective standards for assessing moralities. My thesis is a soberly logical thesis about logical form.

I. INNER JUDGMENTS

We make inner judgments about a person only if we suppose that he is capable of being motivated by the relevant moral considerations. We make other sorts of judgment about those who we suppose are not susceptible of such motivation. Inner judgments include judgments in which we say that someone should or ought to have done something or that someone was right or wrong to have done something. Inner judgments do not include judgments in

which we call someone (literally) a savage or say that someone is (literally) inhuman, evil, a betrayer, a traitor, or an enemy.

Consider this example. Intelligent beings from outer space land on Earth, beings without the slightest concern for human life and happiness. That a certain course of action on their part might injure one of us means nothing to them; that fact by itself gives them no reason to avoid the action. In such a case it would be odd to say that nevertheless the beings ought to avoid injuring us or that it would be wrong for them to attack us. Of course we will want to resist them if they do such things and we will make negative judgments about them; but we will judge that they are dreadful enemies to be repelled and even destroyed, not that they should not act as they do. . . .

Again, suppose that a contented employee of Murder, Incorporated was raised as a child to honor and respect members of the "family" but to have nothing but contempt for the rest of society. His current assignment, let us suppose, is to kill a certain bank manager, Bernard J. Ortcutt. Since Ortcutt is not a member of the "family," the employee in question has no compunction about carrying out his assignment. In particular, if we were to try to convince him that he should not kill Ortcutt, our argument would merely amuse him. We would not provide him with the slightest reason to desist unless we were to point to practical difficulties, such as the likelihood of his getting caught. Now, in this case it would be a misuse of language to say of him that he ought not to kill Ortcutt or that it would be wrong of him to do so, since that would imply that our own moral considerations carry some weight with him, which they do not. Instead we can only judge that he is a criminal, someone to be hunted down by the police, an enemy of peace-loving citizens, and so forth.

It is true that we can make certain judgments about him using the word "ought." For example, investigators who have been tipped off by an informer and who are waiting for the assassin to appear at the bank can use the "ought" of expectation to say, "He ought to arrive soon," meaning that on the basis of their information one would expect him to arrive soon. And, in thinking over how the assassin might carry out his assignment, we can use the "ought" of rationality to say that he ought to go in by the rear door, meaning that it would be more rational for him to do that than to go in by the front door. In neither of these cases is the moral "ought" in question.

There is another use of "ought" which is normative and in a sense moral but which is distinct from what I am calling the moral "ought." This is the use which occurs when we say that something ought or ought not to be the case. It ought not to be the case that members of Murder, Incorporated go around killing people; in other words, it is a terrible thing that they do so. The same thought can perhaps be expressed as "They ought not to go around killing people," meaning that it ought not to be the case that they do, not that they are wrong to do what they do. The normative "ought to be" is used to assess a situation; the moral "ought to do" is used to describe a relation between an agent and a type of act that he might perform or has performed.

The sentence "They ought not to go around killing people" is therefore multiply ambiguous. It can mean that one would not expect them to do so (the "ought" of expectation), that it is not in their interest to do so (the "ought" of rationality), that it is a bad thing that they do so (the normative "ought to be"), or that they are wrong to do so (the moral "ought to do"). For the most part I am here concerned only with the last of these interpretations. . . .

"Right" and "wrong" also have multiple uses; I will not try to say what all of them are. But I do want to distinguish using the word "wrong" to say that a particular situation or action is wrong from using the word to say that it is wrong *of someone* to do something. In the former case, the word "wrong" is used to assess an act or situation. In the latter case it is used to describe a relation between an agent and an act. Only the latter sort of judgment is an inner judgment. Although we would not say concerning the contented employee of Murder, Incorporated mentioned earlier that it was wrong *of him* to kill Ortcutt, we could say that *his action* was wrong and we could say that it is wrong that there is so much killing.

To take another example, it sounds odd to say that Hitler should not have ordered the extermination of the Jews, that it was wrong of him to have

done so. That sounds somehow "too weak" a thing to say. Instead we want to say that Hitler was an evil man. Yet we can properly say, "Hitler ought not to have ordered the extermination of the Jews," if what we mean is that it ought never to have happened; and we can say without oddity that what Hitler did was wrong. Oddity attends only the inner judgment that Hitler was wrong to have acted in that way. That is what sounds "too weak."

It is worth noting that the inner judgments sound too weak not because of the enormity of what Hitler did but because we suppose that in acting as he did he shows that he could not have been susceptible to the moral considerations on the basis of which we make our judgment. He is in the relevant sense beyond the pale and we therefore cannot make inner judgments about him. To see that this is so, consider, say, Stalin, another mass-murderer. We can perhaps imagine someone taking a sympathetic view of Stalin. In such a view, Stalin realized that the course he was going to pursue would mean the murder of millions of people and he dreaded such a prospect; however, the alternative seemed to offer an even greater disaster—so, reluctantly and with great anguish, he went ahead. In relation to such a view of Stalin, inner judgments about Stalin are not as odd as similar judgments about Hitler. For we might easily continue the story by saying that, despite what he hoped to gain, Stalin should not have undertaken the course he did, that it was wrong of him to have done so. What makes inner judgments about Hitler odd, "too weak," is not that the acts judged seem too terrible for the words used but rather that the agent judged seems beyond the pale—in other words beyond the motivational reach of the relevant moral considerations.

Of course, I do not want to deny that for various reasons a speaker might pretend that an agent is or is not susceptible to certain moral considerations. For example, a speaker may for rhetorical or political reasons wish to suggest that someone is beyond the pale, that he should not be listened to, that he can be treated as an enemy. On the other hand, a speaker may pretend that someone is susceptible to certain moral considerations in an effort to make that person or others susceptible to those considerations. Inner judgments about one's children sometimes have this function. So do inner judgments made in political speeches that aim at restoring a lapsed sense of morality in government.

II. THE LOGICAL FORM OF INNER JUDGMENTS

Inner judgments have two important characteristics. First, they imply that the agent has reasons to do something. Second, the speaker in some sense endorses these reasons and supposes that the audience also endorses them. Other moral judgments about an agent, on the other hand, do not have such implications; they do not imply that the agent has reasons for acting that are endorsed by the speaker.

If someone S says that A (morally) ought to do D, S implies that A has reasons to do D and S endorses those reasons—whereas if S says that B was evil in what B did, S does not imply that the reasons S would endorse for not doing what B did were reasons for B not to do that thing; in fact, S implies that they were not reasons for B.

Let us examine this more closely. If S says that (morally) A ought to do D, S implies that A has reasons to do D which S endorses. I shall assume that such reasons would have to have their source in goals, desires, or intentions that S takes A to have and that S approves of A's having because S shares those goals, desires, or intentions. So, if S says that (morally) A ought to do D, there are certain motivational attitudes M which S assumes are shared by S, A, and S's audience.

Now, in supposing that reasons for action must have their source in goals, desires, or intentions, I am assuming something like an Aristotelian or Humean account of these matters, as opposed, for example, to a Kantian approach which sees a possible source of motivation in reason itself. I must defer a full-scale discussion of the issue to another occasion. Here I simply assume that the Kantian approach is wrong. In particular, I assume that there might be no reasons at all for a being from outer space to avoid harm to us; that, for Hitler, there might have been no reason at all not to order the extermination of the Jews; that

the contented employee of Murder, Incorporated might have no reason at all not to kill Ortcutt; that the cannibals might have no reason not to eat their captive. In other words, I assume that the possession of rationality is not sufficient to provide a source for relevant reasons, that certain desires, goals, or intentions are also necessary. Those who accept this assumption will, I think, find that they distinguish inner moral judgments from other moral judgments in the way that I have indicated.

Ultimately, I want to argue that the shared motivational attitudes M are intentions to keep an agreement (supposing that others similarly intend). For I want to argue that inner moral judgments are made relative to such an agreement. That is, I want to argue that, when S makes the inner judgment that A ought to do D, S assumes that A intends to act in accordance with an agreement which S and S's audience also intend to observe. In other words, I want to argue that the source of the reasons for doing D which S ascribes to A is A's sincere intention to observe a certain agreement. I have not yet argued for the stronger thesis, however. I have argued only that S makes his judgment relative to *some* motivational attitudes M which S assumes are shared by S, A, and S's audience.

Formulating this as a logical thesis, I want to treat the moral "ought" as a four-place predicate (or "operator"), "Ought (A, D, C, M)," which relates an agent A, a type of act D, considerations C, and motivating attitudes M. The relativity to considerations C can be brought out by considering what are sometimes called statements of prima-facie obligation, "Considering that you promised, you ought to go to the board meeting, but considering that you are the sole surviving relative, you ought to go to the funeral; all things considered, it is not clear what you ought to do."[2] The claim that there is *this* relativity, to considerations, is not, of course, what makes my thesis a version of moral relativism, since any theory must acknowledge relativity to considerations. The relativity to considerations does, however, provide a model for a coherent interpretation of moral relativism as a similar kind of relativity.

It is not as easy to exhibit the relativity to motivating attitudes as it is to exhibit the relativity to considerations, since normally a speaker who makes a moral "ought" judgment intends the relevant motivating attitudes to be ones that the speaker shares with the agent and the audience, and normally it will be obvious what attitudes these are. But sometimes a speaker does invoke different attitudes by invoking a morality the speaker does not share. Someone may say, for example, "As a Christian, you ought to turn the other cheek; I, however, propose to strike back." A spy who has been found out by a friend might say, "As a citizen, you ought to turn me in, but I hope that you will not." In these and similar cases a speaker makes a moral "ought" judgment that is explicitly relative to motivating attitudes that the speaker does not share.

In order to be somewhat more precise, then, my thesis is this. "Ought (*A, D, C, M*)" means roughly that, given that *A* has motivating attitudes *M* and given *C*, *D* is the course of action for *A* that is supported by the best reasons. In judgments using this sense of "ought," *C* and *M* are often not explicitly mentioned [but] are indicated by the context of utterance. Normally, when that happens, *C* will be "all things considered" and *M* will be attitudes that are shared by the speaker and audience.

I mentioned that inner judgments have two characteristics. First, they imply that the agent has reasons to do something that are capable of motivating the agent. Second, the speaker endorses those reasons and supposes that the audience does too. Now, any "Ought (*A, D, C, M*)" judgment has the first of these characteristics, but as we have just seen a judgment of this sort will not necessarily have the second characteristic if made with explicit reference to motivating attitudes not shared by the speaker. If reference is made either implicitly or explicitly (for example, through the use of the adverb "morally") to attitudes that are shared by the speaker and audience, the resulting judgment has both characteristics and is an inner judgment. If reference is made to attitudes that are not shared by the speaker, the resulting judgment is not an inner judgment and does not represent a full-fledged moral judgment on the part of the speaker. In such a case we have an example of what has been called an inverted-commas use of "ought."[3]

III. MORAL BARGAINING

I have argued that moral "ought" judgments are relational, "Ought (*A, D, C, M*)," where *M* represents certain motivating attitudes. I now want to argue that the attitudes *M* derive from an agreement. That is, they are intentions to adhere to a particular agreement on the understanding that others also intend to do so. Really, it might be better for me to say that I put this forward as a hypothesis, since I cannot pretend to be able to prove that it is true. I will argue, however, that this hypothesis accounts for an otherwise puzzling aspect of our moral views that, as far as I know, there is no other way to account for.

I will use the word "intention" in a somewhat extended sense to cover certain dispositions or habits. Someone may habitually act in accordance with the relevant understanding and therefore may be disposed to act in that way without having any more or less conscious intention. In such a case it may sound odd to say that he *intends* to act in accordance with the moral understanding. Nevertheless, for present purposes I will count that as his having the relevant intention in a dispositional sense.

I now want to consider the following puzzle about our moral views, a puzzle that has figured in recent philosophical discussion of issues such as abortion. It has been observed that most of us assign greater weight to the duty not to harm others than to the duty to help others. For example, most of us believe that a doctor ought not to save five of his patients who would otherwise die by cutting up a sixth patient and distributing his healthy organs where needed to the others, even though we do think that the doctor has a duty to try to help as many of his patients as he can. For we also think that he has a stronger duty to try not to harm any of his patients (or anyone else) even if by so doing he could help five others.[4]

This aspect of our moral views can seem very puzzling, especially if one supposes that moral feelings derive from sympathy and concern for others. But the hypothesis that morality derives from an agreement among people of varying powers and resources provides a plausible explanation. The rich, the poor, the strong, and the weak would all benefit if all were to try to avoid harming one another. So everyone could agree to that arrangement. But the rich and the strong would not benefit from an arrangement whereby everyone would try to do as much as possible to help those in need. The poor and weak would get all of the benefit of this latter arrangement. Since the rich and the strong could foresee that they would be required to do most of the helping and that they would receive little in return, they would be reluctant to agree to a strong principle of mutual aid. A compromise would be likely and a weaker principle would probably be accepted. In other words, although everyone could agree to a strong principle concerning the avoidance of harm, it would not be true that everyone would favor an equally strong principle of mutual aid. It is likely that only a weaker principle of the latter sort would gain general acceptance. So the hypothesis that morality derives from an understanding among people of different powers and resources can explain (and, according to me, does explain) why in our morality avoiding harm to others is taken to be more important than helping those who need help. . . .

Now we need not suppose that the agreement or understanding in question is explicit. It is enough if various members of society knowingly reach an agreement in intentions—each intending to act in certain ways on the understanding that the others have similar intentions. Such an implicit agreement is reached through a process of mutual adjustment and implicit bargaining.

Indeed, it is essential to the proposed explanation of this aspect of our moral views to suppose that the relevant moral understanding is thus the result of *bargaining*. It is necessary to suppose that, in order to further our interests, we form certain conditional intentions, hoping that others will do the same. The others, who have different interests, will form somewhat different conditional intentions. After implicit bargaining, some sort of compromise is reached.

Seeing morality in this way as a compromise based on implicit bargaining helps to explain why our morality takes it to be worse to harm someone than to refuse to help someone. The explanation requires that we view our morality as an implicit agreement about what to do. This sort of explanation

could not be given if we were to suppose, say, that our morality represented an agreement only about the facts (naturalism). Nor is it enough simply to suppose that our morality represents an agreement in attitude, if we forget that such agreement can be reached. . . .

Many aspects of our moral views can be given a utilitarian explanation. We could account for these aspects, using the logical analysis I presented in the previous section of this paper, by supposing that the relevant "ought" judgments presuppose shared attitudes of sympathy and benevolence. We can equally well explain them by supposing that considerations of utility have influenced our implicit agreements, so that the appeal is to a shared intention to adhere to those agreements. Any aspect of morality that is susceptible of a utilitarian explanation can also be explained by an implicit agreement, but not conversely. There are aspects of our moral views that seem to be explicable only in the second way, on the assumption that morality derives from an agreement. One example, already cited, is the distinction we make between harming and not helping. Another is our feeling that each person has an inalienable right of self-defense and self-preservation. Philosophers have not been able to come up with a really satisfactory utilitarian justification of such a right, but it is easily intelligible on our present hypothesis, as Hobbes observed many years ago. You cannot, except in very special circumstances, rationally form the intention not to try to preserve your life if it should ever be threatened, say, by society or the state, since you know that you cannot now control what you would do in such a situation. No matter what you now decided to do, when the time came, you would ignore your prior decision and try to save your life. Since you cannot now intend to do something later which you now know that you would not do, you cannot now intend to keep an agreement not to preserve your life if it is threatened by others in your society. . . .

IV. OBJECTIONS AND REPLIES

. . . A . . . traditional objection to implicit agreement theories is that there is not a perfect correlation between what is generally believed to be morally right and what actually is morally right. Not everything generally agreed on is right and sometimes courses of action are right that would not be generally agreed to be right. But this is no objection to my thesis. My thesis is not that the implicit agreement from which a morality derives is an agreement in moral judgment; the thesis is rather that moral judgments make reference to and are made in relation to an agreement in intentions. Given that a group of people have agreed in this sense, there can still be disputes as to what the agreement implies for various situations. In my view, many moral disputes are of this sort. They presuppose a basic agreement and they concern what implications that agreement has for particular cases.

There can also be various things wrong with the agreement that a group of people reach, even from the point of view of that agreement, just as there can be defects in an individual's plan of action even from the point of view of that plan. Given what is known about the situation, a plan or agreement can in various ways be inconsistent, incoherent, or self-defeating. In my view, certain moral disputes are concerned with internal defects of the basic moral understanding of a group, and what changes should be made from the perspective of that understanding itself. This is another way in which moral disputes make sense with reference to and in relation to an underlying agreement.

Another objection to implicit agreement theories is that not all agreements are morally binding—for example, those made under compulsion or from a position of unfair disadvantage, which may seem to indicate that there are moral principles prior to those that derive from an implicit agreement. But, again, the force of the objection derives from an equivocation concerning what an agreement is. The principle that compelled agreements do not obligate concerns agreement in the sense of a certain sort of ritual indicating that one agrees. My thesis concerns a kind of agreement in intentions. The principle about compelled agreements is part of, or is implied by, our agreement in intentions. According to me it is only with reference to some such agreement in intentions that a principle of this sort makes sense.

Now it may be true our moral agreement in intentions also implies that it is wrong to compel people who are in a greatly inferior position to accept an agreement in intentions that they would not otherwise accept, and it may even be true that there is in our society at least one class of people in an inferior position who have been compelled thus to settle for accepting a basic moral understanding, aspects of which they would not have accepted had they not been in such an inferior position. In that case there would be an incoherence in our basic moral understanding and various suggestions might be made concerning the ways in which this understanding should be modified. But this moral critique of the understanding can proceed from that understanding itself rather than from "prior" moral principles.

In order to fix ideas, let us consider a society in which there is a well-established and long-standing tradition of hereditary slavery. Let us suppose that everyone accepts this institution, including the slaves. Everyone treats it as in the nature of things that there should be such slavery. Furthermore, let us suppose that there are also aspects of the basic moral agreement which speak against slavery. That is, these aspects together with certain facts about the situation imply that people should not own slaves and that slaves have no obligation to acquiesce in their condition. In such a case, the moral understanding would be defective, although its defectiveness would presumably be hidden in one or another manner, perhaps by means of a myth that slaves are physically and mentally subhuman in a way that makes appropriate the sort of treatment elsewhere reserved for beasts of burden. If this myth were to be exposed, the members of the society would then be faced with an obvious incoherence in their basic moral agreement and might come eventually to modify their agreement so as to eliminate its acceptance of slavery.

In such a case, even relative to the old agreement it might be true that slave owners ought to free their slaves, that slaves need not obey their masters, and that people ought to work to eliminate slavery. For the course supported by the best reasons, given that one starts out with the intention of adhering to a particular agreement, may be that one should stop intending to adhere to certain aspects of that agreement and should try to get others to do the same.

We can also . . . envision a second society with hereditary slavery whose agreement has no aspects that speak against slavery. In that case, even if the facts of the situation were fully appreciated, no incoherence would appear in the basic moral understanding of the society and it would not be true in relation to that understanding that slave owners ought to free their slaves, that slaves need not obey their masters, and so forth. There might nevertheless come a time when there were reasons of a different sort to modify the basic understanding, either because of an external threat from societies opposed to slavery or because of an internal threat of rebellion by the slaves.

Now it is easier for us to make what I have called inner moral judgments about slave owners in the first society than in the second. For we can with reference to members of the first society invoke principles that they share with us and, with reference to those principles, we can say of them that they ought not to have kept slaves and that they were immoral to have done so. This sort of inner judgment becomes increasingly inappropriate, however, the more distant they are from us and the less easy it is for us to think of our moral understanding as continuous with and perhaps a later development of theirs. Furthermore, it seems appropriate to make only non-inner judgments of the slave owners in the second society. We can say that the second society is unfair and unjust, that the slavery that exists is wrong, that it ought not to exist. But it would be inappropriate in this case to say that it was morally wrong of the slave owners to own slaves. The relevant aspects of our moral understanding, which we would invoke in moral judgments about them, are not aspects of the moral understanding that exists in the second society. . . .

The vague nature of moral understandings is to some extent alleviated in practice. One learns what can and cannot be done in various situations. Expectations are adjusted to other expectations. But moral disputes arise nonetheless. Such disputes may concern what the basic moral agreement implies for particular situations; and, if so, that can happen either because of disputes over the facts or because

of a difference in basic understanding. Moral disputes may also arise concerning whether or not changes should be made in the basic agreement. Racial and sexual issues seem often to be of this second sort; but there is no clear line between the two kinds of dispute. When the implications of an agreement for a particular situation are considered, one possible outcome is that it becomes clear that the agreement should be modified.

Moral reasoning is a form of practical reasoning. One begins with certain beliefs and intentions, including intentions that are part of one's acceptance of the moral understanding in a given group. In reasoning, one modifies one's intentions, often by forming new intentions, sometimes by giving up old ones, so that one's plans become more rational and coherent—or, rather, one seeks to make all of one's attitudes coherent with each other.

The relevant sort of coherence is not simply consistency. It is something very like the explanatory coherence which is so important in theoretical reasoning. Coherence involves generality and lack of arbitrariness. Consider our feelings about cruelty to animals. Obviously these do not derive from an agreement that has been reached with animals. Instead it is a matter of coherence. There is a prima-facie arbitrariness and lack of generality in a plan that involves avoiding cruelty to people but not to animals.

On the other hand, coherence in this sense is not the only relevant factor in practical reasoning. Another is conservatism or inertia. A third is an interest in satisfying basic desires or needs. One tries to make the least change that will best satisfy one's desires while maximizing the overall coherence of one's attitudes. Coherence by itself is not an overwhelming force. That is why our attitudes towards animals are weak and wavering, allowing us to use them in ways we would not use people. . . .

It should be noted that coherence of attitude provides a constant pressure to widen the consensus and eliminate arbitrary distinctions. In this connection it is useful to recall ancient attitudes toward foreigners, and the ways people used to think about "savages," "natives," and "Indians." Also, recall that infanticide used to be considered as acceptable as we consider abortion to be. There has been a change here in our moral attitudes, prompted, I suggest, largely by considerations of coherence of attitude. . . .

My conclusion is that relativism can be formulated as an intelligible thesis, the thesis that morality derives from an implicit agreement and that moral judgments are in a logical sense made in relation to such an agreement. Such a theory helps to explain otherwise puzzling aspects of our own moral views, in particular why we think that it is more important to avoid harm to others than to help others. The theory is also partially confirmed by what is, as far as I can tell, a previously unnoticed distinction between inner and non-inner moral judgments. . . .

NOTES

1. Bernard Williams, *Morality: An Introduction to Ethics* (New York, N.Y.: Harper & Row, 1972), pp. 20–21; Marcus Singer, *Generalization in Ethics* (New York, N.Y.: Knopf, 1961), p. 332.
2. See Donald Davidson, "Weakness of Will," in Joel Feinberg (ed.), *Moral Concepts* (Oxford: Oxford University Press, 1969).
3. R. M. Hare, *The Language of Morals* (Oxford: Oxford University Press, 1952), pp. 164–168.
4. Philippa Foot, "Abortion and the Doctrine of Double Effect," in James Rachels (ed.), *Moral Problems* (New York, N.Y.: Harper & Row, 1971).

STUDY QUESTIONS

1. Does Harman's version of moral relativism escape the charge of inconsistency?
2. What does Harman mean by an "inner judgment"?
3. What is the best explanation of why we disagree about moral judgments?
4. Could a group consistently hold that slavery is permissible?

Harman and Moral Relativism

Stephen Darwall

Stephen Darwall, Professor of Philosophy at Yale University, attempts to undermine Harman's arguments for moral relativism. Harman's crucial premise is that agents ought to act only when doing so realizes the agent's desires or ends. Harman's main argument for this premise relies on linguistic evidence. He emphasizes the oddness of saying you ought to do something when you do not care about doing it. Darwall maintains, however, that linguistic evidence is often misleading. For example, the oddness of saying "I see you are eating today" does nothing to impugn the truth of the statement. In addition, Darwall argues that the shared intentions of a group are neither necessary nor sufficient for morality. Conventions of the road reflect shared intentions but are not thereby sufficient to be moral principles. And even if we find ourselves in a society of murderers, their agreement is not necessary for murder of the innocent to be immoral. Darwall thus concludes that Harman has failed to make a persuasive case for his version of moral relativism.

I

Gilbert Harman has recently defended a thesis which he characterizes as a version of moral relativism.[1] Though the thesis has the virtue of being internally consistent (unlike some versions of moral relativism) I want to argue that it is unsupported by Harman's arguments.

Harman's claim is that a restricted class of moral judgments, which he terms 'inner judgments,' only make sense (and are true or false) in relation to an agreement or understanding that obtains between the person of whom the judgment is made and some larger group of people. Judgments such as 'it was right (wrong) of S to do X' and 'S ought (not) to have done X' are claimed to be implicitly relational in

that they refer to an agreement in intentions between S and other people. This agreement consists in its being true of each person that he intends to do X (in such circumstances) on the understanding that the others similarly intend. Thus whether or not a given inner judgment is true of someone's doing or failing to do something will depend on whether or not the action in question bears the proper relation to such an agreement; and thus, whether the person shares such an intention. The truth of inner judgments is relative, therefore, to the having of such shared intentions.

Harman's arguments for this view proceed in two different stages. In the first stage Harman is concerned to show that inner judgments are expressed by sentences of the form 'A ought (morally) to have

From Stephen Darwall, "Harman and Moral Relativism," *Personalist* 58 (1977). Reprinted by permission of the publisher.

done D' and that the 'ought' in such judgments is a four-place predicate or operator which relates an agent (A), a type of act (D), considerations (C), and motivating attitudes (M). Thus the truth of the judgment that somebody ought (morally) to have done something depends on the proper relation obtaining between the act in question, various considerations, and motivating attitudes which the agent actually had. If it is false that the agent had the relevant motivating attitudes, then the claim that he (morally) ought to have done something will be false. This is the way in which the truth of such inner judgments is held to be relative to the agent's having the appropriate motivating attitudes. In the second stage Harman argues that the appropriate motivating attitudes to which the truth of inner judgments is relative are agreements or shared intentions. Again, such agreements consist in its being true that each person of a group intends to do something on the understanding that others similarly intend.

II

A. The notion of an inner judgment is introduced by Harman in three rather different ways: (i) It is initially introduced by way of example, "such as the judgment that someone ought or ought not to have acted in a certain way or the judgment that it was right or wrong of him to have done so" (p. 4). (ii) Just after he has given these examples, Harman makes the following claim: "We make inner judgments about a person only if we suppose that he is capable of being motivated by the relevant moral considerations" (p. 4). (iii) Finally, Harman makes the claim that inner judgments are "used to describe a relation between an agent and an act" (p. 7) as opposed to other moral judgments such as that a certain kind of act is wrong or that certain situations ought not to exist.

One is a little puzzled about the status of these different claims about inner judgments. Is the notion ostensively defined *via* the examples and then the remaining two claims offered as substantive truths? Or is the notion introduced through either the second or third claims (or their conjunction) and it then

claimed that (moral) 'ought to do' judgments have the indicated properties? Harman is unclear on this.

Suppose the former. Is it true that moral 'ought to do' judgments always, or even typically, express an assessment of a relation between an agent and his action as opposed to an assessment of his action itself? Consider the use of such judgments in prospect, during the process of deliberation or the giving of advice. To believe, in prospect, that one ought (morally) to do something is to believe that moral considerations are such as to favor (or perhaps require) a particular action. In deciding what to do one is typically more concerned with the grounds that there are for and against a particular action rather than one's actual relation to the action (since this is something which one's accepting or rejecting such grounds will itself establish). Or, correlatively, if someone does the right thing for the wrong reasons, we can sensibly describe what has happened by saying that he did what he ought to have done, though he did it for the wrong reasons. So it is certainly not obvious that all 'ought to do' judgments have the properties indicated in the second two claims.

B. Still, it is arguably the case that if 'ought' entails (presupposes?) 'can,' then if S ought to have done something, then it must be true that he could have done it. And we may take this to imply that the person was capable of being motivated by those considerations which ground the claim that he ought to have done it. If this is true, an 'ought to do' judgment will be true just in case it is true that the agent was such that he was capable of being motivated to perform the action by the relevant considerations. Thus the truth of an 'ought to do' judgment will presuppose that a kind of relation obtains between the agent and the action. Namely, that the agent was capable of being motivated by the relevant considerations to perform the action. It might be thought that to grant Harman this much of an internalist thesis would be to give away the game. I hope to show that this is not the case. Accordingly, I shall assume that if it is true that A ought to have done D because of considerations C, then it is true that A was capable of being motivated by considerations C to do A.

The question now becomes, what does the capacity to be motivated by a consideration consist in?

Harman's explicit answer to this is that no consideration is capable of motivating someone unless it has its "source" in goals, desires, or intentions that the agent has as a matter of fact (p. 9). But what precisely does this come to? Sometimes Harman talks as if a fact can be a reason for someone, and that a person is capable of being motivated by it, only if it would actually weigh with him:

> Now, in this case it would be a misuse of language to say of him that he ought not to kill Ortcutt or that it would be wrong of him to do so, since that would imply that our own moral considerations carry some weight with him (p. 5).

Thus one might suppose Harman to be saying that a person is capable of being motivated by some consideration on the condition that he would be moved by it if certain circumstances were to obtain. But what circumstances? . . .

Harman's view seems to be that a person is capable of being motivated by some consideration just in case the consideration has its source in the person's goals, desires, or intentions, in the following sense: namely, that the consideration is evidence that in acting the person will realize (or tend to realize) some goal, desire, or intention which he has. This, then, specifies how the 'ought' in 'ought to do' judgments is a four-place operator. Unless the relevant considerations show the action to stand in the specified relation to the agent's goals, desires, and intentions (namely that acting will tend to realize them), then it is false that the agent is capable of being motivated by those considerations. And hence false that he ought to perform the indicated action. What are Harman's arguments for this position?

C. There are two rather different arguments. One is an argument from linguistic oddness, the second from an assumption about the nature of practical rationality. Harman notes that it is odd to say that somebody ought to have done something for some reason when the speaker knows that the person cared nothing at all about the consideration in question. For example, according to Harman it would be odd to say that it was wrong of Hitler to have ordered the extermination of the Jews or that he ought not to

have done that. Since such judgments are odd, Harman concludes that they must be false.

But there are many reasons why an utterance may be odd which are quite consistent with the truth of what is said. Indeed, Harman himself offers such an explanation of the present example. To say merely that Hitler ought not to have ordered the extermination of the Jews is to say something which is too weak (p. 7). But from the fact that it is too weak to say merely that Hitler ought not to have done what he did it by no means follows that it is false. It is likewise too weak to say of someone who wins a head to head mile run for the world's championship that he came in next to last in the race, but it is true nonetheless. . . .

Similar remarks apply, for example, to Harman's observation that it would be odd to say of an employee of Murder, Inc. that he ought not to kill Ortcutt. Such an utterance might be odd because it is just too obvious. Much as it would almost always be odd to say to a friend, "I see that you are wearing clothes today."

So even if one accepts Harman's claims of oddness there seem to be other explanations ready at hand which explain that oddness, making the hypothesis that the judgment is false unnecessary.

D. Harman seems to believe that there is a second line of argument to the relativity of inner judgments from a plausible assumption about the nature of practical rationality. And this is just the assumption that reasons for acting must "have their source" in the agent's goals, desires, or intentions:

> Those who accept this assumption will, I think, find that they distinguish inner moral judgments from other moral judgments in the way that I have indicated (p. 9).

If we are to understand this assumption in the way that I suggested earlier, and a look at the surrounding text shows this to be the most natural reading, the assumption is rather strong. It requires that a fact is a reason for someone to do something just in case it shows that action to be such as to realize or to be a means for realizing some desire, intention, or goal that the agent in fact has. This amounts to assuming that the truth of a judgment regarding the reasons that there are for someone to do something has the same relativity as is claimed for inner judgments. It is no surprise that those who accept this assumption should find that they likewise accept the relativity of inner judgments. For all that one needs to derive the relativity of inner judgments from the assumption is the added premise that if it is true that someone ought to do something, then it is true that there is reason for him to do it. And that seems fairly uncontroversial.

The problem with this as an argument, of course, is that it is most unlikely that anyone not already convinced of the relativity of inner judgments will or should be moved by it. Someone who is initially doubtful of Harman's conclusion will probably be equally doubtful of the assumption. Anyone who is inclined to doubt whether the truth of the claim "It was wrong of S to have tapped T's phone" depends on whether S's forbearing such action would have promoted one of his ends will be equally likely to doubt whether the truth of "There was reason for S not to have tapped T's phone" must depend in the same way on whether his forbearance would have promoted one of his ends. . . .

III

A. None of Harman's arguments for the claim that the 'ought' of moral 'ought to do' judgments expresses the stated four-place relation is capable of establishing that claim. Or at any rate, none is thus capable short of making an extraordinarily strong and controversial assumption. Accordingly an important step in his argument for the relativity of moral 'ought to do' judgments to the shared intentions which constitute an agreement among a group of persons is left without much support. To that extent the conclusion of the second stage of the argument, since it depends on the first, is likewise unsupported.

Still, one might advance Harman's claim that "morality arises when a group of people reach an implicit agreement or come to a tacit understanding about their relations with one another" (p. 3)

independently of the considerations advanced in the first stage. Let us then consider independently of Harman's arguments about the relativity of inner judgments, his thesis that morality consists in an implicit agreement in intentions within a group of persons to do something on the understanding that others similarly intend. If this were what morality is, then fairly clearly what is moral (within a group) would depend on the nature of the agreement in such intentions which actually characterizes that group. That is, moral questions could only arise and be settled relative to such an agreement.

B. Clearly not just any such agreement in intentions can yield morality. Two drivers sit at the red light revving up their engines. Each one sees the other and understands that the other will try to get away from the light the fastest on the understanding that the other similarly intends. There is the requisite agreement in intentions, but clearly no moral 'ought' arises. It would not be wrong of either to move slowly away from the light.

Similar examples abound. Harman mentions two himself: conventions of the road and conventions of etiquette. Though he says that these instances of shared intentions are to be distinguished from moral agreements, one wants to know, on what grounds? What are the conditions on agreements in intention which must be satisfied in order for the agreement to give rise to morality?

C. Still, one may wonder, is agreement in intention a necessary condition of morality? The model fits best in cases where a moral 'ought' arises because of considerations of justice. Suppose there is a gasoline crisis and a voluntary program is instituted whereby drivers are only to buy six gallons of gas a week. People are bound by justice (or fairness) to comply on the understanding that others will similarly comply. If as a matter of fact no one (or relatively few others) do in fact comply—that is, if the agreement in intentions to comply on the understanding that others do does not hold—then there is no obligation of justice to comply. One is obligated to do one's fair share on the condition that others will also. But if the agreement in intentions necessary for the functioning of the program does not exist, then one is under no obligation of fairness to do what one would be obligated to do if others were doing their part. Thus, it will in general be true that in order for a moral 'ought' to arise in virtue of considerations of justice (in the sort of case instanced) there will have to be the sort of agreement in intentions that Harman claims. Notice that even here the conditional 'ought' judgment, that one ought do one's part on the understanding that others will, does not itself arise out of an agreement in intentions.

D. Let us consider, though, cases where moral 'oughts' seem to arise without the requisite agreement in intentions. Suppose one finds oneself in an area peopled by wanton murderers, does the wrongness of wantonly murdering someone disappear? One will have increased reasons of self-defense for killing others in such circumstances, and *perhaps* reasons strong enough to justify a preemptive strike. But I take it that it would be wrong in such circumstances wantonly to murder one of them. And furthermore its being wrong could not depend on their agreeing with one in having the intention to forgo wanton murder on the understanding that others will, since *ex hypothesi* there is no such agreement. This sort of example is not offered as a conclusive counterexample to Harman's view. Rather it is intended to show that insofar as Harman offers his view as an hypothesis which is designed to account for various aspects of our moral views there will be some recalcitrant data.

E. Harman's argument that morality does consist in an agreement is that it is such an hypothesis:

> . . . this hypothesis accounts for an otherwise puzzling aspect of our moral views that, as far as I know, there is no other way to account for (p. 12).

The puzzling aspect referred to is that we assign a greater weight to the duty not to harm others than we do to the duty to help them. Harman's hypothesis explains this fact because not everyone, in particular not the wealthy, would agree to do as much as possible to help others (since they would stand to lose, relatively speaking, by such an agreement). However, everyone (rich and poor alike) could agree not to harm other people. Thus regarding morality as an agreement in conditional intentions serves to explain this puzzling fact.

Any inference to the best explanation in this instance depends on the unavailability of other plausible explanations of this feature of our moral view. But surely there are several possible (and less cynical) ones. A rule-utilitarian might explain the asymmetry by considering the utility created by the adopting, respectively, of a stronger and weaker rule for the helping of others (together with a rule against harming others). Coordination problems arise in the helping of others. If there is no scheme allocating particular responsibilities, following the one rule "help others whenever possible" is likely to lead to inefficiencies. A strong rule for the helping of others would undercut each person's own ability to plan and lead his own life (after all, there are always others to be helped). Thus the net effect of having that rule may be worse than would be the net effect of having a weaker rule for the helping of others. More considerations come to mind as soon as one thinks about it. . . .

One could mention other contending moral theories which could provide some explanation of Harman's puzzling fact. However, the [one] mentioned should suffice to show that there are significant theoretical alternatives to Harman's view which explain why we don't think that people ought to direct all of their efforts to the helping of other people. In both instances there will be arguments available to strong rules against harming others, however. Usually one does not have to to go out of one's way to avoid harming others, though often one will have to help them—especially if one is to do all that one can to help them. The presence of alternative explanations of the data together with data which is recalcitrant to Harman's theory suggests that the view that morality consists in an implicit agreement in intentions, and accordingly that what is moral is relative to such an actual agreement, is unsupported.

F. I conclude that the main arguments of both stages of Harman's case for his version of moral relativism are defective. He has not shown that inner moral judgments are relative to the actual motivating attitudes of persons in the way claimed. Nor has he shown that what is moral can only be determined relative to an actual agreement in conditional intentions which holds among a group of people.

NOTE

1. Gilbert Harman, "Moral Relativism Defended," *Philosophical Review*, LXXXIV (1975), 3–22. Further references to this article will occur parenthetically in the text.

STUDY QUESTIONS

1. In what respects, if any, does Darwall fail to do justice to Harman's defense of moral relativism?
2. What are Darwall's major criticisms of Harman's view?
3. If Harman can offer a persuasive reply to Darwall, has Harman thereby proven the truth of moral relativism?
4. If Harman cannot offer a persuasive reply to Darwall, what conclusions, if any, follow about the nature of morality?

Part VII

RESPONSE DEPENDENCE

Dispositional Theories of Value

David Lewis

David Lewis (1941–2001) was Professor of Philosophy at Princeton University. He defends the view that something is valuable if and only if we would be disposed to value it under ideal circumstances. Lewis refines this definition in a couple of respects. Because the definition is obviously circular, he argues that we should replace "value" with "desire to desire." In addition, we need to specify ideal circumstances for valuing. These are ones in which we think hard and imagine vividly and thoroughly, a situation he terms the fullest possible "imaginative acquaintance." With these two clarifications, Lewis's theory is that something is valuable if and only if we would be disposed to desire to desire it under circumstances of the fullest possible imaginative acquaintance. This definition is, he claims, analytic but not obviously so.

Roughly, values are what we are disposed to value. Less roughly, we have this schematic definition: *Something of the appropriate category is a value if and only if we would be disposed, under ideal conditions, to value it.* It raises five questions. (1) What is the favorable attitude of "valuing"? (2) What is the "appropriate category" of things? (3) What conditions are "ideal" for valuing? (4) Who are "we"? (5) What is the modal status of the equivalence?

By answering these questions, I shall advance a version of the dispositional theory of value. I begin by classifying the theory that is going to emerge. First, it is naturalistic: it advances an analytic definition of value. It is naturalistic in another sense too: it fits into a naturalistic metaphysics. It invokes only such entities and distinctions as we need to believe in anyway, and needs nothing extra before it can deliver the values. It reduces facts about value to facts about our psychology.

The theory is subjective: it analyzes value in terms of our attitudes. But it is not subjective in the narrower sense of implying that value is a topic on which whatever we may think is automatically true, or on which there is no truth at all. Nor does it imply that if we had been differently disposed, different things would have been values. Not quite—but it comes too close for comfort.

The theory is internalist: it makes a conceptual connection between value and motivation. But it offers no guarantee that everyone must be motivated to pursue whatever is of value; still less, whatever he judges to be of value. The connection is defeasible, in more ways than one.

The theory is cognitive: it allows us to seek and to gain knowledge about what is valuable. This knowledge is *a posteriori* knowledge of contingent matters of fact. It could in principle be gained by psychological experimentation. But it is more likely

From David Lewis, "Dispositional Theories of Value," *Proceedings of the Aristotelian Society* 63 (1989). Reprinted by permission of the publisher.

to be gained by difficult exercises of imagination, carried out perhaps in a philosopher's or a novelist's armchair.

The theory is conditionally relativist: it does not exclude the possibility that there may be no such thing as value *simpliciter,* just value for this or that population. But it does not imply relativity, not even when taken together with what we know about the diversity of what people actually value. It leaves the question open.

Is it a form of realism about value?—That question is hard. I leave it for the end.

What is "valuing"? It is some sort of mental state, directed toward that which is valued. It might be a feeling, or a belief, or a desire. (Or a combination of these; or something that is two or three of them at once; or some fourth thing. But let us set these hypotheses aside, and hope to get by with something simpler.[1])

A feeling?—Evidently not, because the feelings we have when we value things are too diverse.

A belief? What belief? You might say that one values something just by believing it to be a value. That is circular. We might hide the circularity by maneuvering between near-synonyms, but it is better to face it at once. If so, we have that being a value is some property such that something has it iff we are disposed, under ideal conditions, to believe that the thing has it. In other words, such that we are disposed, under ideal conditions, to be right about whether something has it. That is not empty; but it tells us little, since doubtless there are many properties about which we are disposed to be right.

Further, if valuing something just meant having a certain belief about it, then it seems that there would be no conceptual reason why valuing is a *favorable* attitude. We might not have favored the things we value. We might have opposed them, or been entirely indifferent.

So we turn to desires. But we'd better not say that valuing something is just the same as desiring it. That may do for some of us: those who manage, by strength of will or by good luck, to desire exactly as they desire to desire. But not all of us are so fortunate. The thoughtful addict may desire his euphoric daze, but not value it. Even apart from all the costs and risks, he may hate himself for desiring something he values not at all. It is a desire he wants very much to be rid of. He desires his high, but he does not desire to desire it, and in fact he desires not to desire it. He does not desire an unaltered, mundane state of consciousness, but he does desire to desire it. We conclude that he does not value what he desires, but rather he values what he desires to desire.

Can we do better by climbing the ladder to desires of ever-higher order? What someone desires to desire to desire might conceivably differ from what he does desire to desire. Or. . . . Should we perhaps say that what a person really values is given by his highest order of desire, whatever order that is?—It is hard to tell whether this would really be better, because it is hard to imagine proper test cases.[2] Further, if we go for the highest order, we automatically rule out the case of someone who desires to *value* differently than he does, yet this case is not obviously impossible. I hesitantly conclude we do better to stop on the second rung: valuing is just desiring to desire.

Recall G. E. Moore: "To take, for instance, one of the more plausible, because one of the more complicated, of such proposed definitions, it may easily be thought, at first sight, that to be good may mean to be that which we desire to desire."[3] Of course he does not endorse the definition, but at least he does it the honor of choosing it for his target to display the open question argument. I don't say that everything we value is good; but I do echo Moore to this extent. I say that to be *valued* by us means to be that which we desire to desire. Then to be a value—to be good, near enough—means to be that which we are disposed, under ideal conditions, to desire to desire. Still more complicated, still more plausible. It allows, as it should, that under less-than-ideal conditions we may wrongly value what is not really good. As for Moore's open question, we shall face that later.

We have this much of an "internalist" conceptual connection between value and motivation. If something is a value, and if someone is one of the appropriate "we," and if he is in ideal conditions, then it follows that he will value it. And if he values it, and if he desires as he desires to desire, then he will desire it. And if he desires it, and if this desire is not outweighed by other conflicting desires, and if he has the instrumental rationality to do what serves his desires according to his beliefs, then he will pursue it. And if the relevant beliefs are near enough true, then he will pursue it as effectively as possible. A conceptual connection between value and motivation, sure enough—but a multifariously iffy connection. Nothing less iffy would be credible. But still less is it credible that there is no connection at all.

In general, to find out whether something is disposed to give response R under conditions C, you can put it in C and find out whether you get R. That is a canonical way to learn whether the disposition is present, though surely not the only possible way. If a dispositional theory of value is true, then we have a canonical way to find out whether something is a value. To find out whether we would be disposed, under ideal conditions, to value it, put yourself in ideal conditions, if you can, making sure you can tell when you have succeeded in doing so. Then find out whether you value the thing in question, i.e. whether you desire to desire it. If you do, that confirms that it is a value. (I assume you are one of the appropriate "we" and you know it.) Now we have this much of an "internalist" conceptual connection between value judgements and motivation. It is even iffier than the connection between value itself and motivation; and again I say that if it were less iffy, it would be less credible. If someone believes that something is a value, and if he has come to this belief by the canonical method, and if he has remained in ideal conditions afterward or else retained the desire to desire that he had when in ideal conditions, then it follows that he values that thing. And if he desires as he desires to desire, then he desires that thing; and so on as before.

The connection is not with the judgement of value *per se,* but with the canonical way of coming to it. If someone reached the same judgement in some non-canonical way—as he might—that would imply nothing about his valuing or desiring or pursuing.

What is the "appropriate category"? If values are what we are disposed to desire to desire, then the things that can be values must be among the things that can be desired. Those fall into two classes.

Sometimes, what one desires is that the world should be a certain way: that it should realize one of a certain class of (maximally specific, qualitatively delineated) possibilities for the whole world. This class—a "proposition," in one sense of that word—gives the content of the desire. To desire that the world realize some possibility within the class is to desire that the proposition be true. Call this "desire *de dicto.*"

But sometimes, what one desires concerns not just the world but oneself: one simply desires to *be* a certain way. For instance, Fred might want to be healthy, or wealthy, or wise. Then what he wants is that he himself should realize one of a certain class of (maximally specific, qualitatively delineated) possibilities for an individual—or better, for an individual-in-a-world-at-a-time. This class—a "property" in one sense of that word, or an "egocentric proposition"—gives the content of the desire. To desire to realize some possibility in the class is to desire to have the property, or to desire that the egocentric proposition be true of one. Call this "desire *de se,*" or "egocentric" or "essentially indexical" desire.

You might think to reduce desire *de se* to desire *de dicto,* saying that if Arthur desires to be happy, what he desires is that the world be such that Arthur is happy. (You might doubt that such worlds comprise a qualitatively delineated class, so you might consider dropping that requirement.) But no. That is not exactly the same thing, though the difference shows up only when we imagine someone who is wrong or unsure about who in the world he is. Suppose Arthur thinks he is Martha. If Arthur is self-centered he may desire to be happy, desire that the world be one wherein Martha is happy, but not desire that the world is one wherein Arthur is happy. If instead Arthur is selflessly benevolent he may not desire to be happy, yet he may desire that the world be such that Arthur is happy. If Arthur is so befuddled as not to know whether he is Arthur or Martha, but hopes he is Arthur, he does not just desire that the world be such that Arthur is self-identical! In all these cases, Arthur's desire is, at least in part, irreducibly *de se*.[4]

When we acknowledge desires *de se,* we must distinguish two senses of "desiring the same thing." If Jack Sprat and his wife both prefer fat meat, they *desire alike.* They are psychological duplicates, on this matter at least. But they do not *agree* in their desires, because no possible arrangement could satisfy them both. Whereas if Jack prefers the fat and his wife prefers the lean, then they differ psychologically, they do not desire alike. But they do agree, because if he eats no fat and she eats no lean, that would satisfy them both. In general, they desire alike iff they desire *de se* to have exactly the same properties and they desire *de dicto* that exactly the same propositions hold. They agree in desires iff exactly the same world would satisfy the desires of both; and a world that satisfies someone's desires is one wherein he has all the properties that he desires *de se* and wherein all the propositions hold that he desires *de dicto.* Agreement in desire makes for harmony; desiring alike may well make for strife.

As we can desire *de dicto* or *de se,* so we can desire to desire *de dicto* or *de se.* If desiring to desire is valuing, and if values are what we are disposed to value, then we must distinguish values *de dicto* and *de se.* A value *de dicto* is a proposition such that we are disposed to desire to desire *de dicto* that it hold. A value *de se* is a property such that we are disposed to desire to desire *de se* to have it.

It is essential to distinguish. Consider egoism: roughly, the thesis that one's own happiness is the only value. Egoism is meant to be general. It is not the thesis that the happiness of a certain special person, say Thrasymachus, is the only value. Egoism *de dicto* says that for each person X, the proposition that X is happy is the only value. That is inconsistent, as Moore observed.[5] It says that there are as many different values as there are people, and each of them is the only value. Egoism *de se* says that the property of happiness—in other words, the egocentric proposition that one is happy—is the only value. Moore did not confute that. He ignored it. False and ugly though it be, egoism *de se* is at least a consistent doctrine. What it alleges to be the only value would

indeed be just *one* value *de se,* not a multitude of values *de dicto.*

Insofar as values are *de se,* the wholehearted pursuit by everyone of the same genuine value will not necessarily result in harmony. All might value alike, valuing *de se* the same properties and valuing *de dicto* the same propositions. Insofar as they succeed in desiring as they desire to desire, they will desire alike. But that does not ensure that they will agree in desire. If egoism *de se* were true, and if happiness could best be pursued by doing others down and winning extra shares, then the pursuit by all of the very same single value would be the war of all against all.

Because egoism is false and ugly, we might be glad of a theoretical framework that allowed us to confute it *a priori.* And some of us might welcome a framework that promises us harmony, if only we can all manage to pursue the same genuine values. Was it right, then, to make a place for values *de se*? Should we have stipulated, instead, that something we are disposed to desire to desire shall count as a value only when it is a proposition that we are disposed to desire to desire *de dicto*?

No. Probably it is already wrong to reject egoism *a priori* but, be that as it may, there are other doctrines of value *de se,* more plausible and more attractive. Self-improvement and self-sacrifice are no less egocentric than self-aggrandizement and self-indulgence. Surely we should make a place for putative values *de se* of altruism, of honor, and of loyalty to family, friends, and country. We may entertain the substantive thesis that none of these putative values *de se* is genuine, and that all genuine values are *de dicto.* But even if we believed this—myself, I think it wildly unlikely—we should not beg the question in its favor by building it into our theoretical framework.

What conditions are "ideal"? If someone has little notion what it would be like to live as a free spirit unbound by law, custom, loyalty, or love; or what a world of complete harmony and constant agreement would be like; then whether or not he blindly values these things must have little to do with whether or not they are truly values. What he lacks is imaginative acquaintance. If only he would think harder, and imagine vividly and thoroughly how it would be if these putative values were realized (and perhaps also how it would be if they were not) that would make his valuing a more reliable indicator of genuine value. And if he could gain the fullest imaginative acquaintance that is humanly possible,[6] then, I suggest, his valuing would be an infallible indicator. Something is a value iff we are disposed, under conditions of the fullest possible imaginative acquaintance, to value it.

Compare a version of Intuitionism: by hard thought, one becomes imaginatively well acquainted with X; in consequence, but not as the conclusion of any sort of inference, one intuits that X has a certain unanalyzable, non-natural property; and in consequence of that, one comes to value X. My story begins and ends the same. Only the middle is missing. Again, an exercise of imaginative reason plays a crucial role. Again, its relation to what follows is causal, and in no way inferential. But in my story, the consequent valuing is caused more directly, not via the detection of a peculiar property of X.

Can we say that the valuing ensued because X was a value?—Maybe so, but if we do, we are not saying much: it ensues because there is something about imaginative acquaintance with X that causes valuing.

The canonical way to find out whether something is a value requires a difficult imaginative exercise. And if you are to be sure of your answer, you need to be sure that you have gained the fullest imaginative acquaintance that is humanly possible. A tall order! You had better settle for less. Approximate the canonical test. Try hard to imagine how it would be if the putative value were (or were not) realized. Hope that your acquaintance comes close enough to the fullest possible that getting closer would not change your response. Then you may take your valuing as fallible evidence that you were acquainted with a genuine value, or your indifference as fallible evidence that you were not. You cannot be perfectly certain of your answer, but you can take it as sure enough to be going on with, subject to reconsideration in the light of new evidence. How sure is that?—Well, as always when we acknowledge fallibility, some of us will be bolder than others.

New evidence might be a more adequate imaginative exercise of your own. It might be the testimony of others. It might in principle be a result of scientific psychology—though it is far from likely that any such results will come to hand soon!

A trajectory toward fuller imaginative acquaintance with putative value X is not just a sequence of changes in your imaginative state. It has a direction to it. And that is so independently of my claim that it leads, after a point, to ever-surer knowledge about whether X is a value. For in learning how to imagine X, you gain abilities; later you have all the relevant imaginative abilities you had before, and more besides. And you notice, *a priori,* relationships of coherence or incoherence between attitudes that might figure in the realization of X; later you are aware of all that you had noticed before, and more besides. And you think of new questions to explore in your imagining—what might the life of the free spirit become, long years after its novelty had worn off?—and later you have in mind all the questions you had thought of before, and more besides. Forgetting is possible, of course. But by and large, the process resists reversal.

Our theory makes a place for truth, and in principle for certain knowledge, and in practice for less-than-certain knowledge, about value. But also it makes a place for ignorance and error, for hesitant opinion and modesty, for trying to learn more and hoping to succeed. That is all to the good. One fault of some subjective and prescriptive theories is that they leave no room for modesty: just decide where you stand, then you may judge of value with the utmost confidence!

There is a long history of theories that analyze value in terms of hypothetical response under ideal conditions, with various suggestions about what conditions are ideal. Imaginative acquaintance often gets a mention. But much else does too. I think imaginative acquaintance is all we need—the rest should be in part subsumed, in part rejected.

First, the responder is often called an ideal *spectator.* That is tantamount to saying that conditions are ideal only when he is observing a sample of the putative value in question (or of its absence). If the putative value is *de se,* a property, then a sample can just be an instance. If it is *de dicto,* a proposition, it is hard to say in general what an observable sample could be. But if it is the proposition that a certain property is instantiated sometimes, or often, or as often as possible, or in all cases of a certain kind, then again a sample can just be an instance of the property. Anyone happy may serve as a sample of the proposition that total happiness is maximized.

Observable samples can sometimes prompt the imagination and thereby help us to advance imaginative acquaintance. But they are of limited use. For one thing, observation does not include mind-reading. Also, it does best with short, dramatic episodes. A lifelong pattern of stagnation, exemplifying the absence of various values, goes on too long to be easily observed. Samples are dispensable as aids to imagination, and sometimes they are comparatively ineffective. A novel might be better.

The notion of an ideal spectator is part of a longstanding attempt to make dispositional theories of value and of color run in parallel. But the analogy is none too good, and I doubt that it improves our understanding either of color or of value. Drop it, and I think we have no further reason to say that a disposition to value is a disposition to respond to observed samples.[7]

Second, the ideal responder is often supposed to be well informed. If any item of empirical knowledge would affect his response, he knows it.—But some sorts of knowledge would not help to make your valuing a more reliable indicator of genuine value. Instead they would distract. If you knew too well how costly or how difficult it was to pursue some value, you might reject the grapes as sour, even when imaginative acquaintance with the value itself would have caused you to value it. Genuine values might be unattainable, or unattainable without undue sacrifice of other values. An ideal *balancer* of values needs thorough knowledge of the terms of trade. An ideal valuer may be better off without it. Our present business is not with the balancing, but with the prior question of what values there are to balance.

Another unhelpful sort of knowledge is a vivid awareness that we are small and the cosmos is large; or a vivid awareness of the mortality of mankind, and of the cosmos itself. If such knowledge tends to extinguish all desire, and therefore all valuing, it will not help us to value just what is valuable. Likewise it will be unhelpful to dwell too much on the lowly causal origins of things. If some feature of our lives originated by kin selection, or Pavlovian conditioning, or sublimation of infantile sexuality, that is irrelevant to what it is like in itself. Unless he can overcome the illusion of relevance, a valuer will be more reliable if he remains ignorant of such matters.

However, I grant one case—a common one—in which one does need empirical knowledge in order to gain imaginative acquaintance with a given putative value. It may be "given" in a way that underspecifies it, with the rest of the specification left to be filled in by reference to the actual ways of the world. For instance when I mentioned the life of a free spirit as a putative value, what I meant—and what you surely took me to mean—was the life of a free spirit in a world like ours. In such cases, a valuer must complete the specification by drawing on his knowledge of the world, else he will not know what he is supposed to imagine. To that extent—and only to that extent, I think—being well-informed is indeed a qualification for his job.[8]

Third, it may be said that the ideal responder should not only imagine having (or lacking) a putative value, but also imagine the effect on other people of someone's having (or lacking) it. Thinking what it would be like to live as a free spirit is not enough. You must also think what it would be like to encounter the free spirit and be ill-used.—But again, I think the requirement is misplaced. It is appropriate not to an ideal valuer, but to an ideal balancer who must think through the cost to some values of the realization of others. In addressing the prior question of what values there are, counting the cost is a distraction to be resisted.

Often, however, realizing a putative value *de se* would itself involve imagining the impact of one's conduct on other people. When that is so, imagining realizing the value involves imagining imagining the impact; and that cannot be done without simply imagining the impact. In such cases, imagining the impact does fit in; for it is already subsumed as part of imaginative acquaintance with the value itself.

Fourth, the ideal responder is often said to be dispassionate and impartial, like a good judge.— Once more, the requirement is appropriate not to an ideal valuer but to an ideal balancer. The valuer is not a judge. He is more like an advocate under the adversarial system. He is a specialist, passionate and partial perhaps, in some one of all the values there are. On the present theory, when I say that X is a value iff we are disposed to value X under ideal conditions, I do not mean conditions that are ideal *simpliciter,* but rather conditions that are ideal *for* X. We should not assume that there is any such thing as a condition of imaginative acquaintance with all values at once. (Still less, all putative values.) Imagination involves simulation—getting into the skin of the part. How many skins can you get into all at once? Tranquillity and vigorous activity might both be values; but a full imaginative acquaintance with one might preclude a full imaginative acquaintance with the other. (The incompatibility might even be conceptual, not just psychological.) Then if we value both, as surely many of us do, it is not because of acquaintance with both at once. It might be a lasting effect of past imaginative acquaintance at some times with one and at other times with the other.

A further speculation: it might happen that there were values that could not even be valued all at once. If so, then conflict of values would go deeper than is ever seen in hard choices; because what makes a choice hard is that conflicting values are valued together by the unfortunate chooser. An alarming prospect!—or exhilarating, to those of us who delight in the rich variety of life.

Who are "we"? An *absolute* version of the dispositional theory says that the "we" refers to all mankind. To call something a value is to call it a value *simpliciter,* which means that everyone, always and everywhere, is disposed under ideal conditions to value it. Then there are values only insofar as all mankind are alike in their dispositions.

Maybe all mankind *are* alike. The manifest diversity of valuing between different cultures—or for that matter within a culture, say between colleagues in the same philosophy department is no counterevidence. In the first place, people may not be

valuing as they would be disposed to value under ideal conditions. In the second place, remember that conditions of imaginative acquaintance are ideal for particular values, not *simpliciter.* So even if all are disposed alike, and all value as they would under ideal conditions, that may mean that some people value X as they would under conditions ideal for X, while others, who are no differently disposed, value Y as they would under conditions ideal for Y. If no conditions are ideal at once for X and for Y (still more if X and Y cannot both be valued at once), there could be diversity of valuing even in a population of psychological clones, if different ones had been led into different imaginative exercises.

We saw that it would be no easy job to find out for sure whether a particular person would be disposed to value something under ideal conditions of imaginative acquaintance with it. It would be harder still to find out all about one person's dispositions. And not just because one hard job would have to be done many times over. It might happen that imaginative acquaintance with X would leave traces, in one's valuing or otherwise, that got in the way of afterward imagining Y. To the extent that there was such interference, each new imaginative experiment would be harder than the ones before.

The fallback, if we are wary of presupposing that all mankind are alike in their dispositions to value, is tacit relativity. A *relative* version says that the "we" in the analysis is indexical, and refers to a population consisting of the speaker and those somehow like him. If the analysis is indexical, so is the analysandum. Then for speaker S to call something a value is to call it a value for the population of S and those like him; which means that S and those like him are all disposed, under ideal conditions, to value it.

The relative version is not just one version, but a spectrum. What analysis you get depends on how stringent a standard of similarity you apply to the phrase "the speaker and those somehow like him." At one end of the spectrum stands the absolute version: common humanity is likeness enough, so whoever speaks, all mankind are "we." At the other end, "we" means: "you and I, and I'm none too sure about you." (Or it might be "I, and those who think as I do," which reduces to "I.") In between, "we" means: "I, and all those who are of a common culture with me." Since mankind even at one moment is not made up of isolated and homogeneous tribes, and since we should not limit ourselves to the part of mankind located at one moment, we may haggle endlessly over how much cultural affiliation is meant. . . .

If some relative version were the correct analysis, wouldn't that be manifest whenever people talk about value? Wouldn't you hear them saying "value for me and my mates" or "value for the likes of you"? Wouldn't you think they'd stop arguing after one speaker says X is a value and the other says it isn't?—Not necessarily. They might always presuppose, with more or less confidence (well-founded or otherwise), that whatever relativity there is won't matter in *this* conversation. Even if they accept in principle that people sometimes just differ in their dispositions to value, they may be very reluctant to think the present deadlocked conversation is a case of such difference. However intractable the disagreement may be, they may go on thinking it really *is* a disagreement: a case in which two people are disposed alike, but one of them is wrong about what is a value relative to their shared dispositions, because he is not valuing as he would under ideal conditions. So long as they think that—and they might think it very persistently—they can hold the language of explicit relativity in reserve. It is there as a last resort, if ever they meet with a proven case of ultimate difference. But it will not be much heard, since it is a practical impossibility to prove a case. If the language of absolutism prevails, that is not strong evidence against relativity. . . .

So what version should we prefer, absolute or relative?—Neither; instead, I commend a *wait-and-see* version. In making a judgement of value, one makes many claims at once, some stronger than others, some less confidently than others, and waits to see which can be made to stick. I say X is a value; I mean that all mankind are disposed to value X; or anyway all nowadays are; or anyway all nowadays are except maybe some peculiar people on distant islands; or anyway . . .; or anyway you and I, talking here and now, are; or anyway I am. How much am I claiming?—as much as I can get away with. If my

stronger claims were proven false—though how that could be proven is hard to guess—I still mean to stand by the weaker ones. So long as I'm not challenged, there's no need to back down in advance; and there's no need to decide how far I'd back down if pressed. What I mean to commit myself to is *conditionally relative*: relative if need be, but absolute otherwise.

What is the modal status of the equivalence? The equivalence between value and what we are disposed to value is meant to be a piece of philosophical analysis, therefore analytic. But of course it is not obviously analytic; it is not even obviously true.

It is a philosophical problem how there can ever be unobvious analyticity. We need not solve that problem; suffice it to say that it is everybody's problem, and it is not to be solved by denying the phenomenon. There are perfectly clear examples of it: the epsilon-delta analysis of an instantaneous rate of change, for one. Whenever it is analytic that all A's are B's, but not obviously analytic, the Moorean open question—whether all A's are indeed B's—is intelligible. And not only is it intelligible in the sense that we can parse and interpret it (that much is true even of the question whether all A's are *A*'s) but also in the sense that it makes sense as something to say in a serious discussion, as an expression of genuine doubt.

Besides unobvious analyticity, there is equivocal analyticity. Something may be analytic under one disambiguation but not another, or under one precisification but not another. Examples abound. . . . It is analytic under some precisifications of "mountain" that no mountain is less than one kilometer high. When analyticity is equivocal, open questions make good conversational sense: they are invitations to proceed under a disambiguation or precisification that makes the answer to the question not be analytic. By asking whether there are mountains less than one kilometer high, you invite your conversational partners to join you in considering the question under a precisification of "mountain" broad enough to make it interesting; yet it was analytic under another precisification that the answer was "no." So even if all is obvious, open questions show at worst that the alleged analyticity is equivocal.

I suggest that the dispositional theory of value, in the version I have put forward, is equivocally as well as unobviously analytic. I do not claim to have captured the one precise sense that the word "value" bears in the pure speech, uncorrupted by philosophy, that is heard on the Clapham omnibus. So far as this matter goes, I doubt that speakers untouched by philosophy are found in Clapham or anywhere else. And if they were, I doubt if they'd have made up their minds exactly what to mean any more than the rest of us have. I take it, rather, that the word "value," like many others, exhibits both semantic variation and semantic indecision. The best I can hope for is that my dispositional theory lands somewhere near the middle of the range of variation and indecision—and also gives something that I, and many more besides, could be content to adopt as our official definition of the word "value," in the unlikely event that we needed an official definition.

I've left some questions less than conclusively settled: the matter of absolute versus relative versus wait-and-see versions, the details of "ideal conditions," the question of admitting values *de se,* the definition of valuing as second-order versus highest-order intrinsic desiring. It would not surprise or disturb me to think that my answers to those questions are only equivocally analytic—but somewhere fairly central within the range of variation and indecision—and that the same could be said of rival answers. Even if no version of the dispositional theory is unequivocally analytic, still it's fair to hope that some not-too-miscellaneous disjunction of versions comes out analytic under most reasonable resolutions of indeterminacy (under some reasonable precisification of "most" and "reasonable.")

If the dispositional theory is only unobviously and equivocally analytic, why think that it's analytic at all?—Because that hypothesis fits our practice. (The practice of many of us, much of the time.) It does seem that if we try to find out whether something is a genuine value, we do try to follow—or rather, approximate—the canonical method. We gain the best imaginative acquaintance we can, and see if we then desire to desire it. In investigating values by the canonical method, we ignore any alleged possibility that values differ from what we're disposed to

value. The dispositional theory explains nicely why we ignore it: no such possibility exists. . . .

But is it realism? Psychology is contingent. Our dispositions to value things might have been otherwise than they actually are. We might have been disposed, under ideal conditions, to value seasickness and petty sleaze above all else. Does the dispositional theory imply that, had we been thus disposed, those things would have been values? That seems wrong.

No: we can take the reference to our dispositions as rigidified. Even speaking within the scope of a counterfactual supposition, the things that count as values are those that we are *actually* disposed to value, not those we would have valued in the counterfactual situation. No worries—unless seasickness actually *is* a value, it still wouldn't have been a value even if we'd been disposed to value it.

This is too swift. The trick of rigidifying seems more to hinder the expression of our worry than to make it go away. It can still be expressed as follows. We might have been disposed to value seasickness and petty sleaze, and yet we might have been no different in how we used the word "value." The reference of "our actual dispositions" would have been fixed on different dispositions, of course, but our way of fixing the reference would have been no different. In one good sense—though not the only sense—we would have meant by "value" just what we actually do. And it would have been true for us to say "seasickness and petty sleaze are values."

The contingency of value has not gone away after all; and it may well disturb us. I think it is the only disturbing aspect of the dispositional theory. Conditional relativity may well disturb us too, but that is no separate problem. What comfort would it be if all mankind just *happened* to be disposed alike? Say, because some strange course of cultural evolution happened to be cut short by famine, or because some mutation of the brain never took place? Since our dispositions to value are contingent, they certainly vary when we take *all* of mankind into account, all the inhabitants of all the possible worlds. Given the dispositional theory, trans-world relativity is inevitable. The spectre of relativity within our own world is just a vivid reminder of the contingency of value.

If wishes were horses, how would we choose to ride? What would it take to satisfy us? Maybe this new version of the dispositional theory would suit us better: values are what we're *necessarily* disposed to value. Then no contingent "value" would deserve the name; and there would be no question of something being a value for some people and not for others, since presumably what's necessary is *a fortiori* uniform (unless different dispositions to value are built into different people's individual essences, an unlikely story). . . .

If we amend the dispositional theory by inserting "necessarily," we can be much more confident that the "values" it defines would fully deserve the name—if there were any of them. But it is hard to see how there possibly could be. If a value, strictly speaking, must be something we are necessarily disposed to value, and if our dispositions to value are in fact contingent, then, strictly speaking, there are no values. If Mackie is right that a value (his term is "objective good") would have to be

> sought by anyone who was acquainted with it, not because of any contingent fact that this person, or every person, is so constituted that he desires this end, but just because the end has to-be-pursuedness somehow built into it,

then he is also right to call values "queer" and to repudiate the error of believing in them.[9] (Replacing "sought" by "valued" would not change that.) If we amend the dispositional theory, requiring values to be all that we might wish them to be, we bring on the error theory. The fire is worse than the frying pan.

Is it, after all, out of the question that our dispositions to value might be necessary? If the theory of mind I favor is true, then the platitudes of folk psychology do have a certain necessity—albeit conditional necessity—to them. There are states that play the functional roles specified in those platitudes, and it is in virtue of doing so that they deserve their folk-psychological names. It is not necessary that there should be any states in us

that deserve such names as "pain," "belief," or "desire." But it is necessary that if any states do deserve those names, then they conform to the platitudes. Or rather, they conform well enough. Now suppose that some of the platitudes of folk psychology specified exactly what we were disposed, under ideal conditions, to desire to desire. And suppose those platitudes were non-negotiable: if a system of states did not satisfy them, that would settle that those states did not conform well enough to folk psychology to deserve the mental names it implicitly defines. Then there would be things we were necessarily disposed to value—on condition that we had mental lives at all!

The suggestion is intelligible and interesting, but too good to be true. For one thing, it only spreads the trouble. Instead of losing the risk that nothing deserves the name of value, we gain the added risk that nothing deserves commonplace folk-psychological names. . . . [I]t's not really credible that there might turn out to be no beliefs, no desires, no pains, . . .[10] For another thing, it proves too much. It denies outright that it's possible for someone to differ from others in his dispositions to value. Yet this does seem possible; and we can flesh out the story with plenty of "corroborative detail." This cunning and subtle villain once was as others are; he gained excellent imaginative acquaintance with many values, and valued them accordingly. Now he has gone wrong, and cares not a fig for what he once valued; and yet he has forgotten nothing. (He certainly has not stopped having any mental life deserving of the name.) He hates those who are as he once was, and outwits them all the better because of his superb empathetic understanding of what they hold dear. Could it not happen?—not if the present suggestion were true. So the present suggestion is false. Yet it was the only hope, or the only one I know, for explaining how there might be things we are necessarily disposed to value. The dispositions are contingent, then. And, at least in some tacit way, we know it. If the story of the subtle villain strikes you as a possible story, that knowledge thereby reveals itself.

But if we know better, it is odd that we are disturbed—as I think many of us will be—by a dispositional theory of value, unamended, according to which values are contingent. It feels wrong. Why might that be?—Perhaps because a large and memorable part of our discussion of values consists of browbeating and being browbeaten.[11] The rhetoric would fall flat if we kept in mind, all the while, that it is contingent how we are disposed to value. So a theory which acknowledges that contingency cannot feel quite right. You might say that it is unfaithful to the distinctive phenomenological character of lived evaluative thought. Yet even if it feels not right, it may still be right, or as near right as we can get. It feels not quite right to remember that your friends are big swarms of little particles—it is inadequate to the phenomenology of friendship—but still they are.

I suggested earlier that my version of the dispositional theory of value might be equivocally analytic. So might the amended version, on which values are what we are necessarily disposed to value. Between these two versions, not to mention others, there might be both semantic variation and semantic indecision. If so, it is part of a familiar pattern. One way to create indeterminacy and equivocal analyticity is to define names implicitly in terms of a theory (folk or scientific), and later find out that the theory is wrong enough that nothing perfectly deserves the names so introduced, but right enough that some things, perhaps several rival candidates, deserve the names imperfectly. Nothing perfectly deserves the name "simultaneity," since nothing quite fits the whole of our old conception. So the name will have to go to some imperfect deserver of it, or to nothing. What it takes to deserve this name, not perfectly but well enough, was never officially settled. One resolution of the indeterminacy makes it analytic that simultaneity must be frame-independent; another, that it must be an equivalence relation; a third, that it must be both at once. The third brings with it an error theory of simultaneity.

I suggest that (for some of us, or some of us sometimes) the amended dispositional theory best captures what it would take for something to perfectly deserve the name "value." There are no perfect deservers of the name to be had. But there are plenty of imperfect deservers of the name, and my original version is meant to capture what it takes to be one of the best of them. (But I do not say mine is the only version that can claim to do so. Doubtless there are more dimensions of semantic variation and indeterminacy than just our degree of tolerance for imperfection.) Strictly speaking, nothing shall get the name without deserving it perfectly. Strictly speaking, Mackie is right: genuine values would have to meet an impossible condition, so it is an error to think there are any. Loosely speaking, the name may go to a claimant that deserves it imperfectly. Loosely speaking, common sense is right. There are values, lots of them, and they are what we are disposed *de facto* to value.

Then is my position a form of realism about values?—Irrealism about values strictly speaking, realism about values loosely speaking. The former do not exist. The latter do.

What to make of the situation is mainly a matter of temperament. You can bang the drum about how philosophy has uncovered a terrible secret: there are no values! (Shock horror: no such thing as simultaneity! Nobody ever whistled while he worked!) You can shout it from the housetops—browbeating is oppression, the truth shall make you free. Or you can think it better for public safety to keep quiet and hope people will go on as before. Or you can declare that there are no values, but that nevertheless it is legitimate—and not just expedient—for us to carry on with value-talk, since we can make it all go smoothly if we just give the name of value to claimants that don't quite deserve it. This would be a sort of quasi-realism, not the same as Blackburn's quasi-realism.[12] Or you can think it an empty question whether there are values: say what you please, speak strictly or loosely. When it comes to deserving a name, there's better and worse but who's to say how good is good enough? Or you can think it clear that the imperfect deservers of the name are good enough, but only just, and say that although there are values we are still terribly wrong about them. Or you can calmly say that value (like simultaneity) is not quite as some of us sometimes thought. Myself, I prefer the calm and conservative responses. But so far as the analysis of value goes, they're all much of a muchness.

NOTES

1. The most interesting of the hypotheses here set aside is that an attitude of valuing might be a "besire": a special kind of attitude that is both a belief and a desire and that motivates us, without benefit of other desires, in just the way that ordinary desires do. . . . Valuing X might be the besire that is at once a belief that X is good and a desire for X; where *goodness* just means that property, whatever it may be, such that a belief that X has it may double as a desire for X.

   But we should hesitate to believe in besires, because integrating them into the folk psychology of belief and desire turns out to be no easy thing. . . .

2. It is comparatively easy to imagine *instrumental* third-order desires. Maybe our addict wishes he could like himself better than he does; and not by doing away with his addiction, which he takes to be impossible, but by becoming reconciled to it and accepting himself as he is. Or maybe he just fears that his second-order desire not to be addicted will someday lead him to suffer the pains of withdrawal. Either way, he wants to be rid of his second-order desire not to be addicted, but he wants it not for itself but as a means to some end. This is irrelevant: presumably it is intrinsic, not instrumental, desiring that is relevant to what someone values.

3. *Principia Ethica* (Cambridge University Press, 1903) Section 13.

4. What we can do is to go the other way, subsuming desire *de dicto* under desire *de se*. To desire that the world be a certain way is to desire that one have the property of living in a world that is that way—a property that belongs to all or none of the inhabitants of the world, depending on the way the world is. This subsumption, artificial though it be, is legitimate given a suitably broad notion of property. But for present purposes we need distinction, not unification. So let us henceforth ignore those desires *de se* that are equivalent to desires *de dicto,* and reserve the term "*de se,*" for those that are not.

5. *Principia Ethica,* Section 59.

6. Without in the process having his dispositions to value altered.

7. If we had demanded samples, we would have had a choice about where to locate the disposition. Is it within us or without? Is it a disposition in the samples to evoke a response from spectators?—that is what best fits the supposed parallel with a dispositional theory of color. . . . Or is it a disposition in the spectators to respond to samples? Or is it a disposition of the sample-cum-spectator system to respond to having its parts brought together? For us there is no choice. The propositions and properties that are the values cannot harbor any causal bases for dispositions. Samples could, but there needn't be any samples. Imaginative experiences could, but those are within us, and are not themselves samples of values. So the disposition must reside in us, the responders. Being a value comes out as a dispositionally analyzed property, but not as a disposition of the things that have it. Values themselves are not disposed to do anything.

8. Imaginative acquaintance is sometimes thought to consist in the possession of a special kind of "phenomenal" information. If that is so, of course my own candidate for "ideal conditions" comes down to a special case of being well-informed. But it is not so—not even in the most favorable case, that of imaginative acquaintance with a kind of sense-experience. . . .

9. J. L. Mackie, *Ethics: Inventing Right and Wrong* (Penguin, 1977), p. 40. But note that the queerness Mackie has in mind covers more than just the to-know-it-is-to-love-it queerness described in this passage.

10. As argued in Frank Jackson and Philip Pettit, 'In Defence of Folk Psychology,' forthcoming in *Philosophical Studies.*

11. See Ian Hinckfuss, *The Moral Society: Its Structure and Effects* (Australian National University Discussion Papers in Environmental Philosophy, 1987).

12. Simon Blackburn, *Spreading the Word: Groundings in the Philosophy of Language* (Oxford University Press, 1984), Chapter 6.

STUDY QUESTIONS

1. When we think hard about values, what is the specific nature of that process?
2. How do we go about imagining vividly and thoroughly?
3. Could two people both have full imaginative acquaintance with a situation and yet assess it wholly differently?
4. Does Lewis's theory fall prey to Moore's open-question argument?

Why Idealize?

David Enoch

David Lewis, among others, has emphasized that something is valuable just in case we would be disposed to value it under ideal circumstances. But David Enoch, Professor in the Department of Philosophy and the Faculty of Law at the Hebrew University of Jerusalem, asks what rationale the response dependence theorist like Lewis can supply for idealization. Enoch argues that such theorists are barred from the obvious response that ideal conditions are needed to ascertain the facts. On Lewis's view, for example, desiring to desire under ideal conditions is what *makes* something valuable. Hence the idealization cannot be justified on the ground that it helps us better locate the truth about what is independently valuable. Enoch canvasses alternative ways the response dependence theorist might justify idealization but finds each unsatisfactory.

I. IDEALIZATION

. . . David Lewis thinks that values are not necessarily things we value, but rather things we would value under ideal conditions (conditions of full imaginative acquaintance).[1] More than that, Lewis thinks that something's being of value just is being such that we are disposed to value it under ideal conditions. . . .

In what follows I argue that idealizing views are not likely to be able to motivate the very idealization they employ. If so, such idealization is likely to remain—given the philosophical concerns underlying idealizing views—objectionably ad hoc. And this, I conclude, makes response-dependence theories much less plausible, for they must either embrace the ad-hoc-ness of the idealization or else settle for actual, nonidealized responses. If actual-response-dependence views are as implausible as

they seem, perhaps, then, this should be taken not so much as a reason to idealize, but rather as a reason to reject response-dependence theories of normativity altogether. . . .

II. WHY IDEALIZE—THE NATURAL ANSWER

The challenge, then, is fairly simple. Suppose you want, for whatever reason, to ground . . . values in the state of valuing, or something of that sort. Why not settle . . . for what I actually value? What justifies the move to hypothetical, ideal conditions, however exactly these are characterized?

A natural answer would be to claim that the relevantly ideal conditions are the conditions needed for a reliable tracking of the relevant facts. Suppose that you want to know the time. Looking at a watch

From David Enoch, "Why Idealize?" *Ethics* 115 (2005). Reprinted by permission of the publisher.

293

seems like a good idea. But, of course, looking at your watch may not be such a good idea. This depends on whether your watch keeps reasonably accurate time. What you want, then, is to have a look at a good watch. An ideal watch would be great, but we can settle for one that is less than ideal, so long as it is close enough. So we require, say, that the batteries in your watch be at least almost fully charged. Or consider this: you want to know who is taller, myself or my wife. Having a look seems like a good idea, but of course not just any look will do. What you want is to have a look from a proper angle, from up close, when my wife is not wearing heels.

In these cases, some (very moderate) idealization is called for because otherwise an epistemic procedure—a way of forming beliefs—may very well lead us astray. If the watch is not reasonably accurate, or if you are much closer to me than to my wife, the suggested epistemic procedure will fail; it will not be a reliable indicator of the relevant fact (the time, or my and my wife's relevant height). And this, of course, is one good rationale for idealization: idealization (or its approximation) is called for whenever an actual procedure is fallible in ways (partly) corrected for by the idealization.

Some idealizers sometimes speak as if this rationale holds in the case of their idealization as well. Here, for instance, is Lewis:

> If someone has little notion what it would be like to live as a free spirit . . . or what a world of complete harmony and constant agreement would be like; then whether or not he blindly values these things must have little to do with whether or not they are truly values. . . . If only he would think harder, and imagine vividly and thoroughly how it would be if these putative values were realized . . . that would make his valuing a more *reliable indicator* of genuine value. And if he could gain the fullest possible imaginative acquaintance that is humanly possible, then, I suggest, his valuing would be an *infallible indicator.*[2]

Lewis here seems to suggest that just as a bad angle undermines the reliability of having a look as a way of determining relative height, so too lack of imaginative acquaintance undermines the reliability of the procedure he suggests for finding out whether something is of value.

But . . . this just cannot be right. Lewis—in his more careful moments—does not think of our valuing under ideal conditions as an indicator (fallible or otherwise) of what is of value. He thinks of such valuings as the truth-makers of value claims. For something to be of value just is, so he wants us to believe, for us to be disposed to value it under ideal conditions. . . .

But with the collapse of the reliability and indication rhetoric collapses also the natural rationale for idealization. For when we think of one thing (the watch reading) as a reliable indicator of another (the time), we think of the latter as independent of the former. It is, say, 9:43 p.m. anyway, regardless of the reading of my watch. If my watch keeps accurate time, it will read "9:43." If it does not, it may not. The time, though, does not change together with the reading of my watch. If all goes well, in other words, my watch's reading tracks the time-facts that are independent of it. Similarly, the relative height of me and my wife does not change along with the angle from which you view us. If, say, she is slightly taller than me, she is taller than me independently of how—and even whether—you choose to look at us. When all goes well, your visual impression tracks the truth about relative height that is independent of it.

My point is not the (possible) failure of extensional equivalence, which I am here granting for the sake of argument. Rather, my point is best thought of in terms of priority or dependence relations and best brought out by thinking in terms of the Euthyphro Contrast: a good watch reads "9:43" because it is 9:43. It is not the case that the time is 9:43 because of the watch's reading. In proper conditions you see that, say, my wife is taller than me because she is, not the other way around. And this direction-of-because issue captures an intuitive sense of priority or dependence: even given extensional equivalence, my watch's reading depends on the time, but the time is independent of my watch's reading.

This is why there is, in the time and relative-height examples, room for some idealization. The reading of the watch tracks the time—which is independent of it—only when all goes well[;] the perceptual impression tracks relative height—which is independent of this perception—only when all goes well. So there is reason to make sure—by idealizing—that all does go well. But had we taken the other Euthyphronic alternative regarding these matters things would have been very different. Had the time depended on the reading of my watch, had the reading of my watch made certain time-facts true, there would have been no reason (not this reason, anyway) to "idealize" my watch and see to it that the batteries are fully charged. In such a case, whatever the reading would be, that would be the right reading, because that this is the reading would make it right.

The natural rationale for idealization, the one exemplified by the time and relative-height examples, thus only applies to cases where the relevant procedure or response is thought of as tracking a truth independent of it. This does not necessarily rule out extensional equivalences between normative truths and our relevant responses. One may, for instance, hold a view that is an instance of "tracking internalism,"[3] according to which, necessarily, one cannot have a (normative) reason without being motivated accordingly, not because motivations are part and parcel of (normative) reasons, but rather because our motivations necessarily track the independent truths about (normative) reasons.[4] But typical idealizers do not think of their view in this way; they do not think of the relevant response as (necessarily) tracking an independent order of normative facts. As emphasized above, they think of the relevant response as constituting the relevant normative fact.

This is no coincidence. Idealizers like to think of themselves as naturalists of sorts, indeed often as suggesting a naturalist reduction of the relevant normative facts. And they always want to think of themselves as putting forward an alternative to more robustly, Euthyphronically realist views, such as views that postulate the existence of purportedly queer normative entities that are just as independent

of us and our responses as electrons and planets presumably are. The point I want to make, then, is this: if this is your reason for endorsing a response-dependence view of the normative, you cannot consistently employ the natural rationale for idealization.

III. WHY IDEALIZE—POSSIBLE ANSWERS

But this does not mean that you cannot consistently endorse other rationales for your idealization. In this section I consider two suggestions that are common—if often implicit—among idealizers.

A. Extensional Adequacy

Take an idealizing view and drop the idealization. The view you are left with will be rather obviously extensionally inadequate. Counterexamples—cases where the deliverances of the theory contradict intuitive, pretheoretic judgments that we are rather confident in even upon reflection—are going to be too easy to come by. . . . [I]f I am disposed to value lifelong solitude, then—endorsing something like Lewis's view of values but dropping the idealization—lifelong solitude is of value, even if my valuing it stems merely from my never having thought through what it would be really like. . . .

The point generalizes. No view that ties normative truths to our actual responses is likely to achieve extensional adequacy, because some of our responses are clearly bad, not reason supported, or not in accord with what really is of value, or with what is really good for us. Idealization is called for in order to save even just a possibility of extensional adequacy for response-dependence views.

Why not settle, then, for the following rationale for idealization? We want a theory that is extensionally adequate; we cannot have a response-dependence theory that is extensionally adequate without idealization; presumably, we have independent reasons to go for a response-dependence theory, rather than, say, a more robustly realist one; and so we should idealize.[5]

The problem with this line of thought is that extensional adequacy can be had for cheap. Whenever one puts forward a theory that is found to be extensionally inadequate, one can—in principle, at least, for in practice it may not be an easy task—patch it up and achieve extensional adequacy (say, by using extremely long conjunctions and disjunctions in one's analysans). But such a way of achieving extensional adequacy will be objectionably ad hoc, a case of cheating, really. What would save the theorist is if the patched-up version of the theory still scored reasonably high on the list of theoretical virtues, if it was not too ad hoc, if it had some independent appeal, some rationale distinct from its purported extensional adequacy. This is a perfectly general point about theory choice: scientific theories too attempt more than mere extensional adequacy. If I put forward a scientific theory (say, that water is H_2O), found purported counterexamples, and then patched the theory up in such an ad hoc way (water is H_2O unless it is Tuesday and the water is in a wooden cup, and unless . . .), the resulting theory would be unacceptable even if extensionally adequate. What would save the amended theory would be if it was still simple, explanatory, coherent, predictive, elegant, pragmatically useful, or scored reasonably high on whatever else is on the list of virtues for scientific theories. In the scientific as well as in the philosophical case, then, what is needed for a theory to be attractive is some rationale distinct from its purported extensional adequacy. That such a rationale is needed can also be seen from the obvious fact that there are many—indeed, infinitely many—distinct ways of achieving ad-hoc-extensional adequacy, all internally consistent but mutually inconsistent. Only one of them can be right, and we are going to determine which on grounds independent of extensional adequacy (for ex hypothesi all of them are extensionally adequate). The problem here is not the mere availability of competing ways of achieving extensional adequacy, but rather the fact—exemplified by their availability—that the hope of achieving extensional adequacy cannot on its own motivate an amendment to the original theory, unless the amended theory is still good enough as a theory.

In order to be plausible and avoid being objectionably ad hoc, then, the idealizer must have a further rationale for her idealization, one that is not merely the hope of avoiding obvious counterexamples and thereby achieving extensional adequacy. But this means that we are back at square one: remember, what we set out to find was a plausible rationale for idealization that is consistent with the philosophical concerns underlying response-dependence views. The suggestion was that extensional adequacy could serve as such a rationale. We now see, though, that it cannot do that satisfactorily without some other, independent, rationale for idealization. We are still looking, then, for what we have been looking for all along—a rationale for idealization. . . .

B. Our Justificatory Practices

But perhaps there is another rationale for idealization, one that is consistent with the philosophical motivations underlying idealizing views and that is not disturbingly ad hoc. For the data we can use when philosophizing about these matters include not just straightforwardly normative beliefs (about which actions are right, what is and what is not good for one, what reasons we have, which things are of value, etc.) but also our justificatory practices and our beliefs about them. We think, for instance, that if you say that lifelong solitude is of value, and we show that you do not have a good appreciation of what such life would be like, we have thereby discredited you as a judge of the relevant value claim. . . . Somewhat more generally, we think that we are fallible in our normative judgments and that there is room for genuine normative advice and for coming to see that we were mistaken about our reasons. And so on. The hope is, then, that from our practices of justifying normative claims a rationale for idealization can be extracted.

The idea seems to be this.[6] Characterize our practice of making and justifying reason or value claims, or other relevant normative claims. If we try to correct for false information, this must be because values (say) are not what we value when falsely informed, but what we value when not so mistaken; if we try to put ourselves in the relevant situation and imagine what it is like to be in it, this must be because values are what we value when possessing imaginative acquaintance with the thing being valued; and so on. And this, it is important to notice, is an independent way of motivating the idealization: it does not depend on considerations of extensional adequacy. It relies not on pretheoretic judgments about what is of value, say, or what is good for one, but rather on the standards implicit in our relevant justificatory practices (and perhaps, to an extent, also on our beliefs about them). And notice, of course, that a theory based on the standards of justification implicit in a practice need not be (too) objectionably conservative. It can be critical by exposing tensions within the practice and attempting to settle them in accord with the deeper, more central features of the relevant practice.

Made fully explicit, I think that the argument is an instance of an inference to the best explanation. In attempting to determine whether something is of value we—let us assume—try to put ourselves in conditions of full imaginative acquaintance. Furthermore, we think that this is a good method of inquiry into what is of value. What explains, then, the fact that we put ourselves in conditions of full imaginative acquaintance in order to determine whether something is of value? And what explains the fact that putting ourselves in such conditions (or at least approximating them) is a good method of determining what is of value? Well, it is that the requirement of full imaginative acquaintance is a part of what it takes for something to be of value. The rationale for the idealization is, then, that it best explains important aspects of our relevant justificatory practice.

I want to concede here that if this line can be made to work, it supplies a rationale for idealization of exactly the sort needed. If such inference to the best explanation works, there is nothing ad hoc in the idealization, and the challenge is met. But, I now want to argue, this inference to the best explanation cannot be made to work.

To see that, think of a view of religious obligation I will call "Ideal Prophet Theory." The Ideal Prophet Theorist denies the existence of God and other supernatural entities and properties, perhaps because of his (the theorist's) naturalist leanings. But for some reason he wants to save the truth of

(some) statements about what is religiously required.[7] So he comes up with the following theory: a type of action is religiously required just in case it is sensed-as-required by a prophet in ideal conditions, or by an ideal prophet. The theorist then comes up with a psychological account of sensing-as-required and specifies—in a naturalistically respectable way—the conditions that make a prophet ideal. He decides which conditions to include in this specification on the basis of our practice with religious discourse. If we treat being in a distinct kind of trance as evidence for the reliability of the purported prophet, he includes such conditions in the conditions that make a prophet ideal. If we treat being drugged as undermining the religious force of the trance, he classifies being drugged as a condition that makes a prophet less than ideal. And so on. Of course, the Ideal Prophet Theorist argues not just for an extensional equivalence between being religiously required and being sensed-as-required by an ideal prophet. He argues that being sensed-as-required by an ideal prophet is what the truth of claims about being religiously required consists in, that being religiously required just is being sensed-as-required by an ideal prophet.

Now suppose I put forward to the Ideal Prophet Theorist the challenge of coming up with a rationale for his idealization. Like the metanormative idealizer, he cannot invoke the most natural reply to the challenge because he does not think of the responses of the ideal prophet as tracking an independent order of facts about what is and what is not religiously required, commanded by God, or some such (he is a naturalist, after all). He can, again like the metanormative idealizer, motivate the idealization by considerations of extensional adequacy, but if this is all he can say, this will leave the idealization objectionably ad hoc. Luckily, he can do better than that: he can refer to our religious practice, the practice of talking about what actions are religiously required, of justifying such claims, of discrediting some who make them, and so on. And he can present his argument as an inference to the best explanation: what best explains, he can ask, our practice of justifying claims about what is religiously required by consulting (or approximating) an ideal prophet? And what explains the fact that this is a good way of coming to know which actions are religiously required? The answer is that this is (a part of) what it is to be religiously required.

Ideal Prophet Theory fails for more than one reason, and I do not mean to suggest that metanormative idealizing views fail for all the reasons for which Ideal Prophet Theory fails. . . . I want to highlight one failure of the reasoning above. The problem I want to focus on stems from the gap between the commitments of the Ideal Prophet Theorist and those of the participants in the relevant religious practice. The former is a naturalist, denying the existence of God and other supernatural facts in which religious obligation may be thought to be grounded. But the commitments of the participants in the relevant religious practice are not plausibly understood as consistent with naturalism.[8] They can only be understood as committed to exactly the kind of metaphysics the Ideal Prophet Theorist wants to deny. This gap makes the Ideal Prophet Theorist's argument into a non sequitur: the best explanation of the relevant justificatory practice is not in terms of the theorist's metaphysical beliefs (including the denial of the existence of God), but in terms of the participants' ones. Participants believe in God (or in other supernatural facts), and so the best explanation of the relevant part of religious practice is the obvious one: participants believe that the relevantly ideal conditions are the conditions best suited for the tracking of an independent order of facts regarding religious obligations (say, God's commands).[9] Perhaps they are wrong, perhaps because there is no God. But clearly, their belief that there is a God is very relevant to answering the question of what best explains their religious practice. The theorist's reasons for denying the existence of God—good as they may be—cannot support the claim that what best explains religious practice is the Ideal Prophet Theory and the idealization it employs.

What best explains, then, the relevant part of religious practice is the (false, we're here assuming) belief of participants in God, and their belief that the specified ideal conditions are well suited for finding out about his commands and so about their religious obligations. But earlier on I emphasized that what

needs to be explained is not just the justificatory practices but also the fact that they are good, or justified, methods of forming beliefs about the relevant facts. It should now be clear that this is not quite right. The naturalist who attempts to make sense of the discourse about religious obligation must, if he is honest, concede that the practice is best explained as involving a commitment to some supernatural facts. This means, of course, on this naturalist's assumptions, that the relevant part of religious discourse is systematically erroneous. And this means that the procedures of finding out about religious obligations licensed by the practice are after all not good ones, because they are founded on false beliefs.

Let me summarize, then, the Ideal Prophet Theory detour: an Ideal Prophet Theorist cannot rely, as supplying a rationale for idealization, on standards implicit in our practice of justifying claims about religious obligation. Of the two suggested inferences to the best explanation—one explaining our practices, the other explaining their merit—the former fails because a much better explanation is available (in terms of the participants' false belief in God), and the other fails because the purported explanandum is, in effect, denied by the Ideal Prophet Theorist himself.

I want to suggest that the metanormative idealizer who tries to supply a rationale for her idealization by drawing on our justificatory practices fails in an exactly analogous way. Regardless of how good her (metaphysical, epistemological, or whatever) reasons are for denying a more robustly realist view of the relevant normative truths, still these are not reasons to deny that our justificatory practices are committed to some such realism. This being so, what best explains our justificatory practices is not that an idealized response is what the relevant normative fact consists in. What best explains our justificatory practice is rather our (perhaps implicit) belief, false though it may be, that, say, conditions of full imaginative acquaintance are conducive to the reliable tracking of an independent order of value-facts. And the idealizer cannot consistently require an explanation why it is a good justificatory method, because she believes it is not: she believes that there is no independent order of value-facts that our epistemic methods reliably track.

Perhaps, though, this is too quick. For the idealizer can argue that there is an important disanalogy between her theory and that of the Ideal Prophet Theorist. Whereas it really is highly implausible that the relevant part of religious discourse and practice is not committed to the existence of supernatural facts in which religious obligation is grounded, in the case of normative discourse this is not so. Take God away from talk about what is religiously required, the idealizer can say, and clearly error theory is the way to go. But take a more robust realism away from talk about what actions are right, what is good for one, what reasons we have, or what is of value, and still error theory is not the only—not even the most plausible—way to go. Indeed, the idealizer may argue that assuming otherwise is already assuming that response-dependence views are false, and so that in so assuming I have in effect been begging the question against her.

I agree, of course, that the metanormative case is not as clear-cut as the Ideal-Prophet-Theory case (this, after all, is why I thought it helpful to use the latter as a heuristic device). But this line of thought cannot save the metanormative idealizer. Let me make, then, two points in reply.

First, in assuming that our practice is not best explained by the idealizer's view I have not been assuming that response-dependence views fail. I have not been assuming that some other view—certainly not that a specific other view, such as a robust realism of sorts—is on the whole more plausible than the idealizer's view. All I have been assuming is that as far as fidelity to our practice is concerned response-dependence theories are not as good as some of the alternatives. And making this latter assumption is in no way tantamount to assuming the former one, because for all I have said there may be other considerations—ones not having to do with fidelity to our practice—that count in favor of response-dependence views and, indeed, that outweigh such fidelity considerations, thereby rendering response-dependence views on the whole justified (I return to this point shortly). Indeed, even response-dependence theorists often concede that their view does not capture the commitments of the (relevant part of) normative discourse and practice

as a more robust realism.[10] Typically, they argue for their view by emphasizing some other advantages it has over robust realism—say, by avoiding an ontology of queer entities and a queer epistemology that accompanies it. Consider again Ideal Prophet Theory. The Ideal Prophet Theorist may concede that his theory is not as loyal to the practice as some competing (supernaturalist) view but may argue that his view should still be preferred on the whole because of its naturalist-friendly ontology. I have said nothing incompatible with such a claim. But if it is true that Ideal Prophet Theory is not as loyal to the practice as some supernaturalist view, then the Ideal Prophet Theorist cannot rely on the practice in order to motivate his idealization. Perhaps, in other words, the discrepancy between Ideal Prophet Theory and religious practice cannot all by itself defeat Ideal Prophet Theory (because of its many other advantages), but such discrepancy does prevent the Ideal Prophet Theorist from relying on the commitments of the practice in putting forward a positive defense of his view, for instance, in providing a rationale for his idealization. Analogously, perhaps the discrepancy between idealizing views and (the relevant part of) normative discourse and practice is not sufficient to defeat such views (because of their many other advantages), but such discrepancy certainly does prevent the idealizer from relying on the commitments of the practice in putting forward a positive defense of her view, for instance, in providing a rationale for her idealization.

The dialectical situation, then, is significantly different from the common one where the phenomenology of moral discourse is taken to support a rather robust realism but sensible metaphysical and epistemological considerations are taken to support a different, perhaps response-dependence, view. For we are not at this stage attempting a comprehensive assessment of competing metanormative views. Rather, we are now attempting to evaluate one way in which the idealizer tries to motivate her idealization, namely, by relying on the standards of justification implicit in normative discourse. And in order to evaluate this attempt at addressing the why-idealize challenge, we should focus our attention just on considerations of fidelity to the practice.

My first point, then, is that my assumption regarding fidelity to our relevant practices does not beg the question against the idealizing response-dependence theorist. The second point I want to make is that this assumption is quite plausible. . . . [L]et me make a few preliminary remarks supporting the claim that our normative discourse as a whole does not support the idealizer's argument. First, the point is often made in metaethical discussions—and rightly so, I think—that moral discourse seems to incorporate an objective purport and that for this reason a rather robust realism is the view that best captures the phenomenology of moral discourse. And the analogous point holds, I think, for normative discourse more generally. But it is very hard—perhaps even impossible—to get this kind of objectivity on the basis of a response-dependence view, idealized though it may be. If so, this is some reason to be suspicious of the loyalty of response-dependence views to our relevant justificatory practices. Second, it seems plausible to assume that the history of our practices is relevant to the question of what best explains them. Assuming—as again seems plausible—that our justificatory practices were shaped in eras in which a fairly robust realism was much more in fashion than it is today, this counts against an attempt to argue that the best explanation of these practices is in terms of idealized responses rather than in terms of (the attribution of a belief in) a more robust realism. Third, several idealizers prefer to think of their views as revisionary accounts, not sufficiently loyal to our practices to count as an adequate descriptive theory of the normative . . . This, I think, is . . . evidence that it is not going to be easy to convince us that the best explanation of our justificatory practices is going to yield a rationale for idealization that is consistent with the philosophical concerns typically underlying idealizing views.[11] . . .

VII. CONCLUSION

I conclude, then, that . . . idealizers are not likely to be able to present a rationale for their idealization that is consistent with the philosophical concerns

underlying their views. Of the . . . ways of supplying such a rationale I can think of, none is available to the . . . idealizer. If this is indeed so, we have, I think, a strong reason to reject such idealization. Until the idealizer comes up with such a rationale for her idealization, then, the response-dependence theorist is faced with a choice: settle for actual, nonidealized responses or else abandon response-dependence altogether. If the former is as unattractive as it seems, the prospects for an adequate response-dependence theory of normativity do not seem promising.

NOTES

1. David Lewis, "Dispositional Theories of Value," in his *Papers in Ethics and Social Philosophy* (Cambridge: Cambridge University Press, 2000), 68–94, originally published in *Proceedings of the Aristotelian Society* 63, suppl. (1989): 113–37.
2. Lewis, "Dispositional Theories of Value," 77 (footnote omitted and italics added). . . .
3. See David Sobel, "Explanation, Internalism, and Reasons for Action," *Social Philosophy and Policy* 18 (2001): 218–35, 233 . . .
4. Perhaps Plato's view of the relation between the good and our motivations can serve as an example of tracking internalism.
5. This line of thought is implicit, I think, in . . . Lewis, "Dispositional Theories of Value," 77.
6. I found it made most explicitly in Lewis ("Dispositional Theories of Value," 87), though there it is presented as an argument not so much for the truth of his idealizing view as an argument for its status as analytic. . . .
7. What he wants to save are statements about what is (really, as it were) religiously required, not merely statements about what participants in the relevant religious practice consider religiously required. He wants to argue that some actions (say) really are religiously required.
8. This is so even if some participants endorse Ideal Prophet Theory. The question relevant here is not what (if any) explicit metareligious beliefs participants have (or think they have), but rather what metareligious commitments are embedded (though perhaps implicitly) in their practice.

9. Or that these ideal conditions are indicative of being in such epistemic conditions.

10. See, e.g., Lewis, "Dispositional Theories of Value," 92.

11. Perhaps Lewis's mistake—discussed in Sec. II above—strengthens this point, for it shows that even such a prominent idealizer is tempted by our practice to say things that sound more robustly realist.

STUDY QUESTIONS

1. What are idealizations?
2. What does Enoch believe is the obvious rationale for idealization?
3. According to Enoch, why is the response-dependence theorist barred from this rationale?
4. What point does Enoch seek to establish by the example of the Ideal Prophet Theorist?

Part VIII

CONSTRUCTIVISM

Themes in Kant's Moral Philosophy

John Rawls

John Rawls (1921–2002) was Professor of Philosophy at Harvard University. He offers a constructivist interpretation of Immanuel Kant's moral philosophy, a view that fits well with Rawls's own work in political philosophy. He contrasts constructivism with the rational intuitionism (or non-naturalist realism) of Sidgwick and Moore. Rawls explains that rational intuitionism can be characterized as holding three theses. First, normative concepts are not analyzable in terms of non-normative concepts. Second, foundational normative principles deploying these concepts state truths about which facts count as reasons. Third, the truth of these principles is independent of our conception of persons. Rawls argues that Kant accepts the first two of these theses but rejects the third. The link to persons, however, does not invite relativism or subjectivism. Rather, foundational normative principles are specified by a procedure that reflects our nature as reasonable and rational. Since this procedure, Kant's categorical imperative, expresses requirements constitutive of rational agency as such, all reasonable and rational persons will acknowledge any principles generated as correct. In short, from the nature of persons as such we arrive, via the procedure of the categorical imperative, at objective (in the sense of a shared agreement on) normative principles.

I shall discuss here several connected themes in Kant's moral philosophy, in particular what I shall refer to as moral constructivism and the fact of reason, and how that fact connects with the authentication of the moral law and the moral law as a law of freedom. . . .

To set the background for these topics, I begin with a schematic outline of how Kant understands the moral law, the categorical imperative and the procedure by which that imperative is applied. Some account of that procedure is an essential preliminary to understanding his constructivism. . . .

My discussion has [three] parts: the first covers the procedure for applying the categorical imperative, or the CI-procedure, as I shall call it; the second surveys six conceptions of the good, and how these conceptions are constructed in an ordered sequence; whereas the third, based on the preceding two parts, examines the aspects of Kant's doctrine that make it constructivist and specify a conception of objectivity. . . .

From John Rawls, "Themes in Kant's Moral Philosophy," in *Collected Papers*, ed. Samuel Freeman (Cambridge, MA: Harvard University Press, 1999). Reprinted by permission of the publisher.

1. THE FOUR-STEP
CI-PROCEDURE

1. I begin with a highly schematic rendering of Kant's conception of the categorical imperative. I assume that this imperative is applied to the normal conditions of human life by what I shall call the "categorical imperative procedure," or the "CI-procedure" for short. This procedure helps to determine the content of the moral law as it applies to us as reasonable and rational persons endowed with conscience and moral sensibility, and affected by, but not determined by, our natural desires and inclinations. These desires and inclinations reflect our needs as finite beings having a particular place in the order of nature.

Recall that the moral law, the categorical imperative, and the CI-procedure are three different things. The first is an idea of reason and specifies a principle that applies to all reasonable and rational beings whether or not they are like us finite beings with needs. The second is an imperative and as such it is directed only to those reasonable and rational beings who, because they are finite beings with needs, experience the moral law as a constraint. Since we are such beings, we experience the law in this way, and so the categorical imperative applies to us. The CI-procedure adapts the categorical imperative to our circumstances by taking into account the normal conditions of human life and our situation as finite beings with needs in the order of nature.

Keep in mind throughout that Kant is concerned solely with the reasoning of fully reasonable and rational and sincere agents. The CI-procedure is a schema to characterize the framework of deliberation that such agents use implicitly in their moral thought. He takes for granted that the application of this procedure presupposes a certain moral sensibility that is part of our common humanity. It is a misconception to think of it either as an algorithm that yields more or less mechanically a correct judgment, or on the other hand, as a set of debating rules that will trap liars and cheats, cynics and other scoundrels, into exposing their hand.

2. The CI-procedure has four steps as follows. At the first step we have the agent's maxim, which is, by assumption, rational from the agent's point of view: that is, the maxim is rational given the agent's situation and the alternatives available together with the agent's desires, abilities, and beliefs (which are assumed to be rational in the circumstances). The maxim is also assumed to be sincere: that is, it reflects the agent's actual reasons (as the agent would truthfully describe them) for the intended action. Thus the CI-procedure applies to maxims that rational agents have arrived at in view of what they regard as the relevant features of their circumstances. And, we should add, this procedure applies equally well to maxims that rational and sincere agents might arrive at given the normal circumstances of human life. To sum up: the agent's maxim at the first step is both rational and sincere. It is a particular hypothetical imperative (to be distinguished later from *the* hypothetical imperative) and it has the form:

> (1) I am to do X in circumstances C in order to bring about Y. (Here X is an action and Y a state of affairs.)

The second step generalizes the maxim at the first to get:

> (2) Everyone is to do X in circumstances C in order to bring about Y.

At the third step we are to transform the general precept at (2) into a law of nature to obtain:

> (3) Everyone always does X in circumstances C in order to bring about Y (as if by a law of nature).

The fourth step is the most complicated . . . The idea is this:

> (4) We are to adjoin the law of nature at step (3) to the existing laws of nature (as these are understood by us) and then calculate as best we can what the order of nature would be once the

effects of the newly adjoined law of nature have had a chance to work themselves out.

It is assumed that a new order of nature results from the addition of the law at step (3) to the other laws of nature, and that this new order of nature has a settled equilibrium state the relevant features of which we are able to figure out. Let us call this new order of nature a "perturbed social world," and let's think of this social world as associated with the maxim at step (1).

Kant's categorical imperative can now be stated as follows: We are permitted to act from our rational and sincere maxim at step (1) only if two conditions are satisfied: First, we must be able to intend, as a sincere reasonable and rational agent, to act from this maxim when we regard ourselves as a member of the perturbed social world associated with it (and thus as acting within that world and subject to its conditions); and second, we must be able to will this perturbed social world itself and affirm it should we belong to it.

Thus, if we cannot at the same time both will this perturbed social world and intend to act from this maxim as a member of it, we cannot now act from the maxim even though it is, by assumption, rational and sincere in our present circumstances. The principle represented by the CI-procedure applies to us no matter what the consequences may be for our rational interests as we now understand them. It is at this point that the force of the priority of pure practical reason over empirical practical reason comes into play. . . .

3. To illustrate the use of the four-step procedure, consider the fourth example in the *Grundlegung* [*Groundwork*] (Gr 4:423). The maxim to be tested is one that expresses indifference to the well-being of others who need our help and assistance. We are to decide whether we can will the perturbed social world associated with this maxim formulated as follows.

> I am not to do anything to help others, or to support them in distress, unless at the time it is rational to do so, given my own interests.

The perturbed social world associated with this maxim is a social world in which no one ever does anything to help others for the sake of their well-being. And this is true of everyone, past, present, and future. This is the relevant equilibrium state; and we are to imagine that this state obtains, like any other order of nature, in perpetuity, backwards and forwards in time. Kant takes for granted that everyone in the perturbed social world knows the laws of human conduct that arise from generalized maxims and that everyone is able to work out the relevant equilibrium state. Moreover, that everyone is able to do this is itself public knowledge. Thus, the operation at step (3) converts a general precept at step (2) into a publicly recognized law of (human) nature. That Kant takes these matters for granted is clearest from his second example, that of the deceitful promise.

Now Kant says that we cannot will the perturbed social world associated with the maxim of indifference because many situations may arise in that world in which we need the love and sympathy of others. In those situations, by a law originating from our own will, we would have robbed ourselves of what we require. It would be irrational for us to will a social world in which every one, as if by a law of nature, is deaf to appeals based on this need. Kant does not say much about how the idea of a rational will works in this example. In addition, the test as he applies it to the maxim of indifference is too strong: that is, the same test rejects those maxims that lead to any form of the precept (or duty) of mutual aid. The reason is this: any such precept enjoins us to help others when they are in need. But here also, in the perturbed social world associated with [a] precept to help others in need, situations may arise in which we very much want not to help them. The circumstances may be such that helping them seriously interferes with our plans. Thus, in these cases too, by a law originating from our own will, we would have prevented ourselves from achieving what we very much want. The difficulty is clear enough: in any perturbed social world all moral precepts will oppose our natural desires and settled intentions on at least some occasions. Hence the test of the

CI-procedure, as Kant apparently understands it, is too strong: it appears to reject all maxims that led to moral precepts (or duties).

4. One way out, I think, but I don't say the only one, is to try to develop an appropriate conception of what we may call "true human needs," a phrase Kant uses several times in the *Metaphysics of Morals* (MM 6:393, 432; see also 452–458). Once this is done, the contradiction in the will test as illustrated by the fourth example might be formulated as follows:

> Can I will the perturbed social world associated with the precept of indifference rather than the perturbed social world associated with a precept of mutual aid, that is, a maxim enjoining me to help others in need? In answering this question I am to take account only of my true human needs (which by assumption, as part of the CI-procedure, I take myself to have and to be the same for everyone).

Thus, in applying the procedure as now revised we understand that any general precept will constrain our actions prompted by our desires and inclinations on some and perhaps many occasions. What we must do is to compare alternative social worlds and evaluate the overall consequences of willing one of these worlds rather than another. In order to do this, we are to take into account the balance of likely effects over time for our true human needs. Of course for this idea to work, we require an account for these needs. And here certain moral conceptions, rooted in our shared moral sensibility, may be involved.

I believe that Kant also assumes that the evaluation of perturbed social worlds at step (4) is subject to at least two limits on information. The first limit is that we are to ignore the more particular features of persons, including ourselves, as well as the specific content of their and our final ends and desires (Gr 4:433). The second limit is that when we ask ourselves whether we can will the perturbed social world associated with our maxim, we are to reason as if we do not know which place we may have in that world (see the discussion of the Typic in

The Critique of Practical Reason 5:69–70). The CI-procedure is misapplied when we project into the perturbed social world either the specific content of our final ends, or the particular features of our present or likely future circumstances. We must reason at step (4) not only on the basis of true human needs but also from a suitably general point of view that satisfies these two limits on particular (as opposed to general) information. We must see ourselves as proposing the public moral law for an ongoing social world enduring over time.

5. This brief schematic account of the CI-procedure is intended only to set the background for explaining the sequence of conceptions of the good in Section 2 and Kant's moral constructivism in Section 3. To serve this purpose, the procedure must meet two conditions: (1) it must not represent the requirements of the moral law as merely formal; otherwise, the moral law lacks sufficient content for a constructivist view; and (2) it must have features that enable us to see what Kant means when he says that the moral law discloses our freedom to us . . . ; for this, too, is an essential part of Kant's constructivism, since freedom of moral thought and action is required if the constructivist procedure is to be authenticated as objective, as the work of reason . . .

It turns out that for the second condition to be met, the CI-procedure must display in how it works, on its face as it were, the way in which pure practical reason is prior to empirical practical reason. This enables us to understand the distinctive structure of Kant's moral conception and how it is possible for our freedom to be made manifest to us by the moral law.

What this priority means will become clearer as we proceed. For the present let's say that pure practical reason restricts empirical practical reason and subordinates it absolutely. This is an aspect of the unity of reason. The way in which pure practical reason restricts and subordinates empirical practical reason is expressed in imperative form by the CI-procedure: this procedure represents the requirements of pure practical reason in the manner appropriate for the conditions of human life. Empirical practical reason is the principle of rational deliberation that determines when particular hypothetical imperatives are rational. The CI-procedure restricts empirical practical reason by requiring the agent's rational and sincere deliberations to be conducted in accordance with the stipulations we have just surveyed. Unless a maxim passes the test of that procedure, acting from the maxim is forbidden. This outcome is final from the standpoint of practical reason as a whole, both pure and empirical. The survey of six conceptions of the good in Kant's doctrine in the next part (Section 3) will supplement these remarks about how the two forms of practical reason are combined in the unity of practical reason.

6. Before turning to this survey, a few comments on the sketch of the CI-procedure. In characterizing human persons I have used the phrase "reasonable and rational." The intention here is to mark the fact that Kant uses *vernünftig* to express a full-bodied conception that covers the terms "reasonable" and "rational" as we often use them. In English we know what is meant when someone says: "Their proposal is rational, given their circumstances, but it is unreasonable all the same." The meaning is roughly that the people referred to are pushing a hard and unfair bargain, which they know to be in their own interests but which they wouldn't expect us to accept unless they knew their position is strong. "Reasonable" can also mean "judicious," "ready to listen to reason," where this has the sense of being willing to listen to and consider the reasons offered by others. *Vernünftig* can have the same meanings in German: it can have the broad sense of "reasonable" as well as the narrower sense of "rational" to mean roughly furthering our interests in the most effective way. Kant's usage varies but when applied to persons it usually covers being both reasonable and rational. His use of "reason" often has the even fuller sense of the philosophical tradition. Think of what *Vernunft* means in the title the *Critique of Pure Reason*! We are worlds away from "rational" in the narrow sense. . . .

It is useful, then, to use "reasonable" and "rational" as handy terms to mark the distinction that Kant makes between the two forms of practical reason, pure and empirical. The first is expressed as an imperative in *the* categorical imperative, the second in *the* hypothetical imperative. These forms of practical reason must also be distinguished from

particular categorical and hypothetical imperatives (the particular maxims at step (1)) that satisfy the corresponding requirements of practical reason in particular circumstances. The terms "reasonable" and "rational" remind us of the fullness of Kant's conception of practical reason and of the two forms of reason it comprehends. . . .

2. THE SEQUENCE OF SIX CONCEPTIONS OF THE GOOD

1. In order to understand Kant's constructivism and how he thinks that the moral law discloses our freedom to us, we need to look at the priority of pure practical reason over empirical practical reason, and to distinguish six conceptions of the good in Kant's doctrine. These conceptions are built up in a sequence one by one from the preceding ones. This sequence can be presented by referring to the four steps of the CI-procedure, since each conception can be connected with a particular step in this procedure. This provides a useful way of arranging these conceptions and clarifies the relations between them. It also enables us to explain what is meant by calling the realm of ends the necessary object of a will determined by the moral law, as well as what is meant by saying of this realm that it is an object given a priori to such a pure will (CP 5:4).

The first of the six conceptions of the good is given by unrestricted empirical practical reason. It is the conception of happiness as organized by the (as opposed to a particular) hypothetical imperative. This conception may be connected with step (1) of the CI-procedure, since the maxim at this step is assumed to be rational and sincere given that conception. Thus the maxim satisfies the principles of rational deliberation that characterize the hypothetical imperative, or what we may call "the rational." There are no restrictions on the information available to sincere and rational agents either in framing their conceptions of happiness or in forming their particular maxims: all the relevant particulars about their desires, abilities, and situation, as well as the available alternatives, are assumed to be known.

The second conception of the good is of the fulfillment of true human needs. I have suggested that at the fourth step of the CI-procedure we require some such idea. Otherwise the agent going through the procedure cannot compare the perturbed social worlds associated with different maxims. At first we might think this comparison can be made on the basis of the agent's conception of happiness. But even if the agent knows what this conception is, there is still a serious difficulty, since Kant supposes different agents to have different conceptions of their happiness. On this view, happiness is an ideal, not of reason but of the imagination, and so our conception of our happiness depends on the contingencies of our life, and on particular modes of thought and feeling we have developed as we come of age. Thus, if conceptions of happiness are used in judging social worlds at step (4), then whether a maxim passes the CI-procedure would depend on who applies it. This dependence would defeat Kant's view. For if our following the CI-procedure doesn't lead to approximate agreement when we apply it intelligently and conscientiously against the background of the same information, then that law lacks objective content. Here objective content means a content that is publicly recognized as correct, as based on sufficient reasons and as (roughly) the same for all reasonable and sincere human agents.

Observe that this second conception of the good based on true human needs is a special conception designed expressly to be used at step (4) of the CI-procedure. It is formulated to meet a need of reason: namely, that the moral law have sufficient objective content. Moreover, when this procedure is thought of as applied consistently by everyone over time in accordance with the requirement of complete determination (Gr 4:436), it specifies the content of a conception of right and justice that would be realized in a realm of ends. This conception, as opposed to the first, is restricted: that is, it is framed in view of the restrictions on information to which agents are subject at step (4).

The third conception of the good is the good as the fulfillment in everyday life of what Kant calls "permissible ends" (MM 6:388), that is, ends that respect the limits of the moral law. This means in practice that we are to revise, abandon, or repress desires and inclinations that prompt us to rational and sincere maxims at step (1) that are rejected by the CI-procedure. Here it is not a question of balancing the strength and importance to us of our natural desires against the strength and importance to us of the pure practical interest we take in acting from the moral law. Such balancing is excluded entirely. Rather, whenever our maxim is rejected, we must reconsider our intended course of action, for in this case the claim to satisfy the desires in question is rejected. At this point the contrast with utilitarianism is clear, since for Kant this third conception of the good presupposes the moral law and the principles of pure practical reason. Whereas utilitarianism starts with a conception of the good given prior to, and independent of, the right (the moral law), and it then works out from that independent conception its conceptions of the right and of moral worth, in that order. In Kant's view, however, unrestricted rationality, or the rational, is framed by, and subordinated absolutely to, a procedure that incorporates the constraints of the reasonable. It is by this procedure that admissible conceptions of the good and their permissible ends are specified.

2. The first of the three remaining conceptions of the good is the familiar conception of the good will, This is Kant's conception of moral worth: a completely good will is the supreme (although not the complete) good of persons and of their character as reasonable and rational beings. This good is constituted by a firm and settled highest-order desire that leads us to take an interest in acting from the moral law for its own sake, or, what comes in practice to the same thing, to further the realm of ends as the moral law requires. When we have a completely good will, this highest-order desire, however strongly it may be opposed by our natural desires and inclinations, is always strong enough by itself to ensure that we act from (and not merely in accordance with) the moral law.

The next conception of the good is the good as the object of the moral law, which is . . . the realm of ends. This object is simply the social world that would come about (at least under reasonably favorable conditions) if everyone were to follow the totality of precepts that result from the correct application of the CI-procedure. Kant sometimes refers to the realm of ends as the necessary object of a will, which is determined by the moral law, or alternatively, as an object that is given a priori to a will determined by that law (CP 5:4). By this I think he means that the realm of ends is an object—a social world—the moral constitution and regulation of which is specified by the totality of precepts that meet the test of the CI-procedure (when these precepts are adjusted and coordinated by the requirement of complete determination). Put another way, the realm of ends is not a social world that can be described prior to and independent of the concepts and principles of practical reason and the procedure by which they are applied. That realm is not an already given describable object the nature of which determines the content of the moral law. This would be the case, for example, if this law were understood as stating what must be done in order to bring about a good society the nature and institutions of which are already specified apart from the moral law. That such a teleological conception is foreign to Kant's doctrine is plain from ch. II of the Analytic of the *Critique of Practical Reason*. The burden of that chapter is to explain what has been called Kant's "Copernican Revolution" in moral philosophy (CP 5:62–65).[1] Rather than starting from a conception of the good given independently of the right, we start from a conception of the right—of the moral law—given by pure (as opposed to empirical) practical reason. We then specify in the light of this conception what ends are permissible and what social arrangements are right and just. We might say: a moral conception is not to revolve around the good as an independent object, but around a conception of the right as constructed by our pure practical reason into which any permissible good must fit. Kant believes that once we start from the good as an independent given object, the moral conception must be heteronomous . . . In these cases what determines our will is an object given to it and not principles originating in our pure reason as reasonable and rational beings.

Finally, there is Kant's conception of the complete good. This is the good that is attained when a realm of ends exists and each member of it not only has a completely good will but is also fully happy so far as the normal conditions of human life allow. Here, of course, happiness is specified by the satisfaction of ends that respect the requirements of the moral law, and so are permissible ends. Often Kant refers to this complete good as the highest good. This is his preferred term after the *Grundlegung*, especially when he is presenting his doctrine of reasonable faith in the second *Critique*. I shall use the secular term "realized realm of ends," and I assume that this complete good can be approximated to in the natural world, at least under reasonably favorable conditions. In this sense it is a natural good, one that can be approached (although never fully realized) within the order of nature.

Kant holds that in the complete good, the good will is the supreme good, that is, we must have a good will if the other goods we enjoy are to be truly good and our enjoyment of them fully appropriate. This applies in particular to the good of happiness, since he thinks that only our having a good will can make us worthy of happiness. Kant also believes that two goods so different in their nature, and in their foundations in our person, as a good will and happiness are incommensurable; and, therefore, that they can be combined into one unified and complete good only by the relation of the strict priority of one over the other.

3. The preceding sketch of conceptions of the good in Kant's view indicates how they are built up, or constructed, in an ordered sequence one after the other, each conception (except the first) depending on the preceding ones. If we count the second (that of true human needs) as part of the CI-procedure itself, we can say that beginning with the third (that of permissible ends), these conceptions presuppose an independent conception of right (the reasonable). This conception of right is represented by the CI-procedure as the application of pure practical reason to the conditions of human life. Only the first conception of the good is entirely independent of the moral law, since it is the rational without restriction. Thus the sequence of conceptions beginning with the second exemplifies the priority of pure practical reason over empirical practical reason and displays the distinctive deontological and constructivist structure of Kant's view. We start with two forms of practical reason, the reasonable and the rational. The unity of practical reason is grounded in how the reasonable frames the rational and restricts it absolutely. Then we proceed step by step to generate different conceptions of the good and obtain at the last two steps the conceptions of the good will and of a complete good as a fully realized realm of ends. The contrast between the deontological and constructivist structure of Kant's doctrine and the linear structure of a teleological view starting from an independent conception of the good is so obvious as not to need comment.

3. KANT'S MORAL CONSTRUCTIVISM

1. We are now in a position to see what is meant in saying that Kant's moral doctrine is constructivist, and why the term "constructivist" is appropriate.

One way to bring out the features of Kant's moral constructivism is to contrast it with rational intuitionism. The latter doctrine has, of course, been expressed in many ways; but in some form it dominated moral philosophy from Plato and Aristotle onward until it was challenged by Hobbes and Hume, and, I believe, in a very different way, by Kant. To simplify things, I take rational intuitionism to be the view exemplified in the English tradition . . . by Henry Sidgwick and G. E. Moore, and formulated in its minimum essentials by W. D. Ross. . . .

For our purposes here, rational intuitionism may be summed up in three theses, the first two of which it has in common with a number of other views, including Kant's. These three theses are: *First,* the basic moral concepts of the right and the good, and the moral worth of persons, are not analyzable in terms of nonmoral concepts (although possibly they are analyzable in terms of one another). *Second,* first principles of morals (whether one or many), when correctly stated, are true statements about what kinds of considerations are good reasons for applying one of the three basic moral concepts: that is, for asserting that something is (intrinsically) good, or that a certain institution is just or a certain action right, or that a certain trait of character or motive has moral worth. *Third* (and this is the distinctive thesis for our purposes), first principles, as statements about good reasons, are regarded as true or false in virtue of a moral order of values that is prior to and independent of our conceptions of person and society, and of the public social role of moral doctrines.

This prior moral order is already given, as it were, by the nature of things and is known by rational intuition (or in some views by moral sense, but I leave this possibility aside). Thus, our agreement in judgment when properly founded is said to be based on the shared recognition of truths about a prior order of values accessible to reason. Observe that no reference is made to self-evidence; for although intuitionists have often held first principles to be self-evident, this feature is not essential.

It should be observed that rational intuitionism is compatible with a variety of contents for the first principles of a moral conception. Even classical utilitarianism, which Sidgwick in his *Methods of Ethics* was strongly inclined to favor, was sometimes viewed by him as following from three more fundamental principles, each grasped by rational intuition in its own right. Of the recent versions of rational intuitionism, the appeal to rational intuition is perhaps most striking in Moore's so-called ideal utilitarianism in *Principia Ethica*. A consequence of Moore's principle of organic unity is that his view is extremely pluralistic: there are few if any useful first principles, and distinct kinds of cases are to be decided by intuition as they arise. Moore held a kind of Platonic atomism: moral concepts (along with other concepts) are subsisting and independent entities grasped by the mind. That pleasure and beauty are good, and that different combinations of them alone, or together with other good things, are also good, and to what degree, are truths known by intuition: by seeing with the mind's eye how these distinct objects (universals) are (timelessly) related.

Now my aim in recalling these familiar matters is to indicate how rational intuitionism, as illustrated by Sidgwick, Moore, and Ross, is distinct from a constructivist moral conception. That Kant would have rejected Hume's psychological naturalism as heteronomous is clear. But I believe that the contrast with rational intuitionism, regardless of the specific content of the view (whether utilitarian, perfectionist, or pluralist) is even more instructive. It has seemed less obvious that for Kant rational intuitionism is also heteronomous. Perhaps the reason is that in rational intuitionism basic moral concepts are conceptually independent of natural concepts, and first principles as grasped by rational intuition are viewed as synthetic a priori, and so independent of any particular order of nature. They give the content of an ethics of creation, so to speak: the principles God would use to ascertain which is the best of all possible worlds. Thus, it may seem that for Kant such principles are not heteronomous.

Yet in Kant's moral constructivism it suffices for heteronomy that first principles obtain in virtue of relations among objects the nature of which is not affected or determined by our conception of ourselves as reasonable and rational persons (as possessing the powers of practical reason), and of the public role of moral principles in a society of such persons. Of particular importance is the conception of persons as reasonable and rational, and, therefore, as free and equal, and the basic units of agency and responsibility. Kant's idea of autonomy requires that there exists no moral order prior to and independent of those conceptions that is to determine the form of the procedure that specifies the content of first principles of right and justice among free and equal persons. Heteronomy obtains not only when these first principles are fixed by the special psychological constitution of human nature, as in Hume, but also when they are fixed by an order of universals, or of moral values grasped by rational intuition, as in Plato's realm of forms . . .

Thus an essential feature of Kant's moral constructivism is that the first principles of right and justice are seen as specified by a procedure of construction (the CI-procedure) the form and structure of which mirrors our free moral personality as both reasonable and rational. This conception of the person he regards as implicit in our everyday moral consciousness. A Kantian doctrine may hold (as Kant did) that the procedure by which first principles are specified, or constructed, is synthetic a

priori. This thesis, however, must be properly understood. It simply means that the form and structure of this procedure express the requirements of practical reason. These requirements are embedded in our conception of persons as reasonable and rational, and as the basic units of agency and responsibility. This conception is found in how we represent to ourselves our free and equal moral personality in everyday life, or in what Kant in the second *Critique* calls "the fact of reason."

It is characteristic of Kant's doctrine that a relatively complex conception of the person plays a central role in specifying the content of his moral view. By contrast, rational intuitionism requires but a sparse conception of the person, based on the idea of the person as knower. This is because the content of first principles is already given, and the only requirement is that we be able to know what these principles are and to be moved by this knowledge. A basic psychological assumption is that the recognition of first principles as true of a prior and antecedent order of moral values gives rise, in a being capable of rationally intuiting those principles, to a desire to act from them for their own sake. Moral motivation is defined by reference to desires that have a special kind of causal origin, namely, the intuitive grasp of first principles. This sparse conception of the person together with this psychological assumption characterizes the moral psychology of Sidgwick, Moore, and Ross. Of course, intuitionism is not forced to so sparse a conception. The point is rather that, since the content of first principles is already given, it is simply unnecessary to have a more elaborate moral psychology or a fuller conception of the person of a kind required to specify the form, structure, and content of a constructivist moral view.
2. So much for explaining Kant's moral constructivism by the contrast with rational intuitionism. Let's turn to a more specific account of the constructivist features of his view. . . .

My aim is to see the way in which Kant's moral doctrine has features that quite naturally lead us to think of it as constructivist, and then how this connects with the themes of the unity of reason and the moral law as an idea of freedom. To this end, let's consider three questions.

First, in moral constructivism, *what* is it that is constructed? The answer is: the *content* of the doctrine.[2] In Kant's view this means that the totality of particular categorical imperatives (general precepts at step (2)) that pass the test of the CI-procedure are seen as constructed by a procedure of construction worked through by *rational* agents subject to various *reasonable* constraints. These agents are rational in that, subject to the reasonable constraints of the procedure, they are guided by empirical practical reason, or the principles of *rational* deliberation that fall under *the* hypothetical imperative.

A *second* question is this: Is the CI-procedure itself constructed? No, it is not. Rather, it is simply *laid out.* Kant believes that our everyday human understanding is implicitly aware of the requirements of practical reason, both pure and empirical; . . . this is part of his doctrine of the fact of reason. So we look at how Kant seems to reason when he presents his various examples and we try to *lay out* in procedural form *all* the conditions he seems to rely on. Our aim in doing this is to incorporate into that procedure *all* the relevant criteria of practical reasonableness and rationality, so that the judgments that result from a *correct* use of the procedure are *themselves* correct (given the requisite true beliefs about the social world). These judgments are correct because they meet all the requirements of practical reason.

Third, what, more exactly, does it mean to say, as I said a while back, that the form and structure of the CI-procedure *mirrors* our free moral personality as both reasonable and rational? The idea here is that not everything can be constructed and every construction has a basis, certain materials, as it were, from which it begins. While the CI-procedure is not, as noted above, constructed but laid out, it does have a *basis*; and this basis is the conception of free and equal persons as reasonable and rational, a conception that is *mirrored* in the procedure. We discern how persons are mirrored in the procedure by noting what powers and abilities, kinds of beliefs and wants, and the like, they must have as agents who are viewed as implicitly guided by the procedure and as being moved to conform to the particular categorical imperatives it authenticates. We look at the procedure as laid out, and we consider the use Kant makes of it, and from that we elaborate what his conception of persons must be. This conception, along with the conception of a society of such persons, each of whom can be a legislative member of a realm of ends, constitutes the basis of Kant's constructivism. Thus, we don't say that the conceptions of person and society are constructed. It is unclear what that could mean. Nor do we say they are laid out. Rather, these conceptions are *elicited* from our moral experience and from what is involved in our being able to work through the CI-procedure and to act from the moral law as it applies to us.

To illustrate: that we are both reasonable and rational is mirrored in the fact that the CI-procedure involves both forms of reasoning. We are said to be rational at step (1), and indeed at all steps, since the deliberations of agents within the constraints of the procedure always fall under the rational. We are also said to be reasonable, since if we weren't moved by the reasonable, we would not take what Kant calls a pure practical interest in checking our maxims against the procedure's requirements; nor when a maxim is rejected would we have such an interest in revising our intentions and checking whether our revised maxim is acceptable. The deliberations of agents *within* the steps of the procedure and subject to its reasonable constraints mirror our rationality; our motivation as persons in caring about those constraints and taking an interest in acting in ways that meet the procedure's requirements mirrors our being reasonable.

The conception of free and equal persons as reasonable and rational is the *basis* of the construction: unless this conception and the powers of moral personality it includes—our humanity—are animated, as it were, in human beings, the moral law would have no basis in the world. Recall here Kant's thought that to commit suicide is to root out the existence of morality from the world (MM 6:422–423).

3. It is important to see that the contrast between rational intuitionism and Kant's moral constructivism is not a contrast between objectivism and subjectivism. For both views have a conception of objectivity; but each understands objectivity in a different way.

In rational intuitionism a correct moral judgment, or principle, is one that is true of a prior and independent order of moral values. This order is also prior to the criteria of reasonableness and rationality as well as prior to the appropriate conception of persons as autonomous and responsible, and free and equal members of a moral community. Indeed, it is that order that settles what those reasonable and rational criteria are, and how autonomy and responsibility are to be conceived.

In Kant's doctrine, on the other hand, a correct moral judgment is one that conforms to all the relevant criteria of reasonableness and rationality the total force of which is expressed by the way they are combined into the CI-procedure. He thinks of this procedure as suitably joining together all the requirements of our (human) practical reason, both pure and empirical, into one unified scheme of practical reasoning. As we saw, this is an aspect of the unity of reason. Thus, the general principles and precepts generated by the correct use of that procedure of deliberation satisfy the conditions for valid judgments imposed by the form and structure of our common (human) practical reason. This form and structure is a priori, rooted in our pure practical reason, and thus for us practically necessary. A judgment supported by those principles and precepts will, then, be acknowledged as correct by any fully reasonable and rational (and informed) person.

A conception of objectivity must include an account of our agreement in judgments, how it comes about. Kant accounts for this agreement by our sharing in a common practical reason. For this idea to succeed, we must suppose, as Kant does, that whoever applies the CI-procedure, roughly the same judgments are reached, provided the procedure is applied intelligently and conscientiously, and against the background of roughly the same beliefs and information. Reasonable and rational persons must recognize more or less the same reasons and give them more or less the same weight. Indeed, for the idea of judgment even to apply, as opposed to the idea of our simply giving voice to our psychological state, we must be able to reach agreement in judgment, not of course always, but much of the time. And when we can't do so, we must be able to explain our failure by the

difficulties of the question, that is, by the difficulties of surveying and assessing the available evidence, or else the delicate balance of the competing reasons on opposite sides of the issue, either or both of which leads us to expect that reasonable persons may differ. Or, alternatively, the disagreement arises from a lack of reasonableness or rationality or conscientiousness on the part of one or more persons involved, where of course the test of this lack cannot simply be the fact of disagreement itself, or the fact that other persons disagree with us. We must have independent grounds for thinking these causes of disagreement are at work.

Finally, to prevent misunderstanding, I should add that Kant's constructivism does not say that moral facts, much less all facts, are constructed. Rather, a constructivist procedure provides principles and precepts that specify *which* facts about persons, institutions, and actions, and the world generally, are relevant in moral deliberation. Those norms specify which facts are to *count* as reasons. We should not say that the moral facts are constructed, since the idea of constructing the facts seems odd and may be incoherent; by contrast, the idea of a constructivist procedure generating principles and precepts singling out the facts to count as reasons seems quite clear. We have only to recall how the CI-procedure accepts some maxims and rejects others. The facts are there already, so to speak, available in our everyday experience or identified by theoretical reason, but apart from a constructivist moral conception they are simply facts. What is needed is a way to single out which facts are relevant from a moral point of view and to determine their weight as reasons. Viewed this way, a constructivist conception is not at odds with our ordinary idea of truth and matters of fact. . . .

NOTES

1. John Silber, "The Copernican Revolution in Ethics: The Goad Re-examined," *Kant-Studien,* 51 (1959).
2. It should be noted that this content can never be specified completely. The moral law is an idea of reason, and since an idea of reason can never be fully realized, neither can the content of such an idea. It is always a matter of approximating thereto, and always subject to error and correction.

STUDY QUESTIONS

1. How does Rawls distinguish "rational" and "reasonable"?
2. What is Kant's conception of the complete good?
3. According to Rawls, how does the procedure of the categorical imperative reflect the nature of persons?
4. According to Rawls, how does Kant's conception of "objectivity" differ from that of Sidgwick and Moore?

Self-Constitution

Christine M. Korsgaard

Christine Korsgaard is Professor of Philosophy at Harvard University. She defends constructivism, the view that the formal features of practical rationality are the source of all substantive normative truths. On Korsgaard's Kantian version of constructivism, we start with what it takes to act or make choices as such and move to the claim that we must value humanity in others and ourselves. But how do we make this move from the mere formal features of choice and action to the substantive claim that we must value humanity?

Korsgaard argues that in order to act we need reasons. Absent reasons, what is done is not an action but an involuntary spasm. Reasons for action, however, demand some principle (or law) with which we identify. This identification, in turn, demands a practical identity working as an integrated whole. Agents need a description under which they value themselves, and see actions as worth taking. Absent such an identity they will lack any reasons from which to act. Thus a unified practical identity is a constitutive feature of choice and action. Korsgaard argues that the only identity that could play this unifying role, without another identity-supplying reason to accept it, is the practical identity we have as rational agents—that is, human beings. Accordingly, to value at all, we must value our own humanity.

[1.] AGENCY AND IDENTITY

1.1 Necessitation

1.1.1

Human beings are *condemned* to choice and action. Maybe you think you can avoid it, by resolutely standing still, refusing to act, refusing to move. But it's no use, for that will be something you have chosen to do, and then you will have acted after all. Choosing not to act makes not acting a kind of action, makes it something that you do.

This is not to say that you cannot fail to act. Of course you can. You can fall asleep at the wheel, you can faint dead away, you can be paralyzed with terror, you can be helpless with pain, or grief can turn you to stone. And then you will fail to act. But you can't *undertake* to be in those conditions—if you did, you'd be faking, and what's more, you'd be acting, in a wonderfully double sense of that word. So as long as you're in charge, so long as nothing happens to derail you, you must act. You have no choice but to choose, and to act on your choice.

From Christine Korsgaard, *Self-Constitution: Agency, Identity, and Integrity* (Oxford: Oxford University Press, 2009). Reprinted by permission of the publisher.

So action is necessary. What kind of necessity is this? Philosophers like to distinguish between *logical* and *causal* necessity. But the necessity of action isn't either of those. There's no logical contradiction in the idea of a person not acting, at least on any particular occasion. You could not fail to act, in all the ways I've just described, if there were. And although particular actions, or anyway particular movements, may have causes, the general necessity of action is not an event that is caused. I'm not talking about something that works *on* you, whether you know it or not, like a cause: I am talking about a necessity you are *faced* with.

Now sometimes we also talk about *rational* necessity, the necessity of following the principles of reason. If you believe the premises, then you *must* draw the conclusion. If you will the end, then you *must* will the means. That's rational necessity, and it's a necessity you are faced with, so that comes closer. But the necessity of action isn't quite like that either, for in those cases we have an if-clause, and the necessity of action is, by contrast, as Kant would say, unconditional. The necessity of choosing and acting is not causal, logical, or rational necessity. It is our *plight*: the simple inexorable fact of the human condition.

1.1.2

But once inside that fact, once we face the necessity of acting, we are confronted with a different kind of necessity. We live under the pressure of a vast assortment of laws, duties, obligations, expectations, demands, and rules, all telling us what to do. Some of these demands are no doubt illicit or imaginary—just social pressure, as we say (as if we knew what that was). But there are many laws and demands that we feel we really are bound to obey. And yet in many cases we would be hard pressed to identify the source of what I call the *normativity* of a law or a demand—the grounds of its authority and the psychological mechanisms of its enforcement, the way that it binds you. In philosophy we raise questions about the normativity of highbrow laws like those of moral obligation or theoretical and practical reason. But it is worth remembering that in everyday life the same sort of questions can be raised about the normativity of the laws and demands of professional obligation, filial obedience, sexual fidelity, personal loyalty, and everyday etiquette. And just as we may find ourselves rebelling against, say, the sacrifice of our happiness to the demands of justice, so also, in a smaller, more everyday way, we may find ourselves *bucking* against doing our chores or returning unwanted phone calls or politely thanking a despised host for a dull party.

The surprising thing is not that we resist such demands, but that our resistance so often fails. Sometimes to our own pleasant surprise, sometimes merely with bewilderment or bemusement, we find ourselves doing what we think we ought to do, in the teeth of our own reluctance, and even though nothing obvious forces us to do it. We toil out to vote in unpleasant weather, telephone relatives to whom we would prefer not to speak, attend suffocatingly boring meetings at work, and do all sorts of irksome things at the behest of our families and friends. Part of the lawless charm of a character like W. C. Fields springs from the fact that most of us are almost incapable of ignoring the requests of children, and yet we chafe under the enthrallment. It is a fact worthy of philosophical attention that the wanton disregard of life's little rules makes the people who would never break them laugh. To be sure, there is no question that in what Joseph Butler called "a cool hour," most of us would unhesitatingly choose to be the kinds of people who generally do what they ought.[1] . . . But there is also no question that in those warmer hours when we actually choose the particular actions demanded of us, we often manifestly do not *want* to do them. And yet we do them, all the same: the normativity of obligation is, among other things, a psychological force. Let me give this phenomenon a name, borrowed from Immanuel Kant. Since normativity is a form of necessity, Kant calls its operation within us—its manifestation as a psychological force—*necessitation*.[2]

1.1.3

In recent years, it has become rather unfashionable to focus on the phenomenon of necessitation. It seems to evoke the lugubrious image of the good human being as a Miserable Sinner in a state of eternal reform, who must constantly repress his unruly desires in order to conform to the demands of duty. Necessitation is thus conceived as *repression.* In opposition to this, some recent virtue theorists have offered us the (to my mind) equally rebarbative picture of the virtuous human being as a sort of Good Dog, whose desires and inclinations have been so perfectly trained that he always does what he ought to do spontaneously and with tail-wagging cheerfulness and enthusiasm. The opposition between these two pictures is shallow, for they share the basic intuition that the experience of necessitation is a sign that there is something wrong with the person who undergoes it. The disagreement is only about how inevitable the evil is. It may be natural to think of necessitation as a sign that something is wrong, since necessitation can be painful, and it is natural to interpret pain as a sign that something is wrong. But necessitation is so characteristic, so utterly commonplace a feature of human experience, that we should not be in a hurry to jump to that conclusion. In the *Republic,* Socrates says that the phrases we use to describe necessitation, phrases like "self-control" or "self-mastery" or "self-command," seem absurd on their surface, since the stronger self who imposes the necessity is the same person as the weaker self on whom it is imposed. But Socrates also suggests that these phrases are like "tracks or clues" that virtue has left in the language (R 430e). Necessitation, he thinks, reveals something important about human nature, about the constitution of the human soul. What it reveals—that the source of normativity lies in the human project of self-constitution—is my subject . . .

1.4 Agency and Practical Identity

1.4.1

With that conception of action before us, I am ready to try to state my view. I believe that it is essential to the concept of action that an action is performed by an agent, rather in the same way that it is essential to a thought that it be thought by a thinker. One must be able to attach the "I do" to the action in the same way that, according to Kant, one must be able to attach the "I think" to a thought. As the invocation of Kant here suggests, this is not yet to say whether the agent or the thinker needs to be a separately existing entity . . . But an action requires an agent, someone to whom we attribute the movement in question as its author. And I also believe it is essential to the concept of agency that an agent be unified. That is to say: to regard some movement of my mind or my body as *my action,* I must see it as an expression of my self as a whole, rather than as a product of some force that is at work *on* me or *in* me. Movements that result from forces working *on* me or *in* me constitute things that happen to me. To call a movement a twitch, or a slip, is at once to deny that it is an action and to assign it to some part of you that is less than the whole: the twitch to your eyebrow, or the slip, more problematically, to your tongue. For a movement to be my action, for it to be expressive of *myself* in the way that an action must be, it must result from my entire nature working as an integrated whole.

1.4.2

Now this is where things get complicated. You might suppose that this requires that an action be the effect or result or expression of a *prior* unity in the agent, an integrity already achieved. You first achieve the sort of psychic unity or integrity that makes you the master of your own movements, that is, that makes some of your movements attributable to you as *yours,* and then the choices that lead to your actions express the unified selfhood you have already achieved. But I will argue that this cannot be how it works. This is where the problem of personal identity comes into the picture. . . . [T]here is no *you* prior to your choices and actions, because your identity is in a quite literal way *constituted* by your choices and actions.

1.4.3

The identity of a person, of an agent, is not the same as the identity of the human animal on whom the person normally supervenes. I believe that human beings differ from the other animals in an important way. We are self-conscious in a particular way: we are conscious of the grounds on which we act, and therefore are in control of them. When you are aware that you are tempted, say, to do a certain action because you are experiencing a certain desire, you can step back from that connection and reflect on it. You can ask whether you should do that action because of that desire, or because of the features that make it desirable. And if you decide that you should not, then you can refrain. This means that although there is a sense in which what a non-human animal does is up to her, the sense in which what you do is up to you is deeper. When you deliberately decide what sorts of effects you will bring about in the world, you are also deliberately deciding what sort of a cause you will be. And that means you are deciding who you are. So we are each faced with the task of constructing a peculiar, individual kind of identity—personal or practical identity—that the other animals lack. It is this sort of identity that makes sense of our practice of holding people responsible, and of the kinds of personal relationships that depend on that practice.

You will already see that I think those who claim that judgments of responsibility don't really make sense unless people create themselves are absolutely right—only unlike most people who believe this, I don't think it's a *problem*. It is as the possessor of personal or practical identity that you are the author of your actions, and responsible for them. And yet at the same time it is in choosing your actions that you create that identity. What this means is that you constitute yourself *as* the author of your actions in the very act of choosing them. I am fully aware that this sounds paradoxical. How can you constitute yourself, create yourself, unless you are already there? Call this the paradox of self-constitution. This is a problem to which I will return . . . after I have explained the metaphysical conception which will enable us to grasp the solution. . . .

1.4.7

It will be worth repeating here how. . . the commitment to our own human or rational identity as a form of practical identity . . . is supposed to work. Our practical identities are, for the most part, contingent. We acquire them in various ways. Some we are born into, like being someone's child or neighbor or being the citizen of a certain country. Some we adopt for reasons, like joining a profession that is worthwhile and suits your talents or devoting yourself to a cause in which you ardently believe. Many we adopt voluntarily, but without anything that is in more than a marginal sense a reason. Contrary to romantic notions, you don't marry a person who is made for you. You marry a person who is about your age, lives in your vicinity, and is feeling ready to marry at around the same time that you are. You may drift into a profession by way of a summer job, or champion a moral cause out of fellowship with a friend, or have undying loyalty to a nation because you happened to be born there.

However it goes, reasoned or arbitrary, chosen or merely the product of circumstance, the sorts of identities I am talking about remain contingent in this sense: whether you treat them as a source of reasons and obligations is up to you. If you continue to endorse the reasons the identity presents to you, and observe the obligations it imposes on you, then it's you. Leaving morality aside for the moment—because there may be moral reasons for not doing the things I am about to describe—you can walk out even on a factually grounded identity like being a certain person's child or a certain nation's citizen, dismissing the reasons and obligations that it gives rise to, because you just don't identify yourself with that role. Then it's not a form of *practical* identity anymore: not a description under which you value yourself. On the flip side, you can wholeheartedly endorse even the most arbitrary form of identification, treating its reasons and obligations as inviolable laws. Making the contingent necessary is one of the tasks of human life and the ability to do it is arguably a mark of a good human being. To do your job as if it were the most important thing in the world, love your spouse as if your marriage was made in heaven, treat your friends as if they were the most important people in the world—is to treat your contingent identities as the sources of absolute inviolable laws.

But why should we do that? . . . [T]hese forms of identification are contingent, and we can walk away from them. Their hold on us depends on our own endorsement of the laws they give us. We ratify their laws whenever we act in accordance with them. For us even the reasons that spring from our animal nature are optional—for unlike the other animals, we can choose to turn our backs on our animal identity, and deliberately die. But there is a reason not to abandon all of our identities. The reason is given by the problem I started out from: the human plight. We must act, and we need reasons in order to act. And unless there are *some* principles with which we identify we will have no reasons to act. Every human being must make himself into someone in particular, in order to have reasons to act and to live. Carving out a personal identity for which we are responsible is one of the inescapable tasks of human life.

And that is the point on which the argument turns. Go back for a moment to the case of contingent practical identity. I said that a contingent practical identity was a description under which you value yourself and find your life to be worth living and your actions to be worth undertaking. What does it mean to say that you value yourself under a certain description? The actions or activities that constitute valuing something vary, depending on what sort of thing it is. Valuing doesn't always consist in producing or promoting or even preserving the thing that you value. Valuing beauty, for instance, consists in contemplating it with appreciation. Valuing people consists in respecting their reasons and choices and interests, not in having lots of babies.[3] Valuing yourself under a certain description consists in endorsing the reasons and obligations to which that way of identifying yourself gives rise. To say that a citizen of a certain nation values himself under that description is not to say that his purpose is to be a citizen of that nation. It is to say that he ratifies and endorses the reasons and obligations that go with being a citizen of that nation, because that's how he sees himself.

Suppose now that I conform to my obligations as an American citizen, treating the duties of citizenship as duties to which I must indeed conform. Someone might say to me: okay, sure, I see that you must do that insofar as you identify yourself as an American citizen, but why must you take that way of identifying yourself so seriously? It's only an accident that you were born in America. And here part of the answer is that I must take *some* ways of

identifying myself seriously, or I won't have any reasons at all. Insofar as I take that fact—the fact that I need some way of identifying myself—to be a reason, I express the value I set upon myself as a human and rational being.

So in valuing ourselves as the bearers of contingent practical identities, knowing, as we do, that these identities are contingent, we are also valuing ourselves as rational beings. For by doing that we are endorsing a reason that arises from our rational nature—namely, our need to have reasons. And as I've just said, to endorse the reasons that arise from a certain practical identity just is to value yourself as the bearer of that form of identity. We owe it to ourselves, to our own humanity, to find some roles that we can fill with integrity and dedication. But in acknowledging that, we commit ourselves to the value of our humanity just as such. . . .

[2.] THE METAPHYSICS OF NORMATIVITY

2.1 Constitutive Standards

2.1.1

. . . I proposed that the principles of practical reason serve to unify and constitute us as agents, and that is why they are normative. Behind this thesis lies a more general account of normativity that I believe to be common to the philosophies of . . . three thinkers . . . : Plato, Aristotle, and Kant. According to this account, normative principles are in general principles of the unification of manifolds, multiplicities, or, in Aristotle's wonderful phrase, *mere heaps,* into objects of particular kinds (M 8.6 1045a10).

The view finds its clearest expression in the central books of Aristotle's *Metaphysics,* so that is the place to start.[4] According to Aristotle, what makes an object the kind of object that it is—what gives it its identity—is what it does, its *ergon*: its purpose, function, or characteristic activity. This is clearest in the case of artifacts, which are obviously functionally defined. An artifact has both a form and a matter. The matter is the material, the stuff or the parts, from which the artifact is made. The form of the artifact is its functional arrangement or teleological organization. That is, it is the arrangement of the matter or of the parts which enables the object to serve its function, to do whatever it does that makes it the kind of thing that it is. Say for instance that the function of a house is to serve as a habitable shelter, and that its parts are walls, roof, chimney, insulation, and so on. Then the form of the house is that arrangement of those parts that enables it to serve as a habitable shelter—or rather, to be more precise—it is the *way* the arrangement of those parts enables it to serve as a habitable shelter. The walls are joined at the corners, the insulation goes into the walls, the roof is placed on the top, and so on, so that the weather is kept out, and a comfortable environment is created within. That is the form of a house.

On this view, to be an object, to be unified, and to be teleologically organized, are one and the same thing. Teleological organization is what unifies what would otherwise be a *mere heap* of matter into a particular object of a particular kind. Teleological organization, according to Aristotle, is also the object of knowledge. To know an object, that is, to *understand* it, is to see not only what it does and what it is made of, but also *how* the arrangement of the parts enables it to do whatever it does. After all, anybody knows that a house is a shelter, and anybody knows that its parts are walls and roofs and chimneys and things, and even roughly where they go. What distinguishes the architect is his knowledge of *how* the arrangement of those parts enables the house to serve the purpose of sheltering. And this means that according to Aristotle the form of a thing governs both theory and practice. To understand houses is to have their form in your mind, and to build one is to be guided by that form.

At the same time, it is the teleological organization or form of the object that supports normative judgments about it. A house with cracks in the walls is less good at keeping the weather out, less good at sheltering, and therefore is a less good house. The ancient metaphysical thesis of the identification of the real with the good follows immediately from this conception, for this kind of badness eventually shades off into *literal* disintegration. A house with enough cracks in the walls will crumble, and cease to be a house altogether: it will disintegrate back into a *mere heap* of boards and plaster and bricks.

2.1.2

It is essential here to observe the distinction between being a good or bad *house* in the strict sense and being a house that happens to be a good or bad *thing* for some external reason. The large mansion which blocks the whole neighborhood's view of the lake maybe a *bad thing* for the neighborhood, but it is not therefore a *bad house*. The normative standards to which a thing's teleological organization gives rise are what I will call "constitutive standards," standards that apply to a thing simply in virtue of its being the kind of thing that it is.

An especially important instance of the constitutive standard is what I will call the constitutive *principle,* a constitutive standard applying to an activity. In these cases what we say is that if you are not guided by the principle, you are not performing the activity at all. In the case of essentially goal-directed activities, constitutive principles arise from the constitutive standards of the goals to which they are directed. A house-builder is, as such, trying to build an edifice that will keep the rain and weather out. But all activities—as opposed to mere sequences of events or processes—are, by their nature, directed, self-guided, by those who engage in them, even if they are not directed or guided with reference to external goals. And the principles that describe the way in which an agent engaged in an activity directs or guides himself are the constitutive principles for that activity. So it is a constitutive principle of walking that you put one foot in front of the other, and a constitutive principle of skipping that you do this with a hop or a bounce. . . . And in all these cases, we can say that unless you are guided by the principle in question, you are not performing that activity at all.

2.1.3

The idea of a constitutive standard is an important one, for constitutive standards meet skeptical challenges to their authority with ease. Why shouldn't you build a house that blocks the whole neighborhood's view of the lake? Perhaps because it will displease the neighbors. Now *there* is a consideration that you may simply set aside, if you are selfish or tough enough to brave your neighbors' displeasure. But because it does not make sense to ask why a house should serve as a shelter, it also does not make sense to ask why the corners should be sealed and the roof should be waterproof and tight. I mean, of course you can ask these questions in a technical voice, you can ask how sealed corners and waterproofed roofs serve the function of sheltering. But once you've answered the technical questions, there is no further room for doubting that the constitutive standard has normative force. For if you fall too far short of the constitutive standard, what you produce will simply not be a house. In effect this means that even the most venal and shoddy builder must try to build a good house, for the simple reason that there is no other way to try to build a house. Building a good house and building a house are not different activities: for both are activities guided by the teleological norms implicit in the idea of a house. Obviously, it doesn't follow that every house is a good house, although there is a puzzle about why not. It does, however, follow that building bad houses is not a different activity from building good ones. *It is the same activity, badly done.*

2.1.4

Let's consider that puzzle. If building bad houses is the same activity as building good ones, why are there any bad houses? In the case at hand, we have an object, a house, characterized by certain constitutive standards. It is in terms of those standards that we understand the activity of producing a house. The producer of the house looks to the normative standards that are constitutive of houses—in Aristotle's terms, to its form—and tries to realize that form in appropriate matter—in building materials. Since building is a goal-directed activity, that is what the activity of building essentially is. The description of the form of a house could be read as a sort of recipe, or a set of instructions, for building a house: join the walls at the corners, put the insulation in the walls, put the roof on the top . . . So trying to produce a house is not a different activity from trying to produce a good house. One is trying to build a good

house if one is building a house at all. How then is the shoddy builder even possible? . . .

2.1.5

So we are looking at a quite general problem about finding the conceptual space between performing an activity perfectly and not performing it at all, space into which we can fit the person who does it badly. Among the ancient Greek philosophers this seems to have been one of the standard puzzles about art or craft. At least it comes up in the first book of the *Republic* with respect to the art of ruling. Thrasymachus says that justice is the advantage of the stronger, for the rules of justice are imposed on the weak by the strong, and the strong rule for their own advantage. Socrates pretends to be puzzled by the question where justice lies when the strong make a law that is not *in fact* to their advantage (R 339c-e). Thrasymachus replies that the problem is the result of a loose way of talking. In the *precise sense,* he says, no craftsperson, expert, or ruler, is a craftsperson, expert, or ruler, at the very moment when he makes an error (R 340d–341a). In other words, Thrasymachus concludes you are not practicing an art at all if you practice it badly. Socrates proceeds to make mincemeat of Thrasymachus with this "precise sense" by showing that a ruler, in the *precise sense,* rules for the benefit of whatever he rules, and not for his own benefit (R 341c–343a).

In fact the "precise sense" or perfect version of an activity stands in a complex relation to the activity, because it is at once both normative and constitutive. Although it is not true that you are not performing an activity at all unless you do it precisely, it is true that you have to be *guided by* the precise version of the activity in order to be performing the activity at all. And at the same time the precise sense sets normative standards for the activity. It is tempting to say that the actual activity must *participate* in the perfect or precise one. In other words, Plato's Theory of Forms is true for activities.

The shoddy builder doesn't follow a different set of standards or norms. He may be doing one of two things. He may be guided by the norms, but carelessly, inattentively, choosing second-rate materials in a random way, sealing the corners imperfectly, adding insufficient insulation, and so on. But he may also, if he is dishonest, be doing this sort of thing quite consciously, say in order to save money. In that case, surely we can't say that he is trying to build a good house? No, but now I think we should follow Socrates's lead, and say that he is not trying to build a house at all, but rather a sort of plausible imitation of a house, one he can pass off as the real thing. What guides him is not the aim of producing a house, but the aim of producing something that will fetch the price of a house, sufficiently like a real house that he can't be sued for it afterwards. Socrates . . . makes rather a fuss about this point, insisting that a craftsman in the precise sense is not a money-maker, but simply a practitioner of his craft (R 341c–342a).

2.1.6

So on this conception, every object and activity is defined by certain standards that are both constitutive of it and normative for it. These standards are ones that the object or activity must at least try to meet, insofar as it is to be that object or activity at all. An object that fails to meet these standards is bad in a particular way. It will be useful to give this kind of badness, badness as judged by a constitutive standard, a special name, and in English we have a word that serves the purpose well: *defect*. So in the somewhat special sense that I will be using the term, a house that is so constructed as to be ill-adapted for sheltering is *defective*; while a house that blocks the neighborhood's view, though it may for that reason be a bad thing, is not *a defective house*. . . .

2.1.7

Constitutive standards are important, I claimed above, because they meet skeptical challenges with ease. But the importance of the idea is deeper than that, for I believe—and I know this is more controversial—that the *only* way to establish the authority of any purported normative principle is to establish that it is constitutive of something to which the person whom it governs is committed—something that she either is doing or has to do. . . . The laws of logic govern our thoughts because if we don't follow them we just aren't thinking. Illogical thinking is

not merely bad, it is *defective*, it is bad *as* thinking. The laws of the understanding govern our beliefs because if we don't follow them, we just aren't constructing a representation of an objective world . . . And as I will argue, the laws of practical reason govern our actions because if we don't follow them we just aren't acting, and acting is something that we must do. A constitutive principle for an inescapable activity is unconditionally binding.

How could it be otherwise? Constitutive standards have unquestionable authority, while external standards give rise to further questions, and leave space for skeptical doubt. How then can we ever give authority to an external standard, except by tracing its authority back to a constitutive one? Consider again that house that blocks the neighbors' view of the lake. Why shouldn't the house-builder build it? For I'm supposing that we all do agree that really, after all, he shouldn't do it, in spite of the fact that it wouldn't therefore be a *defective* house. Well, perhaps he identifies himself as a good neighbor, a citizenly type, and doesn't need to ask why he shouldn't build a house that is a blight on the neighborhood. Or perhaps he loves his neighbors, and wouldn't want to harm them. Or perhaps—to anticipate the success of the views we are working on here—it would be morally wrong to build a house that blocks the view of the neighbors, and so although it might be all very well as a bit of *house-building*, it would be *defective* as an *action*. . . .

2.2 The Constitution of Life

2.2.1

In 1.4.3, I mentioned what I called "the paradox of self-constitution." How can you constitute yourself, create yourself, unless you are already there? And how can you need to constitute yourself if you *are* already there? With Aristotle's view before us, we are now ready to start working our way towards the solution of this problem.

Aristotle extended his account of artifactual identity to living things with the aid of the view that a living thing is a thing with a special kind of form.[5] A living thing is a thing so designed as to maintain and reproduce *itself*: that is, to maintain and reproduce its own form. It has what we might call a self-maintaining form. So it is its own end; its *ergon* or function is just to be—and to continue being—what it is. And its organs, instincts, and natural activities are all arranged to that end. The function of a giraffe, for instance, is to be a giraffe, and to continue being a giraffe, and to produce other giraffes. We might therefore say that a giraffe is simply an entity organized to keep a particular instance, a spatio-temporally continuous stream, of giraffeness going— primarily through nutrition—and also to generate other instances of giraffeness, through reproduction. A healthy giraffe is one that is well-organized for keeping her giraffeness going, while an unhealthy giraffe suffers from conditions that tend to her disintegration. So health is not, strictly speaking, a *goal* for giraffes, but rather is our name for the inner condition which enables the giraffe to successfully perform her function—which is to go on being a giraffe. This parallels the way in which . . . goodness is not a goal for people, but rather is our name for the inner condition which enables a person to successfully perform her function—which is to maintain her integrity as a unified person, to be who she is. This is why Plato and Aristotle always compared health to virtue.

It is important to notice the complex role that teleological organization plays with respect to the giraffe's activities and actions. The giraffe's actions are both dictated by, and preservative of, her giraffeness. A good giraffe action, such as nibbling the tender green leaves at the tops of the trees, keeps the giraffe going, for it provides the specific nutrients needed to constantly restore and refurbish her giraffeness through the nutritive processes. Yet the giraffe's action is one to which she is prompted by instincts resulting *from* her giraffe nature. This is related to an apparent difference between living things and artifacts, which is that living things are made of parts that strictly speaking cannot exist independently of the living things themselves. You can't build a giraffe out of tender green leaves, but a giraffe's nutritive processes turn tender green leaves into the kinds of matter out of which a giraffe *is* built—giraffe tissues and giraffe organs and so on. Furthermore, the living tissues that make up organisms are comparatively fragile, and in need of

constant renewal. It follows from all this that if a giraffe ceases her activities—if she stops nibbling the tender green leaves, or stops digesting them when she does—she will fall apart. And this means that, strictly speaking, being a giraffe is not a state, but rather an activity. Being a giraffe is *doing* something: a giraffe is, quite essentially, an entity that is always *making* herself into a giraffe. In fact, the *entity* that I just mentioned is derivative, arrived at only by an artificial freezing of the observer's mental frame, for nothing that stops working at being a giraffe, that stops making herself into a giraffe, will remain a giraffe for long. So to be a giraffe is simply to engage in the activity of constantly making yourself into a giraffe: this is what a giraffe's life consists in. . . .

2.2.3

. . . [Thus] there is no real difference between the activity of living a giraffe's life, and the activity of living a healthy giraffe's life, for in order to live a giraffe's life, you must follow the teleological principles implicit in the form of giraffeness, the constitutive principles of being a giraffe. And so leading the life of an unhealthy giraffe is not a different activity from leading the life of a healthy giraffe. *It is the same activity, badly done.*

2.3 In Defense of Teleology

2.3.1

We are almost ready to solve the paradox of self-constitution, but first I want to address another issue. The account of the normativity of practical reason that I am working on here grounds normative standards in a frankly teleological, Aristotelian, conception of objects and activities. Many philosophers are worried by teleological ways of conceiving the world. Hasn't Aristotle's idea that there are natural purposes, or that the world and the things in it were made for a purpose, long since been discredited by the Modern Scientific World View? My response to these worries will come in three parts: first, I will give an account of the target and scope of the teleological conception I propose to use; second, I will give an account of what justifies its use; and finally I say a few words about the resulting status of teleological claims.

First the target and scope of teleological thinking. The Aristotelian conception that I have just laid out identifies objects as having an internal teleological organization. This is clearest in the case of living things, where the claim is simply about how the living thing's organs and activities are conceived and explained as contributing to its life. A living thing is not assigned a purpose outside of itself—its "purpose," or more properly function, is to be what it is, to live its particular form of life. Thus there are no such claims here as that horses are meant for riding into battle or that cows are meant for human beings to eat or that women are meant for housework or that oil is meant for lamps and automobiles. The teleological claims are made at the level of the individual object: they are claims about its internal organization. It is of course true that we can identify something as having an internal teleological organization only to the extent that we can identify it as *doing something*. Serving a human purpose is one recognizable way of *doing something*; but doing what we ourselves do—namely, living—is another. (Even in the case of an artifact its purpose need not be thought of as external to the object, since in the case of an artifact it is the whole nature of that object to serve the purpose in question.) In fact what I want to claim—although I will have to be a little vague here—is that this is how we pick out the object, how it emerges from what Kant called the sensible manifold as a unified thing. That is to say, we pick out an object as a region of the manifold that appears to be doing something, and we understand it as a single and unified object by understanding it as internally organized for doing whatever it does.

This brings me to the second point—the justification of teleological thinking. That justification falls into two related parts. The first is the claim I have just made. Teleological thinking need not be grounded in a claim about the world. It may be grounded in a claim about how human beings conceptualize the world. The idea, of course a Kantian one, is that human beings are faced with the task of carving the sensible manifold into objects. The claim is that we pick out objects by identifying functional unities. *Very* roughly speaking, the idea is this: in dividing the world into objects, we need

some reason for carving out more particular unities from the sensible manifold. And the kind of unity that grounds the identification of a particular object is a functional unity. To put it a bit fancifully, when a cluster of forces are all contributing to something that we, by our admittedly human standards, would call a *result,* then we bunch these forces together, and call them an object. When a cluster of natural forces works together to produce something I can sit down on, say a flat rock, then I call it a *seat.* When I try to reproduce that cluster of forces, I call the result a *chair.* When a cluster of forces works together to maintain and continually reproduce that same cluster of forces, or a cluster of forces spatio-temporally continuous with itself, thus constantly making itself and copies of itself, then I call it a *living thing.*

And that has implications for the status of the resulting teleological claims. If we are to pick out self-maintaining regions of the manifold as living things, of course, there must be such things, so I do not mean to imply here that living things are merely human constructs, or anything of that sort. Not that that would necessarily be so bad. "Seats" are human constructs, since the concept of a seat is relative to the purposes of an erect-standing creature so constructed as to be able to sit down. "Chairs" like other artifacts are human constructs, but then, no one doubts *that*—the concept and its object are born together in the original craftsman's mind. For all that, however, there are chairs. Why do we pick self-maintainers out of the manifold as a kind of thing? As anyone who watches animals knows, animals or at least middle-sized multicellular animals in fact recognize one another as fellow animals without any fancy powers of conceptualization, so perhaps this question needs no answer. But our later recognition of living things as self-maintainers could have been inspired by the analogy with ourselves. Nothing I'm saying here is incompatible with a Darwinian account of how the world became populated with items fit to be thus conceptualized. And nothing I'm saying here is incompatible with all the ways in which the Darwinian account implies that teleological thinking can be wrong. We can wrongly assign a purpose to a useless vestigial organ, for example. We can conceive of something as relative to our purposes, when it has interests of its own that make a different understanding of its organization available. So there is no claim here that everything has one and only one purpose that is in fact its natural purpose. The claim is simpler—it is that the way we conceptualize the world, the way we organize it into a world of various objects, guarantees that it will appear to be teleologically organized at the level of those objects.

2.3.2

The idea that teleological thinking is inherent in our powers of conceptualization is a development of a point that is implicit in what I have already said. A teleological conception of the world is essential to our functioning as agents. We need the world to be organized into various objects in order to act. To recognize an object as *doing something* or as producing a *result* of some kind is to identify it with reference to our own purposes and powers of action. Since we must act, the world is for us, in the first instance, a world of tools and obstacles, and of the natural objects of desire and fear. An object is identified as a locus, a sort of force field, of particular causal powers, and the causal powers in question are identified as those we might either use or have to work against. And if we did not identify objects in this way, we could not act at all.

Let me put this point more specifically. . . . Kant's hypothetical imperative is a normative principle essential to, constitutive of, action itself . . . . To act is essentially to take the means to your end, in the most general sense of the word "means." And to take the means to your end is, as Kant himself pointed out, to determine yourself to cause the end—that is, to deploy the objects that will bring the end about. Thus action requires a world of objects conceived as the loci of causal powers. You intend to cut, for instance, so you look for a knife, conceiving the knife as the cause of cutting.

Now perhaps some people suppose that as long as you conceive the knife merely as *the cause of the cutting*, rather than as *for the purpose of cutting*, you are not conceiving of the world teleologically. The view that the knife is *the cause of the cutting* is mechanistic. But is it? In the purest form of the mechanistic view, the knife is not the cause of the cutting. It is

rather—say—the knife wielded by the hand directed by the brain operating through the nervous system stimulated by certain forces determined in turn by certain events caused in certain ways. Assuming something like determinism is true at the level of middle-sized objects, the cause of the cutting is the state of the world a nanosecond ago determining the state of the world now. Why then do we say that *the knife,* rather than the state of the world a nanosecond ago, is the cause of the cutting? That is easy—because we can *use* the knife for cutting. From the purely mechanistic point of view, the identification of a particular object or even a particular event as *the cause* of another is artificial, a piece of shorthand, a sort of conception of thumb, if I may put it that way. The teleological view—the view of the world as a realm of tools and obstacles—stands behind the slightly artificial idea that particular objects are "causes." But the teleological conception of the world is essential to creatures who are inside of the world and must act in it.

2.3.3

The teleological view of the world as a realm of tools and obstacles, of objects of desire and fear, the conception of the world from which as agents we must start, is modified by rationality in two ways. One modification occurs within the teleological conception itself, and . . . is an inevitable development of it. It is the moral conception of the world. To act, I have already suggested, is to determine yourself to be the cause of a certain end. So to act *self-consciously* is to conceive of *yourself* teleologically—as the cause—that is, the *first* cause—of a certain end. It is to conceive yourself as an agent, as efficacious to achieve certain subjectively held ends. Thus in addition to tools and obstacles and objects of fear and desire, a rational, self-conscious agent comes to conceive the world as containing agents, with ends of their own. She comes to conceive the world, in Kant's language, as a Kingdom of Ends: a whole of all ends in themselves or first causes, with the ends that each sets before him or herself (G 4:433).

The other modification, which eventually emerges as an alternative conception, is the scientific or mechanistic conception of the world . . . It is a conception that results among other things from pressing the notion of cause, as I did above, until the idea of *a* cause within the world begins to look spurious. Or, to put the same point another way, it is the result of pressing our understanding of the world until the idea of an object, as a unified and independent being within the world, begins to look spurious. You think you're an object, indeed even an agent, but to a flea or a nit you are merely a rather nutritious and specific region of the environment, like a Pacific island. If the flea or nit could think, it would think itself an object, perhaps even an agent, but to the cells in its body it is merely a rather nutritious and specific environment . . . and so on. Even we self-identifying self-conscious and supposedly self-maintaining substances fail to see how thoroughly embedded we are in an environment that supports us from outside, how thoroughly our perceived internal unity and cohesion depends on what goes on around us. A chemical change, a rise in the temperature, a stray bullet, and the transient whirling vortex of forces that thought itself an immortal *thing* puffs away . . .

Are the teleological and moral conceptions of the world then related to the Scientific World View as illusions to fact? If that were so, whose illusions would they be?

2.4 The Paradox of Self-Constitution

2.4.1

Now we are ready to talk about the paradox of self-constitution. According to the Aristotelian picture of the nature of living things, a living thing is engaged in an endless activity of self-constitution. In fact to be a living thing is just to be self-constitutive in this way: a living thing is a thing that is constantly making itself into itself. But notice that the apparent paradox involved in the idea of self-constitution does not seem to arise here. No one is tempted to say: "how can the giraffe make itself into itself unless it is already there?" The picture here is not of a craftsman who is, mysteriously, his own product. The picture here is of the self-constitutive process that is the essence of life. The paradox of self-constitution, in this context, is no paradox at all.

And the same applies to personhood. Aristotle believed that there are three forms of life,

corresponding to what he called three parts of the soul.[6] Each supervenes on the one below it. At the bottom is a vegetative life of nutrition and reproduction, common to all plants and animals. According to Aristotle, animals are distinguished from plants in being alive in a further sense, given by a functionally related set of powers that plants lack. Aristotle emphasizes perception and sensation, but notes that these are necessarily, or at least usually, accompanied by imagination, pleasure and pain, desire, and local movement (OS 2.2 413b22–24). What is distinctive of animals is that they carry out part of their self-constitutive activities through action.

The third form of life, distinctive of human beings, or as I will say, of persons, is the life of rational activity. Rational activity, as I have already suggested, is essentially a form of self-conscious activity, and it is this that leads to the construction of personal identity. Thus personhood is quite literally a form of life, and being a person, like being a living thing, is being engaged in an activity of self-constitution.

In other words, what it is to be a person, or a rational agent, is just to be engaged in the activity of constantly making yourself into a person—just as what it is to be a giraffe is to be engaged in the activity [of] constantly making yourself into a giraffe.

2.4.2

One way to bring out the force of this point is in terms of the idea of practical identity. In 1.4, I proposed that we constitute our own identities in the course of action. In choosing in accordance with the principles of a form of practical identity, I claim, we make that identity our own.

It is sometimes said, in opposition to this sort of point, that it involves an overly voluntaristic conception of identity. I did not choose to be an American citizen, or my parents' daughter. Even many of my personal friendships, the older ones especially, are as much the outcome of circumstance as of choice. So I am these things—this country's citizen, these people's daughter, this person's old friend—*perforce,* and not because I chose to be them. And yet these identities give rise to reasons and obligations, as much as the ones that I do more plainly choose, like a profession or an office or a friendship quite deliberately sought out. But I want to argue that while that is true in one way, in another way it is not. For whenever I act in accordance with these roles and identities, whenever I allow them to govern my will, I endorse them, I embrace them, I affirm once again that I am them. In choosing in accordance with these forms of identity, I make them my own.

The idea that to be a person is to be constantly engaged in making yourself into that person helps to explain what is going on in this debate. To see how this works, consider one of the standard dilemmas of contemporary moral philosophy. Some people have complained that the Kantian self is "empty."[7] If you conceive yourself simply as a pure rational agent, and are not committed to any more specific conception of your identity, you are, as it were, too distant from yourself to make choices. There are two problems here. The more formal problem is that it looks as if your empty self can have no reason to do one thing rather than another. But even if you can find some particular reasons, there is also a problem about wholeheartedness, about commitment. How can you be a true friend, a true citizen, a true Christian, say, if the relevant commitments are always up for question and open to choice? The self, it is argued, must be not empty but rather determinate and full: it must take certain identities and relationships as unquestionable law.

And then of course the other side replies that there are also two problems with the determinate self. In the first place, the determinate self is not free, for its conduct is governed by a principle or a law which is not reason's own. In the second place the determinate self must in the end be unjust. For tolerance requires exactly that distance from our roles and relationships that the defenders of the determinate self deplore. "Christianity is my religion, but just in the same way, Islam is his," says the tolerant person. Tolerance demands that you see your religion not as *you* but as *yours,* yourself not as essentially a Christian but as essentially a person who *has* a religion—and only one of many you might have had. So you cannot identify with your religion all out and still be a tolerant person. Or so says the defender of the empty self.

Now this is a false dilemma, arrived at by an artificial freezing of the observer's mental frame. It assumes that the endorsement of our identities, our self-constitution, is a state rather than an activity. If self-constitution were a state we would be stuck on the horns of this dilemma. Either we must already have constituted ourselves—in which case the self would be full and determinate. Or we must not have done so yet—in which case the self would be empty.

But we don't have to choose between these two options, because self-constitution is not a state that we achieve and from which action then issues. . . .

NOTES

1. Butler, Joseph. *Fifteen Sermons Preached at the Rolls Chapel* (1726). The most influential of these are collected in Butler, *Five Sermons Preached at the Rolls Chapel and a Dissertation upon the Nature of Virtue.* Edited by Stephen Darwall. Indianapolis, IN: Hackett Publishing Company 1983.
2. *Nötigung* (G 4:413).
3. Scanlon, T. M. *What We Owe to Each Other*, 103–7. Cambridge, MA: Harvard University Press, 1998.
4. The views that follow are primarily from *Metaphysics* 7–9.
5. To the aforementioned central books of Aristotle's *Metaphysics*, now add *On the Soul*, especially Book 2. Physics 2 is also helpful.
6. These views are found especially in *On the Soul* 2–3. See also [*Nicomachean Ethics*] 1.7 1097b32–1098a5.
7. Sandel, Michael J. *Liberalism and the Limits of Justice*. Cambridge: Cambridge University Press, 1982.

STUDY QUESTIONS

1. What does Korsgaard mean by "practical identity"?
2. How do practical identities supply us with reasons?
3. What does Korsgaard mean by a "role"?
4. Can a person play multiple roles or none at all?

Coming to Terms with Contingency

Sharon Street

Sharon Street, Associate Professor of Philosophy at New York University, critiques Korsgaard's Kantian constructivism, then forwards a version of constructivism inspired by David Hume. According to Korsgaard, anyone who values is committed to valuing our humanity. Street disagrees. Korsgaard asks, "Need we act as our humanity requires?" And she answers: "You have no option but to say yes." Street responds that the question only makes sense on a realist picture. For the constructivist would be asking: "Does it matter (as judged apart from the standards that determine what matters) whether I take anything to matter?" Thus, Korsgaard's appeal to the value of humanity is, on a constructivist construal, incoherent. Indeed, Street argues that some individuals have values but treat their own lives as of mere instrumental importance.

According to Street's Humean alternative, we cannot stand apart from all our value judgments and ask whether something matters. Instead, once we arrive at a coherent web of interlocking values, the question "Why should I accept this entire set of normative judgments?" does not make sense. Granted, those who think nothing matters are untouched by values. Street concludes, however, that we should accept this possibility as a strength, not a weakness, of constructivism.

1. INTRODUCTION

What is value, and how did it enter the world? Metaethical constructivism gives the following answer: Value is something conferred upon the world by valuing creatures, and it enters and exits the world with them. Causal forces, evolutionary and otherwise, gave rise to conscious living things capable of valuing things—whether it be food or their bodily integrity or each other—and with this state of mind of "valuing" came truths about what *is*

valuable—truths which hold from within the point of view of creatures who are already in that state.

Call the standpoint occupied by any creature who is in the state of mind of "valuing" the *practical point of view.* . . . [M]etaethical constructivism is best understood as claiming the following: The truth of a normative claim consists in that claim's following, as a logical or instrumental matter, from within the practical point of view, where the practical point of view is given a formal characterization. To give the practical point of view a *formal characterization*

From Sharon Street, "Coming to Terms with Contingency: Humean Constructivism about Practical Reason," in *Constructivism in Practical Philosophy*, eds. James Lenman and Yonatan Shemmer (Oxford: Oxford University Press, 2012). Reprinted by permission of the publisher.

is to give an account of the standpoint of valuing *as such,* where this involves giving an account of the attitude of valuing that does not itself presuppose any substantive values but rather merely explicates what is involved in valuing anything at all. Logical and instrumental "requirements," as these govern practical reasoning, are explained not as substantive values, but rather as features constitutive of the attitude of valuing. To ignore these "requirements" in full consciousness of what one is doing is not to make a *mistake* about a normative matter; it is merely to fail to value. Apart from the attitude of valuing, there *is* no such thing as a mistake. Either one values things or one does not, and whether there exist any normative reasons for one to do anything depends upon it.

As this rough characterization suggests, if one accepts metaethical constructivism, then one is an anti-realist about value in an important and traditional sense, holding that value is an *attitude-dependent* property. One regards the attitude of valuing as the more fundamental explanatory notion, and understands value itself as a "construction" of that attitude. Things are valuable ultimately because we value them, not the other way around.

The *realism/anti-realism* debate, understood in this "Euthyphronic" fashion, is a topic I explore elsewhere.[1] In this essay, I wish to set that debate entirely to one side and focus on an intramural debate among metaethical constructivists—what I'll call the debate between *Kantian* versus *Humean* constructivists. As I'll draw the distinction, Kantian and Humean constructivists agree that the truth of a normative claim consists in its following from within the practical point of view, where the practical point of view is given a formal characterization. What separates them is their position on whether *moral* conclusions follow from within the practical point of view given a formal characterization. According to *Kantian* versions of metaethical constructivism, moral conclusions do follow. That is, we may start with a purely formal understanding of the attitude of valuing, and demonstrate that recognizably moral values follow from within the standpoint of any valuer as such. The most prominent

contemporary defender of such a view is Christine Korsgaard.[2]

Humean versions of metaethical constructivism, in contrast, deny that substantive moral conclusions are entailed from within the standpoint of valuing as such. According to the Humean, the substantive content of an agent's normative reasons is a function of his or her particular, contingently given, evaluative starting points. On this view, "pure practical reason"—understood as the standpoint of "valuing," or normative judgment, as such—commits one to no specific substantive values. Instead, the substance of one's normative reasons must ultimately be supplied by the particular, contingent set of values with which one finds oneself alive as an agent. The Humean constructivist accepts the idea that if one had entered the world with a radically different set of values, or were merely causal forces to effect a radical change in one's existing set of values, then one's normative reasons would have been, or would become, radically different in a corresponding way.

The goal of this chapter is to weigh in on the Humean side of this debate, and to sketch the broader picture of practical reason that it involves. The name *Humean constructivism* seems appropriate for a view that draws with equal prominence on both the Kantian tradition, especially as articulated by Rawls,[3] and the Humean tradition. Roughly speaking, from Kant come the ideas of "giving laws to oneself," the "practical point of view," and the associated emphasis on the attitude of *valuing,* as opposed to mere *desiring,* as the key to understanding the phenomenon of normativity and the possibility of truth and falsehood in the normative domain. From Hume, on the other hand, come the skepticism about the ability of "pure" practical reason to tell us how to live and the associated emphasis on the need to look to contingently given, more "passionate" states of mind for the source of the substantive content of our reasons.

. . . [T]he debate between Kantian and Humean constructivism is ultimately just a debate about how to live and why, and about the fundamental nature of our relationship with moral requirements. Is morality something we are bound to by the mere fact that we are valuers at all, or is our relationship with morality more contingent than that, though perhaps no less dear for that fact? I will be arguing for the latter view.

2. THE ATTITUDE OF VALUING

Let's start with a brief look at the attitude of *valuing.* In my view, much of the resistance to attitude-dependent conceptions of normative reasons in general (of which metaethical constructivism is one[4]) is due to a failure, on the part of the view's supporters and opponents alike, to locate accurately enough the type of attitude on which normative reasons are said to depend. It is widely assumed that if an agent's normative reasons are always ultimately a function of his or her attitudes, then the attitudes in question must be the agent's *desires.* While not strictly speaking inaccurate, due to the philosophically cultivated latitude in what may plausibly be labeled a "desire," the language of desire is exceptionally misleading in this context due to its meaning in ordinary speech. I think it is hard to overstate the extent to which the emphasis on "desire" distorts the debate regarding the attitude-dependence of normativity, making the attitude-dependent view seem less plausible than it is.

To see the full attractions of an attitude-dependent account, it is essential to distinguish between what I will call, quite stipulatively, the attitude of *valuing* and the attitude of *mere desire,* and to recognize that if value is indeed conferred upon the world by our attitudes, as the anti-realist claims, then it's the attitude of *valuing,* and not the attitude of *mere desire,* that does the conferring. . . . Here I wish . . . to note three key differences.

First, more is constitutively involved in the attitude of valuing than is constitutively involved in the attitude of mere desiring. As we might also put it: The attitude of valuing is characterized by a "discipline" that the attitude of mere desiring lacks.[5] Consider Korsgaard's example of a Civil War soldier who, if he is to live, must have his leg sawed off without the benefit of anesthetic.[6] Imagine first that the soldier says:

(1) I desire to live, and I know that I must have my leg sawed off without the benefit of anesthetic to do so, but I have no desire to have my leg sawed off.

While the language is of course far too controlled for the circumstances, claim (1) would nevertheless be an entirely coherent and comprehensible thing to say. We all know perfectly well what it's like to *desire* the end but not the means; far too much of life has exactly this structure, and the case of a life-saving amputation is a vivid example. But now imagine the soldier says:

(2) I have most reason to live, and I know that I must have my leg sawed off without the benefit of anesthetic to do so, but I have no reason whatsoever to have my leg sawed off.

In contrast to claim (1), it's hard to make sense of this. The speaker appears to be making some kind of conceptual mistake. It's not that the soldier understands perfectly well the concept of a "reason," and then is making a substantive mistake about the reasons he has; it's that he seems not to know what he's saying.

The lesson, I would argue: The state of mind of *desiring* the end does not constitutively involve *desiring* what one is fully aware is the necessary means to that end. This is so, anyway, in a perfectly familiar sense of the word *desire*—the sense that involves, roughly, a feeling of being pleasantly attracted. This is the state of mind I'll refer to as *mere desire.* In contrast, the state of mind of *taking oneself to have reason* to pursue the end constitutively involves *taking oneself to have reason* to take what one is fully aware is the necessary means to that end. This is the state of mind I'll refer to, interchangeably, as *valuing,* or *taking something to be a reason,* or *normative judgment.* Valuing an end, in contrast to merely desiring it, constitutively involves *valuing* what one is fully aware is the necessary means to that end.

Second, as the idea that one can "*value*" having one's leg sawed off suggests, the state of mind of valuing is characterized by a much broader array of conscious experience than is the attitude of mere desiring. Unlike the state we naturally think of when we hear the word *desire,* which calls to mind paradigmatic examples such as sexual attraction, thirst, a craving for chocolate, and so forth, the state of mind I am stipulatively calling *valuing* is characterized by all the range, nuance, and depth of human emotion and feeling. Consider getting up at 4 a.m. to finish grading papers; breaking bad news to a friend; or risking death to fight an authoritarian regime. We have affective, sometimes intensely emotional, experiences of such things as "demanded" or "called for," but they do not call out to us in a way that is pleasant, as the term *desire* suggests, but rather in a manner that involves something more like anxiety or sickness at the thought of not doing them, feelings of gritty determination to preserve what one cares about most in spite of everything, and so on. The language of *desire* is completely inadequate to capture the kind of emotional and phenomenological complexity involved in the kinds of attitudes that confer value on the world, if any do. The relevant attitude can be directed at things we simultaneously find unpleasant, terrible, anguish-inspiring, and so forth.

Third, the attitude of valuing is characterized by greater structural complexity than the attitude of mere desiring. We tend to think of "desiring" as directed at a single object or state of affairs: I desire a donut, for example, or to be rich or to be liked. Evaluative experience of the kind that confers value if anything does, however, is structurally a great deal more complicated than that. It often involves experiencing very specific features of the world as "calling for" or "demanding" or "counting in favor of" other very specific things. For example, I experience the fact that a friend lent me her car two months ago as counting in favor of saying "yes" to the favor she's asking me now; I experience someone's youth and inexperience as ruling out a harsh reply; and so on. Such states of mind are very different from simply wanting a donut. While no doubt we can speak of desiring things in virtue of specific features they have, there is nevertheless a tendency to think of desiring as involving a simple focus on one object or state of affairs as something to be possessed or brought about. The attitude of valuing involves much more complex attitudes toward the world and one's own potential responses to it.

Attitude-dependent conceptions of normative reasons owe much of their inspiration to the Humean tradition. If we are to see the full promise and plausibility of these views, however, we need to abandon another, much less helpful, element that tends to be associated with the Humean tradition—namely the constant use of the language of *desire,* which fails to draw our attention to the kinds of attitudes we really need to be focusing on, which are characterized by a discipline, a range and subtlety of emotional experience, and a structural complexity that are foreign to the everyday concept of desire.

3. A RECONSTRUCTION OF KORSGAARD'S ARGUMENT FOR KANTIAN CONSTRUCTIVISM

Korsgaard's position . . . is the leading contemporary example of a *Kantian* version of metaethical constructivism. I will assume for the sake of argument that Korsgaard is a metaethical constructivist in the sense I have outlined, holding that normative truth consists in what follows from within the standpoint of a valuing creature, where that standpoint is given a formal characterization. As a specifically *Kantian* metaethical constructivist, Korsgaard holds in addition to this that there are certain substantive values, and in particular *moral* values, that follow from within the standpoint of any valuing creature. In this section I offer a reconstruction of Korsgaard's argument; in subsequent sections I explain where I think the argument goes wrong. . . .

Korsgaard's argument, as I reconstruct it, consists of six steps. We view the argument as starting with a purely formal understanding of the attitude of valuing. We imagine someone who values things, but we assume nothing in particular about *what* he or she values: the individual merely has to be recognizable as valuing something or other. We then seek to show that moral commitments are entailed from within that individual's own evaluative point of view. If we succeed at this, then we will also have shown that morality is entailed from within our point of view, since we are valuing creatures too.

Step 1. Suppose, then, that you take something or other to be valuable; it doesn't matter what. To put it in the language of practical identities: Suppose that you take some practical identity or other (whether it be your identity as a mother or Mafioso or something else) to be normative for you. Since we are assuming nothing about the substantive content of the values in question, we are arguing from within, or addressing, the practical point of view "as such"—the standpoint of anyone who values anything—the standpoint of an agent, any agent.

Step 2. If you do value anything, or if you do embrace any practical identity as normative for you, then you must take your endorsement of that value (or your embrace of that practical identity) to be supported by further reasons. . . .

Discussion of step 2. Why, if one accepts a value or a practical identity (any practical identity), must one take one's acceptance of it to be supported by further reasons? I think this is best read as a point about what is involved, as a constitutive matter, in the attitude of valuing. In particular, we may view it as the same point that Kant is making when he says "we cannot conceive of a reason which consciously responds to a bidding from the outside with respect to its judgments."[7] The idea seems to be: If you value something, then you cannot—simultaneously, in full, conscious awareness—also think that there is *no reason whatsoever* to value it. The force of the "cannot" here is conceptual, not rational. Kant's suggestion seems to be that a faculty isn't recognizable as the faculty of reason at all if that faculty consciously takes itself to have absolutely no reason whatsoever for what it is doing or thinking at that moment.

Step 3. From step 2 it follows that in order to be regarded as normative, every practical identity must be regarded as having a further practical identity—itself also embraced as normative—lying behind it and supplying a reason for accepting it. But such a regressing chain of supporting practical identities cannot extend forever. Therefore, if the original practical identity supposed in step 1 (call it *P*) is to be regarded as normative, then it must—when one

thinks about it—be regarded as ultimately supported by a practical identity that brings the regress of identities to a satisfactory end. If, contrary to this, one thinks the regressing chain bottoms out with no reason, then (in accordance with step 2), one will think one ultimately has no reason for *P* either, and cease to regard *it* as normative. At the bottom of the chain, then, we need a practical identity with the following two characteristics: (a) it must supply a reason for accepting other practical identities; and (b) it must not itself require any further normative practical identity to lie behind it. Call a practical identity that has these two characteristics a *source practical identity* (my term).

Step 4. Our practical identity as human beings, accepted as normative, has these two characteristics.

Step 4a. Our practical identity as human beings, accepted as normative, fulfills the first role of a source identity: it supplies a reason for embracing our other practical identities as normative. What is this reason? According to Korsgaard, one's identity as a human being is one's identity as a creature who is able to distance herself from her impulses and desires, and ask "Should I act?" If (and only if) we embrace this identity as normative, then this sets us up with a problem, according to Korsgaard: we need reasons to act. But we can have reasons to act only if we embrace some particular practical identity or other. Why? As I read it, the idea here is the central metaethical constructivist point that one has reasons to act only if one *takes* something or other to be a reason; this is because "practical identities," or the attitude of "valuing" itself, is what sets the standards determining a creature's reasons. (At work in the background here is the rejection of realism.) Since we need reasons, and we can have reasons only if we endorse some particular practical identity or other, it follows that we have a reason to endorse particular practical identities. Thus, if we take our practical identity as a human being to be normative, then we may say of the original practical identity *P*: one reason that we have to accept this particular identity is that as human beings, we need some reasons or other, and identity *P* supplies us with such reasons if we go ahead and accept it as normative.

Step 4b. Our practical identity as human beings, taken as normative, also fulfills the second role of a source identity: it does not require any further practical identity to lie behind it and impart it with its own normativity in turn. One sees this, according to Korsgaard, when one attempts to continue the regress of questions and asks why one should take one's practical identity as a human being to be normative. Korsgaard writes:

> [N]ow that you see that your need to have a normative conception of yourself comes from your human identity, you can query the importance of that identity. Your humanity requires you to conform to some of your practical identities, and you can question this requirement as you do any other. Does it really matter whether we act as our humanity requires, whether we find some ways of identifying ourselves and stand by them? But in this case you have no option but to say yes. Since you are human you must take something to be normative, that is, some conception of practical identity must be normative for you. If you had no normative conception of your identity, you could have no reasons for action, and because your consciousness is reflective, you could then not act at all. Since you cannot act without reasons and your humanity is the source of your reasons, you must value your humanity if you are to act at all.[8]

Notice what is going on here: I am asking what reason I have to treat my practical identity as a human being as normative, and the answer is that if I do not, then none of my other identities will be normative, and I need some normative conception of my identity. But this reason for treating my practical identity as a human being as normative just springs from the same practical identity that is under question—namely, one's identity as a human being, who needs reasons and who therefore needs some normative conception or other of her identity. In this way, Korsgaard suggests, our practical identity as human beings is self-supporting and so brings our regress of questions to an end: the very reason for embracing it as normative springs from itself.

Step 5. The next step is to claim that our practical identity as human beings, endorsed as normative, is the *only* practical identity capable of serving as a source practical identity. This step involves rejecting all other candidates for the role of bringing the regress of questions to a satisfactory end. Leading contenders for this role include states such as desires or pain, or independent facts about reasons of the kind posited by realists. . . .

Step 6. It follows from all of this that if we are to embrace practical identity *P* (whatever it might be) as normative, then we must accept our practical identity as human beings as normative. Why? From steps 2 and 3, it follows that if one is to regard any given practical identity as normative, then one must regard it as ultimately supported by a source practical identity. From steps 4 and 5, we see that one's practical identity as a human being, if embraced as normative, is not only capable of playing this role but also the *only* thing capable of playing this role. Therefore, if one is to regard any given practical identity as normative, one must also take one's practical identity as a human being to be normative. In other words, if one is committed to the value of anything, then one is committed to the value of one's own humanity.

4. THE PROBLEM WITH KORSGAARD'S ARGUMENT

While suggestive, this argument fails, in my view. My criticisms of Korsgaard's argument will be internal ones, in the sense that my objections will be raised entirely from *within* the larger metaethical constructivist framework. I will argue that Korsgaard's argument does not ultimately remain true enough to the central constructivist point that there are no facts about normative reasons apart from the standpoint of an agent who is already taking things to be reasons. . . .

Let's begin with a look at *Step 4b.* The first sign that something is amiss with this part of the argument is the apparent circularity of the answer that is given to the question of why we should embrace our practical identity as human beings as normative.

The question at hand is: Why should I take my identity as a creature who needs reasons (and hence normative conceptions of my identity) to be normative? And the question-begging reply essentially seems to be: You need reasons (and hence normative conceptions of your identity). This makes it unclear exactly how one's practical identity as a human being is supposed to fulfill the second role of a source identity and bring the regress of questions to a satisfactory end; after all, one could stop at any point in the regress of questions and merely insist upon whatever value is being questioned.

But I don't think circularity or lack thereof is the real problem here. The real problem lies with the question at hand, and with the suggestion that there could be any coherent answer to it. As Korsgaard phrases it, the question is: "Does it really matter whether we act as our humanity requires, whether we find some ways of identifying ourselves and stand by them?" And her reply is: "But in this case you have no option but to say yes." But I think that as a matter of fact we do have an option here, and that the proper answer is not to say yes, but rather to reject the question at hand as ill-formulated. Translated into the language of "mattering" and normative reasons, the question at hand is: Does it really matter whether I take anything at all to matter? Or: Is there any reason why I should take something or other to be a reason? According to metaethical constructivism, however, the standards that determine whether something "really matters" are set by one's own judgments about what matters; the standards that determine one's reasons are ultimately set by one's own judgments about what count as reasons; and there *are* no standards apart from this: this is the rejection of realism. It is therefore illegitimate to stand apart from every last one of one's judgments about what matters, and then to ask whether something further matters; it is illegitimate to stand apart from all of one's judgments about what count as reasons, and then to ask whether one has some further reason. Such questions are ill-formulated in the way that "Is the Empire State Building taller?" is ill-formulated: one has failed to supply the standard that would make the question make sense.[9]

This is precisely the mistake that is involved in the question about the value of humanity, in my view. In asking whether one has reason to take anything at all to be a reason, one is posing a normative question; and yet at the very same time one is stepping back from and suspending one's endorsement of all values, thereby robbing the question of the standards that could make the question make sense. In effect, one is asking: Does it matter (as judged apart from the standards that determine what matters) whether I take anything to matter? Or: Do I have a reason (as judged apart from the standards that determine what counts as a reason) to take anything to be a reason? The proper reply to such questions is not to say yes, but rather to reject the question and say: Either you take something or other to matter or you don't; either you take something or other to be a reason or you don't. If you do, then something matters for you; then you have reasons. If you don't, then nothing matters for you; then you have no reasons.

If this is right, then what Korsgaard calls the "value of humanity" is not a coherent value. For the value of humanity, expressed in various ways, is this:

- I have a reason to have some normative conception or other of my identity.
- I have a reason to take something or other to be a reason.
- It matters that I take something or other to matter.
- It is valuable that I take something or other to be valuable.

In an important sense, such claims do not have meaningful content, any more than "The Empire State Building is taller," for these claims are asserted without reference to any standards which could determine their correctness or incorrectness . . . They are not asserted from any standpoint, but rather from nowhere, and from nowhere there are no normative standards, according to constructivism.

In answer to this criticism, the Kantian constructivist might reply that these claims *are* asserted from somewhere—namely, the standpoint of agency itself. All we have done, the Kantian might say, is to abstract from all *particular* normative commitments; but this still leaves us with an evaluative standpoint that can set a substantive normative standard. What we have arrived at, on this view, is the standpoint of an agent *as such*—i.e. the standpoint of a creature who is able to distance itself from its unreflective evaluative tendencies, and who needs an answer to the question "What should I do?" Such a creature, according to Korsgaard, "needs reasons," and therefore needs some normative conception or other of its identity to supply those reasons. In Kantian language, what we've arrived at is the standpoint of the spontaneous will, which has a problem: it needs some law or other in order to be a will, but if it is to be a free will, this law cannot be supplied by any alien cause.[10]

What makes this idea of the standpoint of "agency as such" sound plausible is the use of words such as *need* and *problem*. Such language makes it sound as though there is indeed a certain universal standpoint that one can identify with, a standpoint that is identified not by any particular normative commitment but rather by the general commitment to having some normative commitment or other. But the language of *need* and *problem* ultimately misleads here by trading on an ambiguity. Consider the basic claim at issue (put in a few different ways):

- An agent needs to take something or other to be a reason.
- A will needs some law or other.
- An animal with a reflective structure to her consciousness needs some normative conception of her identity or other.

There are two different ways to understand such claims about "needs." On one interpretation, such claims state conceptual, "constitutive" truths, such as "To be a parent, one needs to have children." On this interpretation, these claims merely state what is involved in being an agent, a will, or an animal with a reflective structure to her consciousness. On a second interpretation, however, such claims state substantive normative truths, according to which an agent has a *reason* to take something or other to be a reason, or a will has a *reason* to have

some law or other, or an animal with a reflective structure to her consciousness has a *reason* to have some normative conception of her identity or other.

Only the first interpretation of the above claims is proper. On a constructivist picture, an agent is simply defined by the fact that it is a creature that takes something or other to be a reason. Similarly, a will is defined by the fact that it has some law or other (a principle, accepted as normative); and having a reflective structure to one's consciousness is defined by the possession of some normative conception of one's identity or other (i.e. the taking of something or other to be a reason). To advance the second, normative interpretation of these claims is to say something akin to "A parent has a reason to have children." But this is confused: a "parent" who does not have children does not have a reason to have children; rather, he or she is not a parent at all. Similarly, an "agent" who doesn't take anything at all to be a reason does not have a reason to take something or other to be a reason; rather, "he" or "she" is not an agent at all. A will cannot have the *problem* of not having a law. If there is no law, this does not mean there is a will with a need; it means there is no will. If this is right, then the alleged value of "humanity"—i.e. the taking of oneself to have *reason* to take something or other to be a reason—is not a coherent value, and hence cannot bring the regress of questions to a satisfactory end.

5. HOW THE HUMEAN CONSTRUCTIVIST THINKS THE REGRESS ENDS

How then *does* the regress of questions end? According to the Humean constructivist, eventually (at least in theory, if we pursue our reflections far enough) we get to a point where we have arrived at a coherent web of interlocking values. At that point, one can ask: "But why should I endorse this *entire set* of normative judgments? What reason do I have to endorse this set as opposed to some other set, or as opposed to no set at all?"[11]

The proper answer at this point, according to the Humean constructivist, is that the question is ill-formulated. One cannot coherently step back from the entire set of one's interlocking normative judgments at once, and ask, from nowhere, whether this set is correct or incorrect, for on a constructivist view there *are* no independent standards to fix an answer to this question; this is the rejection of realism. It is important to be clear here, lest it sound like the Humean constructivist is ruling out perfectly acceptable questions such as "Do I have a reason to reject the values of the Taliban in favor of my own?" or "Are the normative commitments of Albert Schweitzer superior to my own?" Such questions are entirely in order, according to the Humean constructivist—just so long as one is, at least implicitly, posing them from the standpoint of some further set of values (however vague or inchoate) concerning what makes one set of normative commitments more worthy of endorsement than another. The one thing that one cannot do, coherently, is to step back from every last one of one's normative judgments at once and try to pose such questions from nowhere—asking, while suspending one's acceptance of any value that might be capable of settling the matter, whether one should endorse one's own set of values, or some other set, or none at all. If one tries this, then one has stepped, for the moment, outside the standpoint of agency, into a realm where there are no normative facts, and one's question is ill-formulated. On the Humean constructivist view I am proposing, then, the regress of normative questions comes to an end not with any substantive value, but with an understanding of the exact moment at which normative questions cease to make sense—namely, the moment one divorces oneself from the practical point of view altogether, refusing, for that moment, to take any value for granted.

6. BUT IF I THINK VALUING IS THE SOURCE OF VALUE, MUSTN'T I THINK VALUERS ARE VALUABLE?

But the debate is not over yet. The Kantian constructivist might think that what the Humean

constructivist has said so far is largely correct, but that there is a final implication that the Humean is neglecting. In particular, the Kantian might point out that if you accept metaethical constructivism, then you think, roughly speaking, that the fact that you *take* something to matter is ultimately what *makes* it matter. And this commits you to a further thought, the Kantian may suggest: namely that *you,* as a source of value, are valuable.[11] To argue in this way is to restate the most basic and intuitively appealing point that lies behind Kant's argument for the Formula of Humanity[12] and the "fancy new model" of this argument offered by Korsgaard. As Korsgaard puts it: "Kant saw that we take things to be important because they are important to us—and he concluded that we must therefore take ourselves to be important."[13]

While this thought has some intuitive appeal, I don't think it is correct. One may coherently think that one's attitudes of "valuing" confer value without also thinking that *oneself* has any value; one need only think that this is what value *is*—namely, something that exists from the standpoint of a creature who takes something or other to be valuable, but who need not take herself to be valuable. One thing that makes the Kantian suggestion seem plausible is that as a contingent matter, most actual valuing creatures *do* as a matter of fact take themselves to be valuable. And it is clear, from a biological point of view, why this would be: roughly speaking, creatures who do not value themselves do not look out for themselves, and so they die off. To make clear why the Kantian point doesn't go through, then, it is useful to illustrate with a science fiction example of a creature that does *not* take itself to be valuable.

Consider, then, the case of a reflective social insect, living on another planet in another galaxy. She is a worker in a colony of highly intelligent ant-like creatures, headed by a queen (the worker's mother, and the mother of all members of the colony), who is the only one able to reproduce. The colony is made up of millions upon millions of sisters, all of whom share three-quarters of their genetic material in common.[14] The worker is like us in that she values many things, but she is very unlike us in that she takes her own self to be of only the most trivial and purely instrumental importance. She takes the well-being and survival of her queen and colony to be the most important things in the world, feeling happy and content so long as their future is secure, and feeling horror and anxiety at the very thought of any harm coming to them. When it comes to her own personal welfare and survival, however, she is mostly heedless of these—except as a purely instrumental matter. Though it requires effort and concentration (it doesn't come naturally), she does her best to look out for herself so long as she knows her continued existence is important to her mother and sisters. But the moment she notices that she could help her family more by giving her life (for example, in the service of a construction project), she does so cheerfully and with eagerness—glad to be of some use, and delighted in the knowledge that the colony is flourishing.

Suppose that this worker also takes the pursuit of science and philosophy to be valuable (after all, the colony's success over the generations owes much to its scholarly achievements, and she also views these subjects as worthy in themselves). So in her spare time she studies biology and metaethics, and eventually arrives at the metaethical constructivist conclusion that normative truth consists in what follows from within the practical point of view, given a formal characterization. As part of this, she concludes, for example, that what it *is* for her queen's life to be valuable (for her, the worker) is for this conclusion to follow from within the standpoint of her (the worker's) own set of values. And this it does, she is certain: at every level of her emotional being, she is inclined to regard her mother's life as terribly valuable, and when she subjects her normative judgment to reflective scrutiny, she finds that she is glad to be like this (even when fully aware of the evolutionary origins of this unreflective tendency in herself). As judged from the standpoint of all her other values—such as her love of her sisters, philosophy, science, and so on—she has no reason whatsoever to reject the judgment that her mother's life is valuable and no reason whatsoever to start doing battle with her overwhelming unreflective filial devotion.

The question at issue between the Kantian and Humean constructivists is this. The worker now sees

that what it is for her queen's life to be important is that she (the worker) takes it to be important, and that this judgment follows from within her (the worker's) own set of values. Must the worker now, in light of this realization—that she is a source of value, so to speak—take *herself* to be important? Must she now start treating herself as an end and no longer merely as a means to the welfare of her mother and sisters? I think the answer is clearly no, if we understand "self" in any ordinary sense of the word. The worker has recognized that her own values set the standards determining what is valuable for her, but she need not conclude from this that she herself, as an individual, is of any non-instrumental value. She may quite properly decide to go on as before, treating her own survival and welfare as important only insofar as they tend to promote the survival and welfare of the colony as a whole. To the Kantian theorist who tries to convince her that she must take herself to be non-instrumentally valuable, she might say: "The fact that it is my own values that determine what is valuable (for me) does not imply that *I* am valuable. Rather, this fact implies nothing more than what it says—namely that this is what value *is*—something determined by the normative judgments of valuing creatures like myself. Indeed, I am *not* valuable as legislated by my own normative judgments (except instrumentally). *You* may have strong unreflective tendencies to value yourself non-instrumentally (most animals do)—but I don't: I honestly don't care a hoot for my own survival unless it's clear that it is benefiting these other things (my mother and sisters and the cause of science and so on) that I *do* value so deeply in themselves. And I see no reason to change that about myself, even though now I see that what it is for these other things to *be* valuable is for my own set of values to say so."

I think that the reflective social insect would be right to give such a reply, and that this provides further illustration of the Humean point that nothing substantive—here, nothing substantive about the value of one's *self*—is implied by the mere fact that one takes something or other to be valuable. At this point, the Kantian might grant that the reflective social insect need not take herself to be valuable in the ordinary sense of this expression (a sense we normally take to involve valuing one's own survival, bodily integrity, and so forth), but insist that what the creature *must* do is to take herself to be valuable in the sense of valuing her own valuing. So far as I can see, however, *this* understanding of the "value of self" is empty in the sense that it directs nothing substantive: it just says to value what you value. An agent can embrace any set of values whatsoever and satisfy this "requirement." We have derived no substantive constraints on how the reflective social insect must treat herself, much less all other valuing creatures.

7. MORALITY AND CONTINGENCY

If Humean metaethical constructivism is correct, then morality does not follow from pure practical reason, understood as the standpoint of a valuer as such. Instead, we must conceive of our relationship with morality as more contingent than that. Moral feeling is something that an agent ultimately either has or does not have as part of his nature, and if an agent has no trace of it anywhere in his evaluative makeup, or if that feeling does not run deep enough when push comes to shove, then this is not a mistake in any genuine sense, on the Humean constructivist view; in that case, the agent simply is not, at bottom, a moral agent.[15]

From a Kantian point of view, this thought might seem especially distressing. For on a characteristically Kantian way of thinking about morality, it's part of the very idea of morality that its requirements are categorical—not something whose "bindingness" one may escape merely by failing to care about it. From this point of view, the conclusion that morality is not dictated by pure practical reason could seem tantamount to the conclusion that there is no such thing as morality. Certainly Korsgaard . . . takes her task to be nothing less than showing how morality follows from within the standpoint of any valuer, and it is a plausible interpretation of Kant that he thought morality had to be categorically binding in this way if it was not to be a "phantom."

But we should question this conception of morality. It seems right that it is part of the very idea of morality that its requirements are categorical with respect to *some important parts of our evaluative nature*—for example, that it is categorical with respect to what we *desire* to do in an ordinary sense or what we find most appealing or pleasant. But it seems to me that we have gone too far if we think that it is part of the very idea of morality that its requirements are categorical with respect to *any evaluative nature an agent might have*. Instead, on the view I am suggesting, it is constitutive of being a moral agent that one take certain requirements (of a certain characteristic content concerning the equal treatment of others) to be binding even if carrying them out goes against certain *large aspects* of one's evaluative nature—including what feels easiest, what is pleasant, fun, what one finds most naturally appealing, and so on. But the part of oneself that takes the requirements to be binding in this way is just *another* part of one's evaluative nature, and it goes too far to think that morality is not morality unless it binds us independently of *that part* of our evaluative nature as well. Properly understood, in other words, the requirement to tell the truth, for example, binds us independently of whether we *feel like* telling the truth, or whether we would find it fun or pleasant or easy or to our personal advantage narrowly understood, and so forth. But it is a mistake to think that the requirement must also bind us independently of whether we accept that very requirement.

On this view, the Kantian constructivist is making a mistake a bit analogous to what the Kantian and Humean constructivists both agree is the realist's mistake. The *realist's* mistake is the mistake of thinking that requirements must bind us independently of the evaluative standpoint itself. The Kantian and the Humean constructivists are united on this point against the realist. But the Humean constructivist will think the Kantian constructivist is committing another mistake—less severe than the realist's, but still a mistake, and in the same ballpark. The *Kantian constructivist*'s mistake is the mistake of thinking that moral requirements must bind us independently of the *particular evaluative nature* with which we find ourselves—and in particular, independently of whether we already have moral concerns as a deep part of our nature. But the right view, according to the Humean constructivist, is that moral requirements do not bind us irrespective of our particular evaluative nature. In particular, if one lacks moral concerns altogether, then morality does not bind one. But if one is a moral agent, as opposed to just an agent, then part of what that involves is taking oneself to be bound categorically (in certain cases) with respect to what one feels like doing, what one finds pleasant and attractive, and so forth. Part of the work of standard normative ethics, on this view, is the precise mapping of the contours of the relevant part of our evaluative nature—our moral nature. Depending on one's view, that part of our nature could be characterized as a commitment to living in ways others could not reasonably reject, or to weighing the happiness of all impartially, and so on—and doing so even when it is unpleasant, or indeed much worse. It is important to map out the nature of these commitments as best we can. In so doing, we are mapping out the values that are constitutive of moral agency. But it is a mistake to think that we have to show how these values follow from the standpoint of agency as such, on pain of their not being categorical in the right way. The "categoricity" of moral requirements is with respect to one important part of our contingent evaluative nature, but not the whole of our contingent evaluative nature.

This line of thought raises the worry, though: Can one sustain one's commitment to morality, when (as Korsgaard emphasizes) what it demands is sometimes so hard, and when one comes to view it as a contingent matter that one is a moral agent in the first place? This question raises large issues, and here I will merely offer two brief thoughts.

First, it is and it is not a contingent matter that "I am a moral agent." It *is* a contingent matter in the sense that morality is not required by practical reason as such. It is also a contingent matter in the sense that there is a perfectly intelligible conception of personal identity on which I can imagine myself without moral commitments. But there is another sense in which it is not at all a contingent

matter that I am a moral agent. In a different, deeply intuitive sense of personal identity, commitments like this are constitutive of who I am, such that I would regard myself as having vanished or died were I to lose them. Here the close connection with Korsgaard's own thinking about practical identities is clear. For those of us who have moral commitments as a fundamental part of our evaluative nature, to lose those commitments entirely would be to perish in a deeply intuitive sense: these are the commitments that define ourselves in large part in our own eyes, and so, when we look at ourselves, we cannot just think "It's a contingent matter that I am a moral agent." For if I imagine that, perhaps due to brain injury or illness or just the wear and tear of life, I were to lose my moral commitments entirely, then my view of that hypothetical case is that I, as I think of myself, would be gone from the world—in roughly the same way I think I would be gone from the world were I to develop a severe case of Alzheimer's. Someone else—a person with the same personal identity in one sense, but not the sense that intuitively matters—would have taken my place.

Second, to the extent that our relationship with morality does strike us as contingent, an analogy with love suggests itself.[16] Unless one is a hopeless romantic, one will think that there are any number of human beings running around on the planet today whom one might have, in some very real sense of "might have," met, fallen in love with, married, and built a happy life with, had things gone just a bit differently. But many of us also think that it is possible to acknowledge this contingency fully without having it undermine one's lifelong love and commitment to the person whom one did, as it so happened, actually meet, fall in love with, marry, and build a happy life with. On the contrary, there is a way in which the very contingency of the relationship—the extreme fragility of the whole way things happened, the ease with which they could have gone differently—can be seen as making the relationship all the more dear: *this* is the one, whom, among all the possible ways things could have gone, I *did* meet and become bound to. Our relationship with morality might be seen as similar. . . .

8. CONCLUSION

I will close by discussing a puzzle that might seem to be raised by a Humean, as opposed to a Kantian, version of constructivism. If one accepts Humean constructivism, then one accepts that contingencies—social, historical, biological, and otherwise—have played a crucial role in determining what normative reasons one has.[17] One might wonder how this recognition squares with a point we considered earlier, in the context of the second premise of Korsgaard's argument, according to which (in Kant's words) "we cannot conceive of a reason which consciously responds to a bidding from the outside with respect to its judgments." It might seem that to accept Humean constructivism is to try to do exactly what Kant says is inconceivable, namely consciously to let one's reason be determined "from the outside." Practical reason is being asked to look to a source outside itself for the ultimate substantive content of its reasons.

We may clear up the apparent puzzle by distinguishing between the application of Kant's point at the level of individual values, and the application of the point (or rather the lack thereof) to one's entire set of values taken at once. It is entirely correct, according to the Humean constructivist, that in the case of any individual value, and indeed in the case of any subset of your total set of values, you must (when you think about it) regard yourself as having some reason or other for endorsing them. Such a reason, if one has it, will be supplied by the standards set by one's other values. When it conies to the level of one's entire set of values taken at once, however, the Kantian point no longer holds. One can, and indeed one must, consciously accept that one's starting set of values was given to one "from the outside." This does not mean that one is forced to accept any one of them; by no means. Any one of them may be called into question and subsequently rejected, if one takes oneself to have reason to do so. What it does mean is that there is no escaping the fact that you have to start *somewhere* as an agent—with the acceptance of some values or other—and that this starting point cannot itself be chosen for a reason, since there is no standpoint prior to agency from which one could do this. To put it another way, it is only causes, and not reasons, that can catapult one into agency. Of course, your *parents* and other agents can have reasons for bringing about your birth, and for nurturing you on into reflective agency. The point is that *you* cannot; you must simply come alive. And this is the sense in which you can and must accept direction from the outside with regard to your judgments: you must be born as a reflective creature with some values or other. After that, however, things are very much up to you (for now there is a you). When it comes to the case of any individual value or subset of your values, you cannot consciously let your judgment be directed from the outside. But this is just to say: you cannot consciously let your judgment be directed from outside the further values that *are* you.

NOTES

1. Street 2006, 2008, 2009, 2011, and MS.
2. Korsgaard 1996b.
3. See Rawls 1999.
4. Examples of other attitude-dependent views include Williams 1981; Lewis 1989; and Schroeder 2007.
5. I borrow the language of "discipline" from Wright 1992.
6. Korsgaard 1997
7. Kant 1785/1959. . . .
8. Korsgaard 1996b, p. 123.
9. Recall that here I am taking it as a given—agreed upon between the Kantian and Humean constructivists—that realism is false. Since there are, on the views of both parties to the discussion, no independent normative facts, with standards of correctness for normative judgments existing only from within the standpoint of a valuing creature, *constructivists* can agree that there's a sense in which the question being asked here is ill-formulated. In a broader metaethical context, however—where realism, for example, was still on the table as a live option—it would not be appropriate to put things this way. In other words, the question whether there are independent normative facts *makes sense*; it's just that I think the answer is no. . . .

10. This is Korsgaard's interpretation of Kant in her 1996a.

11. In order to derive *morality,* the Kantian would need to go on to argue that it furthermore follows that *all* valuers (not just you) are valuable. Here . . . I think we need only dwell on the first step of the argument to see why it fails; intuitively, the step to the value of one's own self seems as though it should be the easiest of all, so the prospects for deriving the value of *all* valuers seem especially dim if we can't even get to the value of our own selves.

12. As interpreted by Korsgaard in her 1996a and 1996b, section 3.4.8.

13. Korsgaard 1996b, p. 122.

14. It is this high degree of genetic relatedness that explains how a creature with the set of values I am about to describe could arise via natural selection. Because this creature is more closely related to her sisters than she would be to her own offspring (with whom she would share only one-half of her genetic material), she can actually do "better" (as judged from an "evolutionary point of view") by forgoing reproduction and devoting herself utterly to the promotion of the welfare of her sisters and queen. For a summary of the relevant biology, see Trivers 1985, pp. 169–79. Of course, the *origins* of the creature in my example are really beside the point here—ultimately it does not matter whether such a creature could actually evolve or not. The important point is that such a creature— whether it emerged via natural selection or the handiwork of a god or magician—could value something or other without being rationally required to value its own *self* in addition.

15. The agent might, of course, still be making an *instrumental* mistake as dictated by the terms of his other values. For all the usual Hobbesian reasons, for example, the agent might have self-interested reason to act morally or perhaps even to cultivate moral feeling in himself. The Humean metaethical constructivist can accommodate such thoughts as well as anyone. But the Kantian constructivist, like many theorists, is looking for more.

16. See Lenman 1999, p. 167, for a similar point.

17. Even on a Kantian version of metaethical constructivism, contingency plays a large role in shaping one's reasons. On this point, see Korsgaard 1996b, pp. 241–2. But the point obviously holds even more strongly for Humean versions of metaethical constructivism.

REFERENCES

Kant, I. 1785/1959. *Foundations of the Metaphysics of Morals,* translated by L. W. Beck (New York: Macmillan Library of Liberal Arts).

Korsgaard, C. 1996a. *Creating the Kingdom of Ends* (Cambridge: Cambridge University Press).

Korsgaard, C. 1996b. *The Sources of Normativity* (Cambridge: Cambridge University Press).

Korsgaard, C. 1997. "The Normativity of Instrumental Reason," in *Ethics and Practical Reason,* eds. G. Cullity and B. Gaut (Oxford: Clarendon Press).

Lenman, J. 1999. "Michael Smith and the Daleks: Reason, Morality, and Contingency," *Utilitas* 11, pp. 164–77.

Lewis, D. 1989. "Dispositional Theories of Value," *Proceedings of the Aristotelian Society,* suppl. 63, pp. 113–37.

Rawls, J. 1999. "Kantian Constructivism in Moral Theory," in *Collected Papers,* ed. S. Freeman (Cambridge, MA: Harvard University Press).

Schroeder, M. 2007. *Slaves of the Passions* (Oxford: Oxford University Press).

Street, S. 2006. "A Darwinian Dilemma for Realist Theories of Value," *Philosophical Studies* 127, no. 1, pp. 109–66.

Street, S. 2008. "Reply to Copp: Naturalism, Normativity, and the Varieties of Realism Worth Worrying About," *Philosophical Issues* (a supplement to *Noûs*), vol. 18 on "Interdisciplinary Core Philosophy," ed. W. Sinnott-Armstrong, pp. 207–28.

Street, S. 2009. "In Defense of Future Tuesday Indifference: Ideally Coherent Eccentrics and the Contingency of What Matters," *Philosophical Issues* (a supplement to *Noûs*), vol. 19 on "Metaethics," ed. E. Sosa, pp. 273–98.

Street, S. 2010. "What is Constructivism in Ethics and Metaethics?" *Philosophy Compass* 5, pp. 363–84.

Street, S. 2011. "Mind-Independence Without the Mystery: Why Quasi-Realists Can't Have It Both Ways," *Oxford Studies in Metaethics,* vol. 6, ed. R. Shafer-Landau (Oxford: Clarendon Press).

Street, S. Unpublished ms. "Objectivity and Truth: You'd Better Rethink It."

Trivers, R. 1985. *Social Evolution* (Menlo Park. CA: Benjamin/Cummings Publishing).

Williams, B. 1981. "Internal and External Reasons," in *Moral Luck* (Cambridge: Cambridge University Press).

Wright, C. 1992. *Truth and Objectivity* (Cambridge, MA: Harvard University Press).

STUDY QUESTIONS

1. Why does Street think that Korsgaard's appeal to the value of humanity is incoherent?
2. According to the Humean constructivist, how does the regress of normative questions come to an end?
3. What point does Street seek to establish with the example of a reflective social insect?
4. Do you find compelling Street's appeal to the contingency of love?

Metaphysics and Morals

T. M. Scanlon

T. M. Scanlon, Professor of Philosophy at Harvard University, develops the view that the truth concerning what we owe to each other is determined by an agreement among all those in the moral domain. As Scanlon makes clear, however, he rejects constructivism. He objects to Korsgaard's view on the grounds that whether one has reason to adopt and maintain any particular identity cannot be determined solely by the structure of rationality. Rather, on Scanlon's realist alternative, we need to engage in substantive normative theorizing about the reasons we have. He argues that normative judgments do not need the support of any metaphysical claims. Just as the assertion that "three is a prime number" is licensed by and licenses certain other mathematical claims, so the assertion that "lying is wrong" is licensed by and licenses certain other normative claims.

Judgments about right and wrong and, more generally, judgments about reasons for action, seem, on the surface, to claim to state truths. They obey the principles of standard propositional and quantificational logic, and satisfy (at least most of) the other "platitudes" about truth[1] . . . Moreover, some of these judgments seem to be true, rather than false, if anything is. It would clearly be wrong for me to present, as my Presidential Address, a lecture that was in fact written by someone else, and in light of this I have good reason not to do so (even though in some respects it might have been better if I did). In addition, I find it difficult to resist saying that I believe that these things are so.

I thus find myself strongly drawn to a cognitivist understanding of moral and practical judgments. They strike me as the kind of things that can be true, and their acceptance seems to be a matter of belief.

But strong arguments against accepting these appearances have been offered from several quarters. What I want to do in this lecture is to consider some of these arguments and to try to identify and assess my reasons for resisting them. . . .

When I just said that some moral judgments seem to be clearly true rather than false, what I was claiming is that they are supported by our "ordinary criteria" for answering such questions. Standard ways of arguing about our obligations to one another clearly support these conclusions. So one thing that those who deny that moral judgments should be understood as straightforwardly true may be claiming is that if moral judgments are understood in this way then they claim, or presuppose, more than these "ordinary criteria" can deliver. We might understand moral terms, know how to apply them, and be confident in their applicability to certain situations; yet

From T. M. Scanlon, "Metaphysics and Morals," *Proceedings and Addresses of the American Philosophical Association* 77 (2003). Reprinted by permission of the publisher.

they could still fail to be true because they fail to "describe the world."

Here I think there is some ambiguity in what is meant by "the world." On its most expansive reading, "the world" might be taken to be simply the reflection of those sentences which are true, when judged by the criteria appropriate to sentences of their type. If, according to the best moral criteria, it would be wrong of me to deliver on this occasion a lecture written by someone else, then on this expansive reading it is, trivially, a "truth about the world" that this would be wrong. So if it is claimed that moral judgments do not state truths *because* if taken as true they would not "describe the world," this claim must be understood in terms of some more restrictive idea of "the world." Commonly, I think, this more restrictive sense is "the world as described by science" or "the natural world" where this is understood to include all and only physical and (insofar as they may be different) psychological facts. Thus it is sometimes said that there is a problem about how to fit moral truths into a scientific view of the world. It is, however, not clear what this problem is.

The thought might be that moral judgments endorsed by ordinary moral criteria, understood literally as true, involve claims about the natural world that conflict with those of our best science. Some kinds of (nonmoral) claims do have this problem. Believers in witches, ghosts, and demonic possession may have "ordinary criteria" for telling when these phenomena are present. Yet their claims fail to describe the world accurately, and are literally false. This is because these claims involve claims about events occurring in space and time, and about which things cause or are caused by them. These causal claims are false according to the proper criteria for assessing causal claims.

Do moral judgments, similarly, make claims that conflict with those of science? Moral judgments are often *based on* claims about the occurrence of events in time and space and about causal relations between them. Whether an action is wrong may depend, for example, on whether it causes injury. But these claims are to be assessed according to ordinary empirical criteria, not special moral ones. Moral judgments themselves, I would say, make no *causal* claims beyond these.

It might be replied, however, that even if moral judgments themselves make no special causal claims, claims to know truths about moral matters would involve or presuppose such claims. The idea would be that, if moral judgments express truths, then in arriving at well-founded opinions about moral matters we must be responding to the causal powers of special moral properties in the world. But moral knowledge need not be understood on this perceptual model. There is good reason to understand perceptual beliefs, and other beliefs about the physical world, in this way. It is, after all, part of their content that they are about physical things that exist at a distance from us. How could we be reliably in touch with such things except by being causally affected by them? But moral beliefs, mathematical beliefs, and other beliefs about abstract matters are different. They do not purport to be about things located apart from us is space, or anywhere else. It is therefore plausible (in a way that it is not in the case of beliefs about the physical world) to suppose that these are matters which we can discover the truth about simply by thinking about them in the right way. It may not be easy to say more exactly what this way is, and the answer clearly depends on the concepts involved. In some cases, it may involve the right kind of sequential reasoning, in others, perhaps, the right kind of mental picturing, in others, carefully focusing our attention on the relevant features of the ideas in question and being certain that we have distinguished them from other, irrelevant factors. But as long as there is some way of doing this correctly, there is a difference between getting it wrong and getting it right.

Suppose I am correct that neither moral judgments, understood as true, nor our claims to know such truths involve claims about the natural world that conflict with those of science. Taking moral judgments to be true still might be seen as "incompatible with a scientific view of the world" just because they do *not* make claims about things that exist in space and time and the causal relations between them. But this does not seem to me to be a genuine incompatibility. Science may claim to be a complete account of the occurrence of events in the spatio-temporal world and of the causal relations between them. But accepting this claim does not mean accepting that there are no true statements about anything other than what science deals with.

If science does not claim this, perhaps the best metaphysics does. Metaphysics may make claims about what "the world" is like that go beyond those of science (whether or not it allows that there is more to the world than what science deals with). So it may be that what moral judgments would conflict with if they were understood as being true is not science but metaphysics. It might be said that moral judgments, if they were understood as making truth claims, would involve metaphysical claims that go beyond what is guaranteed merely by their correctness according to ordinary moral criteria: to claim that they are true would be to claim for them an "intrinsic metaphysical *gravitas*."[2] But I do not see why this need be the case. Moral judgments have sometimes been understood as based on a teleological conception of nature in which the world, and some kinds of objects within it, are taken to have certain assigned goals or purposes. But moral judgments as I understand them do not depend on such a view of the world, nor do they need the support of other metaphysical claims.

But this lack of metaphysical import on the part of moral judgments might be held against them. If moral judgments do not make, or need the support of, metaphysical or scientific claims, then what kind of claims "about the world" do they make? Why isn't it idle to take them as true? The answer is that moral judgments are not idle because they make claims about what we have reason to do, and this is something of importance to us, as rational beings. The kind of *gravitas* that they require is thus not metaphysical but normative. This gives rise to at least two problems.

The first is a problem about the adequacy of ordinary moral criteria to deliver the normative significance that moral judgments claim for themselves. To claim that it would be wrong to act in a certain way is to claim that so acting would violate standards that people have strong, normally conclusive, reasons to abide by. If, in deploying our "ordinary criteria" for deciding whether an action is wrong, we are just determining whether that action meets

certain standards, there remains the question what reason people have to take these standards seriously. Indeed, it may be asked whether there, in fact, are any standards that have the authority that moral judgments are normally taken to claim. This question cannot be answered simply by showing that certain actions are wrong according to our "ordinary moral criteria," that is to say, according to the standards we generally accept, since it is a question about the authority of those standards. It seems to follow that these criteria alone do not suffice to establish that judgments about moral wrongness are *true*. To show that they are we would need to meet this challenge by showing that these criteria have the authority claimed for them.

I believe that this challenge can be met. But even if it can, a second, deeper problem remains. Insofar as moral judgments involve claims that we have reasons for acting in certain ways, it may be said that they are not the kind of thing that can be true or false because claims about reasons are not the kind of thing that can be true or false. It seems to me that this is the central issue and that most of the problems that are thought to beset a cognitivist understanding of moral judgments are inherited from, or at least shared by, a cognitivist understanding of practical judgments more generally. Let me turn then, from the question of whether moral judgments can be understood as straightforwardly true to the question of whether judgments about the reasons we have can be so understood.

To begin again at the beginning: I am strongly drawn toward a cognitivist understanding of judgments about the reasons we have. These judgments obey the usual principles of propositional and quantificational logic, and (at least most of) the other platitudes about truth. Moreover, some of these judgments seem clearly to be true rather than false. The fact that jumping into the audience in the middle of my lecture would lead to serious injury and embarrassment is a reason for me not to do this. Some might claim that this is a reason only because I have certain desires. But those who hold that this is so and those who deny it agree that I, in fact, have such a reason. Why not say, then, that the claim that I have this reason is true?

Objections to saying this are of two related kinds. The first holds that judgments about reasons are not true because there is no fact in the world that they describe. The second holds that if we took judgments about reasons merely to describe such facts then we would be unable to account for the practical significance of these judgments. I will comment briefly on the first of these objections, and spend the remainder of my lecture discussing the second.

I said above that moral judgments as I understand them do not conflict with the claims of science, nor do they need the support of, nor could they be supported in a plausible way by, metaphysical claims. The same seems to be true of judgments about reasons. What may lie behind the worry that there are no "facts" that true normative judgments could capture is not this metaphysical worry but two different ones. First, in applying some of our concepts—in identifying objects as chairs, for example—we can be said to be applying relatively clear criteria implicit in our concepts. In the case of reasons, however, it is unclear what these criteria are. Taking *C* to be a reason for *A*, it might be said, is not a matter of applying criteria implicit in our understanding of the relation 'counts in favor of,' but simply a matter of reacting to *C* in a certain way. People can react to the same things in different ways, and there is no basis for counting one of these ways as uniquely correct. I will refer to this as the *problem of insufficiently determinate content* (or, for short, the *problem of content*.)

Second, given the practical significance of recognizing a consideration as a reason, it may seem that the reaction in question is not properly understood as classifying that consideration as one of a certain kind, but rather a reaction of some other, less cognitive sort. This practical significance is often taken to be a matter of motivational force. Since I believe it is better understood in normative terms, I will refer to this problem as the problem of normative significance.

I believe that the problem of content and the problem of normative significance are widely regarded as providing the strongest support for denying that judgments about reasons are true in any substantial sense, despite their apparently assertoric form. These problems may be stated in metaphysical terms. The problem of normative significance might be put by saying that the world does not contain facts with 'oughts' built into them. But in my view neither problem is fundamentally a metaphysical one.

The problem of content arises, rather, from the view that persistent first-order disagreement about reasons is quite legitimate, because the concepts in question provide insufficient structure for us to tell which way of thinking about the reasons we have is thinking about it "in the right way." It is when our understanding of the question gives us insufficient basis for saying why *our* way of assessing matters is the right one that we may have to fall back on a claim "just to see it," which may be characterized as an appeal to "intuition" in a problematic quasi-perceptual sense.

This problem raises difficult issues about which I will confine myself here to two brief remarks. The first is that in the case of practical reasoning, the problem of content can be made to seem more serious than it is by considering it as a problem about reasons in general. It is quite true that the bare concept of a reason—a consideration that counts in favor of some attitude—provides us with very little guidance about how to go about deciding what reasons we have. But it is unrealistic to expect more structure at this level of abstraction. Questions about reasons take on determinate structure only when they are more specific questions about reasons of particular kinds, for particular things (such as my reasons for not jumping into the audience, or breaking into song, in the middle of my lecture). Even at this level there remains room for disagreement in some cases, but in most cases of this kind it no longer seems to be just a matter of "how one reacts."

Second, it should be borne in mind that an understanding of the question being addressed can lend support to one's judgment that a certain consideration is a reason in other ways than by providing substantive grounds for the truth of that claim. An understanding of the concepts involved (for example, of what the consideration in question is supposed to be a reason for) may determine standards of relevance. By helping to identify the kinds of distinctions that need to be made in order to be thinking about the question in the right way, and hence about the kind of errors we might be making, this can give us grounds for confidence that we are not making such errors. Experience in thinking carefully and reflectively about such matters can also provide such support. The fact that a judgment is "intuitive" in the sense being discussed therefore does not mean that it is a guess, or a hunch, or "just a feeling."

Let me turn now to the problem of normative significance, and hence to what I earlier called the second line of objection to construing judgments about reasons as true or false. This is the objection that, if we take judgments about reasons as things that can be true, and understand the acceptance of such a judgment as a belief, we will be unable to account for the practical significance of these judgments.

The difficulty here is not a problem about how to fit the idea of a reason or the relation 'counting in favor of' into a scientific worldview. Our beliefs about reasons, if they are beliefs, need not be caused by interaction with this relation. Nor need this relation be causally active in producing actions. It is an agent's *acceptance* of a judgment about the reasons he or she has that does this. Such acceptance, whether it amounts to belief or not, is a psychological state, and hence the kind of thing that figures in ordinary psychological explanations. The state of accepting a judgment, or having a belief, is just as "naturalistic" as having a desire. Desires may, phenomenologically, present themselves more as "urges" or "tugs" than other intentional states such as beliefs or judgments do. But an explanation of behavior which appeals to factors which have this phenomenological character is not for that reason closer to being a causal explanation. The experience of judging something to be true is a psychological phenomenon just as much as feeling a "desire." Both are, I presume, occurrences with some causal basis. How these experiential states (feeling desire or conviction), and the corresponding enduring states (such as belief) are related to a genuinely causal account of what goes on in us is a deep problem. But a desire (or the feeling of an urge) is not, any more than a belief is, an awareness of a cause. So if there

is a problem, it must lie elsewhere than in the demands of a scientific outlook.

The problem is often put in terms of motivation. The acceptance of a judgment about one's reasons for action cannot be a belief because, it is said, beliefs are not the kind of things that, by themselves, can move one to act. Only desires can do that.[3] I have doubts about the idea of motivation that this statement of the problem appeals to. It seems to me to be troublingly ambiguous between a causal notion and a normative one. But I want to set aside this formulation of the problem. Whether or not there is a problem about how beliefs can motivate, I believe that there is a parallel problem (at least an apparent one) about the requirements of rationality. In what follows I want to describe this problem, discuss its anticognitivist thrust, and consider a possible solution to it. I believe that this solution, if it is one, would bring with it a solution to the problem considered in its motivational form.

The problem I have I mind is this. If a person judges that she has conclusive reason to do X at t, then two things follow. First, insofar as she does not abandon or forget this judgment, she is irrational if she does not intend to do X at t. Second, the fact that she holds this judgment about her reasons can explain her intending to do X at t, and her so acting. The problem is to explain this connection—to explain how a *belief* can rationally require a certain intention to act, and how it can explain this intention and this action.

Before addressing the problem, I want to say something about the idea of rationality in terms of which I am understanding it. We should, I believe, distinguish between two kinds of normative claims. The first kind are claims about the reasons that people have—about what counts in favor of doing what, about what counts in favor of believing what, and about what counts in favor of having other attitudes. The claim that the embarrassment that would result from my singing "The Hills Are Alive with the Sound of Music" right now counts as a reason not to do so is a true claim of this kind.

But not all normative claims are direct substantive claims about reasons. In particular, some claims about what it would be irrational for someone to do are not claims about the reasons that person has. For example, if a person believes that *p,* then it would be irrational for him to refuse to rely on *p* as a premise in further reasoning, and to reject arguments because they rely on it. To say this is not to say that the person has good reason to accept such arguments. Perhaps what he has most reason to do is to give up his belief that *p.* The claim is only that *as long as he believes that p,* it is irrational of him to refuse to accept such arguments. Similar connections hold in practical reasoning: if a person has a certain end, *E,* and believes that *A* would advance *E,* then it is irrational of her not to take this as a reason for doing *A.* This is not to say that she has any reason to do *A.* Perhaps what she has most reason to do is to abandon *E,* or to change her mind about whether doing *A* would promote it. But as long as she does not abandon *E,* and believes that doing *A* would promote *E,* it is irrational for her to deny that she has any reason to do *A.* Normative claims of this kind involve claims about what a person must, if she is not irrational, treat as a reason, but they make no claims about whether this actually *is* a reason.

I will call claims about rationality of this second kind *structural* claims, to distinguish them from *substantive* claims about what is a reason for what. I call these claims structural because they are claims about the relations between an agent's attitudes that must hold insofar as he or she is rational, and because the kind of irrationality involved is a matter of conflict between these attitudes. (For example: a matter of believing something but failing to give it the role in further thinking that believing it involves, or having an end, but failing to give it the role in further thinking that is involved in having it as one's end.) The structural requirements of rationality are, it might be said, requirements that are constitutive of the rational attitudes involved.[4]

In earlier work, I have advocated restricting the term 'irrational' to instances of what I am here calling structural irrationality.[5] I am not relying on that restriction here. My present thesis is just that some claims about rationality are of this kind, and in particular that the claim I have mentioned above, about the connection between judging oneself to have conclusive reason to do *X* at *t* and forming the intention

to do *X* at *t,* is such a claim. It is "structurally irrational" to fail to form an intention do to what one judges oneself to have conclusive reason to do. It is also, I would say, structurally irrational to continue to intend to do what one judges oneself to have conclusive reason not to do.

The question is how this rational requirement is to be explained if a judgment about the strength of the reasons one has is a *belief.* How can having a belief that something is the case make it irrational for someone not to form a certain intention and act on it? Having a belief can, as I have already said, make a difference to what one must do if one is not irrational. If I believe that *p,* then I cannot, without being irrational, refuse to recognize *p* as a valid premise in further reasoning, or form beliefs that I know to be incompatible with *p.* These requirements are, it might be said, partially constitutive of belief.

In particular, if judging that I have conclusive reason to do *X* now is a matter of having a certain belief, and I have that belief, then I must be willing, if I am not to be irrational, to rely on this claim in further reasoning about what reasons I have. But it does not seem to be constitutive of *belief* that, if I believe that I have conclusive reason to do *X* now, I must form the intention to so act.

The idea that there can seem to be a problem here may, I believe, help to explain why there seems to Christine Korsgaard to be a problem with what she calls a substantive realist understanding of judgments about reasons.[6] . . . Korsgaard tends to state this as a problem about *moral* realism, which partially blunts its force. Faced with someone who accepts it as a fact that it would be wrong to act in a certain way but asks why he should do it, Korsgaard sees the (substantive) moral realist as simply insisting that it is obligatory to so act. Her charge that this is unresponsive foot-stomping has merit. It makes sense, as she says, to ask why moral requirements are something we have reason to care about.

But Korsgaard believes that the same problem arises for a (substantive) realist about reasons—that is to say, for a view according to which judging oneself to have a reason to do *X* is a matter of having a certain belief. Here it is less clear what she is claiming. Suppose a person believes that he has conclusive reason to do X at t. How can this fall short of what is required? What is lacking does not seem to be a reason. A person cannot coherently say "Yes, I see that C is a conclusive reason to do X, but what reason do I have to do it?" The problem might be one about motivation. The problem might be that someone might believe that he or she had conclusive reason to do X, but fail to be at all moved by this. This can certainly happen, due to depression, lassitude, or simple irrationality. But the fact that practical realism allows for this does not seem to be an objection to it. A view that ruled out irrationality would be too strong, as Korsgaard herself observes.

I suggest that the problem Korsgaard sees for (substantive) practical realism is better understood in terms of the distinction between substantive and structural normative claims. Suppose you advance some substantive normative claim about the reasons I have. You might say, for example, that the fact that the American Philosophical Association is meeting in Philadelphia is a reason for me to go there. I might ask, "Why is that a reason?" If you offer some further substantive claim in reply, I can again ask for a further reason, and as long as you keep offering further substantive claims I can keep replying in this way. If you stop at some point and say "It just is a reason!" then, Korsgaard might say, you are engaging in unresponsive foot stomping.

What can stop this regress according to Korsgaard is not a claim about what is a reason but a claim about what I must, if I am not irrational, *treat* as a reason. This would be what I am calling a structural normative claim. For example, Kantians like Korsgaard believe that insofar as one is engaged in practical reasoning at all, one must see one's rational nature (and that of others) as an end in itself. It is not that one sees these things as reason-providing *in order* to be engaged in practical reasoning, or that one must take Kant's argument as a *reason* for taking these things to be reasons. Rather, the claim is just that one *will* take them to be reasons insofar as one is rational. This is what I have been calling a structural normative claim rather than a substantive one.

The point is clearest in what Korsgaard says about instrumental rationality.[1] She writes that a realist is unable to account for even instrumental rationality. If the fact that an action's instrumentality to her end constitutes a reason for her to do it is just another fact, which the agent believes, then "[f]or all we can see, an agent may be indifferent" to this fact. So put, this may sound like a problem about motivation. This interpretation is encouraged when Korsgaard puts the point by saying that on a realist interpretation the principle of instrumental reason "fails to meet the internalism requirement," since internalism is generally understood to be a view about motivation. But she goes on to make clear that the problem she sees for realism is not that it cannot explain how an agent could be motivated to take the means to his ends, but rather that it cannot explain why an agent *must* be so motivated. I take her to mean that it cannot explain why being so motivated is a requirement of rationality.

Korsgaard's larger aim seems to be to show that all valid normative claims can be grounded in this way, in claims of structural normativity about what we must do if we are not irrational. This strategy is appealing in part because it seems to offer a solution to the problem of content. The requirements of rational agency provide a framework which structures our thinking about what reasons we have, and provides criteria of the kind that seem to be lacking when we address brute questions of substantive normativity on their own. This is what makes it plausible to call Korsgaard a constructivist about reasons.

Her main device for deriving more substance from the bare structure of rational agency is the idea of a practical identity. Insofar as I see myself as having a certain identity, I must, on pain of structural irrationality, see certain things as reasons. But even if this is accepted, there remains the question what reason one has to adopt and maintain any particular identity. I therefore do not believe that this project of grounding substantive normativity in structural normativity can succeed. It seems to me that there always remain substantive normative questions about "What is a reason for what?" which must be faced, and answered, directly. This is why I am not a Kantian, or a neo-Kantian of Korsgaard's sort.

I do, however, also believe that there are valid claims of structural normativity. For example, as I have said, I believe that it is irrational to fail to form an intention to do what one judges oneself to have conclusive reason to do. The question I want now to address is how this can be so if accepting such judgments about reasons is just having a certain kind of belief. It is worth noting that there is no similar problem about explaining structural connections between intentions and other intentions. If I intend to do X at t and do not change my mind about this, then it is irrational for me not to try to do X at t, and irrational for me not to see myself as having reason to do other things that are necessary to my doing this, such as refraining from other incompatible plans of action. These requirements are part of what it is to intend something. They are, one might say, constitutive of intending, just as a readiness to use what one believes as a premise in further reasoning is constitutive of believing. But giving a belief a special content (making it a belief about my reasons for action) does not turn it into an intention.

It might seem from what I have just said that the problem I am calling attention to concerns the rational links between theoretical and practical reasoning. But this is so only if "practical" is understood in a very broad sense to include all judgments about reasons, including reasons for belief. If I judge that I have conclusive reason to believe that p, then I am irrational if, continuing to hold this judgment, I fail to believe that p. But since this requirement depends on the content of the belief in question (the fact that it is a belief about reasons) it is not captured by the "constitutive" requirements I have mentioned above, such as the requirement that someone who believes that p should be ready to rely on arguments that employ p as a premise. So the problem I have been discussing about reasons for action seems to arise as well about reasons for belief. I will return to this in a moment.

In the case of reasons for action one might conclude, and I think many have concluded, that the only way to account for the intrapersonal rational significance of judgments about reasons is to interpret the acceptance of such judgments as something other than a belief. For example, if judging that C is a reason for A is a matter of adopting a certain policy—a policy of reasoning in a certain way, for example—then it would be easy to explain the

irrationality of accepting such a judgment but not reasoning in accord with the policy it involves. This would be "constitutive" of judgments about reasons, just as a readiness to use p as a premise in further reasoning is constitutive of believing that p.

Given this, why should judgments about reasons be expressed in the form of assertions, which would normally be understood as expressions of belief? Several factors pull us in this direction. First, it makes sense to reason hypothetically about reasons. We can ask ourselves what reasons we would have if our situation were different in certain ways. This is one thing that gives rise to the well-known Frege-Geach problem of embeddings.

Second, we can reach conclusions about what other people have reason to do, or to believe, but we can't, at least in a literal sense, adopt policies for them, although we can make judgments about what policies they have reason to adopt. In fact, since all conclusions about what we have reason to do, or to believe, are conclusions about what someone in a certain situation has reason to do or believe, they are all, implicitly, judgments about what others have reason to believe, insofar as their situations are similar to ours. When you form the belief that p, or the intention to A, you do something that only you can do. But when you and I think about whether C is good reason to do A, or good reason to believe p, we are thinking about the same question, just as when you and I are thinking about whether the sky is blue.

This is how things seem, and it draws me, at least, toward cognitivist understanding of judgments about reasons. The question is whether, in the face of the intrapersonal rational significance of judgments about reasons we must conclude that this is an illusion, and that these judgments must be understood in some other way. What are the possibilities? And how do they fare as accounts of interpersonal normative discourse?

In a recent article, Allan Gibbard suggests that when I form a judgment about what you have reason to do I am "deciding what to do for the case in which I am you" (or in your position).[8] This seems forced to me. Also, the possibility of irrationality makes it implausible. It seems to me that people can (irrationally) believe that they themselves have conclusive reason to do something but fail to decide to do it. It therefore seems implausible to identify the judgment about reasons (whether one's own or someone else's) with such a decision. The solution Gibbard proposed earlier in *Wise Choices, Apt Feelings,* that a judgment that *C* is a reason for *A* expresses one's acceptance of a norm telling us to count *C* in favor of *A,* is more appealing in this score. But even this does not seem to capture the full content of disagreement about reasons.

There is, I believe, an explanation for this. Expressivism arises, initially, as an attempt to explain the special intrapersonal normative significance (or, as expressivists might put it, the special motivational force) of practical judgments. In my terms, it arises as a way to explain phenomena of structural normativity. But *inter*personal disagreement is mainly about claims of *substantive* normativity. Our disagreements are generally about what is a reason for what, such as whether revenge is a good reason to take a certain action in certain circumstances. Disagreements of this kind can arise in many different contexts: when one of us is giving the other advice, or trying to persuade him that he should or should not do something, or when one of us is trying to justify what he has done, or when we are discussing what some third party has reason to do.

The nature of these interpersonal interactions is quite different. But what we are disagreeing about is in fundamental respects the same in each case: whether a certain consideration is or is not a reason for some attitude. The answer to this question is, I am drawn toward saying, something that is properly expressed in the assertoric mode, is capable of being true, and can be the object of belief. It is sometimes suggested that there is something inappropriate, even offensive about this way of putting things. The suggestion is that to assert, in such a disagreement, that one's own claim is *true,* is to claim an inappropriate kind of authority. But insofar as this is so, it is equally so (equally a case of unhelpful foot-stomping) when we are disagreeing about some matter of empirical fact, such as who won the 1948 World Series, and we merely reiterate that the claim we are making *is true*. Moreover, even when it is unclear whether there are any criteria for settling our disagreement

about reasons, there is nothing inappropriate about taking us to be offering contrasting opinions about a matter of fact that we are both inquiring into. So the charge of inappropriate claim to authority is unfair as a general objection to cognitivism about reasons.

On the other side, it might be charged, against the expressivist, that it is inappropriate, in such a case of disagreement, to be issuing commands, or to be making a decision for the other party. But this charge would be equally unfair. In expressing my acceptance of a norm I may be only explaining, in the mode of advice, what I myself would do. A more serious problem is that these ways of understanding what is being claimed fit the case of advice giving better than the other cases I have mentioned, such as offering a defense of one's own actions.

What all this brings out is the fact that when we are disagreeing about a normative question, such as whether revenge is a good reason for taking a certain action, the assertoric or expressivist character of the judgment we are disagreeing *about* is not central. When I defend my action by saying that revenge was a good reason for doing what I did, the normative claim I am making on you is that you *should accept* this view of reasons. Put in the simplest expressivist terms, I am not saying "Take revenge in circumstances like this" but rather "Accept that revenge is a good reason for such actions." The normative appeal I am making is thus not expressed in the first-order judgment we are disagreeing about but (to put it again in expressivist terms) in the higher-order norms about norm acceptance that, I am claiming, support accepting this norm.[9] In this respect, our disagreement is like a disagreement about a question of empirical fact, in which each of us is claiming that there are good reasons to support his view. As an expressivist might describe such a case, we are each expressing our acceptance of norms (in this case epistemic ones) which, we each claim, favor accepting the view we are advancing. In the interpersonal case, then, the normative character of the view we are advancing, or the expressivist character of the way this view is expressed, is not doing any particular work. Even in expressivist terms, normative disagreement looks much like disagreement in belief.

Let me return, then to the intrapersonal case where, as I have said, the appeal of expressivism seems strongest. Is there any way in which the special intrapersonal significance of judgments about reasons might be accounted for other than by interpreting them as something other than the assertoric statements they appear to be? In conclusion, I want to suggest one possible answer, which emerges once we view the problem as one about rationality rather than about motivation.

Recall that, as I indicated above, there is a problem about the significance of judgments about reasons for belief as well as about the significance of judgments about reasons for action. In the case of belief, it seems to me natural to say that it is constitutive of a belief (the one that is to be formed or modified) that it should be responsive to one's judgment about reasons for it. A belief that p is the sort of thing that should be modified if one judges that there is good reason to conclude that p is false, and should be formed if the agent judges there to be conclusive reason for concluding that p is true. This is not to say that a belief that p commonly arises via a prior judgment that p is true. Many, perhaps even most beliefs do not arise in this way, perceptual beliefs being obvious examples.

My claim is only that belief is a judgment-sensitive attitude—a kind of attitude that will, insofar as we are rational, be responsive to our judgments about relevant reasons when we have such judgments. It is the judgment sensitivity of belief, I would argue, that accounts for the significance, for our beliefs, of our judgments about reasons, and thus makes it unnecessary to construe those judgments themselves as something other than beliefs in order to account for their intrapersonal rational significance. This feature of belief also makes it unnecessary to appeal to a special form of motivation, analogous to a desire, to explain how judgments about reasons can lead to changes in belief. If an agent is rational then her beliefs just will be responsive to her other judgments in this way.

The same thing, I would argue, is true of intentions. Although an intention to do some action need not arise from a prior judgment that there is good reason to so act, intention is a judgment-sensitive attitude. If I judge myself to have conclusive reason to do A, then insofar as I am not irrational I will intend to do A, and if I judge myself to have conclusive reason not to do A, then insofar as I am not irrational I will not so intend. These are claims of *structural* rationality. They do not depend on whether I do, in fact, have reason to do A. As in the case of belief, however, these facts about structural rationality explain the special intrapersonal rational significance of judgments about reasons for action, and they do so without supposing that those judgments are anything other than beliefs.

The temptation to think that the explanation for these connections must lie in the noncognitive character of judgments about reasons arises, I believe, from viewing the problem as one of motivation. Insofar as the capacity to motivate is seen as a kind of causal power, it must be attributed to the state that comes first—the desire, or the acceptance of a judgment about reasons—as a power to produce, and to explain, the state that follows. This temporal asymmetry is removed when we view the problem as a question about rationality—about how the acceptance of a judgment about reasons can make it (structurally) irrational to have or not to have another state (a belief, or an intention). Seeing the problem in this way allows us to take a more holistic view. The irrationality of having a certain combination of attitudes can be explained in terms of the relations between those attitudes—the fact that the second is the kind of attitude that must, insofar as the agent is rational, be responsive to the first.

Moreover, once we have this response to the question of rationality, we also have an answer to the corresponding question of motivation. Rationality is, as I have been stressing, a normative idea. But to claim that someone is a rational agent is also in part to claim that that he is so constituted that *in general* though not, of course, invariably, his attitudes fit the patterns required by rationality. They must do so with a certain regularity in order for it to make sense to attribute to him judgments about reasons and beliefs and intentions of the sort that are, ideally, responsive to such judgments. So, in particular, to claim that someone is a rational agent is to claim that he is so constituted that when he judges himself to have conclusive reason to do something he generally responds to this judgment by forming the intention to do it (and, insofar as he is not irrational and does not change this intention, he so acts). Moreover, these things do not just happen, but also seem to him, in the light of his judgment, to be justified.

The normative aspect of the idea of rationality may, however, raise questions about the nature of what I am calling claims of structural normativity. If what is being claimed is that certain beings ought to behave in certain ways (that, for example, the attitudes of rational beings ought to conform to certain principles of rationality) then it may be asked what the basis of these 'oughts' is supposed to be. Worse, it may seem that practical reason, and hence morality, as I am describing them, do after all have troubling metaphysical presuppositions: insofar as they presuppose the existence of rational agents in this sense they may seem to depend on a teleological conception of nature that is incompatible with a modern, scientific view of the world.

To allay this worry, I need to consider in more detail the kind of normativity involved in the ideas of rationality and irrationality as I have been employing them. From the point of view of the deliberating agent, this normativity is self-effacing. A rational person who believes that p does not accept arguments relying on p as a premise because she sees this as required by some principle of rationality to which she must conform. Nor does she do it "in order not [to] be irrational." Rather, she will be willing to rely on p as a premise because this is simply a part of what it is to believe p. Similarly, a person who believes that doing A would advance some end of hers, will see not this as counting in favor of A because doing so is required by a principle, or because she must do this in order to avoid irrationality. Rather, seeing this as a reason for A is part of what is involved for her in having the end in question.

Taking a more "external" view, however, we can say that a person who does not do these things is irrational.[10] This is a normative judgment; irrationality is a kind of fault. What kind of normativity is involved in such a judgment? One plausible idea is that it is a judgment of functional deficiency, of the same kind that that a judgment that a carburetor, or a

kidney, is deficient because it does not operate in the appropriate way. Such judgments are not incompatible with a scientific view of the world. External judgments of this kind are not, however, doing the main work in my account. My argument turns on claims of the first kind, about how rational agents will see things and how they will, as a matter of fact, normally respond.

Even if this response is accepted, the explanation I have offered of the intrapersonal significance of judgments about reasons may seem to put a great deal of weight on the idea of a reason and the idea of rationality. I have tried to defend the idea that the fact that some consideration is a reason (for an action or a belief) can itself be an object of belief. I have not offered an explanation of the content of such beliefs (of the idea of something's being a reason) except by describing how such judgments are linked with other states, such as beliefs and intentions, by requirements of rationality.[11] I have appealed to these requirements to explain how judgments about reasons, even if they are beliefs, can have special intrapersonal normative significance. Here it may seem that I am building a lot into the idea of rationality. So I should stress that I am relying on this idea only to explain claims of what I have called structural normativity. I have not undertaken to build into the idea of rationality, or to derive from it, substantive claims about what is a reason for what. As I have said, I do not believe that this can plausibly be done.

NOTES

1. Crispin Wright, *Truth and Objectivity* (Cambridge: Harvard University Press, 1992), ch. 2, sect. 1 and ch. 3 sect. 1. See also his "Truth in Ethics," in B. Hooker, ed., *Truth in Ethics* (Oxford: Blackwell Publishers, 1996), pp. 7–8. I say "at least most of" because there is some disagreement about the range of platitudes that need to be satisfied in order for a kind of sentence to be "truth apt." See, for example, Frank Jackson, Graham Oppy, and Michael Smith, "Minimalism and Truth Aptness," *Mind,* 103 (1994): 287–302. They argue that these include the platitude that "a sentence counts as truth apt only if it can (barring certain problems about length, etc.) be used to give the content of a belief" (294). It follows that sentences of a certain

kind are truth apt only if they satisfy platitudes about belief. One of these is that beliefs are not conceptually linked to motivation and action. So, if there is such a link between accepting an ethical judgment and being moved to act accordingly, then, if this platitude is accepted, sentences expressing ethical judgments cannot be the contents of beliefs, and hence are not truth apt. In the last part of this lecture, I will try to show how beliefs are in fact linked to motivation and action in a way that derails this argument. I should say that Jackson *et al.* also hold that ethical sentences are truth apt. (299)

2. I take the term from Crispin Wright, *Truth in Ethics,* p. 5. . . .

3. The point is familiar from Hume, *A Treatise of Human Nature,* Book II, Part II, Section III. . . .

4. This way of putting the matter has a Kantian ring, and it is indeed inspired in part by some remarks of Chris Korsgaard's in "The Normativity of Instrumental Reason," in Garrett Cullity and Berys Gaut, eds., *Ethics and Practical Reason* (Oxford: Oxford University Press, 1997), p. 242. But something similar is recognized by non-Kantians as well.

5. *What We Owe to Each Other* (Cambridge: Harvard University Press, 1998), pp. 25–30.

6. In *The Sources of Normativity* (Cambridge: Cambridge University Press, 1996) and in "Realism and Constructivism in 20th Century Moral Philosophy,"

Journal of Philosophical Research, APA Centennial Supplement, "Philosophy in America at the Turn of the Century," (2003): 99–122.

7. In "The Normativity of Instrumental Reason," p. 242.

8. "Normative and Recognitional Concepts," *Philosophy & Phenomenological Research,* 64 (2002), pp. 151–168.

9. This fits with what Gibbard says in his discussion of "normative authority"; Sandel, Michael J. *Liberalism and the Limits of Justice.* Cambridge: Cambridge University Press, 1982

10. I call this view external because it is not the point of view of an agent making a decision but rather a reflection on that process. The quotation marks are a recognition of the fact that agents can take this view of themselves.

11. It might seem that I am here claiming that beliefs about reasons have two "directions of fit": as *beliefs* they must "fit the world" (that is to say be correct), but as beliefs about reasons they are rationally connected with action (and thus demand that the world should fit them). But what I say here does not run afoul of Michael Smith's arguments against this possibility. I explain why it does not, and discuss the relation between my views and Smith's in Scanlon, T. M. 2007. "Structural irrationality." in *Common Minds: Themes from the Philosophy of Philip Pettit* edited by Geoffrey Brennan. Oxford: Oxford University Press: 84-103.

STUDY QUESTIONS

1. According to Scanlon, what is the basis for the truth or falsity of moral claims?
2. How does Scanlon attempt to solve the problem of content?
3. How does Scanlon attempt to solve the problem of normative significance?
4. Why does Scanlon reject constructivism?

Part IX

THEISTIC VOLUNTARISM

The Question: Plato's *Euthyphro*

Steven M. Cahn

According to the divine command theory, ethical requirements are justified because they are God's commands. In Plato's *Euthyphro*, Socrates poses a powerful challenge to this theory. He asks the question that has come to be known as "Euthyphro's dilemma": "Is the pious loved by the gods because it is pious, or is it pious because it is loved by the gods?" In this selection, Steven M. Cahn, co-editor of this book, unpacks the argument Socrates offers to prove that the pious is loved by the gods because it is pious.

To Sherlock Holmes, Irene Adler was always "*the* woman."[1] To philosophers, Plato's *Euthyphro* is the dialogue containing "*the* question." Although the work is one of Plato's most unified and compelling creations, its main point is so famous that references to it appear in countless philosophical contexts.

The situation in the dialogue is that Euthyphro claims to understand the nature of piety and is challenged by Socrates to define the concept. Euthyphro eventually proposes that the pious is what all the gods love. Socrates then asks *the* question: "Is the pious loved by the gods because it is pious, or is it pious because it is loved by the gods?" When Euthyphro replies that he does not understand, Socrates launches into an intricate argument to prove that Euthyphro's definition is unsatisfactory. While the overall import of the argument is clear, some crucial steps are compressed, making it difficult to grasp. I hope the following reconstruction of the logic involved will help clarify the argument's structure and reveal the force and elegance of the proof.

Here is the key passage, as rendered in Maureen Eckert's effective translation:[2]

EUTHYPHRO: Well, I, at least, would say this is the pious, what all the gods love, and the opposite, what all the gods hate, is impious.

SOCRATES: Surely, then, let us examine this again, Euthyphro, if it is well put, or should we consider and so accept our definition and those of others, and if someone should say "it is so," then we should agree that it is so? Should one consider what the speaker means?

EUTHYPHRO: One should consider this, but I certainly think, at the moment, this is well stated.

SOCRATES: Soon we'll know better, good friend. Consider this: Is the pious loved by the gods because it is pious, or is it pious because it is loved by the gods?

EUTHYPHRO: I don't understand what you're saying, Socrates.

SOCRATES: I'll try to explain more clearly. We speak of something being carried and someone carrying, of something being led and someone leading, of something being seen and someone seeing—and you understand that all these are different from one another and how they are different?

EUTHYPHRO: I believe that I understand.

SOCRATES: Very well, then there is something being loved, and someone loving it is a different thing.

EUTHYPHRO: How could it not be so?

SOCRATES: So, tell me then whether something that is being carried is being carried because someone carries it or for some other reason?

EUTHYPHRO: No, that's it.

SOCRATES: And something being led is this way because someone leads it, and something being seen is this way because someone sees it?

EUTHYPHRO: Certainly.

SOCRATES: Well, it's not that something is seen because it has the quality of being seen; but because someone sees it, the thing has this quality of being seen. Nor is something led by someone because it has the quality of being led, but because someone leads it, it has this quality of being led; nor does someone carry something because it has the quality of being carried; but it has this quality of being carried because someone carries it. Well, is what I want to say clear, Euthyphro? I want to say this, if something is produced or affected, it isn't produced because it is being produced, but because it is produced, it has the quality of being produced. Nor is something affected because it's being affected. But because it is affected, it has the quality of being affected. Or do you not agree with this?

EUTHYPHRO: I do.

SOCRATES: All right, then. Is what is loved something that has the quality of either being produced or being affected by someone?

EUTHYPHRO: Certainly.

SOCRATES: Well, then this is like the preceding things; it's not that something is loved by those who love it because it has the quality of being loved, but it has this quality of being loved because they love it?

EUTHYPHRO: Necessarily.

SOCRATES: What do we say about the pious, Euthyphro? So, it is loved by all the gods, as you say?

EUTHYPHRO: Yes.

SOCRATES: Is it pious because of this, or for some other reason?

EUTHYPHRO: No, because of this.

SOCRATES: All right, so, is it loved because it is pious, but it is not pious because it is loved?

EUTHYPHRO: So it seems.

SOCRATES: So then, because it is loved by the gods, it has the quality of being loved and is god-loved?

EUTHYPHRO: How could it not be so?

SOCRATES: The god-loved is not the pious, Euthyphro, nor is the pious god-loved, as you say it is, but one is different from the other.

EUTHYPHRO: How so, Socrates?

SOCRATES: Because we agree that the pious is loved for the reason that it is pious, but it is not pious because it is loved. Is this so?

EUTHYPHRO: Yes.

SOCRATES: So something god-loved is god-loved, meaning it is loved by the gods because of this fact of its being loved, but it is not loved because it is god-loved.

EUTHYPHRO: You speak the truth.

SOCRATES: So, dear Euthyphro, if the god-loved and the pious were the same thing, then the pious would be loved because it was pious, and then the god-loved would be loved because it was god-loved, if the god-loved was god-loved on account of being loved by the gods. And thus, the pious would be pious because it was loved by all the gods; yet now you see that they are opposite to one another, being completely different from each other. For one has the quality of being loved simply because it is loved, while the other is a kind of thing that is loved because it is lovable. I venture to guess, Euthyphro, that when you were asked what piety is, you did not wish to make its nature clear to me, but told me some quality it has, because the pious is affected like this, it is loved by all the gods, but you have not yet said what it is. Therefore, as a friend, do not keep this hidden, but once again from the beginning explain what piety is.

Socrates throughout relies on a common distinction between a thing or person who is receiving love, the loved one, and a person who is giving love, the loving one. To use a more specific example than Plato offers, we can distinguish John, who is loved, from Mary, who is loving him. Mary's loving John is the reason he is loved. That he is loved is not the reason Mary is loving him; rather, she is loving him due to certain lovable characteristics he possesses. In other words, John is loved because he is *being* loved, and he is *being* loved because of his lovable nature. He is not *being* loved because he is loved.

Socrates illustrates this point by a series of analogies. A thing is carried because it is *being* carried; it is not *being* carried because it is carried. A thing is led because it is *being* led; it is not *being* led because it is led. A thing is seen because it is *being* seen; it is not *being* seen because it is seen. This pattern leads to the first step of the argument:

(1) A thing is loved by someone because it is *being* loved; it is not *being* loved because it is loved.

(2) Why is the pious *being* loved? It is not *being* loved because it is loved—that possibility is ruled out by (1); instead, it is *being* loved because it is pious (i.e., of a pious nature).

(3) So restating (2), the pious is *being* loved because it is pious; it is not pious because it is *being* loved.

(4) After substituting in (1) "what is loved by all the gods" for "A thing" and "all the gods" for "someone," the result is: "What is loved by all

the gods is loved by all the gods because it is *being* loved; it is not *being* loved because it is loved."

(5) According to Euthyphro, "the pious" is equivalent to "what is loved by all the gods."

(6) But (3), (4), and (5) are an inconsistent triad; they cannot all be true.

(7) For assuming (3), the pious is *being* loved because it is pious, and (5), the pious is what is loved by all the gods, then after substituting "what is loved by all the gods" for "the pious" twice in (3), the result is: "What is loved by all the gods is *being* loved because it is loved by all the gods."

(8) But, according to (4), what is loved by all the gods is not *being* loved because it is loved; rather, it is loved by all the gods because it is *being* loved. So (3) and (5) together contradict (4).

(9) Similarly, assuming (4), what is loved by all the gods is loved by all the gods because it is *being* loved, and (5) the pious is what is loved by all the gods, then after substituting "the pious" for "what is loved by all the gods," twice in (4), the result is: the pious is pious because it is *being* loved.

(10) But, according to (3), the pious is not pious because it is *being* loved; rather, it is *being* loved because it is pious. So (4) and (5) together contradict (3).

How are these contradictions to be avoided? (3), (4), or (5) has to be abandoned. (4) is unlikely to be abandoned, because (4) follows from (1), and (1) was a distinction accepted as clear from the beginning. To abandon (3) would be to say that the pious is *being* loved by all the gods for no reason at all, an implausible position. So the only recourse is to relinquish (5), thus rejecting Euthyphro's definition of piety as "what is loved by all the gods."

Plato's argument is admittedly complex, but its conclusion is straightforward. God cannot make something right by declaring it right; on the contrary, God declares it right because it *is* right. Thus morality is independent of theism. Those who assume otherwise should be reminded of *the* question.

NOTES

1. Sir Arthur Conan Doyle, *The Complete Sherlock Holmes* (Garden City, NY: Doubleday, n.d.), p. 161. The story cited is "A Scandal in Bohemia."

2. Reprinted from *Philosophical Horizons: Introductory Readings*, eds. Steven M. Cahn and Maureen Eckert (Belmont, CA: Thomson/Wadsworth, 2006), pp. 26–27. Copyright © 2004 by Maureen Eckert and used with her permission.

STUDY QUESTIONS

1. Can God make something right by declaring it right?
2. What is the distinction Socrates draws between a thing that is carried and a thing being carried?
3. According to Socrates, what is the inconsistent triad of claims faced by the divine command theorist?
4. If God didn't exist, would morality collapse?

A Modified Divine Command Theory

Robert M. Adams

A common criticism of divine command theory holds that if it is true, then supposing God commanded cruelty for its own sake, we would be doing wrong by not being cruel. Robert Adams, Recurring Research Professor of Philosophy at Rutgers University, argues that a modified version of divine command theory escapes this objection. He suggests that "it is wrong to act cruelly" means "it is contrary to the commands of a loving, good God to act cruelly." Adams maintains that because a loving, all-good God would not command cruelty for its own sake, the common criticism of divine command theory loses its force. Indeed, Adams believes that if God commanded cruelty, the concept of ethical wrongness itself would break down.

It will be helpful to begin with the statement of a simple, *unmodified* divine command theory of ethical wrongness. This is the theory that ethical wrongness *consists in* being contrary to God's commands, or that the word 'wrong' in ethical contexts *means* 'contrary to God's commands.' It implies that the following two statement forms are logically equivalent.

(1) It is wrong (for A) to do X.

(2) It is contrary to God's commands (for A) to do X.

Of course that is not all that the theory implies. It also implies that (2) is conceptually prior to (1), so that the meaning of (1) is to be explained in terms of (2), and not the other way around. It might prove fairly difficult to state or explain in what that conceptual priority consists, but I shall not go into that here. I do not wish ultimately to defend the theory in its unmodified form, and I think I have stated it fully enough for my present purposes. . . .

The following seems to me to be the gravest objection to the divine command theory of ethical wrongness, in the form in which I have stated it. Suppose God should command me to make it my chief end in life to inflict suffering on other human beings, for no other reason than that he commanded it. (For convenience I shall abbreviate this hypothesis to 'Suppose God should command cruelty for its own sake.') Will it seriously be claimed that in that case it would be wrong for me not to practice cruelty for its own sake? I see three possible answers to this question.

(1) It might be claimed that it is logically impossible for God to command cruelty for its own sake. In that case, of course, we need not worry about whether it would be wrong to disobey if he did command it. It is senseless to agonize about what one should do in a logically impossible situation. This solution to the

From Robert M. Adams, "A Modified Divine Command Theory of Ethical Wrongness," in *Religion and Morality*, eds. G. Outka and J. R. Reeder (Garden City: Anchor Press, 1975). Reprinted by permission of the publisher.

problem seems unlikely to be available to the divine command theorist, however. For why would he hold that it is logically impossible for God to command cruelty for its own sake? Some theologians (for instance, Thomas Aquinas) have believed (a) that what is right and wrong is independent of God's will, *and* (b) that God always does right by the necessity of his nature. Such theologians, if they believe that it would be wrong for God to command cruelty for its own sake, have reason to believe that it is logically impossible for him to do so. But the divine command theorist, who does not agree that what is right and wrong is independent of God's will, does not seem to have such a reason to deny that it is logically possible for God to command cruelty for its own sake.

(2) Let us assume that it is logically possible for God to command cruelty for its own sake. In that case the divine command theory seems to imply that it would be wrong not to practice cruelty for its own sake. There have been at least a few adherents of divine command ethics who have been prepared to accept this consequence. William Ockham held that those acts which we call "theft," "adultery," and "hatred of God" would be meritorious if God had commanded them.[1] He would surely have said the same about what I have been calling the practice of "cruelty for its own sake."

This position is one which I suspect most of us are likely to find somewhat shocking, even repulsive. We should therefore be particularly careful not to misunderstand it. We need not imagine that Ockham disciplined himself to be ready to practice cruelty for its own sake if God should command it. It was doubtless an article of faith for him that God is unalterably opposed to any such practice. The mere logical possibility that theft, adultery, and cruelty might have been commanded by God (and therefore meritorious) doubtless did not represent in Ockham's view any real possibility.

(3) Nonetheless, the view that if God commanded cruelty for its own sake it would be wrong not to practice it seems unacceptable to me; and I think many, perhaps most, other Jewish and Christian believers would find it unacceptable too. I must make clear the sense in which I find it unsatisfactory. It is not that I find an internal inconsistency in it.

And I would not deny that it may reflect, accurately enough, the way in which some believers use the word 'wrong.' I might as well frankly avow that I am looking for a divine command theory which at least might possibly be a correct account of how *I* use the word 'wrong.' I do not use the word 'wrong' in such a way that I would say that it would be wrong not to practice cruelty if God commanded it, and I am sure that many other believers agree with me on this point.

But now have I not rejected the divine command theory? I have assumed that it would be logically possible for God to command cruelty for its own sake. And I have rejected the view that if God commanded cruelty for its own sake, it would be wrong not to obey. It seems to follow that I am committed to the view that in certain logically possible circumstances it would not be wrong to disobey God. This position seems to be inconsistent with the theory that 'wrong' means 'contrary to God's commands.'

I want to argue, however, that it is still open to me to accept a modified form of the divine command theory of ethical wrongness. According to the modified divine command theory, when I say, 'It is wrong to do X,' (at least part of) what I *mean* is that it is contrary to God's commands to do X. 'It is wrong to do X' *implies* 'It is contrary to God's commands to do X.' But 'It is contrary to God's commands to do X' implies 'It is wrong to do X' only if certain conditions are assumed—namely, only if it is assumed that God has the character which I believe him to have, of loving his human creatures. If God were really to command us to make cruelty our goal, then he would not have that character of loving us, and I would not say it would be wrong to disobey him.

But do I say that it would be wrong to obey him in such a case? This is the point at which I am in danger of abandoning the divine command theory completely. I do abandon it completely if I say both of the following things.

(A) It would be wrong to obey God if he commanded cruelty for its own sake.

(B) In (A), 'wrong' is used in what is for me its normal ethical sense.

If I assert both (A) and (B), it is clear that I cannot consistently maintain that 'wrong' in its normal ethical sense for me means or implies 'contrary to God's commands.'

But from the fact that I deny that it would be wrong to disobey God if He commanded cruelty for its own sake, it does not follow that I must accept (A) and (B). Of course someone might claim that obedience and disobedience would both be ethically permitted in such a case; but that is not the view that I am suggesting. If I adopt the modified divine command theory as an analysis of my present concept of ethical wrongness (and if I adopt a similar analysis of my concept of ethical permittedness), I will not hold either that it would be wrong to disobey, or that it would be ethically permitted to disobey, or that it would be wrong to obey, or that it would be ethically permitted to obey, if God commanded cruelty for its own sake. For I will say that my concept of ethical wrongness (and my concept of ethical permittedness) would "break down" if I really believed that God commanded cruelty for its own sake. Or to put the matter somewhat more prosaically, I will say that my concepts of ethical wrongness and permittedness could not serve the functions they now serve, because using those concepts I could not call any action ethically wrong or ethically permitted, if I believed that God's will was so unloving.

NOTE

1. Guillelmus de Occam, *Super 4 libros sententiarum,* bk. II, qu. 19, O, in vol. IV of his *Opera plurima* (Lyon, 1494–6; réimpression en fac-similé, Farnborough, Hants., England: Gregg Press, 1962). I am not claiming that Ockham held a divine command theory of exactly the same sort that I have been discussing.

STUDY QUESTIONS

1. What does Adams mean by an "unmodified divine command theory of ethical wrongness"?
2. What does Adams consider the gravest objection to that theory?
3. What does Adams mean by a "modified divine command theory of ethical wrongness"?
4. Does the modified theory avoid the objection he saw to the unmodified theory?

The Divine Command Theory:
A Reply to Adams

Michael Huemer

Michael Huemer is Professor of Philosophy at the University of Colorado, Boulder. He objects to the modified divine command theory forwarded by Adams. In response to the problem of immoral commands, Adams argues that we are required to obey only the commands of a loving God. And were God to command, for example, cruelty for its own sake, the concept "wrongness" would break down. Huemer, however, maintains that this modification fails to solve the problem. For intuitively, it would be wrong to obey a command to engage in cruelty for its own sake. Yet, on Adams's view, we could not say engaging in such cruelty is wrong, because a necessary condition on an act's being wrong is our being commanded by a loving God to refrain from so acting. In other words, if a loving God did not exist to command a prohibition on cruelty, then cruelty for its own sake could not be said to be wrong. Hence, the modified divine command theory does not solve the problem that plagues its unmodified predecessor, and thus should be abandoned.

Huemer also argues that both modified and unmodified versions of the divine command theory cannot provide a satisfactory answer to the question of why we should do what God commands. Do some of God's characteristics give us reason to obey God? If not, then just as we have no reason to follow the commands of a stranger, so we have no reason to obey God's commands. If, however, God's goodness is supposed to give us reason to obey God's commands, then some moral facts are independent of God's commands. Huemer concludes, therefore, that the divine command theory is false.

We often hear warnings to the effect that the decline of religious belief undermines morality. There is more than one way of interpreting this concern, but here I shall focus on the suggestion that there could be no moral truths if God did not exist—as Dostoyevsky says, if there is no God, everything is permitted.[1]

The Divine Command Theory of ethics holds that an action is morally right if and only if it is of a kind that God commands (or approves of, or wants us to perform).[2] The version of the theory I want to discuss holds a similar view about all other evaluative properties, including goodness, justice, and so on—that is, that all of these properties depend on God in such a way that nothing could have any evaluative property if God did not exist; however, in the following, I shall focus on the property of rightness.

From Michael Huemer, *Ethical Intuitionism* (New York: Palgrave Macmillan, 2005). Reprinted by permission of the publisher.

Since it takes rightness to be reducible and dependent on the attitudes of an observer (God), the Divine Command Theory is a form of subjectivism. This is worth pointing out, since the theory is often seen as the arch-nemesis of cultural relativism, whereas in fact the two are variants on the same basic metaethical approach.

Note that the theory is not merely that it is always right to obey God's commands, or that we can find out what is right by consulting God's commands. Those views would be consistent with the idea that right actions are right independently of God but that God (being all-knowing) always knows which actions are right and (being all-good) always approves of them. Rather, the Divine Command Theory holds that right actions are right only *because* God commands them. . . .

Robert Adams . . . says that the obligation to obey God's commands is contingent on there being a *loving* God. If God were to command the killing of children, this would show that He was not loving as Christians believe him in fact to be. Since the rightness of an action consists in its conforming to the will of a loving God, child killing would *not* be right in that situation.[3] But nor, on Adams' view, would it be wrong. Since on Adams' view, an act's being commanded (forbidden) by a loving God is a necessary condition on its being right (wrong), Adams must say that if God were not loving, if He refrained from forbidding the killing of children, or if He simply did not exist, then there would be *nothing wrong* with killing children. This is hardly more plausible than the position that God's commanding child murder would make it right. . . .

. . . [I]f there is a God, why should we do what He says? Someone's telling you to do something does not in general create a moral obligation to do it. If your next door neighbor tells you to kill your son,[4] this creates no obligation at all, even *prima facie,* for you to do so. If Satan tells you to avoid eating pork, this creates no obligation to obey. There must be something special about God, if *His* commands are to create moral obligations. What is it?

I argue that the divine command theorist has no satisfactory answer to this question. In outline:

(1) If no characteristics of God ground an obligation to obey God's commands, then there is no obligation to obey God's commands.
(2) The morally neutral characteristics of God do not ground an obligation to obey God's commands.
(3) If the morally significant characteristics of God ground an obligation to obey his commands, then some moral facts are independent of God's commands and attitudes.
(4) If either (a) there is no obligation to obey God's commands or (b) some moral facts are independent of God's commands and attitudes, then the divine command theory is false.
(5) Therefore, the divine command theory is false.

Premise (1) has already been motivated. If there is nothing special about God that sets him apart from most other beings, explaining why we must obey him in particular, then, since we are not *in general* obligated to obey other beings, we are not obligated to obey God.

In premises (2) and (3), a "morally neutral" characteristic is one that it is possible to have without having an evaluative property; a morally significant characteristic is one that one cannot have without having an evaluative property. For instance, being powerful and being the creator of the Earth are morally neutral characteristics. Being just and being cruel are morally significant characteristics, since one cannot be just without being good in some respect, nor can one be cruel without being bad in some respect.

[Premise] (2) can be supported by hypothetical examples. For any morally neutral characteristic of God, it is possible to imagine an evil being—Satan, say—having that characteristic. In such a situation, intuitively, there would be no moral obligation to follow Satan's commands. For example, it might be said that we should obey God because He is our creator. But imagine that you found out that you had actually been specially created by Satan. In that case, would you be under a general obligation to follow Satan's will? It is also said that God has unlimited power over us, and can bestow eternal punishments and rewards. Imagine that Satan had unlimited power over you, and could bestow eternal punishments and rewards. In that case, no doubt it would be *prudent* to obey Satan's commands. But would it be *morally obligatory* to do so; would you be *immoral* if you were to resist Satan's evil plans? Lastly, suppose Satan were all-knowing and all-powerful (but still thoroughly evil). Would it then be morally obligatory to follow his will? In all of these cases, the answer is surely that you would not be obligated to follow the will of Satan. Therefore, none of these properties—being our creator, having the ability to reward and punish us, being all-knowing, being all-powerful, or any combination of these—can ground an obligation of obedience on our part towards another being.

There is one crucial respect, or family of respects, in which God differs from Satan in my hypothetical scenarios. This is that Satan is evil, whereas God is purely good, just, benevolent, and so forth. It is plausible that if a *supremely good* being tells you to do something, then you are thereupon obligated to do it. But here is where premise (3) comes in. If the reason we must obey God turns on God's goodness, then some moral facts must exist prior to God's commands. By hypothesis, the capacity of God's commands to generate moral truths depends upon God's goodness; on pain of circularity, therefore, it cannot also be the case that God's goodness is generated by his commands. (It cannot be, for example, that God is good because he approves of himself, or because he commands us to worship him. Imagine Satan likewise approving of himself and commanding us to worship *him*.) God must *already* be good, so there must already be a standard of value in place—for example, that lovingness, mercy, and justice are good—prior to God's commands.

Apropos of this, recall Robert Adams' solution to the problem of God's possible command to kill children. Adams finds God's lovingness relevant to the obligation to obey Him and argues that a loving God could not order such killing. But what motivates Adams to single out *lovingness?* Is it not that he considers this trait a virtue, or in some way *good?*[5] It is hard to imagine someone who placed no value on love giving Adams' reply. Thus, it seems that the ability of a loving God's commands to create obligations depends upon the independently assumed *value* of love.

Finally, premise (4) is true because the divine command theory holds that what is morally obligatory is so in virtue of God's commanding it, and that something similar holds for all other moral properties (such as goodness and wrongness). This implies both that it is obligatory to obey God's commands, and that nothing has any moral property independently of God's commands.

The conclusion (5) follows from premises (1)–(4): God's non-moral characteristics cannot ground an obligation of obedience. God's moral characteristics can ground such an obligation only if there are moral facts independent of God's commands. So either there is no reason to obey God, or there are moral facts independent of God's commands. Either of these alternatives conflicts with the divine command theory. So that theory must be rejected.

A closely related point can be made more succinctly. Why does God command what he does? If God has no moral reasons for his commands, then they are merely arbitrary—and why should we obey arbitrary commands? But if God *has* moral reasons for his commands, then some moral truths must exist independently of his commands. Either way, the divine command theory is false.[6]

One response to this is that God's commands may escape arbitrariness by virtue of God's having *non-moral* reasons for his commands. I don't think this helps, any more than the suggestion that God has *bad* reasons for his commands would help. How would God's having a reason *with no moral weight* for a command serve to render that command non-arbitrary in a morally relevant sense, that is, in such a way that we morally ought to follow it?

NOTES

1. This is a paraphrase of Ivan Karamozov's views in *The Brothers Karamozov.*
2. See Adams (1981); Quinn (2002); Alston (1990); but note that Adams' theory of the good (1999, chapter 1), taking goodness to consist in resemblance to God, is not strictly a form of the divine command theory as I define the latter, since Adams does not take *goodness*

to depend constitutively on God's (or anyone's) commands or attitudes. . . .

3. Adams (1981, pp. 86–8). This is a slight simplification; Adams says that God's lovingness is not explicitly asserted as part of the meaning of a moral statement but is instead *presupposed* by moral statements. But this distinction does not affect my reply.

4. As God reportedly told Abraham (*Genesis* 22:2). The context of the story makes clear that Abraham is to be praised for his willingness to follow this command. Quinn (2002, p. 678) concurs on the rightness of sacrificing Isaac in such a situation.

5. Adams (1999, p. 281) confirms this, affirming that 'the goodness of God' is 'important in accrediting God's commands for their role in constituting obligation'.

6. This is sometimes called 'the Euthyphro Problem' because of its similarity to the problem raised in the *Euthyphro* (Plato 1996, pp. 14–15).

REFERENCES

Adams, Robert Merrihew. 1981. 'A Modified Divine Command Theory of Ethical Wrongness'. Pp. 83–108 in *Divine Commands and Morality*, edited by Paul Helm. Oxford: Oxford University Press.

———. 1999. *Finite and Infinite Goods*. New York, N.Y.: Oxford University Press.

Alston, William. 1990. 'Some Suggestions for Divine Command Theorists'. In *Christian Theism and the Problems of Philosophy*, edited by Michael Beaty. Notre Dame, I.N.: University of Notre Dame Press.

Plato. 1996. *Plato's Euthyphro, Apology, and Crito*. Edited by S. W. Emery. Lanham, M.D.: University Press of America.

Quinn, Philip. 2002. 'God and Morality'. In *Reason and Responsibility*, 11th ed., edited by Joel Feinberg and Russ Shafer-Landau. Belmont, C.A.: Wadsworth.

STUDY QUESTIONS

1. Is the divine command theory a form of subjectivism?
2. According to Huemer, why does Adams's modified divine command theory not succeed?
3. How do God's commands differ from those of a stranger?
4. Why does God command what he does?

Part X

EPISTEMOLOGY

Does Moral Philosophy Rest on a Mistake?

H. A. Prichard

H. A. Prichard (1871–1947) was White's Professor of Moral Philosophy at the University of Oxford. He maintains that moral philosophy has mistakenly been focused on seeking to answer the question: Why should I be moral? In other words, philosophers have tried to supply reasons (or a proof) that we ought to fulfill our obligations. According to Prichard, these attempts are bound to fail, because even if we could demonstrate that fulfilling our duties is in our interest, doing so would not prove that we ought to fulfill them, only that we want to do so. On Prichard's alternative, a moral obligation is not the conclusion of an argument but a self-evident truth, apprehended directly by an act of moral thinking.

Probably to most students of Moral Philosophy there comes a time when they feel a vague sense of dissatisfaction with the whole subject. And the sense of dissatisfaction tends to grow rather than to diminish. It is not so much that the positions, and still more the arguments, of particular thinkers seem unconvincing, though this is true. It is rather that the aim of the subject becomes increasingly obscure. "What," it is asked, "are we really going to learn by Moral Philosophy?" "What are books on Moral Philosophy really trying to show, and when their aim is clear, why are they so unconvincing and artificial?" And again: "Why is it so difficult to substitute anything better?" Personally, I have been led by growing dissatisfaction of this kind to wonder whether the reason may not be that the subject, at any rate as usually understood, consists in the attempt to answer an improper question. And in this article I shall venture to contend that the existence of the whole subject, as usually understood, rests on a mistake, and on a mistake parallel to that on which rests, as I think, the subject usually called the Theory of Knowledge.

If we reflect on our own mental history or on the history of the subject, we feel no doubt about the nature of the demand which originates the subject. Any one who, stimulated by education, has come to feel the force of the various obligations in life, at some time or other comes to feel the irksomeness of carrying them out, and to recognize the sacrifice of interest involved; and, if thoughtful, he inevitably puts to himself the question: "Is there really a reason why I should act in the ways in which hitherto I have thought I ought to act? May I not have been all the time under an illusion in so thinking? Should not I really be justified in simply trying to have a good time?" Yet, like Glaucon, feeling that somehow he ought after all to act in these ways, he asks for a *proof* that this feeling is justified. In other words, he asks *"Why* should I do these things?," and his and other people's moral philosophizing is an attempt to supply

From H. A. Prichard, "Does Moral Philosophy Rest on a Mistake?" *Mind* 21 (1912). Reprinted by permission of the publisher.

the answer, i.e. to supply by a process of reflection a proof of the truth of what he and they have prior to reflection believed immediately or without proof. This frame of mind seems to present a close parallel to the frame of mind which originates the Theory of Knowledge. Just as the recognition that the doing of our duty often vitally interferes with the satisfaction of our inclinations leads us to wonder whether we really ought to do what we usually call our duty, so the recognition that we and others are liable to mistakes in knowledge generally leads us, as it did Descartes, to wonder whether hitherto we may not have been always mistaken. And just as we try to find a proof, based on the general consideration of action and of human life, that we ought to act in the ways usually called moral, so we, like Descartes, propose by a process of reflection on our thinking to find a test of knowledge, i.e. a principle by applying which we can show that a certain condition of mind was really knowledge, a condition which *ex hypothesi* existed independently of the process of reflection.

Now, how has the moral question been answered? So far as I can see, the answers all fall, and fall from the necessities of the case, into one of two species. *Either* they state that we ought to do so and so, because, as we see when we fully apprehend the facts, doing so will be for our good, i.e. really, as I would rather say, for our advantage, or, better still, for our happiness; *or* they state that we ought to do so and so, because something realized either in or by the action is good. In other words, the reason "why" is stated in terms either of the agent's happiness or of the goodness of something involved in the action.

To see the prevalence of the former species of answer, we have only to consider the history of Moral Philosophy. To take obvious instances. Plato, Hutcheson, Paley, Mill, each in his own way seeks at bottom to convince the individual that he ought to act in so-called moral ways by showing that to do so will really be for his happiness. Plato is perhaps the most significant instance, because of all philosophers he is the one to whom we are least willing to ascribe a mistake on such matters, and a mistake on his part would be evidence of the deep-rootedness of the tendency to make it. To show that Plato really justifies morality by its profitableness, it is only

necessary to point out (1) that the very formulation of the thesis to be met, viz, that justice is a ἀλλότριον ἀγαθόν [someone else's good] implies that any refutation must consist in showing that justice is οἰκεῖον ἀγαθόν [one's own good], i.e., really, as the context shows, one's own advantage, and (2) that the term λυσιτελεῖν [to be profitable] supplies the key not only to the problem but also to its solution.

The tendency to justify acting on moral rules in this way is natural. For if, as often happens, we put to ourselves the question "Why should we do so and so?," we are satisfied by being convinced either that the doing so will lead to something which we want (e.g. that taking certain medicine will heal our disease), or that the doing so itself, as we see when we appreciate its nature, is something that we want or should like, e.g. playing golf. The formulation of the question implies a state of unwillingness or indifference towards the action, and we are brought into a condition of willingness by the answer. And this process seems to be precisely what we desire when we ask, e.g., "Why should we keep our engagements to our own loss?"; for it is just the fact that the keeping of our engagements runs counter to the satisfaction of our desires which produced the question.

The answer is, of course, not an answer, for it fails to convince us that we ought to keep our engagements; even if successful on its own lines, it only makes us *want* to keep them. And Kant was really only pointing out this fact when he distinguished hypothetical and categorical imperatives, even though he obscured the nature of the fact by wrongly describing his so-called "hypothetical imperatives" as imperatives. But if this answer be no answer, what other can be offered? Only, it seems, an answer which bases the obligation to do something on the *goodness* either of something to which the act leads or of the act itself. Suppose, when wondering whether we really ought to act in the ways usually called moral, we are told as a means of resolving our doubt that those acts are right which produce happiness. We at once ask: "Whose happiness?" If we are told "Our own happiness," then, though we shall lose our hesitation to act in these ways, we shall not recover our sense that we ought to do so. But how can this result be avoided? Apparently, only by being told one of two things: *either* that anyone's happiness is a thing good in itself, and that *therefore* we ought to do whatever will produce it, *or* that working for happiness is itself good, and that the intrinsic goodness of such an action is the reason why we ought to do it. The advantage of this appeal to the goodness of something consists in the fact that it avoids reference to desire, and, instead, refers to something impersonal and objective. In this way it seems possible to avoid the resolution of obligation into inclination. But just for this reason it is of the essence of the answer, that to be effective it must neither include nor involve the view that the apprehension of the goodness of anything necessarily arouses the desire for it. Otherwise the answer resolves itself into a form of the former answer by substituting desire or inclination for the sense of obligation, and in this way it loses what seems its special advantage.

Now it seems to me that both forms of this answer break down, though each for a different reason.

Consider the first form. It is what may be called Utilitarianism in the generic sense, in which what is good is not limited to pleasure. It takes its stand upon the distinction between something which is not itself an action, but which can be produced by an action, and the action which will produce it, and contends that if something which is not an action is good, then we *ought* to undertake the action which will, directly or indirectly, originate it.[1]

But this argument, if it is to restore the sense of obligation to act, must presuppose an intermediate link, viz. the further thesis that what is good ought to be.[2] The necessity of this link is obvious. An "ought," if it is to be derived at all, can only be derived from another "ought." Moreover, this link tacitly presupposes another, viz. that the apprehension that something good which is not an action ought to be involves just the feeling of imperativeness or obligation which is to be aroused by the thought of the action which will originate it. Otherwise the argument will not lead us to feel the obligation to produce it by the action. And, surely, both this link and its implication are false.[3] The word "ought" refers to actions and to actions alone. The proper language is never "So and so ought to be," but "I ought to do so

and so." Even if we are sometimes moved to say that the world or something in it is not what it ought to be, what we really mean is that God or some human being has not made something what he ought to have made it. And it is merely stating another side of this fact to urge that we can only feel the imperativeness upon us of something which is in our power; for it is actions and actions alone which, directly at least, are in our power.

Perhaps, however, the best way to see the failure of this view is to see its failure to correspond to our actual moral convictions. Suppose we ask ourselves whether our sense that we ought to pay our debts or to tell the truth arises from our recognition that in doing so we should be originating something good, e.g. material comfort in *A* or true belief in *B*, i.e. suppose we ask ourselves whether it is this aspect of the action which leads to our recognition that we ought to do it. We at once and without hesitation answer "No." Again, if we take as our illustration our sense that we ought to act justly as between two parties, we have, if possible, even less hesitation in giving a similar answer; for the balance of resulting good may be, and often is, not on the side of justice.

At best it can only be maintained that there is this element of truth in the Utilitarian view, that unless we recognize that something which an act will originate is good, we should not recognize that we ought to do the action. Unless we thought knowledge a good thing, it may be urged, we should not think that we ought to tell the truth; unless we thought pain a bad thing, we should not think the infliction of it, without special reason, wrong. But this is not to imply that the badness of error is the reason why it is wrong to lie, or the badness of pain the reason why we ought not to inflict it without special cause.[4]

It is, I think, just because this form of the view is so plainly at variance with our moral consciousness that we are driven to adopt the other form of the view, viz. that the act is good in itself and that its intrinsic goodness is the reason why it ought to be done. It is this form which has always made the most serious appeal; for the goodness of the act itself seems more closely related to the obligation to do it than of its mere consequences or results, and therefore, if obligation is to be based on the goodness of something, it would seem that this goodness should be that of the act itself. Moreover, the view gains plausibility from the fact that moral actions are most conspicuously those to which the term "intrinsically good" is applicable.

Nevertheless this view, though perhaps less superficial, is equally untenable. For it leads to precisely the dilemma which faces everyone who tries to solve the problem raised by Kant's theory of the good will. To see this, we need only consider the nature of the acts to which we apply the term "intrinsically good."

There is, of course, no doubt that we approve and even admire certain actions, and also that we should describe them as good, and as good in themselves. But it is, I think, equally unquestionable that our approval and our use of the term "good" is always in respect of the motive and refers to actions which have been actually done and of which we think we know the motive. Further, the actions of which we approve and which we should describe as intrinsically good are of two and only two kinds. They are either actions in which the agent did what he did because he thought he ought to do it, or actions of which the motive was a desire prompted by some good emotion, such as gratitude, affection, family feeling, or public spirit, the most prominent of such desires in books on Moral Philosophy being that ascribed to what is vaguely called benevolence. For the sake of simplicity I omit the case of actions done partly from some such desire and partly from a sense of duty; for even if all good actions are done from a combination of these motives, the argument will not be affected. The dilemma is this. If the motive in respect of which we think an action good is the sense of obligation, then so far from the sense that we ought to do it being derived from our apprehension of its goodness, our apprehension of its goodness will presuppose the sense that we ought to do it. In other words, in this case the recognition that the act is good will plainly *presuppose* the recognition that the act is right, whereas the view under consideration is that the recognition of the goodness of the act *gives rise* to the recognition of its rightness. On the other hand, if the motive in respect of which we think an action good is some intrinsically good desire, such as the desire to help a friend, the recognition of the

goodness of the act will equally fail to give rise to the sense of obligation to do it. For we cannot feel that we ought to do that the doing of which is *ex hypothesi* prompted solely by the desire to do it.[5]

The fallacy underlying the view is that while to base the rightness of an act upon its intrinsic goodness implies that the goodness in question is that of the motive, in reality the rightness or wrongness of an act has nothing to do with any question of motives at all. For, as any instance will show, the rightness of an action concerns an action not in the fuller sense of the term in which we include the motive in the action, but in the narrower and commoner sense in which we distinguish an action from its motive and mean by an action merely the conscious origination of something, an origination which on different occasions or in different people may be prompted by different motives. The question "Ought I to pay my bills?" really means simply "Ought I to bring about my tradesmen's possession of what by my previous acts I explicitly or implicitly promised them?" There is, and can be, no question of whether I ought to pay my debts from a particular motive. No doubt we know that if we pay our bills we shall pay them with a motive, but in considering whether we ought to pay them we inevitably think of the act in abstraction from the motive. Even if we knew what our motive would be if we did the act, we should not be any nearer an answer to the question.

Moreover, if we eventually pay our bills from fear of the county court, we shall still have done *what* we ought, even though we shall not have done it *as* we ought. The attempt to bring in the motive involves a mistake similar to that involved in supposing that we can will to will. To feel that I ought to pay my bills is to be *moved towards* paying them. But what I can be moved towards must always be an action and not an action in which I am moved in a particular way, i.e. an action from a particular motive; otherwise I should be moved towards being moved, which is impossible. Yet the view under consideration involves this impossibility, for it really resolves the sense that I ought to do so and so, into the sense that I ought to be moved to do it in a particular way.[6]

So far my contentions have been mainly negative, but they form, I think, a useful, if not a necessary, introduction to what I take to be the truth. This I will now endeavor to state, first formulating what, as I think, is the real nature of our apprehension or appreciation of moral obligations, and then applying the result to elucidate the question of the existence of Moral Philosophy.

The sense of obligation to do, or of the rightness of, an action of a particular kind is absolutely underivative or immediate. The rightness of an action consists in its being the origination of something of a certain kind A in a situation of a certain kind, a situation consisting in a certain relation B of the agent to others or to his own nature. To appreciate its rightness two preliminaries may be necessary. We may have to follow out the consequences of the proposed action more fully than we have hitherto done, in order to realize that in the action we should originate A. Thus we may not appreciate the wrongness of telling a certain story until we realize that we should thereby be hurting the feelings of one of our audience. Again, we may have to take into account the relation B involved in the situation, which we had hitherto failed to notice. For instance, we may not appreciate the obligation to give X a present, until we remember that he has done us an act of kindness. But, given that by a process which is, of course, merely a process of general and not of moral thinking we come to recognize that the proposed act is one by which we shall originate A in a relation B, then we appreciate the obligation immediately or directly, the appreciation being an activity of *moral* thinking. We recognize, for instance, that this performance of a service to X, who has done us a service, just in virtue of its being the performance of a service to one who has rendered a service to the would-be agent, ought to be done by us. This apprehension is immediate, in precisely the sense in which a mathematical apprehension is immediate, e.g. the apprehension that this three-sided figure, in virtue of its being three-sided, must have three angles. Both apprehensions are immediate in the sense that in both insight into the nature of the subject leads us to recognize its possession of the predicate; and it is only stating this fact from the other side to say that in both cases the fact apprehended is self-evident.

The plausibility of the view that obligations are not self-evident but need proof lies in the fact that an act which is referred to as an obligation may be incompletely stated, what I have called the preliminaries to appreciating the obligation being incomplete. If, e.g., we refer to the act of repaying X by a present merely as giving X a present, it appears, and indeed is, necessary to give a reason. In other words, wherever a moral act is regarded in this incomplete way the question *"Why should I do it?"* is perfectly legitimate. This fact suggests, but suggests wrongly, that even if the nature of the act is completely stated, it is still necessary to give a reason, or, in other words, to supply a proof.

The relations involved in obligations of various kinds are, of course, very different. The relation in certain cases is a relation to others due to a past act of theirs or ours. The obligation to repay a benefit involves a relation due to a past act of the benefactor. The obligation to repay a benefit involves a relation due to a past act of ours in which we have either said or implied that we would make a certain return for something which we have asked for and received. On the other hand, the obligation to speak the truth implies no such definite act; it involves a relation consisting in the fact that others are trusting us to speak the truth, a relation the apprehension of which gives rise to the sense that communication of the truth is something owing by us to them. Again, the obligation not to hurt the feelings of another involves no special relation of us to that other, i.e. no relation other than that involved in our both being men, and men in one and the same world. Moreover, it seems that the relation involved in an obligation need not be a relation to another at all. Thus we should admit that there is an obligation to overcome our natural timidity or greediness, and that this involves no relations to others. Still there is a relation involved, viz. a relation to our own disposition. It is simply because we can and because others cannot directly modify our disposition that it is our business to improve it, and that it is not theirs, or, at least, not theirs to the same extent.

The negative side of all this is, of course, that we do not come to appreciate an obligation by an *argument,* i.e. by a process of nonmoral thinking, and that, in particular, we do not do so by an argument of which a premise is the ethical but not moral activity of appreciating the goodness either of the act or of a consequence of the act; i.e. that our sense of the rightness of an act is not a conclusion from our appreciation of the goodness either of it or of anything else.

It will probably be urged that on this view our various obligations form, like Aristotle's categories, an unrelated chaos in which it is impossible to acquiesce. For, according to it, the obligation to repay a benefit, or to pay a debt, or to keep a promise, presupposes a previous act of another; whereas the obligation to speak the truth or not to harm another does not; and, again, the obligation to remove our timidity involves no relations to others at all. Yet, at any rate, an effective *argumentum ad hominem* is at hand in the fact that the various qualities which we recognize as good are equally unrelated: e.g. courage, humility, and interest in knowledge. If, as is plainly the case, ἀγαθά differ ἦ ἀγαθά [Goods differ *qua* goods], why should not obligations equally differ *qua* their obligatoriness? Moreover, if this were not so there could in the end be only one obligation, which is palpably contrary to fact.[7]

Certain observations will help to make the view clearer.

In the first place, it may seem that the view, being—as it is—avowedly put forward in opposition to the view that what is right is derived from what is good, must itself involve the opposite of this, viz. the Kantian position that what is good is based upon what is right, i.e. that an act, if it be good, is good because it is right. But this is not so. For, on the view put forward, the rightness of a right action lies solely in the origination in which the act consists, whereas the intrinsic goodness of an action lies solely in its motive; and this implies that a morally good action is morally good not simply because it is a right action but because it is a right action done because it is right, i.e. from a sense of obligation. And this implication, it may be remarked incidentally, seems plainly true.

In the second place, the view involves that when, or rather so far as, we act from a sense of obligation, we have no purpose or end. By a "purpose"

or "end" we really mean something the existence of which we desire, and desire of the existence of which leads us to act. Usually our purpose is something which the act will originate, as when we turn round in order to look at a picture. But it may be the action itself, i.e. the origination of something, as when we hit a golf ball into a hole or kill someone out of revenge.[8] Now if by a purpose we mean something the existence of which we desire and desire for which leads us to act, then plainly, so far as we act from a sense of obligation, we have no purpose, consisting either in the action or in anything which it will produce. This is so obvious that is scarcely seems worth pointing out. But I do so for two reasons. (1) If we fail to scrutinize the meaning of the terms "end" and "purpose," we are apt to assume uncritically that all deliberate action, i.e. action proper, must have a purpose; we then become puzzled both when we look for the purpose of an action done from a sense of obligation, and also when we try to apply to such an action the distinction of means and end, the truth all the time being that since there is no end, there is no means either. (2) The attempt to base the sense of obligation on the recognition of the goodness of something is really an attempt to find a purpose in a moral action in the shape of something good which, as good, we want. And the expectation that the goodness of something underlies an obligation disappears as soon as we cease to look for a purpose.

The thesis, however, that, so far as we act from a sense of obligation, we have no purpose must not be misunderstood. It must not be taken either to mean or to imply that so far as we so act we have no *motive*. No doubt in ordinary speech the words "motive" and "purpose" are usually treated as correlatives, "motive" standing for the desire which induces us to act, and "purpose" standing for the object of this desire. But this is only because, when we are looking for the motive of the action, say, of some crime, we are usually presupposing that the act in question is prompted by a desire and not by the sense of obligation. At bottom, however, we mean by a motive what moves us to act; a sense of obligation does sometimes move us to act; and in our ordinary consciousness we should not hesitate to allow that the action we were considering might have had as its motive a sense of obligation. Desire and the sense of obligation are coordinate forms or species of motive.

In the third place, if the view put forward be right, we must sharply distinguish morality and virtue as independent, though related, species of goodness, neither being an aspect of something of which the other is an aspect, nor again a form or species of the other, nor again something deducible from the other; and we must at the same time allow that it is possible to do the same act either virtuously or morally or in both ways at once. And surely this is true. An act, to be virtuous, must, as Aristotle saw, be done willingly or with pleasure; as such it is just not done from a sense of obligation but from some desire which is intrinsically good, as arising from some intrinsically good emotion. Thus, in an act of generosity the motive is the desire to help another arising from sympathy with that other; in an act which is courageous and no more, i.e. in an act which is not at the same time an act of public spirit or family affection or the like, we prevent ourselves from being dominated by a feeling of terror, desiring to do so from a sense of shame at being terrified. The goodness of such an act is different from the goodness of an act to which we apply the term "moral" in the strict and narrow sense, viz. an act done from a sense of obligation. Its goodness lies in the intrinsic goodness of the emotion and of the consequent desire under which we act, the goodness of this motive being different from the goodness of the moral motive proper, viz. the sense of duty or obligation. Nevertheless, at any rate in certain cases, an act can be done either virtuously or morally or in both ways at once. It is possible to repay a benefit either from desire to repay it, or from the feeling that we ought to do so, or from both motives combined. A doctor may tend his patients either from a desire arising out of interest in his patients or in the exercise of skill, or from a sense of duty, or from a desire and a sense of duty combined. Further, although we recognize that in each case the act possesses an intrinsic goodness, we regard that action as the best in which both motives are combined; in other words, we regard as the really best man the man in whom virtue and morality are united.

It may be objected that the distinction between the two kinds of motive is untenable, on the ground that the *desire* to repay a benefit, for example, is only the manifestation of that which manifests itself as the *sense of obligation* to repay whenever we think of something in the action which is other than the repayment and which we should not like, such as the loss or pain involved. Yet the distinction can, I think, easily be shown to be tenable. For, in the analogous case of revenge, the desire to return the injury and the sense that we ought not to do so, leading, as they do, in opposite directions, are plainly distinct; and the obviousness of the distinction here seems to remove any difficulty in admitting the existence of a parallel distinction between the desire to return a benefit and the sense that we ought to return it.[9]

Further, the view implies that an obligation can no more be based on or derived from a virtue than a virtue can be derived from an obligation, in which latter case a virtue would consist in carrying out an obligation. And the implication is surely true and important. Take the case of courage. It is untrue to urge that, since courage is a virtue, we ought to act courageously. It is and must be untrue, because, as we see in the end, to feel an obligation to act courageously would involve a contradiction. For, as I have urged before, we can only feel an obligation to *act;* we cannot feel an obligation to *act from a certain desire,* in this case the desire to conquer one's feelings of terror arising from the sense of shame which they arouse. Moreover, if the sense of obligation to act in a particular way leads to an action, the action will be an action done from a sense of obligation, and therefore not, if the above analysis of virtue be right, an act of courage.

The mistake of supposing that there can be an obligation to act courageously seems to arise from two causes. In the first place, there is often an obligation to do that which involves the conquering or controlling of our fear in the doing of it, e.g. the obligation to walk along the side of a precipice to fetch a doctor for a member of our family. Here the acting on the obligation is externally, though only externally, the same as an act of courage proper. In the second place there is an obligation to acquire courage, i.e. to do such things as will enable us afterwards to act courageously, and this may be mistaken for an obligation to act courageously. The same considerations can, of course, be applied, *mutatis mutandis,* to the other virtues.

The fact, if it be a fact, that virtue is no basis for morality will explain what otherwise it is difficult to account for, viz, the extreme sense of dissatisfaction produced by a close reading of Aristotle's *Ethics.* Why is the *Ethics* so disappointing? Not, I think, because it really answers two radically different questions as if they were one: (1) "What is the happy life?" (2) "What is the virtuous life?" It is, rather, because Aristotle does not do what we as moral philosophers want him to do, viz. to convince us that we really ought to do what in our nonreflective consciousness we have hitherto believed we ought to do, or if not, to tell us what, if any, are the other things which we really ought to do, and to prove to us that he is right. Now, if what I have just been contending is true, a systematic account of the virtuous character cannot possibly satisfy this demand. At best it can only make clear to us the details of one of our obligations, viz. the obligation to make ourselves better men; but the achievement of this does not help us to discover what we ought to do in life as a whole, and why; to think that it did would be to think that our only business in life was self-improvement. Hence it is not surprising that Aristotle's account of the good man strikes us as almost wholly of academic value, with little relation to our real demand, which is formulated in Plato's words: οὐ γὰρ περὶ τοὐπιτυχόντος ο λόγος ἀλλὰ περὶ τοῦ ὄντινα τρόπον χρῆ ζῆν [for no light matter is at stake, nothing less than the rule of human life].

I am not, of course, *criticizing* Aristotle for failing to satisfy this demand, except so far as here and there he leads us to think that he intends to satisfy it. For my main contention is that the demand cannot be satisfied, and cannot be satisfied because it is illegitimate. Thus we are brought to the question: "Is there really such a thing as Moral Philosophy, and, if there is, in what sense?"

We should first consider the parallel case—as it appears to be—of the Theory of Knowledge. As I urged before, at some time or other in the history of all of us, if we are thoughtful, the frequency of our own and of others' mistakes is bound to lead to the reflection that possibly we and others have *always* been mistaken in consequence of some radical defect of our faculties. In consequence, certain things which previously we should have said without hesitation that we *knew,* as e.g. that 4 × 7 = 28, become subject to doubt; we become able only to say that we thought we knew these things. We inevitably go on to look for some general procedure by which we can ascertain that a given condition of mind is really one of knowledge. And this involves the search for a criterion of knowledge, i.e. for a principle by applying which we can settle that a given state of mind is really knowledge. The search for this criterion and the application of it, when found, is what is called the Theory of Knowledge. The search implies that instead of its being the fact that the knowledge that A is B is obtained directly by consideration of the nature of A and B, the knowledge that A is B, in the full or complete sense, can only be obtained by first knowing that A is B, and then knowing that we knew it by applying a criterion, such as Descartes's principle that what we clearly and distinctly conceive is true.

Now it is easy to show that the doubt whether A is B, based on this speculative or general ground, could, if genuine, never be set at rest. For if, in order really to know that A is B, we must first know that we knew it, then really, to know that we knew it, we must first know that we knew that we knew it. But— what is more important—it is also easy to show that this doubt is not a genuine doubt but rests on a confusion the exposure of which removes the doubt. For when we *say* we doubt whether our previous condition was one of knowledge, what we *mean,* if we mean anything at all, is that we doubt whether our previous *belief* was *true,* a belief which we should express as the *thinking* that A is B. For in order to doubt whether our previous condition was one of knowledge, we have to think of it not as knowledge but as only belief, and our only question can be "Was this belief true?" But as soon as we see that we are thinking of our previous condition as only one of belief, we see that what we are now doubting is not what we first *said* we were doubting, viz. whether a previous condition of knowledge was really knowledge. Hence, to remove the doubt, it is only necessary to appreciate the real nature of our consciousness in apprehending, e.g. that $7 \times 4 = 28$, and thereby see that it was no mere condition of believing but a condition of knowing, and then to notice that in our subsequent doubt what we are really doubting is not whether this consciousness was really knowledge, but whether a consciousness of another kind, viz. a belief that $7 \times 4 = 28$, was true. We thereby see that though a doubt based on speculative grounds is possible, it is not a doubt concerning what we believed the doubt concerned, and that a doubt concerning this latter is impossible.

Two results follow. In the first place, if, as is usually the case, we mean by the "Theory of Knowledge" the knowledge which supplies the answer to the question "Is what we have hitherto thought knowledge really knowledge?," there is and can be no such thing, and the supposition that there can is simply due to a confusion. There can be no answer to an illegitimate question, except that the question is illegitimate. Nevertheless the question is one which we continue to put until we realize the inevitable immediacy of knowledge. And it is positive knowledge that knowledge is immediate and neither can be, nor needs to be, improved or vindicated by the further knowledge that it was knowledge. This positive knowledge sets at rest the inevitable doubt, and, so far as by the "Theory of Knowledge" is meant this knowledge, then even though this knowledge be the knowledge that there is no Theory of Knowledge in the former sense, to that extent the Theory of Knowledge exists.

In the second place, suppose we come genuinely to doubt whether, e.g., $7 \times 4 = 28$ owing to a genuine doubt whether we were right in believing yesterday that $7 \times 4 = 28$, a doubt which can in fact only arise if we have lost our hold of, i.e. no longer remember, the real nature of our consciousness of yesterday, and so think of it as consisting in believing. Plainly, the only remedy is to do the sum again. Or, to put the matter generally, if we do come to doubt whether it is true that A is B, as we once thought, the remedy lies not in any process of reflection but in such a reconsideration of the nature of A and B as leads to the knowledge that A is B.

With these considerations in mind, consider the parallel which, as it seems to me, is presented—though with certain differences—by Moral Philosophy. The sense that we ought to do certain things arises in our unreflective consciousness, being an activity of moral thinking occasioned by the various situations in which we find ourselves. At this stage our attitude to these obligations is one of unquestioning confidence. But inevitably the appreciation of the degree to which the execution of these obligations is contrary to our interest raises the doubt whether after all these obligations are really obligatory, i.e. whether our sense that we ought not to do certain things is not illusion. We then want to have it *proved* to us that we ought to do so, i.e. to be convinced of this by a process which, as an argument, is different in kind from our original and unreflective appreciation of it. This demand is, as I have argued, illegitimate.

Hence, in the first place, if, as is almost universally the case, by Moral Philosophy is meant the knowledge which would satisfy this demand, there is no such knowledge, and all attempts to attain it are doomed to failure because they rest on a mistake, the mistake of supposing the possibility of proving what can only be apprehended directly by an act of moral thinking. Nevertheless the demand, though illegitimate, is inevitable until we have carried the process of reflection far enough to realize the self-evidence of our obligations, i.e. the immediacy of our apprehension of them. This realization of their self-evidence is positive knowledge, and so far, and so far only, as the term Moral Philosophy is confined to this knowledge and to the knowledge of the parallel immediacy of the apprehension of the goodness of the various virtues and of good dispositions generally, is there such a thing as Moral Philosophy. But since this knowledge may allay doubts which often affect the whole conduct of life, it is, though not extensive, important, and even vitally important.

In the second place, suppose we come genuinely to doubt whether we ought, for example, to pay our debts, owing to a genuine doubt whether our previous conviction that we ought to do so is true, a doubt which can, in fact, only arise if we fail to remember the real nature of what we now call our past conviction. The only remedy lies in actually getting into a situation which occasions the obligation, or—if our imagination be strong enough—in imagining ourselves in that situation, and then letting our moral capacities of thinking do their work. Or, to put the matter generally, if we do doubt whether there is really an obligation to originate A in a situation B, the remedy lies not in any process of general thinking, but in getting face to face with a particular instance of the situation B, and then directly appreciating the obligation to originate A in that situation.

NOTES

1. Cf. Dr. Rashdall's *Theory of Good and Evil,* I, 138.
2. Dr. Rashdall, if I understand him rightly, supplies this link (cf. ibid., 135–36).
3. When we speak of anything, e.g., of some emotion or of some quality of a human being, as good, we never dream in our ordinary consciousness of going on to say that therefore it ought to be.
4. It may be noted that if the badness of pain were the reason why we ought not to inflict pain on another, it would equally be a reason why we ought not to inflict pain on ourselves: yet, though we should allow the wanton infliction of pain on ourselves: yet, though we should allow the wanton infliction of pain on ourselves to be foolish, we should not think of describing it as wrong.
5. It is, I think, on this latter horn of the dilemma that Martineau's view falls; cf. *Types of Ethical Theory,* Part II, Book I.
6. It is of course not denied here that an action done for a particular motive may be *good;* it is only denied that the *rightness* of an action depends on its being done with a particular motive.
7. Two other objections may be anticipated: (1) that obligations cannot be self-evident, since many actions regarded as obligations by some are not so regarded by others, and (2) that if obligations are self-evident,

the problem of how we ought to act in the presence of conflicting obligations is insoluble.

To the first I should reply:

(a) That the appreciation of an obligation is, of course, only possible for a developed moral being, and that different degrees of development are possible.
(b) That the failure to recognize some particular obligation is usually due to the fact that, owing to a lack of thoughtfulness, what I have called the preliminaries to this recognition are incomplete.
(c) That the view put forward is consistent with the admission that, owing to a lack of thoughtfulness, even the best men are blind to many of their obligations, and that in the end our obligations are seen to be co-extensive with almost the whole of our life.

To the second objection I should reply that obligation admits of degrees, and that where obligations conflict, the decision of what we ought to do turns not on the question "Which of the alternative courses of action will originate the greater good?" but on the question "Which is the greater obligation?"

8. It is no objection to urge that an action cannot be its own purpose, since the purpose of something cannot be the thing itself. For, speaking strictly, the purpose is not the *action's* purpose but *our* purpose, and there is no contradiction in holding that our purpose in acting may be the action.
9. This sharp distinction of virtue and morality as coordinate and independent forms of goodness will explain a fact which otherwise it is difficult to account for. If we turn from books on Moral Philosophy to any vivid account of human life and action such as we find in Shakespeare, nothing strikes us more than the comparative remoteness of the discussions of Moral Philosophy from the facts of actual life. Is not this largely because, while Moral Philosophy has, quite rightly, concentrated its attention on the fact of obligation, in the case of many of those whom we admire most and whose lives are of the greatest interest, the sense of obligation, though it may be an important, is not a dominating factor in their lives?

STUDY QUESTIONS

1. What is the mistake to which Prichard refers in the title of his article?
2. What does Prichard mean by "an act of moral thinking"?
3. Could two people engage in an act of moral thinking and nevertheless disagree about what ought to be done?
4. Does Pritchard's position specify any particular moral duties?

Ethical Intuitionism

P. F. Strawson

P. F. Strawson (1919–2006) was Waynflete Professor of Metaphysical Philosophy at the University of Oxford. He argues against ethical intuitionism of the sort defended by Sidgwick, Moore, and Prichard. Strawson maintains that a serious epistemological problem looms for those who hold both that normative concepts such as goodness and rightness are unanalyzable and that such concepts are known by intuition alone. To illustrate the problem, Strawson returns to Moore's famous analogy with color, another supposedly unanalyzable concept. Strawson suggests that the following claim would be self-contradictory: "I know what 'red' means, but I can't remember ever seeing red and don't know what seeing red is like." After all, if we cannot remember seeing red and do not know what seeing red is like, then it's hard to imagine that we know what "red" means. Of course, in the case of "red," we have had the relevant experiences, so we know what "red" means. Strawson argues, however, that the same is not true of "rightness" and "goodness." At least some of us are unable to remember intuiting goodness or rightness and do not know what doing so would be like. Hence, if goodness or rightness is unanalyzable, at least some of us lack the requisite experience to know what goodness or rightness means. Yet we do know, and thus ethical intuitionism is mistaken.

North.—What is the trouble about moral facts? When someone denies that there is an objective moral order, or asserts that ethical propositions are pseudo-propositions, cannot I refute him (rather as Moore refuted those who denied the existence of the external world) by saying: "You know very well that Brown did wrong in beating his wife. You know very well that you ought to keep promises. You know very well that human affection is good and cruelty bad, that many actions are wrong and some are right"?

West.—Isn't the trouble about moral facts another case of trouble about knowing, about learning?

We find out facts about the external world by looking and listening; about ourselves, by feeling; about other people, by looking and listening *and* feeling. When this is noticed, there arises a wish to say that the facts *are* what is seen, what is heard, what is felt; and, consequently, that moral facts fall into one of these classes. So those who have denied that there are "objective moral characteristics" have not wanted to deny that Brown's action was wrong or that keeping promises is right. They have wanted to point out that rightness and wrongness are a matter of what is felt in the heart, not of what is seen with

From P. F. Strawson, "Ethical Intuitionism," *Philosophy* 24 (1949). Reprinted by permission of the publisher.

the eyes or heard with the ears. They have wanted to emphasize the way in which "Promise-keeping is right" resembles "Going abroad is exciting," "Stories about mothers-in-law are comic," "Bombs are terrifying"; and differs from "Roses are red" and "Sea-water is salt." This does not prevent you from talking about the moral order, or the moral world, if you want to; but it warns you not to forget that the only access to the moral world is through remorse and approval and so on; just as the only access to the world of comedy is through laughter; and the only access to the coward's world is through fear.

North.—I agree, of course, that we cannot see the goodness of something as we see its color, or identify rightness by the sense of touch; though I think you should add that the senses are indispensable as a means of our becoming aware of those characteristics upon which moral characteristics depend. You may be partly right, too, in saying that access to the moral world is obtained through experience of the moral emotions; for it may be that only when our moral feelings have been strongly stirred do we first become clearly aware of the characteristics which evoke these feelings. But these feelings are not identical with that awareness. "Goodness" does not stand to "feeling approval," "guilt" to "feeling guilty," "obligation" to "feeling bound," as "excitingness" stands to "being excited" and "humorousness" to "feeling amused." To use the jargon for a moment: moral characteristics and relations are non-empirical, and awareness of them is neither sensory nor introspectual. It is a different kind of awareness, which the specialists call "intuition": and it is only empiricist prejudice which prevents your acknowledging its existence. Once acknowledged, it solves our problems: and we see that while "Promise-keeping is right" differs from "The sea is salt," this is not because it resembles "Detective-stories are exciting"; it differs from *both* in being the report neither of a sensible nor an introspectible experience, but of an intuition. We may, perhaps, know some moral characteristics mediately, through others. ("Obligation" is, perhaps, definable in terms of "goodness.") But at least one such characteristic—rightness or goodness—is unanalyzable, and known by intuition alone. The fundamental cognitive

situation in morals is that in which we intuit the rightness of a particular action or the goodness of a particular state of affairs. We see this moral characteristic as present in virtue of some other characteristics, themselves capable of being described in empirical terms, which the action or state of affairs possesses. (This is why I said that sense-perception is a necessary, though not a sufficient, condition of obtaining information about the moral order.) Our intuition, then, is not a bare intuition of the moral characteristic, but also the intuition of its dependence on some others: so that this fundamental situation yields us, by intuitive induction, knowledge of moral rules, generalizations regarding the right and the good, which we can apply in other cases, even when an actual intuition is lacking. So much do these rules become taken for granted, a part of our habitual moral life, that most of our everyday moral judgments involve merely an implicit reference to them: a reference which becomes explicit only if the judgment is challenged or queried. Moral emotions, too, assume the character of habitual reactions. But emotions and judgments alike are grounded upon intuitions. Emotion may be the gatekeeper to the moral world; but intuition is the gate.

West.—Not so fast. I understand you to say that at least one fundamental moral characteristic—rightness or goodness—is unanalyzable. Perhaps both are. The experts are divided. In any case, the fundamental characteristic (or characteristics) can be known only by intuitive awareness of its presence in some particular contemplated action or state of affairs. There is, then, a kind of analogy between the word "right" (or "good") and the name of some simple sensible characteristic such as "red."[1] Just as everybody who understands the word "red" has seen some red things, so everybody who understands the word "right" or the word "good" has intuited the character, rightness, in some actions, or the character, goodness, in some states of affairs; and nobody who has not intuited these characters understands the words "right" or "good." But this is not quite enough, is it? In order for me to know *now* the meaning of an indefinable word, it is not enough that a certain perceptual or intuitional event should have occurred at some particular point in my history; for I might not only have forgotten the details of that event; I might have forgotten what *kind* of an event it was; I might not know *now* what it would be like for such an event to occur. If the word "red" expresses an indefinable visual concept, then it is self-contradictory to say: "I know what the word 'red' means, but I can't remember ever *seeing* red and I don't know what it would be *like* to see red." Similarly, if the word "right," or the word "good," expresses an indefinable intuitive concept, then it is self-contradictory to say: "I know what the word 'right' or the word 'good' means, but I can't remember ever *intuiting* rightness or goodness, and I don't know what it would be *like* to intuit rightness or goodness." If your theory is true, then this statement is a contradiction.

But it is not at all obvious to me that it is a contradiction. I should be quite prepared to assert that I understood the words "right" and "good," but that I couldn't remember ever intuiting rightness or goodness and that I couldn't imagine what it would be like to do so. And I think it is quite certain that I am not alone in this, but that there are a large number of people who are to be presumed capable of accurate reporting of their own cognitive experience, and who would find nothing self-contradictory in saying what I say. And if this is so, you are presented with a choice of two possibilities. The first is that the words "right" and "good" have quite a different meaning for one set of people from the meaning which they have for another set. But neither of us believes this. The second is that the intuitionist theory is a mistake; that the phrase "intuitional event having a moral characteristic as its object (or a part of its object)" is a phrase which describes nothing at all; or describes misleadingly the kind of emotional experience we both admit. There is no third possibility. It is no good saying: "All people who succeed in learning the meaning of moral words do as a matter of fact have moral intuitions, but unfortunately many people are inclined to forget them, to be quite unable to remember what they are like." True, there would be nothing self-contradictory in saying this: but it would simply be a variant of the first possibility; for I cannot be said to know *now* the meaning of a word expressing an intuitive concept unless I know now what it would be like to intuit the characteristic of which it is a concept. The trouble with your

intuitionist theory is that, if true, it should be a truism. There should be no doubt about the occurrence of the distinctive experience of intuiting rightness (or goodness), and about its being the only way to learn the meaning of the primary moral words; just as there is no doubt about the occurrence of seeing red (or blue), and about this being the only way to learn the meaning of the primary color words. But there *is* doubt; and over against this doubt there rises a certainty: the certainty that we all know what it is to *feel* guilty, to *feel* bound, to *feel* approving.

North.—What I have said *is* a truism; and that is its strength. It is not I who am inventing a mythical faculty, but you, irritated, perhaps, by the language of intuitionism, who are denying the obvious. When you said that you couldn't *imagine* what it would be like to have moral intuitions, isn't it clear that you wanted "intuiting a moral characteristic" to be like seeing a color or hearing a sound? Naturally you couldn't *imagine* anything of the sort. But I have already pointed out that moral characteristics are dependent on others of which the presence *is* ascertainable by looking and listening. You do not intuit rightness or goodness independently of the other features of the situation. You intuit *that* an action is (or would be) right, a state of affairs good, *because* it has (or would have) certain other empirically ascertainable qualities. The total content of your intuition includes the "because" clause. Of course, our ordinary moral judgments register unreflective reactions. Nevertheless "This act is right (or this state of affairs is good) because it has P, Q, R"—where "P, Q, R" stand for such empirically ascertainable qualities—expresses the type of fundamental cognitive situation in ethics, of which our normal judgments are copies, mediated by habit, but ready, if challenged, to become explicit as their original. Consider what happens when someone dissents from your opinion. You produce reasons. And this is not a matter of accounting for an emotional condition; but of bringing evidence in support of a verdict.

West.—When the jury brings in a verdict of guilty on a charge of murder, they do so because the facts adduced in evidence are of the kind covered by the definition of "murder." When the chemical analyst concludes that the material submitted for analysis is a salt, he does so because it exhibits the defining properties of a salt. The evidence is the sort of thing that is *meant* by "murder," by "salt." But the fundamental moral word, or words, you say, cannot be defined; their concepts are unanalyzable. So it cannot be in this way that the "because" clause of your ethical sentence functions as evidence. "X is a right action because it is a case of promise-keeping" does not work like "X is a salt because it is a compound of basic and acid radicals"; for, if "right" is indefinable, "X is right" does not *mean* "X is an act of promise-keeping or of relieving distress or of telling the truth or . . ."

When I say "It will be fine in the morning; for the evening sky is red," the evidence is of a different sort. For I might observe the fine morning without having noticed the state of the evening sky. But you have rightly stressed the point that there is no *independent* awareness of *moral* qualities: that they are always "seen" as dependent on those other features mentioned in the "because" clause. So it is not in this way, either, that the "because" clause of your ethical sentence functions as evidence. And there is no other way. Generally, we may say that whenever *q* is evidence for *p, either q* is the sort of thing we mean by "*p*" ("*p*" is definable in terms of "*q*") *or* we can have knowledge of the state of affairs described by "*p*" independently of knowledge of the state of affairs described by "*q*." But neither of these conditions is satisfied by the *q,* the "because" clause, of your ethical sentence.

The "because" clause, then, does not, as you said it did, constitute evidence for the ethical judgment. And this, it seems to me, should be a serious matter for you. For where is such evidence to be found? It is no good saying that, after all, the ethical judgments of other people (or your own at other times) may corroborate your own present judgment. They may agree with it: but their agreement strengthens the probability of your judgment only on the assumption that their moral intuitions tend on the whole to be correct. But the only possible evidence for the existence of a *tendency* to have correct intuitions is the correctness of *actual* intuitions. And it is precisely the correctness of actual intuitions for which we are seeking evidence, and failing to find it.

And evidence you must have, if your account of the matter is correct. You will scarcely say that ethical intuitions are infallible; for ethical disagreements may survive the resolution of factual disagreements. (You might, of course, say that *genuine* intuitions were infallible: then the problem becomes one of finding a criterion for distinguishing between the genuine ones and those false claimants that carry the same inner conviction.) So your use of the language of "unanalyzable predicates ascribed in moral judgment to particular actions and states of affairs" leads to contradiction. For to call such a judgment "non-infallible" would be meaningless unless there were some way of checking it; of confirming or confuting it, by producing evidence for or against it. But I have just shown that your account of these judgments is incompatible with the possibility of producing evidence for or against them. So, if your account is true, these judgments are both corrigible and incorrigible; and this is absurd.

But the absurdity points to the solution. Of course these judgments are corrigible: but not in the way in which the diagnosis of a doctor is corrigible; rather in the way in which the musical taste of a child is corrigible. Correcting them is not a matter of *producing evidence* for them or their contraries, though it is (partly) a matter of *giving reasons* for them or their contraries. We say, warningly, that ethical judgments are corrigible, because ethical disagreement sometimes survives the resolution of factual disagreement. We say, encouragingly, that ethical judgments are corrigible, because the resolution of factual disagreement sometimes leads to the resolution of ethical disagreement. But the one kind of agreement leads (when it *does* lead) to the other, not in the way in which agreed evidence leads to an agreed conclusion, but in the way in which common experience leads to sympathy. The two kinds of agreement, the two kinds of judgment, are as different as chalk from cheese. Ordinary language can accommodate the difference without strain: it is the pseudo-precise philosophical use of "judgment" which slurs over the difference and raises the difficulty. Is it not clear, then, what people have meant when they said that ethical disagreements were like disagreements in taste, in choice, in practical attitude?[2] Of course, as you said, when we produce our reasons, we are not often simply giving the causes of our emotional condition. But neither are we producing evidence for a verdict, for a moral diagnosis. We are using the facts to back our attitudes, to appeal to the capacity of others to feel as we feel, to respond as we respond.

North.—I think I see now what you have been leaving out all the time. First, you accused me of inventing a mythical faculty to give us ethical knowledge. Then, when I pointed out that ethical qualities are not intuited out of all relation to other empirically ascertainable features of actions and states of affairs, but are intuited as dependent upon these, you twisted this dependence out of all recognition. You wanted to make it like the causal dependence of a psychological disposition upon some empirical feature of its object: as a child's fondness for strawberries depends upon their sweetness. But the connection between wrongness and giving pain to others is not an accident of our constitution; nor does its perception require any special faculty—but *simply that which we use in all our reasoning.* From the fact that an action involves inflicting needless pain upon others, *it follows* necessarily that the action is wrong, just as, from the fact that a triangle is equilateral, it follows necessarily that its angles are equal. This is the kind of dependence that we intuit; not an analytic dependence, but a synthetic entailment; and this is why the "because" clause of my ethical sentence does, after all, constitute evidence for the ascription of the moral characteristic.

I can anticipate the obvious objection. No moral rule, you will say, no moral generalization concerning the rightness of acts or the goodness of conditions, holds without exception. It is always possible to envisage circumstances in which the generalization breaks down. Or, if the generalization is so wide that no counter-example can be found, if it can be so interpreted as to cover every case, then it has become too wide: it has become tautologous, like "It is always right to do that which will have the best results on the whole," or intolerably vague, like "It is always right to treat people as ends in themselves" or "The greatest good is the greatest general welfare." It is plainly not with the help of such recipes as these that we find out what is right, what is good, in a particular case. There are no criteria for the meaning of "treating a man as an end," for "the greatest general welfare," which do not presuppose the narrower criteria of rightness and

goodness of which I spoke and which seem always to have exceptions. All this is true. But it calls only for a trifling amendment to those narrower criteria. We cannot, for example, assert, as a necessary synthetic proposition, "All acts of promise-keeping are right" or "All states of aesthetic enjoyment are good." But we *can* assert, as a necessary synthetic proposition, "All acts of promise-keeping *tend as such* to be right (or have *prima facie* rightness)"[3] or "All states of aesthetic enjoyment *tend as such* to be good." And we derive our knowledge of such general necessary connections from seeing, in particular cases, that the rightness of an action, the goodness of a state, *follows from* its being an action or state of a certain kind.

West.—Your "trifling amendment" is a destructive one. When we say of swans that they tend to be white, we are not ascribing a certain quality, namely "tending to be white," to each individual swan. We are saying that the number of swans which are white exceeds the number of those which are not, that if anything is a swan, the chances are that it will be white. When we say "Welshmen tend to be good singers," we mean that most Welshmen sing well; and when we say, of an *individual* Welshman, that *he* tends to sing well, we mean that he sings well more often than not. In all such cases, we are talking of a *class* of things or occasions or events; and saying, not that *all* members of the class have the property of *tending-to-have* a certain characteristic, but that *most* members of the class do in fact have that characteristic. Nobody would accept the claim that a sentence of the form "*Most* As are Bs" expresses a necessary proposition. Is the claim made more plausible by re-writing the proposition in the form "*All* As *tend to be* Bs"?

But, waiving this point, there remains the difficulty that the need for such an amendment to our moral generalizations is incompatible with the account you gave of the way in which we come to know both the moral characteristics of individual actions and states, and the moral generalizations themselves. You said that we intuited the moral characteristic as *following from* some empirically ascertainable features of the action or state. True, if we did so, we should have implicitly learnt a moral generalization: but it would be one asserting *without qualification* the entailment of the moral characteristic by these other features of the case. In other words, and to take your instance, if it *ever* follows, from the fact that an act has the empirically ascertainable features described by the phrase "being an act of promise-keeping," that the act is right, then it *always* follows, from the fact that an act is of this kind, that it has this moral quality. If, then, it is true that we intuit moral characteristics as thus "following from" others, it is false that the implied generalizations require the "trifling amendment"; and if it is true that they require the amendment, it is false that we so intuit moral characteristics.[4]

And this is all that need be said of that rationalist superstition according to which a quasi-logical necessity binds moral predicates to others. "Le coeur a ses raisons, que la raison ne connaît pas": this is the whole truth of the matter: but your attention was so riveted to the first half of it that you forgot the second.

Looking for a logical nexus where there was none to be found, you overlooked the logical relations of the ethical words among themselves. And so you forgot what has often enough been pointed out: that for every expression containing the words "right" or "good," used in their ethical senses, it is always possible to find an expression with the same meaning, but containing, instead of these, the word "ought." The equivalences are various, and the variations subtle; but they are always to be found. For one to say, for example, "I know where the good lies, I know what the right course is; but I don't know the end I *ought* to aim at, the course I *ought* to follow" would be self-contradictory. "Right"-sentences, "good"-sentences are shorthand for "ought"-sentences. And this is enough in itself to explode the myth of unanalyzable characteristics designated by the indefinable predicates, "right" and "good." For "ought" is a *relational* word; whereas "right" and "good" are *predicative.* The simplest sentences containing "ought" are syntactically more complicated than the simplest sentences containing "right" or "good." And hence, since the equivalences of meaning hold, the various ethical usages of "right" and "good" *are all definable*: variously definable in terms of "ought."

Of course this last consideration alone is not decisive against intuitionism. If this were all, you could still re-form the ranks: taking your stand on an intuited unanalyzable non-natural *relation* of obligation, and admitting the definability of the ethical predicates in terms of this relation. But the objections I have already raised apply with equal force against this modified position; and, in other ways, its weakness is more obvious. . . .

NOTES

1. Cf. G. E. Moore, *Principia Ethica*, p. 7 et seq.
2. Cf. Charles Stevenson, *Ethics and Language*, Chapter 1.
3. Ross, *Foundations of Ethics*, pp. 83–86 . . .
4. One desperate expedient might occur to North. He might say that it is not the bare presence of the promise-keeping feature that entails the rightness of the act, but the presence of this feature, coupled with the absence of any features which would entail its wrongness. His general rules would then be, not of the form "'χ has ϕ' entails 'χ is right,'" but of the form "'χ has ϕ and χ has no ψ such that "χ has ψ" entails "χ is wrong"' entails 'χ is right.'" But the suggestion is inadmissible, since (i) the establishment of the general proposition "χ has no ψ, etc." would require the enumeration of all those features which would make it wrong to keep a promise, and (ii) any rule of the form "'χ has ψ' entails 'χ is wrong'" would require expansion in exactly the same way as the "right-making" rule; which would involve an infinite regress of such expansions. Besides having this *theoretical* defect, the suggested model is, of course, *practically* absurd.

STUDY QUESTIONS

1. Are all unanalyzable concepts acquired through experience?
2. What is the difference between "seeing" and "intuiting"?
3. Is a contradiction involved in the claim "I know what the number 'three' means, but I can't remember ever intuiting it and don't know what intuiting it would be like"?
4. Is a contradiction involved in the claim "I know what 'goodness' means, but I can't remember ever intuiting it and don't know what intuiting it would be like"?

Moral Epistemology

Alison Hills

Alison Hills is University Lecturer at St. John's College, Oxford. She asks why we take moral advice from others, given that we shouldn't form beliefs about morality on the basis of another's testimony, shouldn't give weight to other people's moral verdicts, and don't recognize any moral experts? She finds the answer by shifting from seeking moral knowledge to seeking moral understanding. Whereas moral knowledge is a matter of knowing facts, moral understanding requires a grasp of the reasons why some action is right or wrong. Such understanding calls for the ability to give explanations and make judgments about similar cases. In this way moral understanding goes beyond merely knowing what is right or wrong.

1. INTRODUCTION

I will begin with a puzzle about moral epistemology. At first sight, the puzzle is primarily a problem for moral realism, since it highlights some ways in which moral epistemology differs from the epistemology of non-moral matters of fact. But I will argue that the problem is much broader, that it affects not just moral realism but other major metaethical theories.

I will set out four features of moral epistemology. Three are related to one another, but the fourth presents a significant problem in that it seems to be inconsistent with the other three. In the next sections I will discuss how moral realism and non-cognitivism might try to account for these four features of moral epistemology. I will show that none of these theories can comfortably accommodate all of them. In the final sections of the paper, I explain how I think that the problem should be solved.

2. FOUR FEATURES OF MORAL EPISTEMOLOGY

The first interesting feature of moral epistemology is the treatment of testimony. Trusting the testimony of other people about non-moral factual matters—what time it is, where the train station is, when the next train is leaving—is acceptable. Indeed, it is a vital way of finding out about the world, one which we could not do without. Of course, you should not trust the word of everyone all of the time. But at least when you have reason to think that the speaker is trustworthy (perhaps even when you have no reason to believe her untrustworthy) you can and should trust her.

Many people think that forming your beliefs about moral matters on the basis of the word of someone else is, by contrast, in many circumstances unacceptable. Of course you may find out factual information from another person and, under special

From Alison Hills, "Moral Epistemology," in *New Waves in Metaethics,* ed. Michael Brady (New York: Palgrave Macmillan, 2011). Reprinted by permission of the publisher.

circumstances, trusting their word on a specifically moral matter may be acceptable. But, in normal circumstances, trusting testimony about a moral question is problematic in a way that trusting testimony about other non-moral matters of fact is not. Suppose that you are not sure what is the right thing to do, or you are not sure how powerful are the moral reasons you have to act. For example, you are wondering whether you should join your union and support your colleagues by going on strike, even though doing so would harm those you usually help and might produce no benefits. You ask a colleague who says: "yes you should." It would be odd simply to take her word for it and do what you were told, even if you thought that she was usually right about such things.

In fact, the status of moral testimony is more complicated. Learning about morality from your parents or peers when you are a child is both normal and perfectly acceptable. It is only when one becomes older and more mature that it seems important not simply to take someone else's word on what you ought to do.

Secondly, deferring to the opinions of experts about non-moral matters of fact is wise. For example, when you buy a house, it is sensible to ask a surveyor whether it is structurally sound and a lawyer to look at your contract, and to defer to their opinions. But deferring to the beliefs or judgments of others about purely moral matters is problematic. There are no moral experts to whom it is rational to defer, as there are experts about other matters of fact.

Thirdly, we tend not to give weight to others' opinions about moral questions as we would about other matters of fact. Many moral issues are extremely controversial, with many sensible people taking opposing views about the morality of euthanasia, abortion and capital punishment, whether it is ever right to lie to someone for her own benefit, to what extent you could be morally required to sacrifice your own interests for the sake of complete strangers, whether animals have similar rights to humans, and so on. A wide variety of different people disagree about these questions, including some whom it is reasonable for you to regard as similar to you in judging these questions, or even better

(that is, as likely as you or more likely to get the answer right). If you took the opinions of others into account, it is likely that you would have to suspend judgment on any controversial moral issue.[1] Most of us do not do this, nor do we think that we should.

These three features of moral epistemology are plainly related. Taking people's words or beliefs or judgments into account on moral matters seems to be problematic, though doing so is perfectly acceptable, even required, with regard to non-moral matters of fact.

The fourth feature of moral epistemology is that taking advice from other people is acceptable and often a very good idea. For example, suppose again that you are considering whether to join the union. Asking your colleagues what they do, asking your friends and family what they think you should do and why, can be an invaluable guide to your own thinking. There is no need for you to try to work out what to do all by yourself and no benefit in doing so—but using what they say as a guide to your own reflections is very different from simply putting your trust in the answer they give you. Taking advice is not the same as trusting testimony.

At first sight, the first three features of moral epistemology seem to be a problem for moral realism, for they are important differences between the epistemology of morality and that of non-moral facts. In the next section, I discuss how moral realists might respond.

3. MORAL REALISM

According to moral realism (as I will understand it here), there are objective facts about morality that do not depend on our beliefs or attitudes about them. Killing the innocent is wrong, for example, no matter whether or not we believe that it is, disapprove of it and so on. There are many challenges that can and have been made to moral realism. But the issues that I have raised in the last section have not been much discussed. Moral realists think that moral questions are similar in important respects to non-moral matters of fact, so they need to explain why the epistemology of the two is so different.

One feature of moral epistemology that I picked out in the last section is easy for moral realists to explain. Taking advice about moral questions is a good idea, if moral realism is true, because others may be better placed than you to recognize the moral facts, and their advice may help you form true beliefs.

But if others can help you form moral beliefs with their advice, why not with their testimony? Why should you not trust their word and take their opinions into account, deferring to them if they are experts? There are some obvious and uncontroversial reasons why we might not defer to moral experts.[2] There are no widely acknowledged moral experts as there are experts in other fields. If you need to find an expert surveyor to assess your house, you can check that she has the appropriate professional qualifications. Not only is there no widely recognized qualification for a moral expert, but it is hard to imagine that one could possibly be devised. There is so much disagreement about who has good judgment about moral matters and what qualities someone needs to have good judgment that no test for moral expertise will ever be widely (let alone universally) accepted.

But, if you cannot identify an appropriate expert, there is no reason for you to defer to anyone else's judgment; you might even think that there was reason not to do so. It might be better to make up your own mind than to rely on someone else whose judgment may be badly flawed.[3]

But, even though it may be difficult to find a moral expert, this is not a strong reason never to accept moral testimony and never to defer to the judgments of others. It is not that difficult to discover someone who has better judgment or more experience than you in some particular area or about some single issue. And there would be no reason not to take their word on at least that moral question.[4] Moral realists tend to be quite optimistic about the possibility of moral knowledge. But, if some people have moral knowledge, why can't they transmit it to others through testimony, or by those others deferring to them?

Moreover, suppose that it was indeed difficult to find anyone whose moral judgment you should trust. What would be the point of asking for their advice?

Either their judgment is no good, in which case there would seem to be no benefit in taking their advice (it might even make things worse). Or if their advice was useful, what could be the problem with trusting their testimony or deferring to their judgment? It is hard for a moral realist to explain why it is not reasonable to trust moral testimony, without claiming that it is hard to find anyone whose judgment you should trust, and therefore without also suggesting that there is no point in taking moral advice.

4. NON-COGNITIVISM

Moral realism has difficulties in explaining why it is a mistake to trust moral testimony or to defer to moral experts. One possible reason for this is its commitment to *cognitivism,* that is, the claim that moral judgments are expressions of belief and that they can be evaluated as true or false. Non-cognitivist accounts of moral judgment, according to which in making a moral judgment you are not representing the world, but are expressing your attitudes towards it, may seem to be well placed to explain why trusting moral testimony and deferring to moral judgments of others is not a good idea. In this section I discuss whether simple or sophisticated versions of non-cognitivism can explain all four features of moral epistemology.

4.1. Simple Non-Cognitivism

According to simple non-cognitivism, moral judgments are expressions of approval or disapproval or combinations of these and other non-cognitive attitudes. Here is Ayer's classic statement of simple non-cognitivism:

> The presence of an ethical symbol in a proposition adds nothing to its factual content. Thus if I say to someone "You acted wrongly in stealing that money" I am not stating anything more than if I had simply said, "You stole that money." . . . If now I generalize my previous statement and say, "Stealing money is wrong," I produce a sentence which has no factual meaning—that is, expresses no proposition which can be either

true or false . . . Another man may disagree with me about the wrongness of stealing, in the sense that he may not have the same feelings about stealing as I have, and he may quarrel with me on account of my moral sentiments. But he cannot, strictly speaking, contradict me. For in saying that a certain type of action is right or wrong, I am not making any factual statement, not even a statement about my own state of mind. I am merely expressing certain moral sentiments. (Ayer, 1936, p. 107)

If moral judgments are all expressions of our attitudes, there is no such thing as moral truth and no such thing as moral knowledge. And if (as is plausible) trusting testimony about matters of fact is reasonable because it can be a source of knowledge, and there is no such thing as moral knowledge, there could be no reason to trust moral testimony.

Since moral judgments are simply expressions of attitudes, according to simple non-cognitivism, and no one's attitudes can be regarded as better in any respect than those of anyone else, we are all equally well placed to make moral judgments. Of course, some of us may have more factual information and could count as experts in that sense. But there would be nothing distinctively moral about our expertise. Indeed, it is hard to see how anyone could distinguish herself as a moral expert, according to simple non-cognitivism. Since there are no moral experts, there is no one to whom it is rational for us to defer.

Similarly, since all you are doing when you make a moral judgment is expressing your attitude, there seems to be no reason why you should suspend judgment when you discover a "disagreement," that is, someone else expressing a different attitude. You are not, as Ayer says, strictly speaking contradicting one another (two propositions can contradict one another, strictly speaking, only if they each can have a truth-value, but of course moral judgments cannot be true or false, according to this view). So there is a good sense in which you are not disagreeing at all. In any case, moral "disagreements" are clearly quite different from ordinary factual disagreements, and it is not surprising that different responses are required in each case.

Simple non-cognitivism gives an account of moral judgments according to which it is easy to see why trusting moral testimony is usually unacceptable, why there are no moral experts to whom one should defer and why you are not required to suspend judgment in response to moral disagreements. It might appear, then, that it gives a better account of moral epistemology than does moral realism. But this is not really so.

In the first place, it cannot give an adequate account of how we make moral judgments. We can and do subject moral claims to scrutiny, we think carefully about them, try to work out which factors are morally relevant and how much they matter and so on, and it certainly seems that our moral beliefs are better justified if we carry these out well. Simple non-cognitivists insist that there are no benefits to thinking carefully about moral matters. But a complete denial that careful deliberation about moral matters has any point is not a very attractive view. It is not very plausible that thinking about moral questions is a complete waste of time.

In the second place, simple non-cognitivism is not able to explain all the features of moral epistemology. For, after all, we do take moral advice, and it is hard to see why we would do so if making a moral judgment were merely expressing an attitude. Why should you regard their expression of an attitude as relevant in any way to your expressing your attitude?

There are reasons why you might be interested in someone else's attitudes. You might simply be curious. You might want to be like that person (and share her attitudes) or unlike her (and develop different attitudes). Discussing moral questions with others may help you to refine your own attitudes, to change them or to endorse them. But this is not a particularly good account of moral advice. In asking for and taking moral advice, you seem to be asking what you should think about moral questions and what you should do. It is not clear that simple non-cognitivism can capture this feature of moral advice.

Moreover, while in many circumstances we do not trust moral testimony, in some situations we do, and we think that doing so is right. Some people—notably children—should listen to moral testimony. The kind of non-cognitivism that insists that there are no better or worse moral opinions, that deliberation and consideration can play no role in ethics, apparently cannot explain why it is ever a good idea to trust moral testimony.

4.2. Sophisticated Non-Cognitivism

Any plausible non-cognitivist theory will be more sophisticated than this very simple non-cognitivism. I will discuss one well-known sophisticated version of non-cognitivism, Simon Blackburn's quasi-realism (Blackburn, 1998).

Blackburn claims that ethical evaluations are typically practical issues on which we want to coordinate or have to coordinate. Initially, therefore, we must understand moral judgments as expressions of non-cognitive attitudes, rather than as attempts to represent the world in any particular way. But moral judgments take on a new form, the moral proposition: a "propositional reflection" of these non-cognitive attitudes.[5]

The moral proposition acquires many features that appear realist. For example, Blackburn also adopts minimalism about truth, the view that to assert "p is true" is to do no more than to assert "p." Since it is proper for us to assert moral propositions such as "murder is wrong," we are also entitled to assert propositions such as "it is true that murder is wrong," which appear to commit us to moral truths. Similarly, there is no problem in talking about moral knowledge. According to Blackburn, we talk of knowledge that p when we are convinced that no improvement has any chance of reversing our commitment to p; we might even find ourselves saying that we know moral propositions to be true.[6] In addition, we can have genuine disagreements, for we are disagreeing about how to coordinate together: obviously, if I want to coordinate with you in a way that is incompatible with the way that you want to coordinate with me, we are disagreeing with one another.[7]

A sophisticated version of non-cognitivism, such as Blackburn's view briefly sketched here, is a much better account than simple non-cognitivism. It allows that thinking through moral questions does have a point, and that some of us have more time, opportunity, relevant experience and perhaps ability, so that

we will do so better than others. It can explain why we sometimes listen to moral testimony and why we take moral advice, because we want to coordinate with other people and the coordination for which we make moral judgments is particularly important.

But, unfortunately, sophisticated non-cognitivism cannot explain all the features of moral epistemology either. Suppose that you are more careful in forming your moral judgments than I am. If there are benefits to careful deliberation in forming your moral beliefs, why can't you share those benefits with me by telling me the results of your deliberation? And why shouldn't people like you, who have spent longer thinking more carefully and more accurately about moral questions, count as moral experts? If there are moral experts, should we not defer to them?

The problem, of course, is that the closer that sophisticated non-cognitivism comes to moral realism, the greater the difficulties it has in retaining the appealing parts of the moral epistemology of simple non-cognitivism.

Neither moral realism nor the versions of non-cognitivism considered here could solve the puzzle about moral epistemology. Indeed, we might be inclined to think that it is not so much a puzzle as an actual inconsistency in moral epistemology. It is simply impossible to reconcile all four features, for any argument in favor of taking moral advice must apply also to trusting moral testimony and deferring to experts; and any argument against trust and deference in ethics also suggests that we should not take moral advice or ever listen to moral testimony. But in the following section I will argue that we can give a coherent account of moral epistemology that accommodates all four features of moral epistemology, one that is compatible with both moral realism and the kind of sophisticated non-cognitivism mentioned above.

5. MORAL UNDERSTANDING

When discussing moral realism, I suggested that, if we could gain moral knowledge through testimony, we would have reasons to trust moral testimony. But that assumes that we want, or have reason to try to gain, moral knowledge. Perhaps we prefer or have stronger reasons to try to gain something else: moral understanding.[8]

If you ask someone else what it is morally permissible or morally right for you to do, and they tell you, you may know what to do and you may as a result do the right action. But you could not give an explanation of the reasons why the action is right—you may have absolutely no idea why it is right. You could not work out what to do in a similar situation in the future. In short, you do not *understand why* your action is right.

Moral understanding, as I conceive of it, is *factive* and it is *not transparent*. You cannot understand why killing the innocent is always morally acceptable, even if you think that you do, because killing the innocent is not always acceptable. In these two important regards it is similar to knowledge. But understanding why p is true is quite different from knowing that p is true. Moral understanding requires a grasp of the reasons why some action is right, or why some policy or practice is morally wrong. This grasp involves a set of abilities, including the ability to give explanations and to make judgments about similar cases. These abilities go beyond what is required to know that some action is right, and even what is needed to know why it is right. If you understand why p (and q is why p), then in the right sort of circumstances you can successfully:

(i) follow an explanation of why p given by someone else
(ii) explain why p in your own words
(iii) draw the conclusion that p (or that probably p) from the information that q
(iv) draw the conclusion that p′ (or that probably p′) from the information that q′ (where p′ and q′ are similar to but not identical to p and q)
(v) given the information that p, give the right explanation, q
(vi) given the information that p′, give the right explanation, q′

To understand why p, you have to have the abilities (i)–(vi) to at least some extent.[9] For example, to understand why killing the innocent is wrong, you might be able to explain that people's lives are valuable, that it is wrong to end their lives prematurely, particularly when they have not given their consent. It follows that you cannot really understand why some isolated fact is true; you need to have a grasp of moral considerations that will have implications for other moral questions (for instance, in this case, the question of whether it is ever morally acceptable to kill someone whose life is no longer worth living and who wishes to die might be relevant).

Since it essentially involves a set of abilities, moral understanding is closer to know-how than to ordinary propositional knowledge.[10] And, like know-how, it is usually not successfully transmissible by testimony. In order to acquire moral understanding, it is important that you develop the abilities to draw conclusions about what is morally right from the reasons why it is morally right. Being told the correct conclusion, or finding out what some expert believes, will usually not help: you need to practice. Of course, you cannot begin to develop moral understanding before you have any moral beliefs at all, because it requires to some extent a systematic grasp of moral considerations. So it is not surprising that we expect children to learn most of their moral beliefs from testimony. It is only when they have acquired sufficient moral beliefs in this way, and have to some extent the ability to give explanations of moral truths and to draw conclusions on the basis of the reasons why certain moral claims are true, that they can develop moral understanding. And, as we would predict, it is at this point that we expect children no longer to trust testimony or defer to moral experts, but to make up their own minds.

I suggest that not only is it important that we acquire the abilities characteristic of moral understanding, but it is also important that we *use* our moral understanding to draw conclusions and to offer explanations (I will be arguing that to do so is an essential part of morally worthy action). If this is right, then not only is it a mistake to fail to acquire moral understanding, but it is also wrong to trust testimony or defer to moral experts when you could have used your own judgment instead.

Now we can also distinguish between taking advice and trusting testimony. When you trust testimony or defer to experts, you base your belief solely on the authority of the other person. You make no attempt to assess whether their reasons for their opinion are any good. It does not, of course, follow that you trust the testimony of anyone or that you treat everyone as an expert. You may take into account how expert and trustworthy the speaker is. You may rate her as a source of moral testimony or of moral expertise. But you are essentially judging the person, not what she says or thinks about this particular issue. So you cannot be responding to the reasons why p is true—you might have no idea of the reasons why it is true, but even if you do (the other person may have offered an explanation) you do not base your belief on that, but on the fact that she said or thought that p.

By contrast, you may take their views as *moral advice,* which you subject to critical scrutiny and then decide whether or not to accept *on its own merits.* Here you take into account what others have said to you as a guide to your own reflections. If you come to the same conclusion (that p), you do so on the basis of the reasons why p—reasons that they may have helped you to become aware of or to appreciate properly—rather than basing your belief on them. Since, when you take moral advice, you develop and use your moral understanding, whereas trusting testimony and deferring to experts is a rival way of forming beliefs, if moral understanding is important in the way I have suggested it is clear why taking moral advice is acceptable when trusting testimony and deferring to others is not. The only exception, I think, is if for some reason you have no moral understanding and could gain none (perhaps you do not have the relevant experience, or you have poor moral judgment), in which case it might be better to trust moral testimony or to defer to someone who was better placed than you.

If I am right that using moral understanding is important, then it also makes sense not to suspend judgment when in moral disagreements, no matter how intractable, and, in general, you have good reason not to give any weight to the opinions of others on moral questions, whatever their level of expertise. For, if you do have moral understanding and they do not, you could have used it to come to the right answer, and paying attention to others would make things worse. On the other hand, if you had got the answer wrong and had no understanding, you would not gain understanding by putting some weight on the fact that others believed that not-p (independently of the weight that you give to their reasons for that belief). For the fact that some people believe that not-p is not usually a reason why not-p is true. So giving weight to that fact is not a way for you to grasp the connection between the reasons why not-p is true and not-p, and to form your belief that not-p on that basis. Treating the opinions of others as having any weight is a different way of forming moral beliefs than using your moral understanding, and, if I am right about the importance of moral understanding, it is a mistake to do so. Since you should not give weight to the moral beliefs of others (independently of their reasons for those beliefs), you should not suspend judgment in response to moral disagreements. If moral understanding is important in the ways that I have suggested, we can explain all four features of moral epistemology.

6. MORAL WORTH

Why does it matter whether or not you have and use your moral understanding? In the first place, moral understanding may be valuable for its own sake. It may simply be worthwhile to grasp the connections between the reasons why p and p (where p is some moral truth), and to form moral beliefs on that basis.

Secondly, moral understanding plays an important role in certain kinds of moral action. If you know what to do, you can do the right action. But what will be your reason for action? That you are doing what you are told? You might do the right action, but you will not be acting for the right reasons. Your action will not be *morally worthy.*

Morally worthy action is right action for the right reasons, that is, for the reasons that make the action right. If you have moral understanding, if you grasp why your action is right, and you act on that basis, you will act for the right reasons.

The most familiar examples illustrating the difference between right action and morally worthy action involve different types of motivation. Recall Kant's well-known two grocers. One treats his customers honestly in order to have a good reputation. He is not really acting well: he is doing what is morally right, but only because it is in his interests to do so, whereas the grocer who gives the right change precisely because doing so is fair is acting well and his action has *moral worth*.[11] But I suggest that, as well as your desires and goals, your beliefs and the ground of those beliefs are also crucial to morally worthy action.

Suppose that you give your customers the right change, not because you realize that doing so is fair and that you should treat your customers with respect, but because you were told by someone whom you trust that doing so is right. Suppose that you reflect on why this might be, and, realizing that all your customers are local, you think that it must be because it is wrong to cheat local people. Unlike the honest shopkeeper who recognizes that all his customers deserve to be treated fairly (no matter where they are from), you do not understand why giving your customers the right change is morally right. You may have good motivations (unlike the selfish shopkeeper) but you did not choose your action on the basis of the reasons that make it right, so you did not act for the right reasons.

I have argued that moral understanding differs from moral knowledge, and that, if you want to acquire and use moral understanding, it does not usually make sense to trust moral testimony, to defer to moral experts, or to suspend judgment on controversial moral issues, but that taking moral advice is worthwhile. I have suggested that having and using moral understanding may be valuable for its own sake, but it is also needed in morally worthy action (of a certain kind). In the next section, I will consider [the objection] to my argument that . . . you can perform morally worthy actions on the basis of moral knowledge rather than moral understanding . . .

7. OBJECTION TO THE ARGUMENT

Moral understanding is not essential for morally worthy action, because you need not act on the basis of explicitly moral beliefs in order to act for the right reasons. But, if you do, then moral understanding is essential.

Why isn't moral knowledge sufficient? Obviously knowledge that some action is right is not sufficient, because you could have that without any idea of why the action is right, and so you would not be able to act for the reasons why it is right. But what about, for example, acting on the basis of testimony that X is right *and* the reasons why it is right?

I do not think that knowing that X is right and knowing why is sufficient for morally worthy action, if you do not have moral understanding. That is because, even if you act on the basis of that knowledge, you are not really responding to moral reasons yourself; you are responding to the testimony or the judgments of others who may be themselves responding to those reasons.

To act for the reason that p, your belief that p must be among the causes of your action. The causal connection is necessary to distinguish the reasons for which you act—your reasons—from all of those for which you might have acted (some or all of which you may be aware of). For example, there might be many reasons to go for a walk: to get some fresh air, to get some exercise, to buy something useful from a shop. But, even if you are aware of these reasons and you go for a walk, they will not be your reasons for going for a walk unless you act because of them. For example, if your belief that going for a walk will give you some exercise is among the causes of your action, that may be among your reasons for action. This causal connection between your belief and your action may not be sufficient, for well-known reasons (the causal connection may be of the "wrong" kind), but I think it is certainly necessary. So, if there is no causal connection between your belief that p and your action, you do not act for p.

Suppose that you have been told that giving the right change to your customers is the right action because doing so treats them with respect. The speaker was someone whose judgment you trust, so you believe them, and as a result you know what it is right to do, and you know why. But, before they had told you what to do, you saw nothing wrong with cheating your customers, provided that you could get away with it and as long as they were not local people. You still have no moral understanding, so you could not draw the conclusion that giving the correct change is right from reasons why it is right on your own, and you certainly could not do so in similar cases (for example, about whether it is acceptable to lie to your non-local customers about the best before dates of your produce). If you give the right change, the explanation of that will be that you believed that doing so is right because you trusted your interlocutor. The explanation will not include: you thought that doing so was right because you would be treating your customers with respect. Of course you now do believe that doing so is right because you would be treating your customers with respect (for you were told so). But that belief is not the cause of your belief that the action is right. Instead, the testimony is a *common cause*: both of your action and of your belief that that the action is right because it treats your customers with respect.

Right action for the right reasons, when it involves explicitly moral belief, also requires moral understanding. You must use your ability to derive a conclusion (of what to do) from the reasons why it is morally right, in order to act for the right reasons. Testimony is a rival way of finding out what to do, but a morally problematic rival, because if you base your moral belief on testimony rather than moral understanding (you trust the testimony, rather than treating it critically as moral advice) you cannot be acting for the right reasons. . . .

8. CONCLUSION

I introduced a puzzle about moral epistemology, which at first sight seemed like a problem for moral realism: how to explain four features of moral epistemology. But I suggested that the problem was much broader, affecting anti-realist theories like non-cognitivism, and that the difficulty in reconciling the four features was serious. But it can be done, provided that we distinguish between moral knowledge and moral understanding and recognize that it is understanding, not knowledge, that we typically seek, and that we have good reasons to do so.

NOTES

1. The rational response to disagreements about ordinary factual matters is itself a matter of considerable disagreement. For example, Elga (2007; forthcoming) argues that it is always rational to suspend judgment when you disagree with an "epistemic peer" (that is, anyone whom, laying aside your current dispute, you judge to be as likely as you to get the answer right). Kelly (2005; forthcoming) defends a different view, according to which suspending judgment is not always rationally required in response to disagreement. Nevertheless, I think that, even if Kelly is right, moral disagreements are of a kind for which suspending judgment is normally appropriate. So in either case, if moral disputes were like ordinary factual disputes, it would be rational to suspend judgment about any controversial moral issue.
2. These reasons are elaborated in Driver (2006).
3. When your decision is particularly important, you may well prefer to trust your own judgment rather than defer to someone who may or may not be an expert. However, this cannot explain why in general we defer to non-moral experts but not moral experts, as Hopkins points out, for some moral truths are trivial, and some non-moral matters (will the house I am going to buy remain upright for the next few years?) are extremely important (see Hopkins, 2007, pp. 621–3).
4. Hopkins makes this argument for gaining moral knowledge by testimony (Hopkins, 2007, pp. 623–6).
5. Blackburn (1998), p. 77.
6. Blackburn (1998), p. 79.
7. In fact, Blackburn claims that, even if we don't have to coordinate together, we cannot tolerate sufficiently serious differences in attitude (Blackburn, 1998, p. 69).
8. The term "understanding" can be used in a variety of ways, including the locutions "understand that p," "understand p" (where p is a proposition) and

"understand X" (where X is a subject matter). I have nothing to say about these uses of the term. My account of moral understanding is restricted to understanding why p (where p is a moral proposition). . . .

9. You can have these abilities to a greater or lesser degree, which may make it tempting to say that moral understanding comes in degrees. You have minimal moral understanding if you correctly believe that q is why p and you can follow an explanation of why p. You have greater understanding if you have (i)–(vi) to some extent and you have full understanding if you have (i)–(vi) to the greatest extent. Alternatively, there might be a cut-off point before which you do not count as having understanding, and after which you do. This cut-off point might be contextually determined.

10. It is, of course, controversial whether know-how is a species of propositional knowledge or not. I think that there are two reasons for thinking that moral understanding is not a type of propositional knowledge. First, unlike propositional knowledge, it requires the abilities mentioned above. Secondly, I think that it is compatible with certain kinds of luck, which knowledge is not. For example, if you learn that q from a source that is usually unreliable but is now telling the truth, and from that you draw the conclusion that p, you can understand why p, though you do not know that p (or know why p).

11. What is it to act for the right reasons? One possibility is that, to do the morally right act for the right reasons, you must choose it under an explicitly moral description, such as "the morally right action." But the use of an explicitly moral concept is not essential to morally worthy action. What matters is that you respond to moral reasons, not that you do so under an explicitly moral description.

REFERENCES

Ayer. (1936) *Language, Truth and Logic* (London: Victor Gollancz).

Blackburn, S. (1998) *Ruling Passions* (Oxford: Oxford University Press).

Driver, J. (2006) "Autonomy and the Asymmetry Problem for Moral Expertise," *Philosophical Studies* 128, 619–44.

Elga, A. (2007) "Reflection and Disagreement," *Noûs* 41, 478–502.

Elga, A. (forthcoming) "How to disagree about how to disagree," in R. Feldman and T. Warfield (eds) *Disagreement* (Oxford: Oxford University Press).

Hopkins, R. (2007) "What is wrong with moral testimony?," *Philosophy and Phenomenological Research* 74, 611–34.

Kelly, T. (2005) "The Epistemic Significance of Disagreement," in J. Hawthorne and T. Gendler (eds) *Oxford Studies in Epistemology*, Volume 1 (Oxford: Oxford University Press).

Kelly, T. (forthcoming) "Peer disagreement and Higher Order Evidence," in R. Feldman and T. Warfield (eds) *Disagreement* (Oxford: Oxford University Press).

STUDY QUESTIONS

1. What is the difference between accepting moral testimony and taking moral advice?
2. Do you recognize any moral experts?
3. Why is moral understanding closer to knowing-how than knowing-that?
4. Should judgments of non-moral value be understood as more akin to moral judgments or scientific judgments?

Moral Disagreement and Moral Expertise

Sarah McGrath

Does widespread moral disagreement undermine the concept of moral knowledge? Sarah McGrath, Professor of Philosophy at Princeton University, distinguishes metaphysical and epistemological variants of the challenge from disagreement. The metaphysical version—found, for example, in Mackie—takes the best explanation of moral disagreement to be that moral facts don't exist. McGrath finds two problems with this argument. First, parallel reasoning would suggest that in view of scientific disagreement, scientific facts don't exist. Second, moral questions may just be especially difficult to resolve. Yet, McGrath finds the epistemological version of the challenge from moral disagreement especially formidable. She notes that we all admit that many, if not all, of our moral beliefs are denied by others whose judgment we believe to be at least as reliable as ours. Why, then, should we suppose our own contested moral beliefs amount to knowledge?

1. INTRODUCTION

The phenomenon of persistent ethical disagreement is often cited in connection with the question of whether there is any "absolute" morality, or whether, instead, morality is in some sense merely "a matter of personal opinion." Citing disagreement, many people who hold strong views about controversial issues such as the permissibility of abortion, eating meat, or the death penalty deny that these views are anything more than "personal beliefs." But while there might be inconsistencies lurking in this position, it is not obviously at fault for according the facts about disagreement some epistemic weight.

This paper addresses the question of whether and to what extent moral disagreement undermines moral knowledge. The most familiar arguments from disagreement in the literature purport to establish conclusions about the metaphysics of morality: that there are no moral facts, or that there are no moral properties, or that the moral facts are relative rather than absolute. Of course, the conclusions of some such metaphysical arguments might be perfectly consistent with the existence of considerable moral knowledge. For example, even if there is some successful argument from disagreement to the conclusion that moral facts are relative rather than absolute, this might very well be consistent with our having just as much moral knowledge as we ordinarily take ourselves to have. . . . On the other hand, a metaphysical argument from disagreement which successfully showed that there are no moral facts would presumably rule out the possibility of moral knowledge.

From Sarah McGrath, "Moral Disagreement and Moral Expertise," in *Oxford Studies in Metaethics* vol. 3, ed. Russ Shafer-Landau (Oxford: Oxford University Press, 2008). Reprinted by permission of the publisher.

By contrast, epistemological arguments from disagreement purport to undermine moral knowledge by showing that, regardless of the metaphysics of the moral facts, we are not in a position to have anything like the amount of moral knowledge that we ordinarily take ourselves to have. For reasons that I explore below, there are various respects in which epistemological arguments from disagreement present a more formidable skeptical challenge than metaphysical ones. My main goal in this paper is to develop an epistemological argument that creates a difficulty for our controversial moral beliefs and to explore the extent to which it succeeds.

2. METAPHYSICAL ARGUMENTS

As a representative metaphysical argument, consider J. L. Mackie's well-known "argument from relativity" (1977: 36–8). According to Mackie, "radical differences between first order moral judgments" provide a compelling reason to doubt "the objectivity of values." While it is not entirely clear what Mackie means when he denies the objectivity of values, he does seem to mean, minimally, that all claims to the effect that something has a certain moral property are false. If Mackie is right about this, then we have very little moral knowledge—far less than we thought we had. Perhaps one could know that nothing is morally wrong, but one could not know of any particular action that it is morally wrong—for all claims to the effect that a particular action is right or wrong are false. (Just as, having learned that there aren't any witches, one could know that Marilyn Manson is not a witch. What one can't know is that anybody *is* a witch.)

Significantly, Mackie does not think that scientific disagreement supports an analogous conclusion about science. He argues that the skeptical inference is compelling in the moral but not in the scientific case because moral and scientific disagreements have different explanations. While scientific disagreement is best explained by the fact that scientists draw different conclusions from inadequate evidence, disagreement about moral codes is better

explained by "people's adherence to and participation in different ways of life" (p. 36). In the moral case, "the causal connection seems to be mainly that way round: it is that people approve of monogamy because they participate in a monogamous way of life rather than that they participate in a monogamous way of life because they approve of monogamy." The hypothesis that moral codes are mere reflections of ways of life better explains the pattern of moral variation than does the hypothesis that different people have different "seriously inadequate and badly distorted" perceptions of objective values (p. 37). Thus, there are no objective values.

One immediate concern about Mackie's argument is that it seems to prove too much: it is not true that, in general, where differences in belief co-vary with differences in ways of life, we ought to draw similar conclusions. For example, within the United States, beliefs about evolutionary theory seem to satisfy the relevant criteria. According to a Harris Poll conducted in the summer of 2005, only one-fifth of Americans believe that human beings evolved from other species; only half think that other plants or animals did; 64 percent believe that "human beings were created directly by God." The poll shows that variation in these beliefs reflects differences in the ways of life of the individuals who hold them, in the sense of reflecting the religious, political, and cultural features of the communities to which they belong: individuals who embrace creationism are more likely to be from the South, to be Republicans, to be religious, and to lack college educations. By contrast, Democrats, those from the Northeast and West, and those with college educations are more likely to believe in evolutionary theory. But while it does seem that people's beliefs about evolutionary theory reflect their ways of life in this sense, this does not support any surprising metaphysical conclusions about the facts at issue. In particular, it does not support the conclusion that there are no truths about the origins of the human species, or that all claims about human origins are false. Perhaps Mackie is correct in holding that the pattern of difference in moral beliefs corresponds to a pattern of difference in the cultural norms prevailing in the communities in which individuals were raised. But even if that is true, it does not show that there are no moral facts.

Of course, more could be said on behalf of Mackie's argument. In particular, one might argue that moral controversy and the controversy about human origins are disanalogous in ways that ultimately prove crucial. I will not explore arguments to that effect here, since I do not claim that the present difficulty is decisive. My purpose in raising this *prima facie* difficulty for Mackie's argument is to highlight a quite general challenge for those who would have us draw conclusions about the metaphysics of morality from the existence of moral disagreement: such arguments naturally invite the charge that they prove too much. In order to successfully respond to this charge, proponents of such arguments must explain why we should not draw the same surprising metaphysical conclusions wherever we find apparently similar phenomena. Why, for example, doesn't widespread religious disagreement show that there is no fact of the matter about whether any gods exist, or that such facts are relative? Notoriously, it is difficult to explain why moral disagreement cries out for the metaethicist's favored metaphysical conclusion while similar disagreement in other domains does not. (Just as we would not want to conclude that all beliefs about human origins are false, so also we would not want to conclude that such beliefs are all relative, or by nature are knowable only by some special faculty of intuition.) Of course, this is not to say that the relevant explanation cannot be provided; only that the task of providing it cannot be avoided, and is far from trivial.

A second potential vulnerability for metaphysical arguments from disagreement is that in general such arguments have the form of inference to the best explanation arguments, according to which the best explanation of the kind of disagreement that we find in the moral domain is the preferred conclusion of the proponent of the argument: that there are no objective values, or, alternatively, that moral facts are relative facts, or that what look like moral claims are really just expressions of emotion, and so on. Because metaphysical arguments are inference to the best explanation arguments, one who offers such an argument must show that her favored conclusion better explains the data than any alternative hypothesis does. One competing hypothesis is the perfectly mundane one that the questions with respect to which we disagree are difficult ones, and at least some of us are getting them wrong; the others include the wide range of surprising candidate metaphysical hypotheses familiar from the metaethics literature. Again, there is no guarantee that such a case cannot be made on behalf of some preferred explanation. The point is just that it is not enough to point to a hypothesis that would adequately explain the relevant features of moral disagreement if it were true: one must show that the hypothesis better explains those features than would any competing hypothesis if *it* were true.

Thus, any metaphysical argument for the skeptical conclusion that we have little or no moral knowledge immediately inherits two potential vulnerabilities. First, to the extent that parallel reasoning applied to other domains would lead to conclusions that we are unwilling to accept, it is potentially vulnerable to the charge that it proves too much or overgeneralizes. Second, inasmuch as such an argument is an inference to the best explanation argument, it is vulnerable to the provision of formidable competing explanations of moral disagreement. In the next section, I consider a line of epistemological argument which possesses neither of these vulnerabilities.

3. AN EPISTEMOLOGICAL ARGUMENT

Consider the following passage from Henry Sidgwick's *The Methods of Ethics*:

> [I]f I find any of my judgments, intuitive or inferential, in direct conflict with a judgment of some other mind, there must be error somewhere: and if I have no more reason to suspect error in the other mind than in my own, reflective comparison between the two judgments necessarily reduces me temporarily to a state of neutrality. (p. 342)

Moreover, according to Sidgwick, "the absence of such disagreement must remain an indispensable negative condition of the certainty of our beliefs" (p. 342).

Let us call a belief ***CONTROVERSIAL*** just in case it satisfies the condition to which Sidgwick draws our attention. Thus your belief that p is CONTROVERSIAL if and only if it is denied by another person of whom it is true that: you have no more reason to think that he or she is in error than you are. Of course, a belief might be controversial without being CONTROVERSIAL. This is the case, for example, when some view that you hold is disputed, but you have reason to think that those who dispute it are more likely to be in error than you are.

As we have noted, Sidgwick holds that no belief that is CONTROVERSIAL can be *certain*. But a parallel claim about *knowledge* also seems attractive. That is, it seems plausible that

> If one's belief that p is CONTROVERSIAL, then one does not know that p.

Suppose that you and your friend Alice intend to take the train together but discover that you have different views about what time it is scheduled to depart: you think that the train departs at a quarter past the hour, while she thinks that it departs at half past. Perhaps you have some good reason to think that Alice is the one who has made a mistake. For example, perhaps you know that she arrived at her view by consulting a train schedule that is out of date, while you arrived at yours by consulting the current schedule. Or perhaps you know that Alice is prone to carelessness with respect to such matters, as she has a past history of having made similar mistakes. But suppose instead that you have no such reason to think that it is Alice who has made the mistake: as far [as] you know, it is just as likely that you are mistaken as that she is. In that case, it seems that your belief about what time the train leaves does not amount to knowledge.[1]

Of course, it's clear enough that your belief does not amount to knowledge if you are in fact the one in error, i.e., if your belief about what time the train leaves is false. But even if your belief is true, and Alice is the one who has misread the schedule, it seems that your belief does not amount to knowledge provided that you have no good reason to think that she is the one who has made the mistake. Even if your belief would amount to knowledge in the absence of Alice's holding a contrary belief, the fact that she believes as she does can preclude your knowing in the circumstances. For plausibly, this would be a case in which misleading evidence undermines knowledge.

This suggests the following epistemological argument for a certain kind of moral skepticism:

> **P1** Our controversial moral beliefs are CONTROVERSIAL.
>
> **P2** CONTROVERSIAL beliefs do not amount to knowledge.
>
> **C** Therefore, our controversial moral beliefs do not amount to knowledge.

The first premise and the conclusion of the argument refer to "our controversial moral beliefs." By this, I mean our beliefs about the correct answers to the kinds of questions that tend to be hotly contested in the applied ethics literature as well as in the broader culture: questions about the circumstances (if any) in which it is morally permissible to administer the death penalty, or to have an abortion, or to eat meat, or about how much money we are morally obligated to donate to those in dire need, and so on. It is clear that our beliefs about the answers to such questions are controversial ones. It is of course much less clear that they are also CONTROVERSIAL, i.e., that P1 is true. A good part of what follows is devoted to scrutinizing this claim. I begin, however, with a few preliminary remarks about the argument.

First, one who endorses the argument might remain studiously agnostic about the metaphysics of morality, and in particular, about whether there are any moral facts. That is, one who endorses the argument need not take a stand on whether such facts exist, or even on what, if anything, the relevant kind of disagreement suggests about their existence. The contention of one who endorses the argument is rather that the kind of disagreement that we find with respect to controversial moral questions precludes our knowing the correct answers to these questions, *regardless* of whether such questions have correct answers.

Second, the conclusion of the argument is that our beliefs about controversial moral matters do not amount to knowledge. The conclusion is not that it is unreasonable to hold those beliefs in the face of disagreement, or that we are rationally required to suspend judgment with respect to controversial moral matters. However, if the argument is successful, then the skeptic would seem to have made significant headway towards establishing these apparently stronger claims. For it has been argued, with considerable plausibility, that if one is not in a position to know whether p, then the reasonable course is to suspend judgment about whether p until further evidence becomes available; that is, one should not believe when one is in no position to know.[2] Thus, if the above argument is sound, then this would at the very least seem to put considerable pressure on the idea that it is rational for us to maintain our controversial moral views.

Third, in the previous section, we noted that metaphysical arguments from disagreement generally take the form of inference to the best explanation arguments, and that this fact presents a potential line of resistance to such arguments. Notice that the epistemological argument presented here is *not* best reconstructed as an inference to the best explanation argument. The suggestion is not that the best explanation of the disagreement is that no one knows; rather, the suggestion is that the circumstances of the disagreement are inconsistent with one's knowing. Thus, the argument does not share at least one of the two potential vulnerabilities characteristic of metaphysical arguments.

It is less clear, however, that the argument avoids the second potential vulnerability of metaphysical arguments: that of susceptibility to the charge of overgeneralizing, or proving too much. This issue is the focus of the next section.

4. DOES THE ARGUMENT OVERGENERALIZE?

. . . One might suspect that the epistemological argument does prove too much. Thus, in responding to a similar line of argument to the one under consideration here, Russ Shafer-Landau poses the following dilemma:

> Either intractable disagreement among consistent intelligent parties forces them to suspend judgment about their contested views, or it doesn't. If it does, then we must suspend judgment about *all* of our philosophical views, as well as our belief that there is an external world, that I am an embodied being, that the earth is older than a second, etc. All of these have been challenged by brilliant, consistent, informed skeptics over the millennia.
>
> Alternatively, if we are warranted in any of our beliefs, despite the presence of such skepticism, then justified belief is possible, even in the face of persistent disagreement. And so we could retain our moral beliefs, especially those we have carefully thought through, despite an inability to convince all of our intelligent opponents. (2004: 108–9)

Here, the suggestion is that our controversial moral beliefs are in the same epistemic boat as our beliefs that *there is an external world* and that *the earth has existed for more than one second*. If this were the case, then we could safely conclude that the argument from disagreement does prove too much, since (I assume) we do know that there is an external world and that the earth has existed for more than one second.

However, the idea that beliefs of this kind and our controversial moral beliefs are equally jeopardized by disagreement seems dubious. After all, my belief that *the earth is older than one second* faces much less opposition than my belief that *the death penalty is morally impermissible*. Even if it is true that brilliant skeptics have disputed the former, they are vastly outnumbered by reasonable people who disagree. By contrast, with respect to, say, the moral permissibility or impermissibilty of the death penalty, the division of opinion is not that of lone geniuses vastly outnumbered by the opposition.

As Shafer-Landau interprets the skeptical challenge, it is the *absence of unanimity* among the relevant class of people which suffices to generate the skeptical conclusion. Even the existence of a single formidable dissenter who cannot be won over would suffice to undermine whatever justification one's belief originally enjoyed. This interpretation allows him to plausibly suggest that such a requirement, if consistently applied, would yield a sweeping and global skepticism. However, this is not the most charitable interpretation of the skeptical challenge. On a more charitable construal of that challenge, it is the fact that there is a substantial division of opinion with respect to controversial moral questions that undermines the possibility of knowing the answers to those questions.

In short, the beliefs that *the earth is older than one second* and that *there is an external world* are not CONTROVERSIAL. Even if these beliefs have on occasion been denied by some, including some of formidable intelligence (etc.), it does not follow that one has no more reason to suspect error in such minds than in one's own. Plausibly, one does have such reasons, reasons provided by facts about the distribution of opinion among the relevant class of people. If you and Alice have conflicting beliefs about what time the train is scheduled to depart, then it might be that both of your beliefs are CONTROVERSIAL. However, if you and Alice subsequently discover that ten other people have independently arrived at your belief while none shares hers, your belief is no longer rendered CONTROVERSIAL by the fact that Alice denies it. For now you do have reason to think that she is the one who has made the mistake. On the other hand, her belief—supposing she maintains it— is CONTROVERSIAL: she lacks any parallel reason.

Of course, it is no objection to the skeptical challenge under consideration that it fails to single out our controversial *moral* beliefs. Parallel arguments might be constructed to show that one lacks knowledge with respect to a significant number of topics—for example, philosophy, public policy, and religion. But this does not show that the argument *over*-generalizes. For it is far from clear that the answers to much disputed questions in such domains are known; in any case, that some of us have such knowledge is not a *datum* to which one might appeal in attempting to discredit the argument.

5. IN SEARCH OF MORAL EXPERTISE

The previous section defended the argument against the charge of overgeneralization. This section addresses the question of why one should think that one's beliefs about disputed moral questions are CONTROVERSIAL in the first place. We have emphasized that, even if a belief is controversial, it might not be CONTROVERSIAL. That is, even if the truth of a given belief is contested, a person who holds that belief might have good reason to think that anyone who thinks otherwise is more likely to be wrong than she herself is. Indeed, some beliefs might be *extremely* controversial without being CONTROVERSIAL. Consider again our earlier example of evolutionary theory. The proposition that *human beings evolved from other species* is vigorously denied by many, but it would be a mistake to conclude that it is therefore not known by any of those who believe it. Indeed, the fact that it is denied by many does not even preclude its being known by some who are relatively unfamiliar with the scientific evidence in its favor. Crucially, the proposition in question is not controversial among those who are known to possess the relevant expertise. Certain scientific questions might be highly controversial among the population as a whole, but when a consensus or near consensus exists among those with the relevant expertise, one need remain in a state of agnosticism only for as long as it takes to discover the content of that consensus. Thus, despite the large number of people who deny that human beings have evolved from other species, awareness of the expert consensus on the opposite side of the issue provides good reason to think that those who deny it are in error.

It might be thought that there is a parallel defense of one's controversial moral beliefs. That is, it might seem plausible that, although many dispute these beliefs, they are not CONTROVERSIAL, because they are not controversial among "the moral experts." This raises two questions. First, are there genuine moral experts? And second, if there are, how can they be recognized—either by themselves or by others—as such? Let us set aside the first question, and concede for the sake of argument that individuals with genuine moral expertise exist. How might they be identified?

The task of identifying those with genuine expertise will be a much less straightforward matter in some domains than in others. For the most part, the epistemology literature devoted to the topic of disagreement has focused on the idealized case, in which facts about relative expertise and "epistemic peerhood" are treated as given; the question that has dominated that literature concerns how we should respond to disagreement with our epistemic peers or equals. But in actual, real-life cases, others do not typically wear their relative levels of competence on their sleeves. Of course, on occasion they do: most of us have good reason to think that the person whose shirt reads "Expert Plumbers" is someone to whose judgment we should defer with respect to whatever plumbing questions might arise. But in other cases, facts about relative levels of expertise and competence are far from transparent.

In general, identifying those with genuine expertise in some domain will be most straightforward when we have some kind of *independent check,* one not itself subject to significant controversy, by which we can tell who is (and who is not) getting things right. In certain domains, it is relatively easy for us to acquire evidence which bears straightforwardly on questions about relative expertise. Consider, for example, weather forecasting. Two weather forecasters might offer what seem to be equally compelling cases for their conflicting predictions about what tomorrow's weather will be like. But once tomorrow's weather rolls in, we will have an answer to the question of which of today's two conflicting predictions was more accurate. Thus, in the weather forecasting case, inductive track record evidence about who is more reliable is relatively easy to acquire. Moreover, crucially, such evidence can be readily assessed and assimilated by the layperson: one need not be an expert weather forecaster in order to reliably identify those who possess genuine expertise with respect to weather forecasting.

But significantly, we possess no similar independent check for moral expertise. If moral expertise stands to morality as weather forecasting expertise stands to weather, then a moral expert would be someone who consistently arrives at the correct answers to non-trivial moral questions (or at least, someone whose reliability with respect to such questions significantly exceeds that possessed by the average person, when the average person does not form his moral opinions by deferring to a moral expert). Given such a straightforward understanding of moral expertise, there is nothing particularly problematic about the idea that some individuals possess such expertise. The difficulty lies in arriving at compelling grounds for attributing such expertise, either to oneself or to others. A natural suggestion is that the possession of certain academic credentials, or professional concern with ethics, is good evidence that one possesses reliable moral judgment. I am acquainted with the ethics literature in a way that my plumber is not; moreover, I have taught ethics classes to college students and attended conferences devoted to the subject. He can claim no similar experiences. But in the absence of an independent check on my relative ability to therefore get the answers right, such facts would seem to constitute a relatively meager basis on which to conclude that I am his superior with respect to the reliability of my moral judgment. Again, contrast a case in which we know that one of two weather forecasters is more reliable than the other on the basis of his superior past track record. It would be a mistake, I think, to suppose that in these circumstances I have anything like the kind of evidence for the superiority of my moral judgment that is available in the weather-forecasting case.

Simply put, there is no obvious way to locate oneself in the space of moral expertise relative to others. It is true that professional philosophers who work in applied ethics have thought about the arguments longer than the average person has. Here, as elsewhere in philosophy, this has not resulted in a convergence of opinion. Yet even if these professionals were to converge on the view that, say, killing is no worse than letting die, on the grounds that no adequate metaphysical basis for imputing moral significance to this distinction could be found, it is not clear that ordinary people of the opposite conviction need treat this as conclusive. For it is less clear in the moral case than in various other cases that reliable judgment with respect to the relevant domain is the typical upshot of formal training. Here again the lack of an independent check seems crucial. If a moral expert is someone who tends to get the hard questions right, then good moral training is presumably whatever confers the relevant capacity. That studying structural engineering at MIT is good training for solving the kinds of problem that confront structural engineers can be more or less readily checked by, for example, examining the stability of bridges built by MIT-trained engineers. But in the moral case, since it is unclear how to check who is getting things right, it is unclear how to check whether MIT is a good place for moral training. Thus, while one might think that good moral training would consist in taking a series of ethics courses devoted to the critical examination of arguments on both sides of divisive issues, an equally plausible answer might be that good moral training consists in being raised by virtuous people who devote relatively little time to scrutinizing arguments for and against their views. Similarly, one might think that the best training for appreciating the permissibility or impermissibility of causing animal suffering would involve, among other things, witnessing such suffering. But we could just as easily imagine that the judgment of those best acquainted with the slaughterhouse tends to become artificially deadened to the thought that animals matter.

If the population is substantially divided about, say, the moral permissibility of abortion in certain circumstances, then, assuming that there is some non-relative fact of the matter, a large number of us are wrong. Unfortunately, we possess no analogue to an eye exam, by which we might determine whose moral vision is askew and whose is in good working order. Thus, the truth about where one stands in the space of moral expertise might prove elusive, even for intelligent, thoughtful people.

The upshot of these considerations is that it is quite unclear how one might argue, in a way that is not transparently question-begging or circular, that one's controversial moral beliefs are uncontroversial among the moral experts. But if, for all one knows, there is no consensus among the moral experts in favor of one's controversial moral beliefs, then one cannot appeal to the existence of such a consensus in order to show that those beliefs are not CONTROVERSIAL. . . .

NOTES

1. Cases broadly similar to this one have recently been discussed in the epistemology literature devoted to the question of how we should respond to "peer disagreement." This literature has not directly addressed the question of how disagreement affects knowledge, which is our primary concern here. Significantly, however, a number of contributors to this literature (notably Feldman 2006, Christensen 2007, and Elga 2007) either endorse or express considerable sympathy for the view that peer disagreement should lead the peers to suspend judgment about the disputed question. Presumably, if one ought to suspend judgment as to whether p, then one does not know that p. . . .

2. This conclusion will be especially attractive to those who take knowledge to be the aim of belief; for defense of this claim, see esp. Williamson 2000.

REFERENCES

Christensen, D. (2007) "Epistemology of Disagreement: the Good News" *Philosophical Review* 116: 187–217.

Elga, A. (2007) "Reflection and Disagreement" *Noûs,* LXI(3): 478–502.

Feldman, R. (2006) "Epistemological Puzzles about Disagreement" in *Epistemology Futures,* ed. S. Hetherington (Oxford: Oxford University Press).

Harris Poll (2005) "Nearly Two-thirds of U.S. Adults Believe Human Beings Were Created by God." Harris Interactive, Inc. http://www.harrisinteractive.com/harris_poll/index.asp?PID=581

Mackie, J. L. (1977) *Ethics: Inventing Right and Wrong* (New York: Penguin).

Shafer-Landau, R. (2004) *Whatever Happened to Good and Evil?* (Oxford: Oxford University Press).

Sidgwick, H. (1907/1981) *The Methods of Ethics* (Indianapolis: Hackett).

Williamson, T. (2000). *Knowledge and its Limits* (Oxford: Oxford University Press).

STUDY QUESTIONS

1. What is the difference between the metaphysical and epistemological challenges from moral disagreement?
2. In Sidgwick's sense, what is a "controversial" belief?
3. Can controversial beliefs be knowledge?
4. Should disagreements about non-moral value judgments—for example, about good restaurants, good quarterbacks, and good computers—undermine claims to knowledge about these matters?

A Darwinian Dilemma for Realist Theories of Value

Sharon Street

We doubt our beliefs if we suppose they have dubious origins. To take an extreme example, learning that our beliefs were produced by brainwashing would cast them into serious doubt. Analogously, recognizing that our beliefs are the product of social, familial, or religious pressures would undermine our confidence in them. But if, as Charles Darwin (1809–1882) proposed, our normative beliefs were partly shaped to aid our chance for survival, are we justified in holding them?

Sharon Street, Professor of Philosophy at New York University, claims not, and she offers the following dilemma for realists. On the one hand, if realists maintain that holding true normative beliefs does not enhance reproductive success, then our beliefs are either wildly off base or just happen by coincidence to reflect the truth. On the other hand, if realists maintain that holding true normative beliefs does enhance reproductive success, then they must reject our best scientific picture of the world. In either case, moral realism is unreasonable. Anti-realism, however, avoids this dilemma by holding that normative truths depend on the psychology of agents.

1. INTRODUCTION

Contemporary realist theories of value claim to be compatible with natural science. In this paper, I call this claim into question by arguing that Darwinian considerations pose a dilemma for these theories. The main thrust of my argument is this. Evolutionary forces have played a tremendous role in shaping the content of human evaluative attitudes. The challenge for realist theories of value is to explain the relation between these evolutionary influences on our evaluative attitudes, on the one hand, and the independent evaluative truths that realism posits, on the other. Realism, I argue, can give no satisfactory account of this relation. On the one hand, the realist may claim that there is *no* relation between evolutionary influences on our evaluative attitudes and independent evaluative truths. But this claim leads to the implausible skeptical result that most of our evaluative judgments are off track due to the distorting pressure of Darwinian forces. The realist's other option is to claim that there *is* a relation between evolutionary influences and independent evaluative truths, namely that natural selection favored ancestors who were able to grasp those truths. But this account, I argue, is unacceptable on scientific grounds. Either way, then, realist theories of value prove unable to accommodate the fact that Darwinian forces have deeply influenced the content of human values. . . . I conclude by sketching how

From Sharon Street, "A Darwinian Dilemma for Realist Theories of Value," *Philosophical Studies* 127 (2006). Reprinted by permission of the publisher.

antirealism is able to sidestep the dilemma I have presented. Antirealist theories of value are able to offer an alternative account of the relation between evolutionary forces and evaluative facts—an account that allows us to reconcile our understanding of evaluative truth with our understanding of the many non-rational causes that have played a role in shaping our evaluative judgments.

2. THE TARGET OF THE ARGUMENT: REALIST THEORIES OF VALUE

The defining claim of realism about value, as I will be understanding it, is that there are at least some evaluative facts or truths that hold independently of all our evaluative attitudes.[1] *Evaluative facts or truths* I understand as facts or truths of the form that X is a normative reason to Y, that one should or ought to X, that X is good, valuable, or worthwhile, that X is morally right or wrong, and so on.[2] *Evaluative attitudes* I understand to include states such as desires, attitudes of approval and disapproval, unreflective evaluative tendencies such as the tendency to experience X as counting in favor of or demanding Y, and consciously or unconsciously held evaluative judgments, such as judgments about what is a reason for what, about what one should or ought to do, about what is good, valuable, or worthwhile, about what is morally right or wrong, and so on.

It is important to note that it is not enough to be a realist to claim that the truth of an evaluative judgment holds independently of one's making *that particular* evaluative judgment. Antirealists can agree with that much. Consider, for example, a constructivist view according to which the truth of "X is a reason for agent A to Y" is a function of whether that judgment would be among A's evaluative judgments in reflective equilibrium. This view is antirealist because it understands truths about what reasons a person has as depending on her evaluative attitudes (in particular, on what those attitudes would be in reflective equilibrium). Yet on this view, it is quite possible for someone to have a reason independently

of whether she thinks she does, for whether she has a reason is not a function of whether she (presently) judges she has it, but rather a function of whether that judgment would be among her evaluative judgments in reflective equilibrium. Antirealists can therefore agree with realists that the truth of a given evaluative judgment holds independently of whether one makes that particular judgment. Where antirealists part ways with realists is in denying that there are evaluative truths which hold independently of *the whole set* of evaluative judgments we make or might make upon reflection, or independently of *the whole set* of other evaluative attitudes we hold or might hold upon reflection. . . .

The kind of independence from our evaluative attitudes that realists endorse is what Russ Shafer-Landau has called *stance-independence*.[3] To illustrate: Realists of course agree that the evaluative truth that "Hitler was morally depraved" depends in part on *Hitler's* evaluative attitudes in the sense that if Hitler had valued peace and universal human rights instead of dictatorial power and genocide, then it would have been false instead of true that he was morally depraved. But given that Hitler *did* value dictatorial power and genocide, value realists think that it is true, independent of all of our (and any of Hitler's other) evaluative attitudes, that Hitler was morally depraved. According to realists, the truth that Hitler was morally depraved holds independently of any stance that we (or Hitler) might take toward that truth, whether now or upon reflection. . . .

4. FIRST PREMISE: THE INFLUENCE OF EVOLUTIONARY FORCES ON THE CONTENT OF OUR EVALUATIVE JUDGMENTS

In its first approximation, the opening premise of the Darwinian Dilemma argument is this: the forces of natural selection have had a tremendous influence on the content of human evaluative judgments. . . . In this section, I make a brief case in support of this view, starting with a highly simplified and idealized evolutionary picture, then discussing two important complications, and ending with a more refined statement of the first premise.

To begin, note the potentially phenomenal costs and benefits, as measured in the Darwinian currency of reproductive success, of accepting some evaluative judgments rather than others. It is clear, for instance, how fatal to reproductive success it would be to judge that the fact that something would endanger one's survival is a reason to do it, or that the fact that someone is kin is a reason to harm that individual. A creature who accepted such evaluative judgments would run itself off cliffs, seek out its predators, and assail its offspring, resulting in the speedy elimination of it and its evaluative tendencies from the world.[4] In contrast, it is clear how beneficial (in terms of reproductive success) it would be to judge that the fact that something would promote one's survival is a reason in favor of it, or that the fact that something would assist one's offspring is a reason to do it. Different evaluative tendencies, then, can have extremely different effects on a creature's chances of survival and reproduction. In light of this, it is only reasonable to expect there to have been, over the course of our evolutionary history, relentless selective pressure on the content of our evaluative judgments, or rather (as I discuss below) "proto" versions thereof. In particular, we can expect there to have been overwhelming pressure in the direction of making those evaluative judgments which tended to promote reproductive success (such as the judgment that one's life is valuable), and against making those evaluative judgments which tended to decrease reproductive success (such as the judgment that one should attack one's offspring).

The hypothesis that this is indeed very roughly what happened is borne out by the patterns of evaluative judgment that we observe in human beings today. There is, of course, a seemingly unlimited diversity to the evaluative judgments that human beings affirm. Yet even as we note this diversity, we also see deep and striking patterns, across both time and cultures, in many of the most basic evaluative judgments that human beings tend to make. Consider, as a brief sampling, the following judgments about reasons:

(1) The fact that something would promote one's survival is a reason in favor of it.

(2) The fact that something would promote the interests of a family member is a reason to do it.

(3) We have greater obligations to help our own children than we do to help complete strangers.

(4) The fact that someone has treated one well is a reason to treat that person well in return.

(5) The fact that someone is altruistic is a reason to admire, praise, and reward him or her.

(6) The fact that someone has done one deliberate harm is a reason to shun that person or seek his or her punishment.

What explains the widespread human acceptance of such judgments? There are so many other possible judgments about reasons we could make—so why these? Why, for instance, do we view the death of our offspring as a horror, rather than as something to be sought after? Why do we think that altruism with no hope of personal reward is the highest form of virtue, rather than something to be loathed and eliminated? Evolutionary biology offers powerful answers to these questions, very roughly of the form that *these* sorts of judgments about reasons tended to promote survival and reproduction much more effectively than the alternative judgments. The details of how survival and reproduction were promoted will vary depending on the evaluative tendency in question. In the case of judgment (1), for instance, the rough explanation is obvious: creatures who possessed this general evaluative tendency tended to do more to promote their survival than those who, say, had a tendency to view the fact that something would promote their survival as counting *against* it, and so the former tended to survive and reproduce in greater numbers. The explanation of evaluative tendencies in the direction of judgments such as (2) and (3) will be somewhat more complicated, drawing on the evolutionary theory of kin selection. The explanation in the case of evaluative tendencies in the direction of judgments (4), (5), and (6), meanwhile, will appeal to the biological theory of reciprocal altruism.

For the sake of contrast, consider the following possible evaluative judgments:

(1′) The fact that something would promote one's survival is a reason against it.

(2′) The fact that something would promote the interests of a family member is a reason not to do it.

(3′) We have greater obligations to help complete strangers than we do to help our own children.

(4′) The fact that someone has treated one well is a reason to do that individual harm in return.

(5′) The fact that someone is altruistic is a reason to dislike, condemn, and punish him or her.

(6′) The fact that someone has done one deliberate harm is a reason to seek out that person's company and reward him or her.

If judgments like these—ones that would, other things being equal, so clearly decrease rather than increase the reproductive success of those who made them—predominated among our most deeply and widely held evaluative judgments across both time and cultures, then this would constitute powerful evidence that the content of our evaluative judgments had not been greatly influenced by Darwinian selective pressures. But these are not the evaluative judgments we tend to see; instead, among our most deeply and widely held judgments, we observe many like those on the first list—many with exactly the sort of content one would expect if the content of our evaluative judgments had been heavily influenced by selective pressures. In this way, the observed patterns in the actual content of human evaluative judgments provide evidence in favor of the view that natural selection has had a tremendous influence on that content. . . .

. . . Darwinian selective pressures on the content of human evaluative judgments is best understood as *indirect*. The most plausible picture is that natural selection has had a tremendous *direct* influence on what I have called our "more basic evaluative tendencies," and that these basic evaluative tendencies, in their turn, have had a major influence on the evaluative judgments we affirm. By this latter claim I do not mean that we automatically or inevitably accept the full-fledged evaluative judgments that line up in content with our basic evaluative tendencies. Certainly not. For one thing, other causal

influences can shape our evaluative judgments in ways that make them stray, perhaps quite far, from alignment with our more basic evaluative tendencies.[5] For another thing, we are reflective creatures, and as such are capable of noticing any given evaluative tendency in ourselves, stepping back from it, and deciding on reflection to disavow it and fight against it rather than to endorse the content suggested by it. My point here is instead the simple and plausible one that had the general content of our basic evaluative tendencies been very different, then the general content of our full-fledged evaluative judgments would also have been very different, and in loosely corresponding ways.[6] Imagine, for instance, that we had evolved more along the lines of lions, so that males in relatively frequent circumstances had a strong unreflective evaluative tendency to experience the killing of offspring that were not his own as "demanded by the circumstances," and so that females, in turn, experienced no strong unreflective tendency to "hold it against" a male when he killed her offspring in such circumstances, on the contrary becoming receptive to his advances soon afterwards. . . . My conclusion: the content of human evaluative judgments has been tremendously influenced—*indirectly* influenced, in the way I have indicated, but nevertheless tremendously influenced—by the forces of natural selection, such that our system of evaluative judgments is saturated with evolutionary influence. The truth of some account very roughly along these lines is all that is required for the Darwinian Dilemma to get off the ground.

5. FIRST HORN OF THE DILEMMA: DENYING A RELATION

The basic problem for realism is that it needs to take a position on what relation there is, if any, between the selective forces that have influenced the content of our evaluative judgments, on the one hand, and the independent evaluative truths that realism posits, on the other. Realists have two options: they may either assert or deny a relation.

Let us begin with the realist's option of claiming that there is *no* relation. The key point to see about this option is that if one takes it, then the forces of natural selection must be viewed as a purely distorting influence on our evaluative judgments, having pushed us in evaluative directions that have nothing whatsoever to do with the evaluative truth. On this view, allowing our evaluative judgments to be shaped by evolutionary influences is analogous to setting out for Bermuda and letting the course of your boat be determined by the wind and tides: just as the push of the wind and tides on your boat has nothing to do with where you want to go, so the historical push of natural selection on the content of our evaluative judgments has nothing to do with evaluative truth. Of course every now and then, the wind and tides might happen to deposit someone's boat on the shores of Bermuda. Similarly, every now and then, Darwinian pressures might have happened to push us toward accepting an evaluative judgment that accords with one of the realist's independent evaluative truths. But this would be purely a matter of chance, since by hypothesis there is no relation between the forces at work and the "destination" in question, namely evaluative truth.

If we take this point and combine it with the first premise that our evaluative judgments have been tremendously shaped by Darwinian influence, then we are left with the implausible skeptical conclusion that our evaluative judgments are in all likelihood mostly off track, for our system of evaluative judgments is revealed to be utterly saturated and contaminated with illegitimate influence. We should have been evolving towards affirming the independent evaluative truths posited by the realist, but instead it turns out that we have been evolving towards affirming whatever evaluative content tends to promote reproductive success. We have thus been guided by the wrong sort of influence from the very outset of our evaluative history, and so, more likely than not, most of our evaluative judgments have nothing to do with the truth. Of course it's *possible* that as a matter of sheer chance, some large portion of our evaluative judgments ended up true, due to a happy coincidence between the realist's independent evaluative truths and the evaluative directions in which natural selection tended to push us, but this would require a fluke of luck that's not only extremely unlikely, in view of the huge universe of logically possible evaluative judgments and truths, but also astoundingly convenient to the realist. Barring such a coincidence, the only conclusion remaining is that many or most of our evaluative judgments are off track. This is the far-fetched skeptical result that awaits any realist who takes the route of claiming that there is no relation between evolutionary influences on our evaluative judgments and independent evaluative truths.

But the realist may not be ready to abandon this route just yet. Let us grant (sticking with this horn of the dilemma) that the distorting influence of natural selection on the content of our evaluative judgments has been tremendous. One might nevertheless object that to draw a skeptical conclusion from this is unwarranted. For the argument so far ignores the power of a very different kind of influence on our system of evaluative judgments—a kind of influence that one might claim *is* related to the truth and that has also been tremendous—namely, the influence of rational reflection. After all, we are not unthinking beings who simply endorse whatever evaluative tendencies were implanted in us by evolutionary forces. Over the course of human history, endless amounts of reflection have gone on and greatly altered the shape of our evaluative judgments. According to the objection at hand, just as a compass and a little steering can correct for the influence of the wind and tides on the course of one's boat, so rational reflection can correct for the influence of selective pressures on our values.

I accept one important point that this objection makes. Any full explanation of why human beings accept the evaluative judgments we do would need to make reference to the large influence of rational reflection. The view I am suggesting by no means involves thinking of us as automatons who simply endorse whatever evaluative tendencies are implanted in us by evolutionary and other forces. On the contrary, the view I am suggesting acknowledges the point that we are self-conscious and reflective creatures, and in a sense seeks to honor that point about us *better* than alternative views, by asking what reflective creatures like ourselves should conclude when we become conscious of what Kant would call this "bidding from the outside" affecting our judgments. . . . The very fact of our reflectiveness implies that something must happen—that something must change—when we become conscious of any foreign influence (such as these Darwinian forces) on our evaluative judgments. What that change should be is exactly what I am exploring in this paper.

Where I think the objection goes wrong, then, is as follows. The objection gains its plausibility by suggesting that rational reflection provides some means of standing apart from our evaluative judgments, sorting through them, and gradually separating out the true ones from the false—as if with the aid of some uncontaminated tool. But this picture cannot be right. For what rational reflection about evaluative matters involves, inescapably, is assessing some evaluative judgments in terms of others. Rational reflection must always proceed from some evaluative standpoint; it must work from some evaluative premises; it must treat some evaluative judgments as fixed, if only for the time being, as the assessment of other evaluative judgments is undertaken. In rational reflection, one does not stand completely apart from one's starting fund of evaluative judgments: rather, one *uses* them, reasons in terms of them, holds some of them up for examination in light of others. The widespread consensus that the method of reflective equilibrium, broadly understood, is our sole means of proceeding in ethics is an acknowledgment of this fact: ultimately, we can test our evaluative judgments only by testing their consistency with our other evaluative judgments, combined of course with judgments about the (non-evaluative) facts. Thus, if the fund of evaluative judgments with which human reflection began was thoroughly contaminated with illegitimate influence—and the objector has offered no reason to doubt *this* part of the argument—then the tools of rational reflection were equally contaminated, for the latter are always just a subset of the former. It follows that all our reflection over the ages has really just been a process of assessing evaluative judgments that are mostly off the mark in terms of others

that are mostly off the mark. And reflection of *this* kind isn't going to get one any closer to evaluative truth, any more than sorting through contaminated materials with contaminated tools is going to get one closer to purity. So long as we assume that there is no relation between evolutionary influences and evaluative truth, the appeal to rational reflection offers no escape from the conclusion that, in the absence of an incredible coincidence, most of our evaluative judgments are likely to be false.[7]

6. SECOND HORN OF THE DILEMMA: ASSERTING A RELATION

So let us now turn to the realist's other option, which is to claim that there *is* indeed some relation between the workings of natural selection and the independent evaluative truths that he or she posits. I think this is the more plausible route for the realist to take. After all, we think that a lot of our evaluative judgments are true. We also think that the content of many of these same evaluative judgments has been influenced by natural selection. This degree of overlap between the content of evaluative truth and the content of the judgments that natural selection pushed us in the direction of making begs for an explanation. Since it is implausible to think that this overlap is a matter of sheer chance—in other words, that natural selection just happened to push us toward true evaluative judgments rather than false ones—the only conclusion left is that there is indeed some relation between evaluative truths and selective pressures. The critical question is what *kind* of relation. Different metaethical views will give different answers, and we may judge them according to those answers.

The realist has a possible account of the relation that might seem attractive on its face. It is actually quite clear, the realist might say, how we should understand the relation between selective pressures and independent evaluative truths. The answer is this: we may understand these evolutionary causes as having *tracked* the truth; we may understand the relation in question to be a *tracking* relation. The realist might elaborate on this as follows. Surely, he or she might say, it is advantageous to recognize evaluative truths; surely it promotes one's survival (and that of one's offspring) to be able to grasp what one has reason to do, believe, and feel. As Derek Parfit has put the point: it is possible that "just as cheetahs were selected for their speed, and giraffes for their long necks, the particular feature for which we were selected was our ability to respond to reasons and to rational requirements." According to this hypothesis, our ability to recognize evaluative truths, like the cheetah's speed and the giraffe's long neck, conferred upon us certain advantages that helped us to flourish and reproduce. Thus, the forces of natural selection that influenced the shape of so many of our evaluative judgments need not and should not be viewed as distorting or illegitimate at all. For the evaluative judgments that it proved most selectively advantageous to make are, in general, precisely those evaluative judgments which are true.

Call this proposal by the realist the *tracking account*. The first thing to notice about this account is that it puts itself forward as a scientific explanation.[8] It offers a specific hypothesis as to how the course of natural selection proceeded and what explains the widespread presence of some evaluative judgments rather than others in the human population. In particular, it says that the presence of these judgments is explained by the fact that these judgments are true, and that the capacity to discern such truths proved advantageous for the purposes of survival and reproduction. So, for instance, if it is asked why we observe widespread tendencies to take our own survival and that of our offspring to be valuable, or why we tend to judge that we have special obligations to our children, the tracking account answers that these judgments are true, and that it promoted reproductive success to be able to grasp such truths.

In putting itself forward as a scientific explanation, the tracking account renders itself subject to all the usual standards of scientific evaluation, putting itself in direct competition with all other scientific hypotheses as to why human beings tend to make some evaluative judgments rather than others. The problem for realism is that the tracking account fares quite poorly in this competition. Even fairly brief consideration suggests that another evolutionary explanation of why we tend to make some evaluative judgments rather than others is available, and that this alternative explanation, or something roughly like it, is distinctly superior to the tracking account.

According to what I will call the *adaptive link account,* tendencies to make certain kinds of evaluative judgments rather than others contributed to our ancestors' reproductive success not because they constituted perceptions of independent evaluative truths, but rather because they forged adaptive links between our ancestors' circumstances and their responses to those circumstances, getting them to act, feel, and believe in ways that turned out to be reproductively advantageous. To elaborate: As a result of natural selection, there are in living organisms all kinds of mechanisms that serve to link an organism's circumstances with its responses in ways that tend to promote survival and reproduction. A straightforward example of such a mechanism is the automatic reflex response that causes one's hand to withdraw from a hot surface, or the mechanism that causes a Venus's-flytrap to snap shut on an insect. Such mechanisms serve to link certain kinds of circumstances—the presence of a hot surface or the visit of an insect—with adaptive responses—the immediate withdrawal of one's hand or the closing of the flytrap. Judgments about reasons— and the more primitive, "proto" forms of valuing that we observe in many other animals—may be viewed, from the external standpoint of evolutionary biology, as another such mechanism. They are analogous to the reflex mechanism or the flytrap's apparatus in the sense that they also serve to link a given circumstance with a given response in a way that may tend to promote survival and reproduction. Consider, for example, the evaluative judgment that the fact that someone has helped one is a reason to help that individual in return. Just as we may see a reflex mechanism as effecting a pairing between the circumstance of a hot surface and the response of withdrawing one's hand, so we may view this evaluative judgment as effecting a pairing between the circumstance of one's being helped and the response of helping in return. Both of these pairings of circumstance and response, at least if the evolutionary theory of reciprocal altruism is correct about the latter case, are ones that tended to promote the reproductive success of ancestors who possessed them.[9]

Now of course there are radical differences between the mechanism of a reflex response and the "mechanism" of an evaluative judgment. The former is a brute, hard-wired physical mechanism, while the latter is a conscious mental state, subject to reflection and possible revision in light of that reflection. But this does not change the fact that there is a deep analogy between their functional roles. From an evolutionary point of view, each may be seen as having the same practical point: *to get the organism to respond* to its circumstances in a way that is adaptive. Something like a reflex mechanism does this through a particular hard-wiring of the nervous system, while an evaluative judgment—or a more primitive evaluative experience such as some other animals are likely to have—does this by having the organism experience a particular response as *called for,* or as *demanded by,* the circumstance in question. In the latter case, the link between circumstance and response is forged by our taking of the one thing to be a *reason* counting in favor of the other—that is, by the experience of normativity or value.[10]

For illustration of the differences between the adaptive link account and the tracking account, consider a few examples. Consider, for instance, the judgment that the fact that something would promote one's survival is a reason to do it, the judgment that the fact that someone is kin is a reason to accord him or her special treatment, and the judgment that the fact that someone has harmed one is a reason to shun that person or retaliate. Both the adaptive link account and the tracking account explain the widespread human tendencies to make such judgments by saying that making them somehow contributed to reproductive success in the environment of our ancestors. According to the tracking account, however, making such evaluative judgments contributed to reproductive success because they are *true,* and it proved advantageous to grasp evaluative truths. According to the adaptive link account, on the other hand, making such judgments contributed to

reproductive success not because they were true or false, but rather because they got our ancestors to respond to their circumstances with behavior that itself promoted reproductive success in fairly obvious ways: as a general matter, it clearly tends to promote reproductive success to do what would promote one's survival, or to accord one's kin special treatment, or to shun those who would harm one.

We now have rough sketches of two competing evolutionary accounts of why we tend to make some evaluative judgments rather than others. For reasons that may already have begun to suggest themselves, I believe that the adaptive link account wins this competition hands down, as judged by all the usual criteria of scientific adequacy. In particular, there are at least three respects in which the adaptive link account is superior to the tracking account: it is more parsimonious; it is much clearer; and it sheds much more light on the explanandum in question, namely that human beings tend to make some evaluative judgments rather than others.

Let me start with the parsimony point. The tracking account obviously posits something extra that the adaptive link account does not, namely independent evaluative truths (since it is precisely these truths that the tracking account invokes to explain why making certain evaluative judgments rather than others conferred advantages in the struggle to survive and reproduce). The adaptive link account, in contrast, makes no reference whatsoever to evaluative truth; rather, it explains the advantage of making certain evaluative judgments directly, by pointing out how they got creatures who made them to act in ways that tended to promote reproductive success. Thus, the adaptive link account explains the widespread presence of certain values in the human population more parsimoniously, without any need to posit a role for evaluative truth.

Second, the adaptive link account is much clearer than the tracking account, which turns out to be rather obscure upon closer examination. As we have seen, according to the tracking account, making certain evaluative judgments rather than others promoted reproductive success *because these judgments were true.* But let's now look at this. How exactly is this supposed to work? Exactly why would it promote an organism's reproductive success to grasp the independent evaluative truths posited by the realist? The realist owes us an answer here. It is not enough to say, "Because they are true." We need to know more about *why* it is advantageous to apprehend such truths before we have been given an adequate explanation.

What makes this point somewhat tricky is that on the face of it, it might seem that *of course* it promotes reproductive success to grasp any kind of truth over any kind of falsehood. Surely, one might think, an organism who is aware of the truth in a given area, whether evaluative or otherwise, will do better than one who isn't. But this line of thought falls apart upon closer examination. First consider truths about a creature's manifest surroundings—for example, that there is a fire raging in front of it, or a predator rushing toward it. It is perfectly clear why it tends to promote reproductive success for a creature to grasp such truths: the fire might burn it to a crisp; the predator might eat it up.[11] But there are many other kinds of truths such that it will confer either no advantage or even a disadvantage for a given kind of creature to be able to grasp them. Take, for instance, truths about the presence or absence of electromagnetic wavelengths of the lowest frequencies. For most organisms, such truths are irrelevant to the undertakings of survival and reproduction; hence having an ability to grasp them would confer no benefit. And then one must also take into account the significant costs associated with developing and maintaining such a sophisticated ability. Since for most organisms, this would be energy and resources spent for no gain in terms of reproductive success, the possession of such an ability would actually be positively *disadvantageous.*

With this in mind, let us look again at the evaluative truths posited by realists. Take first the irreducibly normative truths posited by non-naturalist realists . . . A creature obviously can't run into such truths or fall over them or be eaten by them. In what way then would it have promoted the reproductive success of our ancestors to grasp them? The realist owes us an answer here, otherwise his or her alleged explanation of why it promotes reproductive success to make certain judgments in terms of the *truth* of

those judgments is no explanation at all. To say that these truths could kill you or maim you, like a predator or fire, would be one kind of answer, since it makes it clear how recognizing them could be advantageous. But such an answer is clearly not available in the case of the independent irreducibly normative truths posited by the non-naturalist realist. In the absence of further clarification, then, the non-naturalist's version of the tracking account is not only less parsimonious but also quite obscure.

Value naturalists would appear to have better prospects on this point than non-naturalist realists. Since value naturalists construe evaluative facts as natural facts with causal powers, it is much more comprehensible how grasping such facts could have had an impact on reproductive success. . . . The naturalist's proposed version of the tracking account, so far, is this: making some evaluative judgments rather than others tended to promote reproductive success because those judgments constituted perceptions of evaluative facts, which just are a certain kind of natural fact. At least so far, this isn't much of an explanation either. What kinds of natural facts are we talking about, and exactly why did it promote reproductive success to grasp them? The naturalist can certainly try to develop answers to these questions, but at least on the face of things, the prospects appear dim. Take the widespread judgment that one should care for one's offspring, for example. Exactly what natural fact or facts does the evaluative fact that one should care for one's offspring reduce to, or irreducibly supervene upon, and why would perceiving the natural fact or facts in question have promoted our ancestors' reproductive success? It seems unattractive to get into such complexities when one can just say, as the adaptive link account does, that ancestors who judged that they should care for their offspring met with greater reproductive success simply because *they tended to care for their offspring*—and so left more of them.

I've argued that the adaptive link account is both more parsimonious and clearer than the tracking account. My third and final point is that the adaptive link account does a much better job at actually illuminating the phenomenon that is to be explained, namely why there are widespread tendencies among human beings to make some evaluative judgments rather than others. To return to our original questions, why do we tend to judge that our survival is valuable, rather than worthless? Why do we tend to judge that we have special obligations to care for our children, rather than strangers or distant relatives? Why do we tend to view the killing of other human beings as a much more serious matter than the killing of plants or other animals? The adaptive link account has very good answers to such questions, of the general form that ancestors who made evaluative judgments of these kinds, and who as a result tended to respond to their circumstances in the ways demanded by these judgments, did better in terms of reproductive success than their counterparts. It is quite clear why creatures who judged their survival to be valuable would do much better than those who did not, and so on. Now compare the tracking account's explanation. It tries to answer these same questions by saying that these judgments are *true*: that survival *is* valuable, that we *do* have special obligations to care for our children, that the killing of human beings *is* more serious than the killing of plants or other animals. Such answers do not shed much light. In particular, the tracking account fails to answer three questions.

First, how does the tracking account explain the remarkable coincidence that so many of the truths it posits turn out to be exactly the same judgments that forge adaptive links between circumstance and response—the very same judgments we would expect to see if our judgments had been selected on those grounds alone, regardless of their truth? The tracking account has no answer to this question that does not run right back into the parsimony and clarity problems just discussed.

Second, what does the tracking account have to say about our observed predispositions to make other evaluative judgments which (we may decide on reflection) are *not* true? For instance, we observe in human beings a deep tendency to think that the fact that someone is in an "out-group" of some kind is a reason to accord him or her lesser treatment than those in the "in-group." The adaptive link account offers a promising explanation of this, namely that having this evaluative tendency tended to promote reproductive success because those who possessed it tended to shower their assistance on those with a higher degree of genetic relatedness, or on those most able or likely to reciprocate. The tracking account's preferred explanation, however, falls flat, since in this case it is not plausible to answer that this evaluative predisposition developed because it is *true* that the fact that someone is in an "out-group" is a reason to accord him or her lesser treatment than those in the "in-group." More and more, many of us are coming to think that this is not true. The tracking account is thus left with nothing in the way of an explanation as to why we observe such deep tendencies to make the contrary judgment.

Finally, consider the question of all those normative judgments that human beings *could* make but don't. As I have noted, the universe of logically possible evaluative judgments is huge, and we must think of all the possible evaluative judgments that we *don't* see—from the judgment that infanticide is laudable, to the judgment that plants are more valuable than human beings, to the judgment that the fact that something is purple is a reason to scream at it. Here again the adaptive link account has something potentially informative to point out, namely, that such judgments—or evaluative tendencies in these general sorts of directions—forge links between circumstance and response that would have been useless or quite maladaptive as judged in terms of reproductive success. The tracking account has nothing comparably informative to say. It can just stand by and insist that such judgments are false—reaffirming our convictions but adding nothing to our understanding of why we have them.

To sum up, the set of evaluative judgments that human beings tend to affirm appears to be a disparate mishmash, ranging across all kinds of unrelated spheres and reflecting all kinds of unrelated values—some self-interested, others family-related, still others concerning how we should treat non-relatives and other forms of life, and so on. The power of the adaptive link account is that it exposes much of this seeming unrelatedness as an illusion; it illuminates a striking, previously hidden unity behind many of our most basic evaluative judgments, namely that they forge links between circumstance and response that would have been likely to promote reproductive success in the environments of our ancestors. The tracking account has no comparable explanatory power. Its appeal to the truth and falsity of the judgments in question sheds no light on why we observe the specific *content* that we do in human evaluative judgments; in the end, it merely reiterates the point that we *do* believe or disbelieve these things. When we couple this final point with the points about the parsimony and clarity of the adaptive link account as compared to the tracking account, it is clear which explanation we should prefer. The tracking account is untenable.

One last point remains in order to close off the Darwinian Dilemma. The tracking account was the most obvious and natural account for the realist to give of the relation between selective pressures on our evaluative judgments and the independent evaluative truths that he or she posits. In the wake of the tracking account's failure, one might think that the realist still has the option of developing some alternative account of this relation. But this is not so. Rather, insofar as realism asserts any relation at all between selective pressures on our evaluative judgments and evaluative truths, the position is forced to give a tracking account of this relation. The reason for this stems from the very nature of realism itself. The essence of the realist position is its claim that there are evaluative truths that hold independently of all of our evaluative attitudes. But because it views these evaluative truths as ultimately independent of our evaluative attitudes, the only way for realism *both* to accept that those attitudes have been deeply influenced by evolutionary causes *and* to avoid seeing these causes as distorting is for it to claim that these causes actually in some way *tracked* the alleged independent truths. There is no other way to go. To abandon the tracking account—in other words, to abandon the view that selective pressures pushed us *toward* the acceptance of the independent evaluative truths—is just to adopt the view that selective pressures either pushed us *away from* or pushed us in ways that *bear no relation to* these evaluative truths. And to take *this* view is just to land oneself back in the first horn of the dilemma, in which one claims that there is no relation between

selective pressures on our evaluative judgments and the posited independent truths. Realism about value, then, has no escape: it is forced to accept either the tracking account of the relation or else the view that there is no relation at all, and both of these options are unacceptable. . . .

10. HOW ANTIREALISM SIDESTEPS THE DARWINIAN DILEMMA

Let me now sketch how antirealist views on the nature of value sidestep the dilemma for realism that I have described in this paper. Antirealist views understand evaluative facts or truths to be a function of our evaluative attitudes, with different versions of antirealism understanding the exact nature of this function in different ways. For instance, according to the constructivist view . . . the truth of the evaluative judgment that "X is a reason for agent A to Y" is a function of A's evaluative attitudes—in particular, of whether that judgment would be among A's evaluative judgments in reflective equilibrium. Such a view, as I pointed out earlier, leaves room for the possibility of evaluative error. If, for example, A thinks that the fact that someone is a member of some "out-group" is a reason for him to accord that person lesser treatment, then A's judgment is mistaken if that judgment would not be among his evaluative judgments in reflective equilibrium. It is not my purpose to develop or defend such a view here. The point is to give one example of an antirealist view, and to emphasize that antirealist views can leave room for the possibility of evaluative error, even though the standards determining what counts as an error are understood ultimately to be "set" by our own evaluative attitudes.

What then does an antirealist say about the relation between evaluative truths and the evolutionary influences that have shaped our evaluative judgments? First of all, the antirealist opts for what I have said is the more plausible horn of the Darwinian Dilemma, arguing that *of course* there is some relation at work here—of course it is no coincidence that there is such a striking overlap between the content of evaluative truths and the content that natural selection would have tended to push us toward. Of course it's no coincidence that, say, breaking one's bones *is* bad and that's also exactly what evolutionary theory would have predicted we think. But whereas the realist is forced to offer the scientifically unacceptable tracking explanation of this overlap, the antirealist is able to give a very different account.

According to the antirealist, the relation between evolutionary influences and evaluative truth works like this. Each of us begins with a vast and complicated set of evaluative attitudes. We take the breaking of our bones to be bad, we take our children's lives to be valuable, we take ourselves to have reason to help those who help us, and so on. Our holding of each of these evaluative attitudes is assumed by the antirealist to have some sort of causal explanation, just like anything else in the world. And the antirealist grants without hesitation that one major factor in explaining why human beings tend to hold some evaluative attitudes rather than others is the influence of Darwinian selective pressures. In particular, the antirealist has no problem whatsoever with the adaptive link account, if something along those lines turns out to be the best explanation. These and other questions about the best causal explanations of our evaluative attitudes are left in the hands of scientists. Whatever explanation the natural and social scientists ultimately arrive at is granted, and then evaluative truth is understood as a function of the evaluative attitudes we have, however we originally came to have them. Take the constructivist view I've been mentioning as an example. What exactly is the relation between selective pressures and evaluative truth on this view? It may be put this way: evaluative truth is a function of how all the evaluative judgments that selective pressures (along with all kinds of other causes) have imparted to us stand up to scrutiny in terms of each other; it is a function of what would emerge from those evaluative judgments in reflective equilibrium.

Where the realist's tracking account and the antirealist's account divide, then, is over the *direction of dependence* that they take to be involved in the relation between evaluative truths and the evolutionary causes which influenced the content of our evaluative judgments. The realist understands the *evaluative truths* to be prior, in the sense that evolutionary causes are understood to have selected us to track those independent truths. The antirealist, on the other hand, understands the *evolutionary causes* to be prior, in the sense that these causes (along with many others) gave us our starting fund of evaluative attitudes, and evaluative truth is understood to be a function of those attitudes. Both accounts offer an explanation of why it is no coincidence that there is significant overlap between evaluative truths and the kinds of evaluative judgments that natural selection would have pushed us in the direction of. The difference is that the antirealist account of the overlap is consistent with science. Antirealism explains the overlap not with any scientific hypothesis such as the tracking account, but rather with the metaethical hypothesis that value is something that arises as a function of the evaluative attitudes of valuing creatures—attitudes the content of which happened to be shaped by natural selection. The breaking of our bones *is* bad, in other words, and we're well aware of this. But the explanation is not that it is true independently of our attitudes that the breaking of our bones is bad and we were selected to be able to notice this; the explanation is rather that we were selected to *take* the breaking of our bones to be bad, and this evaluative judgment withstands scrutiny from the standpoint of our other evaluative judgments (to speak, for example, in the voice of the constructivist antirealist).

11. CONCLUSION

By understanding evaluative truth as ultimately prior to our evaluative judgments, realism about value puts itself in the awkward position of having to view every causal influence on our evaluative judgments as either a tracking cause or a distorting cause. In the end, this is a difficult position to be in no matter what kind of causal influence is at issue. I have focused on the case of Darwinian influences on our evaluative judgments because I think it raises the problem for realism in a particularly acute form. In principle, however, an analogous dilemma could be constructed using any kind of causal influence on the content of our evaluative judgments. For the argument to work, two conditions must hold. First, the causal influence in question must be extensive enough to yield a skeptical conclusion if the realist goes the route of viewing those causes as distorting. Second, it must be possible to defeat whatever version of the tracking account is put forward with a scientifically better explanation.

At the end of the day, then, the dilemma at hand is not distinctly Darwinian, but much larger. Ultimately, the fact that there are *any* good scientific explanations of our evaluative judgments is a problem for the realist about value. It is a problem because realism must either view the causes described by these explanations as distorting, choosing the path that leads to normative skepticism or the claim of an incredible coincidence, or else it must enter into the game of scientific explanation, claiming that the truths it posits actually play a role in the explanation in question. The problem with this latter option, in turn, is that they don't. The best causal accounts of our evaluative judgments, whether Darwinian or otherwise, make no reference to the realist's independent evaluative truths. . . .

NOTES

1. More broadly, realism about value may be understood as the view that there are *mind-independent* evaluative facts or truths. I focus on independence from our *evaluative attitudes* because it is independence from this type of mental state that is the main point of contention between realists and antirealists about value.

2. My target in this paper is realism about *practical reasons,* or reasons for action, as opposed to *epistemic reasons,* or reasons for belief. While I actually think the Darwinian Dilemma can be extended to apply against realism about epistemic reasons, that topic is more than I'll be able to pursue here. Throughout the paper, I use the word "reason" in the sense of a normative reason—in other words, in the sense of a consideration that *counts in favor of,* or *justifies,* some action.

3. See Shafer-Landau (2003), p. 15. . . .

4. This assumes that other things are equal—for example, that the effects of these evaluative judgments on the creature's behavior are not cancelled out by other

evaluative judgments that the creature makes. The statement in the text also assumes that a creature is motivated to act in accordance with its evaluative judgments, other things being equal. I do not offer an explicit defense of this internalist assumption in this paper, but I take it to be supported by the plausibility of the overall picture that emerges, and by the hypothesis . . . that the function of evaluative judgments from an evolutionary point of view is not to "track" independent evaluative truths, but rather to *get us to respond* to our circumstances in ways that are adaptive.

5. Indeed, it is likely that we were selected above all else to be extremely flexible when it comes to our evaluative judgments—not locked into any particular set of them but rather able to acquire and adjust them in response to the conditions in which we find ourselves. In suggesting that we possess basic evaluative tendencies, then, I am simply suggesting that when it comes to certain core issues such as our individual survival, the treatment of our offspring, and reciprocal relations with others, there are likely to be strong predispositions in the direction of making some evaluative judgments rather than others, for instance (referring back to my earlier lists) judgments (1) through (6) as opposed to judgments (1′) through (6′).

6. This counterfactual claim is all I need for the purposes of my argument. While one might inquire into the exact causal process by which basic evaluative tendencies have influenced the content of human evaluative judgments, it is not necessary for me to enter into such questions here.

7. If one holds that the assessment of (non-evaluative) factual judgments also proceeds via reflective equilibrium, one might wonder why the points in this paragraph don't apply equally well to rational reflection about scientific matters (for example). The key difference is that in the scientific case, our "starting fund" of (non-evaluative) factual judgments need not be viewed as mostly "off track." For further discussion, see note 11 below.

8. This brings out the interesting way in which non-naturalist versions of value realism, in spite of their insistence that values are *not* the kinds of things that play a role in causal explanations, are ultimately forced (unless they opt for the first horn of the dilemma) to take a stand on certain matters of scientific explanation—in particular, on questions about why human beings tend to make some evaluative judgments rather than others, and on the origins of our capacity to grasp independent evaluative truths.

Indeed, as I'll try to show, these realists are forced (again, unless they opt for the first horn) to posit a causal role for evaluative truths in the course of our species' evolution.

9. In order for a mechanism which *effects a pairing* between the circumstance of a hot surface and the response of withdrawing one's hand to be adaptive, there must of course be a means of *detecting* the presence of a hot surface. Similarly, in order for a "mechanism" which *effects a pairing* between the circumstance of one's being helped and the response of helping in return to be adaptive, there must be a means of *detecting* or *tracking* circumstances in which one is helped. In proposing the adaptive link account, what I mean to be focusing in on are the mechanisms which *effect the pairing* between (perceived) circumstance and response, and *not* the mechanisms which do the (separate) job of *tracking circumstances*. While in the case of an automatic reflex mechanism, it may be hard to pull these mechanisms apart, the two jobs are nevertheless theoretically distinct, and the "mechanisms" clearly do come apart in the case of (non-evaluative) factual judgment versus evaluative judgment. Our capacity for (non-evaluative) factual judgment does the job of *tracking circumstances* (tracking, among innumerable other things, which individuals have helped us), whereas our capacity for evaluative judgment does the job of *effecting pairings of (perceived) circumstance and response* (getting us, among many other things, to respond to those who have helped us with help in return).

10. Here I have suggested that it's a certain kind of *conscious experience*—for example, the conscious experience of the fact that someone has helped you as "counting in favor of" helping in return—that does the work of forging adaptive links between

circumstance and response, and which was selected for. But a qualification is needed here, for it may be that this *conscious experience* was not itself directly selected for, but is rather an incidental byproduct of underlying information-processing and behavior-control systems which *were* selected for. If this is so, it does not pose any problem for my argument, since the only point I need for my argument is that the content of our evaluative judgments has been greatly affected by the influence of natural selection. This point still holds even if what was selected for are certain information-processing and behavior-control systems, which in turn give rise, as an incidental byproduct, to conscious experiences—here, in particular, of some things as "counting in favor of" other things.

11. It is points like this which explain why the Darwinian Dilemma doesn't go through against realism about non-evaluative facts such as facts about fires, predators, cliffs, and so on. In short, the difference is that in the case of such non-evaluative facts, unlike in the case of evaluative facts, the tracking account prevails as the best explanation of our capacity to make the relevant sort of judgment. In order to explain why it proved advantageous to form judgments about the presence of fires, predators, and cliffs, one will need to posit in one's best explanation that there *were indeed* fires, predators, and cliffs, which it proved quite useful to be aware of, given that one could be burned by them, eaten by them, or could plummet over them. . . .

REFERENCES

Kant, I. (1959 [1785]): *Foundations of the Metaphysics of Morals,* L.W. Beck (trans.), New York: Macmillan.
Shafer-Landau, R. (2003): *Moral Realism: A Defence,* Oxford: Oxford University Press.

STUDY QUESTIONS

1. Does evolution pose an epistemic threat to moral realism?
2. Does evolution pose an epistemic threat to moral non-cognitivism?
3. Does evolution pose an epistemic threat to the accuracy of non-moral value judgments?
4. Does evolution pose an epistemic threat to the reliability of our senses?

Debunking Evolutionary Debunking

Katia Vavova

Debunking arguments, such as Street's, hold that belief in evolution undermines moral realism. Katia Vavova, Assistant Professor of Philosophy at Mount Holyoke College, argues that Street's argument is unpersuasive, because, were it sound, it would imply epistemological skepticism with regard to all our beliefs. In other words, if belief in evolution debunks moral realism, it debunks not only moral realism but also all claims to knowledge. Given this unacceptable conclusion, Vavova concludes that arguments like Street's should be rejected.

1. THE EVOLUTIONARY CHALLENGE

Worries about the compatibility of evolution and morality are not new—even Darwin had them. A number of recent arguments revive these concerns. These *evolutionary debunking arguments* take the following form: you just believe what you do because you evolved to, therefore you're not justified in believing what you do. They typically target evaluative realism: the view that evaluative facts are attitude-independent—that what is valuable is valuable whether or not we happen to value it.[1]

The worry is that just as evolutionary forces shaped our eyes and ears, so they shaped our evaluative attitudes. But, the debunker argues, we have no reason to think that these forces would track the attitude-independent evaluative truths that the realist posits.[2] Worse yet, we seem to have a good reason to think that they wouldn't: evolution selects for characteristics that increase genetic fitness—not ones that correlate with evaluative truth. Plausibly, the attitudes and judgments that increase a creature's fitness come apart from the true evaluative beliefs. If this is so, then it seems that evolutionary forces have had a distorting effect on our evaluative attitudes. The debunker concludes, insofar as we are realists and insofar as the evolutionary facts are thus-and-so, we are not justified in our evaluative beliefs.

Evolutionary debunking arguments are sometimes meant to establish just this: evaluative skepticism. Other times the skeptical conclusion is in the service of the greater goal of undermining evaluative realism. In either case, the debunker must first establish that learning about the evolutionary origin of our evaluative beliefs gives us, qua realists, good reason to worry about our evaluative beliefs. I will argue that the considerations she puts forth cannot give us such reason. I will conclude that there is little hope for distinctly evolutionary debunking arguments. This is bad news for the debunker who hoped

From Katia Vavova, "Debunking Evolutionary Debunking," in *Oxford Studies in Metaethics* vol. 9, ed. Russ Shafer-Landau (Oxford: Oxford University Press, 2014). Reprinted by permission of the publisher.

that the cold, hard scientific facts about our origins would undermine our evaluative beliefs.

2. THE DEBUNKER'S ARGUMENT

"[T]here can hardly be a doubt," Darwin speculated, that if we had evolved under the same conditions as hive-bees, "our unmarried females would . . .think it a sacred duty to kill their brothers, and mothers would strive to kill their fertile daughters; and no one would think of interfering" (1871: 73). If instead we had evolved as lions did, Street argues, males would have "a strong unreflective evaluative tendency to experience the killing of [other's] off-spring. . .as 'demanded by the circumstances.'" Not only would females lack an "unreflective tendency to 'hold it against' a male when he killed her off-spring," but would tend to become "receptive to his advances soon afterwards" (2006: 121).

These observations are meant to support this counterfactual: if we had evolved differently, we would have believed differently—our evaluative be-liefs, in particular, would have been different. In turn, this counterfactual is meant to support the claim that the content of human evaluative judg-ments has been "tremendously influenced . . . by the forces of natural selection" (Street 2006: 121).

The debunker hopes to use this story to under-mine our evaluative beliefs. We cannot rationally maintain our opinions about good and bad, right and wrong, reasons and values, she argues, once we real-ize from where they came. The debunker thus aims to get somehow from

> INFLUENCE. Evolutionary forces have influ-enced our evaluative beliefs.

to

> REVISION. We cannot rationally maintain our evaluative beliefs.

To be sure, INFLUENCE is not equally worrying for everyone. Anti-realists take the evaluative truths to be attitude-dependent—somehow a function of our (actual, ideally rational, etc.) beliefs and desires. Since anti-realists hold that our values determine what is valuable, they needn't worry from where those values came. Realists are more vulnerable. Since they take the evaluative truths to be indepen-dent of our beliefs and desires, they are committed to the possibility of evaluative error: what we value and what is valuable can come apart. . . .

. . . [T]he question is how to get from INFLU-ENCE to REVISION. To seal this gap, we need to know what is the epistemic significance of the evo-lutionary story for our evaluative beliefs.

In the next sections, I will consider two ways of filling in the debunker's story. I will extract valid arguments to REVISION from both. The first, which Street suggests, is compelling, but too strong for the debunker's purposes. It collapses her challenge into a more general skeptical challenge. The second is more promising and the right way to understand dis-tinctly empirical debunking arguments.

3. DO WE HAVE GOOD REASON TO THINK WE'RE RIGHT?

The evolutionary debunker claims that in some sense of "evolved" and in some sense of "belief," we evolved to hold our evaluative beliefs. The thought is that just as "creatures inveterately wrong in their in-ductions have a pathetic but praiseworthy tendency to die before reproducing their kind" (Quine 1969: 126), so creatures with deep-rooted inclinations to kill themselves and their offspring tend to have quite short evolutionary histories. Given that different evaluative tendencies can have "extremely different effects on a creature's chances of survival and repro-duction," we should expect "over the course of our evolutionary history, relentless selective pressure on the content of our evaluative judgments" (Street 2006: 114).

This is the evolutionary story. The debunker doesn't suggest, implausibly, that evolution directly shaped our more sophisticated evaluative beliefs. The evolutionary story is meant to undermine directly only more basic and less controversial beliefs, like the belief that the fact that something would promote one's survival is a reason in favor of it, or that we have greater obligations to help our own children than complete strangers. But the evolutionary story is also meant to undermine indirectly the rest of our evaluative beliefs, including our much more sophisticated judgments. If our belief that we have reason to avoid inflicting unnecessary suffering goes, so does the moral theory that rests, partly, on it. Hence, the debunker concludes: "our system of evaluative judgments is thoroughly saturated with evolutionary influence" (Street 2006: 114).

This is the empirical claim. No one, not even the debunker, thinks it conclusive.[3] So, why take it seriously? Because the philosophically interesting question is not whether some empirical claim is true, but what follows about the rationality of our beliefs if something like it were true. This question has implications for our epistemology and our metaethics, but it is also of practical interest. Even if the evolutionary debunker fails, some of our other beliefs might reflect some other suspect influence. We need to know how to respond to such evidence if, or when, we do get it.

Grant the evolutionary story for argument's sake. Why should it worry us? Because if it is true, the debunker argues, then the best explanation for why we hold the evaluative judgments we do is that they are adaptive.[4] And this explanation is epistemically unflattering: that we evolved to hold a judgment is no reason to think that it is true.

The debunker then asks: knowing just about the evolutionary origin of our evaluative beliefs and nothing else, do we have reason to think that those beliefs are true? We know that, by hypothesis, evolution selects for adaptive beliefs regardless of their truth. So it may be that the evaluative beliefs we should hold are such-and-such, but that the ones we do hold are this-and-that, because the latter are adaptive and the former aren't. Our evaluative beliefs may, then, be massively mistaken and our origin story gives us no reason to think that they are not.[5]

This is Street's suggestion. Since we evolved to hold our evaluative beliefs, we have no reason to think they are true. Rationality requires we have good reasons for thinking our beliefs are true. So we cannot rationally maintain our evaluative beliefs. Skepticism follows.

This version of the debunker's story relies on a principle like this:

> NO GOOD. If you have no good reason to think that your belief is true, then you cannot rationally maintain it.

Street explicitly endorses a principle like this. She argues that it captures the difference between being hypnotized to believe that Hayes was the nineteenth US president and learning it in school (Forthcoming: 2). In the former case you have no reason to think that the process by which you gained your belief would have led you to form true beliefs. We don't typically think that magicians use their powers of hypnosis for good—to implant in their victims true beliefs about US history. Competent high school teachers, on the other hand, are concerned with just this task. The explanation of your historical beliefs in terms of hypnosis is thus undermining; the one in terms of education is vindicating.

Street argues that evolution is more akin to a careless hypnotist than a teacher. We have no good reason to think that selective pressures would push us toward the truth. Learning about the influence of evolutionary forces on our evaluative beliefs should thus undermine those beliefs.

Many have found this puzzling, insisting that we have plenty of good reasons to think our evaluative beliefs are true. Even if evolution caused us to believe that "pain and injury are bad, and that we have strong reasons to promote the survival and well-being of ourselves and our children," Parfit writes, "these beliefs are not badly mistaken, but correspond to some of the independent normative truths. Pain is bad, and we do have strong reasons to promote the survival and well-being of ourselves and our children" (2011: 533). . . .

. . . Street argues, however, that such assumptions are illegitimate in this context. To presuppose the truth of particular evaluative judgments is to presuppose exactly what the evolutionary story is meant to bring under scrutiny. This is "trivially question-begging," Street argues. Our reasons for thinking that our judgments are true cannot simply assume "the very thing called into question," namely the truth of those judgments (Street MS: 15-16).

Whatever we think of the best version of this response, we should grant that there is something prima facie fishy about it. . . .

If the onus is on us to demonstrate that we are not mistaken, we cannot simply insist that our beliefs are true and count ourselves lucky. We would be like the dogmatist who reasons that since he knows that *p,* any evidence he gets against *p* must be misleading, so he can ignore it.[6] We cannot safeguard our beliefs from defeating evidence like this. Nor can we dismiss the debunker's challenge so easily.

We can now see what the debunker thinks we need if we are to avoid her challenge: a reason to think that we are not mistaken in our evaluative beliefs that doesn't simply presuppose the truth of those beliefs. This reason is, in some sense, independent of what is called into question.

This explains why the debunker asks us to bracket our evaluative beliefs—even those that we know or rationally believe—and to focus only on the origin story. If we do not do this, we stack the deck in our own favor. The danger, of course, is that if we do, then we may well lack reason to think our beliefs aren't mistaken.

3.1 Why NO GOOD Is No Good

The debunker thus needs a "good" reason to be an appropriately "independent" reason. This stringent understanding allows the debunker to dismiss Parfit and claim that we have no good reason to think our evaluative beliefs are right. But if we understand "good" reason this way here, we must understand it in the same way in NO GOOD. This, I will now argue, entails a skepticism far more pervasive than the debunker ever intended.

Start with an explicit statement of this version of the argument.

(1) INFLUENCE. Evolutionary forces have influenced our evaluative beliefs.

(2) We have no good reason to think that our evaluative beliefs are true. [1]

(3) NO GOOD. If you have no good reason to think that your belief is true, then you cannot rationally maintain it.

(4) REVISION. We cannot rationally maintain our evaluative beliefs. [2, 3]

Every premise in this argument is controversial. I granted the first, and I will momentarily grant, for argument's sake, that it somehow entails the second. Do not worry that this concedes too much to the debunker. Such generosity will not give the game away. Focus instead on the third premise. NO GOOD seems compelling because it raises a familiar sort of skeptical challenge. But it also collapses the debunker's challenge into that more ambitious one for which no empirical premise is necessary and which undermines much more than evaluative realism. To see this, consider:

> *Perception.* We come to hold beliefs about our manifest surroundings on the basis of signals that hit our sensory organs.

Unless we are skeptics, we should grant that sensory perception is a perfectly good belief-forming method. *Ceteris paribus,* if you perceive that *p,* you are rational in concluding that *p.* Do we have good reason to think that perception would lead us to true beliefs about our surroundings? Not if "good" reason is understood as an appropriately independent reason: for if we set aside all that is in question, we must set aside all beliefs gained by perception. This includes all scientific beliefs, like the belief that evolutionary theory is true. Without those, we cannot evaluate the rationality of beliefs formed by perception. We can test the reliability of a particular sense modality by granting the reliability of others. We can test our eyes against our ears, and so on. But if we cannot rely on any of our senses, we have nothing with which to evaluate reliability. We have set aside too much.

This might just be what the skeptic aims to demonstrate: that our justifications eventually run out and our beliefs ultimately rest on nothing. This, however, was never the debunker's point. She aimed to undermine a particular, limited set of our beliefs using good scientific evidence that they are mistaken. NO GOOD commits her to much more. If this argument works, it undermines all that we believe and the evolutionary premise drops out. Worse yet, if we aren't justified in believing *anything,* then everything is awful, but there is no special problem for the evaluative realist.

Some have argued that the evolutionary story is not essential to the argument. This is only true in an uninteresting sense: any suspect influence could do the job. It needn't be evolution. But an empirical claim of some sort is essential—this is the distinctive feature of such arguments.[7]

This isn't always made clear. Elsewhere Street begins by pointing to the phenomenally low "odds that among all the possible coherent normative systems, one's own is the right one" (MS: 21). Since there are infinitely many possible coherent normative systems, she argues, it would be a "striking coincidence" if one's own normative system happened to be the correct one (MS: 21). Given that "one has no non-trivially-question-begging evidence that one's own system is the right one," it is unreasonable to conclude that it is (MS: 21). Street thus concludes that we have no good reason to think that our evaluative beliefs are roughly on-track, for we have no reason that does not assume the very thing called into question: the truth of those beliefs.

This version of the debunker's challenge brings nothing new to the table. It demands that we demonstrate that we aren't massively mistaken about morality. Legitimate or not, this is not the debunker's demand. It is just an instance of a general skeptical worry, suspiciously similar to this one:

> *Possibility of Error.* Some possible states of belief are coherent and stable—they look fine "from the inside"—and yet are mistaken. There are infinitely many of these and just one that is right. Furthermore, we have no good reason to think we're not in such a state. So it would be unreasonable for us to be confident that we're not in such a state.[8]

This challenge doesn't and needn't rely on empirical claims. You are asked to justify your entire body of belief—and, on the relevant understanding of "good reason," you must do it without presupposing the truth of any of the beliefs that have been called into question. But all of your beliefs have been called into question, so the skeptic asks you to put them all aside. She then asks: have you one good reason to think that your beliefs are true? You do not, of course. And it isn't because you have some reasons, but they aren't any good. The problem is that once you put aside all that you believe, you don't have any reasons left.[9] You do not even have beliefs, so how could you have reasons?[10]

This challenge can be raised against any subject matter. It isn't peculiar to the evaluative, it isn't uniquely a problem for realism, and it can be raised without empirical premises. If the debunker accepts NO GOOD, she commits herself to the legitimacy of this reasoning. She thus ends up with the conclusion that we should all—regardless of our metaethics—suspend judgment about everything. But that was never her goal.

Focusing on the many coherent evaluative states that we might be in is thus misleading. That there are many such states, and that we have no good reason to think we are in one of the good ones may be a problem, but it isn't the debunker's problem. Her aim is to show, I will now argue, that we have good reason to think that we are in one of the bad states.

4. WHY GOOD IS GOOD

What is the epistemic significance of the evolutionary story for our evaluative beliefs? I argued that it couldn't be that it leaves us with no good reason to think we are not massively mistaken about the evaluative. If we understand a "good reason" as we must, to avoid begging any questions, then we certainly lack such reason. But we lack it for our entire body of beliefs. While that may be a problem, it isn't the debunker's problem. So her point cannot be that we lack good reason to think we're right.

What is her point? It has something to do with the epistemically unflattering picture the evolutionary story paints. What is epistemically un-flattering, however, isn't that we cannot independently establish that these beliefs are right. Rather, it is that in learning this story about the origin of our evaluative beliefs, we get good reason to think that our beliefs are wrong. Since evolutionary forces select for adaptive beliefs—and not true ones—evolution is a bad, potentially distorting influence on our evaluative beliefs. On this alternative line of thought, the problem is not that we cannot dismiss the possibility of error—it is that good scientific evidence makes this possibility more probable.

This version of the debunker's argument is distinct from traditional skeptical arguments since it rests on an empirical claim. It is more selective than traditional skeptical arguments because it targets all and only the suspiciously influenced beliefs. The epistemic principle it relies on is:

GOOD. If you have good reason to think that your belief is mistaken, then you cannot rationally maintain it.[11]

The difference between GOOD and NO GOOD is subtle but crucial. Roughly, it is the difference between taking our beliefs to be innocent until proven guilty and taking them to be guilty until proven innocent. NO GOOD requires you to launch a defense on behalf of your belief; GOOD requires you to hear out the prosecution. Both of these principles can be used to formulate a valid debunking argument, but the debunker should accept GOOD only.

The debunker's point is that evidence of evolutionary influence is evidence of error. When we get such evidence, we must accommodate it with appropriate revision. This is exactly what GOOD expresses. It rightly shifts the burden to the debunker. It isn't up to us to show her that we aren't mistaken. It is the debunker's job to show us that we are mistaken. GOOD reflects this dialectic and provides a plausible link between the discovery that a belief reflects the influence of a suspect process and the conclusion that we cannot rationally maintain that belief.

Earlier we granted, for the sake of argument, that we have no good (independent) reason to think

our evaluative beliefs are not mistaken. With NO GOOD, this entailed that we could not rationally maintain our evaluative beliefs. If we accept GOOD only, the debunker must do more. Our lack of good (independent) reason to think our evaluative beliefs are right leads nowhere without something like NO GOOD. The onus is now on the debunker to show that the evolutionary story supports something stronger. She must do more than merely demand an explanation and watch us squirm. She must show us that we have good reason to think that our evaluative beliefs are mistaken.

A good reason is here, as before, an appropriately independent one. Your evaluation of whether you have good reason to think that you are mistaken about p should not rely on p or on the evidence or arguments on which p is based. This is for the same reason as before: to block a certain kind of question-begging response. If I can take for granted that pain is bad and survival is good, then I have a quick and easy explanation for why evolution is concerned with exactly the attitude-independent moral truths.

The independence requirement is also important here for another reason. Since the onus is now, rightly, on the debunker to give us evidence of error, this evidence should be good evidence we can recognize as such. It should follow from our other beliefs about reasons and evidence. But notice how odd it would be for her to rely on the beliefs she does not allow us to rely on—the ones we are supposedly mistaken about. Her argument would be something like this one: p is probably false, but it entails q, so you should believe q. The debunker cannot simply rely on the beliefs that are supposed to be mistaken—the very same ones she won't let us take for granted. She must build her case upon solid, independent grounds. She thinks she can, but I will argue to the contrary.[12]

Consider first this revised version of the argument:

(5) INFLUENCE. Evolutionary forces have influenced our evaluative beliefs.

(6) MISTAKEN. We have good reason to think that our evaluative beliefs are mistaken. [1]

(7) GOOD. If you have good reason to think that your belief is mistaken, then you cannot rationally maintain it.

(8) REVISION. We cannot rationally maintain our evaluative beliefs. [2, 3]

Every premise of this argument is also controversial, but GOOD is weaker and more plausible than NO GOOD. It provides a framework within which the debunker can pose an appropriately selective and distinctive challenge. It is at least possible to construct the right kind of debunking argument.

The action is now with the second premise: have we, realists, been given good reason to think that our evaluative beliefs are mistaken? . . . I will argue that . . . the debunker fails to give us good reason to think we are mistaken. Since we can then reject the second premise, we aren't pushed into evaluative skepticism.

5. DEBUNKING EVALUATIVE REALISM

The most familiar evolutionary debunking argument targets moral realism, and aims to undermine our beliefs about what we have reason to do. I will start with a more ambitious argument, which aims to undermine evaluative realism wholesale: not just our beliefs about what we have reason to do, but also our beliefs about what we have reason to believe. This debunker thus targets realism about both practical and epistemic reasons.[13]

To see how the trouble is supposed to arise, consider our belief that frequency facts like

[TIGERS] the fact that all previously encountered tigers were carnivorous,

give us reason to believe inductive claims like

[NEXT TIGER] the next tiger we encounter will also be carnivorous.

It is clear why we evolved a tendency to form beliefs like [NEXT TIGER] on the basis of frequency facts like [TIGERS]: if we hadn't, tigers would have eaten us. But why did we evolve to take frequency facts like [TIGERS] as reasons to believe facts like [NEXT TIGER]? Is it because grasping this attitude-independent normative truth was itself adaptive? Unlikely, Street argues: natural selection favored a tendency to take considerations of truth to bear on what to believe "not because it constituted a perception of an independent fact about reasons, but rather simply because it guided the formation of creatures' beliefs in ways that turned out to be advantageous for the purposes of survival and reproduction—in particular, because it got them to believe things that turned out to be true, or at least roughly true, about tigers and much else" (Forthcoming: 17).

In other words, we wouldn't believe that [TIGERS] is a reason for believing [NEXT TIGER] if concluding [NEXT TIGER] on the basis of [TIGERS] weren't to our evolutionary benefit. Since evolution has no interest in the attitude-independent epistemic truth, the beliefs it influences are likely to be mistaken. Insofar as we are realist, the debunker argues, and continue to maintain that what is epistemically valuable is valuable whether or not we value it, we seem pushed to skepticism.

This argument rests on the claim that the same kinds of considerations meant to undermine beliefs like we have reason to take care of our children would also undermine beliefs such as we have reason to believe this rather than that on this evidence. Even as she launches a formidable defense of this claim, arguing both that evolutionary forces influenced our beliefs and that this should worry us, Street admits that this case is much harder to make.

Grant her the first bit again (namely, INFLUENCE) and ask: if evolution had shaped our beliefs about epistemic reasons, would this give us a good epistemic reason to worry about those beliefs? I will argue that it does not and it cannot, for there is a deep structural problem with an argument this ambitious.

The debunker aims to give us good reason to believe that we cannot trust our beliefs about reasons for belief. But this itself—what the debunker wants to give us—is a reason for belief. So we cannot trust it. We are therefore not permitted to take for granted the very thing we need to call our evaluative beliefs into question. This is because, recall, the debunker must give us good independent reason that is, by our own lights, reason to think we are mistaken. But on this version, what we are supposed to be mistaken about includes, crucially, epistemic principles about how to revise our beliefs in light of evidence. We need to take for granted the truth of GOOD and MISTAKEN. Both of these claims, however, are about what we have reason to believe, which is exactly what we're supposed to be mistaken about.

The debunker thus faces a dilemma. She may relax her standards for what counts as a "good" reason, or she may maintain them. If she maintains them, then she cannot give us good reason to think we are mistaken about the evaluative. In short, this is because to evaluate we must rely on the evaluative. But in aiming to debunk all of our evaluative beliefs, the debunker leaves us with nothing with which to evaluate whether those beliefs have been debunked.

If instead the debunker relaxes her understanding of "good reason," then GOOD is back. But so are our other beliefs about epistemic reasons, like the belief that [TIGERS] really does give us reason to believe [NEXT TIGER], and so on. And if we are allowed these assumptions, then the question-begging response Street blocked is open again. . . .

. . . [T]he debunker is in principle incapable of providing evidence of such global error. The *reductio* thus cannot go through. MISTAKEN is false. We do not have good reason to think we are mistaken. The evolutionary story, at least, hasn't given us any.

. . . But perhaps the debunker can sidestep these difficulties and avoid such a fate, if she can narrow her target.

6. DEBUNKING MORAL REALISM

There is more hope for the debunker who aims only at moral realism. Since she does not target our beliefs about epistemic reasons, both GOOD and MISTAKEN are potentially in play. The question is whether she can actually establish the latter—whether she can use her evolutionary story to give us good reason to think we are mistaken about morality. There are two impediments in her way.

The first is that the debunker must show that evolution causes trouble for our moral beliefs only—that there is some disanalogy between this argument and the previous one. But the two arguments are presented as exactly analogous (Street 2009). If the debunker cannot narrow down her target in a principled way, this less ambitious argument collapses into the previous, thereby sharing its fate.

The second is that even an appropriately narrowed challenge calls too much into question. Since it targets all of our moral beliefs, we are left knowing nothing about morality. But how can we tell if we are likely to be mistaken about morality, if we know nothing about it? This concern will occupy the rest of this section. To see it more clearly we need to zoom in to the first inference of the argument.[14]

So far, we have either granted or glossed over the move from INFLUENCE to MISTAKEN. Now we must look closer, for MISTAKEN simply doesn't follow without, at least, reason to be suspicious of the purported influence. As Street puts it:

> [G]enealogical information by itself implies nothing one way or another about whether we should continue to hold a given belief. Rather, in order validly to draw any conclusions about whether or how to adjust one's belief that p, one must assess the rational significance of the genealogical information, locating it in the context of a larger set of premises about what counts as a good reason for the belief that p. (Forthcoming: 2)

Kahane (2011) suggests, as a possible supplementary premise, that evolution is an "off-track" process since, by hypothesis, it doesn't track the attitude-independent evaluative truths. So long as we think that the adaptive beliefs come apart from true beliefs, we can accept this premise. Expanding the argument thus we get:

(1) Evolutionary forces select for creatures with characteristics that increase fitness.

(2) The true evaluative beliefs and the adaptive evaluative beliefs come apart.

(3) Evolutionary forces are off-track: they do not track the evaluative truth. [1, 2]

(4) INFLUENCE. Evolutionary forces have influenced our evaluative beliefs.

(5) OFF-TRACK. Off-track forces have influenced our evaluative beliefs. [3, 4]

If the debunker can establish OFF-TRACK, she is a short step from MISTAKEN. After all, an off-track influence pushes your beliefs in directions having "nothing whatsoever" to do with the truth. Reason to think your belief reflects the influence of an off-track process thus looks like good reason to worry about the truth of that belief. If the above argument gives us good reason to think that our evaluative beliefs reflect an off-track influence, then it seems that we have good reason to think that those beliefs are mistaken. GOOD then takes the debunker home:

(6) MISTAKEN. We have good reason to think that our evaluative beliefs are mistaken. [5]

(7) GOOD. If you have good reason to think that your belief is mistaken, then you cannot rationally maintain it.

(8) REVISION. We cannot rationally maintain our evaluative beliefs. [6, 7]

We've granted INFLUENCE and GOOD. We could resist the inference from OFF-TRACK to MISTAKEN, but we shouldn't. It isn't so controversial: it doesn't say that learning about an off-track influence should all-things-considered worry you; just that it gives you a reason to worry.

Focus instead on OFF-TRACK. To get there, the debunker needs P2: the claim that the evaluative truths and the adaptive beliefs come apart—that there isn't any helpful overlap between these two sets. Why should the realist accept this? Can't she point to an apparently obvious overlap? Pain is bad, survival is good, and these are exactly the things evolution tracks! It may not track the evaluative truth directly, but evolution tracks it indirectly, by selecting for features with which it correlates (cf. Parfit). . . .

Recall that we are meant to be getting good reason to think that we are mistaken about morality. But we cannot determine if we are likely to be mistaken about morality if we can make no assumptions at all about what morality is like. I argued that the debunker's challenge threatens anyone who holds that the attitude-independent moral truths do not, in any helpful way, coincide with the evolutionarily advantageous beliefs—anyone who accepts P2. But even to make this crucial judgment, that these two sets do not have the same contents, we need to know something about the contents of those sets—what they are or what they are like.

Compare: I cannot demonstrate that I am not hopeless at interacting with external objects in my manifest surroundings without knowing something about what those objects and surroundings are like. Likewise, I cannot show that I am not hopeless at understanding right and wrong without being allowed to make some assumptions about what is right and wrong.

If we can make no moral assumptions, then we cannot get P2: the claim that the true evaluative beliefs and the adaptive evaluative beliefs come apart. Now, I think P2 is plausible, and probably you do too. Certainly any realist should believe it. However, we find P2 plausible against the background of our substantive moral beliefs. For example, we believe it is wrong to discriminate against someone on the basis of race. At the same time, there are evolutionary explanations of racism, on which it is adaptive to be suspicious of those who do not look like you. In this case, then, the adaptive belief and the true moral belief come apart. Thus, to believe P2, one must also believe that the evaluative beliefs are such-and-such, while the evaluative truths are this-and-that. But if we cannot take for granted any of our beliefs about the evaluative truths, then we cannot infer that they come apart from the adaptive beliefs.

Again the debunker faces a dilemma. She may relax her standards for what counts as a "good" reason, or she may maintain them. If she relaxes them, she cannot give us good reason to think we are mistaken. Worse yet, if we are permitted to assume that pain is bad, etc., then we can give her good reason to think we are not mistaken and her purportedly undermining story vindicates our evaluative beliefs.

If, instead, the debunker maintains her standards, she blocks such responses. But she also blocks herself. If we cannot make any moral assumptions—not even that pain is bad—then morality could be about anything.[15] To hold that the moral truths do not coincide with the adaptive judgments, we must assume something about what those moral truths are, or are like. If we may assume nothing about morality, then morality could be about anything. And if morality could be about anything, then we have no idea what morality is about. So we have no reason to think that the attitude-independent truths and the adaptive beliefs don't overlap. But without that, we have no sense of what the chances are that we are mistaken. Therefore, we cannot get to the conclusion that we probably are mistaken. Not, at least, via an evolutionary story. . . .

. . . This is good news for the realist. Whatever her epistemic troubles, this scientifically grounded one is not of them.

NOTES

1. . . . For present purposes, evaluative propositions are of the form: that X is a normative reason to Y, that one should or ought to X, that X is good, valuable, or worthwhile, that X is morally right or wrong, and so on. Evaluative attitudes include (conscious or unconscious) beliefs in evaluative propositions, as well "as desires, attitudes of approval and disapproval, unreflective . . . tendencies such as the tendency to experience X as counting in favor of or demanding Y," etc. (Street 2006: 110).
2. From here on I'll drop the "attitude-independent" qualifier on evaluative attitudes or truths.
3. Cf. Street (2006: §3). . . .
4. Cf. Street (2006) on the adaptive link account.
5. There are two relevant ways of understanding "mistaken" here. On the first, a belief is mistaken just in case it is false. On the second, a belief is mistaken just in case it is not supported by the believer's evidence. What sort of mistake does the debunker point to? That's for her to say. I will follow much of the literature and focus on the first. This mostly won't matter for my purposes, but I will make a note when it does.

6. Cf. Harman (1973: 148) and Kripke (2011: 49).
7. Cf. Bedke (MS: 3) and Street (2006: 155).
8. Elga (MS: 7).
9. Do you have anything left with which to even comprehend the skeptic's question? That is another difficulty. There is a more general anti-skeptical strategy in this spirit, most commonly attributed to Wittgenstein (1969). . . .
10. Of course, there is a sense of "reason" on which I can have one even if I do not or cannot believe I have one. For the record, here and throughout, I will use "having a reason" and "believing you have a reason" interchangeably.
11. The caveat from n. 5 is relevant here. I use "mistaken" to mean "false" here, but these principles could be formulated in terms of rationality, justification, or evidential support. e.g.

    GOOD*. If you have good reason to think that your belief is not supported by your evidence, then you cannot rationally maintain it.

12. This is more controversial. . . .
13. Cf. Street (MS) where she argues that the particular normative assumptions in question are not needed for either raising or responding to the challenge.
14. Cf. Street (2009).
15. In fact, the previous debunker faces an exactly analogous problem: if we know nothing about the evaluative, how can we tell we are likely to be mistaken about it?
16. You might worry here that we are even talking about morality any more. The debunker assumes that morality really could be about anything—it is conceptually possible that morality is about throwing ourselves off of cliffs and causing each other pain. I'm not so sure about this. Cuneo and Shafer-Landau (MS) argue that some of the very basic moral claims (like that pain is bad) are conceptual truths: if we don't have them we don't have our concept of "morality." This seems right to me, but I won't explore it further here.

REFERENCES

Bedke, M. MS. "No Coincidence?" draft for Wisconsin Metaethics Workshop 2012. See Chapter, this volume.
Cuneo, T., and Shafer-Landau, R. MS. "The Moral Fixed Points."
Darwin, C. 1871. *The Works of Charles Darwin*, xxi. Albany, NY: NYU Press, 2010.

Elga, A. MS. "Lucky to be Rational," draft as of 6 June 2008.

Harman, G. 1973. *Thought.* Princeton: Princeton University Press.

Kahane, G. 2011. "Evolutionary Debunking Arguments," *Noûs,* 14(1): 103–25.

Kripke, S. 2011. "On Two Paradoxes of Knowledge," in *Philosophical Troubles: Collected Papers,* i. 27–51. Oxford: Oxford University Press.

Parfit, D. 2011. *On What Matters,* ii. Oxford: Oxford University Press.

Quine, W. 1969. "Natural Kinds," in *Ontological Relativity and Other Essays,* 114–38. New York: Columbia University Press.

Street, S. MS. "Objectivity and Truth: You'd Better Rethink it."

Street, S. 2006. "A Darwinian Dilemma for Realist Theories of Value," *Philosophical Studies,* 127: 109–66.

Street, S. 2009. "Evolution and the Normativity of Epistemic Reasons," *Canadian Journal of Philosophy,* 39, supplement 1: 213–48.

Street, S. Forthcoming. "Does Anything Really Matter or Did We Just Evolve to Think So?" in A. Byrne, J. Cohen, G. Rosen, and S. Shiffrin (eds), *The Norton Introduction to Philosophy.* New York: W. W. Norton.

Wittgenstein, L. 1969. *On Certainty,* ed. G. E. M. Anscombe and G. H. von Wright. Oxford: Basil Blackwell.

STUDY QUESTIONS

1. What is the general form of an evolutionary debunking argument?
2. Is moral realism especially vulnerable to a debunking argument?
3. Are all value judgments more vulnerable to debunking than scientific beliefs?
4. Is our belief that pain is bad subject to debunking?

Part XI

MORAL EXPLANATIONS

The Nature of Morality

Gilbert Harman

Gilbert Harman is Professor of Philosophy at Princeton University. He argues that moral beliefs are incapable of the sort of empirical confirmation characteristic of scientific beliefs. Scientific observations provide evidence for physical theories, because the observations are best explained by the observer's psychology as well as facts about the world. By contrast, moral observations do not provide evidence for ethical theories, because the observations are best explained by the observer's psychology regardless of any moral facts. This asymmetry suggests moral nihilism: the absence of moral facts, moral truths, and moral knowledge. Harman believes, however, that just as non-moral evaluations, such as "a good watch" or "a good teacher," can rest on facts about the world, so moral evaluations may do so also. Yet for Harman, specifying such facts remains problematic.

ETHICS AND OBSERVATION

1. The Basic Issue

Can moral principles be tested and confirmed in the way scientific principles can? Consider the principle that, if you are given a choice between five people alive and one dead or five people dead and one alive, you should always choose to have five people alive and one dead rather than the other way round. We can easily imagine examples that appear to confirm this principle. Here is one:

You are a doctor in a hospital's emergency room when six accident victims are brought in. All six are in danger of dying but one is much worse off than the others. You can just barely save that person if you devote all of your resources to him and let the others die. Alternatively, you can

save the other five if you are willing to ignore the most seriously injured person.

It would seem that in this case you, the doctor, would be right to save the five and let the other person die. So this example, taken by itself, confirms the principle under consideration. Next, consider the following case.

You have five patients in the hospital who are dying, each in need of a separate organ. One needs a kidney, another a lung, a third a heart, and so forth. You can save all five if you take a single healthy person and remove his heart, lungs, kidneys, and so forth, to distribute to these five patients. Just such a healthy person is in Room 306. He is in the hospital for routine tests. Having seen his test results, you know that he is perfectly healthy and of the right

From Gilbert Harman, *The Nature of Morality* (New York: Oxford University Press, 1977). Reprinted by permission of the publisher.

tissue compatibility. If you do nothing, he will survive without incident; the other patients will die, however. The other five patients can be saved only if the person in Room 306 is cut up and his organs distributed. In that case, there would be one dead but five saved.

The principle in question tells us that you should cut up the patient in Room 306. But in this case, surely you must not sacrifice this innocent bystander, even to save the five other patients. Here a moral principle has been tested and disconfirmed in what may seem to be a surprising way.

This, of course, was a "thought experiment." We did not really compare a hypothesis with the world. We compared an explicit principle with our feelings about certain imagined examples. In the same way, a physicist performs thought experiments in order to compare explicit hypotheses with his "sense" of what should happen in certain situations, a "sense" that he has acquired as a result of his long working familiarity with current theory. But scientific hypotheses can also be tested in real experiments, out in the world.

Can moral principles be tested in the same way, out in the world? You can observe someone do something, but can you ever perceive the rightness or wrongness of what he does? If you round a corner and see a group of young hoodlums pour gasoline on a cat and ignite it, you do not need to *conclude* that what they are doing is wrong; you do not need to figure anything out; you can *see* that it is wrong. But is your reaction due to the actual wrongness of what you see or is it simply a reflection of your moral "sense," a "sense" that you have acquired perhaps as a result of your moral upbringing?

2. Observation

The issue is complicated. There are no pure observations. Observations are always "theory laden." What you perceive depends to some extent on the theory you hold, consciously or unconsciously. You see some children pour gasoline on a cat and ignite it. To really see that, you have to possess a great deal of knowledge, know about a considerable number of

objects, know about people: that people pass through the life stages infant, baby, child, adolescent, adult. You must know what flesh and blood animals are, and in particular, cats. You must have some idea of life. You must know what gasoline is, what burning is, and much more. In one sense, what you "see" is a pattern of light on your retina, a shifting array of splotches, although even that is theory, and you could never adequately describe what you see in that sense. In another sense, you see what you do because of the theories you hold. Change those theories and you would see something else, given the same pattern of light.

Similarly, if you hold a moral view, whether it is held consciously or unconsciously, you will be able to perceive rightness or wrongness, goodness or badness, justice or injustice. There is no difference in this respect between moral propositions and other theoretical propositions. If there is a difference, it must be found elsewhere.

Observation depends on theory because perception involves forming a belief as a fairly direct result of observing something; you can form a belief only if you understand the relevant concepts and a concept is what it is by virtue of its role in some theory or system of beliefs. To recognize a child as a child is to employ, consciously or unconsciously, a concept that is defined by its place in a framework of the stages of human life. Similarly, burning is an empty concept apart from its theoretical connections to the concepts of heat, destruction, smoke, and fire.

Moral concepts—Right and Wrong, Good and Bad, Justice and Injustice—also have a place in your theory or system of beliefs and are the concepts they are because of their context. If we say that observation has occurred whenever an opinion is a direct result of perception, we must allow that there is moral observation, because such an opinion can be a moral opinion as easily as any other sort. In this sense, observation may be used to confirm or disconfirm moral theories. The observational opinions that, in this sense, you find yourself with can be in either agreement or conflict with your consciously explicit moral principles. When they are in conflict, you must choose between your explicit theory and observation. In ethics, as in science, you sometimes opt for theory, and say that you made an error in observation or were biased or whatever, or you sometimes opt for observation, and modify your theory.

In other words, in both science and ethics, general principles are invoked to explain particular cases and, therefore, in both science and ethics, the general principles you accept can be tested by appealing to particular judgments that certain things are right or wrong, just or unjust, and so forth; and these judgments are analogous to direct perceptual judgments about facts.

3. Observational Evidence

Nevertheless, observation plays a role in science that it does not seem to play in ethics. The difference is that you need to make assumptions about certain physical facts to explain the occurrence of the observations that support a scientific theory, but you do not seem to need to make assumptions about any moral facts to explain the occurrence of the so-called moral observations I have been talking about. In the moral case, it would seem that you need only make assumptions about the psychology or moral sensibility of the person making the moral observation. In the scientific case, theory is tested against the world.

The point is subtle but important. Consider a physicist making an observation to test a scientific theory. Seeing a vapor trail in a cloud chamber, he thinks, "There goes a proton." Let us suppose that this is an observation in the relevant sense, namely, an immediate judgment made in response to the situation without any conscious reasoning having taken place. Let us also suppose that this observation confirms his theory, a theory that helps give meaning to the very term "proton" as it occurs in his observational judgment. Such a confirmation rests on inferring an explanation. He can count his making the observation as confirming evidence for his theory only to the extent that it is reasonable to explain his making the observation by assuming that, not only is he in a certain psychological "set," given the theory he accepts and his beliefs about the experimental apparatus, but furthermore, there really was a proton going through the cloud chamber, causing the vapor trail, which he saw as a proton. (This is evidence for the theory to the extent that the theory can explain the proton's being there better than competing theories can.) But, if his having made that observation could have been equally well explained by his psychological set alone, without the need for any assumption about a proton, then the observation would not have been evidence for the existence of that proton and therefore would not have been evidence for the theory. His making the observation supports the theory only because, in order to explain his making the observation, it is reasonable to assume something about the world over and above the assumptions made about the observer's psychology. In particular, it is reasonable to assume that there was a proton going through the cloud chamber, causing the vapor trail.

Compare this case with one in which you make a moral judgment immediately and without conscious reasoning, say, that the children are wrong to set the cat on fire or that the doctor would be wrong to cut up one healthy patient to save five dying patients. In order to explain your making the first of these judgments, it would be reasonable to assume, perhaps, that the children really are pouring gasoline on a cat and you are seeing them do it. But, in neither case is there any obvious reason to assume anything about "moral facts," such as that it really is wrong to set the cat on fire or to cut up the patient in Room 306. Indeed, an assumption about moral facts would seem to be totally irrelevant to the explanation of your making the judgment you make. It would seem that all we need assume is that you have certain more or less well articulated moral principles that are reflected in the judgments you make, based on your moral sensibility. It seems to be completely irrelevant to our explanation whether your intuitive immediate judgment is true or false.

The observation of an event can provide observational evidence for or against a scientific theory in the sense that the truth of that observation can be relevant to a reasonable explanation of why that observation was made. A moral observation does not seem, in the same sense, to be observational evidence for or against any moral theory, since the truth or falsity of the moral observation seems to be completely irrelevant to any reasonable explanation of why that observation was made. The fact that an observation of an event was made at the time it was made is evidence not only about the observer but also about the physical facts. The fact that you made a particular moral observation when you did does not seem to be evidence about moral facts, only evidence about you and your moral sensibility. Facts about protons can affect what you observe, since a proton passing through the cloud chamber can cause a vapor trail that reflects light to your eye in a way that, given your scientific training and psychological set, leads you to judge that what you see is a proton. But there does not seem to be any way in which the actual rightness or wrongness of a given situation can have any effect on your perceptual apparatus. In this respect, ethics seems to differ from science.

In considering whether moral principles can help explain observations, it is therefore important to note an ambiguity in the word "observation." You see the children set the cat on fire and immediately think, "That's wrong." In one sense, your observation is that what the children are doing is wrong. In another sense, your observation is your thinking that thought. Moral observations might explain observations in the first sense but not in the second sense. Certain moral principles might help to explain why it was *wrong* of the children to set the cat on fire, but moral principles seem to be of no help in explaining *your thinking* that that is wrong. In the first sense of "observation," moral principles can be tested by observation—"That this act is wrong is evidence that causing unnecessary suffering is wrong." But in the second sense of "observation," moral principles cannot clearly be tested by observation, since they do not appear to help explain observations in this second sense of "observation." Moral principles do not seem to help explain your observing what you observe.

Of course, if you are already given the moral principle that it is wrong to cause unnecessary suffering, you can take your seeing the children setting the cat on fire as observational evidence that they are doing something wrong. Similarly, you can suppose that your seeing the vapor trail is observational evidence that a proton is going through

the cloud chamber, if you are given the relevant physical theory. But there is an important apparent difference between the two cases. In the scientific case, your making that observation is itself evidence for the physical theory because the physical theory explains the proton, which explains the trail, which explains your observation. In the moral case, your making your observation does not seem to be evidence for the relevant moral principle because that principle does not seem to help explain your observation. The explanatory chain from principle to observation seems to be broken in morality. The moral principle may "explain" why it is wrong for the children to set the cat on fire. But the wrongness of that act does not appear to help explain the act, which you observe, itself. The explanatory chain appears to be broken in such a way that neither the moral principle nor the wrongness of the act can help explain why you observe what you observe.

A qualification may seem to be needed here. Perhaps the children perversely set the cat on fire simply "because it is wrong." Here it may seem at first that the actual wrongness of the act does help explain why they do it and therefore indirectly helps explain why you observe what you observe just as a physical theory, by explaining why the proton is producing a vapor trail, indirectly helps explain why the observer observes what he observes. But on reflection we must agree that this is probably an illusion. What explains the children's act is not clearly the actual wrongness of the act but, rather, their belief that the act is wrong. The actual rightness or wrongness of their act seems to have nothing to do with why they do it.

Observational evidence plays a part in science it does not appear to play in ethics, because scientific principles can be justified ultimately by their role in explaining observations, in the second sense of observation—by their explanatory role. Apparently, moral principles cannot be justified in the same way. It appears to be true that there can be no explanatory chain between moral principles and particular observings in the way that there can be such a chain between scientific principles and particular observings. Conceived as an explanatory theory, morality, unlike science, seems to be cut off from observation.

Not that every legitimate scientific hypothesis is susceptible to direct observational testing. Certain hypotheses about "black holes" in space cannot be directly tested, for example, because no signal is emitted from within a black hole. The connection with observation in such a case is indirect. And there are many similar examples. Nevertheless, seen in the large, there is the apparent difference between science and ethics we have noted. The scientific realm is accessible to observation in a way the moral realm is not.

4. Ethics and Mathematics

Perhaps ethics is to be compared, not with physics, but with mathematics. Perhaps such a moral principle as "You ought to keep your promises" is confirmed or disconfirmed in the way (whatever it is) in which such a mathematical principle as "5 + 7 = 12" is. Observation does not seem to play the role in mathematics it plays in physics. We do not and cannot perceive numbers, for example, since we cannot be in causal contact with them. We do not even understand what it would be like to be in causal contact with the number 12, say. Relations among numbers cannot have any more of an effect on our perceptual apparatus than moral facts can.

Observation, however, *is* relevant to mathematics. In explaining the observations that support a physical theory, scientists typically appeal to mathematical principles. On the other hand, one never seems to need to appeal in this way to moral principles. Since an observation is evidence for what best explains it, and since mathematics often figures in the explanations of scientific observations, there is indirect observational evidence for mathematics. There does not seem to be observational evidence, even indirectly, for basic moral principles. In explaining why certain observations have been made, we never seem to use purely moral assumptions. In this respect, then, ethics appears to differ not only from physics but also from mathematics.

In what follows, we will be considering a number of possible responses to the apparent fact that ethics is cut off from observational testing in a way that science is not. Some of these responses claim that there is a distinction of this sort between science and ethics and try to say what its implications are. Others deny that there is a distinction of this sort between science and ethics and argue that ethics is not really exempt from observational testing in the way it appears to be.

NIHILISM AND NATURALISM

1. Moral Nihilism

We have seen that observational evidence plays a role in science and mathematics it does not seem to play in ethics. Moral hypotheses do not help explain why people observe what they observe. So ethics is problematic and nihilism must be taken seriously. Nihilism is the doctrine that there are no moral facts, no moral truths, and no moral knowledge. This doctrine can account for why reference to moral facts does not seem to help explain observations, on the grounds that what does not exist cannot explain anything.

An extreme version of nihilism holds that morality is simply an illusion: nothing is ever right or wrong, just or unjust, good or bad. In this version, we should abandon morality, just as an atheist abandons religion after he has decided that religious facts cannot help explain observations. Some extreme nihilists have even suggested that morality is merely a superstitious remnant of religion.

Such extreme nihilism is hard to accept. It implies that there are no moral constraints—that everything is permitted. As Dostoyevsky observes, it implies that there is nothing wrong with murdering your father. It also implies that slavery is not unjust and that Hitler's extermination camps were not immoral. These are not easy conclusions to accept.

This, of course, does not refute extreme nihilism. Nihilism does not purport to reflect our ordinary views; and the fact that it is difficult to believe does not mean that it must be false. At one time in the history of the world people had difficulty in believing that the earth was round; nevertheless the earth was round. A truly religious person could not easily come to believe that God does not exist; that is no argument against atheism. Extreme nihilism is a possible view and it deserves to be taken seriously.

On the other hand, it is also worth pointing out that extreme nihilism is not an automatic consequence of the point that moral facts apparently cannot help explain observations. Although this is grounds for nihilism, there are more moderate versions of nihilism. Not all versions imply that morality is a delusion and that moral judgments are to be abandoned the way an atheist abandons religious judgments. Thus, a more moderate nihilism holds that the purpose of moral judgments is not to describe the world but to express our moral feelings or to serve as imperatives we address to ourselves and to others. In this view, morality is not undermined by its apparent failure to explain observations, because to expect moral judgments to be of help in explaining observations is to be confused about the function of morality. It is as if you were to expect to explain observations by exclaiming, "Alas!" or by commanding, "Close the door!"

Moderate nihilism is easier to accept than extreme nihilism. It allows us to keep morality and continue to make moral judgments. It does not imply that there is nothing wrong with murdering your father, owning slaves, or setting up extermination camps. Because we disapprove of these activities, we can, according to moderate nihilism, legitimately express our disapproval by saying that they are wrong.

Moderate nihilism, nevertheless, still conflicts with common sense, even if the conflict is less blatant. To assert, as even moderate nihilists assert, that there are no moral facts, no moral truths, and no moral knowledge is to assert something that runs counter to much that we ordinarily think and say. If someone suggests that it was wrong of members of the Oregon Taxpayers Union to have kidnapped Sally Jones in order to get at her father, Austin P. Jones, and you agree, you will express your agreement by saying, "That's *true!*" Similarly, in deciding what to do on a particular occasion, you say such things as this, "I *know* that I should not break my promise to Herbert, but I really would like to go to the beach today." We ordinarily do speak of moral judgments as true or false; and we talk as if we knew certain moral truths but not others.

Nihilism, then, extreme or moderate, is in conflict with ordinary ways of talking and thinking. Although such a conflict does not refute a theory, we must ask whether we can accommodate the point about ethics and observation without having to give up our ordinary views and endorsing some form of nihilism.

2. Reductions

Our previous discussion suggests the following argument for moral nihilism:

Moral hypotheses never help explain why we observe anything. So we have no evidence for our moral opinions.

The argument depends upon this assumption:

We can have evidence for hypotheses of a certain sort only if such hypotheses sometimes help explain why we observe what we observe.

But that assumption is too strong. Hypotheses about the average American citizen never help explain why we observe anything about a particular American, but we can obtain evidence for such hypotheses by obtaining evidence for hypotheses about American citizens. The reason is that facts about the average American citizen are definable in terms of facts about American citizens. Facts of the first sort are constructed out of and therefore reducible to facts of the second sort. Even if assumptions about moral facts do not directly help explain observations, it may be that moral facts can be reduced to other sorts of facts and that assumptions about these facts do help explain observations. In that case, there could be evidence for assumptions about moral facts.

To take another example, we might be able to account for color perception without making the supposition that objects actually have colors. For we might be able to explain how objects whose surfaces have certain physical characteristics will reflect light of a particular wavelength; this light then strikes the retina of an observer's eye, affecting him in a way that might be described by an adequate neuro-physiological psychology. That is, we might be able to explain perception of color entirely in terms of the physical characteristics of the objects perceived and the properties of light together with an account of the perceptual apparatus of the observer. This would not prove that there are no facts about colors; it would only show that facts about colors are not additional facts, over and above physical and psychological facts. If we could explain color perception in this way, we would conclude that facts about color are somehow reducible to facts about the physical characteristics of perceived objects, facts about light, and facts about the psychology and perceptual apparatus of perceivers. We might consider whether moral facts are in a similar way constructible out of or reducible to certain other facts that can help explain our observations.

3. Ethical Naturalism: Functionalism

This is certainly a plausible suggestion for certain nonmoral evaluative facts. Consider, for example, what is involved in something's being a good thing of its kind, a good knife, a good watch, or a good heart. Associated with these kinds of things are certain functions. A knife is something that is used for cutting; a watch is used to keep time; a heart is that organ that pumps the blood. Furthermore, something is a good thing of the relevant kind to the extent that it adequately fulfills its proper function. A good knife cuts well; a good watch keeps accurate time; a good heart pumps blood at the right pressure without faltering. Let us use the letter "K" to stand for a kind of thing. Then, for these cases, a good K is a K that adequately fulfills its function. It is a factual question whether or not something is a good K because it is a factual question whether or not K's have that function and a factual question whether or not this given something adequately fulfills that function.

Moreover, a K ought to fulfill its function. If it does not do so, something has gone wrong. Therefore, it is a factual question whether a given K of this sort is as it ought to be and does what it ought to do, and it is a factual question whether anything is wrong with a K of this sort. A knife ought to be sharp, so that it will cut well. There is something

wrong with a heart that fails to pump blood without faltering.

There are, of course, two somewhat different cases here, artifacts, such as watches and knives, and parts of natural systems, such as hearts. The functions of artifacts are determined by their makers and users. The functions of parts of natural systems are determined by their roles in sustaining those systems. In either case, though, it is a factual question what the relevant function of a K is.

Let us next consider a somewhat different range of cases: a good meal, a good swim, a good time. We might stretch a point and say that meals, swims, and times have functions or purposes; but it would be more accurate to say that they can answer to certain interests. We judge that particular meals, swims, or times are good inasmuch as they answer to the relevant interests. Where different sets of interests are relevant, we get ambiguity: "a good meal" may mean a nourishing meal or a tasty meal.

With this range of cases, "ought" and "wrong" are used as before. A good meal ought to be balanced (or tasty). There is something wrong with a steak that is not tender and juicy.

More complex cases involve roles that a person can have in one way or another: a good farmer, a good soldier, a good teacher, a good citizen, a good thief. A person is evaluated in terms of functions, roles, and various interests in a way that is hard to specify. Here too the words "ought" and "wrong" are relevant as before. During battle, we say, a soldier ought to obey his superior officers without question. It is wrong for a teacher to play favorites. A thief ought to wear gloves.

Some kinds of things are not associated with functions, purposes, or sets of interests; for example, rocks per se are not. Therefore, it does not make sense to ask apart from a specific context whether something is a good rock. We can answer such a question only in relation to interests that we might have in possible uses of the rock. For example, it might be a good rock to use as a paperweight; but, if it is to be used as a doorstop, maybe it ought to be heavier.

The relevant evaluative judgments are factual. The facts are natural facts though somewhat complex facts. We judge that something is good or bad, that it is right or wrong, that it ought or ought not to have certain characteristics or do certain things, relative to a cluster of interests, roles and functions. We can abbreviate this by saying that something X is good to the extent that it adequately answers to the relevant interests. To specify those interests is to specify what X is good as. Similarly, a person P ought to do D if and only if P's doing D would answer to the relevant interests.

This analysis is a realistic one for many cases and it suggests how evaluative facts might be constructed out of observable facts even when the evaluative facts themselves do not figure in explanations of observations. That my watch is a good one may not explain anything about my observations of it; but that it keeps fairly accurate time does help to explain its continual agreement with the announcements of the time on the radio and perhaps the goodness of my watch consists in facts of this sort.

But a problem manifests itself when this sort of analysis is applied in ethics. Consider the case in which you are a doctor who either can save five patients by cutting up the healthy patient in Room 306 and distributing his organs to the other patients or can do nothing and let the five other patients die. The problem is that in either case you would be satisfying certain interests and not others. The interests of the five dying patients conflict with the interests of the healthy patient in Room 306. The moral question is what you ought to do, taking all interests into account. As we saw earlier, our intuitive judgment is that you ought not to sacrifice the one patient in Room 306 to save the five other patients. Is this a factual judgment? If we suppose that it is a fact that you ought not to sacrifice the patient in Room 306, how is that fact related to facts that can help explain observations? It is not at all obvious how we can extend our analysis to cover this sort of case.

Actually, the problem is not peculiar to ethics. Is a heavy, waterproof, shockproof watch that can withstand a considerable amount of pressure a better or worse watch than a lighter, graceful, delicate watch without those features? Is one teacher better or worse than a second if the first teacher makes students unhappy while teaching them more?

To some extent, our difficulty in these cases lies in the vagueness of our standards for watches and teachers. Often we can resolve the vagueness by specifying relevant interests. The heavy watch is a better watch for deep-sea diving. The lighter watch is better for social occasions, out of the water. In the case of evaluating teachers, we must decide what we want from teachers—perhaps that their students should learn a certain minimal amount and, given that they learn at least that much, that they not be made miserable. But even given further specifications of our interests in watches and teachers in this way, there may be no fact of the matter as to which watch or teacher is better—not because these are not factual questions but because of vagueness of standards. Factual questions are still factual even when they cannot be answered because of vagueness. (Is a door open or shut if it is slightly ajar?) Furthermore, even in cases where we feel intuitively that one watch or teacher is clearly better, we may not be able to specify very clearly the interests, functions, and roles with reference to which one is better, as a watch or teacher, than the other. Still, it may well be a fact that one is better—a fact constructed in a way that we can only vaguely specify from facts of a sort that can help explain observations.

Similarly, it *may* be that moral facts, such as the fact that you ought not to sacrifice the healthy patient in Room 306 to save the five other patients, can be constructed in some way or other out of facts of a sort that can explain observations, even though we can only vaguely indicate relevant roles, interests, and functions.

That would vindicate ethical naturalism, which is the doctrine that moral facts are facts of nature. Naturalism as a general view is the sensible thesis that *all* facts are facts of nature. Of course, one can accept naturalism in general without being committed to ethical naturalism, since one can instead be a nihilist and deny that there are any moral facts at all, just as one might deny that there are any religious facts. Naturalists must be either ethical nihilists or ethical naturalists. The question is how do we decide between ethical nihilism and ethical naturalism, and there is no simple answer. If an analysis of moral facts as facts about functions, roles, and interests could be made plausible, that would be a powerful argument for ethical naturalism. But the relevant functions, roles, and interests can at best be only vaguely indicated, so the proposed analysis is difficult to evaluate. Nihilism remains a possibility.

4. The Open Question Argument

On the other hand, general arguments against ethical naturalism, and for nihilism, are also inconclusive. For example, moderate nihilists argue that naturalists misconstrue the function of moral judgments, which is not to describe the facts (they say) but rather to express the speaker's approval or disapproval. Therefore, moderate nihilists say that ethical naturalism involves a "naturalistic fallacy." But as we shall see, the evaluation of this moderate nihilist position is also quite complex.

An ethical naturalist holds that there are moral facts and that these can be "reduced" to natural facts of a sort that might explain observations in the way that facts about color might be reduced to facts about physical characteristics of objects, the properties of light, and the perceptual apparatus of an observer. I have alluded to one way in which an ethical naturalist might attempt such a reduction by appealing to functions, roles, and interests. There are also other ways: he might, for example, try to develop an "ideal observer" theory of moral facts by analogy with the suggested theory of color facts. . . . And other kinds of ethical naturalism are also possible. Now, some moderate nihilists believe that there is a perfectly general argument that can be used once and for all to show that any version of ethical naturalism must fail. This is the so-called "open question argument." Any naturalistic reduction in ethics would have the form, "P ought to do D if and only if P's doing D has characteristics C," in which the characteristics C are naturalistic characteristics of a sort that can help explain observations. Given any such proposed naturalistic reduction, defenders of the open question argument maintain that the following question remains open.

I agree that for P to do D would be for P to do something that is C, but ought P to do D?

This remains an open question, moderate nihilists say, because describing an act is not the same as endorsing it. No matter how you describe it, you have so far not endorsed it and, therefore, have not yet said whether it ought to be done, according to moderate nihilists. Therefore, the displayed question is (they assert) an open question in a way that the following question is not.

I agree that P ought to do D, but ought P to do D?

This question is obviously foolish. Given that something ought to be done, it cannot be an open question whether it ought to be done. And since the first question is an open question but the second is not, we are to conclude that the natural characteristic of being an act that is C cannot be equated with the moral characteristic of being an act that ought to be done.

One problem with this argument is that it has to be shown that the first question is always open. An ethical nihilist is simply begging the question if he only says, in arguing against ethical naturalism, that describing an act as having certain natural characteristics cannot amount to endorsing the act in the sense of saying that it ought to be done. It is not obvious, for example, that the following question is open in the relevant sense.

I agree that, if P does D, P will satisfy the relevant interests, but ought P to do D?

Of course, one part of the problem here is that the "relevant interests" are not specified in a precise naturalistic way. Nevertheless, it is not obvious that, if they are so specified, the question is open.

More important, perhaps, is the fact that as it stands the open question argument is invalid. An analogous argument could be used on someone who was ignorant of the chemical composition of water to "prove" to him that water is not H_2O. This person will agree that it is not an open question whether water is water but it is an open question, at least for him, whether water is H_2O. Since this argument would not show that water is not H_2O, the open question argument in ethics cannot be used as it stands to show that for an act to be an act that ought to be done is not for it to have some natural characteristic C.

The open question argument is often put forward as a refutation, not of ethical naturalism in general, but of a more particular version, which we might call definitional naturalism. Definitional naturalists assume that moral judgments are definitionally equivalent to natural judgments. The open question argument then should show that the proposed definitions must be incorrect.

There are, however, various kinds of definitions and the open question argument is not relevant to most of them. For example, a scientist defines water as H_2O and, as we have seen, the open question argument applied to this definition does not refute it.

Presumably the open question argument is aimed at someone who claims that a naturalistic definition captures the meaning of a moral term in the sense that moral judgments as we ordinarily use them are synonymous with judgments that describe natural facts. If it really is an open question whether an act that is C is an act that ought to be done—an open question even to someone who knows the meanings of "C" and "ought to be done," how can "C" and "ought to be done" be synonymous? It must be shown, not just assumed, however, that the relevant question is always open, no matter what the natural characteristics C.

5. Redefinitional Naturalism

Another kind of definitional naturalism in ethics is actually not a version of ethical naturalism at all. In this view, our moral terminology is so vague, unclear, and confused that we would do well to replace it with better and more precise terminology. For example, someone who was developing the theory that you ought to do what answers to the relevant interests might argue that our view about the example involving the patient in Room 306 shows that our moral views are incoherent. He might go on to suggest that we replace our present notions with clearer concepts, for example, defining "ought" so that an act ought to be done if and only if it would maximize the satisfaction of interests. By this utilitarian criterion, you ought to cut up the patient in Room 306 in

order to save the other patients. It is true that the proposed definition does not capture the ordinary meaning of "ought," since, when we judge intuitively that you ought to protect the healthy patient in Room 306, we are definitely not judging that this would maximize the satisfaction of interests—indeed we see that it would not. But a definition need not capture what we ordinarily mean. We can define our terms however we like, as long as we are willing to use these terms in accordance with our definitions. The suggested definition is relatively clear and precise. What is a better definition?

This line of argument is intelligible and not absurd, although it is also not without its own difficulties. It must be shown and not just assumed that ordinary moral notions are confused. This is a debatable claim. The fact that there is no obvious way to define ordinary moral terminology in a precise way does not show that there is anything wrong with that terminology. Not every term can be defined; it may be that moral terminology cannot be reduced to any simpler terminology.

Furthermore, there is a risk in this line of argument in that someone who takes this line may cheat, using "ought" sometimes as he has defined it and at other times in its ordinary sense. The best way to avoid this problem would be to dispense altogether with moral terminology in favor of utilitarian terminology and, instead of talking about what people ought to do, talk instead about what would satisfy the most interests. But that would be to give up any pretense of ethical naturalism and reveal that you have adopted extreme nihilism. It would involve denying that there are moral facts in the ordinary sense of "moral" and would ask us to abandon morality in the ordinary sense of "morality," just as a general naturalist abandons religion in the ordinary sense of "religion."

6. Why Ethics Is Problematic

Although we are in no position to assume that nihilism, extreme or moderate, is correct, we are now in a position to see more clearly the way in which ethics is problematic. Our starting point in this chapter was that moral judgments do not seem to help explain observations. This led us to wonder whether there are moral facts, moral truths, and moral knowledge. We saw that there could be moral facts if these facts were reducible in some way or other to other facts of a sort that might help explain observations. For we noticed that there are facts about the average American citizen, even though such facts do not themselves help explain observations, because such facts are reducible to facts about American citizens that can help explain observations. Similarly, we noticed that we would not decide that there are no facts about colors even if we were able to explain color perception without appealing to facts about colors; we would instead suppose that facts about colors are reducible to facts about the physical surfaces of objects, the properties of light, and the neurophysiological psychology of observers. So, we concluded that we did not have to accept ethical nihilism simply because moral facts do not seem to help explain observations; instead we might hope for a naturalistic reduction of moral facts.

With this in mind, we considered the possibility that moral facts might be reduced to facts about interests, roles, and functions. We concluded that, if they were to be, the reduction would have to be complex, vague, and difficult to specify. Ethics remains problematic.

It is true that the reduction of facts about colors is also complex, vague, and difficult (probably impossible) to specify. But there is an important difference between facts about colors and moral facts. Even if we come to be able to explain color perception by appeal to the physical characteristics of surfaces, the properties of light, and the neurophysiological psychology of observers, we will still *sometimes* refer to the actual colors of objects in explaining color perception, if only for the sake of simplicity. For example, we will explain that something looks green because it is yellow and the light is blue. It may be that the reference to the actual color of the object in an explanation of this sort can be replaced with talk about the physical characteristics of the surface. But that would greatly complicate what is a simple and easily understood explanation. That is why, even after we come to be able to give explanations without referring to the actual colors of objects, we will still assume that objects have actual colors and that

therefore facts about the actual colors of objects are somehow reducible to facts about physical characteristics of surfaces and so forth, even though we will (probably) not be able to specify the reduction in any but the vaguest way. We will continue to believe that objects have colors because we will continue to refer to the actual colors of objects in the explanations that we will in practice give. A similar point does not seem to hold for moral facts. There does not ever seem to be, even in practice, any point to explaining someone's moral observations by appeal to what is actually right or wrong, just or unjust, good or bad. It always seems to be more accurate to explain moral observations by citing facts about moral views, moral sensibility. So, the reasons we have for supposing that there are facts about colors do not correspond to reasons for thinking that there are moral facts.

It is true that facts about the average American citizen never seem to help explain observations, even in practice. In this respect such facts are like moral facts. But there is this difference. We can give a *precise* reduction of facts about the average American citizen; we cannot for moral facts. We are willing to think that there are facts about the average American citizen because we can explicitly define these facts in terms of facts that are of a sort that can help to explain observations. The trouble with alleged moral facts is that, as far as we can see at present, there is no simple and precise way to define them in terms of natural facts.

We are willing to suppose that there are facts about color, despite our not knowing precisely how to reduce them, because in practice we assume that there are such facts in many of our explanations of color perception, even if in theory this assumption is dispensable. We are willing to suppose that there are facts about the average American citizen, despite our never using such an assumption to explain observations, because we can precisely reduce these facts to facts of a sort that can help explain observations. Since moral facts seem to be neither precisely reducible nor useful even in practice in our explanations of observations, it remains problematic whether we have any reason to suppose that there are any moral facts.

STUDY QUESTIONS

1. According to Harmon, why can't moral claims be tested in the same way as scientific claims?
2. Is the claim that a person is honest more complex, vague, and difficult to specify than the claim that a person is healthy?
3. According to Harman, what is the difference between moral and mathematical explanations?
4. Does the open question argument refute ethical naturalism?

Moral Explanations

Nicholas L. Sturgeon

Nicholas L. Sturgeon is Professor Emeritus of Philosophy at Cornell University. He argues, against the view of Gilbert Harman, that moral facts play an explanatory role in moral observations. Sturgeon maintains that the test of whether moral facts are relevant in a particular situation is whether, had they been different, the observation would have been the same. Given that criterion, Sturgeon believes that the relevance of moral facts is proven by such ordinary observations as that an evil person's actions would have been different if the person had not been evil. Hence moral facts are relevant for explaining our moral observations.

There is one argument for moral skepticism that I respect even though I remain unconvinced. It has sometimes been called the argument from moral diversity or relativity, but that is somewhat misleading, for the problem arises not from the diversity of moral views, but from the apparent difficulty of *settling* moral disagreements, or even of knowing what would be required to settle them, a difficulty thought to be noticeably greater than any found in settling disagreements that arise in, for example, the sciences. This provides an argument for moral skepticism because one obviously possible explanation of our difficulty in settling moral disagreements is that they are really unsettleable, that there is no way of justifying one rather than another competing view on these issues; and a possible further explanation for the unsettleability of moral disagreements, in turn, is moral nihilism, the view that on these issues there just is no fact of the matter, that the impossibility of discovering and establishing moral truths is due to there not being any.

I am, as I say, unconvinced: partly because I think this argument exaggerates the difficulty we actually find in settling moral disagreements, partly because there are alternative explanations to be considered for the difficulty we do find. Under the latter heading, for example, it certainly matters to what extent moral disagreements depend on disagreements about other questions which, however disputed they may be, are nevertheless regarded as having objective answers: questions such as which, if any, religion is true, which account of human psychology, which theory of human society. And it also matters to what extent consideration of moral questions is in practice skewed by distorting factors such as personal interest and social ideology. These are large issues. Although it is possible to say some useful things to put them in perspective,[1] it appears impossible to settle them quickly or in any a priori

From Nicholas L. Sturgeon, "Moral Explanations," in *Morality, Reason, and Truth*, eds. David Copp and David Zimmerman (Totowa, N.J.: Rowman & Allanheld, 1984). Reprinted by permission of the publisher.

way. Consideration of them is likely to have to be piecemeal and, in the short run at least, frustratingly indecisive.

These large issues are not my topic here. But I mention them, and the difficulty of settling them, to show why it is natural that moral skeptics have hoped to find some quicker way of establishing their thesis. I doubt that any exist, but some have of course been proposed. Verificationist attacks on ethics should no doubt be seen in this light, and J. L. Mackie's recent "argument from queerness" is a clear instance.[2] The quicker response on which I shall concentrate, however, is neither of these, but instead an argument by Gilbert Harman designed to bring out the "basic problem" about morality, which in his view is "its apparent immunity from observational testing" and "the seeming irrelevance of observational evidence."[3] The argument is that reference to moral facts appears unnecessary for the *explanation* of our moral observations and beliefs.

Harman's view, I should say at once, is not in the end a skeptical one, and he does not view the argument I shall discuss as a decisive defense of moral skepticism or moral nihilism. Someone else might easily so regard it, however. For Harman himself regards it as creating a strong prima facie case for skepticism and nihilism, strong enough to justify calling it "the problem with ethics."[4] And he believes it shows that the only recourse for someone who wishes to avoid moral skepticism is to find defensible reductive definitions for ethical terms; so skepticism would be the obvious conclusion to draw for anyone who doubted the possibility of such definitions. I believe, however, that Harman is mistaken on both counts. I shall show that his argument for skepticism either rests on claims that most people would find quite implausible (and so cannot be what constitutes, for *them,* the problem with ethics); or else becomes just the application to ethics of a familiar *general* skeptical strategy, one which, if it works for ethics, will work equally well for unobservable theoretical entities, or for other minds, or for an external world (and so, again, can hardly be what constitutes the distinctive problem with *ethics*). . . . [O]ne can . . . be a moral realist, and indeed an ethical naturalist, without believing that we are now or

ever will be in possession of reductive naturalistic definitions for ethical terms.

I. THE PROBLEM WITH ETHICS

Moral theories are often tested in thought experiments, against imagined examples; and, as Harman notes, trained researchers often test scientific theories in the same way. The problem, though, is that scientific theories can also be tested against the world, by observations or real experiments; and, Harman asks, "can moral principles be tested in the same way, out in the world?"

This would not be a very interesting or impressive challenge, of course, if it were merely a resurrection of standard verificationist worries about whether moral assertions and theories have any testable empirical implications, implications stateable in some relatively austere "observational" vocabulary. One problem with that form of the challenge, as Harman points out, is that there are no "pure" observations, and in consequence no purely observational vocabulary either. But there is also a deeper problem that Harman does not mention, one that remains even if we shelve worries about "pure" observations and, at least for the sake of argument, grant the verificationist his observational language, pretty much as it was usually conceived: that is, as lacking at the very least any obviously theoretical terminology from any recognized science, and of course as lacking any moral terminology. For then the difficulty is that moral principles fare just as well (or just as badly) against the verificationist challenge as do typical scientific principles. For it is by now a familiar point about scientific principles—principles such as Newton's law of universal gravitation or Darwin's theory of evolution—that they are entirely devoid of empirical implications when considered in isolation.[5] We do of course base observational predictions on such theories and so test them against experience, but that is because we do *not* consider them in isolation. For we can derive these predictions only by relying at the same time on a large background of additional assumptions, many of which are equally theoretical and equally incapable of being tested in isolation.

A less familiar point, because less often spelled out, is that the relation of moral principles to observation is similar in *both* these respects. Candidate moral principles—for example, that an action is wrong just in case there is something else the agent could have done that would have produced a greater balance of pleasure over pain—lack empirical implications when considered in isolation. But it is easy to derive empirical consequences from them, and thus to test them against experience, if we allow ourselves, as we do in the scientific case, to rely on a background of other assumptions of comparable status. Thus, if we conjoin the act-utilitarian principle I just cited with the further view, also untestable in isolation, that it is always wrong deliberately to kill a human being, we can deduce from these two premises together the consequence that deliberately killing a human being always produces a lesser balance of pleasure over pain than some available alternative act; and this claim is one any positivist would have conceded we know, in principle at least, how to test. If we found it to be false, moreover, then we would be forced by this empirical test to abandon at least one of the moral claims from which we derived it.

It might be thought a worrisome feature of this example, however, and a further opening for skepticism, that there could be controversy about which moral premise to abandon, and that we have not explained how our empirical test can provide an answer to *this* question. And this may be a problem. It should be a familiar problem, however, because the Duhemian commentary includes a precisely corresponding point about the scientific case: that if we are at all cautious in characterizing what we observe, then the requirement that our theories merely be *consistent* with observation is a very weak one. There are always many, perhaps indefinitely many, different mutually inconsistent ways to adjust our views to meet this constraint. Of course, in practice we are often confident of how to do it: if you are a freshman chemistry student, you do not conclude from your failure to obtain the predicted value in an experiment that it is all over for the atomic theory of gases. And the decision can be equally easy, one

should note, in a moral case. Consider two examples. From the surprising moral thesis that Adolf Hitler was a morally admirable person, together with a modest piece of moral theory to the effect that no morally admirable person would, for example, instigate and oversee the degradation and death of millions of persons, one can derive the testable consequence that Hitler did not do this. But he did, so we must give up one of our premises; and the choice of which to abandon is neither difficult nor controversial.

Or, to take a less monumental example, contrived around one of Harman's own, suppose you have been thinking yourself lucky enough to live in a neighborhood in which no one would do anything wrong, at least not in public; and that the modest piece of theory you accept, this time, is that malicious cruelty, just for the hell of it, is wrong. Then, as in Harman's example, "you round a corner and see a group of young hoodlums pour gasoline on a cat and ignite it." At this point, either your confidence in the neighborhood or your principle about cruelty has got to give way. But the choice is easy, if dispiriting, so easy as hardly to require thought. As Harman says, "You do not need to *conclude* that what they are doing is wrong; you do not need to figure anything out: you can *see* that it is wrong" (p. 4). But a skeptic can still wonder whether this practical confidence, or this "seeing," rests in either sort of case on anything more than deeply ingrained conventions of thought—respect for scientific experts, say, and for certain moral traditions—as opposed to anything answerable to the facts of the matter, any reliable strategy for getting it right about the world.

Now, Harman's challenge is interesting partly because it does not rest on these verificationist doubts about whether moral beliefs have observational implications, but even more because what it does rest on is a partial answer to the kind of general skepticism to which, as we have seen, reflection on the verificationist picture can lead. Many of our beliefs are justified, in Harman's view, by their providing or helping to provide a reasonable *explanation* of our observing what we do. It would be consistent with your failure, as a beginning student, to obtain the experimental result predicted by the gas laws, that the laws are mistaken. But a better explanation, in light of your inexperience and the general success experts have had in confirming and applying these laws, is that you made some mistake in running the experiment. So our scientific beliefs can be justified by their explanatory role; and so too, in Harman's view, can mathematical beliefs and many common-sense beliefs about the world.

Not so, however, moral beliefs: they appear to have no such explanatory role. That is "the problem with ethics." Harman spells out his version of this contrast:

> You need to make assumptions about certain physical facts to explain the occurrence of the observations that support a scientific theory, but you do not seem to need to make assumptions about any moral facts to explain the occurrence of the so-called moral observations I have been talking about. In the moral case, it would seem that you need only make assumptions about the psychology or moral sensibility of the person making the moral observation. (p. 6)

More precisely, and applied to his own example, it might be reasonable, in order to explain your judging that the hoodlums are wrong to set the cat on fire, to assume "that the children really are pouring gasoline on a cat and you are seeing them do it." But there is no

> obvious reason to assume anything about "moral facts," such as that it is really wrong to set the cat on fire. . . . Indeed, an assumption about moral facts would seem to be totally irrelevant to the explanation of your making the judgment you make. It would seem that all we need assume is that you have certain more or less well articulated moral principles that are reflected in the judgments you make, based on your moral sensibility. (p. 7)

And Harman thinks that if we accept this conclusion, suitably generalized, then . . . we must conclude that moral theories cannot be tested against

the world as scientific theories can, and that we have no reason to believe that moral facts are part of the order of nature or that there is any moral knowledge (pp. 23, 35).

My own view is that Harman is quite wrong, not in thinking that the explanatory role of our beliefs is important to their justification, but in thinking that moral beliefs play no such role.[6] I shall have to say something about the initial plausibility of Harman's thesis as applied to his own example, but part of my reason for dissenting should be apparent from the other example I just gave. We find it easy (and so does Harman) to conclude from the evidence not just that Hitler was not morally admirable, but that he was morally depraved. But isn't it plausible that Hitler's moral depravity—the fact of his really having been morally depraved—forms part of a reasonable explanation of why we believe he was depraved? I think so, and I shall argue concerning this and other examples that moral beliefs very commonly play the explanatory role Harman denies them. Before I can press my case, however, I need to clear up several preliminary points about just what Harman is claiming and just how his argument is intended to work.

II. OBSERVATION AND EXPLANATION

(1) For there are several ways in which Harman's argument invites misunderstanding. One results from his focusing at the start on the question of whether there can be moral *observations*.[7] But this question turns out to be a side issue, in no way central to his argument that moral principles cannot be tested against the world. There are a couple of reasons for this, of which the more important[8] by far is that Harman does not really require of moral facts, if belief in them is to be justified, that they figure in the explanation of moral observations. It would be enough, on the one hand, if they were needed for the explanation of moral beliefs that are not in any interesting sense observations. For example, Harman thinks belief in moral facts would be vindicated if they were needed to explain our drawing the moral conclusions we do when we reflect on hypothetical

cases, but I think there is no illumination in calling these conclusions observations.[9] It would also be enough, on the other hand, if moral facts were needed for the explanation of what were clearly observations, but not moral observations. Harman thinks mathematical beliefs are justified, but he does not suggest that there are mathematical observations; it is rather that appeal to mathematical truths helps to explain why we make the physical observations we do (p. 10). Moral beliefs would surely be justified, too, if they played such a role, whether or not there are any moral observations.

So the claim is that moral facts are not needed to explain our having any of the moral beliefs we do, whether or not those beliefs are observations, and are equally unneeded to explain any of the observations we make, whether or not those observations are moral. In fact, Harman's view appears to be that moral facts aren't needed to explain anything at all: though it would perhaps be question-begging for him to begin with this strong a claim, since he grants that if there were any moral facts, then appeal to other moral facts—more general ones, for example—might be needed to explain *them* (p. 8). But he is certainly claiming, at the very least, that moral facts aren't needed to explain any nonmoral facts we have any reason to believe in.

(2) Other possible misunderstandings concern what is meant in asking whether reference to moral facts is *needed* to explain moral beliefs. . . . For Harman's question is clearly not just whether there is *an* explanation of our moral beliefs that does not mention moral facts. Almost surely there is. Equally surely, however, there is *an* explanation of our commonsense nonmoral beliefs that does not mention an external world: one which cites only our sensory experience, for example, together with whatever needs to be said about our psychology to explain why with that history of experience we would form just the beliefs we do. Harman means to be asking a question that will lead to skepticism about moral facts, but not to skepticism about the existence of material bodies or about well-established scientific theories of the world.

Harman illustrates the kind of question he is asking, and the kind of answer he is seeking, with an

example from physics that it will be useful to keep in mind. A physicist sees a vapor trail in a cloud chamber and thinks, "There goes a proton." What explains his thinking this? Partly, of course, his psychological set, which largely depends on his beliefs about the apparatus and all the theory he has learned; but partly also, perhaps, the hypothesis that "there really was a proton going through the cloud chamber, causing the vapor trail, which he saw as a proton." We will *not* need this latter assumption, however, "if his having made that observation could have been equally well explained by his psychological set alone, without the need for any assumption about a proton" (p. 6).[10] So for reference to moral facts to be *needed* in the explanation of our beliefs and observations, is for this reference to be required for an explanation that is somehow *better* than competing explanations. Correspondingly, reference to moral facts will be unnecessary to an explanation, in Harman's view, not just because we can find some explanation that does not appeal to them, but because *no* explanation that appeals to them is any better than some competing explanation that does not.

Now, fine discriminations among competing explanations of almost anything are likely to be difficult, controversial, and provisional. Fortunately, however, my discussion of Harman's argument will not require any fine discriminations. This is because Harman's thesis, as we have seen, is *not* that moral explanations lose out by a small margin; nor is it that moral explanations, though sometimes initially promising, always turn out on further examination to be inferior to nonmoral ones. It is, rather, that reference to moral facts always looks, right from the start, to be "completely irrelevant" to the explanation of any of our observations and beliefs. And my argument will be that this is mistaken: that many moral explanations appear to be good explanations, or components in good explanations, that are not obviously undermined by anything else that we know. . . .

(3) It is implicit in this statement of my project, but worth noting separately, that I take Harman to be proposing an *independent* skeptical argument—independent not merely of the argument from the

difficulty of settling disputed moral questions, but also of other standard arguments for moral skepticism. Otherwise his argument is not worth separate discussion. For *any* of these more familiar skeptical arguments will of course imply that moral explanations are defective, on the reasonable assumption that it would be a defect in any explanation to rely on claims as doubtful as these arguments attempt to show all moral claims to be. But if *that* is why there is a problem with moral explanations, one should surely just cite the relevant skeptical argument, rather than this derivative difficulty about moral explanations, as the basic "problem with ethics," and it is that argument we should discuss. So I take Harman's interesting suggestion to be that there is a *different* difficulty that remains even if we put other arguments for moral skepticism aside and *assume,* for the sake of argument, that there are moral facts (for example, that what the children in his example are doing is really wrong): namely, that these assumed facts *still* seem to play no explanatory role.

This understanding of Harman's thesis crucially affects my argumentative strategy in a way to which I should alert the reader in advance. For it should be clear that assessment of this thesis not merely permits, but *requires,* that we provisionally assume the existence of moral facts. I can see no way of evaluating the claim that *even if* we assumed the existence of moral facts they would still appear explanatorily irrelevant, without assuming the existence of some, to see how they would look. So I do freely assume this in each of the examples I discuss in the next section. . . . I grant, furthermore, that if Harman were right about the outcome of this thought experiment—that even after we assumed these facts they still looked irrelevant to the explanation of our moral beliefs and other nonmoral facts—then we might conclude with him that there were, after all, no such facts. But I claim he is wrong: that once we have provisionally assumed the existence of moral facts they *do* appear relevant, by perfectly ordinary standards, to the explanation of moral beliefs and of a good deal else besides. Does this prove that there *are* such facts? Well of course it helps support that view, but here I carefully make no claim to have shown so much. What I *show* is that any remaining

reservations about the existence of moral facts must be based on those *other* skeptical arguments, of which Harman's argument is independent. In short, there may still be a "problem with ethics," but it has *nothing* special to do with moral explanations.

III. MORAL EXPLANATIONS

Now that I have explained how I understand Harman's thesis, I turn to my arguments against it. I shall first add to my example of Hitler's moral character . . . in which it seems plausible to cite moral facts as part of an explanation of nonmoral facts. . . . I shall then argue that Harman gives us no plausible reason to reject or ignore these explanations; I shall claim, in fact, that the same is true for his own example of the children igniting the cat. I shall conclude, finally, by attempting to diagnose the source of the disagreement between Harman and me on these issues.

My Hitler example suggests a whole range of extremely common cases that appear not to have occurred to Harman, cases in which we cite someone's moral character as part of an explanation of his or her deeds, and in which that whole story is then available as a plausible further explanation of someone's arriving at a correct assessment of that moral character. . . .

What is supposed to be wrong with all these explanations? Harman says that assumptions about moral facts seem "completely irrelevant" in explaining moral observations and moral beliefs (p. 7), but on its more natural reading that claim seems pretty obviously mistaken about these examples. For it is natural to think that if a particular assumption is completely irrelevant to the explanation of a certain fact, then that fact would have obtained, and we could have explained it just as well, even if the assumption had been false. But I do not believe that Hitler would have done all he did if he had not been morally depraved, nor, on the assumption that he was not depraved, can I think of any plausible explanation for his doing those things. Nor is it plausible that we would all have believed he was morally depraved even if he hadn't been. Granted, there is a tendency for writers who do not attach much weight to fascism as a social movement to want to blame its evils on a single maniacal leader, so perhaps some of them would have painted Hitler as a moral monster even if he had not been one. But this is only a tendency, and one for which many people know how to discount, so I doubt that our moral belief really is overdetermined in this way. . . .

It is more puzzling, I grant, to consider Harman's own example in which you see the children igniting a cat and react immediately with the thought that this is wrong. Is it true, as Harman claims, that the assumption that the children are really doing something wrong is "totally irrelevant" to any reasonable explanation of your making that judgment? Would you, for example, have reacted in just the same way, with the thought that the action is wrong, even if what they were doing *hadn't* been wrong, and could we explain your reaction equally well on this assumption? Now, there is more than one way to understand this counterfactual question, and I shall return below to a reading of it that might appear favorable to Harman's view. What I wish to point out for now is merely that there is a natural way of taking it, parallel to the way in which I have been understanding similar counterfactual questions about my own examples, on which the answer to it has to be simply: it depends. For to answer the question, I take it, we must consider a situation in which what the children are doing is not wrong, but which is otherwise as much like the actual situation as possible, and then decide what your reaction would be in that situation. But since what makes their action wrong, what its wrongness *consists* in, is presumably something like its being an act of gratuitous cruelty (or, perhaps we should add, of intense cruelty, and to a helpless victim), to imagine them not doing something wrong we are going to have to imagine their action different in this respect. More cautiously and more generally, if what they are actually doing is wrong, and if moral properties are, as many writers have held, supervenient on natural ones,[11] then in order to imagine them not doing something wrong we are going to have to suppose their action different from the actual one in some of its natural features as well. So our question becomes: Even if the children

had been doing something else, something just different enough not to be wrong, would you have taken them even so to be doing something wrong?

Surely there is no one answer to this question. It depends on a lot about you, including your moral views and how good you are at seeing at a glance what some children are doing. It probably depends also on a debatable moral issue: namely, just *how* different the children's action would have to be in order not to be wrong. (Is unkindness to animals, for example, also wrong?) I believe we can see how, in a case in which the answer was clearly affirmative, we might be tempted to agree with Harman that the wrongness of the action was no part of the explanation of your reaction. For suppose you are like this. You hate children. What you especially hate, moreover, is the sight of children enjoying themselves; so much so that whenever you see children having fun, you immediately assume they are up to no good. The more they seem to be enjoying themselves, furthermore, the readier you are to fasten on any pretext for thinking them engaged in real wickedness. Then it is true that even if the children had been engaged in some robust but innocent fun, you would have thought they were doing something wrong; and Harman is perhaps right[12] about you that the actual wrongness of the action you see is irrelevant to your thinking it wrong. This is because your reaction is due to a feature of the action that coincides only very accidentally with the ones that make it wrong. But, of course, and fortunately, many people aren't like this (nor does Harman argue that they are). It isn't true of them, in general, that if the children had been doing something similar, although different enough not to be wrong, they would still have thought the children were doing something wrong. And it isn't true either, therefore, that the wrongness of the action is irrelevant to the explanation of why they think it wrong.

Now, one might have the sense from my discussion of all these examples, but perhaps especially from my discussion of this last one, Harman's own, that I have perversely been refusing to understand his claim about the explanatory irrelevance of moral facts in the way he intends. And perhaps I have not been understanding it as he wishes. In any case, I agree, I have certainly not been understanding the crucial counterfactual question, of whether we would have drawn the same moral conclusion even if the moral facts had been different, in the way he must intend. But I am not being perverse. I believe, as I have said, that my way of taking the question is the more natural one. And, more importantly: although there is, I grant, a reading of that question on which it will always yield the answer Harman wants—namely, that a difference in the moral facts would *not* have made a difference in our judgment—I do not believe this reading can support his argument. I must now explain why.

It will help if I contrast my general approach with his. . . . [W]e have in general no a priori way of knowing which strategies for forming and refining our beliefs are likely to take us closer to the truth. The only way we have of proceeding is to assume the approximate truth of what seems to us the best overall theory we already have of what we are like and what the world is like, and to decide in the light of *that* what strategies of research and reasoning are likely to be reliable in producing a more nearly true overall theory. One result of applying these procedures, in turn, is likely to be the refinement or perhaps even the abandonment of parts of the tentative theory with which we began.

I take Harman's approach, too, to be an instance of this one. He says we are justified in believing in those facts that we need to assume to explain why we observe what we do. But he does not think that our knowledge of this principle about justification is a priori. Furthermore, as he knows, we cannot decide whether one explanation is better than another without relying on beliefs we already have about the world. Is it really a better explanation of the vapor trail the physicist sees in the cloud chamber to suppose that a proton caused it, as Harman suggests in his example, rather than some other charged particle? Would there, for example, have been no vapor trail in the absence of that proton? There is obviously no hope of answering such questions without assuming at least the approximate truth of some quite far-reaching microphysical theory, and our knowledge of such theories is not a priori.

But my approach differs from Harman's in one crucial way. For among the beliefs in which I have enough confidence to rely on in evaluating explanations, at least at the outset, are some moral beliefs. And I have been relying on them in the following way.[13] Harman's thesis implies that the supposed moral fact of Hitler's being morally depraved is irrelevant to the explanation of Hitler's doing what he did. (For we may suppose that if it explains his doing what he did, it also helps explain, at greater remove, Harman's belief and mine in his moral depravity.) To assess this claim, we need to conceive a situation in which Hitler was *not* morally depraved and consider the question whether in that situation he would still have done what he did. My answer is that he would not, and this answer relies on a (not very controversial) moral view: that in any world at all like the actual one, only a morally depraved person could have initiated a world war, ordered the "final solution," and done any number of other things Hitler did. That is why I believe that, if Hitler hadn't been morally depraved, he wouldn't have done those things, and hence that the fact of his moral depravity is relevant to an explanation of what he did.

Harman, however, cannot want us to rely on any such moral views in answering this counterfactual question. This comes out most clearly if we return to his example of the children igniting the cat. He claims that the wrongness of this act is irrelevant to an explanation of your thinking it wrong, that you would have *thought* it wrong even if it wasn't. My reply was that in order for the action not to be wrong it would have had to lack the feature of deliberate, intense, pointless cruelty, and that if it had differed in this way you might very well *not* have thought it wrong. I also suggested a more cautious version of this reply: that since the action is in fact wrong, and since moral properties supervene on more basic natural ones, it would have had to be different in *some* further natural respect in order not to be wrong; and that we do not know whether if it had so differed you would still have thought it wrong. Both of these replies, again, rely on moral views, the latter merely on the view that there is *something* about the natural features of the action in Harman's example that makes it wrong, the former on a more specific view as to which of these features do this.

But Harman, it is fairly clear, intends for us *not* to rely on any such moral views in evaluating his counterfactual claim. His claim is not that if the action had not been one of deliberate cruelty (or had otherwise differed in whatever way would be required to remove its wrongness), you would still have thought it wrong. It is, instead, that if the action were one of deliberate, pointless cruelty, but this *did not make it wrong,* you would still have thought it was wrong. And to return to the example of Hitler's moral character, the counterfactual claim that Harman will need in order to defend a comparable conclusion about that case is not that if Hitler had been, for example, humane and fairminded, free of nationalistic pride and racial hatred, he would still have done exactly as he did. It is, rather, that if Hitler's psychology, and anything else about his situation that could strike us as morally relevant, had been exactly as it in fact was, but this had *not constituted moral depravity,* he would still have done exactly what he did.

Now the antecedents of these two conditionals are puzzling. For one thing, both are, I believe, necessarily false. I am fairly confident, for example, that Hitler really was morally depraved; and since I also accept the view that moral features supervene on more basic natural properties.[14] I take this to imply that there is no possible world in which Hitler has just the personality he in fact did, in just the situation he was in, but is not morally depraved. Any attempt to describe such a situation, moreover, will surely run up against the limits of our moral concepts—what Harman calls our "moral sensibility"—and this is no accident. For what Harman is asking us to do, in general, is to consider cases in which absolutely *everything* about the nonmoral facts that could seem morally relevant to us, in light of whatever moral theory we accept and of the concepts required for understanding that theory, is held fixed, but in which the moral judgment that our theory yields about the case is nevertheless mistaken. So it is hardly surprising that, using that theory and those concepts, we should find it difficult to conceive in any detail what such a situation would be like. It is especially not surprising when the cases in question are as paradigmatic in light of the moral outlook we in fact have as

is Harman's example or is, even more so, mine of Hitler's moral character. The only way we could be wrong about this latter case (assuming we have the nonmoral facts right) would be for our whole theory to be hopelessly wrong, so radically mistaken that there could be no hope of straightening it out through adjustments from within.

But I do not believe we should conclude, as we might be tempted to, that we therefore know a priori that this is not so, or that we cannot understand these conditionals that are crucial to Harman's argument. Rather, now that we have seen how we have to understand them, we should grant that they are true: that if our moral theory were somehow hopelessly mistaken, but all the nonmoral facts remained exactly as they in fact are, then, since we do *accept* that moral theory, we would still draw exactly the moral conclusions we in fact do. But we should deny that any skeptical conclusion follows from this. In particular, we should deny that it follows that moral facts play no role in explaining our moral judgments.

For consider what follows from the parallel claim about microphysics, in particular about Harman's example in which a physicist concludes from his observation of a vapor trail in a cloud chamber, and from the microphysical theory he accepts, that a free proton has passed through the chamber. The parallel claim, notice, is *not* just that if the proton had not been there the physicist would still have thought it was. This claim is implausible, for we may assume that the physicist's theory is generally correct, and it follows from that theory that if there hadn't been a proton there, then there wouldn't have been a vapor trail. But in a perfectly similar way it is implausible that if Hitler hadn't been morally depraved we would still have thought he was: for we may assume that our moral theory also is at least roughly correct, and it follows from the most central features of that theory that if Hitler hadn't been morally depraved, he wouldn't have done what he did. The *parallel* claim about the microphysical example is, instead, that if there hadn't been a proton there, but there *had* been a vapor trail, the physicist would still have concluded that a proton was present. More precisely, to maintain a perfect parallel with Harman's claims about the moral cases, the antecedent must specify that although no proton is present, absolutely *all* the non-microphysical facts that the physicist, in light of his theory, might take to be relevant to the question of whether or not a proton is present, are exactly as in the actual case. (These macrophysical facts, as we may for convenience call them, surely include everything one would normally think of as an observable fact.) Of course, we shall be unable to imagine this without imagining that the physicist's theory is pretty badly mistaken;[15] but I believe we should grant that, *if* the physicist's theory were somehow this badly mistaken, but all the macrophysical facts (including all the observable facts) were held fixed, then the physicist, since he does accept that theory, would still draw all the same conclusions that he actually does. That is, this conditional claim, like Harman's parallel claim about the moral cases, is true.

But no skeptical conclusions follow; nor can Harman, since he does not intend to be a skeptic about physics, think that they do. It does not follow, in the first place, that we have any reason to think the physicist's theory *is* generally mistaken. Nor does it follow, furthermore, that the hypothesis that a proton really did pass through the cloud chamber is not part of a good explanation of the vapor trail, and hence of the physicist's thinking this has happened. This looks like a reasonable explanation, of course, only on the assumption that the physicist's theory is at least roughly true, for it is this theory that tells us, for example, what happens when charged particles pass through a supersaturated atmosphere, what other causes (if any) there might be for a similar phenomenon, and so on. But, as I say, we have not been provided with any reason for not trusting the theory to this extent.

Similarly, I conclude, we should draw no skeptical conclusions from Harman's claims about the moral cases. It is true that if our moral theory were seriously mistaken, but we still believed it, and the nonmoral facts were held fixed, we would still make just the moral judgments we do. But *this* fact by itself provides us with no reason for thinking that our moral theory *is* generally mistaken. Nor, again, does it imply that the fact of Hitler's really having been morally depraved forms no part of a good explanation of his doing what he did and hence, at

greater remove, of our thinking him depraved. This explanation will appear reasonable, of course, only on the assumption that our accepted moral theory is at least roughly correct, for it is this theory that assures us that only a depraved person could have thought, felt, and acted as Hitler did. But, as I say, Harman's argument has provided us with no reason for not trusting our moral views to this extent, and hence with no reason for doubting that it is sometimes moral facts that explain our moral judgments.

I conclude with three comments about my argument.

(1) I have tried to show that Harman's claim—that we would have held the particular moral beliefs we do even if those beliefs were untrue—admits of two readings, one of which makes it implausible, and the other of which reduces it to an application of a general skeptical strategy, a strategy which could as easily be used to produce doubt about microphysical as about moral facts. The general strategy is this. Consider any conclusion C we arrive at by relying both on some distinguishable "theory" T and on some body of evidence not being challenged, and ask whether we would have believed C even if it had been false. The plausible answer, *if* we are allowed to rely on T, will often be no: for if C had been false, then (according to T) the evidence would have had to be different, and in that case we wouldn't have believed C. (I have illustrated the plausibility of this sort of reply for all my moral examples, as well as for the microphysical one.) But the skeptic of course intends us *not* to rely on T in this way, and so rephrases the question: Would we have believed C even if it were false *but* all the evidence had been exactly as it in fact was? Now the answer has to be yes; and the skeptic concludes that C is doubtful. (It should be obvious how to extend this strategy to belief in other minds, or in an external world.) I am of course not convinced: I do not think answers to the rephrased question show anything interesting about what we know or justifiably believe. But it is enough for my purposes here that no such *general* skeptical strategy could pretend to reveal any problems peculiar to belief in *moral* facts.

(2) My conclusion about Harman's argument, although it is not exactly the same as, is nevertheless similar to and very much in the spirit of the Duhemian point I invoked earlier against verificationism. There the question was whether typical moral assertions have testable implications, and the answer was that they do, so long as you include additional moral assumptions of the right sort among the background theories on which you rely in evaluating these assertions. Harman's more important question is whether we should ever regard moral facts as relevant to the explanation of nonmoral facts, and in particular of our having the moral beliefs we do. But the answer, again, is that we should, so long as we are willing to hold the right sorts of *other* moral assumptions fixed in answering counterfactual questions. Neither answer shows morality to be on any shakier ground than, say, physics, for typical microphysical hypotheses, too, have testable implications, and appear relevant to explanations, only if we are willing to assume at least the approximate truth of an elaborate microphysical theory and to hold this assumption fixed in answering counterfactual questions.

(3) Of course, this picture of how explanations depend on background theories, and moral explanations in particular on moral background theories, does show why someone already tempted toward moral skepticism on other grounds (such as those I mentioned at the beginning of this essay) might find Harman's claim about moral explanations plausible. To the extent that you already have pervasive doubts about moral theories, you will also find moral facts nonexplanatory. So I grant that Harman has located a natural symptom of moral skepticism; but I am sure he has neither traced this skepticism to its roots nor provided any independent argument for it. His claim (p. 22) that we do not *in fact* cite moral facts in explanation of moral beliefs and observations cannot provide such an argument, for that claim is false. So, too, is the claim that assumptions about moral facts seem irrelevant to such explanations, for many do not. The claim that we *should* not rely on such assumptions because they *are* irrelevant, on the other hand, unless it is supported by some independent argument for moral skepticism, will just be question-begging: for the principal test of whether they are relevant, in any situation in which it appears they might be, is a counterfactual question

about what would have happened if the moral fact had not obtained, and how we answer that question depends precisely upon whether we *do* rely on moral assumptions in answering it.

My own view I stated at the outset: that the only argument for moral skepticism with any independent weight is the argument from the difficulty of settling disputed moral questions. I have shown that anyone who finds Harman's claim about moral explanations plausible must already have been tempted toward skepticism by some other considerations, and I suspect that the other considerations will typically be the ones I sketched. So that is where discussion should focus. I also suggested that those considerations may provide less support for moral skepticism than is sometimes supposed, but I must reserve a thorough defense of that thesis for another occasion.

NOTES

1. As, for example, in Alan Gewirth, "Positive 'Ethics' and Normative 'Science,'" *The Philosophical Review* 69 (1960), pp. 311–330, in which there are some useful remarks about the first of them.
2. J. L. Mackie, *Ethics: Inventing Right and Wrong* (Harmondsworth, England: Penguin, 1977), pp. 38–42.
3. Gilbert Harman, *The Nature of Morality: An Introduction to Ethics* (New York: Oxford University Press, 1977), pp. vii, viii. Parenthetical page references are to this work.
4. Harman's title for the entire first section of his book.
5. This point is generally credited to Pierre Duhem; see *The Aim and Structure of Physical Theory,* trans. Philip P. Wiener (Princeton, NJ: Princeton University Press, 1954). It is a prominent theme in the influential writings of W. V. O. Quine. For an especially clear application of it, see Hilary Putnam, "The 'Corroboration' of Theories," in *Mathematics, Matter and Method: Philosophical Papers, Volume I,* second ed. (Cambridge: Cambridge University Press, 1977), pp. 250–269.
6. Harman is careful always to say only that moral beliefs *appear* to play no such role, and since he eventually concludes that there *are* moral facts (p. 132), this caution may be more than stylistic. I shall argue that this more cautious claim, too, is mistaken (indeed, that is my central thesis). But to avoid issues about Harmon's intent, I shall simply mean by "Harman's

argument" the skeptical argument of his first two chapters, whether or not be means to endorse all of it. This argument surely deserves discussion in its own right in either case, especially since Harman never explains what is wrong with it.

7. He asks: "Can moral principles be tested in the same way [as scientific hypotheses can], out in the world? You can observe someone do something, but can you ever perceive the rightness or wrongness of what he does?" (p. 4).

8. The other is that Harman appears to use "observe" (and "perceive" and "see") in a surprising way. One would normally take observing (or perceiving, or seeing) something to involve *knowing* it was the case. But Harman apparently takes an observation to be *any* opinion arrived at as "a direct result of perception" (p. 5) or, at any rate (see next footnote), "immediately and without conscious reasoning" (p. 7). This means that observations need not even be true, much less known to be true. A consequence is that the existence of moral observations, in Harman's sense, would not be sufficient to show that there is moral knowledge, although this *would* be sufficient if "observe" were being used in a more standard sense. What I argue in the text is that the existence of moral observations (in either Harman's or the standard sense) is not *necessary* for showing that there is moral knowledge, either.

9. This sort of case does not meet Harman's characterization of an observation as an opinion that is "a direct result of perception" (p. 5), but he is surely right that moral facts would be as well vindicated if they were needed to explain our drawing conclusions about hypothetical cases as they would be if they were needed to explain observations in the narrower sense. To be sure, Harman is still confining his attention to cases in which we draw the moral conclusion from our thought experiment "immediately and without conscious reasoning" (p. 7), and it is no doubt the existence of such cases that gives purchase to talk of a "moral sense." But this feature, again, can hardly matter to the argument: would belief in moral facts be less justified if they were needed only to explain the instances in which we draw the moral conclusion *slowly?* Nor can it make any difference for that matter whether the case we are reflecting on is hypothetical: so my example in which we, quickly or slowly, draw a moral conclusion about Hitler from what we know of him, is surely relevant.

10. It is surprising that Harman does not mention the obvious intermediate possibility, which would occur to any instrumentalist: to cite the physicist's psychological set *and* the vapor trail, but say nothing about protons or other unobservables. It is *this* explanation, as I emphasize below, that is most closely parallel to an explanation of beliefs about an external world in terms of sensory experience and psychological makeup, or of moral beliefs in terms of non-moral facts together with our "moral sensibility."

11. What would be generally granted is just that *if* there are moral properties they supervene on natural properties. But, remember, we are assuming for the sake of argument that there are.

    I think moral properties *are* natural properties; and from this view it of course follows trivially that they supervene on natural properties: that, necessarily, nothing could differ in its moral properties without differing in some natural respect. But I also accept the more interesting thesis usually intended by the claim about supervenience—that there are more basic natural features such that, necessarily, once they are fixed, so are the moral properties. (In supervening on more basic natural facts of some sort, moral facts are like *most* natural facts. Social facts like unemployment, for example, supervene on complex histories of many individuals and their relations; and facts about the existence and properties of macroscopic physical objects—colliding billiard balls, say—clearly supervene on the microphysical constitution of the situations that include them.)

12. Not *certainly* right, because there is still the possibility that your reaction is to some extent overdetermined, and is to be explained partly by your sympathy for the cat and your dislike of cruelty, as well as by your hatred for children (although this last alone would have been sufficient to produce it).

    We could of course rule out this possibility by making you an even less attractive character, indifferent to the suffering of animals and not offended by cruelty. But it may then be hard to imagine that such a person (whom I shall cease calling "you") could retain enough of a grip on moral thought for us to be willing to say he thought the action *wrong,* as opposed to saying that he merely pretended to do so. This difficulty is perhaps not insuperable, but it is revealing. Harman says that the actual wrongness of the action is "completely irrelevant" to the explanation of the observer's reaction. Notice that what is in fact true, however, is that it is *very hard* to imagine someone who reacts in the way Harman describes, but whose reaction is *not* due, at least in part, to the actual wrongness of the action.

13. Harman of course allows us to assume the moral facts whose explanatory relevance is being assessed: that Hitler was depraved, or that what the children in his example are doing is wrong. But I have been assuming something more—something about what depravity *is,* and about what *makes* the children's action wrong. (At a minimum . . . I have been assuming that *something* about its more basic features makes it wrong, so that it could not have differed in its moral quality without differing in those other features as well.)

14. It is about here that I have several times encountered the objection: but surely *supervenient* properties aren't needed to explain anything. It is a little hard, however, to see just what this objection is supposed to come to. If it includes endorsement of the conditional I here attribute to Harman, then I believe the remainder of my discussion is an adequate reply to it. If it is the claim that, because moral properties are supervenient, we can always exploit the insights in any moral explanations, however plausible, without resort to moral *language,* then I have already dealt with it in my discussion of reductionism (see note 8, above): the claim is probably false, but even if it is true it is no support for Harman's view, which is not that moral explanations are plausible but reducible, but that they are totally implausible. And doubts about the causal efficacy of supervenient facts seem misplaced in any case. . . . High unemployment causes widespread hardship, and can also bring down the rate of inflation. The masses and velocities of two colliding billiard balls causally influence the subsequent trajectories of the two balls. There is no doubt some sense in which these facts are causally efficacious *in virtue of* the way they supervene on—that is, are constituted out of, or causally realized by—more basic facts, but this hardly shows them *inefficacious.* (Nor does Harman appear to think it does: for his *favored* explanation of your moral belief about the burning cat, recall, appeals to psychological facts [about your moral sensibility], a biological fact [that it's a cat], and macrophysical facts [that it's on fire]—supervenient facts all, on his physicalist view and mine.) . . .

15. If we imagine the physicist regularly mistaken in this way, moreover, we will have to imagine his theory not just mistaken but hopelessly so. And we can easily reproduce the other notable feature of Harman's claims about the moral cases, that what we are imagining is necessarily false, if we suppose that one of the physicist's (or better, chemist's) conclusions is about the microstructure of some common substance, such as water. For I agree with Saul Kripke that whatever microstructure water has is essential to it, that it has this structure in every possible world in which it exists (Saul Kripke, *Naming and Necessity* [Cambridge, MA: Harvard University Press, 1980]). If we are right (as we have every reason to suppose) in thinking that water is actually H_2O, therefore, the conditional, "If water were not H_2O, but all the observable, macrophysical facts were just as they actually are, chemists would still have come to think it was H_2O," has a necessarily false antecedent; just as, if we are right (as we also have good reason to suppose) in thinking that Hitler was actually morally depraved, the conditional. "If Hitler were just as he was in all natural respects, but not morally depraved, we would still have thought he was depraved," has a necessarily false antecedent. Of course, I am not suggesting that in either case our knowledge that the antecedent is false is a priori.

These counterfactuals, because of their impossible antecedents, will have to be interpreted over worlds that are (at best) only "epistemically" possible; and . . . this helps to explain why anyone who accepts a causal theory of knowledge (or any theory according to which the justification of our belief depends on what explains our holding them) will find their truth irrelevant to the question of how much we know, either in chemistry or in morals. For although there certainly are counterfactuals that are relevant to questions about what causes what (and, hence, about what explains what), these have to be counterfactuals about real possibilities, not merely epistemic ones.

STUDY QUESTIONS

1. What is a "moral fact"?
2. Does a moral fact differ in kind from a fact supporting a non-moral value judgment?
3. Does a moral fact differ in kind from a scientific fact?
4. If we provide reasons why we hold a particular moral judgment, are we thereby committed to the existence of moral facts?

Part XII

REASONS & MOTIVES

The Possibility of Altruism

Thomas Nagel

Metaethical inquiry raises a variety of issues in moral psychology—that is, the study of psychological issues relevant to the practice of morality. For example, do moral judgments motivate action? Do moral judgments express beliefs? How are moral beliefs related to desires? How are desires related to actions?

If normative judgments are necessarily motivating, the theory known as "judgment internalism," and, as Hume maintained, beliefs alone cannot motivate, then how can normative judgments be beliefs? Thomas Nagel, University Professor of Philosophy and Law Emeritus at New York University, responds to this question by accepting judgment internalism but rejecting Hume's theory of motivation. Nagel argues that just as we are motivated to perform an action by believing that it will promote our future interests, so we can be motivated to perform an action by believing that it is morally required. In the first case, our beliefs about our future self-interest produces a desire that motivates us to act; in the second case, our beliefs about what morality requires produces a desire that motivates us to act. In both cases, our beliefs can, albeit indirectly, provide motivation for action.

II. THE TRADITIONAL CONTROVERSY

1. The names "internalism" and "externalism" have been used to designate two views of the relation between ethics and motivation. Internalism is the view that the presence of a motivation for acting morally is guaranteed by the truth of ethical propositions themselves. On this view the motivation must be so tied to the truth, or meaning, of ethical statements that when in a particular case someone is (or perhaps merely believes that he is) morally required to do something, it follows that he has a motivation for doing it.

Externalism holds, on the other hand, that the necessary motivation is not supplied by ethical principles and judgments themselves, and that an additional psychological sanction is required to motivate our compliance. Externalism is compatible with a variety of views about the motivation for being moral. It is even compatible with the view that such a motivation is always present—so long as its presence is not guaranteed by moral judgments themselves, but by something external to ethics. The present discussion attempts to construct the basis of an internalist position.

Internalists appeal to various types of motivation: self-interest, sympathy, benevolence, even the

From Thomas Nagel, *The Possibility of Altruism* (Princeton, NJ: Princeton University Press, 1970). Reprinted by permission of the publisher.

amorphously general "approval" or "pro-attitude." Even emotivism can be counted as an internalist position of sorts, so the conditions which internalism places on the organization of the motivational factor need not be very rigorous. Internalism's appeal derives from the conviction that one cannot accept or assert sincerely any ethical proposition without accepting at least a prima facie motivation for action in accordance with it. Philosophers who believe that there is no room for rational assessment of the basic springs of motivation will tend to be internalists, but at the cost of abandoning claims to moral objectivity. One way to do this is to build motivational content into the meaning of ethical assertions by turning them into expressions of a special sort of inclination, appropriate only when that inclination is present, and rooted only in the motivations of the speaker. The result is a basically anti-rational ethical theory, having as its foundation a commitment, inclination, feeling, or desire that is simply given (though the superstructure may be characterized by a high degree of rational articulation). Motivational content is thereby tied to the meaning of ethical *utterances*—what the speaker means or expresses—rather than to the truth conditions of those utterances, which are left vague or non-existent.

A stronger position, one which ties the motivation to the cognitive content of ethical claims, requires the postulation of motivational influences which one cannot reject once one becomes aware of them. If such influences can be shown to belong to the content of ethics, then someone who recognizes the truth of an ethical claim will have to accept the corresponding motivation.

2. Mill and Moore appear to be externalists. In Moore's case, the attribution is by elimination, for at least in *Principia Ethica,* he does not consider the motivation for being moral at all. Mill devotes a separate chapter of *Utilitarianism* to what he calls the sanctions for the principle of utility. He regards the question as separate from that of the principle's truth, and the answers he provides are unrelated to his arguments for the principle.

On Moore's stated view it can only be regarded as a mysterious fact that people care whether what they do is right or wrong. I suspect, however, that it is really an unrecognized assumption of internalism that underlies Moore's "refutation" of naturalism. The evaluative factor which is always left out by any naturalistic description of the object of ethical assessment is in fact the relevant inclination or attitude. But Moore did not realize this, and consequently did not produce an internalist position but an externalist one in which a peculiar non-natural quality served to flesh out the content of ethical claims.

Such views are, it seems to me, unacceptable on their surface, for they permit someone who has acknowledged that he should do something and has seen *why* it is the case that he should do it to ask whether he has any reason for doing it. Of course one line of retreat from this unacceptable conclusion is to deny that the evaluative portion or aspect of an ethical assertion has any truth value, and to attach the evaluation instead to the individual's expression of the ethical claim.

But if one wishes to tie the requirement of motivational influence to the truth-conditions of moral claims, with the consequence that if someone recognizes their grounds, he cannot but be affected accordingly, then a stricter motivational connection will be required.

3. One example of such a view is provided by Hobbes, whose ethical system is solidly grounded in motivational energies derived from a universal desire for self-preservation. The ethical system is simply a development of certain consequences of that motive in the conduct of a rational and fully informed individual. Human nature is according to Hobbes subject to other, irrational influences as well, so one will not necessarily do what one ought even when one knows what it is; but given the universality and fundamental nature of the desire to live, a recognition of the grounds for one of Hobbes's ethical imperatives cannot fail to move us to some extent.

Hobbes derives the system of moral requirements from the operation of a motivational factor which can be independently understood, together with certain highly general assumptions about the human condition. The basic motive is taken as given, and only its consequences qualify as ethical conclusions. It is not an ethical principle that all men should want to preserve their own lives; so in that sense motivation theory is at the most fundamental level prior to ethics, which constitutes a development of one branch of it. Claims about what we should do simply *are* on this view claims about what we have a certain sort of motivation for doing; ethical arguments are persuasive because, if someone with the assumed desire understands the argument for an ethical conclusion, he must be aware of those circumstances and interconnections which, according to the argument, would motivate him if he were aware of them.

4. The most influential anti-rational internalist is of course Hume. The motivational basis of his ethical system is weaker and less clearly defined than that of Hobbes, since sympathy (later general benevolence), the specifically moral motivation, requires buttressing by self-interest if it is to be sufficiently powerful to resist contrary claims stemming from self-interest directly. But he does make explicit an extremely attractive theory of the justification of action which has had enormous effect on ethical theory. The view is that any justification must appeal to an inclination in the individual to whom it is offered, and that the justification proceeds by drawing connections between that inclination and other things (notably actions) which are means to its satisfaction. The inclination then becomes transferred to these by association, which is what makes persuasive justification possible. If we cast this view in terms of reasons, it will state that among the conditions for the presence of a reason for action there must always be a desire or inclination capable of motivating one to act accordingly.

Hobbes's system satisfies these conditions on justification. In fact he and Hume approach the task in similar ways: both assume that ethics must represent the domain of the objective, the common, in practical matters—i.e., that which all men equally have reason to promote—and both seek a motivational basis for the possibility of such agreement. Hobbes finds it in men's common interest in certain security conditions, social structures, and conventions necessary for the fulfilment of their desire to survive; Hume finds it in the capacity for sympathetic participation in the happiness and unhappiness of others, or even in the mere thought of the likelihood of their happiness or unhappiness. Both regard ethics as a codification of only part of the motivational apparatus; there remains ample room for practical disagreement among men, and, for Hume at least, given the weakness of sympathy in contrast to self-interest, moral considerations alone are by no means decisive.

On Hume's view one begins with psychology, and ethics is an elaboration of it. The basic psychological factors are not themselves brought to light by ethical investigation (though the need for a foundation for ethics may have led to the search for them). And given Hume's famous restrictions on rational assessment of the passions and of preferences, the possibility of justifying morality is strictly limited. Any justification ends finally with the rationally gratuitous presence of the emotion of sympathy; if that condition were not met, one would simply have no reason to be moral. Now it may in fact follow from Hume's theory of imagination that susceptibility to sympathy is a necessary trait of all beings who can think about the feelings of others.[1] But he does not appear to recognize that his psychological factor has this status; so far as he is concerned the edifice of ethics rests on a psychological contingency. In the case of Hobbes, the love of life may be thought somewhat closer to being a necessary motive for human beings. But still the motivational basis is prior to and independent of the ethical system which derives from it. A quite different sort of theory would be necessary to alter that relation of priority.

5. Plato and Aristotle, each in his own way, constitute examples of such a rebellion against the priority of psychology. Both felt, I think, that the motivation for being moral does not come from elsewhere, i.e. from any independently comprehensible desire or feeling. The ethical motivation, even at its most basic level, can on this view be understood only through ethics. But since the issue is not clearly posed by either of these writers, a discussion of their views would require heavier exegetical work than I wish to undertake here.

Fortunately we have a far better example in the person of Kant, who is explicitly and consciously driven by the demand for an ethical system whose motivational grip is not dependent on desires which must simply be taken for granted. His insistence that the imperatives of morality be categorical is essentially an insistence that their application not depend on the presence of a motivational factor prior to ethics, from which they are extracted as consequences. From Kant's efforts one sees what a struggle is required to undercut the priority of ethically neutral motivations, and to put ethical principles themselves at the absolute source of our moral conduct. It seems possible that Kant's postulation of moral interest as the motivating impulse for phenomenal moral behavior compromised the effort. But that need not be settled here. We must try to understand Kant's enterprise.

A hypothetical imperative is the only kind which Hume regards as possible. It states what a given desire provides one with a motivation to do, and it applies only if one is subject to that desire. The desire itself is not commanded by the imperative. Consequently no hypothetical imperative can state an unconditional requirement on action.

Kant's effort to produce a categorical imperative is an attempt to discover requirements on action which apply to a man on no conditions about what he wants, how he feels, etc. They must nevertheless be requirements whose validity involves the capacity to be motivated in accordance with them. Since that motivational factor cannot come from a presupposed motivation which is made a condition of the requirements, it must, if it is to exist at all, come from the requirements themselves. That is, what makes the requirements valid for us must itself determine the capacity of our motivational structure to yield corresponding action. Thus, according to Kant, ethics, rather than appropriating an antecedently comprehensible motivational foundation on which to build its requirements, actually uncovers a motivational structure which is specifically ethical and which is explained by precisely what explains those requirements. It is the conception of ourselves as free which he alleges to be the source of our acceptance of the imperatives of morality, and it is the acceptance of the imperatives thus grounded by which he explains moral motivation. This is moreover not a motivational explanation, since instead of making use of the motivational system, it explains one of its fundamental features.

V. DESIRES

1. Beginning with relatively uncontroversial cases, we must try to arrive at general conclusions about the sources of reasons and their mode of operation. Eventually we shall deal with prudence as a model for the treatment of altruism: the difficulties which arise in the two cases depend on similar arguments and fallacies. Most important, the interpretation of that feature of reasons on which prudence depends provides a model for the parallel enterprise in the case of altruism.

I shall argue that the superficially plausible method of accounting for all motivations in terms of the agent's desires will not work, and that the truth is considerably less obvious and more significant. It is therefore necessary to begin with an investigation of the role of desires in rational motivation generally, in order to demonstrate that what they can explain is limited, and that even in simple cases they produce action by a mechanism which is not itself explicable in terms of desires.

The attempt to derive all reasons from desires stems from the acknowledgment that reasons must be capable of motivating, together with an assumption which I shall attack—that all motivation has desire at its source. The natural position to be opposed is this: since all motivated action must result from the operation of some motivating factor within the agent, and since belief cannot by itself produce action, it follows that a desire of the agent must always be operative if the action is to be genuinely his. Anything else, any external factor or belief adduced in explanation of the action, must on this view be connected with it through some desire which the agent has at the time, a desire which can take the action or its goal as object. So any apparently prudential or altruistic act must be explained by the connection between its goal—the agent's future interest or the interest of another—and a desire which activates him now. Essentially this view denies the possibility of motivational action at a distance, whether over time or between persons. It bridges any apparent gaps with desires of the agent, which are thought to supply the necessary links to the future and to external situations.

Prudence cannot on this view be explained merely by the perception that something is in one's future interest; there must be a desire to further one's future interests if the perception is to have an effect. What follows about altruism is similar: I cannot be motivated simply by the knowledge that an act of mine will have certain consequences for the interests of others; I must care what happens to them if this knowledge is to be effective. There seems little doubt that most people have the desire that makes prudence possible, though it is sometimes overcome by other, more immediate impulses. Altruistic or benevolent desires on the other hand seem less common. In neither case are we in any sense required to possess the desires in question: consequently we are not required to act on the specified considerations. If one lacks the relevant desire, there is nothing more to be said.

The consequence of this view, for a system of normative reasons, is that the interests of others, or his own future interests, cannot themselves provide a person with reasons for action unless we are prepared to admit also that reasons by themselves, or conditions sufficient for their presence, may provide us with no motivation for action whatever. The separation of normative from motivational discourse has of course been attempted. But if one finds that move implausible, and wishes some guarantee that reasons will provide a motive, then one is left with no alternative, on the motivational premises already laid out, but to include a present desire of the agent, one with appropriate scope, among the conditions for the presence of any reason for action whatever. Therefore another's interest, or my own future interest, can provide me with a reason—a reason capable of motivating—only if a desire for that object is present in me at the time.

The consequences for any other-regarding morality are extreme, for if one wishes to guarantee its universal application, one must make the presence of reasons for altruistic behavior depend on a desire present in all men. (No wonder self-interest has so often been preferred to altruism as the foundation for justice and the other social virtues.) This view eliminates the possibility of construing ethical principles so based as requirements on action, unless

one can somehow show that the appropriate underlying *desires* are required of us.

2. The assumption that a motivating desire underlies every intentional act depends, I believe, on a confusion between two sorts of desires, motivated and unmotivated. It has been pointed out before[2] that many desires, like many beliefs, are *arrived at* by decision and after deliberation. They need not simply assail us, though there are certain desires that do, like the appetites and in certain cases the emotions. The same is true of beliefs, for often, as when we simply perceive something, we acquire a belief without arriving at it by decision. The desires which simply come to us are unmotivated though they can be explained. Hunger is produced by lack of food, but is not motivated thereby. A desire to shop for groceries, after discovering nothing appetizing in the refrigerator, is on the other hand motivated by hunger. Rational or motivational explanation is just as much in order for that desire as for the action itself.

The claim that a desire underlies every act is true only if desires are taken to include motivated as well as unmotivated desires, and it is true only in the sense that *whatever* may be the motivation for someone's intentional pursuit of a goal, it becomes in virtue of his pursuit *ipso facto* appropriate to ascribe to him a desire for that goal. But if the desire is a motivated one, the explanation of it will be the same as the explanation of his pursuit, and it is by no means obvious that a desire must enter into this further explanation. Although it will no doubt be generally admitted that some desires are motivated, the issue is whether another desire always lies behind the motivated one, or whether sometimes the motivation of the initial desire involves no reference to another, unmotivated desire.

Therefore it may be admitted as trivial that, for example, considerations about my future welfare or about the interests of others cannot motivate me to act without a desire being present at the time of action. That I have the appropriate desire simply *follows* from the fact that these considerations motivate me; if the likelihood that an act will promote my future happiness motivates me to perform it now, then it is appropriate to ascribe to me a desire for my own future happiness. But nothing follows about the role of the desire as a condition contributing to the motivational efficacy of those considerations. It is a necessary condition of their efficacy to be sure, but only a logically necessary condition. It is not necessary either as a contributing influence, or as a causal condition.

In fact, if the desire is itself motivated, it and the corresponding motivation will presumably be possible for the same reasons. Thus it remains an open question whether an additional, unmotivated desire must always be found among the conditions of motivation by any other factor whatever. If considerations of future happiness can motivate by themselves, then they can explain and render intelligible the desire for future happiness which is ascribable to anyone whom they do motivate. Alternatively, there may be another factor operating in such cases, one which explains both the motivational influence of considerations about the future and the motivated desire which embodies that influence. But if a further, unmotivated desire is always among those further conditions, it has yet to be proved.

If we bring these observations to bear on the question whether desires are always among the necessary conditions of *reasons* for action, it becomes obvious that there is no reason to believe that they are. Often the desires which an agent necessarily experiences in acting will be motivated exactly as the action is. If the act is motivated by reasons stemming from certain external factors, and the desire to perform it is motivated by those same reasons, the desire obviously cannot be among the conditions for the presence of those reasons. This will be true of any motivated desire which is ascribable to someone simply in virtue of his intentional pursuit of a goal. The fact that the presence of a desire is a logically necessary condition (because it is a logical consequence) of a reason's motivating, does not entail that it is a necessary condition of the *presence* of the reason; and if it is motivated by that reason it *cannot* be among the reason's conditions.

3. As I have said earlier, the temptation to postulate a desire at the root of every motivation is similar to the temptation to postulate a belief behind every inference. Now we can see that the reply in both cases is the same: that this is true in the trivial sense that a

desire or belief is always present when reasons motivate or convince—but not that the desire or belief explains the motivation or conclusion, or provides a reason for it. If someone draws conclusions in accordance with a principle of logic such as *modus ponens,* it is appropriate to ascribe to him the belief that the principle is true; but that belief is explained by the *same* thing which explains his inferences in accordance with the principle. The belief that this principle is true is certainly not among the *conditions* for having reasons to draw conclusions in accordance with it. Rather it is the perception of those reasons which explains both the belief and the particular conclusions drawn.

Beliefs provide the material for theoretical reasoning, but finally there is something besides belief, namely reason, which underlies our inferences from one set of beliefs to another, and explains both the conclusions and those logical beliefs which embody our inferential principles in general propositional form. Correspondingly, desires are among the materials for practical reasoning, but ultimately something besides desire explains how reasons function. This element accounts for many of the connections between reasons (including the reasons which stem from desires) and action. It also explains those general desires which embody our acceptance of the principles of practical reason.

The omnipresence of desires in action is misleading, for it suggests that a desire must form the basis of every motivation. But in fact, when we examine the logical reason why desire must always be present, we see that it may often be motivated by precisely what motivates the action. An alternative basis for that motivation must therefore be discovered. The alternative which I . . . defend does not require one to abandon the assumption that reasons must be capable of motivating. It merely points out that they may have this capacity precisely because they are reasons, and not because a motivationally influential factor is among their conditions of application.

An account in terms of the structure of reasons and their relations to their conditions and to each other has the advantage of rendering the motivation of action by those conditions significantly more intelligible than does the mere postulation of intervening desires. It explains the peculiar intelligibility of prudential motivation, and also . . . the possibility of altruistic motivation—both without the assistance of intervening desires for future happiness or the welfare of others.

4. To summarize the argument briefly:
Though all motivation implies the presence of desire, the sense in which this is true does not warrant us in concluding that all motivation requires that desire be operative as a motivational *influence.* To that extent it remains open that there can be motivation without any motivating desire.

Some desires are themselves motivated by reasons. Those desires at any rate cannot be among the conditions of the reasons which motivate them. And since there may in principle be motivation without motivating desires, those reasons may be motivationally efficacious even without the presence of any *further* desires among their conditions.

There are two ways in which this might be so; either some other motivating factor besides desire may be present among the conditions for the existence of those reasons; or else their motivational efficacy may derive not from the conditions themselves, but rather from the principle which governs the derivation of reasons from those conditions.

In the latter event, the motivational efficacy of reasons for action would be due only to the system by which they are derived from their conditions. This would be explained by a connection between the structure of a system of reasons and the structure of human motivation. In that sense it would still be true that a reason is necessarily capable of motivating. . . .

NOTES

1. Because he holds that to imagine the feeling or sensation of another is to have a faint copy of that feeling oneself; hence the imagination of the pain of others will itself be painful.
2. For example by Aristotle: *Nicomachean Ethics,* Book III, Chapter 3.

STUDY QUESTIONS

1. What is the distinction between "internalism" and "externalism"?
2. What is meant by "prudence"?
3. What lessons does Nagel draw from the parallel between prudence and altruism?
4. Can the desire to help others be as strong as the desire to help ourselves?

Moral Cognitivism and Motivation

Sigrún Svavarsdóttir

Nagel and others take judgment (or motivational) internalism as a position to be explained, not justified. Those who question it usually rely on the examples of amoralists or psychopaths, who know they morally ought to act in a certain way yet have no motivation to do so. Intuitions, however, are divided as to whether such cases are possible. Sigrún Svavarsdóttir, Associate Professor of Philosophy at Tufts University, seeks to show that, in this matter, the burden of proof falls on the internalists. She describes the case of Patrick, who asserts that he ought to help a persecuted stranger but appears not motivated to do so. In considering various accounts of this behavior, Svavarsdóttir argues that internalists, by ruling out the case on conceptual grounds, unnecessarily restrict the set of possible explanations. She concludes that the internalists are mistaken in not taking seriously the possibility that Patrick might be making a genuine moral judgment while not motivated in the slightest to conform.

The impact moral judgments have on our deliberations and actions seems to vary a great deal. Moral judgments play a large part in the lives of some people, who are apt not only to make them, but also to be guided by them in the sense that they tend to pursue what they judge to be of moral value, and shun what they judge to be of moral disvalue. But it seems unrealistic to claim that moral judgments play a pervasive role in the lives of all or even most people. There are considerable variations in how strong a tendency people have to think in moral terms, and in how such thoughts affect their decisions and actions. For every moral hero who single-mindedly pursues moral values, there are thousands of less committed people who only do so when it does not cost them too much in material comfort, personal relations, or social standing. And of course, what counts as too much varies from person to person. On top of such variations, there are those who consistently display moral indifference—people who concede, for example, that certain investment policies have morally problematic consequences, but who can readily and without compunction ignore that in their business decisions. There even seem to be moral subversives, people who intentionally and knowingly pursue what they acknowledge to be morally wrong or bad, and do so for that very reason.

Such variations in moral motivation—motivation by moral judgments—strike me as constituting good reasons for thinking, first, that moral judgments need to be supplemented by a distinct conative state (desire in the broadest sense of that term) in order to play a motivational role; second, that this conative attitude is *not* necessarily present in those

From Sigrún Svavarsdóttir, "Moral Cognitivism and Motivation," *The Philosophical Review* 108 (1999). Reprinted by permission of the publisher.

who make moral judgments; and, third, that its motivational strength varies from person to person. Of course, the conceptual content of the judgment and the conative state have to be appropriately related: the judgment has to represent the object of evaluation in a way that engages the conative attitude in question. This suggests that making a moral judgment is a matter of conceiving of something as being a certain way and that this way of conceiving of an object is no more dependent on the motivational states of the thinker than is conceiving, say, of the day as sunny; nor need it affect the motivational states of the thinker any more than the latter judgment does. But although an agent need not be guided in the sense of being motivated by his moral judgment, moral judgments—unlike judgments about the weather—are in some sense invariably action-guiding: for any type of moral judgment, there are fairly determinate ways in which an agent, irrespective of his ends, may act *in accord with* or *contrary to* it. Thus, even when the moral subversive sets the house on fire because she believes it is evil, she acts in some sense contrary to the judgment that it is evil to put the house on fire.[1]

These observations provide, I submit, a good starting point for an inquiry into the nature of moral judgments. In light of them, it seems reasonable to adopt the working hypothesis that moral thought involves conceptual resources employed in the formation both of cognitive states (belief, doubt, worry, etc.) and conative and emotional states (desire, hope, wish, anger, relief, etc.). The challenge is to understand what is distinctive about these conceptual resources and especially in what way they are more intimately bound up with the regulation of conduct than are those involved in conveying information, say, about climatic conditions, given that judgments about both moral and climatic matters motivate only when they engage a desire with appropriately related content.

In taking this approach, I am rejecting the *internalist* thesis that there is a necessary connection between moral judgment and motivation, a thesis that is widely accepted as a constraint of adequacy on accounts of moral judgments. The main goal of the present paper is to undermine this constraint. . . .

1. MOTIVATIONAL INTERNALISM

The internalist thesis in question makes a claim about the connection between the mental act of making a moral judgment and motivation. *Motivational internalism* seems, therefore, an appropriate label; and *motivational externalism* will serve as a name for the opposing view. In its strongest form, motivational internalism states that moral judgments are "intrinsically" motivating; in other words, they motivate on their own rather than in collaboration with a distinct conative state. Although the label 'internalism' suggests this strong version, it is more in line with the existing literature to formulate the thesis as claiming that moral judgments are *necessarily connected* to motivation to pursue or promote what is judged favorably and to shun or prevent what is judged unfavorably. Thus formulated, motivational internalism is compatible with the view that the motivation imported by a moral judgment has its roots in a distinct conative state that is, however, necessarily connected to the moral judgment. The necessity at stake is supposed to be conceptual necessity. Presumably, the idea is that the ascription conditions for moral judgments are such that an agent could not be considered to have made a specific moral judgment unless he were motivated in a specific way—or, some might prefer, the possession conditions for moral concepts are such that an agent could not sincerely and competently apply them without being motivated in a specific way.

Some further modifications of the thesis have been proposed in response to Michael Stocker's observation that under conditions of deep depression, severe cases of weakness of will, and other maladies of the spirit, the connection between moral judgment and motivation is often broken, even in individuals who are normally motivated by their moral judgments.[2] . . .

I am not inclined to resist a modification of the internalist thesis meant to block Stocker's counterexamples. . . . Incorporating this qualification into my statement of motivational internalism, the thesis under scrutiny is that *moral judgments are of conceptual necessity connected to motivation to pursue or promote what is judged favorably and to shun or prevent what is judged unfavorably, except in individuals suffering from motivational disorders that affect them more generally.* (From now on, I will not explicitly state the exception clause, but it should be understood as implicit.)

Notice that motivational internalism, as stated, does not claim that the motivation necessarily accompanying moral judgments overrides all other motivation. Indeed, the position is silent on the strength of the accompanying motivation, and even allows that its strength varies from agent to agent. Internalists will, therefore, acknowledge most of my observations about variations in moral motivation. However, they have to contest my claim that some people, not suffering from general motivational disorders, are unmoved by their moral judgments or are even moved by them to pursue evil and do wrong. This is supposed to be a conceptual impossibility.

The internalist thesis is often invoked in the debate between noncognitivists and cognitivists about moral thought and language. *Cognitivism,* as understood here, maintains that moral judgments employ representational resources, expressible in the moral vocabulary of our public language. Moral judgments are related to moral beliefs in the standard way that beliefs and judgments with the same content are related. Both moral judgments and beliefs, as well as the sentences expressing them, are truth-evaluable.[3] In contrast, *noncognitivism,* as understood here, maintains that moral judgments manifest some sort of conative attitudes taken towards the object of evaluation under a nonmoral mode of presentation.[4] The moral terms of the public language are not representational devices; instead, they function semantically as mood indicators that signal a grammatical mood, employed to express these sorts of conative attitudes. In spite of our frequent use of the truth predicate in moral discourse, neither moral judgments nor moral sentences provide truth-evaluable representations of the object of evaluation. It should be fairly obvious that the internalist constraint prima facie favors noncognitivism: if moral judgments manifest conative states of mind, they will necessarily have some motivational force,

whereas if they manifest beliefs, it needs to be explained why they would—unlike most beliefs—be necessarily motivating. If the internalist constraint is accepted, the burden is on the cognitivists to show that they can meet it.

Indeed, the internalist constraint is often touted as providing conclusive rather than only prima facie support for noncognitivism. But as several cognitivists have pointed out, it can provide conclusive support for noncognitivism only if it is supplemented by the thesis that the motivating power of beliefs invariably relies on the contingent presence of a desire whose content is appropriately related to the belief's content. Many of these cognitivists actually accept the internalist constraint, but reject the Humean view that motivation is always rooted in a desire . . . Some may even attempt to reconcile the internalist constraint, the Humean view of motivation, and moral cognitivism. It might, for example, be argued that although moral judgments are belief-like and therefore—given the Humean thesis—motivationally inert *on their own,* their content is such that they could not be made in the absence of a desire that provided the source of moral motivation.

My working hypothesis that moral thought involves conceptual resources employed in the formation of cognitive, conative, and emotional states clearly puts me in camp with cognitivists. However, I am *not* inclined to take on the burden of explaining how moral cognitivism is to be reconciled with internalism, since I am of a firm externalist conviction and—as explained in the introduction—believe that it helps to provide an interesting starting point for an inquiry into the nature of moral judgments. Instead, I will seek to undermine the internalist thesis as a constraint of adequacy on accounts of moral judgments. . . .

I have a . . . simple-minded proposal: the disposition to be motivated by one's moral judgments is grounded in a conative attitude (desire) taken towards objects under a moral mode of presentation. For convenience, call it *the desire to be moral.* I expect that it varies from agent to agent which other mental states sustain that desire. In some cases, it may be sustained by a healthy dose of sympathy with others, as well as an acceptance of a norm of benevolence. In other cases it will, instead or additionally, be sustained by a desire to be able to justify one's conduct from an impartial standpoint. But undoubtedly, there are also cases in which it is sustained, say, by an awe of God and a theological view of the foundations of morality, or by a fear of punishment. It may also just stand there pretty much on its own, not dependent on any other motive at that particular stage in the person's life. . . .

3. AN ARGUMENT AGAINST THE INTERNALIST CONSTRAINT

Motivational externalists typically argue their case by giving a counterexample to the internalist thesis: they sketch an actual or fictional case of a person described as being adept at making moral judgments but entirely unmoved by them, although not suffering from any general motivational disorder.[5] The problem with such counterexamples is that many people cannot recognize them as such: descriptions of such cases strike them as incoherent. Here intuitions conflict, leading to yet another apparently intractable philosophical disagreement. Externalists and internalists may, therefore, seem to have equal burden to explain the contrary intuition away or support their position with a positive argument. My aim in this section is to show that the burden of argument lies squarely on the internalists' shoulders and that consequently the internalist thesis cannot be invoked as a constraint of adequacy on accounts of moral judgments.

Let's start with an example:

The Example of Patrick: Virginia has put her social position at risk to help a politically persecuted stranger because she thinks it is the right thing to do. Later she meets Patrick, who could, without any apparent risk to himself, similarly help a politically persecuted stranger, but who has made no attempt to do so. Our morally committed heroine confronts Patrick, appealing first to his compassion for the victims. Patrick rather wearily tells her that he has no inclination

to concern himself with the plight of strangers. Virginia then appeals to explicit moral considerations: in this case, helping the strangers is his moral obligation and a matter of fighting enormous injustice. Patrick readily declares that he agrees with her moral assessment, but nevertheless cannot be bothered to help. Virginia presses him further, arguing that the effort required is minimal and, given his position, will cost him close to nothing. Patrick responds that the cost is not really the issue, he just does not care to concern himself with such matters. Later he shows absolutely no sign of regret for either his remarks or his failure to help.

Notice that Patrick has not been described as making a moral judgment without being motivationally affected by it. Nothing has been said about Patrick's mental states. Instead, I have described his overt—verbal and nonverbal—behavior and the features of his situation that would be readily discernible to observers. The description of the case should be readily acceptable to both externalists and internalists.

Patrick's callousness is, of course, baffling, and his exchange with Virginia suggests that he has some major character flaws. But how exactly are we to understand his conduct? Is his assent to Virginia's moral judgment insincere? Is he trying to outrage her? Is he held back by an unreasonable fear of the possible consequences for himself, even if it is obvious that there is no danger to himself involved? Is his moral commitment so weak that the cost in time and energy is enough to override it? Is he hiding his shame and regret? Or is he just callous and cynical about moral matters? It is not clear what to say. However, our epistemic situation in this case is not significantly different from what it is in any other circumstances when we are trying to figure out the psychological states of others. Our understanding of others relies on observations of what they say, their body language, and their overt behavior, preferably over time. . . . And, furthermore, we have to rely heavily on the assumption that there is, typically, a great stability in people's mental lives over time. Although our mental states are subject to various changes, there is a certain consistency for most of us in how easily and under what conditions these changes are effected, which suggests the existence of longstanding mental dispositions on our part: abiding character traits, deep-rooted concerns or attitudes, and fundamental beliefs.

Let's, therefore, add some further information about how Patrick has behaved in the past.

Additional Information about Patrick: Besides being known for courage and conservative estimates of risk to himself, Patrick is independently minded and earnest to a fault—indeed, honest to the point of tactlessness and even cruelty. And in any case, he has nothing to gain from misleading Virginia in the given circumstances. Moreover, Patrick makes claims couched in moral terms infrequently and impassionately, and never gives them as reasons for his actions. He has frequently been observed taking actions that seem pretty uncontroversially wrong (or in other ways morally problematic) without displaying any signs of hesitation or regret. In contrast, he has often displayed obvious signs of regret and shame when his plans have misfired, he has overestimated risk to himself, or he has publicly embarrassed himself in matters he finds important. He has also passed up numerous opportunities to perform obvious and uncostly moral deeds. However, when prodded, he will engage in prolonged and intelligent conversations about moral matters and seemingly take an independent stand on the moral status of a controversial public policy or an action. Nonetheless, he usually ends such conversations by volunteering the opinion that he has long ago rid himself of any aspiration to live by moral standards.

I submit that given this information about Patrick, it would be reasonable to exclude not only the hypothesis that he was overcome by unreasonable fear while too ashamed to admit so, but also the hypotheses that his assent was insincere and that his moral commitment wavered or was very limited to start with. Indeed, it seems most plausible to conclude

that he has no moral commitment and is completely cynical about moral matters: he knew what was right to do in the circumstances, but could not have cared less.

Motivational internalists will tell us that this cannot be the right conclusion to draw under any circumstances. They will insist that Patrick has—in spite of his disavowal—some inkling of motivation to do what he judges morally right or good, or he is not making a sincere and competent moral judgment. Now, I readily grant internalists that in spite of all outer signs of sincerity and competency in judgment and of lack of motivation, it is *possible* that Patrick is—purely on a whim or for some obscure reason—misleading his interlocutor, or that he is constantly fighting, even repressing, inclinations to pursue what he judges to be of moral value. But I would think that the explanation that strikes me as the most plausible one is also in the running. This internalists will deny. Notice that at this point, I am not so much interested in which explanation of Patrick's behavior is the most plausible one, but rather in which explanations cannot be readily ruled out as false or in other ways defective. Internalists and externalists have conflicting intuitions in this matter. But when there is a conflict of intuitions (among intelligent and sensible people) about which hypotheses are in the running as an explanation of some observable phenomenon, the burden of argument is on those who insist on a more restrictive class of explanations. This seems to me entirely reasonable as a methodological principle governing empirical investigation.

An example unrelated to the externalist-internalist dispute might help to make this plausible: Imagine that Alice points out to a fellow microbiologist, Gary, an explanation of his data that competes with the explanation he has advanced. Assuming that Alice is no crackpot but, rather, an intelligent and sensible fellow researcher, Gary cannot responsibly dismiss Alice's challenge without having some reason for ruling out her hypothesis. He might be able to rule out the hypothesis as radically misconceived, as not even being a logically possible explanation. Or, he might be able to rule it out as having bizarre metaphysical commitments, being inconsistent with a well-confirmed background theory, being farfetched, assuming too many coincidences, or overlooking some aspects of the data. But then he might not be able to give any credible reason for ruling out Alice's explanation, in which case he would have to admit that both explanations are in the running, even if he continues to favor his original one and seek evidence to confirm it. It may be objected that Alice has an equal burden to support her contention that the class of explanatory hypotheses in the running needs to be expanded. I readily concede that she would have to support such a general claim by proposing at least one new hypothesis and articulating clearly how it is supposed to account for the data (as she has *ex hypothesi* already done). But Alice does not have any further burden of supporting her claim that the hypothesis is in the running unless she has been given some clearly articulated reasons for dismissing it. It strikes me as reasonable that there is this asymmetry in the burden of argument when the issue is simply what explanations cannot readily be ruled out as false or in other ways defective. A methodological principle that condones this asymmetry in the burden of argument serves to counter our lack of imagination, narrow-mindedness, biases, and intellectual laziness: one cannot responsibly dismiss something that strikes other intelligent and sensible people as a feasible explanation without having some story about why it should be ruled out. There is less danger in overlooking the truth if we hang on to a proposed explanation in face of skepticism from intelligent and sensible people so long as no (unanswered) reasons have been given for dismissing it. The contested explanation will minimally serve as a healthy reminder that the support for favored candidates is still inconclusive.

By casting us in the role of observers trying to understand Patrick's conduct, I have shifted our perspective from a philosophical investigation of moral judgments to an empirical investigation of observable behavior. In this context, the conflicting externalist and internalist intuitions are triggered by the question whether a certain hypothesis is in the running as an explanation of the behavior. This has enabled me to appeal to a methodological principle governing empirical investigations to shift the burden of argument onto the internalists. In order to make my point as forcefully as possible, I have concentrated on a case in which the epistemic possibility in dispute seems to me not only one of the hypotheses that need to be considered, but actually the most plausible one, given the information provided about the agent's past and present behavior. But that intuition need not be universally shared for my point to go through: *it is motivational internalists who are restricting the range of the hypotheses that are in the running for explaining Patrick's conduct, so the burden is on them to justify that restriction.*

Motivational internalists will, of course, claim that the disputed hypothesis is conceptually incoherent. This hardly amounts to meeting the burden of argument, given that intelligent and sensible people in command of the relevant concepts have proposed the explanation and it has the familiar structure of a belief-desire explanation. The conceptual mistake has to be laid bare. At this point, the internalists may elaborate that the hypothesis flies in the face of the conceptual truth that moral judgments necessarily motivate those who make them. It is not question-begging to support the internalist restrictive intuition about the class of feasible explanations by thus invoking the internalist thesis itself. But the move invites the question, Why think this is a conceptual truth? And obviously, it would be question-begging for internalists to appeal to their intuition at that point, since the internalist thesis has already been invoked in defense of that very intuition.

If the internalist thesis is supposed to express a conceptual truth, there must be some concept or concepts that exclude as incoherent the explanatory hypothesis externalists favor. It seems the only way to go for the internalist is to identify these concepts and defend an analysis of them that yields the internalist thesis as a corollary. There are two candidates. One is the class of concepts employed in moral judgments, for example, *good, right, just*. The other is the concept of a *moral* judgment: we simply could not conceive of a mental act as a *moral* judgment unless it had the appropriate motivational impact.[6] If the internalist thesis can be shown to fall out of *the best* account of one or the other of these candidates, externalists will have to acknowledge that they were touting an incoherent explanatory hypothesis. I am not going to argue here that such a defense of motivational internalism is bound to fail. Rather I simply want to emphasize that such a defense would be non-question-begging *only if* the internalist thesis had not been invoked as a criterion for deciding between competing accounts of these concepts. It would be blatantly circular to argue for the internalist constraint on the basis that it falls out of the best account of moral concepts, but then defend that account partly on the ground that it, in contrast with some or all of the contenders, meets the internalist constraint. But then internalists are not in a position to advocate their thesis as a constraint of adequacy on accounts of moral thought and language. Even if we could discover on the basis of an a priori investigation that the internalist thesis is a conceptual truth, it is not an obvious conceptual platitude that can be invoked as a constraint of adequacy on accounts of moral thought and language at this stage of our limited understanding of the relevant conceptual resources.

. . . I would like to supplement my attack on motivational internalism by offering a debunking diagnosis of the internalist intuition.

4. EXPLAINING AWAY THE INTERNALIST INTUITION

Indeed, it does not seem such a hard task to explain away the internalist intuition. First of all, I suspect that in many instances the internalist intuition reflects not a firm grip on moral concepts, but rather a deep moral commitment that makes it hard for the individual in question to imagine how anyone could be motivationally unaffected by his moral judgments. Our attitudes and commitments all too often cloud our imagination in this way. The internalist's mistake is to think that the possibility he cannot envisage is inconceivable. Secondly, the internalist intuition may also reflect the optimism of the overzealous moralist that moral motivation is somehow guaranteed, if only we get people to see moral

matters aright. And thirdly, the internalist intuition may be bred by the wish to close an embarrassing skeptical question. The internalist thesis has the consequence that a certain sort of moral skeptic can simply be dismissed as suffering from conceptual confusion. This is not the skeptic who questions the existence of moral facts or moral properties (call this one a *metaphysical skeptic*), but rather the skeptic who questions our commitment to morality (call this one a *commitment skeptic*). This skeptic does not dispute that there are morally better and worse alternatives, but wonders why that should affect our decision making and action. He need not be cynical about moral judgments; he may be thoroughly committed to morality, but still wonder whether it makes sense—whether there is any justification for being thus committed. But his question presupposes that it is at least conceptually possible to be a moral cynic. So, if internalists are right, this skeptical question can simply be dismissed as an incoherent worry. Now, philosophy is littered with attempts to lay to rest uncomfortable and persistent skeptical questions by unmasking them as based on some conceptual confusion, but most of these have been in vain. A controversial intuition that serves exactly the purpose of closing such a question is extremely suspect.

Although I have much confidence in the above debunking explanations of the internalist intuition, I doubt they give the full story behind the pervasive appeal of internalism. Admittedly, I would probably experience puzzlement upon encountering an individual who made a moral assessment of his circumstances, yet appeared indifferent to moral values. A part of the puzzlement is over a psychological makeup: how could anyone be so emotionally impoverished as not to connect motivationally with the kind of considerations driving moral evaluation? It is somewhat on a par with the puzzlement some of us have experienced over people who seem to be able to recognize the beauty of a rugged landscape without being deeply moved by it: the person who nods with a smile, snaps a picture, and then hurriedly moves on to a more welcoming spot. But the puzzlement seems to run even deeper, especially when the person volunteers the moral judgments:

Why would anyone who is completely indifferent to moral considerations bother to take note of the moral conditions of his surroundings? This perplexity may, however, be traced to the assumption that an individual who bothers to make a moral judgment possesses some degree of moral commitment, an assumption that conflicts with the description of the individual as making a moral judgment and not being in the least motivated by it. For a moral commitment is a commitment to the realization of moral values; and it is a priori true that one could not be committed to something unless one were, *other things equal,* motivated to do what one judges will *best* protect or enhance that something, and abstain from whatever one judges to be detrimental to that something. This, surely, falls out of the concept of a commitment.

It seems reasonable to operate with the assumption that an individual who bothers to make moral judgments is morally committed to some degree, but I see nothing against giving up this assumption when we get significant evidence to the contrary. And once we have done so, there is nothing puzzling about the idea that the person in question fails to be motivated by his sincere and competent moral judgments. It is when we ignore the role of this crucial assumption that we feel the pull toward the internalist position. Put differently: The internalist thesis would be uncontroversial *if* its domain were restricted to morally committed individuals. Those who advocate motivational internalism as a conceptual platitude are ignoring this crucial restriction. Of course, the restriction should be lifted, if it were established that a moral commitment is a precondition for the capacity for making sincere and competent moral judgments. But, given my earlier argument, that would have to be done on grounds that are neutral with respect to the debate between internalists and externalists.

More puzzling than the cynics we have encountered so far is an individual who judges that one course of action is of lesser moral value than another, but is motivated *on account of that very judgment* to take the former alternative. And he is surely rivaled by an agent who becomes all enthused upon judging that an action is of some minor moral value,

but loses considerable interest when realizing that it is of much greater moral value than he initially supposed. But rather than pose problems for externalists, these cases nicely illustrate the strength of the above explanatory framework. The fact that the former character is motivated by his moral judgment enforces our initial assumption that he has a moral commitment of some degree, but that is *other things equal* inconsistent with his being more motivated to pursue what he judges to be the lesser of two moral values. (Of course, our diverse commitments may come into conflict and various other things may interfere with our commitments, with the result that overall we are—notwithstanding our moral commitment—motivated to pursue a thing we judge to be of lesser moral value than something else available to us. But it is particularly puzzling when, as in the above case, the very judgment about the relative value of two alternatives does not motivate an agent, committed to that value, to pursue the one he judges to be the greater of the two.) At the same time, it seems more difficult than in the previous cynic cases to withdraw the assumption that the individual in question is morally committed, given that he is motivationally affected by his moral judgment. Similar observations can be made about the second case above. Both imagined scenarios put us in the paradoxical position of prima facie being able to treat the individual encountered neither as a moral cynic nor as a morally committed person. Thus, this explanatory framework allows us to account for why these two cases are more puzzling than the previous ones. Nevertheless, there is a way of dispelling the puzzlement in both cases—namely, by telling a story that shows that we should give up our (reasonable) assumption that the agent is morally committed. For example: The person in question is a cynic who is normally indifferent to moral values; however, he has made a bet with a friend that he will do something of minor moral value in the next few days, while having avowed not to do anything of great moral value in his life. But although this scenario is possible, it is certainly not the most obvious thing to occur to us, nor is it very likely to be true.

The beauty of the above explanation of our likely puzzlement upon encountering moral cynics is that besides relying on a relatively uncontroversial claim about what it is to be committed to something and making sense of the difference in the degree of puzzlement over the above cases, it enables us to understand the pervasive appeal of internalism. Maybe the internalist intuition is not merely the offspring of wishful thinking, moralistic optimism, and substantive commitments. Its roots probably lie in a perfectly legitimate intuition pertaining to the concept of commitment. . . .

8. IN CLOSING

I hope to have convinced the reader that, regarded as a thesis in motivational theory, internalism is not plausible . . . Motivational internalism probably appeals to many because they think it is a way of rendering more precise the plausible—possibly platitudinous—claim that the point of moral evaluation is distinctively to guide conduct. The distinctive directional role of moral judgments is thus equated with a motivational role. This is too hasty. It is entirely unclear what follows from the rather vague claim concerning the point of moral evaluation. It certainly suggests that the primary use of the conceptual resources involved in moral evaluation is to enable us to think through our circumstances and behavioral options in a distinctive way with an eye to deciding how to act. But it is far from clear whether this means that a competent exercise of the concepts involved is tied to our conative states or sentiments in such a way that sincere moral judgments are intrinsically or necessarily motivating. Indeed, even if our primary interests in employing these conceptual resources were echoed in some of the constraints to which they are subject (as I am inclined to think), it need not follow that it is impossible to exploit these resources in sincere, literal, and competent judgments without taking on these interests or having the underlying concerns. And even if it were necessary to have a rather subtle understanding of these concerns, it is not thereby said that one has to have them. Maybe the presence of these conceptual resources in humans is due to our having certain abiding concerns; and maybe the

nature of these concepts reflects to some extent the nature of these concerns; and maybe the mastery of these concepts requires, or at least is aided by, understanding of these concerns. But nothing of this implies that, in order to use these conceptual resources competently, an *individual* has to be committed to taking sincere judgments employing these concepts as his guide to conduct. Nor does it imply that the application conditions of these concepts are somehow tied to expressions of the concerns in virtue of which we typically have an interest in employing them. . . .

NOTES

1. Here I have in mind Dostoyevsky's fictional character Lisa (the little she-devil) in *The Brothers of Karamazov.*
2. Michael Stocker, "Desiring the Bad: An Essay in Moral Psychology," *Journal of Philosophy* 76 (1979): 738–53.
3. Notice that I have formulated cognitivism so that it does not involve any ontic commitment to moral facts or properties. It is a view about the nature of moral thought and the semantics of moral language. Prima facie, a cognitivist could be either a realist or an error theorist about moral thought and discourse. . . .
4. 'Moral judgment' has become a term of art in the metaethical literature. It is used to refer to the mental and speech acts central to moral evaluation, whatever their nature may be. Since I am concentrating on moral motivation in this paper, I will be mostly using it to refer to the relevant mental acts. . . .
5. Brink's objection against motivational internalism consists essentially in bringing up the case of the amoralist (David O. Brink, *Moral Realism and the Foundations of Ethics* [Cambridge: Cambridge University Press, 1989], 46–48): "someone who recognizes certain considerations as moral considerations and yet remains unmoved by them and sees no reason to act on them" (27).
6. These are genuinely distinct candidates. The best way to appreciate this is to consider the theoretical possibility that moral judgments employ concepts like *good, right,* and *just,* but share these concepts with nonmoral judgments; what distinguishes them from judgments that use the same conceptual resources is their attitudinal force, which is in part motivational. On this view, motivational internalism falls out of the

concept of a moral judgment rather than out of the concepts employed in moral judgments. Noncognitivists would also prefer the former candidate, since they do not think moral judgments employ any distinct concepts (assuming concepts are representational devices). . . .

STUDY QUESTIONS

1. How do moral judgments differ from judgments about the weather?
2. According to judgment (or motivational) internalism, do our moral judgments invariably motivate us?
3. What does Svavarsdóttir aim to show with the case of Patrick?
4. Do you find the case of Patrick to be realistic?

Morality as a System of Hypothetical Imperatives

Philippa Foot

Philippa Foot (1920–2010) was Professor of Philosophy at the University of California, Los Angeles. She argues against the Kantian claim that moral imperatives are distinguished by their categorical structure. Consider, for example, rules of etiquette, which are also categorical, applying to every agent regardless of desires or interests. Yet such rules do not provide reasons regardless of an agent's desires or interests. The question, then, to which Foot finds no answer is why we should think rules of morality differ in their normative authority from rules of etiquette. Just as rules of etiquette do not have binding force and can be disregarded without violating rationality, the same is true of moral rules. Moreover, in both cases, failure to adhere to widely accepted guidelines can undermine a person's ability to work with others and achieve common goals.

There are many difficulties and obscurities in Kant's moral philosophy, and few contemporary moralists will try to defend it all; many, for instance, agree in rejecting Kant's derivation of duties from the mere form of law expressed in terms of a universally legislative will. Nevertheless, it is generally supposed, even by those who would not dream of calling themselves his followers, that Kant established one thing beyond doubt—namely, the necessity of distinguishing moral judgments from hypothetical imperatives. That moral judgments cannot be hypothetical imperatives has come to seem an unquestionable truth. It will be argued here that it is not.

In discussing so thoroughly Kantian a notion as that of the hypothetical imperative, one naturally begins by asking what Kant himself meant by a hypothetical imperative, and it may be useful to say a little about the idea of an imperative as this appears in Kant's works. In writing about imperatives Kant seems to be thinking at least as much of statements about what ought to be or should be done, as of injunctions expressed in the imperative mood. He even describes as an imperative the assertion that it would be "good to do or refrain from doing something"[1] and explains that for a will that "does not always do something simply because it is presented to it as a good thing to do" this has the force of a command of reason. We may therefore think of Kant's imperatives as statements to the effect that something ought to be done or that it would be good to do it.

The distinction between hypothetical imperatives and categorical imperatives, which plays so important a part in Kant's ethics, appears in

---

From Philippa Foot, "Morality as a System of Hypothetical Imperatives," *The Philosophical Review* 81 (1972). Reprinted by permission of the publisher.

480

characteristic form in the following passages from the *Foundations of the Metaphysics of Morals*:

> All imperatives command either hypothetically or categorically. The former present the practical necessity of a possible action as a means to achieving something else which one desires (or which one may possibly desire). The categorical imperative would be one which presented an action as of itself objectively necessary, without regard to any other end.[2]
>
> If the action is good only as a means to something else, the imperative is hypothetical; but if it is thought of as good in itself, and hence as necessary in a will which of itself conforms to reason as the principle of this will, the imperative is categorical.[3]

The hypothetical imperative, as Kant defines it, "says only that the action is good to some purpose" and the purpose, he explains, may be possible or actual. Among imperatives related to actual purposes Kant mentions rules of prudence, since he believes that all men necessarily desire their own happiness. Without committing ourselves to this view it will be useful to follow Kant in classing together as "hypothetical imperatives" those telling a man what he ought to do because (or if) he wants something and those telling him what he ought to do on grounds of self-interest. Common opinion agrees with Kant in insisting that a moral man must accept a rule of duty whatever his interests or desires.[4]

Having given a rough description of the class of Kantian hypothetical imperatives it may be useful to point to the heterogeneity within it. Sometimes what a man should do depends on his passing inclination, as when he wants his coffee hot and should warm the jug. Sometimes it depends on some long-term project, when the feelings and inclinations of the moment are irrelevant. If one wants to be a respectable philosopher one should get up in the mornings and do some work, though just at that moment when one should do it the thought of being a respectable philosopher leaves one cold. It is true nevertheless to say of one, at that moment, that one wants to be a respectable philosopher,[5] and this can be the foundation of a desire-dependent hypothetical imperative. The term "desire" as used in the original account of the hypothetical imperative was meant as a grammatically convenient substitute for "want," and was not meant to carry any implication of inclination rather than long-term aim or project. Even the word "project," taken strictly, introduces undesirable restrictions. If someone is devoted to his family or his country or to any cause, there are certain things he wants, which may then be the basis of hypothetical imperatives, without either inclinations or projects being quite what is in question. Hypothetical imperatives should already be appearing as extremely diverse; a further important distinction is between those that concern an individual and those that concern a group. The desires on which a hypothetical imperative is dependent may be those of one man, or may be taken for granted as belonging to a number of people, engaged in some common project or sharing common aims.

Is Kant right to say that moral judgments are categorical, not hypothetical, imperatives? It may seem that he is, for we find in our language two different uses of words such as "should" and "ought," apparently corresponding to Kant's hypothetical and categorical imperatives, and we find moral judgments on the "categorical" side. Suppose, for instance, we have advised a traveler that he should take a certain train, believing him to be journeying to his home. If we find that he has decided to go elsewhere, we will most likely have to take back what we said: the "should" will now be unsupported and in need of support. Similarly, we must be prepared to withdraw our statement about what he should do if we find that the right relation does not hold between the action and the end—that it is either no way of getting what he wants (or doing what he wants to do) or not the most eligible among possible means. The use of "should" and "ought" in moral contexts is, however, quite different. When we say that a man should do something and intend a moral judgment we do not have to back up what we say by considerations about his interests or his desires; if no such connection can be found the "should" need not be withdrawn. It follows that the agent cannot rebut an assertion about what, morally speaking, he should do by showing that the action is not ancillary to his interests or desires. Without such a connection the "should" does not stand unsupported and in need of support; the support that *it* requires is of another kind.[6]

There is, then, one clear difference between moral judgments and the class of "hypothetical imperatives" so far discussed. In the latter "should" is used "hypothetically," in the sense defined, and if Kant were merely drawing attention to this piece of linguistic usage his point would be easily proved. But obviously Kant meant more than this; in describing moral judgments as non-hypothetical—that is, categorical imperatives—he is ascribing to them a special dignity and necessity which this usage cannot give. Modern philosophers follow Kant in talking, for example, about the "unconditional requirement" expressed in moral judgments. These tell us what we have to do whatever our interests or desires, and by their inescapability they are distinguished from hypothetical imperatives.

The problem is to find proof for this further feature of moral judgments. If anyone fails to see the gap that has to be filled it will be useful to point out to him that we find "should" used non-hypothetically in some non-moral statements to which no one attributes the special dignity and necessity conveyed by the description "categorical imperative." For instance, we find this non-hypothetical use of "should" in sentences enunciating rules of etiquette, as, for example, that an invitation in the third person should be answered in the third person, where the rule does not *fail to apply* to someone who has his own good reasons for ignoring this piece of nonsense, or who simply does not care about what, from the point of view of etiquette, he should do. Similarly, there is a non-hypothetical use of "should" in contexts where something like a club rule is in question. The club secretary who has told a member that he should not bring ladies into the smoking room does not say, "Sorry, I was mistaken" when informed that this member is resigning tomorrow and cares nothing about his reputation in the club. Lacking a connection with the agent's desires or interests, this "should" does not stand "unsupported and in need of support"; it requires only the backing of the rule. The use of "should" is therefore "non-hypothetical" in the sense defined.

It follows that if a hypothetical use of "should" gives a hypothetical imperative, and a non-hypothetical use of "should" a categorical imperative, then "should" statements based on rules of etiquette, or rules of a club, are categorical imperatives. Since this would not be accepted by defenders of the categorical imperative in ethics, who would insist that these other "should" statements give hypothetical imperatives, they must be using this expression in some other sense. We must therefore ask what they mean when they say that "You should answer . . . in the third person" is a hypothetical imperative. Very roughly the idea seems to be that one may reasonably ask why anyone should bother about what should (should from the point of view of etiquette) be done, and that such considerations deserve no notice unless reason is shown. So although people give as their reason for doing something the fact that it is required by etiquette, we do not take this consideration as *in itself giving us reason to act*. Considerations of etiquette do not have any automatic reason-giving force, and a man might be right if he denied that he had reason to do "what's done."

This seems to take us to the heart of the matter, for, by contrast, it is supposed that moral considerations necessarily give reasons for acting to any man. The difficulty is, of course, to defend this proposition which is more often repeated than explained. Unless it is said, implausibly, that all "should" or "ought" statements give reasons for acting, which leaves the old problem of assigning a special categorical status to moral judgment, we must be told what it is that makes the moral "should" relevantly different from the "shoulds" appearing in normative statements of other kinds.[7] Attempts have sometimes been made to show that some kind of irrationality is involved in ignoring the "should" of morality: in saying "Immoral—so what?" as one says "Not *comme il faut*—so what?" But as far as I can see these have all rested on some illegitimate assumption, as, for instance, of thinking that the amoral man, who agrees that some piece of conduct is immoral but takes no notice of that, is inconsistently disregarding a rule of conduct that he has accepted; or again of thinking it inconsistent to desire that others will not do to one what one proposes to do to them. The fact is that the man who rejects morality because he sees no reason to obey its rules can be convicted of villainy but not of inconsistency. Nor will his action necessarily be irrational. Irrational actions are those in which a man in some way defeats his own purposes, doing what is calculated to be disadvantageous or to frustrate his ends. Immorality does not *necessarily* involve any such thing.

It is obvious that the normative character of moral judgment does not guarantee its reason-giving force. Moral judgments are normative, but so are judgments of manners, statements of club rules, and many others. Why should the first provide reasons for acting as the others do not? In every case it is because there is a background of teaching that the non-hypothetical "should" can be used. The behavior is required, not simply recommended, but the question remains as to why we should do what we are required to do. It is true that moral rules are often enforced much more strictly than the rules of etiquette, and our reluctance to press the non-hypothetical "should" of etiquette may be one reason why we think of the rules of etiquette as hypothetical imperatives. But are we then to say that there is nothing behind the idea that moral judgments are categorical imperatives but the relative stringency of our moral teaching? I believe that this may have more to do with the matter than the defenders of the categorical imperative would like to admit. For if we look at the kind of thing that is said in its defense we may find ourselves puzzled about what the words can even mean unless we connect them with the feelings that this stringent teaching implants. People talk, for instance, about the "binding force" of morality, but it is not clear what this means if not that we *feel* ourselves unable to escape. Indeed the "inescapability" of moral requirements is often cited when they are being contrasted with hypothetical imperatives. No one, it is said, escapes the requirements of ethics by having or not having particular interests or desires. Taken in one way this only reiterates the contrast between the "should" of morality and the hypothetical "should," and once more places morality alongside of etiquette. Both are inescapable in that behavior does not cease to offend against either morality or etiquette because the agent is indifferent to their purposes and to the disapproval he will incur by flouting them. But

morality is supposed to be inescapable in some special way and this may turn out to be merely the reflection of the way morality is taught. Of course, we must try other ways of expressing the fugitive thought. It may be said, for instance, that moral judgments have a kind of necessity since they tell us what we "must do" or "have to do" whatever our interests and desires. The sense of this is, again, obscure. Sometimes when we use such expressions we are referring to physical or mental compulsion. (A man has to go along if he is pulled by strong men, and he has to give in if tortured beyond endurance.) But it is only in the absence of such conditions that moral judgments apply. Another and more common sense of the words is found in sentences such as "I caught a bad cold and had to stay in bed" where a penalty for acting otherwise is in the offing. The necessity of acting morally is not, however, supposed to depend on such penalties. Another range of examples, not necessarily having to do with penalties, is found where there is an unquestioned acceptance of some project or role, as when a nurse tells us that she has to make her rounds at a certain time, or we say that we have to run for a certain train. But these too are irrelevant in the present context, since the acceptance condition can always be revoked.

No doubt it will be suggested that it is in some other sense of the words "have to" or "must" that one has to or must do what morality demands. But why should one insist that there must be such a sense when it proves so difficult to say what it is? Suppose that what we take for a puzzling thought were really no thought at all but only the reflection of our *feelings* about morality? Perhaps it makes no sense to say that we "have to" submit to the moral law, or that morality is "inescapable" in some special way. For just as one may feel as if one is falling without believing that one is moving downward, so one may feel as if one has to do what is morally required without believing oneself to be under physical or psychological compulsion, or about to incur a penalty if one does not comply. No one thinks that if the word "falling" is used in a statement reporting one's sensations it must be used in a special sense. But this kind of mistake may be involved in looking for the special sense in which one "has to" do what morality demands. There is no difficulty about the idea that we feel we *have to* behave morally, and given the psychological conditions of the learning of moral behavior it is natural that we should have such feelings. What we cannot do is quote them in support of the doctrine of the categorical imperative. It seems, then, that in so far as it is backed up by statements to the effect that the moral *is* inescapable, or that we *do* have to do what is morally required of us, it is uncertain whether the doctrine of the categorical imperative even makes sense.

The conclusion we should draw is that moral judgments have no better claim to be categorical imperatives than do statements about matters of etiquette. People may indeed follow either morality or etiquette without asking why they should do so, but equally well they may not. They may ask for reasons and may reasonably refuse to follow either if reasons are not to be found.

It will be said that this way of viewing moral considerations must be totally destructive of morality, because no one could ever act morally unless he accepted such considerations as in themselves sufficient reason for action. Actions that are truly moral must be done "for their own sake," "because they are right," and not for some ulterior purpose. This argument we must examine with care, for the doctrine of the categorical imperative has owed much to its persuasion.

Is there anything to be said for the thesis that a truly moral man acts "out of respect for the moral law" or that he does what is morally right because it is morally right? That such propositions are not prima facie absurd depends on the fact that moral judgment concerns itself with a man's reasons for acting as well as with what he does. Law and etiquette require only that certain things are done or left undone, but no one is counted as charitable if he gives alms "for the praise of men," and one who is honest only because it pays him to be honest does not have the virtue of honesty. This kind of consideration was crucial in shaping Kant's moral philosophy. He many times contrasts acting out of respect for the moral law with acting from an ulterior motive, and what is more from one that is self-interested. In the early *Lectures on Ethics* he gave the principle of truth-telling under a system of

hypothetical imperatives as that of not lying *if it harms one* to lie. In the *Metaphysics of Morals* he says that ethics cannot start from the ends which a man may propose to himself, since these are all "selfish."[8] In the *Critique of Practical Reason* he argues explicitly that when acting not out of respect for the moral law but "on a material maxim" men do what they do for the sake of pleasure or happiness.

> All material practical principles are, as such, of one and the same kind and belong under the general principle of self love or one's own happiness.[9]

Kant, in fact, was a psychological hedonist in respect of all actions except those done for the sake of the moral law, and this faulty theory of human nature was one of the things preventing him from seeing that moral virtue might be compatible with the rejection of the categorical imperative.

If we put this theory of human action aside, and allow as ends the things that seem to be ends, the picture changes. It will surely be allowed that quite apart from thoughts of duty a man may care about the suffering of others, having a sense of identification with them, and wanting to help if he can. Of course he must want not the reputation of charity, nor even a gratifying role helping others, but, quite simply, their good. If this is what he does care about, then he will be attached to the end proper to the virtue of charity and a comparison with someone acting from an ulterior motive (even a respectable ulterior motive) is out of place. Nor will the conformity of his action to the rule of charity be merely contingent. Honest action may happen to further a man's career; charitable actions do not *happen* to further the good of others.

Can a man accepting only hypothetical imperatives possess other virtues besides that of charity? Could he be just or honest? This problem is more complex because there is no one end related to such virtues as the good of others is related to charity. But what reason could there be for refusing to call a man a just man if he acted justly because he loved truth and liberty, and wanted every man to be treated with a certain minimum respect? And why should the truly honest man not follow honesty for the sake of the good that honest dealing brings to men? Of course, the usual difficulties can be raised about the rare case in which no good is foreseen from an individual act of honesty. But it is not evident that a man's desires could not give him reason to act honestly even here. He wants to live openly and in good faith with his neighbors; it is not all the same to him to lie and conceal.

If one wants to know whether there could be a truly moral man who accepted moral principles as hypothetical rules of conduct, as many people accept rules of etiquette as hypothetical rules of conduct, one must consider the right kind of example. A man who demanded that morality should be brought under the heading of self-interest would not be a good candidate, nor would anyone who was ready to be charitable or honest only so long as he felt inclined. A cause such as justice makes strenuous demands, but this is not peculiar to morality, and men are prepared to toil to achieve many ends not endorsed by morality. That they are prepared to fight so hard for moral ends—for example, for liberty and justice—depends on the fact that these are the kinds of ends that arouse devotion. To sacrifice a great deal for the sake of etiquette one would need to be under the spell of the emphatic "ought." One could hardly be devoted to behaving *comme il faut.*

In spite of all that has been urged in favor of the hypothetical imperative in ethics, I am sure that many people will be unconvinced and will argue that one element essential to moral virtue is still missing. This missing feature is the recognition of a *duty* to adopt those ends which we have attributed to the moral man. We have said that he *does* care about others, and about causes such as liberty and justice; that it is on this account that he will accept a system of morality. But what if he never cared about such things, or what if he ceased to care? Is it not the case that he *ought* to care? This is exactly what Kant would say, for though at times he sounds as if he thought that morality is not concerned with ends, at others he insists that the adoption of ends such as the happiness of others is itself dictated by morality.[10] How is this proposition to be regarded by one who rejects all talk about the binding force of the moral law? He will agree that a moral man has moral ends and cannot be indifferent to matters such as

suffering and injustice. Further, he will recognize in the statement that one *ought* to care about these things a correct application of the non-hypothetical moral "ought" by which society is apt to voice its demands. He will not, however, take the fact that he ought to have certain ends as in itself reason to adopt them. If he himself is a moral man then he cares about such things, but not "because he ought." If he is an amoral man he may deny that he has any reason to trouble his head over this or any other moral demand. Of course he may be mistaken, and his life as well as others' lives may be most sadly spoiled by his selfishness. But this is not what is urged by those who think they can close the matter by an emphatic use of "ought." My argument is that they are relying on an illusion, as if trying to give the moral "ought" a magic force.[11]

This conclusion may, as I said, appear dangerous and subversive of morality. We are apt to panic at the thought that we ourselves, or other people, might stop caring about the things we do care about, and we feel that the categorical imperative gives us some control over the situation. But it is interesting that the people of Leningrad were not similarly struck by the thought that only the *contingent* fact that other citizens shared their loyalty and devotion to the city stood between them and the Germans during the terrible years of the siege. Perhaps we should be less troubled than we are by fear of defection from the moral cause; perhaps we should even have less reason to fear it if people thought of themselves as volunteers banded together to fight for liberty and justice and against inhumanity and oppression. It is often felt, even if obscurely, that there is an element of deception in the official line about morality. And while some have been persuaded by talk about the authority of the moral law, others have turned away with a sense of distrust.

NOTES

1. *Foundations of the Metaphysics of Morals,* Sec. II, trans. by L. W. Beck.
2. Ibid.
3. Ibid.
4. According to the position sketched here we have three forms of the hypothetical imperative: "If you

want x you should do y," "Because you want x you should do y," and "Because x is in your interest you should do y." For Kant the third would automatically be covered by the second.

5. To say that at that moment one wants to be a respectable philosopher would be another matter. Such a statement requires a special connection between the desire and the moment.

6. I am here going back on something I said in an earlier article ("Moral Beliefs," *Proceedings of the Aristotelian Society, 1958–1959*) where I thought it necessary to show that virtue must benefit the agent. I believe the rest of the article can stand.

7. To say that moral considerations are *called* reasons is blatantly to ignore the problem.

8. Pt. II, Introduction, sec. II.

9. Immanuel Kant, *Critique of Practical Reason,* trans. by L. W. Beck, p. 133.

10. See, e.g., *The Metaphysics of Morals,* pt. II, sec. 30.

11. See G. E. M. Anscombe, "Modern Moral Philosophy," *Philosophy* (1958). My view is different from Miss Anscombe's, but I have learned from her.

STUDY QUESTIONS

1. What is the difference between a hypothetical and a categorical imperative?
2. Do moral rules bind us in ways that rules of etiquette do not?
3. If you don't have a duty to tell the truth, might you still have a good reason to do so?
4. Do you agree with Foot that a person who rejects morality can be convicted of villainy but not of inconsistency?

Internal and External Reasons, with Postscript

Bernard Williams

Some theorists maintain that normative reasons depend on an agent's wants, desires, ends, and interests. In other words, agents have reason to act in particular ways only if their antecedent wants, desires, ends, or interests are thereby promoted. Because reasons must be tied to something within the agent, these accounts are known as "existence internalism," as opposed to "existence externalism."

Bernard Williams (1929–2003), who was Professor of Philosophy at the University of California at Berkeley, defends existence internalism. According to his canonical formulation, we have a reason to act only if a sound deliberative route exists to our action from our motivational set, embodying our desires, loyalties, and projects. Sound deliberation is ensured by complete non-normative information, perfect instrumental rationality, and full imaginative power.

Williams defends existence internalism by arguing that reasons need both to justify and explain our actions. Playing these two roles, and assuming Hume's theory of motivation, requires reasons to connect to our commitments. Hence, as Philippa Foot presumed, although not using this terminology, reasons must be internal.

INTERNAL AND EXTERNAL REASONS

Sentences of the forms "A has a reason to ϕ" or "There is a reason for A to ϕ" (where "ϕ" stands in for some verb of action) seem on the face of it to have two different sorts of interpretation. On the first, the truth of the sentence implies, very roughly, that A has some motive which will be served or furthered by his ϕ-ing, and if this turns out not to be so the sentence is false: there is a condition relating to the agent's aims, and if this is not satisfied it is not true to say, on this interpretation, that he has a reason to ϕ. On the second interpretation, there is no such condition, and the reason-sentence will not be falsified by the absence of an appropriate motive. I shall call the first the "internal," the second the "external," interpretation. . . .

I shall also for convenience refer sometimes to "internal reasons" and "external reasons," as I do in the title, but this is to be taken only as a convenience. It is a matter for investigation whether there are two sorts of reasons for action, as opposed to two sorts of statements about people's reasons for action. Indeed, as we shall eventually see, even the interpretation in one of the cases is problematical.

From Bernard Williams, "Internal and External Reasons, with Postscript," in *Varieties of Practical Reasoning*, ed. Elijah Millgram (Cambridge, MA: MIT Press, 2001). Reprinted by permission of the publisher.

I shall consider first the internal interpretation, and how far it can be taken. I shall then consider, more skeptically, what might be involved in an external interpretation. I shall end with some very brief remarks connecting all this with the issue of public goods and free-riders.

The simplest model for the internal interpretation would be this: A has a reason to ϕ iff A has some desire the satisfaction of which will be served by his ϕ-ing. Alternatively, we might say . . . some desire, the satisfaction of which A believes will be served by his ϕ-ing; this difference will concern us later. Such a model is sometimes ascribed to Hume, but since in fact Hume's own views are more complex than this, we might call it *the sub-Humean model.* The sub-Humean model is certainly too simple. My aim will be, by addition and revision, to work it up into something more adequate. In the course of trying to do this, I shall assemble four propositions which seem to me to be true of internal reason statements.

Basically, and by definition, any model for the internal interpretation must display a relativity of the reason statement to the agent's *subjective motivational set,* which I shall call the agent's *S.* The contents of *S* we shall come to, but we can say:

> (i) An internal reason statement is falsified by the absence of some appropriate element from *S.*

The simplest sub-Humean model claims that any element in *S* gives rise to an internal reason. But there are grounds for denying this, not because of regrettable, imprudent, or deviant elements in *S*—they raise different sorts of issues—but because of elements in *S* based on false belief.

The agent believes that this stuff is gin, when it is in fact petrol. He wants a gin and tonic. Has he reason, or a reason, to mix this stuff with tonic and drink it? There are two ways here (as suggested already by the two alternatives for formulating the sub-Humean model). On the one hand, it is just very odd to say that he has a reason to drink this stuff, and natural to say that he has no reason to drink it, although he thinks that he has. On the other hand, if he does drink it, we not only have an explanation of his doing so (a reason why he did it), but we have such an explanation which is of the reason-for-action

form. This explanatory dimension is very important, and we shall come back to it more than once. If there are reasons for action, it must be that people sometimes act for those reasons, and if they do, their reasons must figure in some correct explanation of their action (it does not follow that they must figure in all correct explanations of their action). The difference between false and true beliefs on the agent's part cannot alter the *form* of the explanation which will be appropriate to his action. This consideration might move us to ignore the intuition which we noticed before, and lead us just to legislate that in the case of the agent who wants gin, he has a reason to drink this stuff which is petrol.

I do not think, however, that we should do this. It looks in the wrong direction, by implying in effect that the internal reason conception is only concerned with explanation, and not at all with the agent's rationality, and this may help to motivate a search for other sorts of reason which are connected with his rationality. But the internal reasons conception is concerned with the agent's rationality. What we can correctly ascribe to him in a third-personal internal reason statement is also what he can ascribe to himself as a result of deliberation, as we shall see. So I think that we should rather say:

> (ii) A member of *S, D,* will not give *A* a reason for ϕ-ing if either the existence of *D* is dependent on false belief, or *A*'s belief in the relevance of ϕ-ing to the satisfaction of *D* is false.

(This double formulation can be illustrated from the gin/petrol case: *D* can be taken in the first way as the desire to drink what is in this bottle, and in the second way as the desire to drink gin.) It will, all the same, be true that if he does ϕ in these circumstances, there was not only a reason why he ϕ-ed, but also that that displays him as, relative to his false belief, acting rationally.

We can note the epistemic consequence:

> (iii) a. *A* may falsely believe an internal reason statement about himself, and (we can add)
>
> b. *A* may not know some true internal reason statement ab out himself.

(b) comes from two different sources. One is that A may be ignorant of some fact such that if he did know it he would, in virtue of some element in S, be disposed to φ: we can say that he has a reason to φ, though he does not know it. For it to be the case that he actually has such a reason, however, it seems that the relevance of the unknown fact to his actions has to be fairly close and immediate; otherwise one merely says that A would have a reason to φ if he knew the fact. I shall not pursue the question of the conditions for saying the one thing or the other, but it must be closely connected with the question of when the ignorance forms part of the explanation of what A actually does.

The second source of (iii) is that A may be ignorant of some element in S. But we should notice that an unknown element in S, D, will provide a reason for A to φ only if φ-ing is rationally related to D; that is to say, roughly, a project to φ could be the answer to a deliberative question formed in part by D. If D is unknown to A because it is in the unconscious, it may well not satisfy this condition, although of course it may provide the reason why he φ's, that is, may explain or help to explain his φ-ing. In such cases, the φ-ing may be related to D only symbolically.

I have already said that

> (iv) internal reason statements can be discovered in deliberative reasoning.

It is worth remarking the point, already implicit, that an internal reason statement does not apply only to that action which is the uniquely preferred result of the deliberation. "A has reason to φ" does not mean "the action which A has overall, all-in, reason to do is φ-ing." He can have reason to do a lot of things which he has other and stronger reasons not to do.

The sub-Humean model supposes that φ-ing has to be related to some element in S as causal means to end (unless, perhaps, it is straightforwardly the carrying out of a desire which is itself that element in S). But this is only one case: indeed, the mere discovery that some course of action is the causal means to an end is not in itself a piece of practical reasoning. A clear example of practical reasoning is that leading to the conclusion that one has reason to φ because φ-ing would be the most convenient, economical, pleasant,

etc. way of satisfying some element in S, and this of course is controlled by other elements in S, if not necessarily in a very clear or determinate way. But there are much wider possibilities for deliberation, such as: thinking how the satisfaction of elements in S can be combined, e.g. by time-ordering; where there is some irresoluble conflict among the elements of S, considering which one attaches most weight to (which, importantly, does not imply that there is some one commodity of which they provide varying amounts); or, again, finding constitutive solutions, such as deciding what would make for an entertaining evening, granted that one wants entertainment.

As a result of such processes an agent can come to see that he has reason to do something which he did not see he had reason to do at all. In this way, the deliberative process can add new actions for which there are internal reasons, just as it can also add new internal reasons for given actions. The deliberative process can also subtract elements from S. Reflection may lead the agent to see that some belief is false, and hence to realize that he has in fact no reason to do something he thought he had reason to do. More subtly, he may think he has reason to promote some development because he has not exercised his imagination enough about what it would be like if it came about. In his unaided deliberative reason, or encouraged by the persuasions of others, he may come to have some more concrete sense of what would be involved, and lose his desire for it, just as, positively, the imagination can create new possibilities and new desires. . . .

We should not, then, think of S as statically given. The processes of deliberation can have all sorts of effect on S, and this is a fact which a theory of internal reasons should be very happy to accommodate. So also it should be more liberal than some theorists have been about the possible elements in S. I have discussed S primarily in terms of desires, and this term can be used, formally, for all elements in S. But this terminology may make one forget that S can contain such things as dispositions of evaluation, patterns of emotional reaction, personal loyalties, and various projects, as they may be abstractly called, embodying commitments of the agent. Above all, there is of course no supposition that the desires or projects of an agent have to be egoistic; he will, one hopes, have non-egoistic projects of various kinds, and these equally can provide internal reasons for action.

There is a further question, however, about the contents of S: whether it should be taken, consistently with the general idea of internal reasons, as containing *needs*. It is certainly quite natural to say that A has a reason to pursue X, just on the ground that he needs X, but will this naturally follow in a theory of internal reasons? There is a special problem about this only if it is possible for the agent to be unmotivated to pursue what he needs. I shall not try to discuss here the nature of needs, but I take it that insofar as there are determinately recognizable needs, there can be an agent who lacks any interest in getting what he indeed needs. I take it, further, that that lack of interest can remain after deliberation, and, also that it would be wrong to say that such a lack of interest must always rest on false belief. (Insofar as it does rest on false belief, then we can accommodate it under (ii), in the way already discussed.)

If an agent really is uninterested in pursuing what he needs; and this is not the product of false belief; and he could not reach any such motive from motives he has by the kind of deliberative processes we have discussed; then I think we do have to say that in the internal sense he indeed has no reason to pursue these things. In saying this, however, we have to bear in mind how strong these assumptions are, and how seldom we are likely to think that we know them to be true. When we say that a person has reason to take medicine which he needs, although he consistently and persuasively denies any interest in preserving his health, we may well still be speaking in the internal sense, with the thought that really at some level he *must* want to be well.

However, if we become clear that we have no such thought, and persist in saying that the person has this reason, then we must be speaking in another sense, and this is the external sense. People do say things that ask to be taken in the external interpretation. In James' story of Owen Wingrave, from which Britten made an opera, Owen's father urges on him the necessity and importance of his joining the army,

since all his male ancestors were soldiers, and family pride requires him to do the same. Owen Wingrave has no motivation to join the army at all, and all his desires lead in another direction: he hates everything about military life and what it means. His father might have expressed himself by saying that *there was a reason for Owen to join the army.* Knowing that there was nothing in Owen's S which would lead, through deliberative reasoning, to his doing this would not make him withdraw the claim or admit that he made it under a misapprehension. He means it in an external sense. What is that sense?

A preliminary point is that this is not the same question as that of the status of a supposed categorical imperative, in the Kantian sense of an "ought" which applies to an agent independently of what the agent happens to want: or rather, it is not undoubtedly the same question. First, a categorical imperative has often been taken, as by Kant, to be necessarily an imperative of morality, but external reason statements do not necessarily relate to morality. Second, it remains an obscure issue what the relation is between "there is a reason for A to . . ." and "A ought to . . ." Some philosophers take them to be equivalent, and under that view the question of external reasons of course comes much closer to the question of a categorical imperative. However, I shall not make any assumption about such an equivalence, and shall not further discuss "ought."

In considering what an external reason statement might mean, we have to remember again the dimension of possible explanation, a consideration which applies to any reason for action. If something can be a reason for action, then it could be someone's reason for acting on a particular occasion, and it would then figure in an explanation of that action. Now no external reason statement could *by itself* offer an explanation of anyone's action. Even if it were true (whatever that might turn out to mean) that there was a reason for Owen to join the army, that fact by itself would never explain anything that Owen did, not even his joining the army. For if it was true at all, it was true when Owen was not motivated to join the army. The whole point of external reason statements is that they can be true independently of the agent's motivations. But nothing can explain an agent's (intentional) actions except something that motivates him so to act. So something else is needed besides the truth of the external reason statement to explain action, some psychological link; and that psychological link would seem to be belief. A's believing an external reason statement about himself may help to explain his action.

External reason statements have been introduced merely in the general form "there is a reason for A to . . . ," but we now need to go beyond that form, to specific statements of reasons. No doubt there are some cases of an agent's ϕ-ing because he believes that there is a reason for him to ϕ, while he does not have any belief about what that reason is. They would be cases of his relying on some authority whom he trusts, or, again, of his recalling that he did know of some reason for his ϕ-ing, but his not being able to remember what it was. In these respects, reasons for action are like reasons for belief. But, as with reasons for belief, they are evidently secondary cases. The basic case must be that in which A ϕ's, not because he believes only that there is some reason or other for him to ϕ, but because he believes of some determinate consideration that it constitutes a reason for him to ϕ. Thus Owen Wingrave might come to join the army because (now) he believes that it is a reason for him to do so that his family has a tradition of military honor.

Does believing that a particular consideration is a reason to act in a particular way provide, or indeed constitute, a motivation to act? If it does not, then we are no further on. Let us grant that it does—this claim indeed seems plausible, so long at least as the connexion between such beliefs and the disposition to act is not tightened to that unnecessary degree which excludes *akrasia*. The claim is in fact *so* plausible, that this agent, with this belief, appears to be one about whom, now, an *internal* reason statement could truly be made: he is one with an appropriate motivation in his S. A man who does believe that considerations of family honor constitute reasons for action is a man with a certain disposition to action, and also dispositions of approval, sentiment, emotional reaction, and so forth.

Now it does not follow from this that there is nothing in external reason statements. What does follow is that their content is not going to be revealed by considering merely the state of one who believes such a statement, nor how that state explains action, for that state is merely the state with regard to which an internal reason statement could truly be made. Rather, the content of the external type of statement will have to be revealed by considering what it is to *come to believe* such a statement—it is there, if at all, that their peculiarity will have to emerge.

We will take the case (we have implicitly been doing so already) in which an external reason statement is made about someone who, like Owen Wingrave, is not already motivated in the required way, and so is someone about whom an internal statement could not also be truly made. . . . The agent does not presently believe the external statement. If he comes to believe it, he will be motivated to act; so coming to believe it must, essentially, involve acquiring a new motivation. How can that be?

This is closely related to an old question, of how "reason can give rise to a motivation," a question which has famously received from Hume a negative answer. But in that form, the question is itself unclear, and is unclearly related to the argument—for of course reason, that is to say, rational processes, can give rise to new motivations, as we have seen in the account of deliberation. Moreover, the traditional way of putting the issue also (I shall suggest) picks up an onus of proof about what is to count as a "purely rational process" which not only should it not pick up, but which properly belongs with the critic who wants to oppose Hume's general conclusion and to make a lot out of external reason statements—someone I shall call "the external reasons theorist."

The basic point lies in recognizing that the external reasons theorist must conceive *in a special way* the connexion between acquiring a motivation and coming to believe the reason statement. For of course there are various means by which the agent could come to have the motivation and also to believe the reason statement, but which are the wrong kind of means to interest the external reasons theorist. Owen might be so persuaded by his father's moving rhetoric that he acquired both the motivation and the belief. But this excludes an element which the external reasons theorist essentially wants, that the agent should acquire the motivation *because* he comes to believe the reason statement, and that he should do the latter, moreover, because, in some way, he is considering the matter aright. If the theorist is to hold on to these conditions, he will, I think, have to make the condition under which the agent appropriately comes to have the motivation something like this, that he should deliberate correctly; and the external reasons statement itself will have to be taken as roughly equivalent to, or at least as entailing, the claim that if the agent rationally deliberated, then, whatever motivations he originally had, he would come to be motivated to φ.

But if this is correct, there does indeed seem great force in Hume's basic point, and it is very plausible to suppose that all external reason statements are false. For, *ex hypothesi,* there is no motivation for the agent to deliberate *from,* to reach this new motivation. Given the agent's earlier existing motivations, and this new motivation, what has to hold for external reason statements to be true, on this line of interpretation, is that the new motivation could be in some way rationally arrived at, granted the earlier motivations. Yet at the same time it must not bear to the earlier motivations the kind of rational relation which we considered in the earlier discussion of deliberation—for in that case an internal reason statement would have been true in the first place. I see no reason to suppose that these conditions could possibly be met.

It might be said that the force of an external reason statement can be explained in the following way. Such a statement implies that a rational agent would be motivated to act appropriately, and it can carry this implication, because a rational agent is precisely one who has a general disposition in his *S* to do what (he believes) there is reason for him to do. So when he comes to believe that there is reason for him to φ, he is motivated to φ, even though, before, he neither had a motive to φ, nor any motive related to φ-ing in one of the ways considered in the account of deliberation.

But this reply merely puts off the problem. It reapplies the desire and belief model (roughly speaking) of explanation to the actions in question, but

using a desire and a belief the content of which are in question. *What* is it that one comes to believe when he comes to believe that there is reason for him to φ, if it is not the proposition, or something that entails the proposition, that if he deliberated rationally, he would be motivated to act appropriately? We were asking how any true proposition could have that content; it cannot help, in answering that, to appeal to a supposed desire which is activated by a belief which has that very content.

These arguments about what it is to accept an external reason statement involve some idea of what is possible under the account of deliberation already given, and what is excluded by that account. But here it may be objected that the account of deliberation is very vague, and has for instance allowed the use of the imagination to extend or restrict the contents of the agent's *S*. But if that is so, then it is unclear what the limits are to what an agent might arrive at by rational deliberation from his existing *S*.

It *is* unclear, and I regard it as a basically desirable feature of a theory of practical reasoning that it should preserve and account for that unclarity. There is an essential indeterminacy in what can be counted a rational deliberative process. Practical reasoning is a heuristic process, and an imaginative one, and there are no fixed boundaries on the continuum from rational thought to inspiration and conversion. To someone who thinks that reasons for action are basically to be understood in terms of the internal reasons model, this is not a difficulty. There is indeed a vagueness about "*A* has reason to φ," in the internal sense, insofar as the deliberative processes which could lead from *A*'s present *S* to his being motivated to φ may be more or less ambitiously conceived. But this is no embarrassment to those who take as basic the internal conception of reasons for action. It merely shows that there is a wider range of states, and a less determinate one, than one might have supposed, which can be counted as *A*'s having a reason to φ.

It is the external reasons theorist who faces a problem at this point. There are of course many things that a speaker may say to one who is not disposed to φ when the speaker thinks that he should be, as that he is inconsiderate, or cruel, or selfish, or imprudent; or that things, and he, would be a lot nicer if he were so motivated. Any of these can be sensible things to say. But one who makes a great deal out of putting the criticism in the form of an external reason statement seems concerned to say that what is particularly wrong with the agent is that he is *irrational.* It is this theorist who particularly needs to make this charge precise: in particular, because he wants any rational agent, as such, to acknowledge the requirement to do the thing in question.

Owen Wingrave's father indeed expressed himself in terms other than "a reason," but, as we imagined, he could have used the external reasons formulation. This fact itself provides some difficulty for the external reasons theorist. This theorist, who sees the truth of an external reason statement as potentially grounding a charge of irrationality against the agent who ignores it, might well want to say that if Wingrave *père* put his complaints against Owen in this form, he would very probably be claiming something which, in this particular case, was false. What the theorist would have a harder time showing would be that the words *meant* something different as used by Wingrave from what they mean when they are, as he supposes, truly uttered. But what they mean when uttered by Wingrave is almost certainly *not* that rational deliberation would get Owen to be motivated to join the army—which is (very roughly) the meaning or implication we have found for them, if they are to bear the kind of weight such theorists wish to give them.

The sort of considerations offered here strongly suggest to me that external reason statements, when definitely isolated as such, are false, or incoherent, or really something else misleadingly expressed. It is in fact harder to isolate them in people's speech than the introduction of them at the beginning of this chapter suggested. Those who use these words often seem, rather, to be entertaining an optimistic internal reason claim, but sometimes the statement is indeed offered as standing definitely outside the agent's *S* and what he might derive from it in rational deliberation, and then there is, I suggest, a great unclarity about what is meant. Sometimes it is little more than that things would be better if the agent so

acted. But the formulation in terms of reasons does have an effect, particularly in its suggestion that the agent is being irrational, and this suggestion, once the basis of an internal reason claim has been clearly laid aside, is bluff. If this is so, the only real claims about reasons for action will be internal claims.

A problem which has been thought to lie very close to the present subject is that of public goods and free riders, which concerns the situation (very roughly) in which each person has egoistic reason to want a certain good provided, but at the same time each has egoistic reason not to take part in providing it. I shall not attempt any discussion of this problem, but it may be helpful, simply in order to make clear my own view of reasons for action and to bring out contrasts with some other views, if I end by setting out a list of questions which bear on the problem, together with the answers that would be given to them by one who thinks (to put it cursorily) that the only rationality of action is the rationality of internal reasons.

1. Can we define notions of rationality which are not purely egoistic?

Yes.

2. Can we define notions of rationality which are not purely means-end?

Yes.

3. Can we define a notion of rationality where the action rational for *A* is in no way relative to *A*'s existing motivations?

No.

4. Can we show that a person who only has egoistic motivations is irrational in not pursuing non-egoistic ends?

Not necessarily, though we may be able to in special cases. (The trouble with the egoistic person is not characteristically irrationality.)

Let there be some good, *G*, and a set of persons, *P*, such that each member of *P* has egoistic reason to want *G* provided, but delivering *G* requires action *C*, which involves costs, by each of some proper sub-set of *P*; and let *A* be a member of *P*: then

5. Has *A* egoistic reason to do *C* if he is reasonably sure either that too few members of *P* will do *C* for *G* to be provided, or that enough other members of *P* will do *C*, so that *G* will be provided?

No.

6. Are there any circumstances of this kind in which *A* can have egoistic reason to do *C*?

Yes, in those cases in which reaching the critical number of those doing *C* is sensitive to his doing *C*, or he has reason to think this.

7. Are there any motivations which would make it rational for *A* to do *C*, even though not in the situation just referred to?

Yes, if he is not purely egoistic: many. For instance, there are expressive motivations—appropriate e.g. in the celebrated voting case. There are also motivations which derive from the sense of fairness. This can precisely transcend the dilemma of "either useless or unnecessary," by the form of argument "somebody, but no reason to omit any particular body, so everybody."

8. Is it irrational for an agent to have such motivations?

In any sense in which the question is intelligible, no.

9. Is it rational for society to bring people up with these sorts of motivations?

Insofar as the question is intelligible, yes. And certainly we have reason to encourage people to

have these dispositions—e.g. in virtue of possessing them ourselves.

I confess that I cannot see any other major questions which, at this level of generality, bear on these issues. All these questions have clear answers which are entirely compatible with a conception of practical rationality in terms of internal reasons for action, and are also, it seems to me, entirely reasonable answers.

POSTSCRIPT: SOME FURTHER NOTES ON INTERNAL AND EXTERNAL REASONS

1

The formulation of the internalist position which I now prefer[1] is: *A* has a reason to φ only if there is *a sound deliberative route* from *A*'s subjective motivational set (which I label "*S*," as in the original article) to *A*'s φ-ing. Whether this is also a sufficient condition of *A*'s having a reason to φ is a question which I have left aside; the essence of the internalist position is that it is a necessary condition. It is natural to take the condition as implying not just that *A* has a reason to φ, but that he or she has more reason to do that than to do anything else. This is the case I shall take as central.

2

There is no attempt to give an account of what counts as "a sound deliberative route" except to the extent that this is required by the demands of internalism. I have assumed that if an agent's conclusion in favor of a certain action is essentially based on a false belief (as in the gin and petrol example) the agent has no reason to do that action, though he thinks that he has. The basis for "correcting" his deliberation in the direction of the truth is that he indeed wants to take the correct means to his ends—this is indeed part of his *S*. In general, the aim of getting things right in such ways is part of any agent's interest as a rational deliberator, and the aim can be assumed to figure in any rational agent's *S* (though there can be exceptional cases in which an agent has a reason to sustain a false belief). However, we cannot simply assume that moral considerations, for instance, or long-term prudential concerns must figure in every agent's *S*. For many agents, as we well know, they indeed do so, if not altogether securely; but a philosophical claim that they are necessarily part of rational agency needs argument.

There is, then, no attempt to exclude altruistic or other ethical considerations from the rational agent's *S*. For most agents, those patterns of motivation appear there together with many others—desires, projects, sympathies and so on. Nor does the account constrain the relation between the action and the agent's *S* to some narrow instrumental connection; actions can express and flow from various elements in the agent's *S* without being means to some separate end. Equally, the account is not committed to the formulations of classical rational decision theory, to the effect that all the input to a decision can be made explicit and is subjected to an algorithmic process. There is room for the imagination in deciding what to do, and correspondingly in saying what someone else has reason to do. Indeed, the stance towards the agent that is implied by the internalist account can be usefully compared to that of an imaginative and informed advisor, who takes seriously the formula "If I were you . . ."

3

It is a consequence of the account that the question whether a given person has a reason to act in a certain way may have no entirely determinate answer. This consequence is entirely welcome: there are indeed many and unclear stages on the path between cases in which it is manifestly and overwhelmingly clear that an agent has reason to do a certain thing, and cases in which my telling him what he has reason to do constitutes influencing him or getting him to see things in a new light. A realistic account should accept that there is an essential indeterminacy in this area.

It follows from the account that in more than one way, an agent may be mistaken about what he has

reason to do (one example we have already noticed is that of false belief). This is essential to preserving the point that statements of what people have reason to do have normative force; no account that excludes this can be adequate. Some writers make a distinction between "normative" and "explanatory" reasons, but this does not seem to me to be helpful, because normative and explanatory considerations are closely involved with one another. On the one hand, if it is said, in the normative mode, that *A* has a reason to φ, the speaker must envisage the possibility of *A*'s φ-ing for that reason, in which case the reason will figure in the explanation of what *A* does. (I appeal to this connection in the argument against external reasons.) On the other hand, if we explain what *A* does in terms of his reason for doing that thing, which is one type of giving a reason why he did it, we rationalize his conduct . . . that is to say, we cite a consideration which was effective in his coming to act because it made normative sense to him. Its making normative sense to him implies that it made normative sense in terms of his *S*. This does not mean that when an agent has a thought of the form "that is a reason for me to φ," he really has, or should really have, the thought "that is a reason for me to φ *in virtue of my S*." The disposition that forms part of his *S* just is the disposition to have thoughts of the form "that is a reason for me to φ," and to act on them.

4

I do not deny, and it would be absurd to deny, that sentences of the form "*A* has a reason to . . ." (or "There is a reason for you to . . ." and so on) are used in ways that do not satisfy the internalist condition. My claim is, first, that when they are so used and are not merely mistaken, the speaker intends some roughly specifiable other thing which does not mean the same in general as "*A* has a reason to . . . ," such as "We have a reason to want *A* to . . ."; and, second, that there is no principled and convincing way of distinguishing the basic sense of "*A* has a reason to . . ." from these other things other than an internalist interpretation.

This raises the question of what an externalist account of such sentences and their truth conditions will be. I say in the article reprinted here that the externalist wants, specifically, to be able to say that someone who resists a correct externalist claim is *irrational*. I accept that this is too strong.[2] But the question remains, of what it is that those who believe in true externalist claims about people's reasons take those claims to say. There seem to be three principal approaches to this question. One is broadly Kantian, to the effect that the structure and not simply the content of practical reason can ground reasons. This is the type of idea which, as I said in discussing the "correction for error" in section 2 above, needs to be made good independently. Moreover, if it could be made good (which I doubt) I think that what it would yield would be a limiting version of internalism. If it were true that the structure of practical reason yielded reasons of a certain kind as binding on every rational agent, then it would be true of every rational agent that there was a sound deliberative route from his or her *S* to actions required by such reasons.[3]

The second approach is very broadly speaking Aristotelian, and constructs a truth condition for externalist claims in terms of the reasons that would be recognized by an ideal, "well brought up," or at least improved, agent—an agent, that is to say, for whom these would indeed be internal reasons. I have argued that this approach gives the wrong answer.[4] Just because I am, and can know myself to be, an imperfect agent, it may be that I have reason not to try things which a better agent would indeed have reason to do; and problems of this type can always in principle arise, until the distance between the actual and the imaginary improved agent has been reduced to zero, and we are back with internalism.

A third line of argument, which has been advanced in various different forms, is roughly to the effect that what counts as a reason for certain actions is an institutional or social question, and not an individual or psychological question as internalism seems to suggest. This line seems to me to take up something true, but not to deliver it at the right place. What can rationalize or render intelligible various kinds of action is certainly a social, and in some part an institutional, matter. It can be a question of historical, anthropological, and philosophical interpretation, how far these various practices are, also,

variable and local. But whether they are local or more widely spread, it will equally be true that they need a basis in individual psychologies. There can be an institution of promising, for example, only because enough people enough of the time have (internal) reason to do something because they have acted in a way that counts as promising to do that thing.[5] There is thus no problem in understanding the exchange of reason claims between people who have internalized the practice. But we are still owed an account of what is being said when the reason claims are directed to people who are known not to have internalized the practice, or to be insufficiently responsive to it—that is to say, in cases where an externalist interpretation is definitively required. It is much too late in the day, historically and politically, to suppose that a socially sanctioned reason gets a hold on a given agent simply because he finds himself within the boundaries of a society in which that reason is widely recognized.

We need a realistic account, social and psychological, of what is going on when seemingly externalist claims, referring to a social or institutional reason, are directed at recalcitrant or unconvinced agents. In the present paper I suggest, vaguely, that those who make claims about people's reasons in such circumstances are often "entertaining an optimistic internal reasons claim." In a later paper[6] I suggested a more detailed account by which seemingly externalist reason claims (I was particularly concerned with blame) work "proleptically": the claim that *A* has a reason to ϕ is not strictly true, by internalist standards, at the moment that it is made, but the very fact that it is made can help to elicit a more general motivation from the agent's *S,* such as the desire to have the respect of people like the speaker, and this motivation together with the recognition of those people's desire or demand that he should ϕ can indeed bring it about that he (now) has a reason to ϕ. This is the merest sketch, but it is only by invoking some such mechanisms that we can bridge the gap between genuinely internalist reason claims, and externalist claims which, unless they can get some help in social and psychological terms, there may be no reason to see as more than bluff and brow-beating.

5

I have made the point that there are many things that critics of an agent may say other than that he has reason to behave differently—for instance, that he is inconsiderate, or cruel, or selfish, or imprudent. In the course of a notably constructive contribution to the discussion,[7] T. M. Scanlon has said:

> These criticisms . . . involve accusing [the agent] of a kind of deficiency, namely a failure to be moved by certain considerations that we regard as reasons. (What else is it to be inconsiderate, cruel, insensitive and so on?) If it is a deficiency for the man to fail to see these considerations as reasons, it would seem that they must be reasons for him. (If they are not, how can it be a deficiency for him to fail to recognize them?)

This is not, and it is not intended to be, a knock-down argument against the internalist position. I agree that the agent's faults can be understood in terms of a failure to see certain considerations as reasons, just as the opposed virtues can be understood as dispositions to see those considerations as reasons. I also agree that if we think of this as a deficiency or fault of this man, then we must think that in some sense these reasons *apply* to him; certainly he cannot head off the criticism by saying that the reasons do not apply to him because he does not have that kind of *S*, as someone else might appropriately say that the fact that a brilliant new opera is being staged in New York is not a reason for him to go there, because a taste for opera is no part of his *S*. This is a point about the (special kind of) universality of (this kind of) reasons.

But none of this implies that these considerations are already the defective agent's reasons; indeed, the problem is precisely that they are not. Let $\lceil N \rceil$ stand in for some normative term: if the critic expresses himself by saying "There is a reason for this man to behave differently to these people," then what he says is of the form "There are considerations about these people's welfare, interests, and so on such that it is $\lceil N \rceil$ that this man should treat those considerations as reasons." What can we take $\lceil N \rceil$ to

be? It does not seem to me that there is anything in this way of putting the situation which takes us beyond understanding $\lceil N \rceil$ as, very roughly speaking, "better." We can make this significantly more determinate by explaining that the improvement would lie in the agent's coming to count as reasons considerations which we, other citizens, humane people in general, count as reasons, but while this may help to explain why we, as critics, express ourselves by saying "There is a reason for *A* to behave differently," it does not make that statement, or the $\lceil N \rceil$ that it implicitly contains, any more a matter of *A*'s reasons.

If we take $\lceil N \rceil$ itself to introduce the notion of a reason, so that we are saying that the agent has a reason to come to treat these considerations as reasons, then we are back with the familiar question of how the project of coming to do that is related to his existing *S*. Scanlon himself has some interesting remarks about the "reflective modification" of one's *S*, which may be controlled by certain dispositions in one's existing *S* without being a deliberative satisfaction of one's *S*. This will be another example of the psychological material that can help, as I put it in the last section, to bridge the gap between internalist claims, and externalist claims which come to no more than bluff and brow-beating. As I believe Scanlon would agree, exploring this territory is an important contribution to breaking down the age-old sharp distinctions between reason on the one hand and force, coercion and mere persuasion on the other—distinctions which in their more extreme forms have been not just philosophically confusing but ethically and politically disastrous.

NOTES

1. As in Williams 1995.
2. Altham and Harrison 1995, p. 192.
3. This was why I said in Williams 1995, at note 3 to p. 37, that in this respect I had "no basic disagreement with Christine Korsgaard's excellent paper 'Skepticism about Practical Reason.'" . . .
4. In Altham and Harrison 1995, against a suggestion of John McDowell's, which I took—perhaps a little simplistically—to be to this effect.

5. I discuss some questions about the individual psychological base of institutional and other socially described actions in "Formal and Substantial Individualism," reprinted in Williams 1995.
6. Williams 1995, esp. pp. 41 ff.
7. Scanlon 1998, pp. 363–373; the cited passage is at p. 367. . . .

BIBLIOGRAPHY

Altham, J. E. J., and Ross Harrison, eds. 1995. *World, Mind, and Ethics: Essays on the Ethical Philosophy of Bernard Williams.* Cambridge: Cambridge University Press.

Scanlon, T. M. 1998. *What We Owe to Each Other.* Cambridge: Harvard University Press.

Williams, Bernard. 1995. *Making Sense of Humanity.* Cambridge: Cambridge University Press.

STUDY QUESTIONS

1. According to Williams, what are the two senses of the sentence "*A* has a reason to ϕ"?
2. Explain the difference between "internal" and "external" reasons.
3. What points does Williams aim to make by citing the story of Owen Wingrave?
4. Must normative reasons be able to motivate?

Internal Reasons and the Motivating Intuition

Julia Markovits

According to Bernard Williams, because reasons both justify and motivate, they must be internal. Julia Markovits, Associate Professor of Philosophy at Cornell University, disagrees. Suppose, for example, you are delusional. You think you are James Bond. Intuitively, you have a reason to seek psychological help so you can come to recognize your delusion. Yet this reason cannot be motivating, for if your being deluded motivates you to seek help, then you no longer need help recognizing that you are deluded. Hence if you have a reason to seek help when you think you are James Bond, your delusion cannot be motivating you. Furthermore, in some cases, you ought not be motivated by your normative reasons. For instance, when you are engaged in landing a plane in an emergency, your being motivated by the facts providing your reason would jeopardize your ability to be successful. Thus the reasons we need to act in a particular way often cannot, and should not, be the reasons that explain why we so act. In short, normative reasons need not be capable of motivating. Markovits maintains, however, that we should not abandon existence internalism, because other arguments, not presented here, can be marshaled in favor of the view.

Internalist theses, as they are usually stated, describe a necessary relation between an agent's having a reason and some other, usually motivational, fact about the agent. So, for example, internalists might claim that an agent can have a reason to perform some act only if he has a relevant desire, or only if he would be motivated to perform it in suitably idealized circumstances. Why should we accept internalism about reasons?

I'll begin by exploring the thought, appealed to by Bernard Williams and often cited in support of internalism, that reasons must be capable of *explaining* action: it must be possible for a fact that is a reason for an agent to act to be *the reason he acts—the reason that motivates him*. I'll call this the *Motivating Intuition*. As I will argue (in Section 1), it represents a key step in Williams' argument for internalism. And (as I will try to show in Section 2), the Motivating Intuition has much to be said for it. The problem is that versions of internalism that reflect the Motivating Intuition are vulnerable to numerous counter-examples, and that attempts to revise the internalist thesis to avoid these counter-examples introduce a divide between normative reasons and possible explanations of action. The result is that workable versions of internalist theses lose the support of the Motivating Intuition, and so begin to appear unmotivated. But the same counter-examples that forced the modification of internalist theses, and others, should also lead us to reconsider the Motivating Intuition itself. Indeed, I will argue (in Sections 3 and 4) that we should reject the Motivating Intuition,

From Julia Markovits, "Internal Reasons and the Motivating Intuition," in *New Waves in Metaethics,* ed. Michael Brady (New York: Palgrave Macmillan, 2011). Reprinted by permission of the publisher.

and that examples of reasons we have to act which cannot, or should not, be the reasons *why* we act are in fact quite common. . . .

1. TWO ARGUMENTS FOR INTERNALISM

According to Bernard Williams's version of *internalism about reasons,* which will serve as the hook on which I hang my own observations, for some agent A to have a reason to perform some action ϕ, that action must be related to A's "motivational set" in a particular way. Specifically, it must be the case that "A could reach the conclusion that he should ϕ . . . by a sound deliberative route from the motivations that he has in his actual motivational set—that is, the set of his desires, evaluations, attitudes, projects, and so on."[1] Williams's formulation is somewhat misleading. One can have a reason to perform an action that is not a "winning" reason—that is, a reason that is outweighed by other reasons not to perform the action. For something to be a reason for an agent to perform an action on the standard internalist picture, it must be the case that the agent would be *motivated to some extent* to perform the action if he deliberated rationally. But it need not be the case that he would be *moved* to perform the action, or that he would reach the conclusion that he should perform the action, *all things considered.*

Put in an oversimplified way, an internal interpretation of reasons is one that takes an agent to have a reason to perform an action only if she has some desire, the satisfaction of which will be served by her doing so.[2] The internalist account of reasons does not entail that any of our desires give us reasons, or that we will always be motivated by our reasons. False beliefs or bad deliberation may cause us to fail to recognize or be motivated by some of our reasons, and can give rise to desires we have no reason to fulfill. But the essential feature of an internalist account of reasons is that it ties the truth of a reasons claim to the presence of a suitable element in an agent's motivational set: according to internalism, what we have reason to do depends fundamentally on what ends, broadly understood, we already have.[3]

The first argument. Williams's argument for internalism about reasons in his seminal article "Internal and External Reasons" seems to *begin* from the assumption that the concept of a reason *is* the concept of a consideration that could explain the actions of a rational agent. Williams thinks that, when we say someone has a reason to ϕ, what we *mean* is that he would be motivated to ϕ if he were rational. Though this claim is sometimes presented as the internalists' *conclusion,* it is in fact the *starting point* of Williams's argument. (For example, Williams claims that an *external* reasons statement (not just an internal reasons statement) "implies that a rational agent would be motivated to act appropriately."[4]) He then points out that it's easy enough to see what it would take for an *internal* reasons statement to be true of an agent. If A has an *internal* reason to ϕ, this means that A would be motivated to ϕ if he deliberated *in a procedurally rational way from his existing ends and motivations* (that's the internalist part), and it's easy enough to see why such procedurally rational deliberation might give rise to a new motivation, derived from one of the old ones. It's no mystery, Williams suggests, to see how an internal reason might serve to explain the actions of an agent who deliberates rationally.

It's much harder, Williams argues, to understand what it would take for an *external* reasons statement to be true of an agent. Because if claiming that an agent has a reason to ϕ amounts to claiming that he would be motivated to ϕ if he were rational, and if claiming the reason is *external* amounts to claiming that it does not apply to the agent in virtue of any of his existing motivations, then the external reasons theorist must explain *how* it could be true of the agent that a process of rational deliberation would motivate him to ϕ, despite the fact that, by hypothesis, he need have no existing motivations from which the new motivation to ϕ could be derived. And Williams finds it hard to imagine a process of rational deliberation that could give rise to a motivation to act, but not by taking any existing motivations as a starting point.

Williams considers the possibility that an external reason could explain the action of the agent whose reason it is, provided the agent is rational, by means of the agent's *coming to believe* he has the reason to act. Rational agents, after all, will form true beliefs about their reasons, and will be motivated to do as they believe they have reason to do, so, if an agent comes to believe an external reason to φ applies to him, then if he is rational he will be motivated to φ, regardless of his former motivations. And this, the thought goes, is enough to establish the truth of the external reasons claim.

An example might make this possibility clearer. The external reasons theorist will want to claim that Jim has a reason to give to charity, say, regardless of whether he has any desire, broadly understood, which might give rise, after procedurally rational deliberation, to a motivation to give to charity. That is to say, Jim has an external reason to give to charity. But if Williams is right about what all reasons claims (including external reasons claims) must mean, than this statement amounts to the claim that Jim would be motivated to give to charity if he were rational, regardless of his actual motivations. How could that be true? The suggestion under consideration is that the external reasons claim is true because, if Jim were rational, he would recognize that he has reason to give to charity, and (because he is rational) this recognition would motivate him to do so (regardless of his prior motivations).

But, Williams asks, what would Jim's "recognition" amount to? If, again, Williams is right about our concept of a reason, it would have to amount to the recognition, on Jim's part, that he would be motivated to give to charity if he were rational (regardless of his existing motivations). It is a *true* belief in this proposition that is supposed to trigger in the rational Jim a motivation to give to charity. But now we do seem to have put the cart before the horse. After all, we were trying to determine how *that* proposition could be true. It doesn't seem to help to say that it can be true, because if it were true, and rational Jim therefore believed it and were motivated accordingly, then it would be true. So, Williams concludes, we can make sense of the idea of a normative reason, which, Williams says, just *is* the idea of a consideration that would motivate a rational agent, only if we accept the internalist thesis: that an agent can have a reason to perform some action only if he could be motivated to perform it by following a

sound deliberative route from his existing ends and motivations.

The second argument. Some of the central claims of Williams's defense of internalism sow the seeds of another argument Williams himself does not make, but which is often attributed to internalists.[5] This argument begins from something like Williams's conceptual claim about reasons: "It must be a mistake," Williams writes, "to simply separate explanatory and normative reasons. If it is true that A has a reason to φ, then it must be possible that he should φ for that reason; and if he does act for that reason, then that reason will be the explanation of his acting." Similarly, the first premise of this second argument claims:

(1) It must be possible for me to be motivated by the reasons that apply to me. So a consideration can be a reason for me to φ only if it can motivate me to φ.

A second premise also looks familiar:

(2) A consideration can motivate me to φ only if it is relevantly connected to my "motivational set"— that is, only if it would motivate me to φ if I were deliberating in a procedurally rational way from my existing ends and motivations.

The internalist conclusion follows from these premises:

(3) Therefore, a consideration can be a reason for me to φ only if it would motivate me to φ if I were deliberating in a procedurally rational way from my existing ends and motivations.

What should we make of this argument? One question it raises immediately is whether the notion of possibility at work in premise (1) is plausibly the same as the notion of possibility at work in premise (2), as it must be if the argument is to go through. The "can" in premise (2) suggests psychological possibility: it identifies the conditions under which an agent who begins with a particular psychological profile might be motivated to perform some action. Is this also a plausible interpretation of the "can" at work in premise (1)? Is it plausibly a conceptual constraint on when a consideration can count as a reason for an agent that there are circumstances in which that agent, burdened, at least at the outset, with his actual psychological profile, might be motivated by that consideration to act? If we take seriously Williams's claim that our concept of a reason is the concept of a conditional explanation of the actions of the agent for whom it is a reason, then this does strike me as a reasonable way of interpreting the argument's first premise. And the premise seems to gain some support from the *ought-implies-can* principle: it's very plausible that we *ought* to be motivated by the reasons that apply to us, so it's also plausible that it must be psychologically possible for us to be motivated by those reasons.

The second premise raises some additional worries. It looks like a version of what is sometimes called the Humean Theory of Motivation. Hume wrote:

> Where . . . objects themselves do not effect us, their connexion [of effect to cause, which reason makes evident to us] can never give them any influence; and 'tis plain, that as reason is nothing but the discovery of this connexion, it cannot be by its means that the objects are able to affect us. . . . [R]eason alone can never produce any action, or give rise to volition. . . . Nothing can oppose or retard the influence of passion, but a contrary impulse. . . . Reason is, and ought only to be the slave of the passions, and can never pretend to any other office than to serve and obey them.[6]

In its crudest form, the Humean Theory of Motivation claims that all motivation depends on a relevant antecedent desire. The argument I've outlined refines this thesis in one important respect: it expands the set of attitudes that can ground motivation to include more than just desires (narrowly understood). Williams makes clear that he means agents' "motivational sets" to include, in addition to straightforward desires, "such things as dispositions of evaluation, patterns of emotional reaction, personal loyalties, and various projects, as they may be abstractly called, embodying commitments of the agent."[7]

Even so, the second premise of the argument is controversial at best. It looks to be making an empirical assertion about psychology—an assertion about what kinds of mental events can trigger the formation of new motivations—without backing it up with empirical research (never a promising strategy in philosophical argument). Why should we believe that the formation of a belief *never* triggers the formation of a new motivation?[8] After all, even a knock on the head could do that.

But we might again revise the premise to make it more plausible. . . .

. . .We might interpret the idea of practical reasoning non-accidentally producing motivation in terms of *rational motivation*—motivation that drives us when and because we are rational. If we amend the premises of the internalist argument accordingly, it reads:

(1*) It must be possible for me to be *rationally* motivated by the reasons that apply to me. So a consideration can be a reason for me to φ only if it can *rationally* motivate me to φ: that is, motivate me to φ *when and because I am rational.*

(2*) A consideration can *rationally* motivate me to φ only if it is relevantly connected to my "motivational set"—that is, only if it would motivate me to φ if I were deliberating in a procedurally rational way from my existing ends and motivations.

(3*) Therefore, a consideration can be a reason for me to φ only if it would motivate me to φ if I were deliberating in a procedurally rational way from my existing ends and motivations.

Our new premise (1*) stays true to the intuition from which we began: that a reasons statement—even a normative reasons statement—must still be able to serve as an explanation. After all, it was never the internalist's claim that any normative reason will serve as the actual explanation of the actions of the agent to whom it applies, since agents frequently fail to act as they have reason to act, whether because of ignorance or poor judgment or weakness of will. Rather, internalists appeal to the intuition that reasons should explain our actions when things go well—when we're not subject to such irrationalities. Reasons must be able to explain how we act when we are rational.

And consider the support the premise got from the *ought-implies-can* principle. I suggested earlier that premise (1) was plausible because it is entailed by *ought-implies-can* and another plausible claim: that we ought to be motivated by the reasons that apply to us. But it seems that we can plausibly claim more than this: it's better to be rationally responsive to our reasons than to be merely accidentally motivated by them. In other words, we ought to be not just motivated by our reasons, but *rationally* motivated by them.

Our new premise (2*) also improves upon the old premise (2). It no longer makes overreaching empirical claims about the conditions under which motivation *of any kind* is possible. And it sticks closer to its Humean origins in its focus on the role *Reason* can play in generating motivation. (3*) is identical to (3): our two new premises issue in the internalist conclusion as surely as the original ones did.

2. MOTIVATING INTUITIONS

Fleshing out the second argument for internalism along these lines brings out a striking similarity between this argument and the argument for internalism that Bernard Williams actually makes in "Internal and External Reasons." For it is now clear that the central premises driving both arguments are the same: both rely, first, on the claim that a consideration could be a reason for me to act only if it would motivate me to act if I was rational, and second on the claim that no process of rational deliberation could produce in me a new motivation to act except by taking my existing motivations as a starting point. Nonetheless, the arguments—at least their first central premises—are powered by different intuitions. Williams takes his first premise to be supported by intuitions about what our reasons statements *mean*. The second argument's first premise is supported by appeal to a conceptual connection between reasons (even normative reasons) and action-explanations, and also, I have suggested, by a plausible assumption about how we ought to be motivated, taken together with the *ought-implies-can* principle.

The argument's second central premise—the Humean one—has been the chief focus of the philosophical disagreement about the nature of reasons for action. Defenders of internalism about reasons have touted their theory's ability to reflect the myriad intuitions captured by the arguments' first premise: that practical reasons must be capable of motivating rational agents. Externalists have defended their view by attempting to block the implication from that first premise to the internalists' conclusion, largely by attacking the Humean Theory of Motivation in its various forms. But the first premise itself, and the intuitions underlying it, have received less scrutiny. . . .

So: why think that some consideration cannot be a reason for us to act unless it could motivate us to act, and would do so if we were rational? I touched on some of the reasons for thinking this in setting out the two arguments for internalism above. I'll begin with the intuition about the *meaning* of our reasons statements that, I have suggested, is the driving force behind the first argument for internalism—the one Williams actually makes explicitly. Why does Williams think that the conception of reasons—as facts that would motivate us if we were rational—is one that internalists and externalists *share*? Williams writes:

> There are of course many things that a speaker may say to one who is not disposed to φ when the speaker thinks that he should be, as that he is inconsiderate, or cruel, or selfish, or imprudent; or that things, and he, would be a lot nicer if he were so motivated. Any of these can be sensible things to say. But one who makes a great deal out of putting the criticism in the form of an external reason statement seems concerned to say that what is particularly wrong with the agent is that he is *irrational*. It is this theorist who particularly needs to make this charge precise: in particular, because he wants any rational agent, as such, to acknowledge the requirement to do the thing in question.[9]

The whole point of ascribing a reason to someone, either internal or external, Williams thinks, is to make clear to them that, if they fail to act accordingly, they are failing by their own lights—they are failing to live up to a standard whose bindingness on them they must themselves, as rational agents, acknowledge: the standard of rationality. This is what makes such a charge different from saying merely that it would be better if they acted this way, or that we would wish them to do so, or would do so in their place. The shared etymology of *reason* and *rationality* is no accident. (Williams's claim is that, on this understanding of what reasons statements mean, only internal reasons statements can be *true*.) Reasons statements aim at objectivity, or at least intersubjectivity, and they add something to our arsenal only if we can use them, in this way, to appeal to the requirements of this shared standard.[10]

Williams's claim about what our reasons statements mean is backed up by an additional claim about the conceptual link between reasons and explanation. It is also no accident of etymology that we use the same word, "reason," to describe both the grounds on which we act—sometimes called motivating reasons—and the reasons *for us* to act—sometimes called normative reasons. In both cases, Williams suggests, reasons statements explain action: motivating reasons explain why we actually act the way we do, and normative reasons statements explain how we would act if all went well—if we did not succumb to weakness of will, or confusion, or ignorance, or poor judgment: if, in other words, we were rational.

So, Williams takes it to be a conceptual truth about reasons that they are the considerations that would move good practical reasoners. This certainly seems plausible, and it is reinforced by a claim that is often made about practical reasons: that they must be *action-guiding*. Reasons, the thought is, are not purposeless: they guide us in how to behave. But a reason that could not motivate us, even if we were perfect practical reasoners, could not play this action-guiding role. So all reasons must be capable of motivating us in so far as we are reasoning well. . . .

Then there is the claim that I appealed to in support of the second argument for internalism, above. Surely, we *ought* to be motivated by any reason that applies to us—indeed, we ought to be so motivated

when and because we are rational. Since *ought* implies *can,* it must follow that we *can* be motivated by any reason that applies to us, when we are rational. This thought becomes all the more forceful if we accept the very plausible claim that *virtue* is a matter of motivational responsiveness to practical reasons. For if we accept that thought, but deny that we ought always to be responsive to our reasons, then we are denying that we ought always to be virtuous.

The power of reasons to motivate rational agents might also help explain another fact that often comes up in the literature on internalism about reasons: that rational agents are reliably motivated to act as they judge they have reason to act. If considerations that provide reasons themselves have the power to motivate rational agents, this fact is neatly explained: rational agents are motivated to act by their judgment that they have reason to act because rational agents' judgments about their reasons are true, and are the discovery of facts that themselves have the power to motivate those agents when they are rational.

Finally, some philosophers have appealed to a somewhat more nebulous idea in support of the claim that our normative reasons must be capable of motivating us, at least when we are rational. They have suggested that a conception of reasons that allows that we might have reasons that could get no motivational grip on us, even when we're reasoning as we should, would unacceptably *alienate* us from our reasons. . . .

It's appealing to think something similar may be true of our reasons more generally. As Williams and others have argued, it may be a limiting condition on our moral obligations that they somehow reflect what *drives* us.[11] And there must be something about the reasons for me to act that makes them *mine.* Shouldn't it be a requirement on some consideration's providing *me* with a reason to φ that *I* can appeal to it to justify myself when I do φ? But I can appeal to such a consideration honestly only if it was one of the (motivating) reasons I *did* φ. If a consideration can't motivate me to φ, than how can I point to it to justify myself for having done so?

Taken together, these considerations provide compelling support for the claim that reasons must be capable of motivating the agents whose reasons they are, and will motivate them if they are rational. I will call this claim the *Motivating Intuition*. As I have argued, the Motivating Intuition plays an essential role in at least two important arguments for internalism about reasons. Unfortunately, as examples will show, the Motivating Intuition is false.

3. COUNTER-EXAMPLES TO THE MOTIVATING INTUITION

The counter-examples to the Motivating Intuition that I will describe fall into three classes. The first, and most commonly discussed, class of counter-examples encompasses reasons we have *because* we are not perfectly rational. Some of these examples put pressure on the idea, which is reflected in part of the Motivating Intuition, that how we *should* act is determined by how we *would* act if we were more ideally rational than we are. Here are two such examples, both of which are, in some version, familiar from the literature on internalism:

> **The student of reasoning.** We surely have reason to take measures to improve our ability to reason: we have reason, for example, to take lessons in chess, or logic, and it is becoming increasingly common for universities to require students to take courses in "reasoning and critical thinking." But, if we were fully rational, we would not be motivated to take any such measures.

Even if our reasoning ability itself is unexceptionable, lack of self-control or weakness of will can also present us with obstacles that we ought to take into account:

> **The sore loser.** A squash player, who, after suffering an embarrassing defeat, rightly believes he will hit his opponent out of anger if he does not leave the court immediately surely has reason to leave, although if he were fully rational, and so not weak-willed, he would be motivated instead to shake his opponent's hand.[12]

As these examples bring out, facts about how we would act if we were ideally rational can seem irrelevant to our actual, non-ideal circumstances, in which we face impediments that our perfectly rational counterparts do not. And we might wonder, more generally, why we should care about the motivations of people who are, after all, quite fundamentally different from us . . .

What can we learn from these examples? They suggest that the Motivating Intuition, as I've stated it, is false; that . . . it is not, after all, a "platitude" about practical reasons that what we have reason to do is what we would be motivated to do if fully practically rational; and certainly that Williams's claim about what our reasons statements *mean* is mistaken: if we think someone has reason to improve his reasoning skills, despite acknowledging that he would not be motivated to do so if he were fully rational, we cannot plausibly *mean* by our reasons claim that he would be motivated to improve his reasoning skills if he were fully rational.

Where does this leave internalism? Examples such as these show that a simple version of the internalist formula, like the one that emerges as the conclusion of the two influential internalist arguments I set out above, is guilty of the "conditional fallacy." Our reasons can't be restricted to what we would be motivated to do if we were perfectly procedurally rational—rational relative to our existing ends and motivations. If we were fully rational relative to our existing ends and motivations, we would not be motivated to do things like taking chess or reasoning lessons, or abruptly walk off the squash court to avoid instigating a fight. So many internalists . . . have replaced the simple internalist thesis with a more complicated thesis that avoids the conditional fallacy: they have suggested, for example, that we have reason to do what our fully procedurally rational *counterparts* would *desire or advise* us to do *in our actual situation*.[13]

Responses of this kind have some virtues. They allow internalism to retain the appeal to the shared standard of rationality that Williams considered so central to understanding reasons claims. . . . But Robert Johnson has argued that revisions like this sacrifice the most appealing feature of internalism about reasons—its accommodation of the intuition that a reason for an agent to act must be capable of serving also as an explanation of how the agent acts, in the right circumstances:

> Once one moves away from [simple internalism about reasons] in such ways in order to avoid the conditional fallacy, an explanatory gap opens up—in this case, between your better self desiring that you should do something and you yourself being motivated to do it. The gap opens because it may be impossible for the desire had by your rationally ideal self to play any role in the explanation of your actions.[14]

Johnson suggests that, if internalists are to retain their advantage over externalists, they must find a way of avoiding the conditional fallacy while continuing to satisfy the "explanatory requirement"— the requirement that an agent's normative reasons be capable of explaining his actions, by serving as his motivating reasons for acting. The two examples I've discussed so far do nothing to undermine the force of that requirement: *we* can be motivated by the reasons we have not to harm people to walk away instead of instigating a fight, and *we* can be motivated by the reasons we have to improve our reasoning skills to take chess lessons or courses in critical thinking, even if our ideally rational counterparts cannot. But, as other counter-examples to the Motivating Intuition show, including the example on which Johnson himself focuses, the case for internalism about reasons would not be strengthened by its satisfying the explanatory requirement, because reasons need not be capable of motivating us, after all.

Let's start with Johnson's own example:

> **"James Bond."** Let's say I become convinced I am James Bond. The fact that I am suffering from such a delusion may give me an excellent reason to see a psychiatrist for treatment. But it cannot motivate me to see the psychiatrist. For if this fact could motivate me to seek help, I would no longer be convinced I was James Bond. Someone who firmly believes he is James

> Bond cannot be motivated to seek a psychiatrist by the fact that his belief is a delusion.

Johnson is right that the versions of internalism about reasons that are revised to avoid the conditional fallacy must allow that "James Bond" has such a reason, since it seems hard to deny that "James's" perfectly rational counterpart would advise him to seek psychiatric help, or would wish that he'd seek help fortuitously, were he to suddenly find himself in "James's" less-than-ideal position. And he is right that this shows that such revised versions of internalism do not satisfy the explanatory requirement. But the "James Bond" example is as much a counter-example to the explanatory requirement itself as it is to simple, unrevised internalism. It suggests that internalists should perhaps not be trying to accommodate the explanatory requirement in the first place. . . .

The [example] I've discussed so far . . . involve[s] reasons we have because we are not perfectly rational. These reasons could not motivate us if we were fully rational, because they would not *apply* to us if we were fully rational. But there are other circumstances in which our reasons might not be capable of motivating us. One interesting class of counter-examples to the Motivating Intuition concerns things we have reason to do (and can do), but which we cannot *do for those reasons,* and so *could* not do if we were fully rational—and so fully responsive to our reasons—even if we wanted to. In a paper investigating some apparent paradoxes of deterrence, Gregory Kavka describes circumstances, which he calls "Special Deterrent Situations" (or SDSs), in which agents would find themselves faced with reasons of this sort. An SDS arises when we have reason to *intend* to apply a very harmful sanction, affecting many innocent people, in retaliation for what would be a similarly extremely harmful and unjust offense, because *intending* to apply such a sanction is the likeliest means of deterring the offense. But, because the sanction is so harmful and its victims innocent, we have no reason to *actually apply* the sanction should the offense occur.[15] Such circumstances are likely not just the stuff of philosophy papers: a plausible real-life SDS (which Kavka discusses) is provided by:

> **Nuclear Deterrence.** Perhaps the most likely way to deter a nuclear attack is to intend to retaliate against any attacking nation by responding in kind.[16] But, if an attack should occur, no good could come of actually retaliating. So, if I am responsible for the defense strategy of a nation threatened by nuclear attack, I have reason to *intend* to retaliate against any such attack with a nuclear attack targeting the aggressor. But I have no reason to actually retaliate. Because of this I cannot be motivated to form the intention to retaliate if I am fully rational: rational agents do not form intentions to act against their own (correct) assessment of the balance of reasons. And, what's more, they cannot intend to perform actions they know they will not perform when the time for performance comes: if the nuclear attack occurs, and I know I have conclusive reason not to retaliate, I won't retaliate. And since I know, now, that I won't retaliate were an attack to occur, I cannot intend to retaliate.

. . . *Nuclear Deterrence* differ[s] from the cases I've already discussed: they do not turn on reasons that I have *because* I am not fully rational. (If anything, the problems of motivation they bring to light afflict us because we are, in a sense, prisoners of our own rationality.) The reasons I have to intend to drink the toxin, or to intend to initiate a retaliatory attack, might not be capable of motivating me even when I'm not fully rational. This is simply not how the process of intention-formation works. The forming of intentions to act is driven by our motivations to perform the intended act. I cannot, through sheer force of will, form an intention to do something I believe I have no reason to do, and conclusive reason not to do, even if I believe I have reason to form the intention. . . .

As Kavka notes, SDSs also bring out the somewhat surprising conclusion that we might sometimes have reason to corrupt ourselves—to bring about in ourselves dispositions to act against the balance of moral reasons, or to fail to be properly motivationally sensitive to some moral reasons. An agent faced with a genuine SDS, like *Nuclear Deterrence,* ought (if she can) to bring it about that she forms the deterrent intention—in this case, to retaliate—even though this means reducing her sensitivity to genuine moral reasons. This has important implications for our consideration of the Motivating Intuition. In particular, it seems to run counter to a thought which played an important role in our defense of the motivating intuition: that we *ought* always to be as virtuous as we can be, and therefore, since it's plausible that being virtuous is a matter of being appropriately motivationally sensitive to our moral reasons, that we ought always to be motivated by the reasons that apply to us. This thought, I argued, underlies the crucial first premise of the second argument for internalism I set out in Section 1. But, as Kavka's SDSs show, we sometimes have reasons to lessen our own sensitivity to reasons.

. . . In *Nuclear Deterrence,* the problem arises because of the partly involuntary nature of intention-formation: we cannot, at will, form the intention to do something we believe we have no reason to do. And cases where we have reason to intend to do something we have no reason to do may be quite rare. But the problem for the Motivating Intuition is in fact much broader than the example of SDSs suggests. It is, in fact, often true that we ought not to be motivated by reasons that apply to us.

Usually, when it is true that we ought not be motivated by our reasons, this is because we are more likely to succeed at doing what we have reason to do if we aren't motivated by those reasons. . . .

Pragmatic grounds not to be motivated by the reasons that apply to us are often generated when we are forced to act in emergency situations and against great odds, a fact that was strikingly demonstrated by post-crash interviews of Captain Chesley Sullenberger, the US Airways pilot who miraculously succeeded in landing a commercial jetliner with no working engines on New York's Hudson River, improbably saving the lives of all 155 passengers and crew on board:

Emergency Landing. On January 15th, 2009, Captain Sullenberger successfully emergency-landed an Airbus A320, which had lost all thrust in both engines due to a double bird strike, in the icy waters of the Hudson River, with no loss of life. Asked, in a *60 Minutes* interview by Katie Couric, whether he had been thinking about the passengers as his plane was descending rapidly towards the waters of the Hudson, Captain Sullenberger replied, "Not specifically. . . . I mean, I *knew* I had to solve this problem. I knew I had to find a way out of this box I found myself in. . . . My focus at that point was so intensely on the landing . . . I thought of nothing else."[17]

While the fact that many lives depended on his successfully landing the aircraft undoubtedly provided Captain Sullenberger with a reason to do so, it is also clear that it was a very good thing that the Captain was not in fact motivated by this reason as he guided the plane onto the water. Indeed, it seems likely that years of training in emergency preparedness coached the Captain, with good reason, not to think about the ultimate reasons for successfully handling a crisis situation when faced with the need to do so.

The [lesson] of . . . *Emergency Landing* generalize[s]. A specialist in a rarely curable disease may be able to cure more patients if she's in it for the social prestige than if she's in it chiefly to save lives, since her low success rate might otherwise drive her to quit. A surgeon may operate more successfully if she learns to suppress some normal sympathy for patients in unavoidable pain,[18] and she may be less likely to make nervous mistakes in delicate procedures if she is not thinking of the life that is at stake. In fact, many of us have found ourselves in situations in which we were fortunate that we were driven by ulterior motives, habit, instinct, or "auto-pilot" rule-following to make decisions or react to threats which we would have likely reacted to less well if we had been responding motivationally to our reasons for doing so. If a child runs into the street right in front of my car, I hit the brakes automatically—I am not motivated by a concern for the well-being of the

child. In a surprising number of cases, there is much to be said for *not* being motivated by our reasons.

4. WHAT THESE COUNTER-EXAMPLES CAN TEACH US

What can we learn from these counter-examples? Has anything survived of the intuitions that supported the Motivating Intuition?

The examples of the *Student of Reasoning* and the *Sore Loser* show us that "A has a reason to φ" cannot *mean* "A would be motivated to φ if she were rational," as Williams suggested . . . We readily ascribe reasons to the *Student of Reasoning* and the *Sore Loser* despite the fact that we are perfectly aware that they would not be motivated to act on those reasons if they were perfectly rational (because they would not have those reasons).

While the *Student of Reasoning* and the *Sore Loser* would not be motivated by their reasons if they were perfectly rational (because the reasons would, in that case, no longer apply), their reasons could nonetheless serve as explanations of their actions in their *actual* circumstances—the circumstances in which they do apply. So does the conceptual link between normative reasons and possible *explanations* of actions, to which Williams also appeals, hold up? No: the [example] of the deluded "*James Bond*" . . . show[s] that we can have reasons for both action and belief that could not possibly serve as explanations of our actions or beliefs, even in the circumstances in which they do apply to us.

Moreover, the problem is not just a result of our imperfect rationality . . . The predicaments presented by *Nuclear Deterrence* . . . show that, even if we're fully rational, we might have reasons to act or believe that could not motivate us to act or believe accordingly. It won't always be possible for us to do as we have reason to do, *for* the reason we have to do it. In other words, it won't always be possible for us to act virtuously.

And finally, as the [case] of . . . the *Emergency Landing* show[s], and as our own experience will confirm, even when we *can* be motivated to do something by the reason we have for doing it, it's not always true that we *ought* to be motivated by that reason. Sometimes, we are significantly more effective in doing what we have reason to do if we train ourselves to be motivated differently. If it's not always true that we *ought* to be (rationally) motivated by the reasons that apply to us, we cannot appeal to the *ought-implies-can* principle to derive the conclusion that we *can* always be (rationally) motivated by the reasons that apply to us.

Remember that the *First Argument* for internalism about reasons, the one explicitly made by Williams in "Internal and External Reasons," depended on the claim that the Motivating Intuition captures what our reasons statements *mean*: that what we *mean* when we ascribe a reason to φ to someone is that they would be motivated to φ if they were rational. And remember my suggestion that the *Second Argument* for internalism about reasons, which also includes the Motivating Intuition as a premise, gained support from the *ought-implies-can* principle. As the counter-examples to the Motivating Intuition show, both of these influential arguments for internalism about reasons fail before we've even considered their controversial Humean premises. If, as Williams and Johnson have suggested and as the structure of the debate about internalism implies, internalism's ability to accommodate the Motivating Intuition were its chief virtue, then considering the counter-examples I've described should lead us to abandon internalism about reasons.

But I don't think we should abandon internalism. I believe internalism still receives some direct support from some of the considerations I appealed to in defense of the Motivating Intuition in Section 2. And I believe we have other good grounds for taking internalism about reasons seriously. . . .

. . . Even without the Motivating Intuition, there is, I believe, plenty to motivate internalism.

NOTES

1. Williams (1995), p. 35.
2. Williams (1981b), p. 101. This way of stating the view oversimplifies the matter in at least two ways: firstly, as I have noted, Williams intends "desires" to be understood broadly—they may include, in addition to ordinary present desires, evaluations, attitudes, projects, commitments, and so on—anything for the sake of which we act. Secondly, the notion of an action's "serving" a desire suggests that reason plays a purely instrumental role. Williams, however, wants to allow for the possibility that we have reason to act in ways that serve our ends non-instrumentally—perhaps the action in question is constitutive of some end or commitment, or expresses that commitment (see p. 104).
3. This dependence does not necessarily rule out the possibility of universal reasons—reasons we all share. Some internalists defend the existence, for example, of universal internal *moral* reasons. . . . What makes such universal reasons *internal* is that they apply to us in virtue of the relation they stand in to our actual ends and desires, whatever those happen to be. But the possibility of such universal internal reasons will not occupy us here.
4. Williams (1981b), p. 109.
5. Thomas Nagel offers it on behalf of internalism (1970, p. 27), although he rejects one of the premises.
6. Hume (1739/1975), pp. 414–15.
7. Williams (1981b), p. 105.
8. That is, one not derived from our existing motivations.
9. Williams (1981b), p. 110.
10. My own view is that thick moral concepts such as *cruel* or *selfish* also aim at objectivity—and so can be appropriately applied only when a reason-ascription is also appropriate. The charge of selfishness, for example, does not merely imply that the selfish person is more protective of her own interests than we would like her to be, say, or than is normal, but rather that she is more protective of her own interests than she has *reason* to be.
11. As Williams puts it, "[t]here can come a point at which it is quite unreasonable for a man to give up, in the name of the impartial good ordering of the world of moral agents, something which is a condition of his having any interest in being around in the world at all" (Williams, 1981a, p. 14).
12. The example is due to Michael Smith (1995, p. 111) . . .
13. See, for example, Smith (1994), p. 151.
14. Johnson (2003). See also Johnson (1999).
15. Kavka (1978)
16. Kavka (1978) notes that "writers on strategic policy frequently assert that nuclear deterrence will be

effective only if the defending nation really intends to retaliate" (p. 287).

17. Katie Couric interviewed Captain Sullenberger on *60 Minutes,* airdate 8 February 2009, copyright CBS News. A summary of the interview that includes the quoted passages can be found at: http://www.cbsnews.com/stories/2009/02/08/60minutes/main4783580_page2.shtml?tag=contentMain;contentBody (accessed 17 September 2009).

18. As Kavka (1978) also suggests—see note 20, p. 287.

REFERENCES

Hume, D. (1739/1975) L.A. Selby-Bigge (ed.) *A Treatise of Human Nature,* 2nd edition, revised by P.H. Nidditch (Oxford: Clarendon Press).

Johnson, R.N. (1999) "Internal Reasons and the Conditional Fallacy," *The Philosophical Quarterly* 49, 53–71.

Johnson, R.N. (2003) "Internal Reasons: Reply to Brady, Van Roojen and Gert," *The Philosophical Quarterly* 53, 573–80.

Kavka, G. (1978) "Some Paradoxes of Deterrence," *Journal of Philosophy* 75, 285–302.

Nagel, T. (1970) *The Possibility of Altruism* (Oxford: Clarendon Press).

Smith, M. (1994) *The Moral Problem* (Oxford: Blackwell Publishers).

Smith, M. (1995) "Internal Reasons," *Philosophy and Phenomenological Research* 55, 109–31.

Williams, B. (1981a) "Persons, Character, and Morality," reprinted in *Moral Luck* (Cambridge: Cambridge University Press), 1–19.

Williams, B. (1981b) "Internal and External Reasons," reprinted in *Moral Luck* (Cambridge: Cambridge University Press), 101–13.

Williams, B. (1995) "Internal Reasons and the Obscurity of Blame," reprinted in *Making Sense of Humanity* (Cambridge: Cambridge University Press), 35–45.

STUDY QUESTIONS

1. According to Markovits, what is the "motivating intuition"?
2. What support does the argument of Williams receive from the principle that ought implies can?
3. What is the "conditional fallacy"?
4. What implications does Markovits draw from the case of "emergency landing"?

The Humean Theory of Reasons

Mark Schroeder

Mark Schroeder, Professor of Philosophy at the University of Southern California, argues that normative reasons must be explained by some psychological state of the agent to whom they apply. His argument eschews reliance on both the Humean theory of motivation and Bernard Williams's claim that reasons must both motivate and justify.

Instead, Schroeder's argument begins with the plausible thought that some reasons are reasons only for some people. For example, imagine we are both sitting outside on a hot day. I love the heat and the feeling of sweat on my skin. You don't. I'm enjoying myself. You're not. We both can retreat to an air-conditioned room. You have a reason to retreat, while I do not. According to Schroeder, we can explain the difference as follows. You desire a room that feels more comfortable. Retreating is an action you can perform to promote the object of your desire. This reason is yours, because you are the one with the desire. If, by contrast, I find the outdoors exactly as I desire it, then I lack a reason to retreat. That you, not I, desire a different environment explains why you have a reason to retreat while I do not. Schroeder concludes that if we want to give a unified account of all reasons, we should, like this case, explain them by the psychological state of the agent to whom they apply.

This paper offers a simple and novel motivation for the Humean Theory of Reasons. According to the Humean Theory of Reasons, all reasons must be explained by some psychological state of the agent for whom they are reasons, such as a desire. This view is commonly thought[1] to be motivated by a substantive theory about the power of reasons to motivate known as *reason internalism,* and a substantive theory about the possibility of being motivated without a desire known as the *Humean Theory of Motivation.* Such a motivation would place substantial constraints on what form the Humean Theory of Reasons might take, and incur substantial commitments in metaethics and moral psychology. The argument offered here, on the other hand, is based entirely on relatively uncontroversial methodological considerations of perfectly broad applicability, and on the commonplace observation that while some reasons are reasons for anyone, others are reasons for only some. The argument is a highly defeasible one, but is supposed to give us a direct insight into what is philosophically deep about the puzzles raised for ethical theory by the Humean Theory of Reasons. I claim that it should renew our interest in the relationship

From Mark Schroeder, "The Humean Theory of Reasons," in *Oxford Studies in Metaethics* vol. 2, ed. Russ Shafer-Landau (Oxford: Oxford University Press, 2007). Reprinted by permission of the publisher.

between these two kinds of reason, and in particular in the explanation of reasons which seem to depend on desires or other psychological states.

1.1 THE HUMEAN THEORY OF REASONS: WHAT

Consider a case like that of Ronnie and Bradley. Ronnie likes to dance, but Bradley can't stand even being around dancing. So the fact that there will be dancing at the party tonight is a reason for Ronnie to go there, but not for Bradley to go there—it is a reason for Bradley to stay away. Ronnie and Bradley's reasons therefore differ—something is a reason for one to do something, but not for the other to do it. And this difference between their reasons seems obviously to have something to do with their psychologies. It may not be ultimately explained by the difference in what they *like,* of course—the explanation may ultimately derive from a difference in what they *value,* or what they *care* about, what they *desire, desire to desire,* what they take or would take *pleasure* in, or what they *believe to be of value.* I'm not claiming that it is uncontroversial that one rather than another of these kinds of psychological states is what really explains the difference between Ronnie and Bradley—after all, many of these psychological characteristics often go hand in hand, and even moderately sophisticated views can make them hard to distinguish simply by considering cases. All I'm claiming is that it should be pretty close to uncontroversial that there are at least some reasons like Ronnie's, in that they are explained by *some* psychological feature.[2]

The *Broad* Humean Theory of Reasons says that all reasons are explained in the same way as Ronnie's—by the same kind of psychological feature:

> **Broad Humean Theory** Every reason is explained[3] by the kind of psychological feature that explains Ronnie's reason in the same way as Ronnie's is.

The Broad Humean Theory of Reasons is really too broad to sound familiar to most readers familiar with the philosophical literature on reasons. That literature is full of references to, and attacks on, a familiar view that is more narrow than the Broad Humean Theory. This view is a *version* of the Broad Humean Theory because it agrees that all reasons must be explained by the same kind of psychological feature as explains Ronnie's. But it is more specific than the Broad Theory, because it takes a view about what kind of psychological state does explain the difference between Ronnie's and Bradley's reasons. It says that it is a *desire,* in the traditional philosophical sense:

> **Narrow Humean Theory** Every reason is explained by a desire in the same way as Ronnie's is.

Even the Narrow Humean Theory of Reasons, of course, is only loosely called "Humean"; there is an excellent case to be made that Hume himself was not a Humean in either sense. Both theories are associated with Hume's name primarily because their proponents have typically been loosely inspired by Hume.

So allow me to reveal my hand. I believe that a version of the Narrow Humean Theory of Reasons is true . . . But in this paper I will not be arguing for the Narrow Humean Theory. The argument of this paper is only a motivation for the Broad Humean Theory. It is my *view* that there are good arguments from the Broad Humean Theory to the Narrow Humean Theory, but I will not advance those arguments in this paper. Indeed, I think that for most of the philosophical reasons for which philosophers have been interested in whether the Humean Theory of Reasons is true, whether the Humean Theory is Narrow or not is beside the point. In the next subsection I will explain why.

1.2 THE HUMEAN THEORY OF REASONS AND MORAL SKEPTICISM

The Broad Humean Theory of Reasons takes no stand on what kind of psychological state it is that explains the difference between Ronnie and Bradley.

It only claims that whatever it is, it is also needed to explain every other reason. But this does not water the Humean Theory down so much as to make it of little interest. On the contrary, it is exactly the right specificity of view that we should be worried about, for exactly the reasons that philosophers have been worried about the Narrow Humean Theory of Reasons all along.

The principal philosophical interest of the Narrow Humean Theory of Reasons, after all, is that it is supposed to play a special role in motivating certain kinds of skepticism about the universality or objectivity of morality. The problem is that according to the Humean Theory, every reason must be explained by a desire of the person for whom it is a reason. But it is hard to see how such an explanation could possibly work for all moral reasons. Consider this case: Katie needs help. So there is a reason to help Katie. It is a reason for you to help Katie, a reason for me to help Katie, and in general, it is a reason for *anyone* to help Katie. Some of the most important moral reasons seem to be like the reason to help Katie—they are reasons for *anyone,* no matter what she is like. But does *everyone* really have some desire that would explain a reason for her to help Katie in the same way that Ronnie's desire to dance explains his reason to go to the party? It seems fairly implausible.

So those who accept versions of the Narrow Humean Theory often take revisionist views about the kind of objectivity that moral claims have. Gilbert Harman, for example, argues for these reasons that moral claims aren't really universally binding, but are only binding on people who have implicitly contracted in certain ways. This is his brand of moral relativism in "Moral Relativism Defended" and subsequently.[4] Philippa Foot argues for almost identical reasons that moral claims don't provide reasons to everyone, but only to those who care about morality. That is her thesis in "Morality as a System of Hypothetical Imperatives."[5] The difference between Harman and Foot is that Foot thinks that there is another, non-reason-giving, sense in which moral claims nevertheless "apply" to everyone, even to those to whom they don't give reasons. John Mackie argues that it is essential to moral claims that moral requirements give reasons to everyone. Since this is incompatible with the Humean Theory of Reasons, he concludes that moral claims are uniformly false.[6] These are all drastic forms of skepticism about the objectivity or universality of morality that are motivated by the Humean Theory of Reasons. And it is these kinds of arguments which give the Humean Theory so much of its interest for moral theorists. It is in order to avoid these kinds of implications that moral philosophers have been so concerned, over so many years, to finally conclusively refute the Humean Theory.

But notice that none of these arguments actually turns on making any particular assumptions about what *kind* of psychological state is necessary in order to explain a reason. No matter what kind of psychological state is necessary in order to explain a reason, it is fairly implausible that we are going to be able to expect that everyone, no matter what she is like, will have some psychological state of the requisite kind in order to explain a reason that is supposed to be a reason for everyone. So the Broad Humean Theory of Reasons best captures what lies at the heart of this kind of worry about the universality or objectivity of morality—the kind of worry that the revisionary Humean takes to be conclusive.

Now if the Narrow Humean Theory of Reasons is the most popular version of the Broad Humean Theory, it is easy to understand for purely sociological reasons why it would receive so much attention. But what we can expect for sociological reasons is quite different from what we should demand of good philosophy. There are any number of supposed refutations of the Narrow Humean Theory of Reasons in the literature, all for the purpose of setting aside the kinds of skeptical arguments run by Harman, Foot, and Mackie. But it's simply faulty reasoning to think that if an argument you want to rebut needs the premise that *p,* you can rebut it by refuting *p+,* a stronger premise. If we're really concerned about the kinds of skeptical arguments raised by Harman, Foot, and Mackie, we have to be concerned about the more general Broad Humean Theory of Reasons.

1.3 THE CLASSICAL ARGUMENT FOR THE HUMEAN THEORY

So why haven't philosophers critical of the skeptical arguments of Harman, Foot, and Mackie been more concerned about this more general view? Are they philosophically lazy? No; a much better explanation is easy to find. The better explanation is that it is widely believed to be common knowledge what the *only motivation* for believing the Broad Humean Theory of Reasons is. And it is an argument which, if it works, also establishes the truth of the Narrow Humean Theory of Reasons. I call it the *Classical Argument* for the Humean Theory.

Elijah Millgram, a critic of the Humean Theory, puts the Classical Argument most succinctly: "How could anything be a reason for action if it could not motivate you to actually *do* something? And what could motivate you to do something, except one of your desires?"[7] Millgram's first rhetorical question states the thesis of *reason internalism* and his second that of the *Humean Theory of Motivation.* If having a reason requires being motivatable, and being motivatable requires having a desire, then having a reason must require having a desire. And that is enough of the Humean Theory of Reasons to motivate the kinds of skepticism just discussed.

A great deal of the abundant literature critical of the Humean Theory of Reasons has focused on rebutting the Classical Argument, and many of the points made there are fairly conclusive. The Classical Argument leaves much to be desired, as a motivation for the Humean Theory of Reasons. But if this is the only motivation for the Broad Humean Theory, then we can straightaway draw two conclusions about the kind of view that the Humean Theory takes about desires. First, they have to be motivating states. And second, they have to be *ubiquitous* motivating states: any action whatsoever has to have one of them in its causal etiology.

These two conclusions set enormous constraints on the kind of shape that the Broad Humean Theory of Reasons might take. If they are sound, then refutations of the Broad Humean Theory of Reasons can take for granted some fairly strong conclusions about

what kind of psychological state explains reasons, according to the Humean: not only that they are *desires,* but what desires, in fact, *are.* But I think that if we are genuinely interested in the kind of view that can motivate Harman's, Foot's, and Mackie's kinds of skepticism about the objectivity of morality, then we should cast our nets wider. In particular, I don't think that the Classical Argument gives the best or most interesting argument for the Broad Humean Theory of Reasons. It is the purpose of this paper to offer a better and more general motivation for the Humean Theory, one which doesn't commit that theory to any particular story about what explains the difference between Ronnie and Bradley. It is my purpose to show how *few* assumptions about the Humean Theory of Reasons are necessary in order to motivate it.

2.1 THE POSITIVE MOTIVATION

It is fairly uncontroversial, as I suggested in section 1.1, that the difference between Ronnie's and Bradley's reasons is due to a difference in their psychologies. It is not uncontroversial, of course, *which* difference in their psychologies it is due to. But the central idea behind my motivation for the Humean Theory is to take what we *do* know about Ronnie and Bradley's case, and to put it to work. If there is *any* uniform explanation of all reasons, then maybe what we know about how *some* explanations of reasons work will help to shed light on how *all* explanations of reasons must work. And that is the idea that I will be pushing. There are broad-based theoretical motivations to hope that there might be some common explanation of why there are the reasons that there are—broad motivations to be in search of a uniform explanation of all reasons. If we are after a uniform explanation of all reasons, I will be suggesting, Ronnie and Bradley's case is where we should look.

This may not move you. You may be thinking, "but maybe there are *two kinds* of reason—one kind that gets explained by psychological states, and one kind that doesn't!" I agree. There *may* be two kinds of reason. But on the face of it, the reason for Ronnie to go to the party and the reason for Ronnie not to murder are both *reasons*—they are both cases of the same general kind of thing. It would be very surprising if these two uses of the word "reason" turned out to be merely homonyms. So, given that they are both cases of the same kind of thing, it is reasonable to wonder whether there is anything to be said about why they are. And it is this reasonable thing to wonder, I will be suggesting, which will lead to the hypothesis that all reasons are explained in the way that Ronnie's is.

Of course, it doesn't follow from the fact that Ronnie's reason is explained, in part, by his psychology, and the hypothesis that there is a common explanation of all reasons, that psychological features figure in all of these explanations. It could be that the feature of Ronnie's psychology plays a *role* in the explanation of his reason that can be filled by other kinds of thing—for example, by promises or special relationships. And in any case, if we really care about finding a common explanation of all reasons, something must motivate us to pay attention to Ronnie and Bradley's case, in particular. After all, there are many cases of reasons, and we might know something about how many of them work. Where does the pressure come from to try to generalize Ronnie and Bradley's case to cover others, rather than trying to generalize other cases to cover Ronnie and Bradley's?

This last question is really what this paper is about. My aim is to give a principled motivation for looking to cases like Ronnie and Bradley's. And it will come in two steps. First I'll give a principled motivation from a broad methodological principle for looking to cases of reasons that are *merely agent-relational,* rather than to reasons that are *agent-neutral,* in a sense that may be unfamiliar, but which I will explain. The second, more controversial, step will be to isolate psychology-explained reasons as a better candidate to generalize from than other categories of merely agent-relational reason, such as those deriving from promises or from special relationships. . . .

2.2 A METHODOLOGICAL PRINCIPLE

The argument that if we are looking for a uniform explanation of all reasons, merely agent-relational reasons are the most methodologically promising place

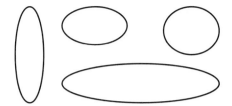

Figure 1

for us to look, trades on what I think should be an uncontroversial methodological principle. I'll uncover this principle in two stages. First, suppose that you start noticing a lot of shapes like the ones depicted in Figure 1. These shapes seem to have something interesting in common, and if you investigate, you will be able to find all kinds of interesting things about them. They are, for example, the shape that objects which are actually circular occupy in our visual fields, and so if you are, for example, a painter, it would behoove you to learn more about what they really have distinctively in common that explains why they are *that* shape, rather than some other. It might, after all (indeed, it will), help you to recreate them accurately.

But you'll be going about things all wrong if you start trying to figure out what these shapes distinctively have in common that distinguishes them simply by looking at *them.* It will put you off on all sorts of wild-goose-chases. For example, one of the first things you're likely to notice about your shapes is that they are all round. But what ellipses all have distinctively in common—for the shapes that you are trying to investigate are ellipses—is not simply that they are all round *plus something else.* You won't ever find something that you can add to their being round, to give you the right account of what sets them aside as a distinctive class of shapes. To discover the answer to that, you have to look not only at ellipses, but at *foils*—shapes that are like ellipses, but not. In particular, you will want to look at egg-shapes and other non-elliptical ovals. Features that are shared by both ellipses and egg-shapes can be quickly set aside as irrelevant. The Methodological Principle, then, is this:

> **MP** If you want to know what makes Ps Ps, compare Ps to things that are not Ps.

I want to take this carefully in order to be perfectly clear how uncontroversial the Methodological Principle should be, because I want to emphasize exactly how natural and forceful my motivation for the Broad Humean Theory of Reasons is. But lest I be accused of belaboring the obvious, the Methodological Principle quickly generalizes once we start paying attention to the case of relations. And here my example will be slightly contrived. Suppose that having discovered what ellipses have in common you notice that some people are the *ancestors* of other people, and decide that you want to discover the same thing about this relation, that you have discovered about the property of being an ellipse. It follows from a generalization of the Methodological Principle that some people are not going to be particularly worth investigating, if you are trying to discover what the common explanation is, of what makes one person the ancestor of another.

Eve, who is the ancestor of everyone . . . [,] will not be a particularly good place to start, in investigating the *ancestor of* relation. Since she is the ancestor of everyone, she has no non-descendants to compare to her descendants as foils. And so you will suffer from an embarrassment of riches, if you try to sort through all of the things that all of Eve's descendants have in common, in search of the one that makes them her descendants. Since every human being is one of Eve's descendants (as I stipulated), any feature that every human being shares will become a candidate, and you will have no way of ruling any of these out. So Eve's case gives you no privileged *insight* into the *ancestor-of* relation. Being descended from Eve is not being human *plus* anything else, any more than being an ellipse is being round plus something else.

So if you really want to investigate the *ancestor of* relation, the generalization of our Methodological Principle tells us that you need to pay more attention to cases like that of Japheth. Japheth is the ancestor of many people, but he is also not the ancestor of many others. And so we have lots of non-descendants of Japheth to compare to lots of descendants of Japheth. With so many foils, we'll be able to rule out many more potential candidates for

what it is that makes Japheth the ancestor of the people who are his descendants. In fact, it is quite likely that there will be *only one* natural candidate for what all of Japheth's descendants have in common but his non-descendants lack: that they are people to whom he stands in the ancestral of the *parent of* relation. So it is quite likely that Japheth's case is going to help you to zero in very quickly on the common explanation of what makes someone the ancestor of someone else. The Generalized Methodological Principle says, then, to pay attention to cases like that of Japheth:

> **GMP** If you want to understand what makes x_1 $\ldots x_n$ stand in relation R, compare cases in which $A_1 \ldots A_n$ stand in relation R but $B_1, A_2 \ldots A_n$ do not, in which $A_1 \ldots A_n$ stand in relation R but A_1, B_2, A_3 $\ldots A_n$ do not, and so on.

Since everyone is a descendant of Eve, Eve's case sets an important *constraint* on a good account of the *ancestor of* relation. The account will be wrong, if it yields the wrong predictions about her case. That is why it is a relief to check and see that Eve does, in fact, stand in the ancestral of the *parent of* relation to everyone. But by the Generalized Methodological Principle, her case is not the right kind of case to give us any particular *insight* into what makes someone the ancestor of someone else. And that is because it leaves us with no useful foils. It allows us to see things that ancestor–descendant pairs have in common, but since it leaves no foils, focusing on this case is like trying to understand ellipses without comparing them to other shapes. It doesn't rule enough out.

2.3 . . . APPLIED TO THE CASE OF REASONS

My *ancestor of* case is . . . slightly contrived. It is highly unlikely, to say the least, that Eve is really the ancestor of *everyone*. To be so, she would have to be her own ancestor, which seems rather unlikely to be the case, stipulations aside. So to that extent, the *ancestor of* relation really only approximates the troubles that beset us when we turn our attention to the *reason* relation. For one of the most philosophically salient features of the *reason* relation—and one that we should have fully in view, if we understand the puzzles about the objectivity of morality raised by the Humean Theory—is that there are some reasons that really *are* reasons for everyone, no matter who she is or what she is like. These *universal,* or *agent-neutral,* reasons of morality, about which the Humean Theory of Reasons is supposed to raise so many puzzles, are supposed to be such reasons. Agent-neutral reasons, in the uncontroversial sense, are like the case of Eve, in that they are reasons for everyone.[8] They may place *constraints* on a good theory about the common explanation of reasons, but they can't give us any important *insight* into what makes some consideration a reason for someone to do something. For in their case we suffer from an embarrassment of riches. There are too many things that everyone has in common for the case to give us any insight into what distinguishes people for whom *R* is a reason to do *A* from those for whom it is not.

So by the Generalized Methodological Principle, it follows that if you want to know what the common explanation of all reasons is, agent-neutral reasons like the reason to help Katie are not going to be a promising place to start. The *promising* place to start is with the case of reasons that are *merely agent-relational*: reasons for some people but not for others. Ronnie and Bradley's is such a case. And so Ronnie and Bradley's case is a much more promising place to look, in order to discover what makes reasons reasons than the case of the agent-neutral reason to help Katie, or any of the other moral reasons.

And that is an interesting result. We might have thought that Humeans are obsessed with cases like that of Ronnie and Bradley because they begin with a pre-theoretic prejudice against reasons like the one to help Katie. . . . But the Generalized Methodological Principle explains why it is natural to be interested in cases like Ronnie and Bradley's. For according to the Generalized Methodological Principle, we *need* to focus on cases of reasons that are merely agent-relational, in order to see what role the agent-place plays in the three-place *reason* relation: *R* is a reason for *X* to do *A*.

But this observation is still insufficient to justify or even motivate the Broad Humean Theory on the basis of our premises. The observation tells us that *merely agent-relational* reasons are the place that we need to look, in order to see what makes reasons reasons, but Ronnie and Bradley's case is only one *kind* of case of merely agent-relational reasons. The observation explains why the efforts of many philosophers to give explanatory accounts of reasons on the basis of paying special or exclusive attention to moral reasons are straightforwardly methodologically unpromising. But it does not justify paying any more attention to psychology-explained agent-relational reasons than to promise-explained agent-relational reasons, special-relation-explained agent-relational reasons, or any number of others, and that is why the methodological principle only gives us the *first* step in our motivation for the Humean Theory.

Compare: Al promises to meet Rose for lunch at the diner. Andy has made no such promise—he's promised his sick mother to visit her at the hospital. The fact that it's time for lunch is a reason for Al to head to the diner. But it's not a reason for Andy to head to the diner—it's a reason for him to head to the hospital. This difference between Al's and Andy's reasons is explained by their respective promises, rather than as a matter of what they like or dislike, want or don't want, care about or not. In another case, Anne is Larry's infant daughter. That is a reason for him to take care of her. But unless you are in Larry's family or a particularly close friend, it isn't a reason for you to take care of Anne. Now, you might have all manner of reasons to take care of Anne—she might, for example, have been abandoned by her father. But the fact that she is Larry's daughter is not among *your* reasons to take care of her. Here it is Larry's relationship to his daughter that seems to make for a difference between his reasons and yours.

So examples of merely agent-relational reasons are ubiquitous. Our Methodological Principle tells us to look at what is distinctive of merely agent-relational reasons, in order to understand reasons in general. But that isn't yet enough to close in on the Humean idea of focusing on Ronnie and Bradley's case, in which the difference in reasons is due to some *psychological* feature. To do that, we need an argument that Ronnie and Bradley's case gives us a *better* insight into what is distinctive of the agent-place in the reason relation than do Al's case or Larry's case. That is, we need to establish an *asymmetry* thesis. My argument for the Broad Humean Theory of Reasons does not rest on ignoring Al's case and Larry's case, or on taking Ronnie's case more seriously. It rests on establishing this Asymmetry Thesis, to which I turn . . .

3.2 THE STANDARD MODEL

Recall that the Methodological Principle does not tell us that cases of agent-neutral reasons *don't matter* for an adequate account of reasons. What it tells us is that like Eve's case, they should operate as a *constraint* on a good account, but they are not likely to give us any particular *insight* into the common explanation of all reasons. . . . My . . . strategy for establishing the Asymmetry Thesis goes the other way around. It is to show that most merely agent-relational reasons can be *subsumed* under the case of agent-neutral reasons, but psychology-explained reasons like Ronnie's and Bradley's plausibly cannot. If that is right, then we can treat Al's case and Larry's case as setting constraints on an adequate account of reasons, but like Katie's case, not being particularly good sources of insight into that relation. But if it is right, then we *can't* treat Ronnie's case in this way. And that will be my argument that if we want to look for a common explanation of all reasons, psychology-explained reasons like Ronnie's and Bradley's are the first place that we should look. And this is my central presumptive argument for the Broad Humean Theory.

So consider the case of Al and Andy. Al promises Rose to meet her for lunch at the diner, and Andy promises his mother to visit her at the hospital. As a result, the fact that it is almost noon is a reason for Al to head to the diner and a reason for Andy to head to the hospital. But plausibly, this difference in Al and Andy's reasons can be traced back to a reason that they have in common—to keep their promises.

One such reason is that breaking promises tends to destroy their usefulness. Another is that breaking promises is a breach of trust. Since this is a reason for Al to keep his promises, the fact that he has promised Rose to meet her at the diner for lunch makes heading for the diner at noon necessary for keeping his promises. And since Andy has promised to visit his mother at the hospital, that makes heading to the hospital at noon necessary for *him* to keep *his* promises. So the facts about what promises they have made explain why going *different* places at noon are *ways* for Al and Andy to do the thing that they both have a reason to do—to keep their promises.[9]

It is non-trivial to hold that the difference in Al and Andy's reasons is explained by a further reason that they both share, in this way. Logically speaking, all that we need in order to explain the difference between Al and Andy, is to appeal to the following *conditional*:

> **Conditional Promise** For all x and a, if x promises to do a, then there is a reason for x to do a.

Logically speaking, no one need have any reasons whatsoever in order for Conditional Promise to be true. But I appealed to something *further* in order to explain Al and Andy's reasons:

> **Categorical Promise** There is a reason r such that for all x, r is a reason for x to keep her promises.

In this case, it does seem like Categorical Promise is true. I named two such reasons, and likely there are more. And in this case, that seems to be *why* Conditional Promise is true. So though Al and Andy's reasons differ, that difference can be traced back to an agent-neutral reason. Some philosophers seem to believe, in fact, that *no* conditional like Conditional Promise could ever be true without being backed up with a categorical reason like that in Categorical Promise. But this would be a bold substantive thesis. Logically speaking, Categorical Promise does not follow from Conditional Promise.

Yet the difference between your reason and Larry's can be explained in this same kind of way. Anne is Larry's infant daughter, and that is a reason for Larry to take care of her, but not a reason for you to take care of her. This, it seems, is because the following conditional is true:

> **Conditional Child**   For all x and y, if y is x's infant child, that is a reason for x to take care of y.

Conditional Child backs up a reason for Larry to take care of Anne, but it doesn't back up a reason for you to take care of her. But in this case, also, it doesn't seem like Conditional Child is true all by itself. Like Conditional Promise, it seems to be backed up by a reason that you and Larry *share*—one to take care of whatever children you *do* have:

> **Categorical Child**   There is a reason r such that for all x, r is a reason for x to take care of whatever children she brings into the world.

Again, it is easy to come up with such reasons. One is that a person's children are moral subjects who cannot provide for themselves, for whom she is causally responsible. This reason seems to back up Larry's reason to take care of Anne, but to avoid backing up the same reason for you to take care of Anne—Anne, after all, is not *your* child.

Cases like these, in which differences in agent-relational reasons are backed up by an agent-neutral reason, follow what I call the *Standard Model* for reason-explanations.[10] The Standard Model is important and interesting, but all that we need to understand about it here is that in a Standard Model explanation, some class of merely agent-relational reasons is collectively subsumed under an agent-neutral reason from which they derive. What I've illustrated here is that merely agent-relative reasons like Al's and like Larry's can be explained in this kind of way, and hence subsumed under the case of agent-neutral reasons. As such, they place *constraints* on a good account of the common explanation of all reasons, but they don't promise to give us any special *insight* into it.

It is natural to think that all cases of merely agent-relational reasons will be like Al's and Larry's cases in this way—that every time some contingent feature of an agent's circumstances plays a role in explaining why something is a reason for *her* to do something, even though it is not a reason for others to do it, it does so by subsuming her case under a more general agent-neutral reason. The theory that all explanations of agent-relational reasons work in this way is the *Standard Model Theory*. According to the Standard Model Theory, though Ronnie's psychological state does play some role in explaining his reason, the role that it plays is a *contingent* one, that can also be played by other kinds of thing. So the possibility of Standard Model explanations is why it doesn't follow from the conjecture that all reasons are explained in fundamentally the same way, and that Ronnie's reason is explained in part by his psychology, that all reasons are in part explained by psychological features. It gives a natural story about how it could be that all reasons really are explained in the same way, and Ronnie's psychological state plays a role in the explanation of his reason, but there are not psychological states in the explanation of every reason. According to the theory, this is because the *role* played by Ronnie's psychology can also be played by other kinds of thing.

But what I'll argue in the next section is that the class of psychology-explained reasons like Ronnie's *can't* be subsumed under agent-neutral reasons in this kind of way. The Standard Model Theory, that is, is false. And that will be the asymmetry that I will argue gives us . . . warrant to hold that Ronnie's case is a more promising place to look in order to see what role the *agent*-place plays in the *reason* relation.

3.3 IS THERE AN AGENT-NEUTRAL REASON TO PROMOTE YOUR DESIRES?

To have a Standard Model explanation of reasons like Ronnie's, we need two things. First, we need an action-type *A* such that in every case like Ronnie's, the action the reason is for is a *way* for the agent to do *A*. And second, we need a reason, *R,* that is a reason for anyone to do *A*. It is easy to see how to construct the appropriate *A* and *R* in the paradigmatic cases in which the Standard Model is motivated. What Rachel has a reason to do on both Monday and Thursday is to write about whatever she is thinking about at the time. And the reason for her to do this is that it has been assigned by her poetry professor. Because this is a reason for Rachel to write about whatever she is thinking about, it follows that no matter what Rachel is thinking about, she has a reason to write about that.

But unfortunately, it is quite difficult to construct the appropriate *A* and *R* for the full range of cases like Ronnie's. Here I will assume for the sake of argument that there *is* some action *A* such that all actions for which there are psychology-explained reasons are *ways* of doing *A*. For the sake of argument, I will assume that this is the action of *doing what you want.* It is unclear, I think, whether any such action-type will do the required work for the Standard Model, but the issues are complicated. I will confine myself to arguing that even if there is some such action *A,* there is no good candidate, *R,* for what the agent-neutral reason is to do this thing. If there is not, then the Standard Model Theory is, I think, wrong, and wrong in an interesting way. The way in which it is wrong leaves a relevant asymmetry between psychology-explained and other merely agent-relational reasons. And from the preceding considerations, that means that reasons like Ronnie's are the most promising place to look for a unified explanation of all reasons.

This may seem like a silly view. It may seem obvious that there is a reason to do what you want. But we have to be careful how we understand that claim, and consequently we should be suspicious about whether the thought supports the Standard Model in any way. Compare the following:

Easy For all *x* and *a,* if doing *a* is what *x* wants, then there is a reason *r* for *x* to do *a.*

Mid For all *x,* there is a reason *r* for *x* to: do what *x* wants.

Hard There is a reason *r* that is a reason for all *x* to: do what *x* wants.

The problem is that in order to get a Standard Model explanation of the full range of cases like Ronnie's, **Hard** must be true. But it is not at all obvious that **Hard** is true (that is why I called it **"Hard"**). At best, it is **Easy** that is obvious.

Consider the case of Brett. Brett wants to finish his Ph.D. in philosophy. Working on his dissertation on the pragmatics of context-dependence promotes finishing his Ph.D. in philosophy, and so there is a reason for Brett to work on his dissertation on the pragmatics of context-dependence. Moreover, it is easy to see what this reason is. It is that working on his dissertation will enable him to finish his Ph.D. But Brett also wants to become a rock star. Recording a new album with his band will promote this aim. And so it seems that there is a reason for Brett to record a new album with his band. Moreover, it is easy to see what this reason is. It is that recording a new album with his band is necessary in order to get picked up by a label, and hence in order to become a rock star.

Obviously, the reasons for Brett to do these two things are different. Examples like this (at least, enough of them—one for every want) are enough to make **Easy** true. But for **Mid** to be true, there must be a *further* reason for Brett to *do what he wants,* some fact about the world that is both a reason for Brett to work on his dissertation and a reason for him to record a new album with his band. And for **Hard** to be true, this reason, whatever it is, must also be a reason for Ronnie to go to the party, for Vera to practice playing chess, for Christina to buy a new cookbook, for Bill to hike the Appalachian Trail, and so on. What single state of the world could possibly tell in favor of such a rich and diverse class of actions? I don't see what it could be, and no one who believes that there is such a reason has ever given me a good answer as to what they think that it is, either. . . .

So despite appearances, it should not be at all obvious that there *must* be *some* agent-neutral reason to do what one likes. What should be obvious is that a Standard Model explanation of psychology-explained reasons like Ronnie's owes us something significant. It is committed to holding that there *is* some such reason. And so it should be able to tell us what this reason is. I myself don't know what this reason is. I have no *proof* that there is no good answer as to what it is, but no one, no matter how confident that there *must* be some such reason, has ever given me a satisfactory answer as to what it is. And so I remain suspicious that their convictions that there is such a reason arise not from knowing what it is, but because they are in the grip of a theory—the Standard Model Theory. . . .

4.1 THE ARGUMENT IN BRIEF

So in sum, this is my argument for the Broad Humean Theory of Reasons:

1 Ronnie's reason is explained by some feature of his psychology.
2 All reasons are, at least at bottom, explained in the same kind of way.
3 From the *Generalized Methodological Principle,* agent-neutral reasons should function as a *constraint* on a good unified explanation of reasons, but they don't give us a promising place to look for how that explanation *works.*
4 From the *Asymmetry Thesis,* all merely agent-relational reasons *other* than the psychology-explained ones can be successfully subsumed under the case of agent-neutral reasons.
C So psychology-explained reasons like Ronnie's are the *most methodologically promising* place to look for features of how the uniform explanation of all reasons must work.

I don't claim that this argument gives more than a presumptive motivation for the Broad Humean Theory of Reasons. All it tells us is that Ronnie and Bradley's case is a *methodologically promising place to look* for an explanation of reasons, *so long as* we aspire for a uniform explanation. But I *do*

claim that this argument gives us a *very good* presumptive motivation for the Humean Theory, which is all that I am after.

Premise **1** is weak enough to be uncontroversial—or at least, to create a quite significant cost to rejecting it. Premise **2** is *not* uncontroversial, but it represents an appropriate and reasonable ambition for philosophical theory. Premise **3** is backed by a genuinely uncontroversial methodological principle. And I've argued carefully for premise **4** in part 3 of this paper—if you think it is false, you're welcome to propose what the action and reason could possibly be that would make a Standard Model explanation of all of the reasons like Ronnie's turn out to work, without raising problems of its own. . . . Once we recognize the Methodological Principle and apply it to reasons, we only need *some* relevant asymmetry in order to generate *some* kind of motivation for the Broad Humean Theory of Reasons. . . .

4.3 CODA: *HOW* IS RONNIE'S REASON EXPLAINED?

One of the principal advantages that I've claimed for my motivation for the Humean Theory of Reasons is that it makes no discriminations among *forms* that the Humean Theory of Reasons might take. It leaves for investigation just *how* the explanation of Ronnie's reason actually works—for example, what kind of psychological state explains it, but also many other questions about how the explanation works. Since we've seen that the Humean Theory cannot accept the Standard Model explanation of Ronnie's reason, and since I've argued in part 3 that this explanation is suspicious anyway, I want to close by offering an alternative way of understanding how Ronnie's reason *does* get explained by his psychology, which leads to an interesting conjecture, which leads to a third, strong, version of the asymmetry thesis, and hence a further, related, argument for the Broad Humean Theory of Reasons.

The fact that there will be dancing at the party tonight is a reason for Ronnie to go there, but not for Bradley to go there. And this is because Ronnie, but not Bradley, desires to dance. For this explanation to be true, something like the following has to be the case:

> **Expl** For all agents x, if R helps to explain why x's doing A promotes p, and p is the object of one of x's desires, then R is a reason for x to do A.

Expl is a generalization under which we can subsume Ronnie's case. In Ronnie's case, the fact that there will be dancing at the party tonight helps to explain why going to the party will promote one of Ronnie's desires. For it helps to explain why going to the party will be a way for Ronnie to go dancing, and dancing is something that Ronnie desires to do. But since Bradley doesn't desire to go dancing, it doesn't follow from **Expl** that this is a reason for Bradley to go to the party.

The Standard Model Theory would have it that positing generalizations like **Expl** is not enough to explain Ronnie's reason. For on the Standard Model Theory, as we have seen, **Expl** itself needs to be explained. *Why* is it that **Expl** is true? On the Standard Model Theory, this question must be answered by appealing to a *further* action that there is a reason for everyone to do. But as I've argued, we *can't* successfully do that in this case.

But that doesn't mean that **Expl** must be unexplained. Compare **Expl** to another explanatory generalization. We can say that the Bermuda Triangle is a triangle, in part, because it has three sides. This is because the following generalization is true:

> **Tri** For all x, if x is a closed plane figure consisting of three straight sides, then x is a triangle.

But no one thinks that for **Tri** to be true, there has to be a further shape, over and above triangularity, that is had by everything, and explains why everything has the conditional property postulated by **Tri**. On the contrary, people are likely to think that **Tri** is true simply because it states *what it is* for something to be a triangle. It is because triangularity *consists* in being a closed plane figure consisting of three straight sides, that **Tri** is true.

So I offer **Tri** to the Humean as a model for how the explanation of how Ronnie's reason works, if it does not follow the Standard Model. On this view, a desire helps to explain Ronnie's reason, because there being such a desire is part of *what it is* for Ronnie to have a reason. That is just what reasons are, just as triangles are simply three-sided plane figures. Like the Standard Model, this is a substantive view about *how* Ronnie's desire helps to explain his reason. But it is an intelligible alternative to the Standard Model. And as such, it suggests the following alternative simple argument for the Humean Theory of Reasons, based on what we might call the *Standard-Constitutive Conjecture*:

> 1 Ronnie's psychology helps to explain his reason.
> 2 The Standard Model does not successfully account for how it does so.
> 3 Conjecture: the constitutive model of **Tri** is the only alternative to the Standard Model.
> **HTR** If so, then being in the kind of psychological state that Ronnie is in must be part of *what it is* to have a reason. So in every case of a reason, there must be some such psychological state.

NOTES

1. See, for example, Williams (1981) . . .
2. Allow me to head off a possible distraction. . . . What I mean, is that it is uncontroversial that at least some reasons *in the objective sense* depend on psychological states.
3. A qualifying note about how to understand this talk about *explanation*. The fact that there will be dancing at the party tonight is a reason for Ronnie to go there, in part *because* Ronnie likes to dance. That must be part of *why* it is a reason for Ronnie to go there, because it is not a reason for Bradley to go there, and liking to dance is precisely what distinguishes Ronnie from Bradley. The Humean Theory of Reasons is a generalization of *this* claim. It is the claim that whenever R is a reason for X to do A, that is in part *because* of something about X's psychology—that this is part of *why* R is a reason for X to do A. I'm using the term "explained by" to cover these kinds of claims about what is so *because* something else is so, and what is part of *why* it is so. This is not intended to import epistemic or pragmatic ideas about what *agents* might be doing when they engage in

the behavior of *explaining* things to one another. In my sense, *X* explains *Y* iff *Y* is the case *because X* is the case, or *X* is part of *why Y* is the case. The explanation is the *content* of the answer to a "why?" question—not the answer itself, nor the process of giving it.

4. Harman (1975). . . .
5. Foot (1975). . . .
6. Mackie (1977). The interpretation of Mackie's argument from "queerness" is controversial, however, since there are at least two other good candidates for the kind of argument that Mackie intended to offer. Richard Joyce, however, does unambiguously endorse this argument as the best argument for a moral error-theory, in the process of motivating his moral fictionalism. See Joyce (2001).
7. Millgram (1997: 3). The classical argument is given in Williams (1981) . . .
8. Unfortunately, both the words "universal" and "agent-neutral" turn out to have misleading associations. See Schroeder (forthcoming-a) and (forthcoming-b), for discussion of the difference between the controversial and uncontroversial senses of "agent-neutral." In essence, in *The Possibility of Altruism* Nagel (although using the terms "objective" and "subjective" at the time) made an uncontroversial distinction between reasons that are reasons for everyone, and reasons that are reasons for only some (1970). . . .

    It is also important to distinguish *universal* reasons from *universalizable* reasons. A reason is *universal* if it is a reason for everyone. A reason is *universalizable,* if its existence follows from a general (universal) principle, of the form, "for all *x,* if *x* is in conditions *C,* then there is a reason for *x* to do *A*." So reasons can be universalizable without being universal. . . .
9. Let me immediately head off one source of misunderstanding. When I say that one reason to keep promises is that breaking promises is a breach of trust, I do *not* mean to be suggesting that there is a *further* agent-neutral reason not to breach trust (but not saying

what that reason is), and that since breaking promises is a breach of trust, this reason transfers its force to a derivative reason to keep promises. All I am saying is that the fact that breaking promises is a breach of trust is an agent-neutral reason to keep promises. So the explanation that I gave *discharged* the obligation to say *what* the agent-neutral reason from which Al and Andy's reasons derive *is*. But the explanation that I did *not* give *failed* to discharge this obligation—it merely passed it on to the further claim that there is an agent-neutral reason not to breach trust.
10. See Schroeder (2005) . . .

REFERENCES

Foot, Philippa (1975) "Morality as a System of Hypothetical Imperatives," reprinted in *Virtues and Vices* (Oxford: Oxford University Press, 2002).

Harman, Gilbert (1975) "Moral Relativism Defended," reprinted in *Explaining Value and Other Essays in Moral Philosophy* (Oxford: Oxford University Press, 2000).

Joyce, Richard (2001) *The Myth of Morality* (Cambridge: Cambridge University Press).

Mackie, J. L. (1977) *Ethics: Inventing Right and Wrong* (New York: Penguin).

Millgram, Elijah (1997) *Practical Induction* (Princeton, NJ: Princeton University Press).

Nagel, Thomas (1970) *The Possibility of Altruism* (Princeton, NJ: Princeton University Press).

Schroeder, Mark (2005) "Cudworth and Normative Explanations," *Journal of Ethics and Social Philosophy,* 1, www.jesp.org.

——— (forthcoming-a) "Reasons and Agent-Neutrality," forthcoming in *Philosophical Studies.*

——— (forthcoming-b) "Teleology, Agent-Relative Value, and 'Good,'" forthcoming in *Ethics.*

Williams, B. (1981) "Internal and External Reasons," in *Moral Luck* (Cambridge: Cambridge University Press).

STUDY QUESTIONS

1. What is the difference between the "broad" and "narrow" Humean Theory of Reasons?
2. What points does Schroeder believe are established by the case of Ronnie and Bradley?
3. Why does Schroeder find "Standard Model" explanations problematic?
4. Why does Schroeder think we should seek a uniform explanation of all reasons?

Against Subjective Theories of Reasons

Derek Parfit

Bernard Williams and Mark Schroeder support subjective theories of reasons, according to which the existence of a reason depends on our commitments, desires, or ends. Derek Parfit, Emeritus Senior Research Fellow at All Souls College, Oxford, argues against subjectivism. He asks us to imagine that we have no desire to avoid future agony. In that case, all subjective theories imply that we lack a reason to avoid agony. But Parfit considers that claim implausible, because given the nature of agony, everyone has reason to avoid it. Hence subjective theories are mistaken. Parfit also notes that if desires are the ultimate source of reasons, then we cannot have reason for our desires. Without such reasons, however, our desires are arbitrary. If reasons are supposed to justify our acting in certain ways, their normative force cannot be arbitrary. Parfit concludes, therefore, that subjectivist theories should be abandoned.

8 SUBJECTIVISM ABOUT REASONS

Subjective theories appeal to facts about our present desires, aims, and choices. On the simplest subjective theory, which we can call

> *the Desire-Based Theory*: We have a reason to do whatever would fulfill any of our present desires.

For subjective theories to be plausible, however, they must admit that some desires do not give us reasons. [Consider a] case in which you want to run away from an angry, poisonous snake because you believe falsely that this act would save your life. If you had reasons to fulfill all of your present desires, your desire to run away would give you a reason for acting. But you have no reason to run away, since standing still is your only way to save your life.

There are two ways to explain why your desire to run away gives you no reason for acting. Subjectivists might claim that

> (A) reasons are provided only by desires that depend on true beliefs.

You have no reason to run away, (A) implies, because your desire depends on the false belief that this act would save your life. . . . [O]ur desires are *telic* when we want some event as an end, or for its own sake, and *instrumental* when we want some event as a means to some end. Our *aims* are often the telic desires that we have decided to try to fulfill.

From Derek Parfit, *On What Matters*, vol. 1 (Oxford: Oxford University Press, 2011). Reprinted by permission of the publisher.

You want to run away merely as a means of saving your life. So Subjectivists might instead claim that

(B) reasons are provided only by telic desires, or aims.

You have no reason to run away, (B) implies, because this act would not help you to fulfill or achieve any such desire or aim. . . .

Subjectivists can defend (B), however, in a different way. Suppose that I want to eat the two remaining apples that are on some tree. I also want to climb a ladder so that I can reach the higher apple. Suppose next that this tree's owner allows me to eat only one of these apples, and lets me choose which apple I shall eat. If instrumental desires gave us reasons, I would have more reason to choose the higher apple. If I chose the lower apple, I would then fulfill only my desire to eat this apple. If I chose the higher apple, I would fulfill not only my desire to eat this other apple, but also my instrumental desire to climb this ladder so that I can reach this apple. But this reasoning is obviously mistaken. Since I want to climb this ladder, not for its own sake, but only as a means of reaching this apple, I have no further, independent reason to fulfill this desire. My reason to climb this ladder derives entirely from, and adds nothing to, my reason to fulfill my desire to eat this higher apple.

As this example shows, instrumental desires do not provide reasons. On the simplest plausible subjective theory, which we can call

the Telic Desire Theory: We have most reason to do whatever would best fulfill or achieve our present telic desires or aims.

This theory correctly implies that you have no reason to run away from the angry snake. Your aim is to save your life, and running away would not achieve this aim. There is no need to appeal to the fact that your desire to run away depends on a false belief. . . .

In some cases, however, our *telic* desires or aims depend on false beliefs. I might want to hurt you, for example, because I falsely believe that you deserve to suffer, or because I want to avenge some injury that I falsely believe you have done me.

Subjectivists ought to deny that this desire gives me a reason. When they consider such cases, many Subjectivists claim that reasons are provided only by telic desires or aims that are *error-free,* in the sense that they do not depend on false beliefs.

If we appeal to what we would want if we knew more, we might next carry this idea to its limit. According to

the Informed Desire Theory: We have most reason to do whatever would best fulfill the telic desires or aims that we would now have if we knew all of the relevant facts.

Any fact counts as *relevant,* some writers claim, if our knowledge of this fact would affect our desires. But this criterion is too wide. . . . [I]f we knew and vividly imagined the full facts about what is going on in the innards of our fellow-diners, we might lose our desire to eat. And if we learnt certain facts about man's inhumanity to man, we might become so depressed that we would lose our desire to live. The Informed Desire Theory would then implausibly imply that, even though we actually want to eat and to stay alive, we have no reason to fulfill these desires. To avoid such implications, some Subjectivists claim that, for some fact to count as *relevant,* it is not enough that our knowledge of this fact would affect our desires. On such views, when we are choosing between several possible acts, what are relevant are only facts about these acts and their possible outcomes.

The Informed Desire Theory needs another revision. It is sometimes true that, if we were fully informed, that would change our situation in some way that altered both our desires and what we had reasons to do. If Subjectivists claim that our reasons are provided, not by our actual desires, but by our hypothetical informed desires, these people may be led in such cases to implausible conclusions. Suppose, for example, that we want to learn certain important facts. If we knew these facts, we would lose this desire. But that should not be taken to imply that we have no reason to act on this desire, by trying to learn these facts. Some Subjectivists therefore claim that we should try to fulfill the desires that, if we were fully informed, we would want ourselves to have in our actual uninformed state.

Some other Subjectivists appeal, not to what would best fulfill or achieve our desires or aims, but to the choices or decisions that we would make after carefully considering the facts. These people also make claims about how it would be rational for us to make such decisions. According to what we can call

> the Deliberative Theory: We have most reason to do whatever, after fully informed and rational deliberation, we would choose to do.

This form of Subjectivism can be easily confused with Objectivism, since such theories can be stated in deceptively similar ways. Subjectivists and Objectivists might both claim that

> (C) what we have most reason to do, or decisive reasons to do, is the same as what, if we were fully informed and rational, we would choose to do.

But this claim is ambiguous. Subjectivists and Objectivists may both claim that, when we are trying to make some important decision, we ought to deliberate in certain ways. We ought to try to imagine fully the important effects of our different possible acts, to avoid wishful thinking, to assess probabilities correctly, and to follow certain other procedural rules. If we deliberate in these ways, we are *procedurally* rational.

Objectivists make further claims about the desires and aims that we would have, and the choices that we would make, if we were also *substantively* rational. These claims are *substantive* in the sense that they [are] not about *how* we make our choices, but about *what* we choose. There are various telic desires and aims, Objectivists believe, that we all have strong and often decisive object-given reasons to have. To be fully substantively rational, we must respond to these reasons by having these desires and aims, and trying to fulfill or achieve them if we can. Deliberative Subjectivists make no such claims. These people deny that we have such object-given reasons, and they appeal to claims that are only about procedural rationality.

Though these two groups of people might both accept (C), they would explain (C) in different ways. According to these Subjectivists, when it is true that

> (D) if we were fully informed and procedurally rational, we would choose to act in some way,

this fact makes it true that

> (E) we have decisive reasons to act in this way.

Objectivists claim instead that, when it is true that

> (E) we have decisive reasons to act in some way,

this fact makes it true that

> (F) if we were fully informed and both procedurally and substantively rational, we would choose to act in this way.

To illustrate these claims, we can suppose that, unless I stop smoking, I shall die much younger, losing many years of happy life. According to all plausible objective theories, this fact gives me a decisive reason to want and to try to stop smoking. If I were fully informed and substantively rational, that is what I would choose to do. What we ought rationally to choose, Objectivists believe, depends on what we have such reasons or apparent reasons to want and to do.

Suppose next that, after fully informed and procedurally rational deliberation—or what we can now call *ideal* deliberation—I would choose to stop smoking. Deliberative Subjectivists would then agree that I have a decisive reason to stop smoking. On this view, however, the inference runs the other way. Instead of claiming that what we ought to choose depends on our reasons, these Subjectivists claim that our reasons depend on what, after such deliberation, we would choose. If I have decisive reasons to stop smoking, that is *because* I would choose to act in this way.

As this example shows, these theories are very different. These Objectivists appeal to normative claims about what, after ideal deliberation, we have *reasons* to choose, and *ought rationally* to choose. These Subjectivists appeal to psychological claims about what, after such deliberation, we *would in fact* choose.

Different subjective theories sometimes disagree about what we have reasons to do. We can here ignore such disagreements, and consider only cases in which these theories agree. In such cases, we know all of the relevant facts, and the act that would best fulfill our present telic desires or aims is also what we would choose to do after ideal deliberation. We can then say that, according to

Subjectivism about Reasons: Some possible act is

what we have most reason to do, and what we should or ought to do in the decisive-reason-implying senses,

just when, and because,

this act would best fulfill our present fully informed telic desires or aims, or is what, after ideal deliberation, we would choose to do. . . .

Subjectivism about Reasons is now very widely accepted. Many people take it for granted that we have subject-given reasons. . . . Williams writes: "Desiring to do something is of course a reason for doing it." In many books and articles, Subjectivism is not even claimed to be the best of several views, but is presented as if it were the only possible view. So it is of great importance whether this view is true.

9 WHY PEOPLE ACCEPT SUBJECTIVE THEORIES

We ought, I believe, to reject all subjective theories, and accept some objective theory. Our practical reasons are all object-given and value-based.

Since so many people believe that *all* practical reasons are desire-based, aim-based, or choice-based, how could it be true that, as objective theories claim, there are *no* such reasons? How could all these people be so mistaken?

There are several possible partial explanations, because there are several ways in which our reasons may seem to be based on some of our desires, aims,

or choices. First, as I have said, what we want is often something that is worth doing or achieving. In such cases, these two kinds of theory at least partly agree, since we have value-based object-given reasons to try to fulfill such desires.

Second, we often have such desires because we believe that we have such reasons. We are often motivated by the belief that some act or outcome would be good or best, in the reason-implying sense. When our desires depend on our beliefs that we have such reasons, we may fail to distinguish between these desires and these beliefs.

Third, some people accept desire-based theories about well-being. According to some of these theories, the fulfillment of some of our present desires would be in itself good for us. If that were true, we would have value-based reasons to fulfill these desires.

Fourth, we can rightly appeal to our desires or aims when we describe our *motivating* reasons, or why we acted as we did. This may lead us to assume that our desires or aims can also give us *normative* reasons. And some people do not distinguish between these two kinds of reason.

Fifth, there is a superficial sense in which our desires or aims can be truly claimed to give us normative reasons. For example, I might truly claim that I have a reason to leave some meeting now, because I want to catch some train, or because my aim is to catch this train, and leaving now is my only way to fulfill this desire, or achieve this aim. But this desire-based or aim-based reason would be *derivative,* since this reason's normative force would derive entirely from the facts that gave me my reasons to want to catch this train, or to have this aim. If I had no reason to want to catch this train, or to have this aim, I would have no reason to leave now. When I claim that no reasons are provided by our desires or aims, I am referring to our primary, non-derivative reasons.

Sixth, when we could fulfill *other people's* desires, or help these people to achieve their aims, these facts may give us *non*-derivative reasons to act in these ways. When other people have some desire or aim that they have no reason to have, these people may have no reason to try to fulfill this desire or achieve this aim. But *we* may have such reasons. In helping other people to fulfill or achieve their desires or aims, we respect these people's autonomy, and avoid paternalism. Other people's desires, aims, or choices are often, in this respect, like votes, which should be given just as much weight even when the voters have no reason to vote as they do. Many people accept desire-based or choice-based theories because they are democrats, liberals, or libertarians, who believe that we should not tell other people what they ought to want, or choose, or do. Nozick, for example, claims that a substantive value-based theory "opens the door to despotic requirements, externally imposed."

Seventh, when we have some aim, and we believe that some possible act would be the only or the best way to achieve this aim, it may be true that we ought rationally to act in this way. Some people assume that, in such cases, we must have a reason to do what we ought rationally to do. But that is not so. When we believe falsely that some act would achieve our aim, we may have no reason to act in this way. Though you ought rationally to run away from the angry snake, you have no reason to run away.

Eighth, when people claim that we have reasons to fulfill our present desires, they are often thinking of our desires for future activities or experiences that we believe we would enjoy. When these beliefs are true, we have reasons to fulfill these desires. But these reasons are provided, not by the fact that we would be fulfilling these desires, but by the fact that we would enjoy these future activities or experiences. If we would *not* enjoy these activities or experiences, we may have no reason to fulfill these desires. When children want something that they later get but don't enjoy, their parents sometimes say, "See! You didn't *really* want that." Such claims are false, since these children *did* want these things, and the truth is rather that their desires didn't give them reasons. Similar claims apply to our desires to avoid what we believe would be painful, or unpleasant. When people claim that our desires give us reasons, it is often such facts about what we would enjoy, or find painful or unpleasant, that they really have in mind. Such facts give us reasons that are *hedonic* rather than *desire-based*.

Ninth, some people mistakenly believe that hedonic reasons *are* desire-based. When these people think about sensations that are painful or unpleasant, they do not distinguish between our dislike of these present sensations and our meta-hedonic desires not to be having sensations that we dislike. It is our dislike, I have claimed, that makes our conscious state bad, and gives us our reason to try to end our pain, or our unpleasant state. Since these people do not distinguish between our dislike and our meta-hedonic desire, they believe that this desire gives us this reason. Similar claims apply to pleasures, and to some other good or bad conscious states.

Tenth, we have many reasons for acting that we wouldn't have if we didn't have certain desires. But these reasons are provided, not by the facts that our acts would fulfill these desires, but by certain other facts that causally depend on our having these desires. When we have some desire, for example, that may cause it to be true that this desire's fulfillment would be pleasant. In many cases, this fact would merely give us a further reason to fulfill this desire, since what we want would be in itself worth achieving. But such cases take their clearest form when we have no such reason to have some desire. When we play some kinds of game, for example, such as games without rewards whose outcomes depend on luck, we have no reason to want to win. But if we do want to win, that may make it true that we would enjoy winning, and this second fact would then give us a reason to try to fulfill this desire.

In describing such cases, we can draw another distinction. According to subjective theories, some facts give us reasons in a way that depends on our having some desire. This dependence is *normative*. On some views, for example, my reason to stop smoking is given by the fact that this act would lengthen my life, but this fact gives me a reason only because I want to achieve this aim. This reason's normative force is claimed to derive from the fact that I have this desire, so this reason is desire-based. The value-based reasons that I have just described are quite different. When the fulfillment of some desire would give us pleasure, this fact gives us a value-based hedonic reason to do what would fulfill this desire. This reason may *causally* depend on our having this desire, since this act may give us pleasure only because we have this desire. But this reason would not *normatively* depend on our having this desire. If some act would give us pleasure, this fact gives us a reason to act in this way, whether or not this pleasure causally depends on our having some desire.

We have many other reasons that causally depend on our having some desire. Unfulfilled desires may, for example, be distressing, or distracting. Such facts give us reasons to fulfill these desires. As before, these would often merely be further reasons, since what we want would often be worth achieving. But such cases may involve desires that we have no such reasons to have. We may be distracted, for example, by wanting to know or remember some trivial fact, or by some obsessive or compulsive desire. I am sometimes distracted by a strangely affectless desire to cut my fingernails. It can be best to get rid of such desires by fulfilling them.

Suppose next that we must choose between two or more good possible aims, none of which would be more worth achieving than any of the others. Some examples are choices between different possible careers, or research projects, or between doing voluntary work for different aid agencies, or political campaigns. If there is one of these possible aims that we most strongly want to achieve, this fact may give us reasons to adopt this aim. But these reasons would again be given, not by the fact that our strongest desire is to achieve this aim, but by certain other facts that would depend on our having this desire. If one of these aims seems most appealing, for example, that may give us reasons to believe that we would find this aim's achievement most rewarding. The thought of this aim's achievement may give us pleasure in advance. And our strongly wanting to achieve this aim may make it easier for us to make the efforts and sacrifices that would be needed to achieve this aim. We may need such desires in our darkest hours, when we are losing energy or hope. As before, it would be these other facts, and not our desire itself, that would give us reasons to adopt and try to achieve this aim.

Similar claims apply to our decisions and aims. When we have decided to try to fulfill some desire, thereby making its fulfillment one of our aims, this decision may give us a further reason to try to fulfill this desire, thereby achieving this aim. But this reason would not be provided merely by the fact that we have made this decision and adopted this aim. This reason would be provided by the fact that, if we do not act on this decision, we shall be less likely to achieve this aim, and more likely to waste our time. In some cases, however, neither is true, since we have nothing better to do than to reconsider some decision. If we have woken up in the middle of the night, for example, reconsidering our decision to adopt some aim may be less boring than simply waiting to drift back to sleep. In such cases, the fact that we have adopted some aim gives us no reason to keep and to try to achieve this aim, since this fact gives us no reason not to change our mind, and adopt some other aim instead.

We have many reasons to fulfill our desires or aims that are provided, not by the fact that we would be fulfilling these desires or aims, but by such other *desire-dependent* or *aim-dependent* facts. As before, when people claim that our desires or aims give us reasons, it is often such other facts that they really have in mind.

Since there are all these many ways in which our desires, aims, or choices can seem to give us reasons for acting, it is not surprising that so many people accept subjective theories. Many of these people have various true or plausible beliefs about which are the facts that give us reasons, and they have merely failed to see that these beliefs do not in fact support any subjective theory. Though these people may believe that they are Subjectivists, that is not really true. When these people make Subjectivist claims, they are misdescribing their view. . . .

11 THE AGONY ARGUMENT

Subjective theories can have implausible implications. Suppose that, in

Case One, I know that some future event would cause me to have some period of agony. Even after ideal deliberation, I have no desire to avoid this agony. Nor do I have any other desire or aim whose fulfillment would be prevented either by this agony, or by my having no desire to avoid this agony.

Since I have no such desire or aim, all subjective theories imply that I have no reason to want to avoid this agony, and no reason to try to avoid it, if I can.

This case might be claimed to be impossible, because my state of mind would not be *agony* unless I had a strong desire *not* to be in this state. But this objection overlooks the difference between our attitudes to present and future agony. Though I know that, when I am later in agony, I shall have a strong desire not to be in this state, I might have no desire now to avoid this future agony.

It might next be claimed that my predictable future desire not to be in agony gives me a desire-based reason now to want to avoid this future agony. But this claim cannot be made by those who accept subjective theories of the kind that we are considering. These people do not claim, and given their other assumptions they could not claim, that facts about our *future* desires give us reasons. . . .

. . . We are supposing that, in *Case One,* I have carefully considered all of the relevant facts about my possible future period of agony. Since I have no present desire or aim whose fulfillment would be prevented either by this agony, or by my having no desire to avoid this agony, all subjective theories imply that I have no reason to want to avoid this agony. Similar claims apply to my acts. Even if I could easily avoid this agony—perhaps by moving my hand away from the flames of some approaching fire—I have no reason to act in this way. Such a reason would have to be provided by some relevant present desire, and I have no such desire. . . .

We can now argue:

We all have a reason to want to avoid, and to try to avoid, all future agony.

Subjectivism implies that we have no such reason.

Therefore

Subjectivism is false.

We can call this the Agony Argument.

Some Subjectivists might claim that we can ignore this argument, because my example is purely imaginary. Every actual person, they might say, wants to avoid all future agony.

This reply would fail. First, we are asking whether subjective theories imply that we all have a *reason* to want to avoid all future agony. To support the claim that we all have such a reason, it is not enough to claim that everyone *has* this desire. These Subjectivists would also have to claim that, when we have some desire, this fact gives us a reason to have it. As we shall see, that is an indefensible claim.

Second, it seems likely that some actual people do not want to avoid all future agony. Many people care very little about pain in the further future. Of those who have believed that sinners would be punished with agony in Hell, many tried to stop sinning only when they became ill, and Hell seemed near. And when some people are very depressed, they cease to care about their future well-being.

Third, even if there were no such actual cases, normative theories ought to have acceptable implications in merely imagined cases, when it is clear enough what such cases would involve. Subjectivists make claims about which facts give us reasons. These claims cannot be true in the actual world unless they would also have been true in possible worlds in which there were people who were like us, except that these people did not want to avoid all future agony, or their desires differed from ours in certain other ways. So we can fairly test subjective theories by considering such cases.

Subjectivists might reply that, even in such possible worlds, there would be some telic desires that everyone must have, because without these desires these people could not even be rational agents, who can act for reasons. To be such agents, Williams suggests, we must have "a desire not to fail through error," and some "modest amount of prudence." But such claims are irrelevant here. We could be agents who act for reasons without wanting to avoid all future agony.

Subjectivists might next claim that, if some theory has acceptable implications in all or most actual cases, this fact may give us sufficient reasons to accept this theory. We might justifiably accept such a theory even if there are some unusual or imagined cases in which this theory's implications seem to be mistaken.

Many theories of many kinds can be plausibly defended in this way. For such a defense to succeed, however, we must be able to claim that there are no other, competing theories which have more acceptable implications. And Subjectivists cannot make that claim. When subjective theories are applied to actual people, these theories often have plausible implications. But that is because most actual people often have desires that they have object-given reasons to have, because they want things that are in some way good, or worth achieving. In many such cases, subjective theories have the same implications as the best objective theories. In trying to decide which theories are best, we must consider cases in which these two kinds of theory disagree. That is how, for similar reasons, we must decide between different scientific theories. Such disagreements take their clearest form in some unusual actual cases and some imaginary cases. So Subjectivists cannot claim that we can ignore these cases, or that we can give less weight to them. On the contrary, these are precisely the cases that we have *most* reason to consider. In their claims about such cases, subjective theories are, I am arguing, much less plausible than the best objective theories. And if these objective theories are more plausible whenever these two kinds of theory disagree, these objective theories are clearly better.

There is another possible reply. Deliberative Subjectivists appeal to what we would want and choose after some process of informed and *rational* deliberation. These people might argue:

(A) We all have reasons to have those desires that would be had by anyone who was fully rational.

(B) Anyone who was fully rational would want to avoid all future agony.

Therefore

We all have a reason to want to avoid all future agony.

As I have said, however, such claims are ambiguous. Objectivists could accept (B), because these people make claims about *substantive* rationality. According to objective theories, we all have decisive reasons to have certain desires, and to be substantively rational we must have these desires. These reasons are given by the intrinsic features of what we might want, or might want to avoid. We have such a decisive object-given reason to want to avoid all future agony. If we did not have this desire, we would not be fully substantively rational, because we would be failing to respond to this reason.

Subjectivists cannot, however, make such claims. On subjective theories, we have no such object-given reasons, not even reasons to want to avoid future agony. Deliberative Subjectivists appeal to what we would want after deliberation that was *merely procedurally* rational. On these theories, *if* we have certain telic desires or aims, we may be rationally required to want, and to do, what would best fulfill or achieve these desires or aims. But, except perhaps for the few desires without which we could not even be agents, there are no telic desires or aims that we are rationally required to have. We can be procedurally rational whatever else we care about, or want to achieve. . . . So Subjectivists cannot claim that anyone who is fully rational would want to avoid all future agony. . . .

There are other problems. If we don't care about some of our future agony, our desires would be more coherent if we didn't care about any of our future agony. For all these reasons, Subjectivists cannot claim that, if we were procedurally rational, we would want to avoid all future agony.

Since Subjectivists cannot defend this claim, my earlier conclusion stands. Subjectivists must claim that, in *Case One,* I would have no reason to want to avoid my future period of agony. As I have said, we can argue:

> We all have a reason to want to avoid, and to try to avoid, all future agony.
>
> Subjectivism implies that we have no such reason.

Therefore

> Subjectivism is false.

Some Subjectivists might now bite the bullet, by denying that we have this reason. In *Case One,* these people might say, though the approaching flames threaten to cause me excruciating pain, this fact does not count in favor of my wanting and trying to move my hand away. But that is hard to believe.

We can next remember why Subjectivism has these implications. Since Subjectivists deny that we have object-given reasons, they must agree that, on their view,

> (E) the nature of agony gives us no reason to want to avoid being in agony.

We can argue:

> The nature of agony does give us such a reason.

Therefore

> Subjectivism is false.

These arguments are, I believe, decisive.

Subjectivists might protest that, in denying (E), we are not *arguing* against their view, but are merely rejecting this view. If that is so, our claim could instead be that everyone ought to reject this view, since (E) is a very implausible belief. Subjectivists are not *Nihilists,* who deny that we have any reasons. These people believe that we have reasons for acting. If we can have some reasons, nothing is clearer than the truth that, in the reason-implying sense, it is bad

to be in agony. It can be hard to remember accurately what it was like to have sensations that were intensely painful. Some of the awfulness disappears. But we can remember such experiences well enough. According to Subjectivists, what we remember gives us no reason to want to avoid having such intense pain again. If we ask "Why not?," Subjectivists have, I believe, no good reply.

12 THE ALL OR NONE ARGUMENT

We have reasons, I have claimed, to have certain telic desires, such as a reason to want to avoid all future agony. We can now ask whether, as Subjectivists claim, our telic desires give us reasons. Suppose that, in

> *Case Two,* I want to *have* some future period of agony. I am not a masochist, who wants this pain as a means to sexual pleasure. Nor am I repentant sinner, who wants this pain as deserved punishment for my sins. Nor do I have any other present desire or aim that would be fulfilled by my future agony. I want this agony as an end, or for its own sake. I have no other present desire or aim whose fulfillment would be prevented either by this agony, or by my having my desire to have this agony. After ideal deliberation, I decide to cause myself to have this future agony, if I can.

Subjective theories here imply that I have a decisive reason to fulfill my desire and act on my decision, by causing myself to be in agony. If there is a fire nearby, and I shall have no other way to fulfill my desire, I would have a decisive reason to thrust my hand into this fire. That is hard to believe.

In response to this objection, Subjectivists might reply that *Case Two* cannot be coherently imagined. Some writers claim that, if we really believed that it would be *us* who would later be in agony, and we also understood what this agony would be like, it is inconceivable that we might want ourselves to be later in this state. But this claim is false. We can want what we know will be bad for us.

It makes sense to suppose that someone wants to have some future period of agony, for its own sake. Nor could Subjectivists claim that, if we had this desire, that would make it impossible for us to be rational agents, who act for reasons.

Though it is conceivable that someone might want future agony for its own sake, this case *is* hard to imagine. This fact may seem to weaken this objection to subjective theories.

The opposite is true. This fact *strengthens* this objection. If we find it hard to imagine that anyone might have this desire, that is because we assume what objective theories claim. The nature of agony, we believe, gives everyone very strong reasons to want *not* to be in this state. According to subjective theories, we have no such object-given reasons. If that were true, it would *not* be hard to imagine that someone might want, for its own sake, to have some future period of agony. We could at most claim that this desire would be unusual, like the bizarre sexual desires that some people have. This case is hard to imagine because the awfulness of agony gives everyone such clear and strong reasons *not* to have this desire. It is hard to believe that anyone could be so irrational.

In an attempt to answer this objection, Subjectivists might now revise their view. They might claim that

(F) for some desire or aim to give us a reason, we must have some reason to have this desire or aim.

If Subjectivists could appeal to (F), they could claim that, since I have no reason in *Case Two* to want to have some future period of agony, their theory does not imply that I have any reason to fulfill this desire.

To assess this reply, we can suppose that, in

Case Three, I want to *avoid* some future period of agony.

Could Subjectivists claim that I have some reason to have this desire? We are supposing that, in our examples, we know all of the relevant facts, and we have gone through some process of ideal deliberation. Subjective theories imply that, in such cases,

(G) for us to have a reason to have some desire or aim, we must have some present desire or aim that gives us this reason.

There is one straightforward way in which we might be claimed to have some desire-based or aim-based reason to want to avoid some future period of pain. Subjective theories imply that

(H) if some possible event would have effects that we want, or would help us to achieve some aim, this fact gives us a reason to want this event as a means to these effects, or to the achievement of this aim.

Suppose that, if I have a headache while I am playing in some chess match this afternoon, my pain would distract me, and would deny me the victory that I want. Subjective theories then imply that I have a reason to want to avoid this headache as a means of helping me to win this game, thereby fulfilling my desire. But we can suppose that, in *Case Three,* I have no such instrumental reason to want to avoid my future period of agony. Since this period would be fairly brief, my avoiding this agony would not have any other effects that I want, or help me to fulfill or achieve any of my other present desires or aims. On these assumptions, (H) does not imply that I have any reason to want to avoid this agony.

Subjectivists might also claim that

(I) when it is true either that

(a) our *having* some desire or aim would have effects that we want,

or that

(b) we *want* to have this desire or aim,

these facts give us a reason to have this desire or aim, or at least give us a reason to cause ourselves to have or to keep this desire or aim, if we can.

But in *Case Three* I might have no such reasons. Suppose first that I cannot avoid my future period of agony.

Partly for this reason, my desire to avoid this agony has no effects that I want. And this desire has some effects that I don't want, since it fills me with anxiety about what lies ahead. For these reasons, I don't want to have this desire. On these assumptions, (I) does not imply that I have any reason to have or to keep this desire.

Since I have no *other* present desire or aim that gives me any desire-based or aim-based reason to want to avoid this agony, Subjectivists might now claim that this desire *itself* gives me such a reason. To defend this claim, Subjectivists might say that

> (J) when we have some present fully informed desire or aim, this fact gives us a reason to have this desire or aim.

If (J) were true, all such desires or aims would be rationally self-justifying. My desire to avoid this agony would give me a reason to have this desire. But if I wanted to *be* in agony, this fact would give me a reason to want to be in agony. If I wanted to waste my life, this fact would give me a reason to want to waste my life. *Whatever* we want, our having such informed desires would give us reasons to have them. Since these claims are clearly false, Subjectivists must reject (J). Because Subjectivists cannot appeal to (J), these people must agree that, in this version of *Case Three*, my desire to avoid my future agony gives me no reason to have this desire. Since I have no other present desire or aim that gives me any reason to have this desire, these people must now admit that, on their view, I have no reason to want to avoid this agony.

Suppose next that, in a different version of this case, I *could* avoid this future agony. My having this desire would then lead me to do what would avoid this agony, thereby fulfilling this desire. This fact might be claimed to give me a desire-based reason to have this desire. Subjectivists might say that

> (K) if our having some fully informed desire would lead us to do what would fulfill this desire, this fact would give us a reason to have this desire.

But if (K) were true, all such fulfillable desires would be rationally self-justifying. If our wanting to be in agony would lead us to thrust our hand into some fire, this fact would give us a reason to want to be in agony. If our wanting to waste our lives would lead us to waste our lives, this fact would give us a reason to want to waste our lives. Since these claims are clearly false, Subjectivists must reject (K). These people must again admit that, on their view, I have no reason to want to avoid my future period of agony. So subjective theories imply that, in both versions of *Case Three*, I have no reason to have this desire.

There are many actual cases of this kind. When we want to avoid some future period of agony, or lesser pain, it is often true that, even after ideal deliberation, we would have no other present desire or aim whose fulfillment would be prevented by this future pain, and no present desire or aim that could be claimed to give us a desire-based or aim-based reason to want to avoid this pain. So subjective theories imply that we often have no reason to want to avoid some future period of pain.

Similar claims apply to many other kinds of case. When we want ourselves or others to have some future period of happiness, or we have other good or rational aims, it is often true that, even after ideal deliberation, we would have no other present desire or aim that would be fulfilled by the achievement of these aims, and no other desire or aim that could be claimed to give us a reason [to] have these aims. That is often true because we want such things for their own sake, not as a means of fulfilling other desires. So subjective theories imply that we often have no reason to want ourselves or others to have such periods of happiness, and no reason to have several other good or rational aims.

Return now to the claim that

> (F) for some desire or aim to give us a reason, we must have some reason to have this desire or aim.

We have seen that, in *Case Three*, I have no desire-based or aim-based reason to have my desire to avoid my future agony. So if Subjectivists accepted (F), they would have to claim that my desire to avoid this agony does not give me any reason for acting. Even if I could easily fulfill this desire by moving my hand away from the flames of some approaching fire,

I would have no reason to act in this way. This claim contradicts all subjective theories, and is clearly false. So Subjectivists cannot appeal to (F).

There is another reason why Subjectivists cannot claim that, for some desire to give us a reason, we must have some reason to have this desire. On these people's theories, as we have seen, any such reason would have to be provided by some other desire. For this other desire to give us this reason, (F) implies, we must have some reason to have this desire. On subjective theories, this reason would also have to be provided by some *other* desire, and so on for ever. We could not have any such beginningless chain of desire-based reasons and desires. Any such chain must begin with, or be grounded on, some desire that, according to these theories, we have no reason to have. So if these Subjectivists appealed to (F), they would have to conclude that none of our desires give us reasons, thereby denying their theory's main claim.

Since Subjectivists cannot appeal to (F), they must admit that, on their theories,

> (L) we have most reason to do what would best fulfill or achieve our present fully informed telic desires or aims, *whatever* we want, and whether or not we have *any reason* to have these desires or aims.

Similar claims apply to the choices that we would make after ideal deliberation.

We can now return to *Case Two,* in which I want to have some future period of agony, not as a means, but as an end, or for its own sake. I have no other present desire or aim that would be either fulfilled or prevented by this future agony, or by my desire to have this agony. After ideal deliberation, I have decided to cause myself to have this agony, if I can. Since Subjectivists must accept (L), they must admit that, on their view, I have most reason to cause myself to be in agony for its own sake. This act would best fulfill my present fully informed telic desires, and is what, after ideal deliberation, I have chosen to do. If there is a fire nearby, and I have no other way to fulfill my desire, I would have a decisive reason to thrust my hand into this

fire. That is very hard to believe. Given my description of this case, there are, I believe, no facts that count even weakly in favor of my thrusting my hand into this fire. And I would have decisive reasons not to cause myself to be in agony in this way.

There could be many other, similar cases. According to subjective theories, if we had such informed desires to hit our howling baby, or to smash some malfunctioning machine, these facts would give us reasons to hit our baby and smash this machine. If what we most wanted and chose was to frustrate all of our future desires, this fact would give us a decisive reason to frustrate all of these desires. If what we most wanted and chose was to waste our lives, and to achieve other bad or worthless aims, these facts would give us decisive reasons to waste our lives, and to try to achieve these bad or worthless aims. These claims are also very hard to believe. These implications of subjective theories give us decisive reasons, I believe, to reject all such theories.

Subjectivists might reply that, though *these* desires and choices would not give us any reasons for acting, that does not show that *no* desires or choices give us reasons. These people must admit that, in *Case Two,* my desire to be in agony gives me no reason for acting. But Subjectivists might claim that, in *Case Three,* my desire *not* to be in agony *does* give me a reason. These people might similarly claim that, though we would have no reasons to fulfill our desires if what we wanted was to suffer in other ways, to waste our lives, or to achieve other bad or worthless aims, we *do* have reasons to fulfill our desires when what we want is to be happy, to live productive and worthwhile lives, or to achieve other good aims.

Subjectivists *cannot,* however, make such claims. These claims appeal to differences between the reason-giving features of the *objects* of these desires or aims. If we make such claims, we have moved to an objective theory, which appeals to such object-given reasons. Subjectivists cannot distinguish in these ways between desires or aims that do or don't give us reasons. We are considering cases in which we know all the relevant facts. In such cases, we can argue:

> If we have desire-based reasons for acting, all that would matter is *whether* some act would

fulfill the telic desires that we now have after ideal deliberation. It would be irrelevant *what* we want, or would be trying to achieve.

Therefore

Either all such desires give us reasons, or none of them do.

If all such desires gave us reasons, our desires could give us decisive reasons to cause ourselves to be in agony for its own sake, to waste our lives, and to try to achieve countless other bad or worthless aims.

We could not have such reasons.

Therefore

None of these desires gives us any reason. We have no such desire-based reason to have any desire, or to act in any way.

We can call this *the All or None Argument.* Similar arguments apply to aim-based and choice-based reasons.

When we want to avoid agony, or to be happy, or we have other good or rational aims, we do indeed have reasons to try to fulfill these desires and achieve these aims. But these reasons are provided, not by the facts that these acts would fulfill or achieve these desires or aims, but by the features of what we want, or have as our aims, that make these events good or worth achieving.

Here is an overlapping argument for this conclusion. According to Objectivists, we have instrumental reasons to want something to happen, or to act in some way, when this event or act would have effects that we have some reason to want. As that claim implies, every instrumental reason gets its normative force from some other reason. This other reason may itself be instrumental, getting its force from some third reason. But at the beginning of any such chain of reasons, there must be some fact that gives us a reason to want some possible event as an end, or for its own sake. Such reasons are provided by the intrinsic features that would make this possible event in some way good. It is from such telic value-based object-given reasons that all instrumental reasons get their normative force.

Subjectivists must reject these claims. According to these people, instrumental reasons get their force, not from some telic reason, but from some telic desire or aim. We can have desire-based reasons to have some desire, and we can have long chains of instrumental desire-based reasons and desires. But at the beginning of any of *these* chains, as we have seen, there must always be some desire or aim that we have no such reason to have. And as my examples help us to see, we cannot defensibly claim that such desires or aims give us reasons. I would have no reason to thrust my hand into the fire. We would have no reason to hit our howling baby, or to waste our lives, or to try to achieve countless other bad or worthless aims. So subjective theories are built on sand. Since all subject-given reasons would have to get their normative force from some desire or aim that we have no such reason to have, and such desires or aims cannot be defensibly claimed to give us any reasons, we cannot be defensibly claimed to have any subject-given reasons. We cannot have any such reasons to have any desire or aim, or to act in any way.

STUDY QUESTIONS

1. What is the difference between "subjective" and "objective" theories of reasons?
2. Do we have reason to want to avoid agony regardless of our desires?
3. How does Parfit distinguish between "procedural" and "substantive" rationality?
4. Do we have reason to seek happiness regardless of our desires?

Grounding Practical Normativity: Going Hybrid

Ruth Chang

What is the source of normative reasons? Over the course of our readings, we have seen three answers. Plato, Moore, Scanlon, Prichard, and Parfit believe that the existence of reasons is explained by facts external to us. Hobbes, Kant, Rawls, and Korsgaard hold that the existence of reasons is explained by our voluntary acts of will. Smith, Foot, Williams, and Schroeder hold that the existence of reasons is explained by our own psychology. Ruth Chang, Professor of Philosophy at Rutgers University, argues that we should take an ecumenical approach. She believes that all these views contain an element of truth. Some reasons are given to us; these can be either internal, desire-based reasons or external, value-based reasons. Some reasons are the product of our own will; these arise in special circumstances. As Chang explains, we can create will-based reasons in those cases in which our given reasons leave indeterminate a question concerning what to do. For example, if the desire-based and value-based reasons for becoming a painter are balanced with the desire-based and value-based reasons for becoming a lawyer, choosing one career path over the other will provide an additional will-based reason. It tips the balance, dictating what, all things considered, you have the strongest reason to do.

In virtue of what is something a reason for an agent to perform some action? In other words, what *makes* a consideration a reason for an agent to act?

This is a prima facie metaphysical or metanormative question about the grounding of reasons for action and not a normative question about the circumstances or conditions under which, normatively speaking, one has a reason to do something. The normative question is answered by normative theory, as when one says that such-and-such feature of an action is a reason to perform that action because bringing about that feature would maximize happiness. The metaphysical question asks instead for the metaphysical determinant of something's being a reason. When we ask for the ground of a reason's normativity, we ask what metaphysically makes something have the action-guidingness of a reason: where does the normativity of a practical reason come from? As Christine Korsgaard puts it somewhat more poetically what is the "source" of a reason's normativity?

This paper takes a synoptic approach to the question of source, and from this broad perspective explores the idea that the source of practical normativity might best be understood as a hybrid of more traditional views of source.

From Ruth Chang, "Grounding Practical Normativity: Going Hybrid," *Philosophical Studies* 164 (2013). Reprinted by permission of the publisher.

The paper begins with a survey of three leading non-hybrid answers to the question of a practical reason's normative ground or source (Sect. 1). It then recapitulates one or two of the supposedly most difficult problems for each, suggesting along the way a new objection to one of the leading views (Sect. 2). It ends with a sketch of an alternative, hybrid view about source—what I call "hybrid voluntarism"—(Sect. 3) which, as it turns out, avoids each of the main problems faced by the three leading "pure" views (Sect. 4).

Hybrid voluntarism grounds practical normativity in a structured relation of two sources, one of which is *willing*. The view that willing is a ground of normativity has not had many defenders because it is widely thought to suffer from two fatal flaws. As we will see, however, by "going hybrid" and making willing the ground of only some, but not all, of practical normativity, we avoid not only these fatal flaws but also what are arguably the most difficult problems for the other leading views. Unlike most hybrid theories, then, which inherit the central flaws of the views they combine, hybrid voluntarism cures the main flaws of its component views taken in their "pure" form. . . .

1 THREE VIEWS ABOUT NORMATIVE SOURCE

We should start by distinguishing the grounding question from others in the neighborhood. When we ask for the ground of something's being a reason, we are not asking what causes something to be normative, if indeed that question makes sense. We are looking for something deeper, for what metaphysically determines something's being a reason.

Nor are we asking for the subvening base of something's being a reason, that is, which facts modally covary with the fact that something has the action-guidingness of a reason. The source of normativity isn't what modally covaries with something's being a reason since the explanation provided by source is asymmetric. Consider the case of morality. Suppose God's will is the source of morality; God's commands—or a supernatural realm—is where morality comes from. While God's commands may modally covary with the moral facts,

there is more to his being the source of these moral facts than simply modally covarying with them. God's commands explain the moral facts but are not explained by them. So the source of moral facts is one thing and their subvening base another.

A third question asks what general principle or law subsumes the fact that something is a reason. There is a sense in which the normativity of particular reasons may "come from" more general normative principles, if the most extreme forms of particularism are mistaken. But when we wonder about the grounds of normativity, our question is not about the subsumption of particular reasons, such as that it hurts Jane, under general normative reasons or principles, such as that one shouldn't hurt others unnecessarily, but rather about one fact being the metaphysical fount of another.

Intuitively when we ask about the source of normativity, we are asking what "makes" something normative, what it is "in virtue of which" something has the normativity of a practical reason. For simplicity, we can assume that all reasons are facts and that their grounds are also facts. If we trace the normativity of a reason back to its fount, we will reach what "makes" that fact a reason in the first place— its metaphysical source or ground.[1] . . . [W]e can work with the basic idea that fact y grounds fact x when y gives a metaphysically necessary explanation of x that is not causation, modal covariation, or subsumption.

Now there is more than one way in which one fact can make something the case, different ways in which a fact can be grounded. The most natural way one fact can ground another is by constituting it, or, equivalently, by the one fact consisting in the other. The fact that p or the fact that q grounds the fact that p or q in that the former facts constitute the latter fact, and the latter fact consists in the former. The fact that it's H_2O grounds the fact that it's water in that its being H_2O constitutes its being water, and its being water consists in its being H_2O. . . .

So one way to answer the question, "What is the source of x?" is by saying what constitutes the fact that x. And thus one way of answering the source question about normativity is by saying what constitutes the fact that something is a reason.

Another way something can—perhaps degenerately—be grounded is by being "self-grounded," that is, by being its own fount. Consider . . . the case of cause. If we ask, "Where does a law that constitutes the fact that one event causes another come from?," the answer may be "Nowhere" or, as I will treat as equivalent, "From itself."[2] . . . Facts that are explanatorily primitive are self-grounded; they cannot be accounted for in any other terms and represent the end of the line in explanation. Hence, we might say, they are their own ground.

Thus another way to answer the source question is by appealing to the fact whose source we are seeking in the first place—the fact is its own source. If we ask where the normativity of a reason comes from, one possible answer is that the fact that something is a reason is, in a degenerate sense, its own source.

There is, I believe, a third way in which one fact can intuitively "make" or "ground" another that is neither a case of constitution nor one of self-grounding . . . This is a relation of metaphysical creation or construction. Consider, again, the case of cause. The fact that the striking of the match causes the lighting may be constituted by a law of causation, but what is the source of this nomological law? Where does it come from? As we've already seen, one answer might be "Nowhere"—it is its own ground. But there is another possible answer. Perhaps God metaphysically creates the law of causation by commanding that it exist. What makes the fact that there is a law of causation is the fact that God willed such a law. Metaphysical creation is not creation in the ordinary, causal sense, as when you or I might create a sculpture. God does not cause the law of causation to come into existence in the way that an ordinary person might cause an artwork to come into being. For one thing, he is, by hypothesis, outside of the domain of the causal laws. For another, there doesn't seem to be enough of a gap between the event of God's commandment and the existence of the law for the case to be one of cause and effect. The law seems to come into existence by the command in some more direct way. Moreover, his command doesn't seem to constitute the law—the law is constituted, for example, by certain nomological necessities. Rather, God's command seems

metaphysically to create the law without constituting it. (And if you don't like God, substitute the Big Bang).

Or consider the naming of your newborn. What makes it the case that your little bundle of joy is called "Winston"? The fact that you have named him "Winston." The fact that he is called "Winston" doesn't consist in the fact that you so named him—rather, the fact that you so named him metaphysically creates the fact that his name is "Winston." Nor does your naming him "Winston" cause the fact that his name is Winston—to be a case of cause, the effect must be distinct from the cause, but there doesn't seem to be enough distance between your dubbing him "Winston" and the fact that his name is "Winston" for the relation to be one of cause and effect. Nor must a naming convention be in place in order for his name to be what you dub it to be. You might grow up alone on a deserted island and start calling a mysterious orange-colored ball that washes ashore "Winston." By calling it by that name, you metaphysically create the fact that its name is Winston. . . .

There are thus three ways in which the question, "What makes something a reason for action?" can be answered. The fact that something is a reason can, degenerately, be its own ground or source; its ground can be what constitutes the fact that it is a reason; and finally, the source of a reason can be what metaphysically creates the fact that it is a reason.

Philosophers can be seen as having offered three main answers to the source question, each of which broadly corresponds to one of the three ways the source question can be answered. "Source externalists" . . . think that normative facts make some fact, like the fact that it is painful, a reason. So the source of normativity is external normative facts. These facts are "external" in the sense that they lie outside of us as agents.

Some source externalists think that the normative facts that ground the fact that something is a reason are those very facts; when we ask what "makes" something a reason, our answer is "nothing," or, equivalently for our purposes, "the fact itself." In this way, the fact that something is a reason is self-grounded. Put another way, when we contemplate the fact that something is a reason, we are already at the source of the normativity of that reason. Other source externalists think that the normative facts that ground the fact that something is a reason are other normative facts, facts not about reasons but about values, for example, evaluative facts about the goodness of things, where value is not simply a matter of being reason-providing. The constitutive ground of the fact that being painful is a reason to avoid it is the badness of the experience, and hence it is the disvalue of the experience that is the source of the reason's normativity. So the source of the normativity of your reason—"it's painful!"— to avoid touching the hot poker is either the fact that its being painful is such a reason or the fact that pain is bad.

While normative externalists can be said to locate the source of normativity outside of us, in a realm of normative facts, "normative internalists" . . . think normativity has its source inside of us, and in particular, in desires and dispositions—the mental states towards which we are largely passive. If the fact that an experience is painful gives you a reason to avoid it, it does so in virtue of the fact that you want—or would want under certain evaluatively neutral conditions—to avoid pain. What constitutes the fact that something is a reason is thus some relation between that thing and one's desires or dispositions. One way something might relate to your desires is by being constitutive of its satisfaction. Suppose you want pleasurable experiences. What constitutes the fact that being pleasurable is a reason for you to pursue it? The fact that you want pleasure and that being pleasurable is constitutive of satisfaction of that desire. Another way something can relate to your desires is by being instrumental to its satisfaction. What constitutes the fact that being painful is a reason to avoid it? The fact that you want to concentrate on writing your paper, and the pain would be distracting.

Source externalism and internalism occupy the bulk of discourse about the source of normativity. Each appeals to one or the other of the first two explanatory connections of grounding— self-grounding and constitution. Together they offer a neat dichotomy in thinking about normative source—it is grounded either in facts external to us or in our internal dispositions, desires, and motivations.

There is, however, a third view, what we might call "source voluntarism."[3] According to voluntarism, normativity comes from an act of will. Like internalism, voluntarism locates the source of normativity inside of us—but not in passive states like desiring but rather in the active state of willing. Divine command theory offers the earliest example of such a view; by willing it, God can ground the fact that being a hoofed animal is a reason not to eat it. Post-enlightenment philosophers replaced God's will with our own; through an act of will, a rational agent can lay down laws for herself. A rational agent's own legislation can ground the fact that something is a reason. Kant's revolutionary account of normativity . . . is the most developed defense we have of voluntarism . . .

An interesting feature of source voluntarism is that, unlike both source externalism and source internalism, voluntarism can in principle provide an answer to the source question via either constitution or metaphysical creation. An act of will can be the constitutive ground of something's being a reason and it can also be what creates, as opposed to constitutes, the fact that it is a reason. The fact that something is a reason could consist in the fact that God, or a rational agent, wills something; perhaps there is nothing more to being a reason than being willed by God or a rational agent. More strikingly, the fact that an agent wills something could metaphysically create the fact that something is a reason. By willing something, you may metaphysically create the fact that something is a reason in much the same way that by "willing" your newborn to be called "Winston," you metaphysically create the fact that his name is Winston.

Exactly how source voluntarism is understood also depends on how "willing" is understood. "Willing" in contemporary parlance is usually taken to be a conscious deliberate decision to do something, as when you "steel your will" and do something you don't want to do, or, as captain, "willingly" go down with your ship. . . .

But "the will" is also sometimes taken to be shorthand for the agent herself and "willing" correspondingly taken to be an activity constitutive of either rational agency or agency itself. You might consciously and deliberately decide or intend to exercise every day, but your will—your agency—is not cooperating. Willing is thus sometimes understood not as a conscious, deliberate decision to do something but as the activity of (rational) agency as such. Perhaps willing in this sense is what grounds the fact that something is a reason. Kant, by the lights of certain modern interpreters, had such a view: a will constrained by rationality is that in virtue of which something is a reason.[4]

Or we might understand willing as the activity of agency involved in putting yourself—your agency—behind something. By willing something, you give it your agential stamp of approval. And perhaps this agential stamp of approval can confer normativity. Indeed, as I'll be suggesting later, by willing something *to be a reason*—by putting your agency behind it as a reason—you can make or create the fact that it is a reason in something like the way your willing that the name of your newborn be "Winston" makes or creates the fact that his name is Winston. Willing—putting your agency behind a fact—I suggest, can be that in virtue of which that fact is a reason.

2 PROBLEMS WITH EXTERNALISM, INTERNALISM, AND VOLUNTARISM

Objections to the three standard views of source are familiar, and what follows is largely a potted survey of what is widely considered to be one or two of the most serious difficulties for each view.

2.1 A Problem with Source Externalism

The main problem with source externalism, I suggest, is what we might call the *Problem of Explanatory Shortfall*. Source externalism can offer no explanation *just where* further explanation seems to be needed. . . .[5]

Consider the fact that a certain consideration has a particular normative weight against other considerations in a particular set of circumstances. How is this fact to be explained? There are many cases in which the right thing to say will reasonably be: "There is no more explanation to be had—that's just how things are." In most circumstances, if you can save a drowning stranger at the cost of ruining your new shoes, the answer to the question, "Why does the fact that the act would save her life have greater normative weight than the fact that it would ruin your shoes?" can reasonably be "Those are just the normative facts."

There are other cases—"hard cases"—however, in which further explanation—explanation beyond "that's just how things are"—is reasonably demanded, and the source externalist cannot provide it. This is because in at least some cases, the source externalist must hold that the fact that some reason is stronger or more significant than another is self-grounded—there is no further answer to the question, "Why is this reason stronger than that one?" other than "That's just how things are." In hard cases, the normative relations among the reasons at stake is a highly nuanced and circumstance-sensitive matter, it is very unclear how to go about determining what those relations are, and the resolution of the case is of great importance. How much should you give to charity? Should you have one child, two, five, or none? Which of two careers should you pursue, all things considered—one in the arts or one in finance? . . . These are the cases of interest to philosophers because of their importance to human lives and the epistemic challenge they pose. Much of first-order normative theorizing is taken up with proposals as to why the normative relations in hard cases such as these are one way rather than another.

Now it is a fact about hard cases that people can reasonably differ about how such cases should be resolved. Some might reasonably believe that you have most reason to x while others reasonably believe that you have most reason to not-x, or they might reasonably disagree in other ways. If source externalism is not to be completely anodyne, claiming only that what we have most reason to do is whatever reasonable people agree we have most reason to do, it will sometimes claim that we have most reason to x when at least some reasonable people believe we have most reason to not-x. Suppose that Jane is deciding between a career in painting and one on Wall Street. Suppose too that the case is hard—reasonable people differ about what Jane has most reason to do. Finally, suppose that Jane reasonably believes that she has most reason to be a painter, but the normative facts are that she has most reason to be a banker.

Jane believes she has most reason to spend her life as an artist but the externalist tells her that she has most reason to spend her life as a banker. Jane is puzzled. Why does she have most reason to spend her life on Wall Street? The need for further explanation here is acute, but all the externalist can say is: "These are the normative facts: you have most reason to spend your life on Wall Street and that's just how things are. We have hit rock-bottom and there is no more explanation to be had." Of course not all hard cases need be ones in which we have hit rock bottom, but source externalists must hold that *some* are, and for those that are, we will have run out of explanation just where it is most needed.

It might be thought that, although the source externalist cannot give a direct explanation of why we have most reason to x though we might reasonably believe we have most reason to not-x, she can give an "indirect" explanation. She might indirectly explain why we have most reason to x in a given hard case by pointing out how those reasons and similar ones relate in other cases. Instead of saying to Jane "That's just how things are," she might say "That's just how things are, and you can see why they are that way by looking at how the reasons relate in these other cases." And this indirect explanation, though not as good as a direct one, is good enough; it is all that can be reasonably expected in such hard cases. So perhaps there is no explanatory shortfall after all.

This strategy, however, is problematic because it is doubtful that all hard cases are amenable to indirect explanation. In attempting to give an indirect explanation as to why Jane has most reason to be a banker, the source externalist will need to appeal to general normative considerations, such as *principles, aims, policies, values,* and the like, which provide the normative relations of the reasons relevant in the case and other related ones across a range of cases. But general considerations are by their nature general and don't deliver answers as to what one has most reason to do in every possible circumstance. Take the principle "You should aid victims of harm unless the cost is too high." Such a principle can indirectly explain why you have most reason to save a drowning stranger when the cost is your shoes or your coat or your laptop—all easy cases—but can't plausibly explain, indirectly or otherwise, why you have most reason to save the stranger, assuming that you do, when the cost is your leg or your life's work or the life of a severely disabled person—all hard cases. Which costs are "too high"? The general principle doesn't tell us. Hard cases are very plausibly those that fall between the boundaries of straightforward application of general, abstract principles and so their resolution cannot be explained by those principles. . . . The relation among reasons in hard cases thus explains and is not explained by general principles. Jane is again left without an explanation.

Now the source externalist could turn instead to very specific and detailed "principles" that determine what one has most reason to do [in] every hard case in which one has most reason to do something. These wouldn't be principles of the ordinary kind because so specific, and since they cover every case, each might be thought of as a chapter of the Book of Reasons, with each chapter laying out the way some subset of reasons relate to one another in every possible circumstance. It is unlikely that we could grasp any such "principles," but the externalist might nevertheless vaguely point to such "principles" as providing an indirect explanation as to why one has most reason to x in a given case. That we can't grasp them is a deficiency in us, not in the explanation they provide.

But a "principle" laying out how every subset of reasons relates in every circumstance is highly implausible as a brute normative truth. What's more plausible is that this "principle" gets its content at least in part via more specific truths of the form "in such-and-such hard case, the reasons relate in such-and such a way." The relations among reasons in hard cases seem explanatorily prior to any "principle" laying out how reasons relate across all circumstances. And so the Problem of Explanatory Shortfall remains. . . .

2.2 A Problem with Source Internalism

The main difficulty with source internalism has been forcefully pressed by Derek Parfit in his magisterial *On What Matters*. Source internalism fails to guarantee the right substantive results about what reasons we have because the constraints it puts on desires are purely formal in nature. No formal constraint, however intricate, can *guarantee* the intuitively right answer as to what reasons we have. If what makes something a reason is some formal relation with our desires and dispositions then, given the right desires, it could turn out that an agent has most reason to want agony—an intensely disliked sensation—for its own sake because having such a desire satisfies other desires the agent has. But, the agony argument goes, everyone has a reason not to want agony for its own sake, even if agony is what she most wants or wanting agony would satisfy other desires she has. For the most part, the various ingenious ways that source internalists have tried to deliver reasons not to want agony for its own sake either fail on their own merits or end up smuggling substantive constraints that presuppose normative resources beyond what the internalist can legitimately help herself to. Call this the *Right Reasons Problem*. . . .

2.3 Two Problems with Voluntarism

Voluntarism is widely supposed to suffer from two fatal flaws. First, if what makes a consideration a reason is some act of willing, what prevents us from willing reasons willy-nilly? . . . This is a version of the Right Reasons Problem already encountered. Kant's answer was that *rational* agents could not will reasons willy-nilly; rational agents are bound by purely formal laws that govern the autonomous, rational will, and these laws guarantee that a

rational agent can will reasons only in accord with the moral law. But Kant's argument notoriously fails, and ingenious attempts to rescue Kant on this score have fallen short of the mark.

There is a second, related difficulty. Voluntarists try to constrain willing by appealing to what the rational agent *must* will in order to be a rational agent in the first place. The strongest sense of "must" they are in the ballpark of defending, however, is only the "must" of structural—or what is sometimes misleadingly called "subjective"—rationality. So willing is a source of normativity that is constrained by structural requirements of consistency and coherence on attitudes. But now we can ask, "Why should the rational agent be bound by such structural requirements?" This question asks what *reason* an agent has to bind her will in this way. And this appeal to a *reason* requires further normative materials beyond those that the voluntarist is plausibly able to provide. Either the voluntarist must admit that her reason to follow structural requirements has its source in something other than structural requirements and so willing is not the only source of normativity, or she is faced with an unhappy endless regress of structural requirements that provide reasons to conform to other structural requirements. In short, willing cannot be the source of normativity because it leaves open the question, "What reason do we have to will in conformity with the requirements of structural rationality?" Call this *The Regress Problem.*[6]

Modern-day voluntarists have tried to respond to this difficulty by suggesting that it is constitutive of agency that one's will conform to certain requirements. Korsgaard has ingeniously suggested that the principles willed by a rational agent are those that solve a practical problem the agent actually confronts. That is, the principles that a rational agent "must" will are those that provide an answer to a practical problem to which she needs to have a solution. Thus, insofar as she is to be a rational agent in response to the practical problem she faces, she must will certain principles rather than others. Those principles provide a solution to her problem, so of course she "must" will them if she is to respond to her problem as a rational agent.[7] But as William

Fitzpatrick has carefully argued, the "must" her arguments deliver fall short of the "must" of being an agent at all.[8] Instead, Korsgaard at best shows that in order to conform to the requirements of structural rationality—to be a structurally rational agent—an agent "must" will certain principles and not others. And since it makes sense to ask, "Why be structurally rational?," the problem remains.

More recently, Korsgaard has developed her constitutivist argument by focusing on the metaphysics of action. You can't act unless your will is guided by the Categorical Imperative, among other principles. This is not to say that your will must conform to the requirements in order to act at all but only that it must conform to them if you are to act well. But you won't even count as acting unless what you're doing is guided by these requirements.[9] Korsgaard's argument here is complex and provocative but, I believe, the fundamental problem remains. The essential difficulty is that our concept of a reason is not beholden to action or agency—it permits us to reach beyond action or agency to ask, "Why act?" Korsgaard tells us that we can't help but act because acting is in our natures, but this does not stop the reasons question from rearing its inquiring head. Consider an analogy. Perhaps Rousseau was right: we can't help but make invidious discriminations among people because invidious discrimination is in our natures. But this does not block the question, "What reasons [are there] for us to make such discriminations?" In the same way, even if we can't help but act, we can still ask, "Why act?" Insofar as the question makes sense, the Regress Problem remains.

3 HYBRID VOLUNTARISM

Source externalism and source internalism occupy the bulk of both contemporary and historical debate about the source of normativity, despite their known difficulties. Normativity either comes from outside of us, from a realm of normative facts, or from inside us, from passive states such as desires, dispositions, and motivations we have or would have under certain evaluatively neutral conditions.

That the debate about source has long had this focus—with voluntarism getting short shrift—seems to me unfortunate. The most profound—and interesting—divide in the debate is not between those who think normativity derives from normative facts (externalists) on the one hand, and those who think that it derives from a relation with our desires (internalists), on the other, but rather between those who think that normativity is *given* to us, either by normative facts or relations to passive states, like desires (externalists and internalists), on the one hand, and those who think that we can *create* it (voluntarists), on the other. Is normativity given to us or do we make it?

Hybrid voluntarism offers a way of understanding how these two fundamentally opposed approaches to the source of normativity—each boasting a persistent history of endorsement by distinguished thinkers—could each contain an important truth. If hybrid voluntarism is correct, sometimes the fact that a consideration has the normativity of a reason is given to us, while other times it is a fact of our own making.

Unlike the traditional views about source, hybrid voluntarism maintains that there is no univocal answer the question, What metaphysically makes a fact have the normativity of a reason? Sometimes the fact that a consideration is a reason is given to us and sometimes it is of our own making.

The hybrid view crucially turns on a distinction between two kinds of reasons: "given" reasons, on the one hand, and "will-based," or "voluntarist," ones, on the other. "Given" reasons are considerations that are reasons in virtue of something that is not a matter of our own making. They are given to us and not created by us and thus are a matter of recognition or discovery of something independent of our own volition or agency. Both source externalism and source internalism might best be understood as accounts of our given reasons: our given reasons might be "value-based" or "desire-based": that in virtue of which they are reasons is either a normative fact or some relation to our desires or dispositions. My own preferred view, for reasons that will become apparent later, is to understand "given" reasons as being grounded in normative facts rather than desires.

"Will-based" reasons, by contrast, are considerations that are reasons in virtue of some act of will; they are a matter of our creation. They are voluntarist in their normative source. In short, we create will-based reasons and receive given ones.

While standard forms of voluntarism hold that all reasons are will-based, hybrid voluntarism maintains that not all of our reasons are a matter of acts of will. Like traditional views about source, however, the hybrid view holds that *each* reason has a single normative source, and in this way, although it is pluralist about the sources of normativity writ large, it is univocal about the source of the normativity of each reason. Hybrid voluntarism's pluralism about normative source is not, moreover, one of coeval considerations each taking turns being that in virtue of which a reason has its action-guiding force. The sources of normativity are *structured*. In answer to the question, "What is the source of normativity?" hybrid voluntarism answers that the source of normativity is a *structured* hybrid of two sorts of consideration, sometimes given to us and sometimes of our own making. This structure has two aspects.

Most importantly, given reasons operate as *metaphysical* constraints on voluntarist ones; we cannot bring voluntarist reasons into existence unless our given reasons fail *fully* to determine what we should do. Given reasons have, as it were, "first dibs" in determining what we should do. As I will put it, we can create will-based reasons only when our given reasons have "run out."

Reasons run out when they fail fully to determine what one has most reason to do. More precisely, they run out when (1) one fails to have more, less, or equal reason to choose one alternative over the other—what we might call a state of "equipoise," or (2) one has most reason to choose one alternative over the other but it is indeterminate how much more—what we might call a state of "indeterminate most reason." Alternatives are in equipoise when they are incomparable or "on a par"—that is, comparable, but neither is better than the other and nor are they equally good.[10] And one alternative is supported by indeterminate most reason if there is more reason to choose it, but it is indeterminate what the overall normative

difference is between it and its alternative. That is, one alternative is better, but to an indeterminate degree—it is this indeterminateness that precludes "full determination" by one's reasons.[11] With respect to ordinary given reasons, the latter condition is plausibly very common. And . . . so is the former. According to hybrid voluntarism, the scope of normativity grounded in our wills is a direct function of the scope of equipoise and indeterminate most reason. This scope is plausibly both very wide—covering a wide range of choices—and very deep—covering some of the most important choices we might make.

Our given reasons, however, determine not only when voluntarist reasons can be created but also what role such reasons can play in determining what we should do. They operate not only as metaphysical constraints but also as *normative* ones. Whenever our given reasons have a *valence,* that is, whenever they determine that we have most reason to do one thing rather than another, our voluntarist reasons cannot alter that valence in the all-things-considered truth about what we have most reason to do; they cannot make it the case that the disfavored alternative is now better supported by reasons, nor can they make it the case that the alternatives are equally good or in equipoise. All they can do is change the degree or extent to which the favored alternative is supported by most reason.

Why these constraints? . . . The metaphysical and normative constraints on voluntarist reasons derive from an independently attractive, plausible view about the role of our agency in the world. Metaphysically speaking, if we have the freedom to create reasons, we have it only within the confines of the reasons we have no freedom to create, our given reasons. So we can create reasons only when our given reasons run out. Normatively speaking, just as our freedom to change the nonnormative facts of the world is constrained by the nonnormative facts given to us—we can't change the fact that there is a wall in front of us—so too our freedom to change the normative facts of the world is constrained by the normative facts given to us—we can't make ourselves have most reason x if the normative facts given to us are that we have most reason not to x.

The valence of given reasons is a non-negotiable wall around which we must exercise our agency.

If hybrid voluntarism is right, willing has an important, though constrained, role to play in determining what we have most reason to do. If you have most indeterminate given reason to x but will yourself a voluntarist reason not to x, you may now have *more* reason not to x than you had before you willed yourself a reason to x. In this way, through an exercise of your will, you can create reasons for yourself, thereby giving yourself more reason than you had before, though the normative upshot of those reasons is constrained by the valence of your given reasons.[12] If, instead, your given reasons are in equipoise—if there is no valence to be disrupted—then through an exercise of your will, you can make it the case that you have most all-things-considered—given and voluntarist—reason to choose one alternative over the other. In this way, by willing yourself a voluntarist reason, you can directly determine what you have most reason to do.

Here is an example. Suppose your boss gives you a holiday bonus, and as the circumstances have it, you can either donate it to Oxfam or buy yourself a new laptop. The case can be filled out in one of two ways. You might have most given reason to donate the money to Oxfam. In this case, you can, according to hybrid voluntarism, will yourself a reason to buy the laptop.

Now part of the plausibility of your being able to will yourself a voluntarist reason turns on what is involved in so willing. . . . [H]ybrid voluntarism maintains that what you will is itself normative: you will some consideration *to be a reason*. This willing a consideration to be a reason is not simply deciding, or believing, or wishing, or wanting it to be a reason; it is akin to a *stipulation* that something be a reason in much the way that you might "stipulate" that your newborn be called "Winston." But when you will something to be a reason, something further beyond mere stipulation is involved: your agency is implicated. Very roughly, when you will something to be a reason, you *put yourself* behind some consideration that, as a logical matter, counts in favor of one of the alternatives. You take an agential stand of the sort: "Having a few extra seconds of speed on my computer matters to me!" When you will yourself a voluntarist reason, you will a consideration, such as having a few extra seconds of speed, to be reason-providing for you. Having willed such a voluntarist reason, the difference in strength of the reasons to give the money to Oxfam and the reasons to buy the laptop will be less than it would have been had you not so willed. But this does not change the fact that what you should do is to give the money to Oxfam.

The case can be filled out in another way. Perhaps the given reasons to donate to Oxfam or to buy a new computer are in equipoise: the reasons for donating and for buying the laptop are neither stronger than one another and nor are they equally strong. By willing the extra speed of a new laptop to be a reason for you to buy one, you can create a voluntarist reason to buy the laptop and perhaps thereby give yourself most all-things-considered reason to do so. Whether you do have most reason to do so depends on the substantive question of how the voluntarist reason relates to the given reasons. . . .

4 HOW HYBRID VOLUNTARISM AVOIDS THE PROBLEM OF EXPLANATORY SHORTFALL, THE RIGHT REASONS PROBLEM, AND THE PROBLEM OF REGRESS

Recall that in hard cases, the need for an explanation of the resolution is especially acute and it won't do to rest with "That's just how things are." Source externalism is, I have suggested, committed to saying that in at least some such cases, there is no further explanation to be had.

If, however, as hybrid voluntarism might suppose, externalism accounts for the source of only some and not all of our reasons—if it accounts for the normative source of only our given reasons—then we can cure the Problem of Explanatory Shortfall by understanding externalism as a partial theory of source. Source externalism goes only so far providing reasons in normative explanation, leaving a gap that voluntarist reasons can fill.[13]

Hard cases are ones in which reasonable people can differ as to what one has most reason to do. This reasonable disagreement may at least sometimes indicate that the given reasons are in equipoise. If the given reasons are in equipoise, then individual agents are free to create voluntarist reasons that may make it the case that for that agent, she has most all-things-considered reasons to choose one way rather than another. This freedom to create voluntarist reasons when given reasons are in equipoise can explain both why reasonable people disagree about what one has most reason to do in hard cases and why one might nevertheless have all-things-considered most reason to choose one way rather than another.

Return to the case of Jane. Reasonable people disagree about whether she has most reason to be a painter or a banker. The hybrid voluntarist can explain this reasonable disagreement as follows: The given reasons for pursuing one career over the other are in equipoise. When one person reasonably insists that Jane has most reason to be a banker, this is because that person is putting himself in Jane's shoes and were he Jane, he would will some feature of the banking career to be normative for him. When someone disagrees, maintaining that Jane has most reason to be a painter, he again puts himself in Jane's shoes, and were he Jane, he would will some feature of being a painter as normative for him. One person says, "Were I Jane, I would have most reason to be a banker," while the other says "Were I Jane, I would have most reason to be a painter." This is one way to understand disagreements about what career Jane has most reason to pursue, or for that matter, about whether one should give to Oxfam or buy a new laptop . . . and so on. The source externalist, by contrast, cannot allow for reasonable disagreement. Instead, he would have to explain away the appearance of reasonable disagreement by insisting, for example, that at least one party is making an *epistemic* mistake. But we can imagine cases in which there is no reason to think that one party to the disagreement is epistemically less well-placed than the other.

The hybrid voluntarist can explain why Jane has most all-things-considered reasons to be a banker. The externalist, recall, has to settle with "That's just how things are" because we have hit bedrock. The hybridist maintains that Jane has most reason to be a banker because the given reasons are in equipoise, and Jane has willed a voluntarist reason in favor of banking. We can explain why Jane has most reason by appealing to the voluntarist reasons she has created as a matter of will. Thus hard cases are typically ones in which one's given reasons are in equipoise, and insofar as one has most reason to choose one option over the other, it is because one has voluntarist reasons that fill the gap left by one's given reasons. . . .

But hybrid voluntarists need never rest with "That's just how things are" in a hard case because voluntarist reasons are in play even when one has (indeterminate) most given reason to do one thing rather than another.[14] If Jane wills a voluntarist reason in favor of banking, the fact that she has most all-things-considered reasons to be a banker can be explained by both her given and voluntarist reasons to take up that career. If, alternatively, she wills a voluntarist reason in favor of the visual arts, that reason will be part of the story as to why she has most reason to be a banker. It is informative to be told that despite having a voluntarist reason in favor of a career in painting, one has most all-things-considered reasons to be a banker. This is because "That's just how things are" is a fully passive explanation of why we have the reasons we do while appeal to voluntarist reasons, even if they can't change the valence of our given reasons, introduces our agency into the explanation. By appealing to reasons the agent actively puts herself behind, we no longer rest with reasons passively given to us—the explanation of why we have most reason to do what we have most reason to do always involves appeal to something other than the normative facts simply given to us. That is enough to avoid the Problem of Explanatory Shortfall faced by the source externalist.

In short, when you have most all-things-considered reason to do one thing rather than another in a hard case, voluntarist reasons provide an additional resource with which to fill the explanatory gap left by one's externalist given reasons. In this way, hybrid voluntarism provides the resources—arguably just where they are needed—for avoiding the explanatory shortfall of source externalism.[15]

Hybrid voluntarism also avoids the Right Reasons Problem that plagues both pure forms of voluntarism and source internalist views. One of the difficulties with voluntarism, recall, is that it cannot block the Mafioso from willing into existence all-things-considered reasons to shoot the kneecaps off his enemy. Purely formal constraints on willing, like those suggested by Kant and his followers, are insufficient to prevent the willing of reasons willy-nilly. If, however, hybrid voluntarism is true, then voluntarism accounts for the source of only our voluntarist reasons. And since will-based reasons cannot change the valence established by one's given—source externalist—reasons, the Mafioso is unable to create the reasons that make it permissible for him to shoot the kneecaps off his enemy. This is because he has all-things-considered most given reasons not to do so, and his will-based reasons cannot change the valence established by these reasons. Of course, according to hybrid voluntarism, the Mafioso may have *more* reason to shoot the kneecaps off his enemy if he has created a voluntarist reason than if he had not created such a reason. But since reasons can be regarded as cheap—there might, arguably, not be much difference in there being a reason that cannot change the valence and there being no reason at all—this is arguably as it should be.[16]

Finally, hybrid voluntarism sidesteps the Regress Problem. The Regress Problem maintains that in order to answer the open question, "What *reason* does a rational agent have to will a principle of action?," the voluntarist must either appeal to resources beyond voluntarist reasons or be faced with an endless regress of willings.

To see how the hybrid view escapes the Regress Problem, consider the following scenario. Suppose you are faced with a choice between x and y, and your given reasons for choosing either have run out. According to the hybrid view, you have the normative power to create a new voluntarist reason through some act of will, which may then give you most all-things-considered reason to choose x over y.

Now if we ask, "What reason do you have to exercise your normative power, that is, to will a voluntarist reason as opposed to, say, employ the decision procedure 'eeny, meany, miney moe. . . .' or toss a coin between them?," we can appeal to given reasons. You might have a given reason to will a voluntarist reason because it's a good thing to exert one's agency in making it true that one has most reason to do things. Or you could have a given reason to exercise your will in order to achieve control over what you have most reason to do instead of leaving your reasons to the vagaries of a coin toss. There are many other possible given reasons that justify the activity of creating voluntarist reasons. Because hybrid voluntarism does not attempt to make willing the source of all of practical normativity, it can allow that given reasons are deployed in answer to the question, "Why go in for the activity of creating voluntarist reasons?" These additional resources—given reasons—block the Regress Problem faced by standard forms of voluntarism. So while the question, "What reason does one have to create a voluntarist reason?" is open, hybrid voluntarism has the resources to answer it.

There is another regress lurking in the area. We might ask, "What reason is there to will *this* rather than *that* to be a voluntarist reason?" Creating voluntarist reasons is something rational agents *simply do,* and by definition this activity of creating voluntarist reasons is not itself guided by reasons, given or otherwise. It is in the very nature of creating voluntarist reasons that doing so is not guided by reasons. This has an important implication. If the activity of willing reasons is not open to being guided by reasons, then it makes no sense to ask, "What reason is there to will this rather than that to be a reason?" Put another way, when your given reasons run out, your willing reasons to x instead of y (or vice versa), while open to assessment by given reasons, cannot itself be guided by given reasons. Which reasons you will, then, is quite literally up to you.

Note that hybrid voluntarism's ability to dodge the regress cannot be transferred over to the constitutivist accounts favored by "pure" voluntarists, such as Korsgaard. The hybrid voluntarist says that it is constitutive of the activity of willing reasons that this activity is not guided by reasons, and the pure voluntarist says it is constitutive of action itself (or of agency or of rational agency) that one's will be guided by certain requirements. Why is one view subject to regress and the other not?

In the former case, it makes no sense to ask of an activity that is by its nature not governed by reasons what reason one has to engage in that activity in one way rather than another. But it does make sense to ask of an activity that is by its nature governed by certain requirements—by hypothesis, action itself—what reasons we might have to engage in that activity (or indeed to engage in it one way rather than another). Put another way, our concept of a normative practical reason applies to action: "what reason is there to perform actions?" makes sense, even if we can't help but act, but it does not apply to the activity of willing this rather than that to be a reason: "what reason is there to will this rather than that to be a reason?" does not make sense. This is because asking what reason we have to will this rather than that is, in this one respect, like asking what reason we have to flinch rather than laugh when we are startled—one's reaction to being startled is by its nature an activity not guided by reasons. Of course flinching is arguably not an intentional action but a reflex while willing is something that one does intentionally, perhaps for a given reason. But while there may be given reasons to engage in an act of willing, what one wills is not a matter guided by reason. Since willing this rather than that to be a reason is by its nature not something guided by reasons but simply something one does, there is no regress.

5 CONCLUSION

My aim here has been to sketch an alternative view about the sources of practical normativity and to show how, by going hybrid, we can avoid some of the main difficulties that plague more familiar ways of grounding practical reasons. My aim has also been to try to bolster and reinvigorate the relatively neglected view that willing can be a ground of normativity. Many philosophers have dismissed the view as absurd, and it has few contemporary adherents. My suggestion in this paper is that if willing can be a ground of normativity, then it might plausibly be a ground in the way hybrid voluntarism suggests.

NOTES

1. The idea of "ground" was explicitly introduced into the contemporary scene by Kit Fine 2001. See also Rosen (2010).

2. Of course "Nowhere" and "From itself" are not in fact equivalent, but for the purposes of the present discussion, they can be treated as such. Externalists who balk at the description of their views as ones in which certain normative facts are self-grounded can substitute "ungrounded" for "self-grounded" without any substantive loss in the subsequent argument of the paper. It is, I suspect, the externalist's insistence that there are no metaphysical grounds of normative facts that has helped to obscure the importance and legitimacy of the source question in the debate about practical reasons.

3. Source voluntarist views should be distinguished from the many normative views according to which an act of will—such as making a promise—can result in having reasons. . . . Christine Korsgaard, and perhaps Mary Clayton Coleman (Manuscript), are the only nontheistic contemporary philosophers I am aware of (besides myself) who think that willing can be a metaphysical ground of normativity.

4. See Korsgaard (1996, 2008, 2009) for a development of this view.

5. Strictly speaking, there are forms of source externalism for which this problem does not arise, but they are all ones in which hard cases never arise. For example, source externalist theories that think all values or reasons can be represented by some function over the reals that is easy to manipulate (e.g., involving only addition or multiplication) would always deliver a determinate answer as to what one has most reason to do and would preclude hard cases. But since it is clear that there are hard cases, such theories are substantively implausible. I assume such views should be rejected on other grounds and do not discuss them here.

6. This objection is formulated in general terms by Railton (2004) and specifically against Korsgaard's voluntarism by Scanlon (2003) . . .

7. Korsgaard (2003).
8. Fitzpatrick (2005).
9. Korsgaard (2009) . . .
10. See Chang (2002).
11. It may seem odd to say that reasons "run out" when they determine what one has most reason to do but to an indeterminate degree, after all, they determine what one has most reason to do. But they "run out" in the sense of interest—the normative criteria at stake do not admit of fully determinate measurement of degrees of difference. See Parfit (Manuscript) for further thoughts along these lines. Some normative criteria—such as number of lives saved—arguably allow fully determinate measurement of degrees of difference—e.g., saving two lives may be twice as good as saving one—and where such normative criteria, if there are any, are at stake, voluntarist reasons have no place. My own view is that there are few, if any, normative considerations that admit of either ratio or interval cardinal measurement, but if it turns out that all do—if standard expected utility models of value are true to the facts and not mere idealizations—then hybrid voluntarism has no application.
12. Some might find the idea that the Mafioso has more reason to harm his enemy simply by willing problematic, but having "a reason" is a relatively cheap matter, especially if that reason can never make it the case that he has all-things-considered reasons to harm his enemy. As those who have pressed the Right Reasons Problem most forcefully have noted, the real problem arises when a view leads to the result that he has most all-things-considered reasons to harm his enemy.
13. This gap in externalist reasons is not, strictly speaking, only in hard cases or ones in which the given reasons are in equipoise. For even easy cases might involve voluntarist reasons. It might be obviously true that I have most indeterminate reason to save 5 lives at the cost of my new shoes. But there might be a difference in the relations among the reasons in the case in which I have willed the importance of those lives to be reasons for me and the case in which I have not. Nor should willing reasons be thought to be something that happens only after we are stymied by our given reasons. We are willing reasons—putting our agency behind certain considerations—all the time and succeed in giving ourselves voluntarist reasons when the given reasons have run out. The priority of given over voluntarist reasons is metaphysical and normative but not temporal.
14. Here I assume that the view of value as "precise"—admitting of cardinal representation by the reals (or utility functions mapping value onto the reals) is a nonstarter and so the second condition for the existence of voluntarist reasons is very broadly satisfied. . . .
15. Note that the explanation that hybrid voluntarism makes possible is normative. The Problem of Explanatory Shortfall is a problem of shortfall in normative explanation—we run out of reasons too soon if source externalism is true. Hybrid voluntarism provides additional normative resources—voluntarist reasons—in the normative explanation of why you have most reason to x rather than y.
16. The importance of voluntarist reasons in cases where there is indeterminate most reason to do one thing rather than another is a complicated matter that I cannot go into here. In brief: they have little significance within a choice situation but great significance for what they suggest for the agent's "rational identity" over time.

REFERENCES

Chang, R. (2002). The possibility of parity. *Ethics, 112,* 659–688.

Coleman, M. C. Exploring Meta-Normative Constitutivism, (Manuscript).

Fine, K. (2001). The question of realism. *Philosophers' Imprint, 1*(1), 1–30.

Fitzpatrick, W. (2005). The practical turn in ethical theory: Korsgaard's constructivism, realism, and the nature of normativity. *Ethics, 115*(4), 651–691.

Korsgaard, C. (1996). *The sources of normativity.* Cambridge: Cambridge University Press.

Korsgaard, C. (2003). Realism and constructivism in 20th century moral philosophy. *Journal of Philosophical Research, 28,* 99–122.

Korsgaard, C. (2008). *The constitution of agency: Essays on practical reason and moral psychology.* Oxford: Oxford University Press.

Korsgaard, C. (2009). *Self-constitution: Agency, identity, and integrity.* Oxford: Oxford University Press.

Parfit, D. On How to Avoid the Repugnant Conclusion, Draft, (Manuscript).

Railton, P. (2004). How to engage reason: The problem of regress. In Wallace et al. (Eds.), *Reasons and values: Themes from the philosophy of Joseph Raz.* Oxford: Oxford University Press.

Rosen, G. (2010). Metaphysical dependence: Grounding and reduction. In B. Hale & A. Hoffman (Eds.), *Modality: Metaphysics, logic & epistemology.* Oxford: Oxford University Press.

Scanlon, T. (2003). Metaphysics and morals. *Proceedings and Addresses of the American Philosophical Association, 77,* 7–22.

STUDY QUESTIONS

1. What are the strengths and weaknesses of externalism?
2. What are the strengths and weaknesses of internalism?
3. What are the strengths and weaknesses of voluntarism?
4. Does "going hybrid" retain the strengths and avoid the weaknesses of the three other approaches?

Glossary

A posteriori **proposition**   A proposition whose truth-value can be known only through experience. For example, "some swans are black" is true *a posteriori*, because we need to examine the swans in the natural world to discover if some of them are black.

A priori **proposition**   A proposition whose truth-value can be known independently of experience. For example, "triangles have three sides" is true *a priori*, because we do not need to examine any triangles in the natural world to discover that they have three sides.

Absolutism   The view that certain types of acts are impermissible no matter the consequences.

Abstract Entities   Entities that are not part of the spatiotemporal world and do not enter into causal relations.

Act-consequentialism   The view that, for all persons, each person is permitted to do (of the available actions) only what will bring about the most good-simpliciter.

Act-utilitarianism   Act-consequentialism combined with a hedonistic theory of value. The view that, for all persons, each person is permitted to do (of the available actions) only what will bring about the most utility, where "utility" is pleasure and the absence of pain.

Agency   To be an agent is to have the capacity to recognize and respond to reasons.

Agent-neutral reasons   Reasons that do not make essential reference to the agent; reasons for everyone.

Agent-relative reasons   Reasons that make essential reference to the agent; reasons for a particular person.

Amoralist   People who know that they are ethically required to act in certain ways yet have no motivation whatsoever to act in these ways. The possibility of amoralists, it is argued, calls into question the truth of judgment internalism.

Analytic proposition   A proposition whose truth-value depends solely on the meaning of the terms with which it is expressed. For example, "all bachelors are unmarried men" is analytically true, because the predicate concept is contained within the sub-ject concept.

Autonomy   Having control over one's life. For Kant, autonomy is a property of the will—namely, to be a law unto oneself.

Belief-desire psychology   Agents act in order to satisfy their desires based on their beliefs. Beliefs, on this picture, are representational mental states that the agent adjusts to fit the world, whereas desires are pro-attitudes, which the agent tries to adjust the world to fit. That is, agents try to get their beliefs to conform to the world and the world to conform to their desires.

Categorical reasons   Reasons whose grounds are not conditional on the agent's commitments (desires, ends, interests, etc.).

Closed question   A question that it is not possible for a competent speaker to understand and yet not know its answer.

Cognitivism   The view that ethical judgments are beliefs and, hence, are truth-apt.

Concepts   Contents of thoughts; ways of conceiving of things as being.

Concrete entities   Entities that are part of the spatiotemporal world and enter into causal relations.

Consistency   A set of claims is consistent if it is logically possible for all of the claims in the set to be true at the same time.

Constitutive rule   A rule that must be followed in order to engage in the activity in the first place.

Constructivism   The view that holds there are ethical truths, but that these truths are the product of the practical point of view or some hypothetical procedure. According to Rawls' Kantian constructivism, ethical objectivity is to be understood in terms of a constructed point of view that all can accept. Apart from this procedure, there are no ethical facts.

Contingent   A claim that is true in the actual world, but there exists at least one possible world where the claim is false.

Cornell realism   A version of ethical realism that holds ethical properties exist as *sui generis* natural properties—that is, a form of non-reductive naturalism.

Decisive (or conclusive) reasons   Reasons to act in a certain way that outweigh any other reason (or combination of reasons) not to act in this way.

Deontic verdict   A claim about the normative status of an action—for example, impermissible, permissible, required, optional, supererogatory.

Descriptivism   The view that holds that ethical utterances attempt to accurately describe reality and, hence, maintains that ethical utterances are truth-apt.

Derivative reasons   Reasons that are parasitic on other reasons—in other words, reasons that are not ultimate. Derivative reasons do not supply additional justificatory weight for a particular deontic verdict.

Divine command theory   The view that, for all persons, each person, S, is required to do whatever God commands S to do.

Emotivism   A species of Non-Descriptivism/Non-Cognitivism that holds ethical utterances express the speaker's emotions. For example, when we say "lying is wrong," we are really saying "lying—booo!"

Expressivism   A species of Non-Descriptivism/Non-Cognitivism that holds ethical utterances express the speaker's non-cognitive attitudes.

Error theory   The view that holds ethical thought and talk express beliefs that ascribe normative properties but no such properties exist.

Ethical functionalism   A form of analytic naturalism that holds ethical terms are defined by the roles they play in the system of which they are a part. According to Jackson and Pettit, to be ethically right is to have the property that plays the rightness role in folk morality.

Existence externalism   It is possible for an agent to have a reason to φ, even if φ-ing does not connect to the agent's (perhaps idealized) motivational set (broadly construed). That is, it is not the case that what agents have reason to do depends on their existing wants, ends, or desires. See *Reasons, Parfit*.

Existence internalism   The view that holds an agent's having a reason to act in a certain way depends on the agent's (perhaps idealized) motivational set (broadly construed). That is, what agents have reason to do depends on their existing wants, ends, or desires. See *Reasons, Schroeder*; *Reasons, Smith*; and *Reasons, Williams*.

Extension   Everything to which a concept or term applies. For example, the extension of the term "red" is everything that is red.

Fact   A true proposition.

Fictionalism   The view that holds that, though ethical discourse is systematically in error, we can treat such discourse as a useful fiction. For Joyce, when we make ethical utterances, we put them forward in a non-assertoric way. For example, when we say "lying is wrong," we are merely fictively asserting that lying is wrong; we do not literally believe it.

Folk morality   The network of ethical opinions, intuitions, principles, and concepts whose mastery is part of having a sense of what is right and wrong and of being able to engage in meaningful ethical debate.

Frege-Geach problem   Narrowly, how can Non-Cognitivism/Non-Descriptivism keep meaning fixed across asserted and unasserted contexts? Broadly, why do ethical and descriptive terms have identical semantic properties despite, according to Non-Cognitivism/Non-Descriptivism, having different meanings?

Good-for   Personally good. Good for some group or particular person—for example, "College was good for her."

Good-simpliciter   Impersonally good. Good, period—for example, "It was good that the beautiful painting was saved from the fire."

Good will   A will that is able to reliably identify and carry out its duty for its own sake.

Grounding   The giving of a metaphysically necessary explanation. If p grounds q, then we are saying what it is in virtue of which something is q—in this case, p. For example, being water is grounded in being H_2O.

Humean theory of motivation   Beliefs and desires are distinct existences: desires are not the product of beliefs, and beliefs are not the product of desires. All motivation depends on a relevant antecedent desire. No belief could motivate us unless it is combined with some independent desire. Beliefs, alone, are motivationally inert.

Hybrid (or ecumenical) expressivism   The view that holds normative utterances express both cognitive and non-cognitive mental states. An analogy to slurs—given that they have both a factual and emotional component—is often made in defending the view. For Ridge, an ethical utterance about an action expresses both a general attitude concerning such actions insofar as they have a certain property and a belief that this property applies to this specific action. For example, a utilitarian who utters "ϕ-ing is impermissible" expresses a general disapproval of actions insofar as they fail to be pleasure maximizing and a belief the ϕ-ing fails to be pleasure maximizing.

Hypothetical imperative   An imperative that is conditional, depending on the agent's contingent aims, desires, or ends.

Hypothetical reasons   Reasons whose grounds are conditional on the agent's commitments: desires, ends, interests, etc.

Iff   Shorthand for "if and only if." A sentence containing "iff" thus states a necessary and sufficient condition: a biconditional.

Inference to the best explanation   Tells us to infer the truth of a given hypothesis from the fact that this hypothesis would explain the available evidence better than any other available hypotheses.

Instrumental reasons   Reasons that are merely means to accomplishing something we have ultimate reason to accomplish. Instrumental reasons do not supply additional justificatory weight for a particular deontic verdict.

Instrumental value   Something's having value because of what it brings about via its consequences—for example, money.

Intrinsic value   Something's having value in and of itself, or for its own sake—for example, pleasure.

Intuitionism   The view that ethical truths are self-evident, known by direct apprehension. Intuitions are intellectual seemings analogous to perceptual seemings. For Sidgwick, self-evident ethical axioms must meet four conditions: (1) the terms must be clear and precise, (2) it must be ascertained by careful reflection, (3) it must be mutually consistent with other self-evident truths, and (4) it must attract general consensus.

Judgment externalism   The view that holds that it is not the case that if a person makes an ethical judgment that she is required to act in some way, then it is conceptually necessary that the person is (somewhat) motivated to act in conformity with this judgment (if she is rational). Instead, judgment externalism holds that the connection between ethical judgment and motivation is psychological—for example, a product of a person's desire to be ethical—and so contingent.

Judgment internalism   The view that holds that if a person makes an ethical judgment that she is required to act in some way, then it is conceptually necessary that the person is (somewhat) motivated to act in conformity with this judgment (if she is rational).

Kantianism   The view that, for all persons, each person, S, is required to refrain from acting according to a maxim S could not rationally will as a universal law. Alternatively, for all persons, each person, S, is required to refrain from acting according to a maxim that treats humanity (rational nature), whether in S's own person or in the person of another rational agent, as a mere means and not as an end.

Maxim   A subjective principle of action that consists of the actor's intention and reason for so intending.

Minimalism about truth   The view that the truth predicate comes with no ontological commitments; it merely serves as a device for quotation and disquotation.

Moral rationalism   The view that holds if one has a moral obligation to act in a certain way, then one has a reason to act in this way. Moral obligations entail reasons for action.

Moral worth   The praiseworthy feature of an action associated with the motive that led the agent to perform the action. For Kant, an action has moral worth if and only if it is a dutiful action done from the motive of duty.

Motivating reasons   Reasons that explain why an agent acted in a certain way. They are what causally bring agents to do certain things—for example, the desire-belief pair.

Naturalism   The natural world is the whole of reality; roughly, all facts and properties are features of the empirically discoverable, spatiotemporal world.

Non-Cognitivism   The view that it is not the case that ethical judgments are beliefs and, hence, ethical judgments are not truth-apt.

Non-derivative reasons   Reasons that are neither instrumental nor derivative; the ultimate reasons that supply justificatory weight for our deontic verdicts.

Non-Descriptivism   The view that it is not the case that ethical utterances attempt to accurately describe reality and, hence, ethical utterances are not truth-apt.

Non-Naturalism   Rejects naturalism about reality; some truths—for example, some ethical truths—are made true by correctly describing how things are in some non-spatiotemporal realm.

Normative (as opposed to descriptive) claims   A claim that tells us what should, ought, or must be the case. By contrast, a descriptive claim tells us what is, was, or will be the case.

Normative reason   A consideration that counts in favor of, or justifies, acting in certain ways. Contrast with motivating reasons.

Object-given reasons   Reasons that are provided by facts that make certain outcomes worth producing or preventing, or make certain things worth doing for their own sake. Contrast with *Subject-given reasons*.

Objective claim   A claim that depends on how things are, independent of the speaker's psychology.

Ontological reductionism   The view that ethical facts and properties are identical to certain non-ethical facts and properties. Denies the autonomy of ethics. Comes in both analytic and non-analytic forms. See also *Reductive naturalism*.

Open question   A question that it is possible for a competent speaker to understand and yet not know its answer.

Predicate   A term that tells us something about the subject of the sentence. For example, in the sentence "The cat is fat," the portion "is fat" is the predicate. The predicate here tells us that the subject (the cat) possesses a certain attribute (fatness). But predicates can also be used to tell us that there is a certain relation between two things.

For instance, in the sentence "The cat is north of New York City," the portion "is north of" is the predicate.

Prescriptivism   A species of Non-Descriptivism/Non-Cognitivism that holds ethical utterances aim to direct, not describe, action. For example, when we say "lying is wrong," we are really issuing the imperative "Don't lie!"

***Pro tanto* reason**   A consideration that counts in favor of acting in a certain way but may not do so decisively.

Property   Ways things might be. Or, alternatively, features that things have in common. For example, my cat has the property of being fat, and my neighbor's dog shares this property.

Psychological egoism   The view that all human actions are motivated by self-interest.

Quasi-realism   A program that jettisons the metaphysical commitments of realism but nonetheless attempts to capture those features that make realism the default position in metaethics.

Realism   The view that holds moral properties and facts exist. More precisely, our ethical thought and talk is truth-apt—that is, it tries to accurately describe reality—and sometimes we succeed; our thought and talk are sometimes true. (Some add that realism is committed to these facts being subject-independent.)

Reasons, Parfit   An agent's having a reason to ϕ-ing is provided by the fact that ϕ-ing promotes what is good or valuable.

Reasons, Schroeder   For R to be a reason for S to ϕ is for there to be some p such that S has a desire whose object is p, and the truth of R is part of what explains why S's ϕ-ing promotes p.

Reasons, Smith S has a reason to ϕ in C means that if S were fully rational, she would desire that in C she ϕs.

Reasons, Williams A has a reason to ϕ only if there is a sound deliberative route from S's subjective motivational set to S's ϕ-ing.

Reductive naturalism   The view that denies the autonomy of ethics; ethical facts and properties just consist in certain naturalistic facts and properties. Reduction thus takes the form of a biconditional with some ethical property on one side and some uncontroversially natural property (or properties) on the other. If this biconditional is true in virtue of its meaning, in the same way we think of "being a bachelor" as just consisting in "being an unmarried male," then the reduction is analytic. This view is called *analytic naturalism*. If the reduction is based on grounding, in the way "being water" is grounded in "being H_2O," the reduction is non-analytic. This view is called *non-analytic naturalism*.

Referent   The object denoted by a term. For example, if we say "Mark Schroeder is a metaethicist," we use the name "Mark Schroeder" to refer to a particular person: Mark Schroeder.

Regulative rule   A rule that serves as guidelines for improving an activity but, if violated, do not disqualify the activity as an activity of the kind. Contrast with *constitutive rule*.

Relativism The view that ethical thought and talk is truth-apt but truth or falsity is indexed to a certain frame of reference—for example, indexed to the speaker, to the agent, or to a group. Often, an analogy is drawn to the rejection of absolute motion in physics.

Response-dependent theories of value The view that holds values are explained in terms of our responses. Often, an analogy is drawn between evaluative properties and secondary qualities, such as colors. For Lewis, X is valuable if and only if we would be disposed to desire to desire X under circumstances of fullest possible imaginative acquaintance with X.

Semantic Having to do with meaning.

Semantic externalism The meaning of a term is environmentally determined—for example, by natural features of the world or experts in society.

Semantic internalism The meaning of a term is psychologically determined—for example, by the speaker's intentions.

Semantic reductionism The view that the meaning of ethical terms is identical to the meaning of certain non-ethical terms.

Subject-given reasons Reasons provided by facts about what would fulfill or achieve our desires or aims. Contrast with *Object-given reasons*.

Subjective claim A claim that depends on the speaker's psychology, independently of how things are.

Subjectivism The view that ethical utterances and judgments report certain aspects of our psychology—for example, our being for or against some actions.

***Sui generis* properties** Properties that are irreducible. They are of their own kind, forming an autonomous domain.

Supervenience, ethical If two actions are identical in natural respects, then they are identical in ethical respects. There cannot be an ethical difference without a natural difference.

Synthetic proposition A proposition that is not analytic. For example, "all creatures with hearts have kidneys" is true because of the way the world is, not because the predicate concept is contained within the subject concept.

Thick concepts Concepts that are both descriptive and evaluative—for example, loyalty.

Truth-apt An utterance or judgment that is capable of being true or false.

Universality The view that deontic verdicts must not be relative to a particular culture but apply to all persons in relevantly similar circumstances.

Voluntarist reasons Reasons that are the product of our own will. For Chang, such will-based reasons arise in cases where our given reasons leave indeterminate a question concerning what to do.

Index